Tenth Edition

HUMAN RELATIONS

Interpersonal Job-Oriented Skills

Andrew J. DuBrin

College of Business
Rochester Institute of Technology

PEARSON

Prentice
Hall

Upper Saddle River, New Jersey
Columbus, Ohio

Library of Congress Cataloging-in-Publication Data

DuBrin, Andrew J.
    Human relations : interpersonal job-oriented skills / Andrew J. DuBrin.—10th ed.
        p. cm.
    ISBN-13: 978-0-13-501944-3
    ISBN-10: 0-13-501944-3
    1. Industrial sociology.   2. Personnel management.   3. Organizational behavior.
I. Title.

HD6955.D82 2009
658.3—dc22   2008011953

Editor in Chief: Vernon R. Anthony
Senior Acquisitions Editor: Gary Bauer
Editorial Assistant: Megan Heintz
Project Manager: Stephen C. Robb
Production Coordination: Sarvesh
    Mehrotra/Aptara, Inc.
Senior Art Director: Diane Y. Ernsberger
Text Designer: Kristina D. Holmes
Cover Designer: Kristina D. Holmes
Cover images: Mike Kemp/Rubberball/Jupiter
    Images, Inc., Photodisk® by Getty Images,®
    and Corbis
Senior Operations Supervisor: Pat Tonneman

Director, Image Resource Center: Melinda
    Patelli
Manager, Rights and Permissions: Zina Arabia
Manager, Visual Research: Beth Brenzel
**Manager, Cover Visual Research &
    Permissions:** Karen Sanatar
Image Permission Coordinator: Nancy Seise
Director of Marketing: David Gesell
Campaign Marketing Manager: Leigh Ann Sims
Curriculum Marketing Manager: Thomas
    Hayward
Senior Marketing Coordinator: Alicia Dysert
Marketing Assistant: Les Roberts

This book was set in Sabon by Aptara, Inc. It was printed and bound by Courier Kendallville, Inc.
The cover was printed by Phoenix Color Corp.

Photo Credits: p. 2 Jupiter Images – Rubberball; p. 7 Photodisc/Getty Images; p. 11 Photolibrary.com;
p. 20 Jupiter Images – Rubberball; p. 23 Getty Images – Stockbyte; p. 33 Corbis/Image Source/Royalty
Free; p. 44 Jupiter Images – Rubberball; p. 49 Photos.com; p. 57 Getty Images, Inc.- Photodisc; p. 64
Corbis RF; p. 70 Getty Images, Inc.; p. 79 © Daly & Newton / Getty Images; p. 88 Jupiter Images –
Rubberball; p. 93 Getty Images – Stockbyte; p. 103 Photodisc/Getty Images; p. 110 Getty
Images/Digital Vision; p. 113 © Keith Dannemiller/CORBIS SABA; p. 120 Getty Images, Inc.; p. 130
Rubberball Productions; p. 135 Getty Images, Inc. – PhotoDisc; p. 137 Jose Luis Pelaez, Inc.; p. 152
Dream Pictures/Stone/Getty Images; p. 159 Photodisc/Getty Images; p. 169 -PhotoEdit Inc.; p. 176
Jupiter Images – Rubberball; p. 183 Photodisc/Getty Images; p. 185 Greg Miller Photography; p. 200
Jupiter Images – Rubberball; p. 208 © Colin Hawkins / Getty Images; p. 210 Getty Images, Inc. – Taxi;
p. 218 Corbis RF; p. 221 Getty Images – Stockbyte; p. 225 Getty Images – Stockbyte; p. 242 Hans
Neleman/Stone/Getty Images; p. 245 Getty Images – Stockbyte; p. 261 Corbis/Image Source/Royalty
Free; p. 270 Jupiter Images PictureArts Corporation/Brand X Pictures Royalty Free; p. 278 Getty
Images Editorial; p. 284 Getty Images – Stockbyte; p. 294 Photodisc/Getty Images; p. 297 AP Wide
World Photos; p. 307 © Jon Feingersh/Masterfile – www.masterfile.com;
p. 318 Jupiter Images – Rubberball; p. 324 PhotoEdit Inc.; p. 334 Chabruken/Taxi/Getty Images; p. 346
Jupiter Images – Rubberball; p. 349 Andrew DuBrin; p. 368 Paul Barton.

Pearson Education Ltd., London
Pearson Education Singapore Pte. Ltd.
Pearson Education Canada, Inc.
Pearson Education—Japan

Pearson Education Australia Pty. Limited
Pearson Education North Asia Ltd., Hong Kong
Pearson Educación de Mexico, S.A. de C.V.
Pearson Education Malaysia Pte. Ltd.

10 9 8 7 6 5 4 3 2 1
ISBN-13: 978-0-13-501944-3
ISBN-10:   0-13-501944-3

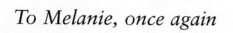

To Melanie, once again

Brief Contents

Contents

Chapter 3   Building Self-Esteem and Self-Confidence 44

CONTENTS

Preface

Welcome to the tenth edition of *Human Relations: Interpersonal Job-Oriented Skills.* Success in any position involving interaction with people requires two broad sets of competencies: functional skills and generic skills. *Functional skills* refer to knowledge of one's discipline (or organizational function), technical skills, specialty skills, or simply details of the job. *Generic skills* refer to competencies important in a variety of jobs. Among these generic skills are good work habits and time management, information technology skills, high ethics, and interpersonal skills.

My purpose in writing this book is to help readers enhance their interpersonal skills, including ethical behavior, in the workplace. By enhancing interpersonal skills, a person has a better chance of capitalizing upon his or her other skills. Two primary approaches are used in this text to achieve the lofty goal of improving interpersonal skills. First, basic concepts are introduced to enhance understanding of key topics in interpersonal relations in organizations.

Second, skill-building suggestions, exercises, and cases are presented that are designed to improve interpersonal skills related to the topic. Chapter 5, for example, presents general information about the nature of teamwork, followed by suggestions for improving teamwork. The chapter also includes several exercises or experiential activities and two case problems—all designed to improve teamwork skills.

Third, examples and box inserts provide insight into how a particular skill is applied on the job. For example, in Chapter 7, I describe how call center operators learn another culture so they can relate effectively to their customers.

AUDIENCE FOR THIS BOOK

The primary audience for this book is people taking courses that emphasize the development of interpersonal skills. Such courses typically include the term *human relations.* Because interpersonal relations contribute so heavily to effective leadership, the text is suited for participants in leadership and supervisory training courses that emphasize interpersonal skills, rather than leadership theory and research.

FRAMEWORK FOR THIS BOOK

The book is a blend of current and traditional topics dealing with interpersonal relations in organizations with a heavy component of skill development and self-assessment. The information is organized into chapters, all emphasizing interpersonal relations between two or more people. Chapter 1, "A Framework for Interpersonal Skill Development," sets the stage for improving one's interpersonal skills on the job. Chapter 2, "Understanding Individual Differences," presents information that is the foundation of effective interpersonal relations. Chapter 3, "Building Self-Esteem and Self-Confidence," describes how to develop self-esteem and self-confidence both for oneself and to improve relationships with others. Chapter 4, "Interpersonal Communication," deals with skills in sending and receiving messages.

Chapter 5, "Developing Teamwork Skills," sensitizes the reader to a vital set of skills in the workplace. Chapter 6, "Group Problem Solving and Decision Making," provides additional skill in collaborative effort. Chapter 7, "Cross-Cultural Relations and Diversity," is about developing cross-cultural skills in a diverse workforce. Chapter 8, "Resolving Conflicts with Others," helps readers develop skills in finding constructive solutions to differences of opinion and disputes with others.

Four consecutive chapters deal with exerting influence over others. Chapter 9, "Becoming an Effective Leader," presents information relevant to exercising leadership in the workplace. Chapter 10, "Motivating Others," emphasizes skills in getting others to work hard to achieve goals. Chapter 11, "Helping Others Develop and Grow," is about coaching, counseling, and teaching other. Chapter 12, "Positive Political Skills," describes how to use power and influence for constructive purposes.

Chapter 13, "Customer Satisfaction Skills," describes several approaches to enhancing skills to achieve the critically important goal of pleasing customers. Chapter 14, "Enhancing Ethical Behavior," translates ethical principles into usable skills. The rationale is that an ethical base is important for achieving career-long effectiveness in interpersonal relations. Chapter 15, "Stress Management and Personal Productivity," supports development of interpersonal skills by showing that productive people who have stress under control can relate more effectively to others. Chapter 16, "Job Search and Career Management Skills," includes information about the application of interpersonal skills (such as networking) to enhance one's career.

CHANGES IN THIS EDITION

The new edition of *Human Relations* adds three new features and expands upon two others in response to reviewer suggestions. These enhancements included the following:

- A brief section, Self-Assessment Quizzes in Overview, that provides more insight into the self-quizzes and explains how the quizzes relate to each other
- An Internet Skill-Building exercise placed in the Web Corner that gives students an opportunity to search for a particular type of interpersonal skill building related to the chapter subject (for example, a Website for enhancing listening skills that is described in Chapter 4)
- Photos throughout the text
- Twenty-one new figures, many of which include drawings to symbolize a key point
- Twelve new skill-building exercises and five new self-assessment quizzes

New information, research findings, and examples appear throughout the text. Fourteen of the case openers and nineteen of the cases are new. Chapter 3, about building self-esteem and self-confidence, is new. Material that may have lost some of its relevance has been selectively pruned. The new topics in the text are as follows:

- A section about personality types and cognitive styles that has been revamped in line with the suggestions of the distributor of the Myers-Briggs Type Indicator (Chapter 2)
- More information about the implications of emotional intelligence (Chapter 2)
- A complete chapter on building self-esteem and self-confidence (Chapter 3)
- The importance of voice quality when being interviewed on the phone (Chapter 4)
- Suggestions for becoming an effective meeting participant (Chapter 6)
- Political correctness as part of cross-cultural relations (Chapter 7)
- Employee network groups (Chapter 7)
- A revamped section on cultural dimensions (Chapter 7)
- Reframing by asking questions as a technique for conflict resolution (Chapter 8)
- Understanding the other party's perspective as a negotiating technique (Chapter 8)
- Question-and-answer sessions with the team as a method of team development (Chapter 9)
- A brief discussion about whether leaders are born or made (Chapter 9)
- Political skill and social intelligence (Chapter 12)
- A revamped section on impression management including these subtopics: being visible and creating a strong presence, minimizing yes-person behavior, and creating a healthy image (Chapter 12)

- Etiquette for working in a cubicle (Chapter 12)
- Understanding unwritten boundaries (Chapter 12)
- The impact on career of indiscreet behavior in private life (Chapter 12)
- The three components of customer experience (or service) (Chapter 13)
- New research about the importance of smiling at customers (Chapter 13)
- Building a relationship by interacting with customers (Chapter 13)
- Ethical problems with cronyism (Chapter 14)
- Developing virtuousness (Chapter 14)
- Being environmentally conscious as ethical behavior (Chapter 14)
- Upward leadership to encourage ethical behavior (Chapter 14)
- Challenge versus hindrance stressors (Chapter 15)
- Extreme jobs as a potential stressor (Chapter 15)
- Environmentally induced attention deficit disorder (Chapter 15)
- Perfecting skills and productivity through deliberate practice (Chapter 15)
- Social networking Websites for job hunting (Chapter 16)
- Video résumés and creative (but honest) résumés (Chapter 16)
- Avoidance of overtalking during job interviews (Chapter 16)
- Capitalizing on your strengths and building your personal brand (Chapter 16)

Experience the DuBrin Total Learning System

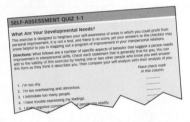

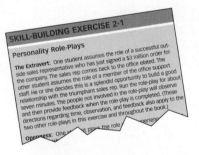

Human Relations: Interpersonal Job-Oriented Skills, Tenth Edition, is not just a textbook. The tenth edition includes a wealth of experiential exercises, including new cases and self-assessment quizzes that can be completed in class or as homework.

CHAPTER OPENING CASES SET THE STAGE

Following a listing of the chapter objectives and chapter outline. All chapters begin with a case scenario that deals with the chapter topic and sets the stage for the chapter narrative.

PEDAGOGICAL FEATURES RELATE CONCEPTS TO WHAT'S HAPPENING TODAY, PERSONALLY AND IN THE WORKPLACE

- **Back to the Opening Case** boxes within the chapter provide further insight into the situation posed in the chapter opening case related to chapter content.

- **Self-Assessment Exercises** give students the opportunity to explore their own opinions, feelings, and behaviors patterns related to chapter topics. All chapters include one or more self-assessment quizzes with a summary overview of assessment outcomes included at the end of the chapter.

- **Job-Oriented Interpersonal Skills in Action** in all chapters illustrate a real human relations business practice in today's business world.

- **Skill-Building Exercises** provide students with opportunities to apply concepts at the point at which they are being discussed in the textbook.

NEW, EXPANDED ASSIGNMENT MATERIAL

End-of-chapter assignment material has been reorganized and expanded into two sections: **Concept Review and Reinforcement** featuring exercises that focus on concept retention and developing critical thinking skills and **Developing Your Human Relations Skills** focusing on developing skills that can be used immediately in life and on the job.

Concept Review and Reinforcement	**Key Terms** alert readers about critical terminology.
	Summary of Key Concepts provides an excellent detailed review of key chapter concepts.
	Check Your Understanding objective questions review key chapter topics.
	The **Web Corner** provides informational Websites and asks students to use the power of the web in researching outside resources.

Developing Your Human Relation Skills	**Two Human Relations Case Studies** put students into a realistic scenario so they can practice making decisions in tough situations.
	Interpersonal Skills Role-Play exercises provide students with the opportunity to develop personal insight through interactive exercises.

Supplemental Materials

COMPANION WEBSITE

Students can access a wealth of study aids at **http://www.prenhall.com/dubrin**. The online Companion Website includes the following: chapter learning objectives; test-prep quizzes for each chapter, including true/false, multiple choice, and short essay questions; immediate feedback to all questions; Web exercises for each chapter; and online resource links to additional Websites.

INSTRUCTOR'S MANUAL WITH TEST ITEM FILE

The Instructor's Manual for this text is available as a downloadable Word document at **http://www.pearsonhighered.com** under Instructor's Resource Center. It contains 800 multiple-choice and true/false test questions, chapter outlines and lecture notes, answers to discussion questions and case problems, and comments about the exercises.

To access supplementary materials online, instructors need to request an instructor access code. Go to **www.pearsonhighered.com**, click the **Instructor Resource Center** link, and then click **Register Today** for an instructor access code. Within 48 hours after registering you will receive a confirming e-mail including an instructor access code. Once you have received your code, go the site and log on for full instructions on downloading the materials you wish to use.

PRENTICE HALL TESTGEN

This computerized text generation system is available as a downloadable file at **http://www.prenhall.com** under Download Instructor Resources. The program gives the instructor maximum flexibility in preparing tests. It can create custom tests and print scrambled versions of a test at one time, as well as build tests randomly by chapter, level of difficulty, or question type. The software also allows online testing and record-keeping and the ability to add problems to the database.

POWERPOINT LECTURE PRESENTATION PACKAGE

Lecture Presentation screens for each chapter are available online at **http://pearsonhighered.com** under Instructor's Resource Center.

JWA HUMAN RELATIONS VIDEOS

JWA Videos on human relations and interpersonal communication topics are available to qualified adopters. Contact your local Prentice Hall representative for details.

DISTANCE LEARNING AND OTHER ONLINE SUPPLEMENTS
BlackBoard, WebCT, and CourseCompass Courses

Ready-made courses in these popular distance learning platforms are available. Please contact your local Prentice Hall representative for more information.

CourseSmart

An electronic version of this text can be purchased at **www.coursesmart.com**.

Prentice Hall's Self-Assessment Library (SAL)

SAL is an online product developed by Steve Robbins that contains 51 research-based self-assessments that provide students with insights into their skills, abilities, and interests. It is easy to use, self-scoring, and can be packaged with this text at a discounted price. Instructors: Please contact your Prentice Hall representative to obtain a review copy. Students: Purchase SAL at **www.prenhall.com**.

ACKNOWLEDGMENTS

My appreciation goes to the many people who contributed to the development and production of this book. I extend special thanks to the reviewers for this edition: Tim Blood, Lane Community College; Jane Bowerman, University of Oklahoma; Robert G. DelCampo, University of New Mexico; Abhirjun Dutta, Bainbridge College; Tommy Gilbreath, The University of Texas at Tyler; and Dr. David W. Robinson, Malaspina University College.

I also thank the reviewers for previous editions of the text: John Adamski II, Ivy Tech State College; Patricia Lynn Anderson, Valdosta State University; Judy Bowie, DeVry Institute of Technology; Robert A. Herring III, Winston–Salem State University; H. Frederick Holmes, Ogeechee Technical Institute; Ruth V. Kellar, Ivy Tech State College; Nancy Kriscenski, Manchester Community College; Diane Paul, TVI Community College; Lou Jean Peace, Valdosta Technical Institute; Gary W. Piggrem, Ph.D., DeVry Institute of Technology; Dean Weeden, Utah Career College; and James E. Wetz, Central Florida Community College.

My family members give me an additional reason for writing, so I extend my appreciation to Drew, Douglas, Melanie, Gizella, Will, Rosie, Clare, Camila, Sofia, and Eliana.

Andrew J. DuBrin
Rochester, New York

CHAPTER 1

....

A Framework for Interpersonal Skill Development

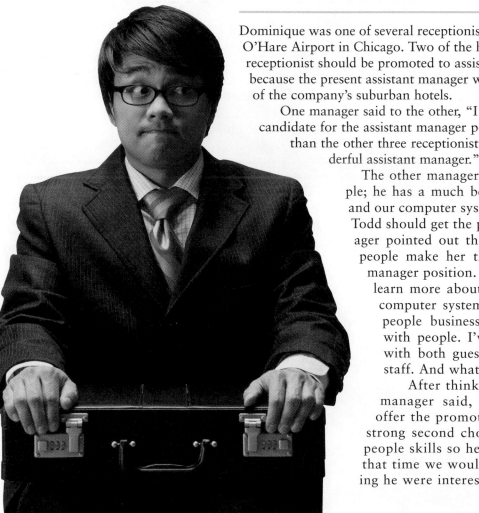

Dominique was one of several receptionists at a large hotel not located far from O'Hare Airport in Chicago. Two of the hotel executives were discussing which receptionist should be promoted to assistant hotel manager, a vacancy created because the present assistant manager was being promoted to manager of one of the company's suburban hotels.

One manager said to the other, "I think that Dominique is the strongest candidate for the assistant manager position. She has a little less experience than the other three receptionists, but I think she would make a wonderful assistant manager."

The other manager replied, "But take Todd, for example; he has a much better knowledge of hotel operations and our computer system than does Dominique. So maybe Todd should get the promotion this time." The first manager pointed out that Dominique's superior skills with people make her the best candidate for the assistant manager position. "I think that in time Dominique can learn more about our operations, including the new computer system. We can't forget that hotels are a people business, and Dominique gets along great with people. I've seen her resolve tough problems with both guests and other members of the hotel staff. And what a warm smile she has."

After thinking for a few moments, the second manager said, "You've got a good point. Let's offer the promotion to Dominique, with Todd as a strong second choice. We'll also coach Todd on his people skills so he can be promoted in the future. At that time we would offer him the promotion, assuming he were interested."

Learning Objectives

After reading and studying this chapter and doing the exercises, you should be able to

1. Explain how interpersonal skills are learned.
2. Explain the model for interpersonal skills improvement.
3. Pinpoint your needs for improvement in interpersonal relations.
4. Describe potential opportunities for developing interpersonal skills on the job.

Scenarios similar to this one take place often in the workplace. Many people are promoted to a supervisory position because they have good human relations skills combined with adequate technical skills. As the Dale Carnegie organization states, "To achieve success in today's work world—with its emphasis on collaboration, teamwork, motivation, and leadership—you need to perfect your interpersonal skills."[1]

Effective interpersonal relations must be combined with technical knowledge and good work habits to achieve success in any job involving interaction with people. Workers at all levels are expected not only to solve problems and improve processes (how work is performed), but also to interact effectively with other employees.[2] Many employers, including Southwest Airlines, emphasize hiring people with positive attitudes rather than focusing strictly on technical skills. And another airline, JetBlue, refuses to hire pilots who are arrogant or nasty despite their piloting skills.

Furthermore, the lack of good interpersonal skills can adversely affect a person's career. A study found that 90 percent of firings results from poor attitudes, inappropriate behavior, and problems in interpersonal relationships rather than substandard interpersonal skills.[3] An example of poor interpersonal relations that led to job loss was a receptionist at a boat dealer who told several potential customers something to the effect, "Are you just here to look? You don't look like you could afford one of our speed boats."

This chapter explains how people develop interpersonal skills and presents a model that can serve as a foundation for improving your interpersonal skills. In addition, the chapter explains how the workplace can be a natural setting for developing interpersonal skills.

> 66 For employers, interpersonal and technical skills go hand-in-hand. 99
>
> —Linda Leung, *Network World IT Education and Training Newsletter*

PLAN OF THE BOOK

This entire book is devoted to many different ways of improving interpersonal relations in organizations. A three-part strategy is presented for achieving the high level of effectiveness in interpersonal relations required in today's workplace. First, each chapter presents key concepts required for understanding a particular aspect of interpersonal relations, such as resolving conflict. Second, the chapter provides specific suggestions or

LEARNING OBJECTIVE 1

FIGURE 1-1 Plan for Achieving Effectiveness in Interpersonal Relations

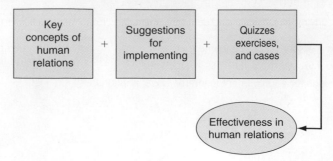

behavioral guidelines for improvement in the aspect of interpersonal relations under consideration.

Third, a variety of exercises gives you the opportunity to work on and improve your skills. Among these exercises are self-assessment quizzes, skill-building exercises, and cases for analysis. In addition, the questions at the end of each chapter give you an opportunity to think through and apply the key ideas in the chapter. Figure 1-1 illustrates the plan of the book.

Much of this book is concerned with **interpersonal skill training**, the teaching of skills in dealing with others so they can be put into practice. Interpersonal skills training is referred to as *soft-skills* training to differentiate it from technical training. (Technical skills training is referred to as *hard-skills* training.) Soft-skills training builds interpersonal skills, including communication, listening, group problem solving, cross-cultural relations, and customer service. Several specific competencies related to soft skills are as follows:

- Effectively translating and conveying information
- Being able to accurately interpret other people's emotions
- Being sensitive to other people's feelings
- Calmly arriving at resolutions to conflicts
- Avoiding negative gossip
- Being polite[4]
- Being able to cooperate with others to meet objectives (teamwork)

Soft-skills training is more important than ever as organizations realize that a combination of human effort and technology is needed to produce results. Multiple studies have shown that soft skills can compensate for more traditional cognitive (or analytical) intelligence. For example, a supervisor with good interpersonal skills might perform well even if he or she is not outstandingly intelligent. The statement does not mean, however, outstanding soft skills will compensate for high cognitive intelligence when doing highly analytical work such as analyzing the value of a company.

Soft skills are often the differentiating factor between adequate and outstanding performance because dealing with people is part of so many jobs.[5] Assume that a company establishes an elaborate intranet system to enable employees to exchange work-related information with each other. The system will not achieve its potential unless employees are motivated to use it properly and they develop a spirit of cooperation. The employees must also be willing to share some of their best ideas with each other. Consider this example also:

> *Sara, a newly hired intake receptionist in a cardiac clinic, notices that too often the patients present incomplete or inaccurate information, such as omitting data about the next of kin. Sara spends considerable amounts of time reworking forms with the patients, until she begins using soft skills more effectively. With coaching from her supervisor, Sara learns that if she attempts to calm down a patient first, the patient is more likely to complete the intake form accurately. The accompanying box illustrates the importance of interpersonal skills for a business executive.*

interpersonal skill training

The teaching of skills in dealing with others so they can be put into practice.

4 CHAPTER 1

Executive Learns About the Importance of Interpersonal Skills

Several years ago, while visiting a regional branch of Lee Hecht Harrison, a global management services company, then-president Stephen Harrison was stopped short by Ray, his chief operating officer (CEO). "You didn't greet the receptionist," said Ray, who proceeded to show Harrison how to do what he called the "two-minute schmooze." Introducing himself, Ray inquired about the receptionist's commute and impressions of the company.

Ray explained to Harrison: "A receptionist is a corporate concierge. He or she will talk to more important people in a day—suppliers, customers, even CEOs—than you will talk to all year."

"Decency is not just about being nice," noted Harrison, author of *The Manager's Book of Decencies*. Rather, it is about creating a "bubble wrap" of good deeds that will protect a company in hard times. "Our willingness to be decent at work cannot depend on whether business is up or whether we're in a bad mood or whether it's raining. Decencies don't amount to anything unless we take the trouble to make them come alive through concrete acts in all kinds of weather."

Questions

1. Why might an executive chatting with a receptionist be considered an interpersonal skill?
2. In what way might being *decent* to employees help make a company more profitable?

Source: "Talking with the Receptionist, Pausing When You Speak, and Other Secrets of Leadership Success," Knowledge@Wharton (*http://knowledge.wharton.upenn.edu/article.cfm?articleid=1792*), p. 1.

A MODEL FOR IMPROVING INTERPERSONAL SKILLS

LEARNING OBJECTIVE 2

Acquiring and improving interpersonal skills is facilitated by following a basic model of learning as it applies to changing your behavior. Learning is a complex subject, yet its fundamentals follow a five-part sequence, as shown in Figure 1-2. To change your behavior, and therefore improve, you need a goal and a way to measure your current reality against this goal. You also need a way to assess that reality and a way to obtain feedback on the impact of your new actions.[6]

Goal or Desired State of Affairs

Changing your behavior, including enhancing your interpersonal relations, requires a clear goal or desired state of affairs. Your goal can also be regarded as what you want to accomplish as a result of your effort. A major reason that a goal is important is that having a specific goal improves performance. With a goal in mind, a person will usually not be satisfied until the goal is attained. So he or she keeps plugging away until the goal is attained, thereby increasing both personal satisfaction and performance on the task. Goals are also important because where people perceive that they have not attained their goal, they typically increase their effort or modify their strategy for reaching the goal.[7]

As a concrete example, let us take the common problem of a person who nibbles his fingernails during tense situations, such as being called on in a meeting. The nibbler might say, "My hopes [a goal] are to be able to sit in a meeting and not nibble my nails even though I know I might be called on." This man's desired state of affairs (his goal) is to avoid putting his nails in his mouth in order to appear calm and professional. Having a goal helps provide motivation and makes it possible to exercise the self-discipline necessary to follow through on your plans. In short, the goal focuses your effort on acquiring the improvements in behavior you seek.

FIGURE 1-2 A Model for Improving Interpersonal Skills

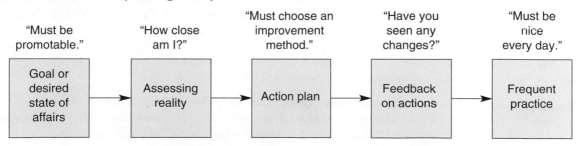

A FRAMEWORK FOR INTERPERSONAL SKILL DEVELOPMENT

Here we turn to Sean, a credit analyst who is being blocked from promotion because his manager perceives him as having poor interpersonal skills. After a discussion with his manager, Sean recognizes that he must improve his interpersonal relations if he wants to become a team leader.

Sean's goal is to be considered promotable to a leadership position. To achieve his goal, he will have to achieve the general goal of improving his interpersonal relations. By conferring with the human resources director, Sean learns that his broad goal of "improving my interpersonal relations" will have to be supported by more specific goals. Having poor interpersonal relations or "rubbing people the wrong way" includes many different behaviors. To begin, Sean selects one counterproductive behavior to improve: He is exceptionally intolerant of others and does not hide his intolerance. Sean's goal is to become less intolerant and more patient in his dealings with others on the job.

BACK TO THE OPENING CASE

When Todd learned that he was turned down for the promotion, he could have become upset and quit or taken some other form of revenge. Instead, he decided to take constructive action by further developing his interpersonal skills. The manager's constructive attitude was helpful to Todd, who was told that with a little more polish in dealing with people, he would be a logical choice for an assistant manager position. Todd's starting point in developing his human relations skills would be to consult with the human resources manager of the hotel.

Assessing Reality

The second major requirement for a method of changing behavior is to assess reality. Sean needs a way to assess how far he is from his goal of being eligible for promotion and how intolerant he is perceived to be. Sean has already heard from his manager, Alison, that he is not eligible for promotion right now. Sean might want to dig for more information by finding answers to the following questions:

"If I were more tolerant, would I be promoted now?"

"How bad are my interpersonal relations in the office?"

"How many people in the office think I rub them the wrong way?"

"How many deficiencies do my manager and coworkers perceive me to have?"

A starting point in answering these questions might be for Sean to confer with Alison about his behavior. To be more thorough, however, Sean might ask a friend in the office to help him answer the questions. A coworker is sometimes in an excellent position to provide feedback on how one is perceived by others in the office. Sean could also ask a confidant outside the office about his intolerance. Sean could ask a parent, a significant other, or both about the extent of his intolerance.

An Action Plan

action plan

A series of steps to achieve a goal.

The learning model needs some mechanism to change the relationship between the person and the environment. An **action plan** is a series of steps to achieve a goal. Without an action plan, a personal goal will be elusive. The person who sets the goal may not initiate steps to make his or her dream (a high-level goal) come true. If your goal is to someday become a self-employed business owner, your action plan should include saving money, establishing a good credit rating, and developing dozens of contacts.

Sean has to take some actions to improve his interpersonal relations, especially his intolerance. The change should ultimately lead to the promotion he desires. Sean's action plan for becoming more tolerant includes the following:

- Pausing to attempt to understand why a person is acting the way he or she does. An example would be attempting to understand why a sales representative wants to extend credit to a customer with a poor credit rating.

- Learning to control his own behavior so he does not make intolerant statements just because he is experiencing pressure.
- Taking a course in interpersonal skills or human relations.
- Asking Alison to give him a quick reminder whenever she directly observes or hears of him being intolerant toward customers or workmates.

In addition to formulating these action plans, Sean must have the self-discipline to implement them. For example, he should keep a log of situations in which he was intolerant and those in which he was tolerant. He might also make a mental note to attempt to be cooperative and flexible in most of his dealings at work. When a customer does not provide all the information Sean needs to assess his or her creditworthiness, Sean should remind himself to say, "I want to process your credit application as quickly as possible. To do this, I need some important additional information." Sean's reflex in the same situation had been to snap, "I can't read your mind. If you want to do business with us, you've got to stop hiding the truth."

Feedback on Actions

The fourth step in the learning model is to measure the effects of one's actions against reality. You obtain feedback on the consequences of your actions. When your skill-improvement goal is complex, such as becoming more effective at resolving conflict, you will usually have to measure your progress in several ways. You will also need both short- and long-term measures of the effectiveness of your actions. Long-term measures are important because skill-development activities of major consequence have long-range implications.

To obtain short-range feedback, Sean can consult with Alison to see whether she has observed any changes in his tolerance. Alison can also collect any feedback she hears from others in the office. Furthermore, Sean will profit from feedback over a prolonged period of time, perhaps one or two years. He will be looking to see whether his image has changed from an intolerant person who rubs people the wrong way to a tolerant person who has cordial interactions with others.

Frequent Practice

The final step in the learning model makes true skill development possible. Implementing the new behavior and using feedback for fine-tuning is an excellent start in acquiring a new interpersonal skill. For the skill to be long lasting, however, it must be integrated into your usual way of conducting yourself. In Sean's case, he will have to practice being tolerant regularly until it becomes a positive habit.

After a skill is programmed into your repertoire, it becomes a habit. This is important because a skill involves many habits. For example, good customer service skills include the habits of smiling and listening carefully. After you attempt the new interpersonal skills described in this book, you will need to practice them frequently to make a noticeable difference in your behavior.

A sports analogy is appropriate here. Assume that Marisa, a tennis player, takes a lesson to learn how to hit the ball with greater force. The instructor points out that the reason Marisa is not hitting with much force is that she is relying too much on her arm and not enough on her leg and body strength. To hit the ball with more force, Marisa is told that she must put one foot out in front of her when she strikes the ball (she must "step into" the ball).

Under the watchful eye of the coach, Marisa does put a foot out in front when she strikes the ball. Marisa is excited about the good results. But if Marisa fails to make the same maneuver with her feet during her tennis matches, she will persist in hitting weakly. If Marisa makes the effort to use her legs more effectively on almost every shot, she will soon integrate the new movement into her game.

In summary, the basics of a model for learning skills comprise five steps: goal or desired state of affairs   assessing reality   an action plan   feedback on actions   frequent practice. You must exercise self-discipline to complete each step. If you skip a step, you will be disappointed with the results of your interpersonal skill-development program.

Applying the Model for Improving Interpersonal Skills

The model for improving interpersonal skills is aimed at developing skills. At the same time, becoming effective in applying the model is a valuable skill within itself. You will need to apply the model perhaps a few times before you can become effective at developing an interpersonal skill when you want to. To get started with the model, attempt to develop an important yet basic interpersonal skill. For illustrative purposes, begin with enhancing your ability to give recognition to others for actions and words you consider meritorious. If you are already good at giving recognition, you can enhance your skill even further. For additional information, you might want to refer to the discussion about giving recognition in Chapter 10. The exercise under discussion should take a few minutes here and there spread out over several weeks.

Step 1: Goal or Desired State of Affairs

Your goal here is to learn how to give recognition, or to further enhance your skill in giving recognition. You want to recognize others in such a way that they are encouraged to keep up the good work. (Or, perhaps you have another related goal.)

Step 2: Assessing Reality

Ask a few confidants how good you already are in giving recognition. Ask questions such as "How good have I been in saying thank you?" "When you have done something nice for me, how did I react to you?" "How many thank-you notes have I sent you since you've known me?" Also, reflect on your own behavior in such matters as giving a server a big tip for exceptional service, or explaining to a tech specialist how much or he or she has helped you. Ask yourself whether you have ever thanked a teacher for an outstanding course, or explained to a coach how much his or her advice helped you.

Step 3: Action Plan

What are you going to do in the next few weeks to recognize the meritorious behavior of others? Will you be sending thank-you e-mail messages; warmly worded postcards; giving smiles and handshakes to people who help you; or larger-than-usual tips for excellent service with an explanation of why the tip is so large? Part of the action plan will be *who* are you going to recognize, *where* you are going to recognize them, *when* you will be giving recognition, and *how* (what form) of recognition will you be giving.

Step 4: Feedback on Actions

Observe carefully how people react to you recognition. Do they smile? Do they shrug off your form of recognition? It is especially important to observe how the person reacts to you during your next interaction. For example, does the server who you tipped so generously give you a big welcome? Does the bank teller who you thanked so sincerely seem eager to cash your next check? If you do not get the intended result from your recognition efforts, you might need to fine-tune your sincerity. Maybe when you sent a recognition e-mail you did not mention the person's name, and just wrote "Hey." Maybe you did not combine a thank you with a smile. Analyze carefully the feedback you receive.

Step 5: Frequent Practice

For this exercise perhaps you can only practice giving recognition in one or two settings. Yet if this exercise appears promising, you might continue to practice in the future. Should you continue to practice, you will be taking personal steps to make the world a better place.

BACK TO THE OPENING CASE

If Todd wanted to be promoted to assistant manager, he needed to refine his interpersonal skills. After being declined for promotion, Todd was a little despondent. However, he did work hard at developing his interpersonal skills, including taking a course in business communications. Eighteen months later the hotel chain acquired another hotel in the area, and Todd was promoted to assistant manager at the newly acquired hotel.

IDENTIFICATION OF DEVELOPMENTAL NEEDS

LEARNING OBJECTIVE 3

An important concept in skill development is that people are most likely to develop new skills when they feel the need for change. The importance of the perceived need for change is reflected in a variation of an old joke:

Question: How many psychologists does it take to change a light bulb?

Answer: None, if the light bulb wants to change.

As you read this book and do the experiential exercises, you will probably be more highly motivated to follow through with skill development in areas in which you think you need development. A specific area in which a person needs to change is referred to as a **developmental need**. For instance, some people may be too shy, too abrasive, or too intolerant, and some may not give others the encouragement they need.

developmental need

A specific area in which a person needs to change or improve.

To improve interpersonal skills, we must first be aware of how we are perceived by other people who interact with us.[8] Developmental needs related to interpersonal skills can be identified in several ways. First, if you are candid with yourself, you can probably point to areas in which you recognize that change is needed. You might reflect on your experiences and realize that you have had repeated difficulty in resolving conflict. Second, a related approach is to think of feedback you have received. If there has been consistency in asking you to improve in a particular area, you could hypothesize that the feedback has merit. Perhaps five different people have told you that you are not a good team player. "Becoming a better team player" might therefore be one of your developmental needs.

A third approach to assessing developmental needs is to solicit feedback. Ask the opinion of people who know you well to help you identify needs for improvement with respect to interpersonal skills. Present and previous managers are a valuable source of this type of feedback. A fourth approach to pinpointing developmental needs is closely related to the previous three: feedback from performance evaluations. If you have worked for a firm that uses performance evaluations to help people develop, you may have received constructive suggestions during the evaluation. For example, one manager told his assistant: "You need to project more self-confidence when you answer the phone. You sound so unsure and vague when you talk on the telephone. I have noticed this, and several customers have joked about it." The recipient of this feedback was prompted to participate in assertiveness training where she learned how to express herself more positively.

Self-Assessment Quiz 1-1 gives you the opportunity to identify your developmental needs. The same exercise is a first step in improving your interpersonal relations on the job because identification of a problem is the first—and most important—step toward change. For example, if you cite improving your relationships with people from cultures different from your own, you have planted the seeds for change. You are then more likely to seek out people from other cultures in the workplace or at school and cultivate their friendship.

Now that you (and perhaps another person) have identified specific behaviors that may require change, you need to draw up an action plan. Proceed with your action plan even though you have just begun studying this text, but peek ahead to relevant chapters if you wish. Describe briefly a plan of attack for bringing about the change you hope to achieve for each statement that is checked. Ideas for your action plan can come from information presented anywhere in this text, from outside reading, or from talking to a person experienced in dealing with people. A basic example would be to study materials about customer service and observe an effective model if you checked "I feel awkward dealing with a customer."

UNIVERSAL NEEDS FOR IMPROVING INTERPERSONAL RELATIONS

LEARNING OBJECTIVE 4

I have just described how understanding your unique developmental needs facilitates improving your interpersonal skills. There are also areas for skill improvement in interpersonal relations that are shared by most managerial, professional, technical, and sales personnel. These common areas for improvement are referred to as **universal training needs**. Almost any professional person, for example, could profit from enhancing his or her negotiation and listening skills.

universal training needs
An area for improvement common to most people.

This book provides the opportunity for skill development in a number of universal training needs. In working through these universal training needs, be aware that many of them will also fit your specific developmental needs. A given universal training need can be an individual's developmental need at the same time. It is reasonable to expect that you will be more strongly motivated to improve skills that relate closely to your developmental needs.

The major universal training needs covered in this text are as follows:

1. **Understanding individual differences.** To deal effectively with others in the workplace, it is necessary to recognize that people have different capabilities, needs, and interests.

What Are Your Developmental Needs?

This exercise is designed to heighten your self-awareness of areas in which you could profit from personal improvement. It is not a test, and there is no score, yet your answers to the checklist may prove helpful to you in mapping out a program of improvement in your interpersonal relations.

Directions: What follows are a number of specific aspects of behavior that suggest a person needs improvement in interpersonal skills. Check each statement that is generally true for you. You can add to the validity of this exercise by having one or two other people who know you well answer this form as they think it describes you. Then compare your self-analysis with their analysis of you.

*Place checkmark
in this column*

1. I'm too shy.	_____
2. I'm too overbearing and obnoxious.	_____
3. I intimidate too many people.	_____
4. I have trouble expressing my feelings.	_____
5. I make negative comments about people too readily.	_____
6. I have a difficult time solving problems when working in a group.	_____
7. I'm a poor team player.	_____
8. Very few people listen to me.	_____
9. It is difficult for me to relate well to people from different cultures.	_____
10. When I'm in conflict with another person, I usually lose.	_____
11. I hog too much time in meetings or in class.	_____
12. I'm very poor at office politics.	_____
13. People find me boring.	_____
14. It is difficult for me to criticize others.	_____
15. I'm too serious most of the time.	_____
16. My temper is too often out of control.	_____
17. I avoid controversy in dealing with others.	_____
18. It is difficult for me to find things to talk about with others.	_____
19. I don't get my point across well.	_____
20. I feel awkward dealing with a customer.	_____
21. I am a poor listener.	_____
22. I don't get the point of the importance of ethics in business.	_____
23. My attempts to lead others have failed.	_____
24. I rarely smile when I am with other people.	_____
25. I multitask when people are talking to me.	_____
26. _____ (Fill in your own statement.)	_____

2. **Interpersonal communication.** Effective communication with people is essential for carrying out more than 50 percent of the work conducted by most professional and managerial workers.

3. **Self-esteem and self-confidence.** To function effectively with people in most work and personal situations, people need to feel good about themselves and believe they can accomplish important tasks. Although self-esteem and self-confidence are essentially attitudes about the self, they also involve skills such as attaining legitimate accomplishments and using positive self-talk.

4. **Developing teamwork skills.** The most sweeping change in the organization of work in the past 30 years has been a shift to teams and away from traditional departments. Knowing how to be an effective team player therefore enhances your chances for success in the modern organization.

5. **Group problem solving and decision making.** As part of the same movement that emphasizes work teams, organizations now rely heavily on group problem solving. As a consequence, being an above-average contributor to group problem solving is a key part of effective interpersonal relations on the job. In addition to solving the problem, a decision must be made.

6. **Cross-cultural relations.** The modern workplace has greater cultural diversity than ever before. Being able to deal effectively with people from different cultures, from within and outside your own country, is therefore an important requirement for success.

7. **Resolving conflicts with others.** Conflict in the workplace is almost inevitable as people compete for limited resources. Effective interpersonal relations are therefore dependent upon knowing how to resolve conflict successfully.

8. **Becoming an effective leader.** In today's organizations a large number of people have the opportunity to practice leadership, even if on temporary assignment. Enhancing one's leadership skills is therefore almost a universal requirement.

9. **Motivating others.** Whether you have the title of manager or leader or are working alone, you have to know how to motivate the people whom you depend on to get your work accomplished. Given that few people are gifted motivators, most people can profit from skill development in motivation.

10. **Helping others develop.** As power is shared in organizations among managers and individual contributors (non-managers) alike, more people are required to help each other grow and develop. To carry out this role, most of us need skill development in coaching and mentoring.

11. **Positive political skills.** Whether you work in a small or large firm, part of having effective interpersonal relations is being able to influence others so your interests are satisfied. Positive political skills help you satisfy your interests without being unethical or devious.

12. **Customer service skills.** The current emphasis on customer satisfaction dictates that every worker should know how to provide good service to customers. Most people can benefit from strengthening their skills in serving both external and internal customers. (*Internal customers* are the people with whom you interact on the job.)

13. **Enhancing ethical behavior.** Although most workers in their heart know right from wrong, we can all sharpen our ability to make ethical decisions. By consistently making highly ethical decisions, people can improve their interpersonal relations.

14. **Personal productivity and stress management.** Having good work habits and time-management skills contributes to relating well to others even though they are not interpersonal skills themselves. By being efficient and productive and having your stress under control, you are in a better position to relate comfortably to others. Coworkers enjoy relating to a person who does not procrastinate and who is not visibly stressed.

15. **Job search and career-management skills.** Finding an outstanding job for yourself, holding on to the job, and moving ahead are not specifically interpersonal skills. However, both finding the right job for yourself and managing your career rely heavily on good interpersonal skills. Two basic examples are conducting yourself well in an interview and developing a network of contacts that can help you advance.

DEVELOPING INTERPERSONAL SKILLS ON THE JOB

The primary thrust of this book is to teach interpersonal skills that can be applied to the job. As part of enhancing your skills, it is essential to recognize that opportunities also exist in the workplace for developing interpersonal skills. This dual opportunity for learning soft skills is similar to the way hard skills are learned both inside and outside the classroom. Studying a text and doing laboratory exercises, for example, will help you learn useful information technology skills. On the job, one day you might be asked to insert a video on a Web site. Having never performed this task before, you may search a computer manual, ask questions of coworkers, telephone a help desk, and use trial and error. Within an hour, you have acquired a valuable new skill. The information technology skills you learned in the course facilitated learning new computer tasks, yet the actual learning of how to download the video was done on the job.

Here we look at two related aspects of learning interpersonal skills on the job: informal learning and specific developmental experiences.

Informal Learning

Business firms, as well as nonprofit organizations, invest an enormous amount of money and time in teaching interpersonal skills. Teaching methods include paying for employees to take outside courses; conducting training on company premises; using videoconferencing or courses on DVD; offering computer-assisted training; and reimbursing for distance learning courses on the Internet. Workers also develop interpersonal skills by interacting with work associates and observing how other people deal with interpersonal challenges. Figure 1-3 presents a summary of how people learn on the job. Observe that the learning experiences are a mixture of formal learning, such as that from company-provided training, and informal learning, which occurs from interaction with coworkers. Much of the learning shown in Figure 1-3 refers to technical skills and knowledge, but learning about interpersonal skills is also included.

informal learning

The acquisition of knowledge and skills that takes place naturally outside a structured learning environment.

Informal learning is the acquisition of knowledge and skills that takes place naturally outside a structured learning environment. In the context of the workplace, informal learning takes place without being designed by the organization. Learning can take place informally in such ways as speaking to the person in the next cubicle, asking a question of a coworker while in the hall, or calling the tech support center. A study of more than 1,000 employees at seven companies in seven states found that up to 70 percent of learning takes place informally. Another researcher reported about the same figure more recently.[9] The director of the first study emphasizes that formal training includes both a goal stated by the organization and a defined method or process. Informal learning can occur whether or not a goal is stated or the method is defined.

A trend in business is for employees to integrate formal classroom learning with informal learning. Boeing and the Bank of Montreal are two examples of major firms that have invested in facilities that provide formal and informal learning under one roof.[10]

FIGURE 1-3 Sources of Learning on the Job

Capital Works reported that we learn at work through the following means:

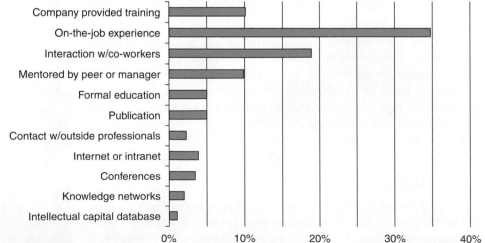

Source: Reprinted with permission. Capital Works, LLC, *http://agelesslearner.com/intros/informal.html.*

Top-level managers at both companies support the idea that formal and informal learning support rather than compete with each other.

Learning interpersonal skills informally can take place through such means as observing a coworker, manager, or team leader deal with a situation. A newly hired assistant store manager could not help seeing and overhearing a customer screaming at the store manager about a defective space heater. The manager said calmly, "It appears you are pretty upset about your heater that caused a short circuit in your house. What can I do to help you?" The customer calmed down as quickly as air being released from a balloon. The assistant store manager thought to herself, "Now I know how to handle a customer who has gone ballistic. I'll state what the customer is probably feeling, and then offer to help."

Informal learning can also occur when another person coaches you about how to handle a situation. The store manager might have said to the new assistant manager, "Let me tell you what to do in case you encounter a customer who goes ballistic. Summarize in a few words what he or she is probably feeling, and then offer to help. The effect can be remarkable." (This incident is classified as informal learning because it takes place outside a classroom.)

Formal and informal learning of interpersonal skills are useful supplements to each other. If you are formally learning interpersonal skills, your level of awareness for enhancing your interpersonal skills will increase. By formally studying interpersonal skills, you are likely to develop the following attitude: "What hints about dealing more effectively with people can I pick up on the job?" You may have noticed that if you are taking lessons in a sport, you become much more observant about watching the techniques of outstanding athletes in person or on television.

Specific Developmental Experiences

Another perspective on developing interpersonal skills in the workplace is that certain experiences are particularly suited to such development. Coping with a difficult customer, as previously suggested, would be one such scenario. Morgan W. McCall, Jr., for many years has studied ways in which leaders develop on the job. Contending with certain challenges is at the heart of these key learning experiences. Several of the powerful learning experiences that McCall has identified are particularly geared toward developing better interpersonal skills.[11]

- **Unfamiliar responsibilities.** The person has to handle responsibilities that are new, very different, or much broader than previous ones. Dealing with these unfamiliar responsibilities necessitates asking others for help and gaining their cooperation. For example, being assigned to supervise a group doing work unfamiliar to you would put you in a position of gaining the cooperation of group members who knew more about the work than you.

- **Proving yourself.** If you feel added pressure to show others that you can deal effectively with responsibilities, you are likely to develop skills in projecting self-confidence and persuading others.

- **Problems with employees.** If you supervise employees, or have coworkers, who lack adequate experience, are incompetent, or are poorly motivated, you need to practice such skills as effective listening and conflict resolution to work smoothly with them.

- **Influencing without authority.** An excellent opportunity for practicing influence skills is being forced to influence coworkers, higher management, company outsiders, and other key people over whom you have no control. Team leaders typically face the challenge of needing to influence workers whom they lack the authority to discipline or grant raises for. (The reason is that a team leader usually does not have as much formal authority as a traditional manager.)

- **Difficult manager.** If you and your manager have different opinions on how to approach problems, or if your manager has serious shortcomings, you will have to use your best human relations skills to survive. You will need to develop such subtle skills as using diplomacy to explain to your manager that his or her suggestion is completely unworkable.

The general point to be derived from these scenarios is that certain on-the-job challenges require a high level of interpersonal skill. Faced with such challenges, you will be prompted to use the best interpersonal skills you have. Formal training can be a big help because you might remember a skill that should be effective in a particular situation. Assume that you are faced with an overbearing manager who belittles you in front of others. You might be prompted to try a conflict-resolution technique you acquired in class.

SELF-ASSESSMENT QUIZ IN OVERVIEW

Self-Assessment Quiz 1-1, What Are Your Developmental Needs?, if answered accurately then acted upon, will help you considerably in your job performance and your career. However, capitalizing on your strengths is even more important for your personal growth, and these topics are discussed in Chapter 3 about building self-esteem, and Chapter 16 about advancing your career.

Concept Review and Reinforcement

Key Terms

interpersonal skill training, 4
action plan, 6

developmental need, 8
universal training needs, 9

informal learning, 12

Summary of Key Concepts

Effective interpersonal relations must be combined with technical knowledge to achieve success in any job involving interactions with people. This book presents a three-part strategy for achieving a high level of interpersonal skill. Each chapter presents concepts related to an area of interpersonal skill, behavioral guidelines, and experiential exercises. Interpersonal skill training is also referred to as soft-skills training to differentiate it from technical training.

A five-part model of learning can be applied to improving interpersonal skills. First, state a goal or desired state of affairs. Second, assess the reality of how far you are from your goal. Third, develop an action plan to change the relationship between the person and the environment. Self-discipline is required to implement the action plan. Fourth, solicit feedback on actions to measure the effects of your actions against reality. Fifth, continue to practice your newly learned skill.

People are most likely to develop new skills when they feel the need for change. A developmental need is the specific area in which a person needs to change. Identifying

your developmental needs in relation to interpersonal relations can be achieved through self-analysis and feedback from others. You can also solicit feedback and make use of the feedback you have received in performance appraisals.

Universal training needs are those areas for improvement that are common to most people. The major topics in this text reflect universal training needs because they are necessary for success in most positions involving interaction with people.

Opportunities exist in the workplace to develop interpersonal skills. A general approach to developing these skills is informal learning, whereby you acquire skills naturally outside a structured work environment. Informal learning of interpersonal skills often takes place through such means as observing a coworker, manager, or team leader cope with a situation. Certain workplace experiences are particularly well suited to developing interpersonal skills. These include unfamiliar responsibilities, proving oneself, having problems with employees, influencing without authority, and having a difficult manager.

Check Your Understanding

1. In recent years, several of the most prestigious business schools, such as those at Wharton, Massachusetts Institute of Technology (MIT), and the University of Virginia, have placed much more emphasis on teaching soft skills. Why do you think this change might have come about?

2. In your opinion, do supervisors of entry-level workers rely more on soft skills or hard skills to accomplish their work?

3. Why do people need soft skills in an era of high technology?

4. A recent article about conducting yourself well at meetings recommended that people do not chew gum or accept cell phone calls during a business meeting. Why are some intelligent and well-educated people so rude on the job? (Or is the writer of the article simply out of touch with the modern world?)

5. How does a person know whether the feedback he or she receives from another person is accurate?

6. How could doing a thorough job with Self-Assessment Quiz 1-1 have a major impact on a person's career?

7. Many business executives, as well as people in public office, have been forced out of their positions because they made "inappropriate sexually oriented comments" to young workers on their staff. What do you think is wrong with these executives and politicians with respect to interpersonal skills?

8. Based on what you have learned so far in this book, and your own intuition, how would you respond to the statement, "You can't learn how to get along with people from reading a book"?

9. Give an example of a skill you might have learned informally at any point in your life.

10. Why are soft skills alone usually not sufficient for building a successful career?

The Web Corner

http://www.internettime.com/Learning
(Informal learning.)

http://members.aol.com/chass522/
(Interpersonal skill development.)

http://www.cdevelop.com/Ropes.htm
(Developing interpersonal skills through a challenge course.)

Internet Skill Builder: The Importance of Interpersonal Skills

One of the themes of this chapter as well as the entire book is that interpersonal skills are important for success in business. But what do employers really think? To find out, visit the Web sites of five of your favorite companies, such as *http://www.Starbucks.com* or *http://www.ge.com*. Go to the employment section and search for a job that you might qualify for now or in the future. Investigate which interpersonal or human relations skills the employer mentions as a requirement, such as "Must have superior spoken communication skills." Make up a list of the interpersonal skills you find mentioned. What conclusion or conclusions do you reach from this exercise?

Developing Your Human Relations Skills

Interpersonal Relations Case 1.1

Nobody Likes Me

Marge Caitlin, the supervisor of inventory control, was walking down the aisle with BlackBerry in hand, ruminating about the major inventory-reduction program taking place at the company. She thought to herself, "The CEO is putting a lot of pressure on us to trim inventory to the bone. Yet the manufacturing and sales groups want enough inventory available so they can do their job. We really have to get focused and creative to satisfy everybody."

As Caitlin hurried down the aisle thinking about the inventory challenge, she still kept a watchful eye on her staff working in their cubicles. She noticed that Phil Baxter, one of the inventory control analysts, was looking even more discouraged than usual. Caitlin put aside her BlackBerry, and tapped on the entrance to Baxter's cubicle. "Can we talk?" said Caitlin with a reassuring smile on her face.

"Sure," said Baxter. "Did I screw up again?"

"Phil, there you go putting yourself down again," said Caitlin. "I just noticed that you look a little glum today. I want to know if you are having a problem that I could help with."

"Thanks, Marge, for being interested in my problems. It's really nothing new—just the same old problem that I have had in school and on the job. Nobody likes me. Nobody wants me. It gets sickening after a while."

"What makes you so sure that nobody likes you and that nobody wants you?" asked Caitlin.

Baxter responded, "First of all, almost nobody asks me to go out to lunch with him or her. Second, when you asked us to form our own teams, no team invited me to join them. I was finally chosen to be on one of the three teams because I was the last person not assigned."

"What do you think is your problem?" asked Caitlin.

"Maybe you could tell me. I think people see me as kind of a nerd. Maybe I'm just not likeable. I don't think I'm special in any way."

"Just hang in there for a while," said Caitlin. "After this big inventory overhaul is completed, I will get back to you with some suggestions."

"I'll be waiting for your magic bullet," said Baxter with a dejected look.

Case Questions

1. What developmental needs does Phil Baxter appear to have?
2. If you were Marge Caitlin, what would your recommend that Baxter do?
3. From the little evidence that you have, what is your opinion of Caitlin's interpersonal skills?

Interpersonal Relations Case 1.2

How Do You Say No to Girl Scout Cookies?

Bok Lei Goodman finds it hard to say no to a colleague selling Girl Scout cookies. "I know it's a good cause, but it can make you feel uncomfortable," said Goodman, of Greenville, Delaware, who is a real estate agent.

Goodman is not the only one who sometimes resents being put on the spot at work by fund-raising coworkers or folks pushing cosmetics, vitamins, or cleaning products. Because of what many see as an increase in at-work solicitations, several employers now ban selling in the office with explicit written antisolicitation policies to eliminate

the sale or distribution of materials on behalf of another organization, according to Jen Jorgensen, spokesperson for the Society for Human Resource Management.

The society's sample "NO solicitations" policy available to members states, in part, that solicitations for money, products, services, and memberships are not permitted on company property except in nonwork areas during nonwork time.

"I do think that more companies are putting in place policies to limit it," said John A. Challenger, chief executive of the Challenger, Gray & Christmas outplacement firm. "The solicitations at work seem to be getting more prevalent. Each office has one or two people who seem to inflict their charities on their coworkers."

"Some people are less able to stand up for themselves than others," said Devona E. G. Williams, president of an organizational performance firm.

Case Questions

1. What developmental needs might workers such as Bok Lei Goodman have in relation to their dealing with charity appeals at the office?

2. What developmental needs might the workers have who sell products for charity at the office?
3. Why might this case about soliciting for charity be considered a human relations problem?

Source: Maureen Milford, "Selling at Work Frowned Upon," Gannett News Service, March 21, 2005.

Interpersonal Skills Role-Play 1.1

Selling at the Office

One student plays the role of Kristina, who sells wellness products such as vitamins and food supplements for a direct sales company. (Direct sales are from person to person, and not distributed through stores.) Kristina is working hard to reach her goal for the month, and she just needs to sell $75 more of products to attain her goal. Another student plays the role of Ricardo, who enjoys working with Kristina but thinks that wellness products are overrated. During lunch in the company cafeteria, Kristina approaches Ricardo and begins her sales pitch about her wonderful life-enhancing products.

Run the role-play for about six minutes, while other class members observe the interactions, and later provide feedback about the interpersonal skills displayed by Kristina and Ricardo.

CHAPTER 2

Understanding Individual Differences

At Intuit, the Mountain View, California, maker of Quicken, TurboTax, and other money-management software, CEO Steve Bennett understands that employees who are unhappy at work won't contribute their best efforts—on the job or even at home. "It will cause trouble in their personal relationships," he says. He tells his Intuit managers to create a "psychological contract" with every employee, spelling out what is expected of them, how well they are performing, and what they must do to advance.

When he joined Intuit six years ago, Bennett found a company where employees didn't know how to handle differing emotions and opinions. They were afraid to counter one another at meetings and they couldn't make decisions without spending hours trying to reach a consensus. He subsequently urged all employees to voice their views and without fear of offending anyone.

"We want everyone to aim for what we call True North objectives—or better short-term as well as long-term results—and we want everyone to feel enthused and connected at work," says Bennett, who spends half his time coaching employees. "If you accept this contract and want to learn but aren't getting good results, we'll find you a job at the company where you can perform better."[1]

The scenario that took place at Intuit illustrates how the ability to manage emotions on the job can contribute to business and individual success. One of the many topics about individuals we study in this chapter concerns emotional intelligence, or managing emotions. The major theme of this chapter deals with how people vary in a wide range of personal factors.

Learning Objectives

After reading and studying this chapter and doing the exercises, you should be able to

1. Make adjustments for the individual differences among people in dealing with them on the job.
2. Develop insight into how your personality, mental ability, emotional intelligence, and values differ from others.
3. Respond to personality differences among people.
4. Respond to mental ability differences among people.
5. Respond to differences in values among people.

Individual differences exert a profound effect on job performance and behavior. Such differences refer to variations in how people respond to the same situation based on personal characteristics. One of hundreds of possible examples is that some people can concentrate longer and harder on their work, thereby producing more and higher quality work than others.

This chapter describes several of the major sources of individual differences on the job. It also gives you the chance to measure your standing on several key dimensions of behavior and helps you develop skill in responding to individual differences. Knowing how to respond to such differences is the cornerstone of effective interpersonal relations.

> **individual differences**
>
> Variations in how people respond to the same situation based on personal characteristics.

PERSONALITY

LEARNING OBJECTIVE 1

LEARNING OBJECTIVE 2

"We're not going to promote you to department head," said the manager to the analyst. "Although you are a great troubleshooter, you've alienated too many people in the company. You're too blunt and insensitive." As just implied, most successes and failures in people-contact jobs are attributed largely to interpersonal skills. And personality traits are important contributors to interpersonal, or human relations, skills.

Personality refers to persistent and enduring behavior patterns and tend to be expressed in a wide variety of situations. A person who is brash and insensitive in one situation is likely to behave similarly in many other situations. Your personality is what makes you unique. Your walk, your talk, your appearance, your speech, and your inner values and conflicts all contribute to your personality. Have you ever noticed that when you know a person well, you can identify that person by his or her footsteps even though you do not see the individual? This is true because many people have a distinctive gait.

I illustrate the importance of personality to interpersonal relations in organizations by describing eight key personality traits and personality types related to cognitive styles. In addition, you are given guidelines for dealing effectively with different personality types.

> **personality**
>
> Persistent and enduring behavior patterns that tend to be expressed in a variety of situations.

Eight Major Personality Factors and Traits

Many psychologists believe that the basic structure of human personality is represented by five broad factors, known as the Big Five: neuroticism, extraversion (the scientific

FIGURE 2-1 Eight Personality Factors Related to Interpersonal Skills

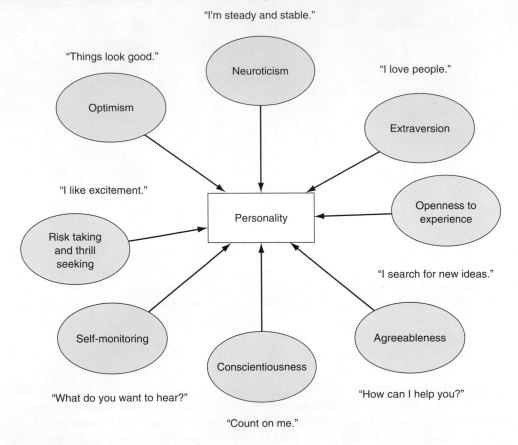

"I'm steady and stable."

"Things look good."

Neuroticism

"I love people."

Optimism

Extraversion

"I like excitement."

Personality

Openness to experience

Risk taking and thrill seeking

"I search for new ideas."

Self-monitoring

Agreeableness

Conscientiousness

"What do you want to hear?"

"How can I help you?"

"Count on me."

spelling of *extroversion*), openness, agreeableness, and conscientiousness. This approach to understanding personality is often referred to as the Five-Factor Model. Three more key personality factors—self-monitoring of behavior, risk taking and thrill seeking, and optimism—are so important for human relations that they are considered here.

All eight factors have a substantial impact on interpersonal relations and job performance. The interpretations and meanings of these factors provide useful information because they help you pinpoint important areas for personal development. Although these factors are partially inherited, most people can improve them, providing they exert much conscious effort over a period of time. For example, it usually takes a minimum of three months of effort before a person is perceived to be more agreeable. The eight factors, shown in Figure 2-1, are described in the following list.

1. *Neuroticism* reflects emotional instability and identifies people prone to psychological distress and coping with problems in unproductive ways. Traits associated with this personality factor include being anxious, insecure, angry, embarrassed, emotional, and worried. A person of low neuroticism—or high emotional stability—is calm and confident, and usually in control.

2. *Extraversion* reflects the quantity or intensity of social interactions, the need for social stimulation, self-confidence, and competition. Traits associated with extraversion include being sociable, gregarious, assertive, talkative, and active. An outgoing person is often described as extraverted, whereas introverted persons are described as reserved, timid, and quiet.

3. *Openness* reflects the proactive seeking of experience for its own sake. Traits associated with openness include being creative, cultured, intellectually curious, broad-minded, and artistically sensitive. People who score low on this personality factor are practical, with narrow interests.

4. *Agreeableness* reflects the quality of one's interpersonal orientation. Traits associated with the agreeableness factor include being courteous, flexible, trusting,

good-natured, cooperative, forgiving, softhearted, and tolerant. The other end of the continuum includes disagreeable, cold, and antagonistic people.

5. *Conscientiousness* reflects organization, self-restraint, persistence, and motivation toward attaining goals. Traits associated with conscientiousness include being hardworking, dependable, well organized, and thorough. The person low in conscientiousness is lazy, disorganized, and unreliable.

6. *Self-monitoring* of behavior refers to the process of observing and controlling how we are perceived by others. Self-monitoring involves three major and somewhat distinct tendencies: (1) willingness to be the *center of attention*, (2) *sensitivity* to the reactions of others, and (3) ability and willingness to a*djust* behavior to induce positive reactions in others. High self-monitors are pragmatic and even chameleonlike actors in social groups. They often say what others want to hear. Low self-monitors avoid situations that require them to adapt to outer images. In this way their outer behavior adheres to their inner values. Low self-monitoring can often lead to inflexibility. Take Self-Assessment Quiz 2-1 to measure your self-monitoring tendencies.

7. *Risk taking and thrill seeking* refer to the propensity to take risks and pursue thrills. Persons with high standing on this personality trait are sensation-seekers who pursue novel, intense, and complex sensations. They are willing to take risks for the sake of such experiences. The search for giant payoffs and daily thrills motivates people with an intense need for risk taking and thrill seeking.[2] Take Self-Assessment Quiz 2-2 to measure your propensity for risk taking and thrill seeking.

8. *Optimism* refers to a tendency to experience positive emotional states, and to typically believe that positive outcomes will be forthcoming from most activities. The other end of the scale is *pessimism*—a tendency to experience negative emotional states, and to typically believe that negative outcomes will be forthcoming from most activities. Optimism versus pessimism is also referred to in more technical terms as *positive affectivity versus negative affectivity*, and is considered a major personality trait. A person's tendency toward having positive affectivity (optimism) versus negative affectivity (pessimism) also influences job satisfaction. Being optimistic, as you would suspect, tends to enhance job satisfaction.[3]

Evidence for the relevance of the Five-Factor Model (traits one through five of the previous list) of personality in understanding human behavior comes from a cross-cultural study involving 7,134 individuals. The five-factor structure of the American personality was also found to hold true for German, Portuguese, Hebrew, Chinese, Korean, and Japanese samples when the personality test questions were translated into each of these languages. Based on this extensive study, it was concluded that personality structure is universal, much like the structure of the brain or the body.[4] Another look at the evidence found that extraversion, agreeableness, and conscientiousness are major personality factors in most cultures. Neuroticism and openness are more dependent on the culture and are particularly relevant in the United States.[5]

The Eight Factors and Traits and Job Performance

Depending on the job, any one of the preceding personality factors can be important for success. One explanation for personality being tied to performance is that a particular personality trait gives us a bias or positive spin to certain actions.[6] A person high in conscientiousness, for example, believes that if people are diligent they will accomplish more work and receive just rewards. Conscientiousness relates to job performance for many different occupations, and has proven to be the personality factor most consistently related to success. However, there are a few instances in which being highly conscientious can interfere with job success. If the job requires considerable spontaneity and imagination, a highly conscientious person might perform poorly because he or she dislikes breaking the rules or straying from conventional thinking.[7] For example, a conscientious

The Self-Monitoring Scale

Directions: The statements below concern your personal reactions to a number of different situations. No two statements are exactly alike, so consider each statement carefully before answering. If a statement is true or mostly true as applied to you, *circle the "T"* next to the question. If a statement is false or not usually true as applied to you, *circle the "F"* next to the question.

(T) (F) 1. I find it hard to imitate the behavior of other people.

(T) (F) 2. My behavior is usually an expression of my true inner feelings, attitudes, and beliefs.

(T) (F) 3. At parties and social gatherings, I do not attempt to do or say things that others will like.

(T) (F) 4. I can only argue for ideas which I already believe.

(T) (F) 5. I can make impromptu speeches even on topics about which I have almost no information.

(T) (F) 6. I guess I put on a show to impress or entertain people.

(T) (F) 7. When I am uncertain how to act in a social situation, I look to the behavior of others for cues.

(T) (F) 8. I would probably make a good actor.

(T) (F) 9. I rarely seek the advice of my friends to choose movies, books, or music.

(T) (F) 10. I sometimes appear to others to be experiencing deeper emotions than I actually am.

(T) (F) 11. I laugh more when I watch a comedy with others than when alone.

(T) (F) 12. In groups of people, I am rarely the center of attention.

(T) (F) 13. In different situations and with different people, I often act like very different persons.

(T) (F) 14. I am not particularly good at making other people like me.

(T) (F) 15. Even if I am not enjoying myself, I often pretend to be having a good time.

(T) (F) 16. I'm not always the person I appear to be.

(T) (F) 17. I would not change my opinions (or the way I do things) in order to please someone else or win their favor.

(T) (F) 18. I have considered being an entertainer.

(T) (F) 19. In order to get along and be liked, I tend to be what people expect me to be rather than anything else.

(T) (F) 20. I have never been good at games like charades or improvisational acting.

(T) (F) 21. I have trouble changing my behavior to suit different people and different situations.

(T) (F) 22. At a party, I let others keep the jokes and stories going.

(T) (F) 23. I feel a bit awkward in company and do not show up quite as well as I should.

(T) (F) 24. I can look anyone in the eye and tell a lie with a straight face (if for a right end).

(T) (F) 25. I may deceive people by being friendly when I really dislike them.

Scoring and Interpretation: Give yourself one point each time your answer agrees with the key. A score that is between 0-12 would indicate that you are a relatively low self-monitor; a score that is between 13-25 would indicate that you are relatively high self-monitor.

1. F	10. T	19. T
2. F	11. T	20. F
3. F	12. F	21. F
4. F	13. T	22. F
5. T	14. F	23. F
6. T	15. T	24. T
7. T	16. T	25. T
8. T	17. F	
9. F	18. T	

Source: Mark Snyder, Professor of Psychology, University of Minnesota.

advertising worker might hesitate to develop a television advertisement that depicts a woman jumping out of a building onto a United Parcel Service (UPS) delivery truck.

As explained in the previous discussion, each of the Big Five factors is composed of more narrow or specific traits. With respect to conscientiousness, the specific trait of *dependability* may be the most important contributor to job performance.[8]

Another important research finding is that extraversion is associated with success for managers and sales representatives. The explanation is that managers and salespeople are required to interact extensively with other people.[9] For people who want to advance in their careers, being a high self-monitor is important. An analysis was made of the self-monitoring personality by combining 136 studies involving 23,101 people. A major finding was that high self-monitors tend to receive better performance ratings than low self-monitors. High self-monitors were also more likely to emerge as leaders and work their way into top management positions.[10]

Another advantage to being a high self-monitor is that the individual is more likely to help out other workers, even when not required.[11] An example would be helping a worker outside your department with a currency exchange problem even though this was not your responsibility. The willingness to go beyond one's job description without a specific reward apparent is referred to as **organizational citizenship behavior.** Good organizational citizens are highly valued by employers. A recent perspective on organizational citizenship behavior is that an employee will make a short-term sacrifice that leads to long-term benefits to the organization.[12] An example would be an employee voluntarily working from home to deal with customer confusion about a product recall, which would lead to more loyal and appreciative customers.

A study with 141 customer service employees demonstrated that having low standing on the Big Five personality factors is associated with counterproductive work behavior such as (a) taking property without company permission and (b) playing a mean prank on a coworker. The customer service employees most likely to engage in these behaviors scored low on agreeableness and conscientious, and high on neuroticism. The same study

organizational citizenship behavior

The willingness to go beyond one's job description without a specific reward apparent.

showed that when employees were more satisfied with their job, they were less likely to be counterproductive.[13] Experienced workers are likely to be aware of this fact, and a scientific study like this would reinforce their observations.

A combination of personality factors will sometimes be more closely associated with job success than one factor alone. A study about personality and job performance ratings was conducted with diverse occupations, including clerical workers and wholesale appliance sales representatives. A key finding was that conscientious workers who also scored high on agreeableness performed better than conscientious workers who were less agreeable.[14] (Being agreeable toward your manager helps elevate performance evaluations!) A study with experienced pharmaceutical sales representatives found that the combination of extraversion and conscientiousness was associated with higher sales. However, being conscientious was the personality factor most closely associated with growth in sales over several years for the experienced sales representatives.[15]

Optimism and pessimism also can be linked to job performance. Optimism can be quite helpful when attempting such tasks as selling a product or service or motivating a group of people. Yet psychologist Julie Normen has gathered considerable evidence that pessimism can sometimes enhance job performance. Pessimists usually assume that something will go wrong, and will carefully prepare to prevent botches and bad luck. A pessimist, for example, will carefully back up computer files or plan for emergencies that might shut down operations.[16]

Personality Types and Cognitive Styles

People go about solving problems in various ways. You may have observed, for example, that some people are more analytical and systematic while others are more intuitive. The most widely used method of classifying problem-solving styles is the Myers-Briggs Type Indicator (MBTI®). Many readers of this book will have already taken the MBTI. Modes of problem solving are referred to as **cognitive styles**. According to this method of understanding problem-solving styles, your personality traits strongly influence how you approach problems, such as being introverted gives you a preference for working with ideas. Knowledge of these cognitive styles can help you relate better to people because you can better appreciate how they make decisions.

The MBTI is a self-report questionnaire designed to make the theory of psychological types developed by psychoanalyst Carl Jung applicable to everyday life. Jung developed the theory of psychological types, but he did not develop the measuring instrument in question. Katharine Cook Briggs and Isabel Briggs Myers are the authors of the MBTI.

More than 2 million assessments are administered to individuals annually—including many employees of Fortune 500 companies. The purposes of using the MBTI include team building, career exploration, conflict management, leadership development and coaching, retention, and exploring the world of work. The administrations must be given by a certified MBTI administrator. The developers of the MBTI caution that the instrument should be taken voluntarily, and should not be used in the hiring or firing process.

As measured by the MBTI instrument, four separate dichotomies direct the typical use of perception and judgment by an individual. The four dichotomies can also be considered a person's cognitive style.

1. **Extraversion–Introversion dichotomy of attitudes or orientations of energy.** Extraverts direct their energy primarily toward the outer world of people and objects. In contrast, introverts direct their energy primarily toward the inner world of experiences and ideas.

2. **Sensing–Intuition dichotomy of functions or processes of perception.** People who rely on sensing focus primarily on what can be perceived by the five primary senses of vision, touch, sight, sound, and smell. People who rely on intuition focus primarily on perceiving patterns and interrelationships.

3. **Thinking–Feeling dichotomy of functions or processes of judgment.** People who rely primarily on thinking base conclusions on logical analysis and emphasize objectivity and detachment. People who rely on feelings base conclusions on personal or social values, and focus on understanding and harmony.

cognitive style

Mental processes used to perceive and make judgments from situations.

FIGURE 2-2 Four Cognitive Styles of the Myers-Briggs Typology

ENTP (Conceptualizer)	ISTJ (Traditionalist)	INTJ (Visionary)	ESTJ (Organizer)
Quick, ingenious, will argue either side of issue for fun, may neglect routine assignments. (Good for creative work where deadlines are not crucial.)	Serious, quiet, practical, logical, dependable. (Good for work requiring careful attention to detail such as accountant or auditor.)	Original thinking, determined to implement, skeptical, critical, independent, and high standards. (Good for major leadership role such as CEO.)	Practical, realistic, has a natural mind for business or mechanics, likes to organize and run activities. (Good for manufacturing supervisor.)

Note: I = Introvert, E = Extravert, T = Thinking, F = Feeling, S = Sensing, N = Intuitive, J = Judging, and P = Perceiving.

Source: Modified and reproduced by special permission of the Publisher, CPP, Inc., Mountain View, CA 94043. From *Introduction to Type*, 6th ed., by Isabel Briggs Myers and Katharine D. Myers, p. 13. All rights reserved. Further reproduction is prohibited without the Publisher's written consent.

4. **Judging–Perceiving dichotomy of attitudes or orientations toward dealing with the outside world.** People who use the judging process prefer to use the judging processes of Thinking or Feeling because the processes lead to decisiveness and closure. People who use one of the Perceiving processes (Sensing or Intuition) do so because they prefer the flexibility and spontaneity that results from using these processes.[17]

Combining the four types with each other results in 16 personality types, such as ISTJ people who I (draw energy from and pay attention to their inner world); S (like information that is real and factual); T (use logical analysis in decision making); and J (like a structured and planned life). Four of the personality types relate directly to cognitive styles as shown in Figure 2-2. People with different cognitive styles prefer different occupations.[18]

You might want to take the MBTI in an authorized center such as a counseling center to discover your type. CPP, Inc., can refer customers to the organization that can offer qualification and certification programs at http://www.cpp.com. You can also study these four types and make a tentative judgment as to whether one of them fits your problem-solving style. Recognizing your problem-solving style can help you identify work that you are likely to perform well, as detailed in Figure 2-2. For example, the ENTP cognitive type is labeled the "conceptualizer." He or she is passionate about new opportunities and dislikes routine, and is more likely to be an entrepreneur than a corporate manager. The ISTJ cognitive type is labeled the "traditionalist," and will often become an accountant or financial analyst. The INJT type is labeled the "visionary." Although a small proportion of the population, these individuals are often chief executives of business firms. One of the most common types among people in general, as well as among managers, is the ESTJ, labeled the "organizer."

Far too many people overinterpret Myers-Briggs personality types as being definitive indicators of an individual's personality, and therefore pigeonhole that person. In contrast, the founders of the MBTI caution us: "You may use type to understand and forgive yourself, but not as an excuse for doing or *not* doing anything. Type should *not* keep you from considering any career, activity, or relationship."[19]

An interpersonal skills application of understanding the Myers-Briggs personality types is to help people get along better within a work group. All the group or team members would have their types assessed using the MBTI, and all members would be made aware of each other's type or working style. Knowing your type among the 16 types, and the type of the other group members would give you some clues for working smoothly together.

To illustrate, I will use a couple of the types shown in Figure 2-2. Visualize yourself as a member of a work group. You know that Nick is a visionary (INTJ). The group has an assignment that calls for creating something new, so you consult with Nick to capitalize on his original thinking, high standards, and determination to follow through. Yet you know that you and Margot are organizers (ESJT), so you two will play a heavy role in helping translate Nick's plan into action. And you, Nick, and Margot know that Jason is a traditionalist (ISTJ), so you will have to work slowly with him to get him involved in the new project. The reason is that Jason is quiet and likes to focus on details.

Guidelines for Dealing with Different Personality Types

LEARNING OBJECTIVE 3

A key purpose in presenting information about a sampling of various personality types is to provide guidelines for individualizing your approach to people. As a basic example, if you wanted to score points with an introvert, you would approach that person in a restrained, laid-back fashion. In contrast, a more gregarious, lighthearted approach might be more effective with an extravert. The purpose of individualizing your approach is to build a better working relationship or to establish rapport with the other person. To match your approach to dealing with a given personality type, you must first arrive at an approximate diagnosis of the individual's personality. The following suggestions are therefore restricted to readily observable aspects of personality:

1. When relating to a person who appears to be neurotic based on symptoms of worry and tension, be laid back and reassuring. Do not attempt to project your own anxiety and fears. Be a good listener. If possible, minimize the emphasis on deadlines and the dire consequences of a project's failing. Show concern and interest in the person's welfare.

2. When relating to an extraverted individual, emphasize friendliness, warmth, and a stream of chatter. Talk about people more than ideas, things, or data. Express an interest in a continuing working relationship.

3. When relating to an introverted individual, move slowly in forming a working relationship. Do not confuse quietness with a lack of interest. Tolerate moments of silence. Emphasize ideas, things, and data more heavily than people.

4. When relating to a person who is open to experience, emphasize information sharing, idea generation, and creative approaches to problems. Appeal to his or her intellect by discussing topics of substance rather than ordinary chatter and gossip.

5. When relating to a person who is closed to experience, stick closely to the facts of the situation at hand. Recognize that the person prefers to think small and deal with the here and now.

6. When relating to an agreeable person, just relax and be yourself. Reciprocate with kindness to sustain a potentially excellent working relationship.

7. When relating to a disagreeable person, be patient and tolerant. At the same time, set limits on how much mistreatment you will take. Disagreeable people sometimes secretly want others to put brakes on their antisocial behavior.

8. When relating to a conscientious person, give him or her freedom and do not nag. The person will probably honor commitments without prompting. Conscientious people are often taken for granted, so remember to acknowledge the person's dependability.

9. When relating to a person of low conscientiousness, keep close tabs on him or her, especially if you need the person's output to do your job. Do not assume that because the person has an honest face and a pleasing smile he or she will deliver as promised. Frequently follow up on your requests, and impose deadlines if you have the authority. Express deep appreciation when the person does follow through.

10. When dealing with a person whom you suspect is a high self-monitor, be cautious in thinking that the person is really in support of your position. The person could

Personality Role-Plays

The Extravert: One student assumes the role of a successful outside sales representative who has just signed a $3 million order for the company. The sales rep comes back to the office elated. The other student assumes the role of a member of the office support staff. He or she decides this is a splendid opportunity to build a good relationship with the triumphant sales rep. Run the role-play for about seven minutes. The people not involved in the role-play will observe and then provide feedback when the role-play is completed. (These directions regarding time, observation, and feedback also apply to the two other role-plays in this exercise and throughout the book.)

Openness: One student plays the role of an experienced worker in the department who is told to spend some time orienting a new co-op student or intern. It appears that this new person is open to experience. Another student plays the role of the co-op student who is open to experience and eager to be successful in this new position.

Sensing and Intuiting Types: One student plays the role of a sensing-type individual who is responsible for reviewing the company expense accounts. The other student plays the role of a manager in whose department many expense account abuses (such as lack of documentation and high expenses) have been uncovered. This manager is an intuitive type. The person in charge of the accounts is visiting the manager in the latter's office to discuss this problem.

just be following his or her natural tendency to appear to please others, but not really feel that way.

11. When relating to a person with a high propensity for risk taking and thrill seeking, emphasize the risky and daring aspects of activities familiar to you. Talk about a new product introduction in a highly competitive market, stock options, investment in high-technology start-up firms, skydiving, and race car driving.

12. When relating to a person with a low propensity for risk taking and thrill seeking, emphasize the safe and secure aspects of activities familiar to you. Talk about the success of an established product in a stable market (like pencils and paper clips), investment in U.S. Treasury bonds, life insurance, camping, and gardening.

13. When dealing with a sensing-type person, emphasize facts, figures, and conventional thinking without sacrificing your own values. To convince the sensing type, emphasize logic more than emotional appeal. Focus on details more than the big picture.

14. When dealing with an intuiting-type individual, emphasize feelings, judgments, playing with ideas, imagination, and creativity. Focus more on the big picture than details.

To start putting these guidelines into practice, do the role-plays in Skill-Building Exercise 2-1. Remember that a role-player is an extemporaneous actor. Put yourself in the shoes of the character you play and visualize how he or she would act. Because you are given only the general idea of a script, use your imagination to fill in the details.

MENTAL ABILITY

Mental ability, or intelligence, is one of the major sources of individual differences that affects job performance and behavior. **Intelligence** is the capacity to acquire and apply knowledge, including solving problems. Intelligent workers can best solve abstract problems. In an exceedingly simple job, such as packing shoes into boxes, having below-average intelligence can be an advantage because the employee is not likely to become bored.

intelligence

The capacity to acquire and apply knowledge, including solving problems.

Understanding the nature of intelligence contributes to effective interpersonal relations in the workplace. Your evaluation of a person's intelligence can influence how you relate to that person. For example, if you think a person is intelligent, you will tend to seek his or her input on a difficult problem. If you realize that different types of intelligence exist, you are more likely to appreciate people's strengths. You are thus less likely to judge others as being either good or poor problem solvers.

Four important aspects of mental ability include: (1) the components of traditional intelligence, (2) practical intelligence, (3) multiple intelligences, and (4) emotional intelligence. (This fourth type of intelligence can also be regarded as personality, not mental ability.) Knowledge of the four aspects will enrich your understanding of other workers and yourself.

Components of Traditional Intelligence

Intelligence consists of more than one component. A component of intelligence is much like a separate mental aptitude. Evidence suggests that intelligence consists of a **g (general) factor** and **s (special) factors** that contribute to problem-solving ability. Scores of tests of almost any type (such as math, aptitude for spatial relations, or reading skill) are somewhat influenced by the *g* factor. The *g* factor helps explain why some people perform well in so many different mental tasks. Substantial evidence has accumulated over the years indicating that workers with high intelligence tend to perform better. The relationship between *g* and job performance is likely to be strongest for those aspects of jobs that involve thinking and knowledge, such as problem solving and technical expertise.[20]

Over the years, various investigators have arrived at different special factors contributing to overall mental aptitude. The following seven factors have been identified consistently:

1. **Verbal comprehension.** The ability to understand the meaning of words and their relationship to each other and to comprehend written and spoken information.
2. **Word fluency.** The ability to use words quickly and easily, without an emphasis on verbal comprehension.
3. **Numerical acuity.** The ability to handle numbers, engage in mathematical analysis, and to do arithmetic calculations.
4. **Spatial perception.** The ability to visualize forms in space and manipulate objects mentally, particularly in three dimensions.
5. **Memory.** Having a good rote memory for symbols, words, and lists of numbers, along with other associations.
6. **Perceptual speed.** The ability to perceive visual details, to pick out similarities and differences, and to perform tasks requiring visual perception.
7. **Inductive reasoning.** The ability to discover a rule or principle and apply it in solving a problem and to make judgments and decisions that are logically sound.

Being strong in any of the preceding mental aptitudes often leads to an enjoyment of work associated with that aptitude. The reverse can also be true: enjoying a type of mental activity might lead to the development of an aptitude for the activity.

Practical Intelligence

Many people, including psychologists, are concerned that the traditional way of understanding intelligence inadequately describes mental ability. An unfortunate implication of intelligence testing is that intelligence as traditionally calculated is largely the ability to perform tasks related to scholastic work. Thus, a person who scores very high on an intelligence test could follow a complicated instruction manual, but might not be street smart.

To overcome the limited idea that intelligence mostly involves the ability to solve abstract problems, the **triarchic theory of intelligence** has been proposed. See Figure 2-3. The theory holds that intelligence is composed of three different subtypes: analytical, creative, and practical. The *analytical* subtype is the traditional intelligence needed for solving difficult problems. Analytical intelligence is required to perform well in most school subjects. The *creative* subtype is the type of intelligence required for imagination and combining things in novel ways. The *practical* subtype is the type of intelligence required for adapting your environment to suit your needs.[21] The idea of practical intelligence helps explain why a person who has a difficult time getting through school can still be a successful businessperson, politician, or athlete. Practical intelligence incorporates the ideas of common sense, wisdom, and street smarts.

A person with high practical intelligence would also have good **intuition**, an experience-based way of knowing or reasoning in which the weighing and balancing of evidence are done automatically. Examples of good intuition include a merchandiser who develops a hunch that a particular style will be hot next season, a basketball coach who sees the possibilities in a gangly youngster, and a supervisor who has a hunch that a neighbor would be a great fit for her department. Intuition is also required for creative intelligence.

FIGURE 2-3 The Triarchic Theory of Intelligence

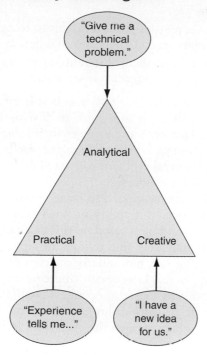

An important implication of practical intelligence is that experience is helpful in developing intellectual skills and judgment. At younger ages, raw intellectual ability such as required for learning information technology skills, may be strongest. However, judgment and wisdom are likely to be stronger with accumulated experience. This is why people in their forties and older are more likely to be chosen for positions such as the CEO of a large business or a commercial airline pilot. Poor judgment is *sometimes* associated with inexperience and youth. Several years ago in Amagasaki, Japan, a commuter train derailed and hit the parking garage of a nine-story building, killing 73 people and injuring 441. Investigators focused on excessive speed and a 23-year-old train conductor's lack of experience after the train jumped the track and plowed into the apartment building garage a few yards from the tracks.[22]

One major reservation some have about practical intelligence is the implication that people who are highly intelligent in the traditional sense are not practical thinkers. In truth, most executives and other high-level workers score quite well on tests of mental ability. These tests usually measure analytical intelligence.

Multiple Intelligences

Another approach to understanding the diverse nature of mental ability is the theory of **multiple intelligences.** According to Howard Gardner, people know and understand the world in distinctly different ways and learn in different ways. Individuals possess the following eight intelligences, or faculties, in varying degrees:

1. **Linguistic.** Enables people to communicate through language, including reading, writing, and speaking.
2. **Logical-mathematical.** Enables individuals to see relationships between objects and solve problems, as in calculus and statistics.
3. **Musical.** Gives people the capacity to create and understand meanings made out of sounds and to enjoy different types of music.
4. **Spatial.** Enables people to perceive and manipulate images in the brain and to recreate them from memory, as is required in making graphic designs.
5. **Bodily-kinesthetic.** Enables people to use their body and perceptual and motor systems in skilled ways such as dancing, playing sports, and expressing emotion through facial expressions.

multiple intelligences

A theory of intelligence contending that people know and understand the world in distinctly different ways and learn in different ways.

6. **Intrapersonal.** Enables people to distinguish among their own feelings and acquire accurate self-knowledge.

7. **Interpersonal.** Makes it possible for individuals to recognize and make distinctions among the feelings, motives, and intentions of others as in managing or parenting.

8. **Naturalist.** Enables individuals to differentiate among, classify, and utilize various features of the physical external environment.

Your profile of intelligences influences how you best learn and to which types of jobs you are best suited. Gardner believes it is possible to develop these separate intelligences through concentrated effort. However, any of these intelligences might fade if not put to use.[23] The components of multiple intelligences might also be perceived as different talents or abilities. Having high general problem-solving ability (g) would contribute to high standing on each of the eight intelligences.

The three types of intelligence mentioned so far (cognitive, practical, and multiple) all contribute to but do not guarantee our ability to think critically. Critical thinking is the process of evaluating evidence, and then based on this evaluation, making judgments and decisions. Through critical thinking, we find reasons to support or reject an argument.[24]

The various types of intelligence, particularly the cognitive type, give us the capacity to think critically. Personality factors heavily contribute to whether we choose to use these skills. For example, the personality factor of openness facilitates critical thinking because the individual enjoys gathering evidence to support or refute an idea. Also, conscientiousness also facilitates critical thinking because the individual feels compelled to gather more facts and think harder.[25]

Emotional Intelligence

emotional intelligence

Qualities such as understanding one's own feelings, empathy for others, and the regulation of emotion to enhance living.

Later research has updated and expanded the idea of practical intelligence, suggesting that how effectively people use their emotions has a major impact on their success. **Emotional intelligence** refers to qualities such as understanding one's own feelings, having empathy for others, and regulating one's emotion to enhance living. A person with high emotional intelligence would be able to engage in such behaviors as sizing up people, pleasing others, and influencing them. Four key factors included in emotional intelligence are as follows[26]:

1. **Self-awareness.** The ability to understand your moods, emotions, and needs as well as their impact on others. Self-awareness also includes using intuition to make decisions you can live with happily. A person with good self-awareness knows whether he or she is pushing other people too far. Imagine that Amanda is an assistant to the food service manager at a financial services company. Amanda believes strongly that the cafeteria should ensure that no food served on company premises contains trans fats. However, the food services manager seems lukewarm to the idea. So instead of badgering the manager, Amanda decides to fight her battle bit by bit with by presenting facts and reminders in a friendly way. Eventually the manager agrees to have a meeting on the subject with an invited nutritionist. Amanda's self-awareness has paid off.

2. **Self-management.** The ability to control one's emotions and act with honesty and integrity in a consistent and acceptable manner. The right degree of self-management helps prevent a person from throwing temper tantrums when activities do not go as planned. Effective workers do not let their occasional bad moods ruin their day. If they cannot overcome the bad mood, they let coworkers know of their problem and how long it might last. A person with low self-management would suddenly decide to drop a project because the work was frustrating.

   Imagine that Jack is an assistant to the export sales manager, and today is a big day because a company in Russia appears ready to make a giant purchase. The export sales manager says, "Today we need peak performance from everybody. If we nail down this sale, we will exceed our sales quota for the year." Unfortunately, Jack is in a grim mood. His favorite NFL team was eliminated from the playoffs the night before, and his dog has been diagnosed as having a torn abdominal muscle. Jack would like to lash out in anger against everybody he meets today, but instead he focuses his energy on getting the job done and does not let his personal problems show through.

3. **Social awareness.** Includes having empathy for others and having intuition about work problems. A team leader with social awareness, or empathy, would be able to assess whether a team member has enough enthusiasm for a project to assign him to that project. Another facet of social awareness is the ability to interpret nonverbal communication, such as frowns and types of smiles.[27] A supervisor with social awareness, or empathy, would take into account the most likely reaction of group members before making a decision affecting them.

Imagine that Cindy has been working as an assistant purchasing manager for six months. Company policy prohibits accepting "lavish" gifts from vendors or potential vendors attempting to sell the company goods or services. Cindy has been placed in charge of purchasing all paper toweling for the company. Although most of the purchasing is made over the Internet, sales representatives still make the occasional call. The rep from the paper towel company asks Cindy if she would like an iPhone as a token gift for even considering his company. Cindy really wants an iPhone, but it is not yet in her budget. After thinking through the potential gift for five minutes, Cindy decides to refuse. Perhaps an iPhone is not really a lavish gift, but her intuition tells her it would appear to be a conflict of interest if she accepted the iPhone.

4. **Relationship management.** Includes the interpersonal skills of being able to communicate clearly and convincingly, disarm conflicts, and build strong personal bonds. Effective workers use relationship management skills to spread their enthusiasm and solve disagreements, often with kindness and humor. A worker with relationship management skills would use a method of persuasion that is likely to work well with a particular group or individual.

Much of this book is about relationship management, but here is yet another example. Donte is an information technology (IT) specialist. His assignment for the first six months is to visit users at their workplace to help them with any IT problems they might be experiencing. In discussing his role with his supervisor, Donte begins to realize that helping with technical problems is not his only job. He is an ambassador of goodwill for the IT department. He and his manager want to build a network of support for the efforts of the department. So when Donte visits the various departments he is courteous and friendly, and asks about how an IT rep could make work easier for the person in question.

Two researchers who study emotion emphasize that the idea behind emotional intelligence is that it represents a skill through which employees treat emotions as valuable information in navigating a situation.

An example follows:

Let's say a sales manager has come up with an amazing idea that will increase corporate revenues by up to 200%, but knows that his boss tends to be irritable and short-tempered in the morning. Having emotional intelligence means that the manager will first recognize and consider this emotional fact about his boss. Despite the stunning nature of the idea—and his own excitement—he will regulate his own emotions, curb his enthusiasm, and wait until the afternoon to approach the boss.[28]

Emotional intelligence thus incorporates many of the skills and attitudes necessary to achieve effective interpersonal relations in organizations. Most of the topics in this book, such as resolving conflict, helping others develop, and possessing positive political skills, would be included in emotional intelligence. As mentioned earlier, emotional intelligence might also be regarded as a major aspect of personality rather than true intelligence. For example, if you can read the feelings of other people, aren't you just being smart?

To achieve the objectives sought by CEO Steve Bennett, most workers and managers at Intuit would have to develop their emotional intelligence. Among these competencies would be expressing their feelings explicitly in resolving conflict without throwing a tantrum, or becoming so angry that a useful solution could not be reached. Expressing enthusiasm also requires some emotional intelligence because many people are too emotionally flat in the workplace. Enthusiasm is contagious, so it helps Intuit when workers spread their enthusiasm.

LEARNING OBJECTIVE 4

Guidelines for Relating to People of Different Levels and Types of Intelligence

Certainly you cannot expect to administer mental ability and emotional intelligence tests to all your work associates, gather their scores, and then relate to associates differently based on their scores. Yet it is possible to intuitively develop a sense for the mental quickness of people and the types of mental tasks they perform best. For example, managers must make judgments about mental ability in selecting people for jobs and assigning them to tasks. Following are several guidelines worth considering for enhancing your working relationships with others:

1. If you perceive another worker (your manager included) to be mentally quick, present your ideas in technical depth. Incorporate difficult words into your conversation and reports. Ask the person challenging questions.

2. If you perceive another worker to be mentally slow, present your ideas with a minimum of technical depth. Use a basic vocabulary, without going so far as to be patronizing. Ask for frequent feedback about having been clear. If you have supervisory responsibility for a person who appears to be below average in intelligence, give that person the opportunity to repeat the same type of task rather than switching assignments frequently.

3. If you perceive a work associate to relish crunching numbers, use quantitative information when attempting to persuade that person. Instead of using phrases such as "most people," say "about 65 percent of people."

4. If you perceive a work associate to have high creative intelligence, solicit his or her input on problems requiring a creative solution. Use statements such as "Here's a problem that requires a sharp, creative mind, so I've come to you."

5. If you perceive a work associate to have low emotional intelligence, explain your feelings and attitudes clearly. Make an occasional statement such as "How I feel about his situation is quite important" to emphasize the emotional aspect. The person may not get the point of hints and indirect expressions.

To start putting these guidelines into practice, do the role-plays in Skill-Building Exercises, 2-2 and 2-3.

SKILL-BUILDING EXERCISE 2-2

Adapting to People of Different Mental Abilities

The Mentally Sharp Coworker: One student plays the role of a worker who needs to learn a new software package in a hurry. This person intends to approach a particular coworker who is known for having a sharp mind. The worker wonders whether this highly intelligent person will be interested in your problem. The other person plays the role of the computer whiz who ordinarily does not like to solve problems for people that they should be able to solve themselves. The first worker meets with the second to discuss loading the software.

The Mentally Average Team Member: One student plays the role of a supervisor who needs to explain to a team member how to calculate discounts for customers. To the supervisor's knowledge, the team member does not know how to calculate discounts, although it will be an important part of the team member's new job. The supervisor and the team member get together for a session on calculating discounts.

VALUES AS A SOURCE OF INDIVIDUAL DIFFERENCES

Another group of factors influencing how a person behaves on the job is that person's values and beliefs. A **value** refers to the importance a person attaches to something. Values are also tied to the enduring belief that one's mode of conduct is better than another mode of conduct. If you believe that good interpersonal relations are the most important part of your life, your humanistic values are strong. Similarly, you may think that people who are not highly concerned about interpersonal relations have poor values.

Values are closely tied in with **ethics**, or the moral choices a person makes. A person's values influence which kinds of behaviors he or she believes are ethical. Ethics convert values into action. An executive who strongly values profits might not find it unethical to raise prices higher than needed to cover additional costs. Another executive who strongly values family life might suggest that the company invest money in an on-site child care center. Ethics is such an important part of interpersonal relations in organizations that the topic receives separate mention in Chapter 14.

Differences in values among people often stem from age, or generational, differences. Workers over age 50, in general, may have different values than people who are much younger. These age differences in values have often been seen as a clash between Baby Boomers and members of Generation X and Generation Y. According to the stereotype, Boomers see Generation Xers and Yers as disrespectful of rules, not willing to pay their dues, and being disloyal to employers. Generation Xers and Yers see Boomers as worshipping hierarchy (layers of authority), being overcautious, and wanting to preserve the status quo.

Table 2-1 summarizes these stereotypes with the understanding that massive group stereotypes like these are only partially accurate because there are literally millions of exceptions. For example, many Baby Boomers are fascinated with technology, and many Generation Yers like hierarchy.

How Values Are Learned

People acquire values in the process of growing up, and many values are learned by the age of 4. One important way we acquire values is through observing others, or modeling. Models can be teachers, friends, brothers, sisters, and even public figures. If we identify with a particular person, the probability is high that we will develop some of his or her major values.

Derek, a restaurant owner, was known for his ability to offer employment to troubled teenagers and then help them get back on their feet. Asked why he put so much effort into helping youths in trouble, he explained, "I was greatly influenced as a boy by my Uncle Clarence. I was going through troubled times—stealing from a variety store and getting drunk on beer.

"Uncle Clarence took me under his wing and spent hours listening to my problems. He would take me fishing and ask if there was anything he could do to help me. Finally, I straightened out. I decided that I would be like Uncle Clarence if someday I had a chance to help young people."

value

The importance a person attaches to something.

ethics

The moral choices a person makes. Also, what is good and bad, right and wrong, just and unjust, and what people should do.

TABLE 2-1 Value Stereotypes for Several Generations of Workers

Baby Boomers (1946–1964)	Generation X (1961–1980)	Generation Y (1981–2002) (Millennials)
Uses technology as necessary tool	Techno-savvy	Techno-savvy
Appreciates hierarchy	Teamwork very important	Teamwork very important
Tolerates teams but values independent work	Dislikes hierarchy	Dislikes hierarchy; prefers participation
Strong career orientation	Strives for work–life balance but will work long hours for now	Strives for work–life balance but will work long hours for now
More loyalty to organization	Loyalty to own career and profession	Loyal to own career and profession and feels entitled to career growth
Favors diplomacy	Candid in conversation	Ultracandid in conversation
Favors old economy	Appreciates old and new economy	Prefers the new economy
Seeks long-term employment	Will accept long-term employment if situation is right	Looks toward each company as a stepping-stone to better job in another company
Believes that issues should be formally discussed	Believes that feedback can be administered informally	Believes that feedback can be given informally, even on the fly
Somewhat willing to accept orders and suggestions	Often questions why things should be done in a certain way	Frequently asks why things should be done in a certain way, and asks loads of questions

Source: Several of the ideas in this table are from Robert McGarvey, "The Coming of Gen X Bosses," *Entrepreneur*, November 1999, pp. 60–64; Joanne M. Glenn, "Teaching the Net Generation," *Business Education Forum*, February 2000, pp. 6–14; Gregg Hammill, "Mixing and Managing Four Generations of Employees," *FDUMagazine Online*, Winter/Spring 2005, p. 5; Sommer Kehrli and Trudy Sopp, "Managing Generation Y: Stop Resisting and Start Embracing the Challenges Generation Y Brings to the Workplace," *HR Magazine*, May 2006, pp. 113–119.

Note: Disagreement exists about which age bracket fit Baby Boomers, Generation X, and Generation Y, with both professional publications and dictionaries showing slight differences.

Another major way values are learned is through the communication of attitudes. The attitudes that we hear expressed directly or indirectly help shape our values. Assume that using credit to purchase goods and services was considered an evil practice among your family and friends. You might therefore hold negative values about installment purchases. Unstated but implied attitudes may also shape your values. If important people in your life showed no enthusiasm when you talked about work accomplishments, you might not place such a high value on achieving outstanding results. If, however, your family and friends centered their lives on their careers, you might develop similar values. (Or you might rebel against such a value because it interfered with a more relaxed lifestyle.) Many key values are also learned through religion and thus become the basis for society's morals. For example, most religions emphasize treating other people fairly and kindly. To "knife somebody in the back" is considered immoral both on and off the job.

Although many core values are learned early in life, our values continue to be shaped by events later in life. The media, including the dissemination of information about popular culture, influence the values of many people throughout their lives. The aftermath of Hurricane Katrina intensified a belief in the value of helping less fortunate people. Volunteers from throughout the United States and several other countries invested time, money, and energy into helping rebuild New Orleans and several other Gulf Coast cities. Influential people, such as NBA players, were seen on television building houses for Katrina victims. Such publicity sent a message that helping people in need is a value worth considering.

The media, particularly advertisements, can also encourage the development of values that are harmful to a person intent on developing a professional career. People featured in advertisements for consumer products, including snack food, beer, and vehicles, often flaunt rudeness and gross grammar. The message comes across to many people that such behavior is associated with success.

Changes in technology can also change our values. As the world has become increasingly digitized, more and more people come to value a *digital lifestyle* as the normal way of life. Many people would not think of leaving their electronic gadgets behind when spending time away from the house, even while participating in sports or watching sports. Being part of the digital lifestyle is therefore an important value for many people of all ages.

Clarifying Your Values

The values that you develop early in life are directly related to the kind of person you are and to the quality of the relationships you form.[29] Recognition of this has led to exercises designed to help people clarify and understand some of their own values. Self-Assessment Quiz 2-3 gives you an opportunity to clarify your values.

The Mesh between Individual and Job Values

Under the best of circumstances, the values of employees mesh with those required by the job. When this state of congruence exists, job performance is likely to be higher. Suppose that Jacquelyn strongly values giving people with limited formal education an

---

SELF-ASSESSMENT QUIZ 2-3

Clarifying Your Values

Directions: Rank from 1 to 20 the importance of the following values to you as a person. The most important value on the list receives a rank of 1; the least important a rank of 20. Use the space next to "Other" if the list has left out an important value in your life.

_____ Having my own place to live

_____ Having one or more children

_____ Having an interesting job and career

_____ Owning a car

_____ Having a good relationship with coworkers

_____ Having good health

_____ Sending and receiving e-mail messages, and using the Web

_____ Being able to stay in frequent contact with friends by cell phone and text messaging

_____ Watching my favorite television shows

_____ Participating in sports or other pastimes

_____ Following a sports team, athlete, music group, or other entertainer

_____ Being a religious person

_____ Helping people less fortunate than myself

_____ Loving and being loved by another person

_____ Having physical intimacy with another person

_____ Making an above-average income

_____ Being in good physical condition

_____ Being a knowledgeable, informed person

_____ Completing my formal education

_____ Other

1. Discuss and compare your ranking of these values with the person next to you.

2. Perhaps your class, assisted by your instructor, can arrive at a class average on each of these values. How does your ranking compare to the class ranking?

3. Look back at your own ranking. Does it surprise you?

4. Are there any surprises in the class ranking? Which values did you think would be highest and lowest?

opportunity to work and avoid being placed on welfare. So she takes a job as a manager of a dollar store that employs many people who would ordinarily have limited opportunity for employment. Jacquelyn is satisfied because her employer and she share a similar value.

When the demands made by the organization or a superior clash with the basic values of the individual, he or she suffers from **person–role conflict**. The individual wants to obey orders, but does not want to perform an act that seems inconsistent with his or her values. A situation such as this might occur when an employee is asked to produce a product that he or she feels is unsafe or of no value to society.

> A manager of a commercial weight-reduction center resigned after two years of service. The owners pleaded with her to stay, based on her excellent performance. The manager replied, "Sorry, I think my job is immoral. We sign up all these people with great expectations of losing weight permanently. Most of them do achieve short-term weight reduction. My conflict is that over 90 percent of our clientele regain the weight they lost once they go back to eating standard food. I think we are deceiving them by not telling them up front that they will most likely gain back the weight they lose."

Guidelines for Using Values to Enhance Interpersonal Relations

LEARNING OBJECTIVE 5

Values are intangible and abstract, and thus not easy to manipulate to help improve your interpersonal relations on the job. Despite their vagueness, values are an important driver of interpersonal effectiveness. Ponder the following guidelines:

1. Establish the values you will use in your relationships with others on the job, and then use those values as firm guidelines in working with others. For example, following the Golden Rule, you might establish the value of treating other people as you want to be treated. You would then not lie to others to gain personal advantage, and you would not backstab your rivals.

2. Establish the values that will guide you as an employee. When you believe that your values are being compromised, express your concern to your manager in a tactful and constructive manner. You might say to your manager, "Sorry, I choose not to tell our customers that our competitor's product is inferior just to make a sale. I choose not to say this because our competitor makes a fine product. But what I will say is that our service is exceptional."

3. Remember that many values are a question of opinion, not a statement of being right versus wrong. If you believe that your values are right, and anybody who disagrees is wrong, you will have frequent conflict. For example, you may believe that the most important value top managers should have is to bring shareholders a high return on their investment. Another worker believes that profits are important, but providing jobs for as many people as possible is an equally important value. Both of you have a good point, but neither is right or wrong. So it is better to discuss these differences rather than hold grudges because of them.

4. Respect differences in values and make appropriate adjustments when the value clash is reasonable. If you are an older person, recognize that you may have to win the respect of a younger coworker rather than assume that because you are more experienced, or a manager, that respect will come automatically.[30] If you are a younger person, recognize that an older person might be looking for respect, so search for something you can respect right away, such as his or her many valuable contacts in the company.

5. Recognize that many people today are idealistic about their jobs, and want to have an impact on the lives of others.[31] In the meantime, you might feel that you need that person's cooperation to get an important task done right now, such as fulfilling a larger order. Invest a couple of minutes in helping that person understand how an ordinary task might be having an impact on the lives of others—such as earning money to feed a hungry baby at home!

The Value-Conflict Role-Play

One student plays the role of a company CEO who makes an announcement to the group that the company must soon lay off 10 percent of the workforce to remain profitable. The CEO also points out that the company has a policy against laying off good performers. He or she then asks four of the company managers to purposely give below-average performance ratings to 10 percent of employees. In this way, laying them off will fit company policy.

Four other students play the role of the company managers who receive this directive. If such manipulation of performance evaluations clashes with your values, engage in a dialogue with your manager expressing your conflict. Remember, however, that you may not want to jeopardize your job.

Conduct this group role-play for about seven minutes, with other class members observing and being prepared to offer feedback.

To help you put these guidelines into practice, do Skill-Building Exercise 2-4. Remember, however, that being skilled at using your values requires day-by-day monitoring.

SELF-ASSESSMENT QUIZZES IN OVERVIEW

The several self-assessment quizzes presented in this chapter taken collectively will help you paint a verbal portrait of your personality. Self-Assessment Quiz 2-1, The Self-Monitoring Scale, gives you insight into how much you go out of your way to please others, often by telling them what they want to hear. Self-Assessment Quiz 2-2, The Risk-Taking Scale, looks at a dimension of personality that could lead you toward being adventuresome and innovative. Quite often people who are high risk takers are low self-monitors because they risk telling people what they do not want to hear, such as pointing out flaws in a company product.

Self-Assessment Quiz 2-3 gives you a chance to reflect on what is important to you. Your values are linked to the first two scales in that some people want to please others, and therefore would place a high premium on values like "helping people less fortunate than myself" and "loving and being loved by another person." Examples of strong values for a high risk taker would be "having an interesting job and career" and "making an above-average income."

Concept Review and Reinforcement

Key Terms

individual differences 21
personality 21
organizational citizenship
behavior 25
cognitive style 26

intelligence 29
g (general) factor 30
s (special) factors 30
triarchic theory of intelligence 30
intuition 30

multiple intelligences 31
emotional intelligence 32
value 35
ethics 35
person–role conflict 38

Summary of Key Concepts

Individual differences are among the most important factors influencing the behavior of people in the workplace. Knowing how to respond to such differences is the cornerstone of effective interpersonal relations.

Personality is one of the major sources of individual differences. The eight major personality factors described in this chapter are neuroticism, extraversion, openness, agreeableness, conscientiousness, self-monitoring of behavior, risk taking and thrill seeking, and optimism. Depending on the job, any one of these personality factors can be important for success; they also affect interpersonal relations. Conscientiousness relates to job performance for many different occupations, and has proved to be the personality factor most consistently related to success.

Personality also influences a person's cognitive style, or modes of problem solving. According to the Myers-Briggs Type Indicator (MBTI), four separate dichotomies direct the typical use of perception and judgment by the individual: Extraversion–Introversion; Sensing–Intuition; Thinking–Feeling; and Judging–Perceiving. Combining the four types results in 16 personality types, such as a person being a conceptualizer, traditionalist, visionary, or organizer. For example, the organizer (ESTJ) scores high on extraversion, sensing, thinking, and judging.

Mental ability, or intelligence, is one of the major sources of individual differences that affect job performance and behavior. Understanding the nature of intelligence contributes to effective interpersonal relations in organizations. For example, understanding that different types of intelligence exist will help a person appreciate the strengths of people.

Intelligence consists of many components. The traditional perspective is that intelligence includes a general factor (g) along with special factors (s) that contribute to problem-solving ability. A related perspective is that intelligence consists of seven components: verbal comprehension, word fluency, numerical acuity, spatial perception, memory, perceptual speed, and inductive reasoning.

To overcome the idea that intelligence involves mostly the ability to solve abstract problems, the triarchic theory of intelligence has been proposed. According to this theory, intelligence has three subtypes: analytical, creative, and practical (street smarts included). Another approach to understanding mental ability contends that people have multiple intelligences, or faculties, including linguistic, logical-mathematical, musical, spatial, bodily-kinesthetic, intrapersonal, interpersonal, and naturalist.

Emotional intelligence refers to factors other than traditional mental ability that influence a person's success. The four components of emotional intelligence are (1) self-awareness, (2) self-management, (3) social awareness, and (4) relationship management. Emotional intelligence is a skill through which employees treat emotions as valuable information in navigating a situation.

Values and beliefs are another set of factors that influence behavior on the job, including interpersonal relations. Values are closely tied in with ethics. People acquire values in the process of growing up and modeling others, and in the process of communicating attitudes. Later, life influences such as the media also shape values. The values a person develops early in life are directly related to the kind of adult he or she becomes and to the quality of relationships formed. Values-clarification exercises help people identify their values. Person–role conflict occurs when the demands made by an organization or a superior clash with the basic values of an individual.

Check Your Understanding

1. Why is responding to individual differences considered the cornerstone of effective interpersonal relations?

2. How can knowledge of major personality factors help a person form better interpersonal relations on the job?

3. Identify two job situations (or entire jobs) in which being pessimistic might be an asset.

4. Suppose a high self-monitoring person is attending a company-sponsored social event and that person dislikes such events. How is he or she likely to behave?

5. Identify two business occupations for which a high propensity for risk taking and thrill seeking would be an asset.

6. What kind of problems would individuals who rely on *feelings* prefer to tackle?

7. Which of the seven components of traditional intelligence represents your best mental aptitude? What is your evidence?

8. How could you use the concept of multiple intelligences to raise the self-esteem of people who did not consider themselves to be very smart?

9. Suppose a person is quite low in emotional intelligence. In what type of job is he or she the most likely to be successful?

10. How can you use information about a person's values to help you relate more effectively to him or her?

The Web Corner

http://myskillsprofile.com
(This site provides many self-quizzes, including emotional intelligence, sports mental skills, and spiritual intelligence. Several of the tests are free.)

http://www.queendom.com
(This site provides many tests and quizzes related to cognitive factors, personality, and emotional IQ.)

Internet Skills Builder: Boosting Your Mental Ability

Do you want to be smarter? Thousands of specialists think they have developed intelligent ways of making people more intelligent. You will find at least one million Web sites that provide information about improving brain functioning through such methods as practice in problem solving and taking food supplements. Try out one of these sights. Evaluate the suggestions for plausibility. You might even try the exercises for a couple of weeks and observe if you become smarter. Ask somebody close to you if have become smarter. You might also see if you do better on tests with the same amount of study and classroom attentiveness.

Developing Your Human Relations Skills

Interpersonal Relations Case 2.1

Capitalizing on Hidden Talent at Westmont Center

Ginette Gagnon is the director of Westmont Center, a residential center for older persons who require assisted living, such as being served meals, help with taking baths, and supervision for taking daily medication. Many of the residents also need readily available professional health care provided by physicians or nurses. Westmont takes care of an average of 125 guests on a given month.

At a recent meeting with the Westmont board of directors, Gagnon addressed the center's most critical problem. She explained, "We are in good shape financially. Because of the aging population in the area we serve, there is a never-ending supply of people who want entrance to Westmont. I say with pride that the good reputation of our staff and our comfortable physical facilities have enhanced our reputation.

"Our biggest need is to attract staff who will stick around long enough after they are trained and experienced. You will recall that we used to emphasize hiring young people. We still hire young people, but they tend not to stay very long. Many of them see taking care of older people as a stepping-stone to other work. Our program of recruiting young retirees has worked somewhat. The older folks usually have developed nurturing skills, and that is exactly what our residents need. The big problem is that we cannot find enough retirees who want to take care of people not much older than themselves."

"Ginette, please get to the point," said Karl Adams, one of the board members.

"OK, here's what I am proposing. I would like to start a pilot program of hiring about five workers with developmental disabilities to work on our staff. Our local university has a program of preparing people with light intellectual deficiencies for the workforce. The people in the program are not college students, but individuals whose parents or guardians have enrolled them in this cooperative program between the psychology department and a community agency.

"We would assign these workers to basic jobs like baking bread and muffins, folding laundry, and bringing meals to residents. Running the dishwashing machine would be another possibility, as would be trimming bushes. We would make sure that the workers in the pilot program perform the same task everyday. McDonald's has had a program like this for years, and both the workers and the restaurants have benefited quite well."

"Hold on," said Jean Weiss. "When the word gets out that we are staffing our center with mentally unstable people, we will be in big trouble. I can imagine headlines in the newspapers and the blogs."

Ginette responded with a tone of anger. "I must say, Jean, you do not understand the meaning of an intellectual deficiency, or I am not making myself clear. A developmental disability such as having difficulty learning has nothing to do with mental instability, which refers to emotional problems. Emotional stability and IQ are not particularly related."

The discussion with the board lasted another hour. Ralph Goodwin, the chairperson of the board, concluded the meeting in these words: "I think we see advantages and disadvantages in hiring about five people with intellectual deficiencies to work at Westmont. We would be doing a social good, we would have a new source of dependable workers. Yet, we have some concerns about hiring people who might not be able to think well in emergencies. Also, maybe some of our constituents would think that we are hiring mentally unstable people."

"I am disappointed that we could not reach an approval of my plan today," said Gagnon. "However, with more study, I think the board will see the merit in my plan of hiring a group of workers who have mild intellectual deficiencies."

Case Questions

1. What do you recommend that the board should do in terms of approving Gagnon's plan for hiring about five people with intellectual deficiencies to work at Westmont?

2. Assuming that the workers with mild intellectual deficiencies are hired, what recommendations can you make to the supervisors for their training and supervision?

3. Gagnon mentioned a few potential jobs at the center for workers with light intellectual deficiencies. What other tasks would you recommend?

"We've Got to Make Our Numbers"

Bruce Malone works as an account manager for an office-supply company with branches in most cities of the United States. The company has two lines of business, retail and commercial. Among the many products the company sells are computers and related equipment, office furniture, copy paper, and other basic office supplies.

The retail trade is served by customers walking directly into the store or ordering online. Many of the customers are small business owners or corporate employees who work at home part of their work week. The commercial trade also does some walk-in purchasing and online ordering. However, each large customer is also assigned an account manager who calls on them periodically to discuss their needs for larger purchases such as office furniture and multiple copiers and desktop computers.

Malone is meeting his sales targets for the year despite a flat economy in the city where the office supplier is located. Shortly before Thanksgiving, Malone was analyzing his sales to estimate his performance for the year. According to his projections, his total sales would be 1 percent beyond his quota, giving him a satisfactory year. Making his quota would qualify him for a year-end bonus.

The Friday after Thanksgiving, Malone received an e-mail message from his boss Lucille Whitman requesting that the two meet Monday morning before Bruce began working with his customers. At the start of the meeting, Whitman told Malone that she had something very important to discuss with him. "Bruce, we're getting a lot of heat from corporate headquarters," Whitman began. "If we don't make our numbers [attaining the sales goals] the stock price could dip big time, and the home office executives will be in trouble. Even their bonuses will be at risk."

"I've done what I can," responded Malone. "I'm going to make my quota for the year plus a little extra margin. So I guess I'm covered. There isn't much I can do about the company as a whole."

"Let me be a little more specific," replied Whitman. "The company is in trouble, so we all have to pitch in and show better numbers for the year. What we need our account managers to do is to pump up the sales figures a little. Maybe you could count as December sales a few of the purchases your customers have planned for early January. Or maybe you could ship extra-large orders at a discount, and tell your customers they can pay as late as February or March.

"You're smart, Bruce. Beef up your sales figures for the year a little because we have got to make our numbers."

"Lucille, maybe I could work extra hard to pull in a few more sales in the next four weeks. But I would feel rotten faking my sales figures for December. I'm a professional."

With an angry tone, Whitman responded, "I don't care what you call yourself; we have got to make our numbers. Get back to me soon with your plan for increasing your numbers for December."

Case Questions

1. What type of values is Lucille Whitman demonstrating?
2. What do you recommend Bruce should have done to work his way out of the problem he was facing?
3. Is Bruce too naïve for a career in business?

The "Making the Numbers" Conundrum

Here is an opportunity to practice dealing with the type of conflict facing Bruce Malone. One person plays Bruce, who has a follow-up conversation with Lucille Whitman about improving his December sales figures by less than straightforward means. Another student plays the role of Lucille Whitman, who is focused on the corporate demands of "making the numbers." Bruce wants to communicate clearly how uncomfortable he feels about fudging the facts, while Lucille feels enormous pressure to meet the demands of the executive group. Ideally, the two role-players will reach a solution acceptable to both sides.

CHAPTER 3

Building Self-Esteem and Self-Confidence

Susan Chapman, age 37, is the Global Head of Operations, Citigroup Reality Services. She oversees 14,000 properties representing 90 million square feet of space in 96 countries. Chapman talks about herself and her career in an interview with *Black Enterprise* magazine.

BE: What obstacles have you faced in your career?

SE: There were times when I wasn't given opportunities because of my gender or the color of my skin. Part of me wanted to stay and stick it out because that's what we do, we don't quit. But then the other part of me realized that I needed to make a change. When I did, the whole world opened up to me.

BE: What strategies have you employed?

SC: Having people around me who are willing to tell you the truth is key. Oftentimes it's very hard to get feedback from those who are culturally different from you. But it's critically important to develop relationships so that others feel comfortable telling you where you need to improve.

BE: How do you handle constructive feedback?

SC: I seek it. Early in my career, I didn't really seek out feedback. One day a mentor told me, "You need to get a lot more quality feedback because something's going on that you don't know about."

BE: What was the problem?

SC: There were a couple of problems in terms of not getting promoted and in being in an environment where people weren't engaging me the way I needed in order for me to be successful in my job. I hadn't built the relationships the way I needed to. I have to go out of my way to build the relationships.

BE: What traits or skills do you think are most important in overcoming obstacles?

SC: Be ambitious about setting goals, and do a self-check regularly. Ask yourself: Who am I? What am I doing? Why am I doing this? And is it working for me? You also have to be very giving, which allows a channel of things to come back to you

Learning Objectives

After reading and studying this chapter and doing the exercises, you should be able to

1. Describe the nature, development, and consequences of self-esteem.
2. Explain how to enhance self-esteem.

3. Describe the importance of self-confidence and self-efficacy.
4. Pinpoint methods of enhancing and developing your self-confidence.

when you really need it. When you're trying to overcome an obstacle and you need some help, it's hard to ask for help if you've never given it."[1]

One of many possible interpretations of this executive's answers to the interview questions is that she scores high in self-esteem and self-confidence. She thinks highly enough about herself to believe that she can advance to great heights in her career. At the same time she has the self-confidence to ask for and handle feedback that can set her in the right direction. Many other people you will meet in this book score high in self-esteem and self-confidence—otherwise they would never have been so successful. In this chapter we focus on two of the biggest building blocks for more effective human relations: the nature and development of self-esteem and self-confidence. The development of both self-esteem and self-confidence includes refining certain skills.

LEARNING OBJECTIVE 1

THE MEANING OF SELF-ESTEEM AND ITS DEVELOPMENT AND CONSEQUENCES

Understanding the self from various perspectives is important because who you are and what you think of you influences many different facets of your life both on and off the job. A particularly important role is played by **self-esteem**, the overall evaluation people make about themselves, whether positive or negative.[2] A useful distinction is that our self-concept is what we *think* about ourselves, whereas self-esteem is what we *feel* about ourselves.[3] People with positive self-esteem have a deep-down, inside-the-self feeling of their own worth. Consequently, they develop a positive self-concept. Before reading further, you are invited to measure your current level of self-esteem by doing Human Relations Self-Assessment Quiz 3-1. We look next at the development of self-esteem and many of its consequences.

self-esteem

The overall evaluation people make about themselves, whether positive or negative.

How Self-Esteem Develops

Part of understanding the nature of self-esteem is to know how it develops. Self-esteem develops and evolves throughout our lives based on interactions with people, events, and things.[4] As an adolescent or adult, your self-esteem might be boosted by a key accomplishment. A 44-

The Self-Esteem Checklist

Indicate whether each of the following statements is Mostly True or Mostly False as it applies to you.

	Mostly True	Mostly False
1. I am excited about starting each day.	____	____
2. Most of any progress I have made in my work or school can be attributed to luck.	____	____
3. I often ask myself, "Why can't I be more successful?"	____	____
4. When my manager or team leader gives me a challenging assignment, I usually dive in with confidence.	____	____
5. I believe that I am working up to my potential.	____	____
6. I am able to set limits to what I will do for others without feeling anxious.	____	____
7. I regularly make excuses for my mistakes.	____	____
8. Negative feedback crushes me.	____	____
9. I care very much how much money other people make, especially when they are working in my field.	____	____
10. I feel like a failure when I do not achieve my goals.	____	____
11. Hard work gives me an emotional lift.	____	____
12. When others compliment me, I doubt their sincerity.	____	____
13. Complimenting others makes me feel uncomfortable.	____	____
14. I find it comfortable to say, "I'm sorry."	____	____
15. It is difficult for me to face up to my mistakes.	____	____
16. My coworkers think I am not worthy of promotion.	____	____
17. People who want to become my friends usually do not have much to offer.	____	____
18. If my manager praised me, I would have a difficult time believing it was deserved.	____	____
19. I'm just an ordinary person.	____	____
20. Having to face change really disturbs me.	____	____
21. When I make a mistake, I have no fear owning up to it in public.	____	____
22. When I look in the mirror, I typically see someone who is attractive and confident.	____	____
23. When I think about the greater purpose in my life, I feel like I am drifting.	____	____
24. When I make a mistake, I tend to feel ashamed and embarrassed.	____	____
25. When I make a commitment to myself I usually stick to it with conviction and await the rewards that I believe will come from it.	____	____

Scoring and Interpretation: The answers in the high self-esteem direction are as follows:

1. Mostly True	8. Mostly False	15. Mostly False	22. Mostly True
2. Mostly False	9. Mostly False	16. Mostly False	23. Mostly False
3. Mostly False	10. Mostly False	17. Mostly False	24. Mostly False
4. Mostly True	11. Mostly True	18. Mostly False	25. Mostly True
5. Mostly True	12. Mostly False	19. Mostly False	
6. Mostly True	13. Mostly False	20. Mostly False	
7. Mostly False	14. Mostly True	21. Mostly True	

20–25 You have very high self-esteem. Yet if your score is 25, it could be that you are denying any self-doubts.

14–19 Your self-esteem is in the average range. It would probably be worthwhile for you to implement strategies to boost your self-esteem (described in this chapter) so that you can develop a greater feeling of well-being.

0–13 Your self-esteem needs bolstering. Talk over your feelings about yourself with a trusted friend or with a mental health professional. At the same time, attempt to implement several of the tactics for boosting self-esteem described in this chapter.

year-old woman who was studying to become a licensed practical nurse (LPN) said that her self-esteem increased when she received an A in a pharmacology course. Self-esteem can also go down in adulthood by means of a negative event such as being laid off and not being able to find new employment.

Early life experiences have a major impact on self-esteem. People who were encouraged to feel good about themselves and their accomplishments by family members, friends, and teachers are more likely to enjoy high self-esteem. Early life experiences play a key role in the development of both healthy self-esteem and low self-esteem, according to research synthesized at The Counseling and Mental Health Center of the University of Texas.[5] Childhood experiences that lead to health self-esteem include

- Being praised
- Being listened to
- Being spoken to respectfully
- Getting attention and hugs
- Experiencing success in sports or school

In contrast, childhood experiences that lead to low self-esteem include

- Being harshly criticized
- Being yelled at or beaten
- Being ignored, ridiculed, or teased
- Being expected to be "perfect" all the time
- Experience failures in sports or school
- Often being given messages that failed experiences (losing a game, getting a poor grade, and so forth) were failures of their whole self

A widespread explanation of self-esteem development is that compliments, praise, and hugs alone build self-esteem. Yet many developmental psychologists seriously question this perspective. Instead, they believe that self-esteem results from accomplishing worthwhile activities and then feeling proud of these accomplishments. Receiving encouragement, however, can help the person accomplish activities that build self-esteem.

Leading psychologist Martin Seligman argues that self-esteem is caused by a variety of successes and failures. To develop self-esteem, people need to improve their skills for dealing with the world.[6] Self-esteem therefore comes about by genuine accomplishments, followed by praise and recognition. Heaping undeserved praise and recognition on people may lead to a temporary high, but it does not produce genuine self-esteem. The child develops self-esteem not from being told he or she can score a goal in soccer, but from scoring that goal.

In attempting to build the self-esteem of children and students, many parents and teachers give children too many undeserved compliments. Researchers suggest that inappropriate compliments are turning too many adults into narcissistic praise-junkies. As a result, many young adults feel insecure if they do not receive compliments regularly.[7]

As mentioned earlier, experiences in adult life can influence the development of self-esteem. David De Cremer of the Tilburg University (Netherlands) and his associates conducted two studies with Dutch college students about how the behavior of leaders, and fair procedures, influence self-esteem. The focus of any given leader's behavior was whether he or she motivated the workers–students to reward *themselves* for a job well done, such as a self-compliment. Procedural fairness was measured in terms of whether the study participants were given a voice in making decisions. Self-esteem was measured by a questionnaire somewhat similar to Self-Assessment 3-1 in this chapter. The study questionnaire reflected the perceived value that individuals have of themselves as organizational members.

The study found that self-esteem was related to procedural fairness and leadership that encourages self-rewards. When leadership that encouraged rewards was high, procedural fairness was more strongly related to self-esteem. The interpretation given of the findings is that a leader or supervisor can facilitate self-esteem when he or she encourages self-rewards and uses fair procedures. Furthermore, fair procedures have a stronger impact on self-esteem when the leader encourages self-rewards.[8] A takeaway from this study would that rewarding yourself for a job well done, even in adult life, can boost your self-esteem a little.

The Consequences of Self-Esteem

No single factor is as important to career success as self-esteem, as observed by psychologist Eugene Raudsepp. People with positive self-esteem understand their own competence and worth, and a positive perception of their ability to cope with problems and adversity.[9]

One of the major consequences of high self-esteem is good mental health. People with high self-esteem feel good about themselves and have a positive outlook on life. One of the links between good mental health and self-esteem is that high self-esteem helps prevent many situations from being stressful. Few negative comments from others are likely to bother you when your self-esteem is high. A person with low self-esteem might crumble if somebody insulted his or her appearance. A person with high self-esteem might shrug off the insult as simply being the other person's point of view. If faced with an everyday setback, such as losing keys, the high self-esteem person might think, "I have so much going for me, why fall apart over this incident?"

Positive self-esteem also conributes to good mental health because it helps us ward off being troubled by feelings of jealousy and acting aggressively toward others because of our jealousy. Particularly with adolescents, lower self-worth leads to jealousy about friends liking other people better.[10]

Although people with high self-esteem can readily shrug off undeserved insults, they still profit well from negative feedback. Because they are secure, they can profit from the developmental opportunities suggested by negative feedback. Workers with high self-esteem develop and maintain favorable work attitudes and perform at a high level. These positive consequences take place because such attitudes and behavior are consistent with the personal belief that they are competent individuals. Mary Kay Ash, the legendary founder of a beauty-products company, put it this way: "It never occurred to me I couldn't do it. I always knew that if I worked hard enough, I could." Furthermore, research has shown that high-self-esteem individuals value reaching work goals more than do low-self-esteem individuals.[11]

The combined effect of workers having high self-esteem helps a company prosper. Long-term research by Nathaniel Branden, as well as more recent studies, suggests that self-esteem is a critical source of competitive advantage in an information society. Companies gain the edge when, in addition to having an educated workforce, employees have high self-esteem, as shown by such behaviors as the following:

- Being creative and innovative
- Taking personal responsibility for problems
- A feeling of independence (yet still wanting to work cooperatively with others)
- Trusting one's own capabilities
- Taking the initiative to solve problems[12]

Behaviors such as these help workers cope with the challenge of a rapidly changing workplace where products and ideas become obsolete quickly. Workers with high self-esteem are more likely to be able to cope with new challenges regularly because they are confident they can master their environment.

High self-esteem can sometimes have negative consequences, particularly because individuals with high self-esteem work hard to preserve their high status relative to others. When people with high self-esteem are placed in a situation where undermining others helps them maintain their status, they will engage in behaviors that diminish others. In one study it was shown that high self-esteem individuals who are also a little neurotic (somewhat emotionally unstable) will often engage the following undermining behaviors: Criticizing group members in front of others, intentionally ignoring others, talking down to other group members, going back on their word, giving others the silent treatment, belittling others, and not listening to people.[13]

Another potential danger exists in having highly inflated self-esteem. A controversial study conducted in England found that people with high self-esteem might have an unrealistic sense of themselves. "They expect to do well at things, discount failure, and feel beyond reproach." Furthermore, people with exaggerated self-esteem are sometimes intolerant of people who are different from them.[14]

A potential negative consequence of low self-esteem is envying too many people. If you perceive that many individuals have much more of what you want, and are more worthwhile than you, you will suffer from enormous envy. To decrease pangs of envy, it is best to develop realistic standards of comparison between you and other people in the world. If high school basketball player Joshua measures his self-esteem in terms of how well he stacks up with basketball superstar and supermillionaire LeBron James, young Joshua will take a lot of blows to his self-esteem. However, if Joshua compares himself to other players on his team and in his league, his self-esteem will be higher because he has chosen a more realistic reference group.

According to economist Robert H. Frank of Cornell University, our own reference group has the biggest impact on self-esteem. He writes: "When you see Bill Gates' mansion, you don't actually aspire to have one like it. It's who is local, who is near you physically and who is most like you—your family members, coworkers and old high school classmates—with whom you compare yourself. If someone in your reference group has a little more, you get a little anxious."[15]

Low self-esteem can have negative consequences for romantic relationships because people with self-doubts consistently underestimate their partners' feelings for them. People with low self-respect distance themselves from the relationship—often devaluing their partner—to prepare themselves for what they think will be an inevitable breakup. John G. Holmes, a psychologist at the University of Waterloo in Ontario, Canada, says, "If people think negatively about themselves, they think their partner must think negatively about them—and they're wrong."[16]

The consequences of self-esteem are related to its source. People who evaluate their self-worth on how others perceive them and not on their value as human beings often suffer negative mental and physical consequences. In a series of studies, developmental psychologist Jennifer Crocker found that college students who based their self-worth on external sources reported more stress, anger, academic problems, and interpersonal conflicts. In addition, these students had higher levels of drug and alcohol use and symptoms of eating disorders. (External sources of self-worth include appearance, approval from others, and grades in school.) Students who based their self-esteem (or self-worth) on internal sources generally received higher grades and were less likely to consume alcohol and drugs or develop eating disorders.[17] (An internal source would be thinking of yourself as a kind and charitable person.)

LEARNING OBJECTIVE 2

ENHANCING SELF-ESTEEM

Improving self-esteem is a lifelong process because self-esteem is related to the success of your activities and interactions with people. Following are approaches to enhancing self-esteem that are related to how self-esteem develops (see also Figure 3-1). Each of these approaches has a skill component, such as learning to avoid situations that make you feel incompetent.

FIGURE 3-1 Methods of Enhancing Self-Esteem

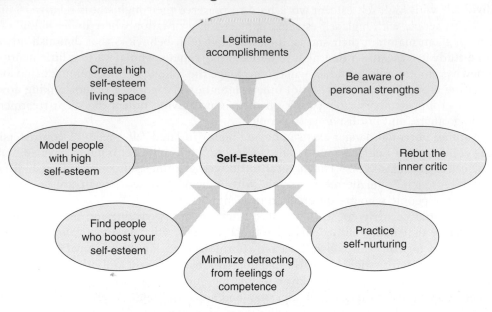

Attain Legitimate Accomplishments

To emphasize again, accomplishing worthwhile activities is a major contributor to self-esteem (as well as self-confidence) in both children and adults. Social science research suggests this sequence of events: Person establishes a goal; person pursues the goal; person achieves the goal; person develops esteem-like feelings.[18] The opposite point of view is this sequence: Person develops esteem-like feelings; person establishes a goal; person pursues the goal; person achieves the goal. Similarly, giving people large trophies for mundane accomplishments is unlikely to raise self-esteem. More likely, the person will see through the transparent attempt to build his or her self-esteem and develop negative feelings about the self. What about you? Would your self-esteem receive a bigger boost by (1) receiving an A in a course in which 10 percent of the class received an A or by (2) receiving an A in a class in which everybody received the same grade?

Be Aware of Personal Strengths

Another method of improving your self-esteem is to develop an appreciation of your strengths and accomplishments. Research a while back with over 60 executives has shown that their self-concepts become more positive after one month of practicing this exercise for a few minutes every day.[19] A good starting point is to list your strengths and accomplishments on a word processing document or paper. This list is likely to be more impressive than you expected.

You can sometimes develop an appreciation of your strengths by participating in a group exercise designed for such purposes. A group of about seven people meet to form a support group. All group members first spend about 10 minutes answering the question, "What are my three strongest points, attributes, or skills?" After each group member records his or her three strengths, the person discusses them with the other group members.

Each group member then comments on the list. Other group members sometimes add to your list of strengths or reinforce what you have to say. Sometimes you may find disagreement. One member told the group, "I'm handsome, intelligent, reliable, athletic, self-confident, and very moral. I also have a good sense of humor." Another group member retorted, "And I might add that you're unbearably conceited."

Skill-Building Exercises 3-1 and 3-2 provide additional ways of developing self-esteem, both of which focus on appreciation of strengths.

Reinforcing a Positive Self-Image

To do this exercise, you will need a piece of paper and a pencil or pen or a word processor, and a timer or clock.

Set a timer for 10 minutes or note the time on your watch, cell phone, or a clock. Write your name across the top of the document. Then write everything positive and good you can think of about yourself. Include special attributes, talents, and achievements. You can use single words or sentences. You can write the same things over and over if you want to emphasize them. Your ideas do not have to be well organized. Write down whatever comes to mind. You are the only one who will see this document. Avoid using any negative words. Use only positive ones.

When the 10 minutes are up, read the document over to yourself. You may feel sad when you read it over because it is a new, different, and positive way of thinking about yourself. Your document will con-

tradict some of the negative thoughts you have had about yourself. Those feelings will diminish as you reread this document. Read the document over again several times. Print the document if written by computer, and put it in a convenient place, such as in your pocket, purse, wallet, or your bedside table. Read it over at least once a day to keep reminding yourself of how great you are! Find a private space and read it aloud. If you have a good friend or family member who is supportive, read it to that person. Maybe your confidant can think of a positive attribute that you have missed.

Source: Adapted from "Building Self-esteem: A Self-Help Guide," http://mentalhealth.samhsa.gov/, accessed September 7, 2007.

The Self-Esteem Building Club

You and your classmates are invited to participate in one of the most humane and productive human-relations skill-building exercises, membership in the "self-esteem building club." Your assignment is, for three consecutive weeks, to help build the self-esteem of one person. Before embarking upon the exercise, review the information about self-esteem development in this chapter. One of the most effective tactics would be to find somebody who has a legitimate accomplishment, and give that person a reward or thank you. Record carefully what the person did, what you did, and any behavioral reactions of the person whose self-esteem you attempted to build. An example follows, written by a 46-year old student of human relations:

Thursday night two weeks ago I went to the athletic club to play racquetball. Different than usual, I had a date after the club. I wanted to look good, so I decided to wear my high school class ring. The ring doesn't have much resale value, but I was emotionally attached to it, having worn it for special occasions for 28 years. I stuffed the ring along with my watch and wallet in my athletic bag.

When I was through with racquetball, I showered and got dressed. My ring was missing from my bag, but my wallet and watch were still there. I kind of freaked out because I hate to lose a prized possession.

I shook the bag out three times, but no luck. Very discouraged, I left my name, telephone number, and e-mail address at the front desk just in case somebody turned in the ring. I kept thinking that I must have lost the ring when I stopped at the desk to check in.

The next morning before going to class, I got a phone call from a front-desk clerk at the club. The clerk told me that Karl, from the housekeeping staff, heard a strange noise while he was vacuuming near the front desk. He shut off the vacuum cleaner immediately, and pulled out my ring. To me, Karl was a hero. I made a special trip to the club that night to meet with Karl. I shook his hand, and gave him a $10 bill as a reward. I also explained to Karl what a difference he had made in my mood. I told him that honest, hardworking people like him who take pride in their work make this world a better place. It made my day when Karl smiled and told me it was a pleasure to be helpful.

Your instructor might organize a sharing of self-esteem building episodes in the class. If the sharing does take place, look for patterns in terms of what seemed to work in terms of self-esteem building. Also, listen for any patterns in failed attempts at self-esteem building.

Rebut the Inner Critic

Another early step in attaining better self-esteem is to rebut your inner critic—the voice inside you that sends negative messages about your capabilities. Rebutting critical statements about you might also be considered another way of appreciating your strengths. Two examples of rebutting your inner critic follow[20]:

Your unfairly harsh inner critic says: "People said they liked my presentation, but it was nowhere as good as it should have been. I can't believe no one noticed all the places I messed up. I'm such an imposter."

Your reassuring rebuttal: "Wow, they really liked it. Maybe it wasn't perfect, but I worked hard on that presentation and did a good job. I'm proud of myself. This was a great success."

Your harsh inner critic makes leaps of illogic: "He is frowning. He didn't say anything, but I know it means that he doesn't like me!"

Your rebuttal that challenges the illogic: "Okay, he's frowning, but I don't know why. It could have nothing to do with me. Maybe I should ask."

These are but two examples of the type of put-downs we often hear from our inner critic. To boost your self-esteem in spite of such criticism, you need to develop the skill of rebuttal by rebutting your inner critic frequently.

Practice Self-Nurturing

Although you may be successful at pointing to your strengths and rebutting the inner voice that puts you down, it is also helpful to treat yourself as a worthwhile person. Start to challenge negative experiences and messages from the past by nurturing and caring for yourself in ways that show how valuable, competent, deserving, and lovable you really are. Self-nurturing is often referred to "as treating yourself well" or "spoiling yourself." Here are two suggestions for self-nurturing, both of which involve a modest amount of skill development.

- **Administer self-rewards for a job well done.** When you have carried out an activity especially well in relation to your typical performance, reward yourself in a small, constructive way. You might dine at a favorite restaurant, take an afternoon off to go for a nature walk, or spend an hour at a Web site you usually do not have the time to visit.
- **Take good care of yourself mentally and physically.** Make sure you get enough sleep and rest, eat nutritious foods, avoid high-bacteria environments such as a public keyboard unless you use a bacteria spray, and participate in moderate physical exercise. Even taking an extra shower or bath can give you a physical and mental boost. The suggestions just mentioned are also part of stress management.

Real estate agent Laura provides a helpful example of how self-nurturing can help bolster self-esteem. While watching her son play soccer at four in the afternoon, she was asked by another soccer parent, "How's business?" Laura replied, "I haven't made a deal in two weeks, but I know times will get better. So for now, I'm enjoying myself watching Todd [her son] play his little heart out. Afterwards we are going for pizza, and a few video games. My soul will be energized again."

Minimize Settings and Interactions That Detract from Your Feelings of Competence

Most of us have situations in our work and personal lives that make us feel less than our best. If you can minimize exposure to those situations, you will have fewer feelings of incompetence. The problem with feeling incompetent is that it lowers your self-esteem. An office supervisor said she detested company picnics, most of all because she was forced into playing softball. At her own admission, she had less aptitude for athletics than any able-bodied person she knew. In addition, she felt uncomfortable with the small-talk characteristic of picnics. To minimize discomfort, the woman attended only those picnics she thought were absolutely necessary. Instead of playing on the softball team, she volunteered to be the equipment manager.

A problem with avoiding all situations in which you feel lowly competent is that it might prevent you from acquiring needed skills. Also, it boosts your self-confidence and self-esteem to become comfortable in a previously uncomfortable situation.

Get Help from Others

Self-esteem is strongly shaped by how others perceive us, so getting help from others is a major step a person can take to improve his or her self-esteem. However, getting help from others can also be difficult. People with low self-esteem often do not ask for help because they may not think they are worthy of receiving help. Yet help from others is effective in overcoming the negative messages received from others in the past.

Asking for support from friends can include such basic steps as these: (1) Ask friends to tell you what they like about you or think that you do well. (2) Ask someone who cares about you to listen to you complain about something without offering a solution to your problem. (3) Ask for a hug. (4) Ask someone who loves you to remind you that he or she does.

Getting help from teachers and other helpers can include these steps: (1) Ask professors or tutors for help with work you find challenging. (2) If you lack self-confidence in certain areas, take classes or attempt new activities to increase your self of competence. An increasing number of retired people today are taking classes in such subjects as computer utilization and digital photography to help catch up with younger people whose skills have challenged their self-esteem.[21]

Another way of getting help from others is to talk and socialize frequently with people who can boost your self-esteem. Psychologist Barbara Ilardie says that the people who can raise your self-esteem are usually those with high self-esteem themselves. They are the people who give honest feedback because they respect others and themselves. Such high self-esteem individuals should not be confused with yes-people who agree with others just to be liked. The point is that you typically receive more from strong people than weak ones. Weak people will flatter you but will not give you the honest feedback you need to build self-esteem.[22]

For many people with low self-esteem, casual help with others will not increase self-esteem. In these situations, discussing low self-esteem with a mental health specialist might be the most effective measure.

Model the Behavior of People with High Self-Esteem

Observe the way people who you believe to have high self-esteem stand, walk, speak, and act. Even if you are not feeling so secure inside, you will project a high self-esteem image if you act assured. Eugene Raudsepp recommends, "Stand tall, speak clearly and with confidence, shake hands firmly, look people in the eye and smile frequently. Your self-esteem will increase as you notice encouraging reactions from others."[23] (Notice here that self-esteem is considered to be about the same idea as self-confidence.)

Choose your models of high self-esteem from people you know personally, as well as celebrities you might watch on television news and interview shows. Observing actors on the large or small screen is a little less useful because they are guaranteed to be playing a role. Identifying a teacher or professor as a self-esteem model is widely practiced, as is observing successful family members and friends.

Create a High Self-Esteem Living Space

A panel of mental health specialists recommends that to enhance your self-esteem you should make your living space one that honors the person you are.[24] Whether you live in a single room, a small apartment, or a large house, make that space comfortable and attractive for you. If you have a clean, inviting living space, others are likely to treat you with more respect, which will contribute to your self-esteem. If you share your living space with others, dedicate some space just for you—a place where you can keep your things and know that they will not be disturbed and that you can decorate any way you choose.

Your living space is part of your self-image, so you want to ask yourself if your living space projects the right self-image. Also, if you arrange your living space to fit your preferences, you will feel better about yourself.

LEARNING OBJECTIVE 3

THE IMPORTANCE OF SELF-CONFIDENCE AND SELF-EFFICACY

Although self-confidence can be considered part of self-esteem (or almost its equivalent), it is important enough to study separately. **Self-efficacy** is confidence in your ability to carry out a specific task, in contrast to generalized self-confidence. Various studies have shown that people with a high sense of self-efficacy tend to have good job performance, so being self-confident is important for your career. They also set relatively high goals for themselves.[25] Self-confidence has also long been recognized as a trait of effective leaders. A straightforward implication of self-efficacy is that people who think they can perform well on a task do better than those who think they will do poorly.

self-efficacy

The confidence in your ability to carry out a specific task.

Research by college professors and psychological consultants George P. Hollenbeck and Douglas T. Hall suggests that our feelings of self-confidence stem from five sources of information.[26] The first source is the *actual experience*, or *things we have done.* Having done something before and succeeded is the most powerful way to build self-confidence. If you successfully inserted a replacement battery into your watch without destroying the watch, you will be confident to make another replacement.

The second source of self-confidence is the *experiences of others*, or *modeling.* You can gain some self-confidence if you have carefully observed others perform a task, such as resolving conflict with a customer. You might say to yourself, "I've seen Tracy calm down the customer by listening and showing sympathy, and I'm confident I can do the same thing." The third source of self-confidence is *social comparison*, or *comparing yourself to others.* If you see other people with capabilities similar to your own perform a task well, you will gain in confidence. A person might say to him- or herself, "If that person can learn how to work with enterprise software, I can do it also. I'm just as smart."

The fourth source of self-confidence is *social persuasion, the process of convincing another person.* If a credible person convinces you that you can accomplish a particular task, you will often receive a large enough boost in self-confidence to give the task a try. If the encouragement is coupled with guidance on how to perform the task, your self-confidence gain will be higher. So the boss or teacher who says, "I know you can do it, and I'm here to help you," knows how to build self-confidence.

The fifth source of information for making a self-confidence judgment is *emotional arousal,* or *how we feel about events around us and manage our emotions.* We rely somewhat on our inner feelings to know if we are self-confident enough to perform the task. Imagine a person standing on top of a high mountain ready to ski down. However, he is she is trembling and nauseated from fear. Contrast this beginner to another person who simply feels mildly excited and challenged. Skier number one has a self-confidence problem, whereas skier number two has enough confidence to start the descent. (Have your emotional sensations ever influenced your self-confidence?)

The more of these five sources of self-confidence are positive for you, the more likely your self-confidence will be positive. A subtle point about self-confidence is that being too low in self-confidence is a problem yet being too high is also a problem. The overly self-confident person may not listen carefully to the suggestions of others, and may be blind to criticism.

Human Relations Self-Assessment Exercise 3-2 provides some insight into your level of self-confidence.

LEARNING OBJECTIVE 4

TECHNIQUES FOR DEVELOPING AND ENHANCING YOUR SELF-CONFIDENCE

Self-confidence is generally achieved by succeeding in a variety of situations. A confident civil engineering technician may not be generally self-confident unless he or she also achieves success in activities such as forming good personal relationships, navigating complex software, writing a letter, learning a second language, or displaying athletic skills.

Although this general approach to self-confidence building makes sense, it does not work for everyone. Some people who seem to succeed at everything still have lingering self-doubt. Low self-confidence is so deeply ingrained in this type of personality that success in later life is not sufficient to change things. Following are seven specific strategies and tactics for building and elevating self-confidence, as outlined in Figure 3-2. They will generally work unless the person has deep-rooted feelings of inferiority. The tactics and strategies are arranged approximately in the order in which they should be tried to achieve best results.

Develop a Solid Knowledge Base

A bedrock strategy for projecting self-confidence is to develop a base of knowledge that enables you to provide sensible alternative solutions to problems. Intuition is very important,

How Self-Confident Are You?

Indicate the extent to which you agree with each of the following statements. Use a 1–5 scale: (1) disagree strongly (DS); (2) disagree (D); (3) neutral (N); (4) agree (A); (5) agree strongly (AS).

	DS	D	N	A	AS
1. I frequently say to people, "I'm not sure."	5	4	3	2	1
2. I perform well in most situations in life.	1	2	3	4	5
3. I willingly offer advice to others.	1	2	3	4	5
4. Before making even a minor decision, I usually consult with several people.	5	4	3	2	1
5. I am generally willing to attempt new activities for which I have very little related skill or experience.	1	2	3	4	5
6. Speaking in front of the class or other group is a frightening experience for me.	5	4	3	2	1
7. I experience stress when people challenge me or put me on the spot.	5	4	3	2	1
8. I feel comfortable attending a social event by myself.	1	2	3	4	5
9. I'm much more of a winner than a loser.	1	2	3	4	5
10. I am cautious about making any substantial change in my life.	5	4	3	2	1

Total score: _____

Scoring and Interpretation: Calculate your total score by adding the numbers circled. A tentative interpretation of the scoring is as follows:

45–50 Very high self-confidence with perhaps a tendency toward arrogance.

38–44 A high, desirable level of self-confidence.

30–37 Moderate, or average, self-confidence.

10–29 Self-confidence needs strengthening.

Questions:

1. How does your score on this test fit with you evaluation of your self-confidence?

2. What would it be like working for a manager who scored 10 on this quiz?

FIGURE 3-2 Boosting Your Self-Confidence

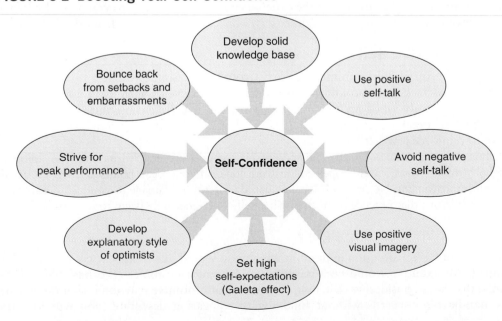

Develop solid knowledge base

Bounce back from setbacks and embarrassments

Use positive self-talk

Strive for peak performance

Self-Confidence

Avoid negative self-talk

Develop explanatory style of optimists

Set high self-expectations (Galeta effect)

Use positive visual imagery

but working from a base of facts helps you project a confident image. Formal education is an obvious and important source of information for your knowledge base. Day-by-day absorption of information directly and indirectly related to your career is equally important. A major purpose of formal education is to get you in the right frame of mind to continue your quest for knowledge. In your quest for developing a solid knowledge base to project self-confidence, be sensitive to abusing this technique. If you bombard people with quotes, facts, and figures, you are likely to be perceived as an annoying know-it-all.

Use Positive Self-Talk

A basic method of building self-confidence is to engage in **positive self-talk**, saying positive things about yourself. The first step in using positive self-talk is to objectively state the incident that is casting doubt about self-worth.[27] The key word here is *objectively*. Terry, who is fearful of poorly executing a report-writing assignment, might say, "I've been asked to write a report for the company, and I'm not a good writer."

The next step is to objectively interpret what the incident *does not* mean. Terry might say, "Not being a skilled writer doesn't mean that I can't figure out a way to write a good report or that I'm an ineffective employee."

Next, the person should objectively state what the incident *does* mean. In doing this, the person should avoid put-down labels such as "incompetent," "stupid," "dumb," "jerk," or "airhead." All these terms are forms of negative self-talk. Terry should state what the incident does mean: "I have a problem with one small aspect of this job."

The fourth step is to objectively account for the cause of the incident. Terry would say, "I'm really worried about writing a good report because I have very little experience in writing along these lines."

The fifth step is to identify some positive ways to prevent the incident from happening again. Terry might say, "I'll get out my textbook on business communications and review the chapter on report writing" or "I'll enroll in a course or seminar on business report writing."

The final step is to use positive self-talk. Terry imagines his boss saying, "This report is really good. I'm proud of my decision to select you to prepare this important report."

Positive self-talk builds self-confidence and self-esteem because it programs the mind with positive messages. Making frequent positive statements or affirmations about the self creates a more confident person. An example would be, "I know I can learn this new equipment rapidly enough to increase my productivity within five days."

Business coach Gary Lockwood emphasizes that positive self-talk is also useful for getting people past difficult times. "It's all in your head," he said. "Remember, you are in charge of your feelings. You are in control of your attitude." Instead of berating yourself after making a mistake, learn from the experience and move on. Say to yourself, "Everyone makes mistakes," "Tomorrow is another day," or "What can I learn from this?"[28]

Avoid Negative Self-Talk

As implied, you should minimize negative statements about yourself to bolster self-confidence. A lack of self-confidence is reflected in statements such as "I may be stupid, but ...," "Nobody asked my opinion," "I know I'm usually wrong, but ...," "I know I don't have as much education as some people, but ..." Self-effacing statements like these serve to reinforce low self-confidence.

It is also important not to attribute to yourself negative, irreversible traits, such as "idiotic," "ugly," "dull," "loser," and "hopeless." Instead, look on your weak points as areas for possible self-improvement. Negative self-labeling can do long-term damage to your self-confidence. If a person stops that practice today, his or her self-confidence may begin to increase.

Use Positive Visual Imagery

Assume you have a situation in mind in which you would like to appear confident and in control. An example would be a meeting with a major customer who has told you by e-mail that he is considering switching suppliers. Your intuitive reaction is that if you cannot handle his concerns without fumbling or appearing desperate, you will lose the account. An important technique is this situation is **positive visual imagery**, or picturing a positive outcome in your mind. To apply this technique in this situation, imagine yourself engaging in a convincing argument about why your customer should retain your company as the primary supplier. Imagine yourself talking in positive terms about the good service your company offers and how you can rectify any problems.

Visualize yourself listening patiently to your customer's concerns and then talking confidently about how your company can handle these concerns. As you rehearse this moment of truth, create a mental picture of you and the customer shaking hands over the fact that the account is still yours.

Positive visual imagery helps you appear self-confident because your mental rehearsal of the situation has helped you prepare for battle. If imagery works for you once, you will be even more effective in subsequent uses of the technique.

positive visual imagery

Picturing a positive outcome in your mind.

Set High Expectations for Yourself (the Galeta Effect)

If you set high expectations for yourself and you succeed, you are likely to experience a temporary or permanent boost in self-confidence. The **Galeta effect** is a type of self-fulfilling prophecy in which high expectations lead to high performance. Similar to positive self-talk, if you believe in yourself, you are more likely to succeed. You expect to win, so you do. The Galeta effect does not work all the time, but it does work some of the time for many people.

Workplace behavior researchers D. Brian McNatt and Timothy A. Judge studied the Galeta effect with 72 auditors within three offices of a major accounting firm over a three-month period. The auditors were given letters of encouragement to strengthen their feelings of self-efficacy. Information in the letters was based on facts about the auditors, such as information derived from their résumés and company records. The results of the experiment showed that creating a Galeta effect bolstered self-efficacy, motivation, and performance. However, the performance improvement was temporary, suggesting that self-expectations need to be boosted regularly.[29]

Galeta effect

A type of self-fulfilling prophecy in which high expectations lead to high performance.

Develop the Explanatory Style of Optimists

According to the research and observations of consultant and trainer Price Pritchett, optimism is linked to self-confidence. Explaining events in an optimistic way can help preserve self-confidence and self-esteem. When experiencing trouble, optimists tend to explain the problems to themselves as temporary. Bad events are expected to be short-lived, and optimists look to the future when times will be better. Another aspect of optimists' explanatory style protects their self-confidence. Rather then condemn themselves for failures, they look for how other factors or circumstances have contributed to the problem. Optimists, then, do not take all the blame for a problem, but look to external factors to help explain what went wrong.

Interpreting difficulties in this way gives the optimists a sense of control. Instead of looking at the unfortunate situation as hopeless, they have faith in their ability to deal with the problem.[30] Suppose an optimist purchases a computer workstation that comes packed in a box with many parts along with directions. A problem arises: some of the screws and dowels do not fit, and the directions are unclear. A pessimist might suffer a drop in self-confidence and self-esteem, saying to himself or herself, "What a fool I am. I can't even assemble a piece of office furniture." In contrast, the optimist might say, "I'm doing something wrong here, and I will get a buddy to help show me my mistake. But the manufacturer can also be blamed. The instructions are terrible, and all the parts may not fit together." In this way the optimist does not take such a big hit to self-confidence and self-esteem.

Strive for Peak Performance

A key strategy for projecting self-confidence is to display **peak performance**, or exceptional accomplishment in a given task. The experience is transient but exceptionally meaningful. Peak performance refers to much more than attempting to do your best.

peak performance

Exceptional accomplishment in a given task.

Experiencing peak performance in various tasks over a long time period would move a person toward self-actualization.[31] To achieve peak performance, you must be totally focused on what you are doing. When you are in the state of peak performance, you are mentally calm and physically at ease. Intense concentration is required to achieve this state. You are so focused on the task at hand that you are not distracted by extraneous events or thoughts. To use an athletic analogy, you are *in the zone* while you are performing the task. In fact, many sport psychologists and other sports trainers work with athletes to help them attain peak performance.

The mental state achieved during peak performance is akin to a person's sense of deep concentration when immersed in a sport or hobby. On days when tennis players perform way above their usual game, they typically comment, "The ball looked so large today, I could read the label as I hit it." On the job, focus and concentration allow the person to sense and respond to relevant information coming both from within the mind and from outside stimuli. When you are at your peak, you impress others by responding intelligently to their input. While turning in peak performance, you are experiencing a mental state referred to as *flow*.

Although you are concentrating on an object or sometimes on another person during peak performance, you still have an awareness of the self. You develop a strong sense of the self, similar to self-confidence and self-efficacy, while you are concentrating on the task. Peak performance is related to self-confidence in another important way. Achieving peak performance in many situations helps you develop self-confidence.

Skill-Building Exercise 3-3 gives you and opportunity to work on enhancing your self-confidence.

Bounce Back from Setbacks and Embarrassments

Resilience is a major contributor to personal effectiveness. Overcoming setbacks also builds self-confidence, as implied from the description of the explanatory style of optimists. An effective self-confidence builder is to convince yourself that you can conquer adversity such as setbacks and embarrassments, thus being resilient. The vast majority of successful leaders have dealt successfully with at least one significant setback in their careers, such as being fired or demoted. In contrast, crumbling after a setback or series of setbacks will usually lower self-confidence. Two major suggestions for bouncing back from setbacks and embarrassments are presented next.

Get Past the Emotional Turmoil   Adversity has enormous emotional consequences. The emotional impact of severe job adversity can rival the loss of a personal relationship. The stress from adversity leads to a cycle of adversity followed by stress, followed by more adversity. A starting point in dealing with the emotional aspects of adversity is to

---

HUMAN RELATIONS SKILL-BUILDING EXERCISE 3-3

Building Your Self-Confidence and Self-Efficacy

Most people can use a boost to their self-confidence. Even if you are a highly confident individual, perhaps there is room for building your feelings of self-efficacy in a particular area, such as a proud and successful business owner learning a new skill such as editing digital photos or speaking a foreign language. For this skill-building exercise, enhance your self-confidence or self-efficacy in the next two weeks by trying out one of the many suggestions for self-confidence building described in the text.

As part of planning the implementation of this exercise, think about any area in which your self-confidence could use a boost. A candid human relations student, who was also a confident cheerleader, said, "Face it. I'm terrible at PowerPoint presentations. I put up so many details on my slides that the audience is trying to read my slides instead of looking at me. I have to admit that my PowerPoint presentation consists mostly of my reading my slides to the audience. I'm much better at cheerleading." So this student studied information in her human relations text about making better graphic presentations. She revamped her approach to using her slides as headlines and talking points. She tried out one presentation in class, and one at her church. She received so many compliments about her presentations that she now has much higher self-efficacy with respect to PowerPoint presentations.

Your instructor might organize a sharing of self-confidence building episodes in the class. If the sharing does take place, look for patterns in what seemed to work for self-confidence or self-efficacy building. Also, listen for any patterns in failed attempts at self-confidence building.

accept the reality of your problem. Admit that your problems are real and that you are hurting inside. A second step is *not to take the setback personally*. Remember that setbacks are inevitable so long as you are taking some risks in your career. Not personalizing setbacks helps reduce some of the emotional sting. If possible, *do not panic*. Recognize that you are in difficult circumstances under which many others panic. Convince yourself to remain calm enough to deal with the severe problem or crisis. Also, *get help from your support network*. Getting emotional support from family members and friends helps overcome the emotional turmoil associated with adversity.

Find a Creative Solution to Your Problem   An inescapable part of planning a comeback is to solve your problem. You often need to search for creative solutions. Suppose a person faced the adversity of not having enough money for educational expenses. The person might search through standard alternatives such as applying for financial aid, looking for more lucrative part-time work, and borrowing from family members. Several students have solved their problem more creatively by asking strangers to lend them money as intermediate-term investments. An option the investors have is to receive a payback based on the future earnings of the students.

SELF-ASSESSMENT QUIZZES IN OVERVIEW

The two self-assessment quizzes presented in this chapter support each other well. Self-Assessment Quiz 3-1 is a self-esteem checklist. People who score high on The Self-Esteem Checklist should theoretically score high on Self-Assessment Quiz 3-2, How Self-Confident Are You? The reason is that self-esteem and self-confidence are closely related and may be part of the same concept. An exception is that some people might like themselves even though they are not particularly self-confident in many situations. Perhaps their attitude is, "So who cares if I am not self-confident? I like me anyway."

Concept Review and Reinforcement

Key Terms

self-esteem 45
self-efficacy 53

positive self-talk 56
positive visual imagery 57

Galeta effect 57
peak performance 57

Summary of Key Concepts

Self-esteem refers to the overall evaluation people make about themselves. People with high self-esteem develop a positive self-concept. Self-esteem develops from a variety of early-life experiences. People who were encouraged to feel good about themselves and their accomplishments by key people in their lives are more likely to enjoy high self-esteem. Of major significance, self-esteem also results from accomplishing worthwhile activities, and then feeling proud of these accomplishments. Praise and recognition for accomplishments also help develop self-esteem.

Self-esteem is important for career success. Good mental health is another major consequence of high self-esteem. One of the links between good mental health and self-esteem is that high self-esteem helps prevent many situations from being stressful. Workers with high self-esteem develop and maintain favorable work attitudes and perform at a high level. A company with high self-esteem workers has a competitive advantage.

High self-esteem can sometimes have negative consequences, such as undermining others to preserve one's own status. A potential negative consequence of low self-esteem is envying too many people. Our own reference group has the biggest impact on self-esteem. Low self-esteem can have negative consequences for romantic relationships because people with self-doubts consistently underestimate their partners' feelings for them. A series of studies showed that students who based their self-esteem on internal sources generally received higher grades and were less likely to consume alcohol and drugs or develop eating disorders.

Self-esteem can be enhanced in many ways: (a) attain legitimate accomplishments; (b) be aware of your personal strengths; (c) rebut the inner critic; (d) practice self-nurturing; (e) minimize settings and interactions that detract from your feelings of competence; (f) get help from others, including talking and socializing frequently with people who boost your self-esteem; (g) model the behavior of people with high self-esteem; and (h) create a high self-esteem living space.

Various studies have shown that people with a high sense of self-efficacy tend to have good job performance, so self-confidence is important for your career. Our feelings of self-confidence stem from five sources of information: actual experiences, or things that we have done; experiences of others, or modeling; social comparison, or comparing yourself to others; social persuasion, the process of convincing another person; and emotional arousal, or how we feel about events around us and manage our emotions.

A general principle of boosting your self-confidence is to experience success (goal accomplishment) in a variety of situations. The specific strategies for building self-confidence described here are (a) develop a solid knowledge base, (b) use positive self-talk, (c) avoid negative self-talk, (d) use positive visual imagery, (e) set high expectations for yourself (the Galeta effect), (f) develop the explanatory style of optimists, (g) strive for peak performance, and (h) bounce back from setbacks and embarrassments.

Check Your Understanding

1. Why does holding an important job contribute to a person's self-esteem?

2. A study by economists indicated that workers with higher levels of self-esteem tended to be more productive. What would be an explanation for this finding?

3. Having workers with high self-esteem is supposed to give a company a competitive edge. If you were responsible for hiring a few new workers, how would you evaluate a given applicant's level of self-esteem?

4. Exercises to boost self-esteem and self-confidence often emphasize focusing on your positive qualities. Why might it also be important to be aware of your weak points to develop self-esteem?

5. A study mentioned in this chapter showed that people with high self-esteem are sometimes intolerant of people quite different from themselves. How would you explain these findings?

6. When you meet another person, on what basis do you conclude that he or she is self-confident?

7. What positive self-talk can you use after you have failed on a major assignment?

8. In what way does your program of studies contribute to building your self-esteem and self-confidence?

9. Many pharmaceutical firms actively recruit cheerleaders as sales representatives to call on doctors to recommend their brand of prescription drugs. The firms in question say that cheerleaders make good sales reps because they are so self-confident. What is your opinion on this controversial issue?

10. Interview a person whom you perceive to have a successful career. Ask that person to describe how he or she developed high self-esteem. Be prepared to discuss your findings in class.

The Web Corner

http://www.more-self-esteem.com
(Measuring and building your self-esteem.)

http://www.self-confidence.co.uk
(Developing your self-confidence.)

http://www.mindtools.com/selfconf.html
(The difference between self-confidence and low self-confidence.)

Internet Skills Builder: Learning More About Your Self-Esteem

The Self-Esteem Checklist in this chapter gave you one opportunity to assess you self-esteem. To gain additional insights into your self-esteem, visit http://www.more-selfesteem.com. Go to "Quizzes" under Free Resources, and take the self-esteem test. How does your score on this quiz compare to your score on The Self-Esteem Checklist? If your level of self-esteem as measured by the two quizzes is quite different (such as high vs. low), explain why this discrepancy might occur.

Developing Your Human Relations Skills

Interpersonal Relations Case 3.1

The Confetti Man

Nick Jablonski works for a manufacturer of property maintenance and recreational vehicles such as lawn mowers, snowblowers, and all-terrain vehicles. The company prospers even during downturns in the economy. This is true because when economic conditions are worrisome, many people invest more money in taking care of their property and enjoying themselves close to home instead of traveling. Nick holds the job title "celebrations assistant" as part of his work duties. The more traditional part of his job is to organize company events like picnics, sales meetings, and shareholder meetings.

When asked to explain the celebrations assistant part of his job in more detail, Nick replied with a smile, "My job is to help workers throughout the company celebrate accomplishments that help the company reach its goals. I'll give you a couple of examples. Suppose I learn that a production technician has exceeded quota on inserting dashboards on riding mowers. I will visit the factory floor and help the technician celebrate. Sometimes I will attach a smiley face to his or her work area. I might shake his or her hand or pat the person on the back. Yet to be dramatic, I will shower the person with confetti.

"Just last week I was told by her supervisor that one of our customer service reps was working on the phone with a woman suffering from arthritis. The customer was having a difficult time starting one of our lawn mowers. The rep stayed on the phone 20 minutes with the lady until she could pull the start cord correctly. The customer was so pleased that she wrote a letter to the CEO praising the helpfulness of the rep.

"My response was to visit the customer service rep's area and have a little celebration. Not only did I throw two bags of confetti, I blew a fog horn. I could tell the rep became a little embarrassed because she blushed. Yet I knew that I really boosted her self-esteem."

When Nick was asked why his work as a celebrations assistant boosted worker self-esteem, he answered as follows: "My job is to make our employees feel good about themselves. My smiley faces, my encouraging message, and especially my confetti throwing make people feel great. If people feel great about themselves and their accomplishments, their self-esteem heads north. It's that simple."

Case Questions

1. To what extent do you think that the celebrations assistant is really boosting the self-esteem of workers?
2. Assume that Nick is successful in boosting worker self-esteem. How might this help the company?
3. Advise the CEO of the company in question as to whether having a celebrations assistant on the payroll is a good investment of company money.

Source: Several facts in this case are based on Jeffrey Zaslow, "The Most-Praised Generation Goes to Work," *The Wall Street Journal*, April 20, 2007, pp. W1, W7.

Interpersonal Relations Case 3.2

Building Up Kristina

Kristina Wright entered the front door of the half of a house she was sharing with Wendy Lopez. Her housemate said, "I don't see a smile on your face. How did the job hunt go today?"

"Not too well," replied Wright. "I had two interviews, but I doubt I'll be called back. After all, there are dozens of applicants looking for administrative assistant positions with better qualifications than mine. In this economy you really have to know the right people to land a job."

"Will you please stop it, Kristina? You're as good or better than the competition. You have your degree, and you have experience as an administrative intern. Besides that, you look great."

"That's easy for you to say, Wendy. You have a good job, and people like you. I'm just average, average, average. Even Lucky [Kristina's cocker spaniel] has an average name. And thousands of girls are named Kristina."

"With an attitude like that," replied Wendy, "you won't get hired. Be proud of who you are. You're somebody special."

"Thanks for the ego boost, my ever faithful friend. But I almost don't have the courage to go back out there tomorrow and face any more interviews."

Case Questions

1. What seems to be Kristina's problem based on the brief information you have been given?
2. What recommendations can you make to Kristina to boost her self-confidence enough to get through any upcoming job interviews she might have?
3. How helpful might be the words of encouragement and advice that Wendy has given Kristina so far?

CHAPTER 4

··

Interpersonal Communication

Mike Dionne epitomized the hotshot sales rep of the late-'90s info tech boom. A master of the frontal assault, Dionne, who works for Altera Corp., juggled 25 accounts, winning customers on complex features that only an engineer could love. But when the bubble burst in 2000, Dionne's sales dried up fast, and no amount of wheedling could persuade many of his customers to meet with him. He talked a lot but listened for the wrong things. The market had changed, but Dionne hadn't.

Six years later, he handles only seven accounts and often takes four times as long to close a deal. He listens more, too. For example, Dionne met with an exec at a medical firm for the first time. He reiterated what he had said on the phone: Altera was looking at how it should invest in the medical field. For 90 minutes, Dionne sat quietly as the potential customer described the technology he planned to buy and the obstacles he expected. Dionne never said Altera wanted to sell him chips. "You could tell the IT exec was jazzed," says Dionne. "He was comfortable, leaning back in his chair and talking freely."

The meeting did not close with a sale, but Altera Chief Executive John P. Danne couldn't be happier with Dionne's approach. The transformation is exactly what Danne hope to see from a three-year effort to create a more empathetic workforce. In the last four years, Danne has spent nearly $11 million on training, using self-proclaimed "empathy consultants" to help his sales force identify with customer situations, feelings, and motives.[1]

The story about the high-tech sales representative and his careful

Learning Objectives

After reading and studying this chapter and doing the exercises, you should be able to

1. Explain the basic steps in the communication process.
2. Explain the relationship-building aspect of interpersonal communication.
3. Understand nonverbal communication and improve your nonverbal communication skills.

4. Understand barriers to communication, including gender differences, and know how to overcome them.
5. Enhance your listening skills.

listening illustrates the importance of effective interpersonal communication skills in business. (Empathetic listening is a key part of face-to-face communication.) **Communication** is the sending, receiving, and understanding of messages. It is also the basic process by which managers, customer contact workers, and professionals accomplish their work. For example, a customer service representative cannot resolve a thorny customer problem without carefully receiving and sending information. Communication is also important because communication skills are a success factor for workers in a variety of jobs.

The subject of this chapter is interpersonal, or face-to-face, communication rather than electronic communication such as e-mail, instant messaging, text messaging, and videoconferencing. However, almost all principles of interpersonal communication also apply to electronic communication. The importance of face-to-face communication has increased in the age of electronic communication. Many companies have discovered that the subtle aspects of communication possible in face-to-face communication can help productivity. A key example would be talking to a person to help build a good working relationship. A concern expressed by management advisors recently is that too many electronic messages are misinterpreted, and that e-mail messages have become a substitute for the nuanced conversations critical in the workplace.[2]

The information in this chapter is aimed at reducing communication problems among people and helping you enhance your communication effectiveness. The chapter approaches these ends in two ways. First, it explains the nature of a few key facets of interpersonal communication. Second, it presents guidelines for improving your effectiveness, along with skill-building exercises. Keep in mind that communication underlies almost every human relations activity, as much as running supports almost every sport. You need good communication skills to get through job interviews, perform well on the job, and get promoted.

communication

The sending, receiving, and understanding of messages.

STEPS IN THE COMMUNICATION PROCESS

LEARNING OBJECTIVE 1

One way to understand how people communicate is to examine the steps involved in transmitting and receiving a message, as shown in Figure 4-1. For effective communication to take place, six components must be present: a sender, a message, a channel, a receiver, feedback, and the environment. In addition, a seventh component, noise, affects the entire communication process. To help understand the communication process,

FIGURE 4-1 A Basic Model of the Communication Process

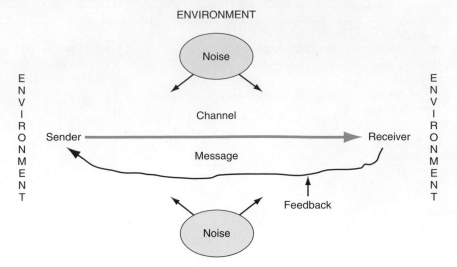

assume that a production manager in a bicycle factory wants to inform a team leader that productivity in her department slipped last month.

1. **Sender (or source).** The sender in a communication event is usually a person (in this case, the production manager) attempting to send a spoken, written, sign language, or nonverbal message to another person or persons. The perceived authority and credibility of the sender are important factors in influencing how much attention the message will receive.

2. **Message.** The heart of the communication event is the **message**, a purpose or idea to be conveyed. Many factors influence how a message is received. Among them are clarity, the alertness of the receiver, the complexity and length of the message, and how the information is organized. The production manager's message will most likely get across if he says directly, "I need to talk to you about last month's below-average productivity figures."

3. **Channel (medium).** Several communication channels, or media, are usually available for sending messages in organizations. Typically, messages are written (usually electronically), spoken, or a combination of the two. Some kind of nonverbal signal such as a smile or hand gesture accompanies most spoken messages. In the production manager's case, he has chosen to drop by the team leader's office and deliver his message in a serious tone.

4. **Receiver.** A communication event can be complete only when another party receives the message and understands it properly. In the example here, the team leader is the receiver. Perceptual distortions of various types act as filters that can prevent a message from being received as intended by the sender. If the team leader is worried that her job is at stake, she might get defensive when she hears the production manager's message.

5. **Feedback.** Messages sent back from the receiver to the sender are referred to as **feedback**. Without feedback, it is difficult to know whether a message has been received and understood. The feedback step also includes the reactions of the receiver. If the receiver takes action as intended by the sender, the message has been received satisfactorily. The production manager will know his message got across if the team leader says, "OK, when would you like to review last month's productivity reports?" Effective interpersonal communication therefore involves an exchange of messages between two people. The two communicators take turns being receiver and sender.

6. **Environment.** A full understanding of communication requires knowledge of the environment in which messages are transmitted and received. The organizational culture (attitudes and atmosphere) is a key environmental factor that influences

message

A purpose or idea to be conveyed.

feedback

In communication, messages sent back from the receiver to the sender.

communication. It is easier to transmit controversial messages when trust and respect are high than when they are low.

7. **Noise.** Distractions such as noise have a pervasive influence on the components of the communication process. In this context, **noise** is anything that disrupts communication, including the attitudes and emotions of the receiver. Noise includes such factors as stress, fear, negative attitudes, and low motivation.

noise

Anything that disrupts communication, including the attitudes and emotions of the receiver.

RELATIONSHIP BUILDING AND INTERPERSONAL COMMUNICATION

Another way of understanding the process of interpersonal communication is to examine how communication is a vehicle for building relationships. According to Ritch Sorenson, Grace DeBord, and Ida Ramirez, we establish relationships along two primary dimensions: dominate–subordinate, and cold–warm. In the process of communicating we attempt to dominate or subordinate. When we dominate, we attempt to control communication. When we subordinate, we attempt to yield control, or think first of the wishes and needs of the other person. Dominators expect the receiver of messages to submit to them; subordinate people send a signal that they expect the other person to dominate.[3]

LEARNING OBJECTIVE 2

We indicate whether we want to dominate or subordinate by the way we speak or write, or by the nonverbal signals we send. The dominator might speak loudly or enthusiastically, write forceful messages filled with exclamation points, or gesture with exaggerated, rapid hand movements. He or she might write a harsh e-mail message, such as "It's about time you started taking your job seriously, and put in some real effort."

In the subordinate mode, we might speak quietly and hesitantly, in a meek tone, apologetically. A subordinate person might ask, "I know you have better things on your mind than to worry about me, but I was wondering when I can expect my reimbursement for travel expenses?" In a work setting, we ordinarily expect people with more formal authority to have the dominant role in conversations. However, in more democratic, informal companies, workers with more authority are less likely to feel the need to dominate conversations.

The *cold–warm dimension* also shapes communication because we invite the same behavior that we send. Cold, impersonal, negative messages evoke similar messages from others. In contrast, warm verbal and nonverbal messages evoke similar behavior from others. Getting back to the inquiry about the travel-expense check, here is a colder versus warmer response by the manager:

Colder: Travel vouchers really aren't my responsibility. You'll just have to wait like everybody else.

Warmer: I understand your problem. Not getting reimbursed on time is a bummer. I'll follow up on the status of your expense check sometime today or tomorrow.

The combination of dominant and cold communication sends the signal that the sender of the message wants to control and to limit, or even to withdraw from a personal relationship. A team leader might say that she cannot attend a Saturday morning meeting because she has to go out of town for her brother's wedding. A dominant and cold manager might say, "I don't want to hear about your personal life. Everyone in this department has to attend our Saturday meeting."

Subordinate actions combined with warm communication signal a desire to maintain or build the relationship while yielding to the other person. A manager communicating in a warm and subordinate manner in relation to the wedding request might say, "We'll miss you on Saturday morning because you are a key player in our department. However, I recognize that major events in personal life sometimes take priority over a business meeting."

Figure 4-2 summarizes how the dual dimensions of dominate–subordinate and cold–warm influence the relationship-building aspects of communication. Rather than regarding these four quadrants of relationships as good or bad, think of your purposes.

FIGURE 4-2 Communication Dimensions of Establishing a Relationship

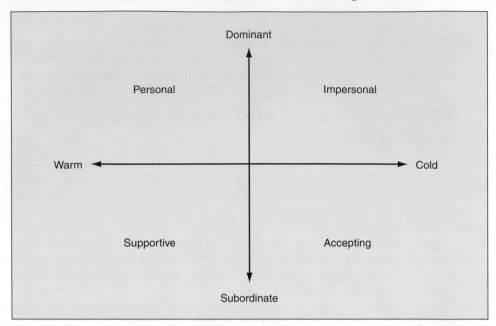

Source: Ritch Sorenson, Grace Debord, and Ida Ramirez, *Business and Management Communication: A Guide Book*, 4th ed., © 2001. Adapted by permission of Pearson Education, Inc., Upper Saddle River, NJ.

In some situations you might want to dominate and be cold, yet in most situations you might want to submit a little and be warm in order to build a relationship. For example, being dominant and cold might be necessary for a security officer who is trying to control an unruly crowd at a sporting event.

Observe that the person in the *dominant–cold* quadrant has an impersonal relationship with the receiver, and the person in the *warm–subordinate* quadrant has a supportive relationship with the receiver. Being *dominant and warm* leads to a personal relationship, whereas being *subordinate and cold* leads to an accepting relationship. The combinations of *dominant–cold* and *warm–subordinate* are more likely to produce the results indicated.

Harvard psychologist Steven Pinker adds additional insight into how warm acquaintances communicate. They go out of their way not to look as if they are presuming a dominant–subordinate relationship but instead a relationship of equals.[4] Your friend who values your relationship might say, "If you're going to the recycling center today, is there any chance you could take along my old cell phone and laptop with you?"

LEARNING OBJECTIVE 3

An acquaintance not interested in maintaining a relationship with you might communicate in a cold, dominant–subordinate fashion by saying, "When you visit the recycling center today, take along my old cell phone and laptop with you."

NONVERBAL COMMUNICATION IN ORGANIZATIONS

nonverbal communication

The transmission of messages through means other than words.

A substantial amount of communication between people takes place at the nonverbal level. **Nonverbal communication** refers to the transmission of messages through means other than words. These messages accompany verbal messages or sometimes stand alone. The general purpose of nonverbal communication is to communicate the feeling behind a message. For instance, you can say no with either a clenched fist or a smile to communicate the intensity of your negative or positive feelings.

The following paragraphs summarize the major modes of transmission of nonverbal communication and provide guidelines for improving nonverbal communication. Chapter 7, about cross-cultural relations, describes cultural differences in nonverbal communication.

Modes of Transmission of Nonverbal Communication

Nonverbal communication can be transmitted in many modes. You may be surprised that certain factors, such as dress and appearance, are considered part of nonverbal communication.

Environment The setting or environment in which you send a message can influence how that message is received. Assume that your manager invites you out to lunch at an upscale restaurant to discuss a problem. You will think it is a more important topic under these circumstances than you would if the manager had lunch with you in the company cafeteria.

Other important environmental silent messages include room color, temperature, lighting, and furniture arrangement. A person who sits behind a large, uncluttered desk, for example, appears more powerful than a person who sits behind a small, messy desk.

Interpersonal Distance The placement of one's body in relation to someone else is widely used to transmit messages (see Figure 4-3). In general, getting physically close to another person conveys a positive attitude toward that person. Putting your arm around someone is generally interpreted as a friendly act. (Some people, however, recoil when touched by someone other than a close friend. Touching others on the job can also be interpreted as sexual harassment.) Watch out for cultural differences in preferences for interpersonal distance, such as French people standing much closer to each other while conversing than do Americans.

Closely related to interpersonal distance is where and how you sit in relation to another person during a meeting. Sitting across the table from a person during a negotiation session creates a defensive, competitive atmosphere, often leading to each party taking a firm stand on his or her point of view. The table becomes a tangible and psychological barrier between both parties. Recognition of this observation leads many a manager or salesperson to meet another person with neither a conference table nor coffee table between them. Even when seated on separate chairs instead of a sofa, removal of a large table or desk separating the two parties leads to a friendlier, more open negotiation or sales discussion.[5]

Posture Posture communicates a variety of messages. Standing erect usually conveys the message that the person is self-confident and experiencing positive emotion. Slumping makes a person appear to be lacking in self-confidence or down in the dumps. Another

FIGURE 4-3 Four Circles of Intimacy

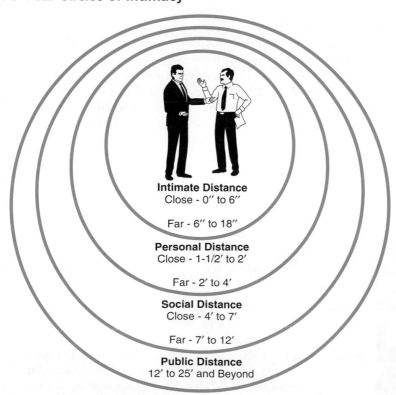

Intimate Distance
Close - 0″ to 6″

Far - 6″ to 18″

Personal Distance
Close - 1-1/2′ to 2′

Far - 2′ to 4′

Social Distance
Close - 4′ to 7′

Far - 7′ to 12′

Public Distance
12′ to 25′ and Beyond

interpersonal message conveyed by posture involves the direction of leaning. Leaning toward the sender suggests that you are favorably disposed toward his or her message; leaning backward communicates the opposite. Openness of the arms or legs serves as an indicator of liking or caring. In general, people establish closed postures (arms folded and legs crossed) when speaking to people they dislike.

Can you think of an aspect of your posture that conveys a specific message?

Hand Gestures   Frequent hand movements show positive attitudes toward another person. In contrast, dislike or disinterest usually produces few gestures. An important exception is that some people wave their hands furiously while arguing. Gestures are also said to provide clues to a person's levels of dominance and submission. The gestures of dominant people are typically directed outward toward the other person. Examples include a steady, unwavering gaze and touching one's partner. Submissive gestures are usually protective, such as touching oneself or shrugging one's shoulders.

Facial Expressions and Eye Contact   Using your head, face, and eyes in combination provides the clearest indications of interpersonal attitudes. Looking at the ceiling (without tilting your head), combined with a serious expression, almost always communicates the message "I doubt what you're saying is true." Maintaining eye contact with another person improves communication. To maintain eye contact, it is usually necessary to move your face and eyes with the other person. Moving your face and eyes away from the other person is often interpreted as defensiveness or a lack of self-confidence.

The face is often used as a primary source of information about how we feel. We look for facial clues when we want to determine another person's attitude. You can often judge someone's current state of happiness by looking at his or her face. The term *sourpuss* attests to this observation. Happiness, apprehension, anger, resentment, sadness, contempt, enthusiasm, and embarrassment are but a few of the emotions that can be expressed through the face.

Voice Quality   Often more significance is attached to the *way* something is said than to *what* is said. A forceful voice, which includes a consistent tone without vocalized pauses, connotes power and control. Closely related to voice tone are volume, pitch, and rate of speaking. Anger, boredom, and joy often can be interpreted from voice quality. Anger is noted when the person speaks loudly, with a high pitch and at a fast rate. Boredom is indicated by a monotone. Joy is indicated by loud volume. Avoiding an annoying voice quality can make a positive impact on others. The research of voice coach Jeffrey Jacobi provides some useful suggestions. He surveyed a nationwide sample of 1,000 men and women and asked, "Which irritating or unpleasant voice annoys you the most?" The most irritating was a whining, complaining, or nagging tone.

Jacobi notes that we are judged by the way we sound. He also notes that careers can be damaged by voice problems such as those indicated in the survey. "We think about how we look and dress," says Jacobi, "and that gets most of the attention. But people judge our intelligence much more by how we sound than how we dress."[6] Do Self-Assessment Quiz 4-1 to apply Jacobi's findings to your development.

Voice quality can be even more important over the phone because you cannot rely on facial expressions and eye contact to improve your message. Ed Barks, who trains public speakers, says that small-business owners need to make effective use of their vocal pitch, articulation, volume, and rate of speech. Furthermore, "Paying attention to all of these factors is essential if a small-business owner has any hope of capturing the fancy of his or her attendant at the other end of the line."[7] The same suggestions would apply to anyone trying to create a favorable impression in other work environments.

Personal Appearance   Your external image plays an important role in communicating messages to others. Job seekers show recognition of the personal appearance aspect of nonverbal communication when they carefully groom for a job interview. People pay more respect and grant more privileges to those they perceive as being well dressed and neatly groomed. The meaning of being well dressed depends heavily on the situation. In an IT firm, neatly pressed jeans, a stylish T-shirt, and clean sport shoes might

Voice-Quality Checkup

The voice-quality study cited in the text ranked voice quality in decreasing order of annoyance, as follows:

- Whining, complaining, or nagging tone—44.0 percent
- High-pitched, squeaky voice—15.9 percent
- Mumbling—11.1 percent
- Very fast talking—4.9 percent
- Weak and wimpy voice—3.6 percent
- Flat, monotonous tone—3.5 percent
- Thick accent—2.4 percent

Directions: Ask yourself and two other people familiar with your voice whether you have one or more of the preceding voice-quality problems. If your self-analysis and feedback from others does indicate a serious problem, get started on self-improvement. Record your voice on tape and attempt to modify the biggest problem. Another avenue of improvement is to consult with a speech coach or therapist.

qualify as being well dressed. The same attire worn in a financial service firm would qualify as being poorly dressed.

A recent tendency is a return to more formal business attire, to suggest that a person is ambitious and successful. The best advice for using appearance to communicate non-verbal messages is to size up the environment to determine what type of appearance and dress connotes the image you want to project.

Attention Paid to Other Person   The more attention paid to the other person during face-to-face interaction, the more valued and important that person feels. Paying attention to another individual includes other modes of nonverbal communication such as eye contact, an interested facial expression, and moving toward the other person. In a society that increasingly accepts and values multitasking, a natural tendency is to divide your attention between the person you are communicating and a computer screen, cell phone message, or a text message. Such multitasking is acceptable and natural to some people, yet makes many others feel unimportant and marginalized. Communication consultant Ericc Krell writes, "A CEO who checks her BlackBerry during a meeting can give the impression that the session is unimportant."[8]

Guidelines for Improving Nonverbal Communication

Nonverbal communication, like verbal communication, can be improved. Here are six suggestions to consider.

1. **Obtain feedback on your body language by asking others to comment on the gestures and facial expressions you use in conversations.** Be videotaped conferring with another individual. After studying your body language, attempt to eliminate those mannerisms and gestures that you think detract from your effectiveness. Common examples include nervous gestures such as moving knees from side to side, cracking knuckles, rubbing the eyes or nose, head scratching, and jingling coins.

2. **Learn to relax when communicating with others.** Take a deep breath and consciously allow your body muscles to loosen. Tension-reducing techniques should be helpful here. A relaxed person makes it easier for other people to relax. You are likely to elicit more useful information from other people when you are relaxed.

3. **Use facial, hand, and body gestures to supplement your speech, but don't overdo it.** A good starting point is to use hand gestures to express enthusiasm. You can increase the potency of enthusiastic comments by shaking the other person's hand, nodding approval, or smiling.

4. **Avoid using the same nonverbal gesture indiscriminately.** If you want to use nodding to convey approval, do not nod with approval when you dislike what somebody else is saying. Also, do not pat everybody on the back. Nonverbal gestures that are used indiscriminately lose their communication effectiveness.

The Mirroring Technique

To practice mirroring, during the next 10 days each class member schedules one mirroring session with an unsuspecting subject. An ideal opportunity would be an upcoming meeting on the job. Another possibility would be to practice interviewing techniques with a friend—but do not mention the mirroring technique. A third possibility would be to sit down with a friend and conduct a social conversation.

While holding an interview or discussion with the other party, use the mirroring technique. Imitate the person's breathing pattern, rate of speech, hand movements, eye movements, leg movements, or any other noticeable aspect of behavior.

After the mirroring sessions have been conducted, hold a class discussion about the results. Questions include the following:

1. Did the other person notice the mirroring and comment on the behavior of the person doing the mirroring?

2. Was the rapport enhanced (or hindered) by the mirroring?

3. How many of the students intend to repeat the mirroring technique in the future?

5. **Use role-playing to practice various forms of nonverbal communication.** A good starting point would be to practice selling your ideas about an important project or concept to another person. During your interchange, supplement your spoken messages with appropriate nonverbal cues such as posture, voice intonation, gestures, and so forth. Later, obtain the other person's perception of the effectiveness of your nonverbal communication.

mirroring
Subtly imitating someone.

6. **Use mirroring to establish rapport.** Nonverbal communication can be improved through **mirroring**, or subtly imitating someone. The most successful mirroring technique is to imitate the breathing pattern of another person. If you adjust your own breathing rate to match someone else's, you will soon establish rapport with that individual. Another effective mirroring technique is to adopt the voice speed of the person with whom you are communicating. If the other person speaks more slowly than you typically do, slow down to mirror him or her.

You can also use mirroring by imitating a manager to win favor. Many subordinates have a relentless tendency to copy the boss's mannerisms, gestures, way of speaking, and dress. As a consequence, without realizing why, your manager may think more favorably of you.

Caution: Do not use mirroring to the extent that you appear to be mocking another person, thereby adversely affecting rapport. Do Skill-Building Exercise 4-1 to get started developing your mirroring skills.

GUIDELINES FOR OVERCOMING COMMUNICATION PROBLEMS AND BARRIERS

LEARNING OBJECTIVE 4

Communication problems in organizations are ever present. Some interference usually takes place between ideation and action, as suggested earlier by the noise factor in Figure 4-1. The type of message influences the amount of interference. Routine or neutral messages are the easiest to communicate. Interference is most likely to occur when a message is complex, emotionally arousing, or clashes with a receiver's mental set.

An emotionally arousing message deals with topics such as money or a relationship between two people. A message that clashes with a receiver's mental set requires the person to change his or her typical pattern of receiving messages. Try this experiment. The next time you visit a restaurant, order dessert first and the main meal second. The server probably will not receive your dessert order because it deviates from the normal sequence.

Here we describe strategies and tactics for overcoming some of the more frequently observed communication problems in the workplace, as outlined in Figure 4-4.

FIGURE 4-4 Overcoming Communication Problems and Barriers

1. Understand the receiver.
2. Minimize defensive communication.
3. Repeat message and use multiple channels
4. Check comprehension and feelings and use verbal and nonverbal feedback.
5. Display a positive attitude.
6. Use persuasive communication.
7. Engage in active listening.
8. Prepare for stressful conversations.
9. Engage in metacommunication.
10. Recognize gender differences in communication.

Understand the Receiver

Understanding the person you are trying to reach is a fundamental principle of overcoming communication barriers. The more you know about your receiver, the better able you are to deliver your message effectively. Three important aspects of understanding the receiver are (1) developing empathy, (2) recognizing his or her motivational state, and (3) understanding the other person's frame of reference.

Developing **empathy** requires placing yourself in the receiver's shoes. To accomplish this, you have to imagine yourself in the other person's role and assume the viewpoints and emotions of that individual. For example, if a supervisor were trying to communicate the importance of customer service to sales associates, the supervisor might ask himself or herself, "If I were a part-time employee being paid close to the minimum wage, how receptive would I be to messages about high-quality customer service?" To empathize, you have to understand another person. *Sympathy* means that you understand and agree.

Recent research suggests subtle patterns of brain cells, called *mirror neurons,* help us empathize with others. These brain circuits reflect the actions and intentions of others as if they were our own. Neuroscientist Marco Iacoboni explains that the mirror system gives us an open-mindedness, and a propensity to understand others and cultures. The cells work in this manner: When another person smiles or wrinkles his or her nose in distaste, motor cells in your own brain linked to those expressions resonate in response like a tuning fork. As a result, you get a hint of the feeling itself. The more empathy you have, the stronger the motor neuron response.[9]

The biological component to empathy should not lead you to conclude that empathy is not a skill that can be acquired. It is conceivable that as you develop empathy, your mirror neurons grow in number or become better developed, just as your calf muscles become better defined if you run frequently.

The receiver's **motivational state** could include any active needs and interests operating at the time. People tend to listen attentively to messages that show promise of satisfying an active need or interest. Management usually listens attentively to a suggestion framed in terms of cost savings or increased profits. A coworker is likely to be attentive to your message if you explain how your idea can lead to a better year-end financial bonus for the group.

People perceive words and concepts differently because their vantage points and perspectives differ. Such differences in **frame of reference** create barriers to communication. A frame of reference can also be considered a lens through which we view the world. A manager attempted to chastise a team member by saying, "If you keep up your present level of performance, you'll be a repair technician all your life." The technician replied, "That's good news," because he was proud of being the first person in

empathy

In communication, imagining oneself in the receiver's role, and assuming the viewpoints and emotions of that individual.

motivational state

Any active needs and interests operating at a given time.

frame of reference

The fact that people perceive words and concepts differently because their vantage points and perspectives differ.

his family to hold a skilled job. Understanding another person's frame of reference requires empathy.

On a day-by-day basis, understanding another person's frame of reference often translates into figuring out his or her mind-set. A woman telephoned a call center located in India with a sense of frustration in her voice. She said she was instructed by her computer to "press any key to continue," and was upset that her keyboard didn't have an "any" key. The caller's mind-set was such that she had to search for the "any" key.[10] (Of course, a more perceptive person might have noticed that the instructions did not say, press *the* any key to continue, but *any key*.)

BACK TO THE OPENING CASE

The chief executive of Altera believed strongly that empathy is a key interpersonal skill for a sales representative, especially in a competitive sales situation. Perhaps during the high-tech boom of years ago customers would line up to order a product even if the sales rep did not take the time to understand him or her. In today's world, however, empathizing with the situations, feelings, and motives of customers is a critical interpersonal skill for closing sales.

Minimize Defensive Communication

defensive communication

The tendency to receive messages in such a way that our self-esteem is protected.

An important general communication barrier is **defensive communication**—the tendency to receive messages in such a way that our self-esteem is protected. Defensive communication is also responsible for people sending messages to make them look good. For example, when being criticized for low production, a financial sales consultant might blame high interest rates, which are drawing customers away from stocks and mutual funds.

Overcoming the barrier of defensive communication requires two steps. First, people have to recognize the existence of defensive communication. Second, they have to try not to be defensive when questioned or criticized. Such behavior is not easy because of the unconscious or semiconscious process of **denial**—the suppression of information we find uncomfortable. For example, the sales consultant just cited would find it uncomfortable to think of himself or herself as being responsible for below-average performance.

denial

The suppression of information we find uncomfortable.

Repeat Your Message Using Multiple Channels

Repetition enhances communication, particularly when different channels are used to convey the same message. Effective communicators at many job levels follow spoken agreements with written documentation. Because most communication is subject to at least some distortion, the chances of a message being received as intended increase when two or more channels are used. Many firms have a policy of using a multiple-channel approach to communicate the results of a performance evaluation. The worker receives an oral explanation from the manager of the results of the review. The worker is also required to read the form and indicate by signature that he or she has read and understands the meaning of the review. Another useful way of using multiple channels is to follow up a telephone call or in-person conversation with an e-mail message summarizing key facts or agreements.

Check Comprehension and Feelings via Verbal and Nonverbal Feedback

Ask for feedback to determine whether your message has been received as intended. A frequent managerial practice is to conclude a meeting with a question such as "OK, what have we agreed upon?" Unless feedback of this nature is obtained, you will not know whether your message has been received until the receiver carries out your request. If the request is carried out improperly, or if no action is taken, you will know that the message was received poorly.

Obtaining feedback is important because it results in two-way communication in which people take turns being sender and receiver, thereby having a dialogue. Dialogues take time because they require people to speak more slowly and listen more carefully. The results of having employees engage in dialogue are said to include a deeper sense of community (a feeling of belongingness) and greater trust among employees.[11] Relate this finding to your own experiences. Do you trust people more when you both exchange ideas and listen to each other?

Feedback is also important because it provides reinforcement to the sender, and few people will continue to communicate without any reinforcement. The sender is reinforced when the receiver indicates understanding of the message. When the original receiver indicates that he or she understands the message, that person becomes the sender. A nod of approval would be an appropriate type of nonverbal reinforcement for the sender to receive.

In addition to looking for verbal comprehension and emotions when you have delivered a message, check for feelings after you have received a message. When a person speaks, we too often listen to the facts and ignore the feelings. If feelings are ignored, the true meaning and intent of the message is likely to be missed, thus creating a communication barrier. Your boss might say to you, "You never seem to take work home." To clarify what your boss means by this statement, you might ask, "Is that good or bad?" Your boss's response will give you feedback on his or her feelings about getting all your work done during regular working hours.

When you send a message, it is also helpful to express your feelings in addition to conveying the facts. For example, "Our defects are up by 12 percent [fact], and I'm quite disappointed about those results [feelings]." Because feelings contribute strongly to comprehension, you will help overcome a potential communication barrier.

Display a Positive Attitude

Being perceived as having a positive attitude helps melt communication barriers. This is true because most people prefer to communicate with a positive person. According to Sharon Lund O'Neil, you must establish credibility and trustworthiness if you expect others to listen, let alone get them to react positively to your communication.[12] Being positive helps make you appear more credible and trustworthy, whereas being consistently negative makes you less credible and trustworthy. As one coworker said about a chronic complainer in his office, "Why take Margot seriously? She finds something wrong with everybody and everything."

Communicate Persuasively

A powerful tactic for overcoming communication barriers is to communicate so persuasively that obstacles disappear. *Persuasiveness* refers to the sender convincing the receiver to accept his or her message. Persuasion thus involves selling to others. Hundreds of articles, books, audiotapes, and videos have been developed to help people become more persuasive. The following are some representative suggestions for becoming a more persuasive communicator, both in speaking and in writing.[13]

1. **Know exactly what you want.** Your chances of selling an idea increase to the extent that you have clarified the idea in your own mind. The clearer and more committed you are at the outset of a selling or negotiating session, the stronger you are as a persuader.

2. **Never suggest an action without telling its end benefit.** In asking for a raise, you might say, "If I get this raise, I'll be able to afford to stay with this job as long as the company likes."

3. **Get a yes response early on.** It is helpful to give the persuading session a positive tone by establishing a "yes pattern" at the outset. Assume that an employee wanted to convince the boss to allow the employee to perform some work at

> "If you want to get to a certain level, especially in a professional environment like most businesses, you have to project the right image. You have to speak the way people you aspire to be speak. Your speech is related to status."
> —Dian DiResta, speech pathologist who runs her own consulting firm in New York. Quoted in Alyssa Danigelis, "Like, Um, You Know," *Fast Company*, May 2006, p. 99.

home during normal working hours. The employee might begin the idea-selling questions with "Is it important for the company to obtain maximum productivity from all its employees?"

4. **Use power words.** An expert tactic for being persuasive is to sprinkle your speech with power (meaning *powerful*) words. Power words stir emotion and bring forth images of exciting events. Examples of power words include *decimating the competition, bonding with customers, surpassing previous profits, sustaining customer loyalty,* and *attaining the unattainable.* Using power words is part of having a broad vocabulary.

5. **Minimize raising your pitch at the end of sentences.** Part of being persuasive is to not sound unsure and apologetic. In English and several other languages, a convenient way to ask a question or to express doubt is to raise the pitch of your voice at the end of a sentence or phrase. As a test, use the sentence "You like my ideas." First say *ideas* using approximately the same pitch and tone as with every other word. Then say the same sentence by pronouncing *ideas* with a higher pitch and louder tone. By saying *ideas* loudly, you sound much less certain and are less persuasive.

6. **Talk to your audience, not the screen.** Computer graphic presentations have become standard practice even in small-group meetings. Many presenters rely so heavily on computer-generated slides and transparencies that they basically read the slides and transparencies to the audience. Jean Mausehund and R. Neil Dortch remind us that in an oral presentation, the predominant means of connection between sender and receiver should be eye contact. When your audience is frequently distracted by movement on the screen, computer sounds, garish colors, or you looking at the screen, eye contact suffers. As a result, the message is weakened, and you are less persuasive.[14]

7. **Back up conclusions with data.** You will be more persuasive if you support your spoken and written presentations with solid data. You can collect the data yourself or quote from a printed or electronic source. Relying too much on research has a potential disadvantage, however. Being too dependent on data could suggest that you have little faith in your intuition. For example, you might convey a weak impression if, when asked your opinion, you respond, "I can't answer until I collect some data."

8. **Minimize "wimp" phrases and words.** Persuasive communicators minimize statements that make them appear weak and indecisive. Such phrases convey the impression that they are not in control of their actions. Wimp phrases include "It's one of those days," "I'm not sure about that," "Don't quote me on that," and "I'll try my best to get it done." (It is better to commit yourself forcibly by saying, "I'll get it done.") Wimpy words include *sort of, hopefully,* and *maybe.* Although wimp phrases and words should be minimized, there are times when they reflect honest communication, such as a team leader saying to the manager, "Maybe we can get this crash project completed by the end of the month."

9. **Avoid or minimize common language errors.** You will enhance your persuasiveness if you minimize common language errors because you will appear more articulate and informed. Here are several common language errors:

   a. "Just between you and I" is wrong. "Just between you and me" is correct.

   b. *Irregardless* is not a word; *regardless* is correct.

   c. Avoid double negatives when you want to express the negative, despite the increasing popularity of double negatives. Common examples of double negatives are "I got no nothing from my best customer this week" and "We don't have no money in the budget for travel." If expressed with the right inflection, a double negative can be correct. For example, to say "We don't have no money" with an emphasis on *no money* means that the budget is not completely depleted. Yet in general, double negatives make the sender appear so ill-informed that they fail to persuade.

    d. "We are customer oriented" is correct. "We are customer orientated" is wrong. Here is an example of an error so widely committed that it would be fair to wonder if dictionaries will soon include *orientated*.

10. **Avoid overuse of jargon and clichés.** To feel "in" and hip many workers rely heavily on jargon and clichés, such as referring to their "fave" (for *favorite*) product, or that "At the end of the day" something counts, or that software is "scalable" (meaning it can get bigger). Add to the list "a seamless company," to mean the various departments cooperate with one another. The caution is that if a person uses jargon and hip phrases too frequently, the person appears to be too contrived and lacking in imagination.[15]

If you can learn to implement most of the preceding 10 suggestions, you are on your way toward becoming a persuasive communicator. In addition, you will need solid facts behind you, and you will need to make skillful use of nonverbal communication. If you are looking for an example of a persuasive communicator in business, check out David Brandon, the CEO of Domino's Pizza. Brandon is such a great motivator and communicator that many people have encouraged him to run for public office. See if you can find a video of Brandon on YouTube or Facebook.

Skill-Building Exercise 4-2 provides you an opportunity to practice persuasive communication.

Engage in Active Listening

LEARNING OBJECTIVE 5

Persuasion deals primarily with sending messages. Improving one's receiving of messages is another part of developing better communication skills. Unless you receive messages as they are intended, you cannot perform your job properly or be a good companion. A major challenge in developing good listening skills is that we process information much more quickly than most people speak. The average speaking rate is about 130 words per minute. In contrast, the average rate of processing information is about 300 words per minute.[16] So, you have to slow down mentally to listen well.

Listening can be even more essential than talking when engaged in face-to-face communication. Listening is a particularly important skill for anybody whose job involves troubleshooting, as one needs to gather information to solve problems. Another reason that improving the listening skills of employees is important is because insufficient listening is extraordinarily costly. Listening mistakes lead to reprocessing letters, rescheduling appointments, reshipping orders, and recalling defective products. Effective listening also improves interpersonal relations because the people listened to feel understood and respected.

SKILL-BUILDING EXERCISE 4-2

I Want a Raise

The purpose of this exercise is to practice your persuasive skills using a topic of interest to many people—obtaining a salary increase. One by one, students make a presentation in front of the class, presenting a persuasive argument for why they merit a salary increase. The instructor will decide whether to use a handful of volunteers or the entire class. The audience represents the boss. The student will first explain his or her job title and key responsibilities. (Use your imagination here.) Next, make a three-minute convincing argument as to why you merit a salary increase, and perhaps indicate how much you want. You will probably have about 15 minutes for preparation, inside or outside of class.

After the presentations, volunteers will offer feedback on the effectiveness of selected presentations. During the presentations of the other students, make a few notes about the presenter's effectiveness. You may need a couple of minutes between presenters to make your notes. Consider these factors:

- Overall, how convincing was the presenter? If you were the boss, would you give him or her the requested salary increase?
- Which techniques of persuasion did he or she use?
- What aspect of the presentation was unconvincing or negative?

What lessons did you take away from this exercise about persuasive communication?

A major component of effective listening is to be an **active listener**. The active listener listens intensely, with the goal of empathizing with the speaker. As a result of listening actively, the listener can feed back to the speaker what he or she thinks the speaker meant. Feedback of this type relies on both verbal and nonverbal communication. Active listening also involves **summarization**. When you summarize, you pull together, condense, and thereby clarify the main points communicated by the other person. Summarization is also referred to as *paraphrasing* because you repeat in your own words what the sender says, feels, and means. Here are three examples of summarization (or paraphrasing) statements:

"What I heard you say during our meeting is that ."

"As I understand it, your position is that ."

"Your major objection, then, is that ."

Another component to active listening is to indicate by your body language that you are listening intently. When a coworker comes to you with a question or concern, focus on that person and exclude all else. If you tap your fingers on the desk or glance around the room, you send the message that the other person and his or her concerns do not warrant your full attention. Listening intently through nonverbal communication also facilitates active listening because it demonstrates respect for the receiver.

Observing nonverbal communication is another important part of active listening. Look to see if the speaker's verbal communication matches his or her nonverbal communication. Suppose you ask another person if he or she would like to join your committee. If the person says yes, but looks bored and defensive, he or she is probably not really interested in joining your committee. Quite often a person's nonverbal communication is more indicative of the truth than is verbal communication.[17]

Specific suggestions for improving active listening skills are summarized in Figure 4-5. These suggestions relate to good listening in general, as well as active listening. As with any other suggestions for developing a new skill, considerable practice (with some supervision) is needed to bring about actual changes in behavior. One of the problems

FIGURE 4-5 Suggestions for Active Listening

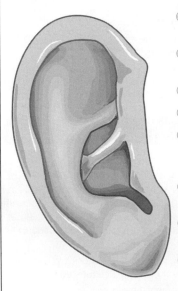

- *While your target is talking, look at him or her intently.* At the same time, maintain steady eye contact.

- *Be patient about your turn to speak.* A common barrier to effective listening is to mentally prepare an answer while another person is speaking.

- *Nod your head in agreement from time to time.*

- *Mutter "mmh" or "uh-huh" periodically but not incessantly.*

- *Ask open-ended questions to encourage the other person to talk.* For example, you encourage more conversation by saying "What do you think of . . . ?" rather than asking "Do you agree that . . . ?"

- *Reflect your target's content or meaning.* Rephrase and summarize concisely what the other person is saying.

- *Reflect the other person's feelings.* Reflection-of-feeling responses typically begin with "You feel that . . . "

- *Keep your ratio of talking to listening down to about one to five.* In other words, spend 20 percent of your time talking, and 80 percent listening to be perceived as a great listener.

- *Ask yourself whether anything the other person is saying could benefit you.* Maintaining this perspective will enable you to benefit from most listening episodes and will motivate you to listen intently.

a poor listener would encounter is the difficulty of breaking old habits to acquire new ones. Self-Assessment Quiz 4-2 gives you an opportunity to think about bad listening habits you may have acquired. To practice your listening skills, do Skill-Building Exercise 4-3.

Prepare for Stressful Conversations

Communication barriers will frequently surface when two or more people are engaged in conversation fraught with emotion, such as giving highly negative performance feedback, rejecting a person for membership in your team, or firing an employee. Giving praise is another exchange that can make both or either parties uncomfortable. The sender might feel that he or she is patronizing the receiver, and the receiver might feel unworthy of the praise. One technique for reducing the stress in potentially stressful conversations is to prepare for them in advance.

A starting point in preparing for a stressful conversation is self-awareness about how you react to certain uncomfortable exchanges. For example, how do you feel when the

SELF-ASSESSMENT QUIZ 4-2		

Listening Traps

Communication specialists at Purdue University have identified certain behavior patterns that interfere with effective hearing and listening. After thinking carefully about each trap, check how well the trap applies to you: not a problem or need improvement. To respond to the statements accurately, visualize how you acted when you recently were in a situation calling for listening.

	Not a problem	Need improvement
Mind reader. You will receive limited information if you constantly think, "What is this person really thinking or feeling?"	____	____
Rehearser. Your mental rehearsals for "Here's what I'll say next" tune out the sender.	____	____
Filterer. You engage in selective listening by hearing only what you want to hear. (Could be difficult to judge because the process is often unconscious.)	____	____
Dreamer. You drift off during a face-to-face conversation, which often leads you to an embarrassing "What did you say?" or "Could you repeat that?"	____	____
Identifier. If you refer everything you hear to your experience, you probably did not really listen to what was said.	____	____
Comparer. When you get sidetracked sizing up the sender, you are sure to miss the message.	____	____
Derailer. You change the subject too quickly, giving the impression that you are not interested in anything the sender has to say.	____	____
Sparrer. You hear what is said, but quickly belittle or discount it, putting you in the same class as the derailer.	____	____
Placater. You agree with everything you hear just to be nice or to avoid conflict. By behaving this way you miss out on the opportunity for authentic dialogue.	____	____

Interpretation: If you checked *need improvement* for five or more of the above statements, you are correct—your listening needs improvement! If you checked only two or fewer of the above traps, you are probably an effective listener and a supportive person.

Source: Listening Traps Quiz from *Messages: The Communication Skills Handbook* (Oakland, CA: New Harbinger Publications, 1983).

receiver of the negative feedback reacts with hostility? Do you clam up, or do you become counterhostile? If you anticipate a hostile reception to an upcoming conversation, rehearse the scenario with a neutral friend. Deliver the controversial content that you will be delivering during the real event. Practice the body language you will use when you deliver a phrase such as, "As team leader, I must tell you that you have contributed almost nothing of value to our current project." Another part of the rehearsal is to practice delivering clear content—be explicit about what you mean. "Almost nothing of value to our current project" is much more explicit than, "Your contribution has much room for improvement."

Also, practice *temperate phrasing*, or being tactful while delivering negative feedback. Communications specialist Holly Weeks suggests the following: Instead of snapping at someone, "Stop interrupting me," try this: "Can you hold on a minute? I want to finish before I lose my train of thought." Temperate phrasing will take some of the sting out of a stressful conversation.[18]

Engage in Metacommunication

Sometimes the best way to overcome a communication barrier with another person is to describe the nature of the relationship between you two at the moment. **Metacommunication** means to communicate about your communication to help overcome barriers or resolve a problem. If you as a team leader were facing heavy deadline pressures, you may say to a team member, "I might appear brusque today and tomorrow. Please don't take it personally. It's just that I have to make heavy demands on you because the team is facing a gruesome deadline." A more common situation is when the person with whom you are attempting to communicate appears angry or indifferent. Instead of wasting the communication event, it would be better to say, "You do not seem receptive to listening to me now. Are we having a problem? Should I try again later?"

metacommunication

To communicate about your communication to help overcome barriers or resolve a problem.

Recognize Gender Differences in Communication Style

A trend in organizations for many years has been to move toward gender equality. Despite this trend, substantial interest has arisen in identifying differences in communication styles between men and women. People who are aware of these differences face fewer communication barriers between themselves and members of the opposite sex. As we discuss these differences, recognize that they are group stereotypes. Please do not be offended by these stereotypes; they are exaggerations noticed by some researchers and observers. To cite one example that runs counter to the stereotype, some women dominate meetings whereas some men focus on listening to and supporting others during a meeting. Individual differences in communication style usually are more important than group (men versus women) differences. Here we will discuss the major findings of gender differences in communication patterns.[19]

SKILL-BUILDING EXERCISE 4-3

Listening to a Coworker

Before conducting the following role-plays, review the suggestions for effective listening presented in the text and Figure 4-5. Restating what you hear (summarization) is particularly important when listening to a person who is talking about an emotional topic.

The Elated Coworker: One student plays the role of a coworker who has just been offered a six-month assignment to the Rome, Italy, unit of the company. She will be receiving a 30 percent pay increase during the assignment plus a supplementary living allowance. She is eager to describe full details of her good fortune to a coworker. Another student plays the role of the coworker to whom the first worker wants to describe her good fortune. The second worker decides to listen intently to the first worker. Other

class members will rate the second student on his or her listening ability.

The Discouraged Coworker: One student plays the role of a coworker who has just been placed on probation for poor job performance. His boss thinks that his performance is below standard and that his attendance and punctuality are poor. He is afraid that if he tells his girlfriend, she will leave him. He is eager to tell his tale of woe to a coworker. Another student plays the role of a coworker he corners to discuss his problems. The second worker decides to listen intently to his problems but is pressed for time. Other class members will rate the second student on his or her listening ability.

Concept Review and Reinforcement

Key Terms

communication 65
message 66
feedback 66
noise 67
nonverbal communication 68

mirroring 72
empathy 73
motivational state 73
frame of reference 73
defensive communication 74

denial 74
active listener 78
summarization 78
metacommunication 80

Summary of Key Concepts

Communication is the basic process by which managers, customer contact workers, and professionals accomplish their work, yet many communication problems exist in organizations. Communication among people is a complex process that can be divided into six components: sender or source, message, channel (or medium), receiver, feedback, and environment. Noise, or interference, can disrupt communication within any component.

Nonverbal communication plays an important part in sending and receiving messages and is especially important for imparting the emotional aspects of a message. The modes of nonverbal communication include the environment in which the message is sent, interpersonal distance, posture, gestures, facial expressions, voice quality, and personal appearance.

Nonverbal communication can be improved through such means as obtaining feedback, learning to relax, using gestures more discriminately, role playing, and mirroring. The latter refers to subtly imitating someone.

Methods of overcoming communication barriers include the following: (1) understand the receiver, (2) minimize defensive communication, (3) repeat your message using multiple channels, (4) check comprehension and feelings via verbal and nonverbal feedback, (5) display a positive attitude, (6) communicate persuasively, (7) engage in active listening, (8) prepare for stressful conversations, (9) engage in metacommunication (communicating about your communication), and (10) recognize gender differences in communication style.

Check Your Understanding

1. Why are communication skills important in the field you are in or intend to enter?
2. How can knowing the steps in the communication process help a person become a more effective communicator?
3. How can people use their automobiles as a form of nonverbal communication?
4. What type of voice quality do you think would be effective in most work situations?
5. Should a person use power words when he or she is not in a powerful job? Explain.
6. Why does giving employees training in listening often lead to increased productivity and profits?
7. Why is summarization such a powerful communication technique?
8. Identify three scenarios in the workplace that are likely to result in stressful conversations.

9. Suppose your manager does not listen to your suggestions for job improvements. How would you meta-communicate to deal with this problem?

10. What are the implications of gender differences in communication for conducting meetings?

The Web Corner

http://www.optimalthinking.com/
quiz-communication-skills.asp
(Rate your level of communication.)

http://www.queendom.com
(Look for the Communication Skills Test.)

http://nonverbal.ucsc.edu
(Explore nonverbal communications, and test your ability to read nonverbal communication.)

http://members.aol.com/nonverbal2/diction1.htm
(Nonverbal dictionary of gestures, signs, and body language cues.)

Internet Skill Builder: Practicing Listening Skills

Infoplease offers some practical suggestions for improving your listening skills that both support and supplement the ideas offered in this chapter. Infoplease divides listening into three basic steps: hearing, understanding, and judging. Visit the site at www.infoplease.com/homework/listeningskills1.html.

Developing Your Human Relations Skills

Interpersonal Relations Case 4.1

Karl Walks Around

Karl Bennett, a supervisor in a call center located in Iowa, was urged by his manager to walk around the center from time to time to chat informally with the call center workers. His boss said to Karl, "It's always good to know what the call center specialists are feeling and thinking. You might pick up some good ideas." Bennett had studied the technique of *management by walking around* in a human relations course, so he was enthused about the idea.

Karl chose a Tuesday evening to conduct his walk around, and decided to stop by the cubicles of four call center operators to test the technique. If it worked well, he would walk around again in another week.

Karl first stopped by the cubicle of Mandi, making sure first that she was not on the telephone with a customer. "I just dropped by to say hello, and see how things are going," said Karl. "I take it everything is going fine, and that you have no problems," he continued. "Am I right?"

Mandi answered, "Yes, no real problems. Thanks for stopping by."

Next, Karl stopped by the cubicle of Pete, a relatively new operator. "How's it going Pete?" asked Karl. "What kind of problems might you be facing?"

Pete answered, "I'm having trouble understanding the accent of some of my customers. And some of the customers say I talk too fast. Other than that, the job is going well."

"That's interesting," said Karl. "But I see I have a couple of e-mails waiting for me on my BlackBerry. Maybe you do talk too fast. I'll get back to you later."

Karl thought to himself that the walk around was going fine so far. He then dropped by Brittany's cubicle. "What's happening, Brittany?" asked Karl as Brittany was completing a customer inquiry about a defective piece of equipment. Brittany raised the palm of her right hand to signal that she was not quite finished with the call.

Karl then asked, "Are your wedding plans going along OK?"

Brittany replied, "Yes, Karl. Everything is fine. Thanks for stopping by."

A few minutes later, Karl completed his walk around by stopping to visit Derek, a rabid Chicago Bears fan. "Hey Derek, how goes it?" said Karl. "I think the Bears are headed to the league championship this year. What do you think?"

Derek answered, "Oh yes, the Bears are strong this season, and I'm optimistic. But so long as you have dropped by, I wanted to mention that our instruction manuals seem to be too complicated. People are calling in again and again with the most basic questions, like how to find the serial number."

"Don't worry too much about that," replied Derek. "A lot of our customers can hardly read these days. I think the term is *functional illiterate*," said Karl with a smile.

Case Questions

1. How successful is Karl in using his walk around to uncover useful information?
2. What can Karl do to increase his questioning effectiveness?
3. What can Karl do to increase his listening effectiveness?

Interpersonal Relations Case 4.2

The Dental Floss Communication Challenge

Claudia Telfair has worked as a dental hygienist for five years in the same large dental practice in suburban Columbus, Ohio. She treats patients about 25 hours per week. In her words, "If I work too much—more than 25 hours per week—I'm liable to get tendonitis and carpal tunnel syndrome. All that precision scraping takes a toll on my right hand, and to some extent on my left hand. Hovering over patients can also give me back pains, if I do it for too long each week.

"I feel that my work is so important that I am willing to put up with a little physical pain to help my patients have healthy teeth and gums."

"You would say, then, that the biggest frustration in your work is its physical demands?" asked the case researcher.

"I never said that. You said that," replied Telfair. "The part of my job with the biggest impact on the health of patients is getting across my message about healthy habits to prevent tooth decay and gum disease. I lecture my patients. I demonstrate how they should be brushing and flossing, and how they should use soft wood plaque removers [such as Stim-u-Dents]. I give out samples.

"I do everything I can think of to convince my patients to take good care of their teeth and gums between cleaning appointments."

"What's so frustrating about what you've just described?"

"The frustration is that my patients don't seem to listen. They smile, they nod in agreement, and they pack the samples. Yet four months later when the patients return, it appears that most of them are engaging in the same old sloppy dental habits. They continue with superficial brushing with an old toothbrush instead of using a battery-powered or electric one. It looks like they forgot my message about using wooden plaque removers. Yet flossing is the least used preventive treatment of them all."

"When you ask patients why they neglect flossing between their cleaning appointments, what do they say?" asked the case researcher.

"I hear more excuses than you get from violators in traffic court," said Telfair. Some of the typical excuses are that the patients forget, that they are too busy, and that flossing is too painful. A patient told me the other day that he dislikes flossing because the ritual is so ugly and weird."

"What do you tell the patients when you observe that they are not following your advice?"

"I usually just tell them that are doing a poor job of taking care of their teeth and gums. Also, I will usually give them more samples of floss and plaque remover so they will be reminded to do better. Sometimes I give them another brochure about a battery-powered toothbrush.

"I guess you could say that I'm doing a much better job treating tooth and gum problems than preventing them."

Case Questions

1. What communication problems is Claudia Telfair facing in her role as a dental hygienist?
2. What communication errors might Telfair be making?
3. Offer Telfair a couple of suggestions to help her accomplish her goal of being more effective at preventing dental and gum problems, based on your knowledge of interpersonal communication.

Interpersonal Skills Role-Play 4.1

The Dental Hygienist and Dental Patient Role-Play

One student sits on a chair pretending to be a dental patient who does a sloppy job of dental care, such as brushing regularly and flossing. Another student plays the role of dental hygienist Claudia. (She can use a pencil or pen to simulate a metal gum scraper.) With the patient in the chair, engage in a dialogue about the importance of using dental floss. Claudia wants this patient to practice much better dental hygiene, whereas the patient is somewhat skeptical about her advice. Perhaps two or three different pairs can conduct the role-play in front of the class. Other class members will observe the effectiveness of the communication episode in terms of Claudia getting her message across.

CHAPTER 5

Developing Teamwork Skills

It seemed like a typical company holiday party. The brandy and eggnog flowed freely, although it didn't seem to loosen up any of the attendees. "Smile and make pleasant talk while you serve, please," instructed the fellow who had cast himself as Santa. There were plenty of gag gifts: a luxury flat overlooking the Kremlin for Victoria, who was moving to Moscow; growth-enhancing supplements for Domas, who hovers at 6-foot-4. And of course, the requisite tasteless humor. All standard fare for an office party—except that there was no office. Thomas Basil, director of support at MySQL, a $40 million software maker, staged the event online, playing Santa while dispensing virtual drinks and gifts to staffers scattered in such outposts as Russia, England, and Germany.

To accommodate the different geographics, Basil started the festivities on a December day at 10 a.m. in Baltimore, where he lives. (His clocks are actually set seven hours ahead to Helsinki time, the time zone of many of his team members.) "When a company is as spread out as this one," Basil explains, "you have to think of virtual ways to imitate the dynamics of what goes one in a more familiar employment situation."[1]

The activities of the executive just described are directed toward nurturing a bond among workers who, as participants on a virtual team, rarely, if ever, meet. The reason Basil bothers attempting to create bonds among team members is that bonds enhance teamwork, and the modern organization depends on teamwork throughout the company. Many firms rely more on teamwork than on individuals acting alone to accomplish work. To be successful in the modern organization, it is therefore necessary to be an effective team player. You have to work smoothly with other members of the team to accomplish your goals. Teamwork is more important as people work their way up through the organization. Executives, such as CEOs, preach teamwork but tend to dominate meetings and make more decisions by themselves.[2]

Learning Objectives

After reading and studying this chapter and doing the exercises, you should be able to

1. Identify several types of teams in organizations.
2. Understand the advantages and disadvantages of teams.
3. Identify various team member roles.
4. Apply interpersonal-related tactics for effective team play.
5. Apply task-related tactics for effective team play.

The challenges a team member faces come to light when the true nature of a team is recognized. A **team** is a special type of group. Team members have complementary skills and are committed to a common purpose, a set of performance goals, and an approach to the task. In other words, the members of a team work together smoothly, and all pull in the same direction. A workplace team should be more like an effective athletic team than a group of individuals out for individual glory.[3]

This chapter gives you the information, insights, and preliminary practice necessary to develop effective teamwork skills. Self-Assessment Quiz 5-1 will help you assess your current mental readiness to be a contributing team member.

team

A small number of people with complementary skills who are committed to a common purpose, set of performance goals, and approach for which they hold themselves mutually accountable.

TYPES OF TEAMS

All teams in the workplace have the common element of people working together cooperatively and members possessing a mix of skills. Nevertheless, many specific types of work teams can be identified. Successful people will usually have the opportunity to be a member of several different types of teams.

Four representative work teams are self-managing work teams, cross-functional teams, virtual teams and crews. Projects, task forces, and committees are similar in design to cross-functional teams, so they do not receive separate mention here. No matter what label the team carries, its broad purpose is to contribute to a *collaborative workplace* in which people help each other achieve constructive goals. The idea is for workers to collaborate (a high level of cooperation) rather than compete with or prevent others from getting their work done.

As teams have become more common in the workplace, effort has been directed toward specifying the skills and knowledge a person needs to function effectively on a team, particularly a self-managing work team. Self-Assessment Quiz 4-2 presents a representative listing of team skills as perceived by employers.

Self-Managing Work Teams

The best-known work team is a group of workers who take much of the responsibility for managing their own work. The same type of team is referred to as a self-managing work

self-managing work team

A small group of employees responsible for managing and performing technical tasks to deliver a product or service to an external or internal customer.

team, a self-directing work team, a production work team, or a team. A **self-managing work team** is a small group of employees responsible for managing and performing technical tasks to deliver a product or service to an external or internal customer.[4] The majority of large- and medium-size firms make some use of self-managing work teams. Work teams are used in a variety of activities including the production of motorcycles, telephone directories, or a major component for a large computer.

Members of a self-managing work team typically work together on an ongoing, day-by-day basis, thus differentiating it from a task force or a committee. The work team is often given total responsibility for or "ownership" of an entire product or service, such as producing a telephone directory. At other times, the team is given responsibility for a major chunk of a job, such as building an airplane engine (but not the entire airplane).

A major hurdle in forming self-managing teams is to help employees overcome the attitude reflected in the statement "I'm not paid to think." Work teams rely less on supervisors and more on the workers assuming more responsibilities for managing their own activities. For example, work team members may be required to discipline other team members who have attendance, performance, or behavioral problems.[5]

As with all teams, mutual trust among members contributes to team effectiveness. A study conducted with business students, however, showed that if the members trust each other too much they may not monitor (check up on) each other's work enough. As a result, group performance will suffer. This problem of too much trust surfaces primarily when the team members have individual assignments that do not bring them into frequent contact with each other.[6] An example of an individual, or autonomous, project would be preparing a statistical report that would later be given to the group.

Team Skills

A variety of skills is required to be an effective member of various types of teams. Several different business firms use the skill inventory here to help guide team members toward the competencies they need to become high-performing team members.

Directions: Review each team skill listed and rate your skill level for each one using the following classification:

S = strong (capable and comfortable with effectively implementing the skill)

M = moderate (demonstrated skill in the past)

B = basic (minimum ability in this area)

N = not applicable (not relevant to the type of work I do)

Communication skills	*Skill level (S, M, B, or N)*
Speak effectively	_____
Foster open communications	_____
Listen to others	_____
Deliver presentations	_____
Prepare written communication	_____
Self-management skills	
Act with integrity	_____
Demonstrate adaptability	_____
Engage in personal development	_____
Strive for results	_____
Display a commitment to work	_____
Thought process skills	
Innovate solutions to problems	_____
Use sound judgment	_____
Analyze issues	_____
Think "outside the box"	_____
Organizational skills	
Know the business	_____
Use technical/functional expertise	_____
Use financial/quantitative data	_____
Strategic (broad business perspective) skills	
Recognize "big picture" impact	_____
Promote corporate citizenship	_____
Focus on customer needs	_____
Commit to quality	_____
Manage profitability	_____

Interpretation: There is no scoring key for this questionnaire. Its purpose is to raise your awareness of the types of skills that are required to be a successful team member in business.

Cross-Functional Teams

It is common practice for teams to be composed of workers from different specialties. A **cross-functional team** is a work group composed of workers from different specialties, who come together to accomplish a task. The purpose of the cross-functional team is to get workers from different specialties to blend their talents toward accomplishing a task that requires such a mix.

A typical application of a cross-functional team would be to develop a new product such as a video cell phone. Among the specialties needed on such a team would be computer science, engineering, manufacturing, industrial design, marketing, and finance. (The finance person would help guide the team toward producing a video cell phone that could

cross-functional team

A work group composed of workers from different specialties, and about the same organizational level, who come together to accomplish a task.

be sold at a profit.) When members from different specialties work together, they can take into account each other's perspectives when making their contribution. For example, if the manufacturing representative knows that a video cell phone must sell for about one-half the price of a plasma screen TV, then he or she will have to build the device inexpensively. A major advantage of cross-functional teams for product development is that they enhance communication across groups, thereby saving time. In addition to product development, cross-functional teams are used for such purposes as improving quality, reducing costs, and running a company (in the form of a top management team).

To perform well on a cross-functional team, a person would have to think in terms of the good of the larger organization, rather than in terms of his or her own specialty. For example, a manufacturing technician might say, "If I proposed using expensive components for the video phone, would the product cost too much for its intended market?"

Virtual Teams

Some teams conduct most of their work by sending electronic messages to each other rather than conducting face-to-face meetings. A **virtual team** is a small group of people who conduct almost all of their collaborative work by electronic communication rather than face-to-face meetings. E-mail, including IM (instant messaging), is the usual medium for sharing information and conducting meetings. *Groupware* is another widely used approach to conducting an electronic meeting. Using groupware, several people can edit a document at the same time, or in sequence. Desktop videoconferencing is another technological advance that facilitates the virtual team.

Most high-tech companies make some use of virtual teams and electronic meetings. Strategic alliances in which geographically dispersed companies work with each other are a natural for virtual teams. It is less expensive for the field technician in Iceland to hold an electronic meeting with her counterparts in South Africa, Mexico, and California than it is to bring them all together in one physical location. Virtual teams are sometimes the answer to the challenge of hiring workers with essential skills who do not want to relocate. With team members geographically dispersed, precise communications are all the more important for virtual teams. The virtual team members usually need a formal document outlining the objectives, job responsibilities, and team goals. Another communication problem takes place when the virtual team is composed of both in-house workers and those in remote locations. The office-bound members become jealous of the seemingly cushy setup enjoyed by the telecommuters. One solution to this problem is for every member of the team to be given a chance to prove he or she can work off-site.[7]

Establishing trust is a major challenge in a virtual team because the team members have to rely on people they never see to carry out their fair share of the workload, and to exchange reliable information. Trust is also needed in terms of what information should be shared outside of the team. For example, if the team is behind schedule on a project, can each member be trusted not to inform outsiders about the problem? For example, one virtual team had an external communication norm that prohibited team members from conveying negative information to anyone outside the team.[8]

Despite the efficiency of virtual teams, there are times when face-to-face (or at least telephone) interaction is necessary to deal with complex and emotional issues. Negotiating a new contract between management and a labor union, for example, is not well suited to an electronic meeting.

BACK TO THE OPENING CASE

The software company executive believed strongly that a feeling of teamwork is not easy to accomplish among workers who are geographically dispersed. So instead of going to the expense and difficulty of have a physical holiday party, he held a virtual party. Although a virtual holiday party may not be a substitute for the real thing, it reflected a sincere effort on the executive's part to help enhance team spirit. Because almost all of the workers attended the holiday party from their homes, the company did not have to worry about employees driving home from the party under the influence of alcohol.

Crews

We are all familiar with common use of the term *crew* in relation to such groups as those who operate airplanes, boats, and firefighting equipment. The technical meaning of the term means virtually the same thing. A **crew** is a group of specialists each of whom have specific roles, perform brief events that are closely synchronized with each other, and repeat these events under different environmental conditions. A crew is identified by the technology it handles, such as an aircraft crew, or a deep-sea salvage operation. The crew members rarely rotate specialties, such as the flight attendant taking over for the chief pilot. (Special training and licensing would be required.) The following are several criteria of a group qualifying as a crew[9]:

- Clear roles and responsibilities
- Work flow well established before anyone joins the team
- Careful coordination required with other members to perform the task
- Group needs to be in a specific environment to complete its task
- Different people can join the group without interfering with its operation or mission

Because of the specialized roles they play and the essential tasks they perform, much is expected of crews. The future of crews is promising. For example, computer-virus-fighting crews would be a welcome addition to business and society. Mutual trust is especially important in a crew because good cooperation could save one's life, such as in a firefighting crew. Experience with sailing crews strongly suggests that team members should be technically excellent and have good personal chemistry with each other.[10] Under life-threatening circumstances, such as navigating a storm, it is best to have strong bonds with each other.

crew

A group of specialists each of whom have specific roles, perform brief events that are closely synchronized with each other, and repeat these events under different environmental conditions.

THE ADVANTAGES AND DISADVANTAGES OF TEAMS AND TEAMWORK

Groups have always been the building blocks of organizations. Yet groups and teams have recently grown in importance as the basic unit for organizing work. In an attempt to cope with numerous changes in the outside world, many organizations have granted teams increased independence and flexibility. Furthermore, teams are often required to work more closely with customers and suppliers.

The increased acceptance of teams suggests that group work offers many advantages. Nevertheless, it is useful to specify several of these advantages and examine the potential problems of groups. Being aware of these potential pitfalls can often help a person avoid them. These same advantages and disadvantages also apply to group decision making, to be described in Chapter 6.

LEARNING OBJECTIVE 2

synergy

A situation in which the group's total output exceeds the sum of each individual's contribution.

Advantages of Group Work and Teamwork

Group work and group decision making offer several advantages over individual effort. If several knowledgeable people are brought into the decision-making process, a number of worthwhile possibilities may be uncovered[10] It is also possible to gain **synergy**, whereby the group's total output exceeds the sum of each individual's contribution. For example, it would be a rare person working alone who could build a racing car.

Group decision making is also helpful in gaining acceptance and commitment. The argument is that people who contribute to making a decision will feel some ownership about implementing the decision. Team members often evaluate each other's thinking, so the team is likely to avoid major errors. An advertising specialist was developing an advertising campaign to attract seniors to live in a retirement community. The proposed ads had photographs of senior citizens engaged in playing shuffleboard, visiting the pharmacy, and sleeping in a hammock. Another team member on the project pointed out that many seniors perceive themselves to be energetic and youthful. Ads emphasizing advanced age might

therefore backfire. A successful advertising campaign was then developed that featured seniors in more youthful activities such as jogging and dancing.

A major justification for relying on teams in the workplace is that under the right circumstances, they can enhance productivity and profitability. The right circumstances include an atmosphere that promotes teamwork and financial bonuses for high-performing teams. A classic example is American steelmaker Nucor Corp. The company is committed to the spirit of teamwork, and bonuses for teams of steelworkers average 170 percent to 180 percent. Since Nucor implemented its team incentive plan in 1966, the company has been profitable each quarter through 2007 despite foreign competition.[11]

Working in teams and groups also enhances the job satisfaction of members. Being a member of a work group makes it possible to satisfy more needs than working alone. Among these needs are affiliation, security, self-esteem, and self-fulfillment. (Chapter 10 provides more details about psychological needs.)

Disadvantages of Group Work and Teamwork

Group activity has some potential disadvantages for both individuals and the organization. Teams and other groups often waste time because they talk too much and act too little. Committees appear to suffer from more inaction than teams. Abigail Johnson, president of Fidelity Employer Services Co. (Fesco), says that committees are not effective decision makers. "They have tended to be slow and overly risk averse. Even worse, I believe, they can drain an organization of talent, because the group can only be as good as the average."[12] A major problem is that members face pressures to conform to group standards of performance and conduct, as just implied. Some teams might shun a person who is much more productive than his or her coworkers. Shirking of individual responsibility is another problem frequently noted in groups. Unless work is assigned carefully to each team member, an undermotivated person can often squeeze by without contributing his or her fair share to a group effort.

social loafing

The psychological term for shirking individual responsibility in a group setting.

Social loafing is the psychological term for shirking individual responsibility in a group setting. The social loafer risks being ostracized (shunned) by the group but may be willing to pay the price rather than work hard. Loafing of this type is sometimes found in groups such as committees and project teams. Have you ever encountered a social loafer on a group project at school?

At their worst, teams and other groups foster conflict on the job. People within the work group often bicker about such matters as doing a fair share of the undesirable tasks within the department. Cohesive work groups can also become xenophobic (fearful of outsiders). As a consequence, they may grow to dislike other groups and enter into conflict with them. A customer service group might put considerable effort into showing up a sales group because the latter makes promises to customers that the customer service group cannot keep. For example, a sales representative might promise that a customer can get a loaner if his or her equipment needs repair, although customer service has no such policy.

groupthink

A deterioration of mental efficiency, reality testing, and moral judgment in the interest of group solidarity.

A well-publicized disadvantage of group decision making is **groupthink**, a deterioration of mental efficiency, reality testing, and moral judgment in the interest of group solidarity. Simply put, groupthink is an extreme form of consensus. The group atmosphere values getting along more than getting things done. The group thinks as a unit, believes it is impervious to outside criticism, and begins to have illusions about its own invincibility. As a consequence, the group loses its powers of critical analysis.[13] Groupthink appears to have contributed to several of the major financial scandals of the previous decade. Members of top management got together to vote themselves huge bonuses just before filing bankruptcy for their company. Several of the executives, including a few from Enron Corporation, were later sent to prison for their outrageous decisions.

Related to groupthink is the idea that groups often breed conformity in thinking and behavior. In an effort to be accepted by members of the group, some members will attempt

FIGURE 5-1 Key Characteristics of Effective Teams and Work Groups

- The team has clear-cut goals linked to organizational goals so that group members feel connected to the entire organization. Group members are empowered so they learn to think for themselves rather than expecting a supervisor to solve all the difficult problems. At the same time, the group believes it has the authority to solve a variety of problems without first obtaining approval from management.

- Group members are assigned work they perceive to be challenging, exciting, and rewarding. As a consequence, the work is self-rewarding.

- Members depend on one another to accomplish tasks, and work toward a common goal.

- Members learn to think "outside the box" (are creative).

- Members receive extensive training in technical knowledge, problem-solving skills, and interpersonal skills.

- Members inspect their own work for quality.

- Members receive part of their pay related to team or group incentives rather than strictly based on individual performance.

- Group size is generally about 6 people, rather than 10 or more.

- Team members have good intelligence and personality factors such as conscientiousness, openness to experience, collectivism (as opposed to individualism), and pride that contribute to good performance.

- There is honest and open communication among group members and with other groups in the organization.

- Members have the philosophy of working as a team—25 brains, not just 50 hands.

- Members are familiar with their jobs, coworkers, and the work environment. This experience adds to their expertise. The beneficial effects of experience may diminish after awhile because the team needs fresh ideas and approaches.

- The team has emotional intelligence in the sense that it builds relationships both inside and outside the team. Included in emotional intelligence are norms that establish mutual trust among members, a feeling of group identity, and group efficacy.

Sources: Gerben S. Van Der Vegt et al., "Patterns of Interdependence in Work Teams: A Two-Level Investigation of the Relations with Job and Team Satisfaction," *Personnel Psychology,* Spring 2001, pp. 51–69; Shawn L. Berman, Vanessa Urch Druskat, and Steven B. Wolff, "Building the Emotional Intelligence of Groups," *Harvard Business Review,* March 2001, pp. 80–90; Claus W. Langred, "Too Much of a Good Thing? Negative Effects of High Trust and Individual Autonomy in Self-Managing Work Teams," *Academy of Management Journal,* June 2004, pp. 385–389; Suzanne T. Bell, "Deep Level Composition Variables as Predictors of Team Performance: A Meta-Analysis," *Journal of Applied Psychology,* May 2007, pp. 595–615.

to think and act like other members in terms of speech, thinking, and even dress. This tendency is pronounced among teenagers, and takes place on the job as well. You might want to examine a photo of Google, Microsoft, or Apple employees and observe how much conformity in dress you find. Self-Assessment Quiz 5-3 gives you an opportunity to think about your tendencies toward conformity.

Two conditions are important for overcoming the potential disadvantages of teams and groups. First, the members must strive to act like a team,[14] following some of the suggestions given in the upcoming pages. Second, the task given to the group should require collective effort instead of being a task that could better be performed by individuals. For example, an international business specialist would probably learn to conjugate verbs in a foreign language better by working alone than on a team. What is your opinion on this issue? Figure 5-1 presents more information about key factors associated with effective work teams and groups. The more of these factors that are present, the more likely it is that a given team or group will be productive.

The Conformity Quiz

Directions: Circle the extent to which each of the following statements describes your behavior or attitude: agree strongly (AS); agree (A); neutral (N); disagree (D); disagree strongly (DS). You may have to respond in terms of any team or group experience you have had if you are not currently a member of a work team, a class project team, or a sports team. Consider having someone who is familiar with your behavior and attitudes help you respond accurately.

	AS	A	N	D	DS
1. I rarely question the decision reached by the team.	5	4	3	2	1
2. Whatever the group wants is fine with me.	5	4	3	2	1
3. My clothing distinguishes me from the other members of the team.	1	2	3	4	5
4. I consider myself to be one of the gang.	5	4	3	2	1
5. I rarely express disagreement during a group discussion.	5	4	3	2	1
6. I routinely have lunch with other members of the team.	5	4	3	2	1
7. My teammates sometimes complain that I think too independently.	1	2	3	4	5
8. My preference is to piggyback on the ideas of others rather than contribute the ideas of my own.	5	4	3	2	1
9. When I notice that the other members of the team make the same error in speech, I will copy them rather than sound different.	5	4	3	2	1
10. I am often the first person to get up at the scheduled ending of the meeting.	1	2	3	4	5
11. I do almost all of my creative thinking for the team task when I'm with the team.	5	4	3	2	1
12. I'm particularly careful not to criticize an idea submitted by the team leader.	5	4	3	2	1
13. The number of hours I work per week corresponds closely to the number worked by my teammates.	5	4	3	2	1
14. When I think it is necessary, I bring information to the group conflicting with the path we are following.	1	2	3	4	5
15. I would rather keep my mouth closed than point out weaknesses in a teammate's ideas.	5	4	3	2	1
16. I've been called a maverick on more than one occasion by teammates.	1	2	3	4	5
17. I encourage team members to express doubts about proposed solutions to problems.	1	2	3	4	5
18. I invite criticism of my ideas.	1	2	3	4	5
19. When the team laughs at a comment, I laugh too even if I don't think the comment was funny.	5	4	3	2	1
20. Most of my social life centers around activities with my teammates.	5	4	3	2	1

Interpretation: Calculate your score by adding the numbers you have circled, and use the following guide:

80–100 You are a high-conforming individual who readily goes along with the team without preserving your individuality. In an effort to be liked, you might be overcompromising your thinking.

40–79 You have probably achieved the right balance between following group norms (standards of conduct) and expressing your individuality. With actions and attitudes like this, you are on your way to becoming a good team player, yet also in a position to attain individual recognition.

20–29 You are highly individualistic, perhaps to the point of not working smoothly in a team setting. Be careful that you are not going out of your way to be a nonconformist, thereby interfering with your ability to be an effective team player.

Skill Development: Examine your responses to the 20 questions because the response might give you a clue to needed development, often just by making a subtle change within your control. Here are two examples: If you answered agree strongly or agree to Question 8, you might work toward contributing ideas of your own. If you answered disagree or disagree strongly to Question 14, you might work toward helping the team think more critically about the path it is following.

TEAM MEMBER ROLES

LEARNING OBJECTIVE 3

A major challenge in learning to become an effective team member is to choose the right roles to occupy. A role is a tendency to behave, contribute, and relate to others in a particular way. If you carry out positive roles, you will be perceived as a contributor to team effort. If you neglect carrying out these roles, you will be perceived as a poor contributor. Self-Assessment Quiz 5-4 will help you evaluate your present inclinations toward occupying effective roles as a team member. In this section we describe a number of the most frequently observed positive roles played by team members.[15] We also mention a group of negative roles. The description is followed by an activity in which the roles can be practiced.

SELF-ASSESSMENT QUIZ 5-4

Team Player Roles

Directions: For each of the following statements about team activity, check *mostly agree* or *mostly disagree*. If you have not experienced such a situation, imagine how you would act or think if placed in that situation. In responding to the statements, assume that you are taking the questionnaire with the intent of learning something about yourself.

	Mostly agree	Mostly disagree
1. It is rare that I ever miss a team meeting.	___	___
2. I regularly compliment team members when they do something exceptional.	___	___
3. Whenever I can, I avoid being the note taker at a team meeting.	___	___
4. From time to time, other team members come to me for advice on technical matters.	___	___
5. I like to hide some information from other team members so I can be in control.	___	___
6. I welcome new team members coming to me for advice and learning the ropes.	___	___
7. My priorities come first, which leaves me with very little time to help other team members.	___	___
8. During a team meeting, it is not unusual for several other people at a time to look toward me for my opinion.	___	___
9. If I think the team is moving in an unethical direction, I will say so explicitly.	___	___
10. Rarely will I criticize the progress of the team even if I think such criticism is deserved.	___	___
11. It is typical for me to summarize the progress in a team meeting, even if not asked.	___	___
12. To conserve time, I attempt to minimize contact with my teammates outside our meetings.	___	___
13. I intensely dislike going along with a consensus decision if the decision runs contrary to my thoughts on the issue.	___	___
14. I rarely remind teammates of our mission statement as we go about our work.	___	___
15. Once I have made up my mind on an issue facing the team, I am unlikely to be persuaded in another direction.	___	___
16. I am willing to accept negative feedback from team members.	___	___
17. Just to get a new member of the team involved, I will ask his or her opinion.	___	___
18. Even if the team has decided on a course of action, I am not hesitant to bring in new information that supports another position.	___	___
19. Quite often I talk negatively about one team member to another.	___	___
20. My teammates are almost a family to me because I am truly concerned about their welfare.	___	___

(Continued)

21. When it seems appropriate, I joke and kid with teammates. ____ ____
22. My contribution to team tasks is as important to me as my individual work. ____ ____
23. From time to time I have pointed out to the team how we can all improve in reaching our goals. ____ ____
24. I will fight to the last when the team does not support my viewpoint and wants to move toward consensus. ____ ____
25. I will confront the team if I believe that the members are thinking too much alike. ____ ____

Total Score: _____

Scoring and Interpretation: Give yourself one point (+1) for each statement you gave in agreement with the keyed answer. The keyed answer indicates carrying out a positive, as opposed to a negative, role.

Question number	Positive role answer		Question number	Positive role answer
1.	Mostly agree		14.	Mostly disagree
2.	Mostly agree		15.	Mostly disagree
3.	Mostly disagree		16.	Mostly agree
4.	Mostly agree		17.	Mostly agree
5.	Mostly disagree		18.	Mostly agree
6.	Mostly agree		19.	Mostly disagree
7.	Mostly disagree		20.	Mostly agree
8.	Mostly agree		21.	Mostly agree
9.	Mostly agree		22.	Mostly agree
10.	Mostly disagree		23.	Mostly agree
11.	Mostly agree		24.	Mostly disagree
12.	Mostly disagree		25.	Mostly agree
13.	Mostly disagree			

20–25 You carry out a well-above-average number of positive team roles. Behavior of this type contributes substantially to being an effective team player. Study the information in this chapter to build upon your already laudable sensitivity to occupying various positive roles within the team.

10–19 You carry out an average number of positive team roles. Study carefully the roles described in this chapter to search for ways to carry out a greater number of positive roles.

0–9 You carry out a substantially above average number of negative team roles. If becoming an effective team player is important to you, you will have to diligently search for ways to play positive team roles. Study the information in this chapter carefully.

According to the role theory developed by R. Meredith Belbin and his group of researchers, there are nine frequent roles occupied by team members. All of these roles are influenced to some extent by an individual's personality.

1. **Creative problem solver.** The creative problem solver is creative, imaginative, and unorthodox. Such a person solves difficult problems. A potential weakness of this role is that the person tends to ignore fine details and becomes too immersed in the problem to communicate effectively.

2. **Resource investigator.** The resource investigator is extraverted and enthusiastic, and communicates freely with other team members. He or she will explore opportunities and develop valuable contacts. A potential weakness of this role is that the person can be overly optimistic and may lose interest after the initial enthusiasm wanes.

3. **Coordinator.** The coordinator is mature, confident, and a natural team leader. He or she clarifies goals, promotes decision making, and delegates effectively. A downside to occupying this role is that the person might be seen as manipulative

and controlling. Some coordinators delegate too much by asking others to do some of the work they (the coordinators) should be doing.

4. **Shaper.** The shaper is challenging, dynamic, and thrives under pressure. He or she will use determination and courage to overcome obstacles. A potential weakness of the shaper is that he or she can be easily provoked and may ignore the feelings of others.

5. **Monitor-evaluator.** The monitor-evaluator is even tempered, engages in strategic (big picture and long-term) thinking, and makes accurate judgments. He or she sees all the options and judges accurately. A potential weakness of this role occupant is that he or she might lack drive and the ability to inspire others.

6. **Team worker.** The team worker is cooperative, focuses on relationships, and is sensitive and diplomatic. He or she is a good listener who builds relationships, dislikes confrontation, and averts friction. A potential weakness is that the team worker can be indecisive in a crunch situation or crisis.

7. **Implementer.** The implementer is disciplined, reliable, conservative, and efficient. He or she will act quickly on ideas, and convert them into practical actions. A potential weakness is that the implementer can be inflexible and slow to see new opportunities.

8. **Completer-finisher.** The completer-finisher is conscientious and eager to get the job done. He or she has a good eye for detail, and is effective at searching out errors. He or she can be counted on for finishing a project and delivering on time. A potential weakness is that the completer-finisher can be a worrier and reluctant to delegate.

9. **Specialist.** The specialist is a single-minded self-starter. He or she is dedicated and provides knowledge and skill in rare supply. A potential weakness of the specialist is that he or she can be stuck in a niche with little interest in other knowledge and may dwell on technicalities.

The weaknesses in the first nine roles point to problems the team leader or manager can expect to emerge, and therefore an allowance should be made. Belbin refers to these potential problems as *allowable weaknesses* because an allowance should be made for them. To illustrate, if a team worker has a tendency to be indecisive in a crisis, the team should not have high expectations of the team worker when faced with a crisis. Team workers will be the most satisfied if the crisis is predicted and decisions involving them are made before the pressure mounts.[16]

Another perspective on team roles is that team members will sometimes engage in *self-oriented roles*. Members will sometimes focus on their own needs rather than those of the group. The individual might be overly aggressive because of a personal need such as wanting a bigger budget for his or her project. The individual might hunger for recognition or power. Similarly, the person might attempt to dominate the meeting, block others from contributing, or serve as a distraction. One of the ploys used by distracters recently is to engage in cell phone conversations during a meeting, blaming it on "those people who keep calling me."

The many roles just presented overlap somewhat. For example, the implementer might engage in specialist activities. Do not be concerned about the overlap. Instead, pick and choose from the many roles as the situation dictates—whether or not overlap exists. Skill-Building Exercise 5-1 gives you an opportunity to observe these roles in action. The behavior associated with the roles just described is more important than remembering the labels. For example, remembering to be creative and imaginative is more important than remembering the specific label "creative problem solver."

GUIDELINES FOR THE INTERPERSONAL ASPECTS OF TEAM PLAY

The purpose of this and the following section is to help you enhance your effectiveness as a team player by describing the skills, actions, and attitudes required to be an effective team player. You can regard these behaviors (the collective term for skills, actions, and attitudes) as goals for personal improvement. Identify the actions and attitudes for which

LEARNING OBJECTIVE 4

Team Member Roles

A team of approximately six people is formed to conduct a 20-minute meeting on a significant topic of their choosing. The possible scenarios follow:

Scenario A: Management Team. A group of managers are pondering whether to lay off one-third of the workforce to increase profits. The company has had a tradition of caring for employees and regarding them as the company's most precious asset. However, the CEO has said privately that times have changed in our competitive world, and the company must do whatever possible to enhance profits. The group wants to think through the advisability of laying off one-third of the workforce, as well as explore other alternatives.

Scenario B: Group of Sports Fans. A group of fans have volunteered to find a new team name to replace "Redskins" for the local basketball team. One person among the group of volunteers believes that the name "Redskins" should be retained because it is a compliment, rather than an insult to Native Americans. The other members of the group believe that a name change is in order, but they lack any good ideas for replacing a mascot team name that has endured for over 50 years.

Scenario C: Community Group. A community group is attempting to launch an initiative to help battered adults and children. Opinions differ strongly as to what initiative would be truly helpful to battered adults and children. Among the alternatives are establishing a shelter for battered people, giving workshops on preventing violence, and providing self-defense training. Each group member with an idea strongly believes that he or she has come up with a workable possibility for helping with the problem of battered people.

While the team members are conducting their heated discussion, other class members make notes on which team members carry out which roles. Students should watch for the different roles as developed by Belbin and his associates, as well as the self-oriented roles. For example, students in the first row might look for examples of the creative problem solver.

Use the role worksheet that follows to help make your observations. Summarize the comment that is indicative of the role. An example would be noting in the shaper category: "Linda said naming the team the 'Washington Rainbows' seems like too much of an attempt to be politically correct."

Creative Problem Solver _____

Resource Investigator _____

Coordinator _____

Shaper _____

Monitor-Evaluator _____

Team Worker _____

Implementer _____

Completer-Finisher _____

Specialist _____

Self-Oriented Roles _____

Understanding team member roles will contribute to working effectively as a member of a team. However, a contributor to the foundation of effective team play is recognizing individual differences and having good communication skills. The same two factors are fundamental for effectiveness in any setting involving interaction between and among people. Here is an example of how recognizing individual differences and having effective communication skills can help in a team setting: Max and Beth are teammates, and Max notices that Beth is shy and somewhat sullen. (He observes individual differences.) Max gives Beth a playful fist in the air, and says, "Come on Beth, we need your contribution in the 10 o'clock meeting. You have one of the sharpest minds on the team, and you're hiding it from us." With such warm encouragement, Beth then has the courage to contribute more to the morning meeting.

you need the most improvement, and proceed accordingly with self-development. Apply the model for skill development presented in Chapter 1.

One convenient method for classifying team activities in pursuit of goals is to categorize them as people related or task related. Remember, however, that the categorization of people- versus task-related activities is not entirely accurate. For example, if you are challenging your teammates with a difficult goal, are you focusing more on the people (offering them a motivational challenge) or the task (achieving the goal)? We begin first with people-related actions and attitudes (see also Figure 5-2), followed in the next section by task-related actions and attitudes.

FIGURE 5-2 Interpersonal Aspects of Team Play

> 1. Trust team members.
> 2. Display a high level of cooperation and collaboration.
> 3. Recognize the interests and achievements of others.
> 4. Give and receive helpful criticism.
> 5. Share the glory.
> 6. Take care not to rain on another person's parade.

Trust Team Members

The cornerstone attitude of an outstanding team player is to trust team members, including the leader. Working on a team is akin to a small business partnership. If you do not believe that the other team members have your best interests at heart, it will be difficult for you to share opinions and ideas. You will fear that others will make negative statements behind your back.

Trusting team members also includes believing that their ideas are technically sound and rational until proven otherwise. Another manifestation of trust is taking risks with others. You can take a risk by trying out one of their unproved ideas. You can also take a risk by submitting an unproved idea and not worrying about being ridiculed.

Display a High Level of Cooperation and Collaboration

Cooperation and collaboration are synonymous with teamwork. If you display a willingness to help others by working cooperatively with them, you will be regarded as a team player. If you do not cooperate with other team members, the team structure breaks down. Collaboration at a team level refers to working jointly with others to solve mutual problems. Although working with another person on a given problem may take longer than working through a problem alone, the long-term payoff is important. You have established a climate favorable to working on joint problems where collective action is necessary.

Achieving a cooperative team spirit is often a question of making the first move. Instead of grumbling about poor teamwork, take the initiative and launch a cooperative spirit in your group. Target the most individualistic, least cooperative member of the group. Ask the person for his or her input on an idea you are formulating. Thank the person, then state that you would be privileged to return the favor.

Another way of attaining good cooperation is to minimize confrontations. If you disagree with the opinion of another team member, patiently explain the reasons for your differences and look for a workable way to integrate both your ideas. A teammate might suggest, for example, that the team stay until midnight to get a project completed today.

SKILL-BUILDING EXERCISE 5-2

The Scavenger Hunt

The purpose of this teamwork exercise is to demonstrate the importance of cooperation and collaboration in accomplishing a task under pressure. The class is divided into teams of about five students. How much time you can devote to the task depends upon your particular class schedule. The instructor will supply each team with a list of items to find within a prescribed period of time—usually about 35 minutes. Given the time constraints, the group will usually have to conduct the hunt on campus. What follows is a representative list of items to find in an on-campus scavenger hunt:

- A floppy disk
- A tie
- A brick
- A cap from a beer bottle
- A pocket knife
- A flash drive

When the groups return within 30 minutes, you hold a public discussion about what you learned about teamwork and what insights you acquired.

You have plans for the evening and are angered by the suggestion. Instead of lashing out at your teammate, you might say, "I agree we need to put in extra time and effort to get the job done. But why can't we spread out this extra effort over a few days? In this way those of us who cannot work until midnight this evening can still contribute."

Skill-Building Exercise 5-2 is a widely used technique for demonstrating the importance of cooperation and collaboration.

Recognize the Interests and Achievements of Others

A fundamental tactic for establishing yourself as a solid team player is to actively recognize the interests and achievements of others. Let others know you care about their interests.

After you make a suggestion during a team meeting, ask: "Would my suggestion create any problems for anybody else?" or "How do my ideas fit into what you have planned?"

Recognizing the achievements of others is more straightforward than recognizing interests. Be prepared to compliment any tangible achievement. Give realistic compliments by making the compliment commensurate with the achievement. To do otherwise is to compromise your sincerity. For example, do not call someone a genius just because he or she showed you how to compute an exchange rate from one currency to another. Instead, you might say, "Thank you. I am very impressed by your knowledge of exchange rates."

A technique has been developed to enable the entire team to recognize the interests and achievements of others. Playing the anonymous praise game, each team member lists what he or she admires about a specific coworker. The team leader collects the responses and sends each team member the comments made about him or her. Using this technique, team members see a compilation of praise based on how coworkers perceive them. The anonymous praise game helps overcome the hesitancy some people have to praise another person face-to-face.[17]

Give and Receive Helpful Criticism

The outstanding team player offers constructive criticism when needed, but does so diplomatically. To do otherwise is to let down the team. A high-performance team demands sincere and tactful criticism among members. No matter how diplomatic you are, keep your ratio of criticism to praise small. Keep two time-tested principles in mind. First, attempt to criticize the person's work, not the person. It is better to say "The conclusion is missing from your analysis" than "You left out the conclusion." (The latter statement hurts because it sounds like your teammate did something wrong.)

Another key guideline for criticism is to ask a question rather than to make a declarative statement. By answering a question, the person being criticized is involved in improving his or her work. In the example at hand, it would be effective to ask, "Do you think your report would have a greater impact if it contained a conclusion?" In this way, the person being criticized contributes a judgment about the conclusion. The person has a chance to say, "Yes, I will prepare a conclusion."

Criticism works both ways, so the effective team player is willing to accept helpful criticism, such as "You are speaking too fast for several of our team members for whom English is their second language." Becky Blalock, the vice president and chief information officer (CIO) of the electric utility, the Southern Company, regards being open to feedback as one of the core principles of teamwork.[18]

Share the Glory

An effective team player shares praise and other rewards for accomplishment even if he or she is the most deserving. Shared praise is usually merited to some extent because teammates have probably made at least some contribution to the achievement that received praise. For example, if a team member comes up with a powerful suggestion for cutting costs, it is likely that somebody else in the group sparked his or her thinking. Effective examples of sharing glory are easy to find. Think back to watching athletes and other entertainers who win a title or an award. Many of them are gracious enough to share the glory. Shortly after he retired, hockey legend Wayne Gretzky told a television reporter, "I never would have accomplished what I did if I hadn't played with such a great group of guys."

Take Care Not to Rain on Another Person's Parade

As teamwork specialist Pamela Lovell observes, we all have achievements and accomplishments that are sources of pride. Belittling the achievements of others for no legitimate reason brings about tension and anger. Suppress your feelings of petty jealousy.[19] An example would be saying to someone who is proudly describing an accomplishment, "Don't take too much credit. It looks to me like you were at the right place at the right time." If you support teammates by acknowledging their accomplishments, you are more likely to receive their support when needed.

FIGURE 5-3 Task Aspects of Team Play

1. Provide technical expertise (or knowledge of the task).
2. Assume responsibility for problems.
3. See the big picture.
4. Believe in consensus.
5. Focus on deadlines.
6. Help team members do their jobs better.
7. Be a good organizational citizen.

GUIDELINES FOR THE TASK ASPECTS OF TEAM PLAY

LEARNING OBJECTIVE 5

The task aspects of team play also make a key contribution to becoming an effective team player. Here we describe six major task-related tactics, as outlined in Figure 5-3. As mentioned earlier, a task aspect usually has interpersonal consequences.

Provide Technical Expertise (or Knowledge of the Task)

Most people are selected for a work team primarily because of their technical expertise. *Technical* refers to the intimate details of any task, not just tasks in engineering, physical science, and information technology. The sales promotion specialist on a product development team has technical expertise about sales promotion, whether or not sales promotion requires knowledge of engineering or computers.

As team consultant Glenn Parker observes, to use your technical expertise to outstanding advantage you must have the willingness to share that expertise.[20] Some experts perceive their esoteric knowledge as a source of power. As a consequence, they are hesitant to let others share their knowledge for fear of relinquishing power. It is also necessary for the technical expert to be able to communicate with team members in other disciplines who lack the same technical background. The technical person who cannot explain the potential value of his or her contribution may fail to receive much attention.

Assume Responsibility for Problems

The outstanding team player assumes responsibilities for problems. If a problem is not yet assigned to anybody, he or she says, "I'll do it." One team member might note that true progress on the team's effort is blocked until the team benchmarks (compares itself) with other successful teams. The effective team player might say, "You are right, we need to benchmark. If it's okay with everybody else, I'll get started on the benchmarking project tomorrow. It will be my responsibility." Taking responsibility must be combined with dependability. The person who takes responsibility for a task must produce, time after time.

See the Big Picture

Effective team players need to think conceptually, or see the big picture. A trap in team effort is that discussion can get bogged down in small details and the team might lose sight of what it is trying to accomplish. The team player (including the team leader) who can help the group focus on its broader purpose plays a vital role. The following case history illustrates what it means to see the big picture.

A group of retail sales associates and customer service representatives were sent to a one-day seminar about customer-service training. The group was sent to training because customer-service ratings at their store were below the level store executives thought acceptable. During the lunch breaks, the conversation quickly turned to

the fact that the coffee was not as hot as desired, the snacks were mediocre, the restrooms were too far from the meeting room, and the presenter had a phony smile and told goofy jokes. Next came a few complaints about a couple of the PowerPoint slides having too much detail.

Alyssa, an experienced sales associate, stepped in with a comment. She noted, "I think all of you have valid complaints, but your points are minor. We are here to learn how to improve customer service. If we want our store to survive, and for us to earn bigger bonuses, we have to learn what we can to help us do our jobs better. Whether or not you like our trainer's smile or jokes, he is trying to be helpful." The group returned after lunch with a more determined effort to focus on the purpose of the seminar—picking up ideas to improve customer service.

Believe in Consensus

consensus

General acceptance by the group of a decision.

A major task-related attitude for outstanding team play is to believe that consensus has merit. **Consensus** is general acceptance of a decision by the group. Every member may not be thrilled about the decision, yet they are unopposed and are willing to support the decision. Believing that consensus is valuable enables you to participate fully in team decisions without thinking that you have sacrificed your beliefs or the right to think independently. To believe in consensus is to believe that the democratic process has relevance for organizations and that ideal solutions are not always possible.

Focus on Deadlines

A notable source of individual differences among work group members is how much importance they attach to deadlines. Some work group members may regard deadlines as a moral contract, to be missed only in case of emergency. Others may view deadlines as an arbitrary date imposed by someone external to the group. Other work group members may perceive deadlines as moderately important. Differences in perception about the importance of deadlines influence the group's ability to meet deadlines.[21]

Keeping the group focused on the deadline is a valuable task behavior because meeting deadlines is vital to team success. Discussing the importance of the deadlines is helpful because of the varying attitudes about deadlines likely to be found among group members.

Help Team Members Do Their Jobs Better

Your stature as a team player will increase if you take the initiative to help coworkers make needed work improvements. Helping other team members with their work assignments is a high-level form of cooperation. Make the suggestions in a constructive spirit rather than displaying an air of superiority. Identify a problem that a coworker is having, and then suggest alternatives he or she might be interested in exploring. Avoid saying to team members that they "should" do something, because many people become defensive when told what they should do. The term *should* is usually perceived as a moral judgment given to one person by another, such as being told that you should save money, should learn a second language, or should improve your math skills.

Be a Good Organizational Citizen

A comprehensive way of carrying out the task aspects of team play (as well as relationship aspects) is to help out beyond the requirements of your job description. As discussed in Chapter 2, such extra-role activity is referred to as "organizational citizenship behavior"—working for the good of the organization even without the promise of a specific reward. As a result of many workers being good organizational citizens, the organization functions more effectively in such ways as improved product quantity and quality.[22] Good citizenship on the job encompasses many specific behaviors, including helping a coworker with a job task and refraining from complaints or petty grievances. A good organizational citizen would carry out such specific acts as picking up litter in the company parking lot. He or she would also bring a reference to the office that could help a coworker solve a job problem. Most of the other team player tactics described here are related to organizational citizenship behavior.

Habitat for Homeless People

Organize the class into teams of about six people. Each team takes on the assignment of formulating plans for building temporary shelters for homeless people. The task will take about one hour and can be done inside or outside the class. The dwellings you plan to build, for example, might be two-room cottages with electricity and indoor plumbing.

During the time allotted to the task, formulate plans for going ahead with Habitat for Homeless People. Consider dividing up work by assigning certain roles to each team member. Sketch out tentative answers to the following questions:

1. How will you obtain funding for your venture?
2. Which homeless people will you help?
3. Where will your shelters be located?
4. Who will do the actual construction?

After your plan is completed, evaluate the quality of the teamwork that took place within the group. Specify which team-work skills were evident and which ones did not surface. Search the chapter for techniques you might use to improve teamwork. The skills used to accomplish the habitat task could relate to the team skills presented in Self-Assessment Quiz 4-2, the interpersonal aspects of team play, the task aspects of team play, or some team skill not mentioned in this chapter. Here is a sampling of the many different skills that might be relevant in this exercise:

- Speaks effectively
- Listens to others
- Innovates solutions to problems
- Thinks outside the box
- Displays a high level of cooperation and collaboration
- Provides knowledge of the task
- Sees the big picture
- Focuses on deadlines

Two experiments, one with business students and one with managers, suggested that organizational citizenship behavior is even more important when people depend on each other to accomplish a task.[23] An example is filling an order with components from different departments. Given that most tasks on a team are interdependent, organizational citizenship behavior is quite important for effective teamwork.

Skill-Building Exercise 4-3 will help you integrate the many suggestions presented here for developing teamwork skills.

SELF-ASSESSMENT QUIZZES IN OVERVIEW

Self-Assessment Quiz 5-1 gave you an opportunity to think through the extent to which you really enjoy, or are interested, in teamwork. Being part of a close-knit team is important for many types of work, but there is always room for some people who prefer to work alone doing analytical or creative work. For example, at Microsoft Corp. the office layout gives space to people who want to work alone and not be distracted by other people. Self-Assessment Quiz 5-2 follows up your interests and attitudes about teamwork with an opportunity to review your skills. Interest and skills are not the same. A given individual who likes the idea of skydiving might lack the eye—hand coordination to pull the cord under pressure, and therefore would be a disaster as a skydiver.

If you have the attitudes for teamwork, another subtle factor about teamwork can influence your effectiveness. As measured in Self-Assessment Quiz 5-3, your level of conformity can influence your effectiveness. Too much or too little conformity can detract from your effectiveness. Self-Assessment Quiz 5-4 takes you even further into the intricacies of teamwork by measuring your tendency to play positive team roles. With few exceptions, a person needs to focus on positive team roles to be a successful team member.

Concept Review and Reinforcement

Key Terms

team, 89
self-managing work team, 90
cross-functional team, 91

virtual team, 92
crew, 93
synergy, 93

social loafing, 94
groupthink, 94
consensus, 104

Summary of Key Concepts

To be successful in the modern organization it is necessary to be an effective team player. Team members have complementary skills and are committed to a common purpose. All teams have some elements in common, but four key types of teams are self-managing work teams, cross-functional teams, virtual teams, and crews. (A virtual team does most of its work electronically instead of in face-to-face meetings.)

Groups and teams offer such advantages as gaining synergy, avoiding major errors, and gaining increased acceptance of and commitment to decisions. Working in groups can also enhance job satisfaction. Groups and teams also have disadvantages, such as more talk than action, conformity in thinking and action, social loafing, and the creation of conflict. A serious potential problem is groupthink, whereby bad decisions are made as a by-product of strong consensus. Key characteristics of effective work groups are outlined in Figure 5-1.

An important part of being an effective team player is to choose effective roles. The roles studied here are: creative problem solver, resource investigator, coordinator, shaper, monitor-evaluator, team worker, implementer, completer-finisher, and specialist. Self-oriented roles are less effective and detract from group productivity. Understanding roles does not supplant the need for recognizing individual differences and communicating well.

Guidelines for effectively contributing to the interpersonal aspects of team play include (1) trusting team members, (2) displaying a high level of cooperation and collaboration, (3) recognizing the interests and achievements of others, (4) giving and receiving helpful criticism, (5) sharing the glory, and (6) taking care not to rain on another person's parade.

Guidelines for effectively contributing to the task aspects of team play include (1) providing technical expertise, (2) assuming responsibility for problems, (3) seeing the big picture, (4) believing in consensus, (5) focusing on deadlines, and (6) helping team members do their jobs better.

Check Your Understanding

1. Part of being a good team player is helping other members. How can members of a workplace team help each other?

2. How do team members know when they have achieved synergy?

3. What should the other team members do when they uncover a social loafer?

4. What is the potential downside of heavily emphasizing the *specialist* role?

5. How can the *monitor-evaluator* role backfire for a person?

6. Assume that you are a team member. What percent of your pay would you be willing to have based on a group reward? Explain your reasoning.

7. Many retail companies, banks, and medical offices require customer-contact employees to wear the same uniform. In what ways might these uniforms enhance teamwork?

8. A number of companies have sent employees to a team-building exercise in which they prepare a gourmet meal. Why would preparing a gourmet meal help build teamwork?

9. The "little picture" in studying this chapter is learning details about teamwork skills. What is the "big picture"?

10. How can a person achieve individual recognition yet still be a team player?

The Web Corner

http://www.adventureassoc.com/workshops/teamwork.html

(Development of teamwork skills, including the use of the MBTI.)

http://www.quintcareers.com/team_player_quiz.html

(Take the quiz, "Are You a Team Player? A Quintessential Careers Quiz.")

Internet Skill Builder: Becoming a Better Team Player

The purpose of this exercise duplicates the major purpose of the chapter—finding practical suggestions for improving your teamwork skills. Visit several Web sites that deal with enhancing teamwork skills from the standpoint of the individual, not the manager. An example of such a Web site is http://www.confidencecenter.com. Write down at least three concrete suggestions you find, and compare these suggestions to those made in this chapter. If the opportunity arises, practice one of these skills in the next 10 days and observe the results.

Developing Your Human Relations Skills

Interpersonal Relations Case 5.1

Mark Wants to Look Good

Certified public accountant (CPA) Mark was looking for a way to document his contribution to a team whose work directly supported the mission of his firm. Mark's firm was experiencing a business plateau. As more large business firms gobbled up smaller companies, the demand for accounting services decreased. (Fewer companies were available to hire accountants.) In addition, more companies were doing their work internally and using software to replace some of the contributions of outside accountants.

Mark served on a client-development team that uncovered several productive ways of expanding the firm's practice. Among these initiatives was to advertise and hold tax seminars free to the public. The team received ample credit from the senior partners for helping the accounting practice grow. However, Mark believed that he deserved more credit than several of the other team members. Nevertheless, he did not want to appear tacky by stating this observation to the senior partners. Instead, he wrote an e-mail message describing his contribution without asking for credit. His e-mail stated:

Hello Senior Partners,

Thanks for the opportunity to serve on the client-development team. I'm pleased that the team accomplished its mission. My major assignment was to conduct tax seminars for the public. I am so pleased that the team accomplished its mission. I found that to be a professionally rewarding experience. Should the opportunity arise to help the firm again by conducting seminars, please consider me a candidate.

Sincerely,

Mark Davenport

Mark thought to himself, "This e-mail should work. I'll be seen as a fine team player and a great individual contributor at the same time."

Case Questions

1. What is your evaluation of Mark as a team player?
2. If Mark had asked your advice about sending this e-mail, what would you have told him?
3. If you were a senior partner in Mark's firm, how would you reply to his memo?

Interpersonal Relations Case 5.2

Ruth Waves a Red Flag

Carlos is the team leader of a cost-reduction team within a well-established baked-goods company that produces bakery products under its own label, as well as private labels for grocery-store chains such as Giant and Winn-Dixie. Top-level management formed the team to arrive at suggestions for reducing costs throughout the organization. A transcript of one of the meetings is presented next.

Carlos: We've been gathering information for a month now. It's about time we heard some specific suggestions.

Jack: At the top of my list is cutting pension benefits. Our pension payments are higher than the minimum required by law. Our medical benefits are way above average. If we cut back on pension benefits, no current employees would be adversely affected.

Melissa: I like your analysis, Jack. No sense risking laying off employees just to keep retirees happy.

Jordan: We should make absolutely certain there are no legal complications here. Then we can sharpen our cost-cutting knives and dig right in.

Gunther: I'd support cutting pension benefits. It would probably reduce expenses more dramatically than the ways I have uncovered.

Carlos: There seems to be consensus so far that we should considered making recommendations about cutting pension benefits. Ruth, what do you think?

Ruth: I think it is much too early to reach consensus on such a sensitive issue. Cutting pension benefits would create panic among our retirees. Our older employees would be screaming as well. We'll have an avalanche of negative publicity in the media.

Jordan: Hold on, Ruth. I said the team should first check out this idea with the legal department.

Ruth: Just because cutting pension benefits could squeeze by legally doesn't mean that it's a good idea. We haven't examined the negative ramifications of cutting pension benefits. Let's study this issue further before word leaks out that we're taking away the golden egg.

Carlos: Maybe Ruth has a point. Let's investigate this issue further before making a recommendation.

Case Questions

1. What role, or roles, is Ruth occupying on the cost-reduction team?
2. How effective does she appear to be in her role?
3. What role, or roles, is Jack occupying on the cost-reduction team?
4. How effective does he appear to be in his role?
5. How effective is Carlos in his role as a team leader?

CHAPTER 6

Group Problem Solving and Decision Making

Jim Graf has his sights set on a target 100 million miles away. Sometimes it's closer. Sometimes it's farther. Mars. The target is moving. So is he. Each morning he leads a team of several managers in a standup meeting in his office at NASA's [National Aeronautics and Space Administration] Jet Propulsion Laboratory on the top floor of a sprawling, four-story building tucked into the foothills above Pasadena, California. Sitting is not allowed. All the meeting's participants are constantly in motion, changing positions with respect to one another, even as their target changes position with respect to Earth.

"We have a daily standup so we can talk about things," said Graf. "We physically stand up here. I want everybody a little uncomfortable so they get right to the point." Usually these meetings last about 15 minutes. Some mornings, they go longer. "It's important to communicate," said Graf. "You wouldn't think a team member working on one thing would need to know about another team working on another thing, until suddenly you hear someone say, 'Wow, that impacts me!' The standup meetings are essential to our success."[1]

Standup meetings are but one way in which groups solve many key problems. Part of having high-level interpersonal skills is the ability to work closely with others in solving problems and making decisions. This

Learning Objectives

After reading and studying this chapter and doing the exercises, you should be able to

1. Understand the difference between rational and political decision making.
2. Use the general approach to problem-solving groups.
3. Use brainstorming effectively.
4. Use the nominal group technique effectively.

5. Understand how to increase the efficiency of group problem solving through e-mail and groupware.
6. Pinpoint several suggestions for being an effective meeting participant.

chapter will enhance your group problem-solving and decision-making skills. You will receive guidelines for applying several major group problem-solving methods, along with suggestions for being an effective contributor at meetings. As a starting point in studying these techniques, first think through your present level of receptiveness toward group problem solving by doing Self-Assessment Quiz 6-1.

RATIONAL VERSUS POLITICAL DECISION MAKING IN GROUPS

LEARNING OBJECTIVE 1

Group decision making is the process of reaching a judgment based on feedback from more than one individual. Most people involved in group problem solving may share the same purpose in agreeing on a solution and making a decision. Nevertheless, they may have different agendas and use different methods. Two such different approaches to group decision making are the rational model and the political model.

group decision making

The process of reaching a judgment based on feedback from more than one individual.

The **rational decision-making model** is the traditional, logical approach to decision making, based on the scientific method. It is grounded in establishing goals, establishing alternatives, examining consequences, and hoping for optimum results. The search for optimum results is based on an economic view of decision making—the idea that people hope to maximize gain and minimize loss when making a decision. For example, a work team would choose the lowest cost, highest quality supplier even though the team leader may be a good friend of the sales representative of a competitor.

rational decision-making model

The traditional, logical approach to decision making based on the scientific method.

The rational model also assumes that each alternative is evaluated in terms of how well it contributes to reaching the goals involved in making the decision. For example, if one of the goals in relocating a factory were to reduce energy costs and taxes, each alternative would be carefully examined in terms of its tax and energy consequences. A team member might say, "Setting up a factory in the Phoenix area sounds great. It's true that taxes are low, the labor market is wonderful, and we won't lose any days to snow emergencies. But did you know that the energy costs are very high because of the amount of air-conditioning required?"

The **political decision-making model** assumes that people bring preconceived notions and biases into the decision-making situation. Because the decision makers are politically motivated (a focus on satisfying one's own interests), the individuals often do not make the most rational choice. In the relocation example at hand, two of the members may say, "Thumbs up to Phoenix," for reasons that satisfy their own needs. One team member

political decision-making model

The assumption about decision making that people bring preconceived notions and biases into the decision-making situation.

might be fascinated with the American Indian culture so prevalent in Arizona and therefore want to move to Phoenix. Another member might have retired parents living in Phoenix and be interested in living near them.

People who use the political model may operate on the basis of incomplete information. Facts and figures that conflict with personal biases and preferences might get blocked out of memory or rationalized away. A team member might say, "Those air-conditioning costs are exaggerated. I've heard that if you use thermal pumps in a factory, the cooling costs go way down."

In practice, it is sometimes difficult to determine whether a decision maker is being rational or political. Have you ever noticed that many hotels do not have a 13th floor? The reason is both rational and political. The hotel manager might say rationally, "Many people are superstitious about the number 13, so they will refuse to take a room on the 13th floor. So if we want to maximize room use, the rational decision for us is to label the 13th floor as 14. In this way we will avoid the irrational [political] thinking of guests."

GUIDELINES FOR USING GENERAL PROBLEM-SOLVING GROUPS

LEARNING OBJECTIVE 2

Solving problems effectively in groups requires skill. The effort is often worthwhile because participation in group decision making frequently leads to better acceptance of the decision and stronger commitment to the implications of the decision. For example, a group involved in making decisions about cost cutting might be more willing to carry through with the suggestions than if participants had not made the decision. Group decision making can also lead to higher quality decisions and innovations because the group collectively has more information than might individuals.[2] Similarly, the group might come up with better suggestions for cost cutting because of group members sharing information.

Here we examine three aspects of group problem solving useful in making more effective decisions: working through the group problem-solving steps, managing disagreement about the decision, and aiming for inquiry rather than advocacy.

Working through the Group Problem-Solving Steps

When team members get together to solve a problem, they typically hold a discussion rather than rely on formal problem-solving techniques. Several team members might attempt to clarify the true nature of the problem, and a search then begins for an acceptable solution. Although this technique can be effective, the probability of solving the problem well (and therefore making the right decision) increases when the team follows a systematic procedure. The following guidelines represent a time-tested way of solving problems and making decisions within a group.[3] You may recognize these steps as having much in common with the scientific method. The same steps are therefore ideal for following the rational decision-making model. Two other aspects of group decision making will be described here: managing disagreement and inquiry versus advocacy. Assume that you are a team member of a small business that distributes food supplies to hospitals, nursing homes, and schools. Your business volume is adequate, but you have a cash-flow problem because some of your customers take over 30 days to pay their bills. Here is how problem solving would proceed following the steps for effective group problem solving and decision making:

Step One. *Identify the problem.* Describe specifically what the problem is and how it manifests itself. The surface problem is that some customers are paying their bills late. Your company's ultimate problem is that it does not have enough cash on hand to pay expenses.

Step Two. *Clarify the problem.* If group members do not see the problem the same way, they will offer divergent solutions to their own individual perceptions of the problem. To some team members, late payments may simply mean the company has less cash in the bank. As a result, the company earns a few dollars less in interest. Someone else on the team might perceive the problem as mostly an annoyance and inconvenience. Another person may perceive late payers as being immoral and therefore want to penalize them. The various perceptions of the problem solvers contribute to their exercising a political model of decision making. It is important for the group to reach consensus that the ultimate problem is not enough cash on hand to run the business, as explained in Step 1.

Step Three. *Analyze the cause.* To convert what exists into what they want, the group must understand the cause of the specific problems and find ways to overcome the causes. Late payment of bills (over 30 days) can be caused by several factors. The customers may have cash-flow problems of their own, they may have slow-moving bureaucratic procedures, or they may be understaffed. Another possibility is that the slow-paying customers are dissatisfied with the service and are holding back on payments in retaliation. Research, including interviewing customers, may be needed to analyze the cause or causes.

Step Four. *Search for alternative solutions.* Remember that multiple alternative solutions can be found to most problems. The alternative solutions you choose will depend on your analysis of the causes. Assume that you did not find customers to be dissatisfied with your service, but that they were slow in paying bills for a variety of reasons. Your team then gets into a creative mode by developing a number of alternatives. Among them are offering bigger discounts for quick payment, dropping slow-paying customers, sending out your own bills more promptly, and using follow-up e-mail messages and phone calls to bring in money. For regular customers, you might try for

automatic withdrawals from their checking account. Another possibility would be to set up a line of credit that would enable your firm to make short-term loans to cover expenses until your bills were paid.

Step Five. *Select alternatives.* Identify the criteria that solutions should meet, then discuss the pros and cons of the proposed alternatives. No solution should be laughed at or scorned. Specifying the criteria that proposed solutions should meet requires you to think deeply about your goals. For example, your team might establish the following criteria for solutions, such as that they (a) improve cash flow, (b) do not lose customers, (c) do not cost much to implement, and (d) do not make the company appear desperate. The pros and cons of each proposed alternative can be placed on a flip chart, board, or computer screen.

Step Six. *Plan for implementation.* Decide what actions are necessary to carry out the chosen solution to the problem. Suppose your group decides that establishing a bank line of credit is the most feasible alternative. The company president or the chief financial officer might then meet with a couple of local banks to apply for a line of credit at the most favorable rate. Your group also chooses to initiate a program of friendly follow-up telephone calls to encourage more rapid payment.

Step Seven. *Clarify the contract.* The contract is a restatement of what group members have agreed to do and deadlines for accomplishment. In your situation, several team members are involved in establishing a line of credit and initiating a system of follow-up phone calls.

Step Eight. *Develop an action plan.* Specify who does what and when to carry out the contract. Each person involved in implementing alternatives develops an action plan in detail that stems logically from the previous steps.

Step Nine. *Provide for evaluation and accountability.* After the plan is implemented, reconvene to discuss progress and to hold people accountable for results that have not been achieved. In the situation at hand, progress will be measured in at least two objective ways. You can evaluate by accounting measures whether the cash-flow problem has improved and whether the average cycle time on accounts receivable has decreased.

The steps for effective group problem solving are best applied to complex problems. Straightforward problems of minor consequence (such as deciding on holiday decorations for the office) do not require all the steps. Nevertheless, remember that virtually every problem has more than one feasible alternative. A classic example of searching for the best alternative to a problem is as follows:

At one time complaints of late room service were plaguing a Ritz-Carlton hotel, a chain known for its superior service. To solve the problem, president Horst Schulze dispatched a team composed of a room-service order taker, a waiter, and a cook. Everything seemed fine except that the service elevator took a long time. Next, the group consulted with the engineers in charge of the elevator. Neither the engineers nor the elevator company representative could find a technical problem with the elevator.

Next, team members took turns riding the elevators at all hours for a week. Finally, one of them observed that every time the elevator made its trip from the first floor to the twenty-fourth, it stopped four or five times. At each step, housemen (who assisted the housekeepers) got on the elevators to different floors. The housemen were taking towels from other floors to bring them to housekeepers on their own floors who were short of towels. Foraging for towels was slowing down the elevators.

The team discovered that the Ritz-Carlton didn't really have a room-service problem or an elevator problem; it had a towel shortage. As the hotel bought more towels, room-service complaints dropped 50 percent.[4]

For practice in using the problem steps described above, do Skill-Building Exercise 6-1. Skill-Building Exercise 6-2 gives you an opportunity to solve a few more of the perplexing type of problems that the Ritz-Carlton faced.

A General Problem-Solving Group

The class is divided into groups of about six people. Each group takes the same complicated problem through the nine steps for effective group decision making. Several of the steps will be hypothetical because this is a simulated experience. Pretend you are a task force composed of people from different departments in the company. Choose one of the following possibilities:

Scenario 1: Your company wants your task force to decide whether to purchase a corporate jet for members of senior management or require them to continue flying on commercial airlines.

Scenario 2: You are employed by Hewlett Packard Corp., the IT giant that specializes in computers and printers. Data supplied by the marketing research department indicates that the consumption of HP inkjet cartridges by consumers worldwide is declining more rapidly than anticipated. At the same time, private label refill cartridges are selling at a pace much faster than forecasted. Your task force is asked to recommend a plan for increasing the consumption of HP ink cartridges.

Managing Disagreement about Group Decision Making

A major reason that group decision making does not proceed mechanically is that disagreement may surface. Such disagreement is not necessarily harmful to the final outcome of the decision because those who disagree may have valid points and help prevent groupthink. The idea is to manage disagreement so the decision-making process does not break down and the dissenters are not squelched. Conflicts about decisions were studied among 43 cross-functional teams engaged in new product development. Disagreeing about major issues led to positive outcomes for team performance (as measured by ratings made by managers) under two conditions.[5]

First, the dissenters have to feel they have the freedom to express doubt. To measure such freedom, participants in the study responded to such statements as "I sometimes get the feeling that others are not speaking up although they harbor serious doubts about the direction being taken." (Strongly disagreeing with this statement would suggest that group members had the freedom to express doubt.)

Second, doubts must be expressed collaboratively (trying to work together) rather than contentiously (in a quarrelsome way). An example of collaborative communication would be having used the following statement during decision making: "We will be working together for a while. It's important that we both [all] feel comfortable with a solution to this problem." An example of contentious communication would be high agreement with the statement "You're being difficult and rigid."

Solving a Few Unusual Problems

Use group problem solving to find a solution to the three problems described next. Each problem is designed to capitalize on the group's ability to search for creative alternatives and think flexibly. Answers to the three problems follow the Chapter 6 references, which can be found in the References section toward the end of the book.

Problem 1: Seven Tennis Balls in a Tube

Seven tennis balls are located at the bottom of a 6-foot vertical pipe with a diameter of 4 inches, bolted securely to the floor. Your job is to remove the balls without destroying the pipe.

Problem 2: The Too-Low Truck

A couple has rented a large truck to move their belongings to a new house in the country. As they are driving down a country road, they encounter an overhead bridge that appears somewhat low. Before barreling through the bridge, the couple climbs up on the hood to discover that indeed the bridge is 1.5 inches too low

for the truck. Ten minutes later, the couple drives right under the bridge. What solution did they find to the problem of their rented truck being too tall?

Problem 3: The Aging Members of HOG

A few years ago, managers at Harley-Davidson recognized that they were losing a lot of their members of HOG (Harley Owner's Group) because many Harley drivers had reached the age whereby they perceived driving a traditional motorcycle to be too dangerous. A problem-solving group was formed, and they arrived at a solution that prevented a lot of older HOG members from slipping away, especially in Florida. Some of those HOG members are now as happy as a pig dipped in mud. What product do you think the Harley-Davidson problem-solving group developed?

Source: The seven-ball problem is from Dodge Fernald, Psychology (Upper Saddle River, NJ: Prentice Hall, 1997), p. 288.

More recent research lends strength to the idea that teams are more likely to make optimal decisions when they take the time to debate the issues and thoughtfully discuss alternative solutions. A study about hiring pilots for long-distance flights found that when groups disagreed over who to hire, there was more information sharing. Also, the strong disagreement led to more intense discussions that prompted participants to repeat their reasoning in front of other group members. A debate over which candidate to hire encourages team members to focus on information that may be inconsistent with how they formed their original opinion.[6]

Conflict-resolution techniques, as described in Chapter 8, are another potentially useful approach to managing disagreement about decision making.

Aiming for Inquiry versus Advocacy in Group Decision Making

Another useful perspective on group decision making is to compare the difference between group members involved in *inquiry* (looking for the best alternative) versus *advocacy* (or fighting for one position). Inquiry is an open process designed to generate multiple alternatives, encourage the exchange of ideas, and produce a well-reasoned solution. Decision makers who care more about the good of the firm than personal gain are the most likely to engage in inquiry. According to David A. Garvin and Michael A. Roberto, this open-minded approach does not come easily to most people.[7]

Instead, most groups charged with making a decision tend to slip into the opposite mode, called advocacy. The two approaches look similar because under either mode the group members are busily immersed in work and appear to be searching for the best alternative. Yet the results from the two modes are quite different. Using an advocacy approach, participants approach decision making as a contest with the intent of selecting the winning alternative. One member of the group might be trying to gain the largest share of the budget, and become so passionate about winning budget share that he loses objectivity. Advocates might even withhold important information from the group, such as not revealing that their budget is big enough considering their decreased activity.

With an advocacy approach, the disagreements that arise tend to separate the group and are antagonistic. Personality conflicts come into play, and one person might accuse the other side of not being able to see the big picture. In contrast, an inquiry-focused group carefully considers a variety of alternatives and collaborates to discover the best solution.

Conflict-resolution methods can be useful in helping the decision makers overcome the advocacy approach. As part of resolving the conflict, the group leader must make sure everyone knows that his or her viewpoint is being carefully considered.

GUIDELINES FOR BRAINSTORMING

brainstorming

A group problem-solving technique that promotes creativity by encouraging idea generation through noncritical discussion.

In many work situations, groups are expected to produce creative and imaginative solutions to problems. When the organization is seeking a large number of alternatives for solving the problems, **brainstorming** is often the technique of choice. Brainstorming is a group problem-solving technique that promotes creativity by encouraging idea generation through noncritical discussion. Alex Osborn, who developed the practice of brainstorming, believed that one of the main blocks to organizational creativity was the premature evaluation of ideas.[8] The basic technique is to encourage unrestrained and spontaneous participation by group members. The term *brainstorm* has become so widely known that it is often used as a synonym for a clever idea.

Brainstorming is used both as a method of finding alternatives to real-life problems and as a creativity-training program. In the usual form of brainstorming, group members spontaneously call out alternative solutions to a problem facing them. Any member is free to enhance or "hitchhike" upon the contribution of another person. At the end of the session, somebody sorts out the ideas and edits the more unrefined ones.

Brainstorming is widely used to develop new ideas for products, find names for products, develop advertising slogans, and solve customer problems. For instance, the idea for luxury sport utility vehicles (SUVs) emerged from a brainstorming session. Brainstorming has also been used to develop a new organizational structure in a government agency, and it is now widely used in developing software.

Adhering to a few simple rules or guidelines helps ensure that creative alternative solutions to problems will be forthcoming. The brainstorming process usually falls into place without frequent reminders about guidelines. Nevertheless, here are nine rules to improve the chances of having a good session. Unless many of these rules are followed, brainstorming becomes a free-for-all, and is not brainstorming in its original intent.

1. **Group size should be about five to seven people.** If there are too few people, not enough suggestions are generated; if there are too many people, the session becomes uncontrolled. However, brainstorming can be conducted with as few as three people.

2. **Everybody is given the chance to suggest alternative solutions.** Members spontaneously call out alternatives to the problem facing the group. (Another approach is for people to speak in sequence.)

3. **No criticism is allowed.** All suggestions should be welcome; it is particularly important not to use derisive laughter.

4. **Freewheeling is encouraged.** Outlandish ideas often prove quite useful. It's easier to tame a wild idea than to originate one.

5. **Quantity and variety are very important.** The greater the number of ideas put forth, the greater the likelihood of a breakthrough idea.

6. **Combinations and improvements are encouraged.** Building upon the ideas of others, including combining them, is very productive. Hitchhiking or piggybacking is an essential part of brainstorming.

7. **Notes must be taken during the session by a person who serves as the recording secretary.** The session can also be taped, but this requires substantial time to retrieve ideas.

8. **Invite outsiders to the brainstorming session.** Inviting an outsider to the brainstorming session can add a new perspective that the "insiders" might not think of themselves. (Such is the argument for having a diverse problem-solving group.)

9. **Do not overstructure by following any of the first eight ideas too rigidly.** Brainstorming is a spontaneous group process.

According to one observer, the most productive brainstorming sessions take place in physically stimulating environments as opposed to a drab conference room. Natural light may stimulate thinking, so work in a room with windows or outside if weather permits. Changing from a seated position to walking around from time to time can be mentally stimulating. Food and drink also contribute to an enhanced environment for brainstorming.[9]

Brainstorming is an effective technique for finding a large number of alternatives to problems, particularly when the list of alternatives is subsequently refined and edited. Brainstorming in groups is also valuable because it contributes to job satisfaction for many people. Skill-Building Exercise 6-3 gives you an opportunity to practice a commercially useful application of brainstorming.

A curious feature of brainstorming is that individuals working alone typically produce more useful ideas than those placed in a group. Brainstorming by individuals working alone is referred to as **brainwriting**. Skill-Building Exercise 6-4 gives you a chance to compare brainstorming with brainwriting.

brainwriting

Brainstorming by individuals working alone.

The full potential of brainstorming has been held back by three forces that block production of ideas: evaluation apprehension, free riding, and inhibiting procedures.[10] Being aware of these production-blocking mechanisms can help you improve your skill in brainstorming.

Evaluation apprehension means that many people are unwilling to come forth with some of their ideas because they fear being critically evaluated. This fear may be intensified when people are told that the group is being observed and rated or that experts are in the group. (Did you notice any evaluation apprehension in the brainstorming exercise?) When people work by themselves—and do not have to present their ideas to the larger group—they will have less evaluation apprehension.

Free riding is just about the same behavior as social loafing. Free riders do not work as hard in a group as they would if they worked alone. They are willing to let the next person do the heavy thinking. A reason offered for free riding is that being an outstanding

Choosing an Effective Domain Name

Using brainstorming, huddle in small groups. Your task is to develop original domain names for several products or services. An effective domain name is typically one that is easy to remember and will capture potential customers in an uncomplicated Web search. One reason this exercise is difficult is that "cybersquatters" grab unclaimed names they think business owners might want, and then sell these names later. For example, a cybersquatter (or domain name exploiter) might develop or buy the domain name *www.retro-clothing.com*, hoping that an e-tailer of retro clothing will want this name in the future. The owner of retroclothing.com would charge a company like Macy's every time a surfer looking to purchase retro clothing over the Internet, entered *www.retroclothing.com*, and was then linked to Macy's.

After your team has brainstormed a few possible domain names, search the Internet to see if your domain name is already in use. Simply enter *www* plus the name you have chosen into your browser. Or visit the site of a company like DomainCollection.com, Inc. After you have developed your list of domain names not already in use, present your findings to the rest of the class.

Here are some alternatives for constructing domain names:

- Hair salons
- Replacement parts for antique or classic autos
- A used-car chain
- Organic food stores
- Personal loans for people with poor (subprime) credit ratings
- Recycled steel for manufacturers
- One of your own choice

Brainstorming Versus Brainwriting

Half the class is organized into brainstorming groups of about six people. The rest of the class works by themselves. Groups and individuals then work on the same problems for 10 minutes. The brainstorming groups follow the aforementioned guidelines. Individuals jot down as many alternatives as come to mind without interacting with other people. After the problem-solving sessions are completed, compare the alternatives developed by the groups and individuals. Groups and individuals choose one of the following problems so that solutions can be compared to the same problems:

1. How might we reduce the carbon dioxide emissions in our community?
2. How can we earn extra money, aside from holding a regular job?
3. How can we find new people to date?
4. How can we save money on food costs?
5. How can we save money on gasoline?

contributor in a group carries no larger reward than being a noncontributor. A person generating ideas alone would not have the opportunity to free ride. Have you ever encountered a free rider in a group class project?

An *inhibiting procedure* in spoken (or verbal) brainstorming is that only one person can speak at a time. This limits the idea generation and production time available to group members. As a result, some people forget what they wanted to say because they were listening to others. They might also ignore the ideas of others because they are rehearsing what they want to say. Furthermore, they will hold back on ideas that are redundant.

GUIDELINES FOR THE NOMINAL GROUP TECHNIQUE

LEARNING OBJECTIVE 4

A team leader or other manager who must make a decision about an important issue sometimes needs to know what alternatives are available and how people will react to them. In such cases, group input may be helpful. Spoken brainstorming is not advisable because the problem is still in the exploration phase and requires more than a list of alternative solutions.

nominal group technique (NGT)

A group problem-solving technique that calls people together in a structured meeting with limited interaction.

A problem-solving technique called the **nominal group technique (NGT)** was developed to fit the situation. The NGT is a group problem-solving technique that calls people together in a structured meeting with limited interaction. The group is called nominal (in name only) because people first present their ideas without interacting with each other, as they would in a real group. However, group discussion does take place at a later stage in the process. Figure 6-1 outlines the NGT.

FIGURE 6-1 The Nominal Group Technique

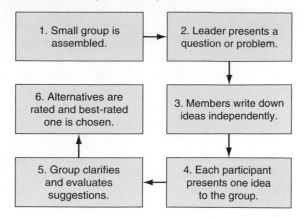

A problem that is an appropriate candidate for NGT is a decision about which suppliers or vendors should be eliminated. Many companies are shrinking their number of suppliers because they believe that working with a smaller number of suppliers can lead to higher quality components. It is easier to train a small number of suppliers, and it is also possible to build better working relationships when fewer people are involved.

A decision of this type can lead to hurt feelings and breaking up of old friendships. Suppose Pedro Ortiz, the team leader, is empowered to make this decision about reducing the number of suppliers. The NGT involves a six-step decision process:

1. Work-team members are assembled because they will all participate in the decision to reduce the number of companies that serve as suppliers to the team. All team members are told in advance of the meeting and the agenda. The meeting is called, and an office assistant is invited to help take care of the administrative details of the meeting.

2. The team leader presents a specific question. Ortiz tells the group, "Top management says we have to reduce our number of suppliers by two-thirds. It's too difficult to keep track of all these different suppliers and train them to meet our quality specs. I dislike terminating a supplier as much as anybody, but I can understand the logic of top management. Right now our team is doing business with 12 suppliers, and we should shrink that number to 4. Your assignment is to develop criteria for choosing which suppliers to eliminate. I also need to know how you feel about the decision you make on supplier reduction and how it might affect the operations of our team."

3. Individual team members write down their ideas independently, without speaking to other members. Using notepads, e-mail, or word processors, the five team members write down their ideas about reducing the number of suppliers by two-thirds.

4. Each team member in turn presents one idea to the group. Sometimes these ideas are presented to the group by the team leader without identifying which person contributed the idea. In this way, ideas are submitted anonymously. The group does not discuss the ideas. The office assistant summarizes each idea by writing it on a flip chart. Here are the ideas submitted by each team member:

   Alternative A. We'll carefully study the prices offered by all 12 suppliers. The 8 suppliers with the highest average prices for comparable goods are given the boot. I like this idea because our team will save the company a bundle of money.

   Alternative B. Let's keep the 4 suppliers who have the best quality record. We'll ask each supplier if they have won a quality award. If a supplier has won a quality award, the company is put on the retained list. We'll include awards from their customers or outside standards such as ISO [International Standards Organization] 9000. If we find more than 4 of the suppliers have won awards, we'll retain those with the most impressive awards.

Alternative C. I say we reward good service. We keep the 4 suppliers among the 12 who have been the most prompt with deliveries. We'll also take into account how good the suppliers have been about accepting returns of damaged or defective merchandise.

Alternative D. Here's an opportunity to get in good with top management. Stop kidding each other. We know that the plant's general manager [Jake] has his favorite suppliers. Some of them are his fishing and golfing buddies. The suppliers who are friends with Jake get our vote. In this way, Jake will think our team shows really good judgment.

Alternative E. Let's reward the suppliers who have served us best. We'll rate each supplier on a 1 to 10 scale on three dimensions: the quality of goods they have provided us, price, and service in terms of prompt delivery and returns policy. We could do the ratings in less than one hour.

5. After each team member has presented his or her idea, the group clarifies and evaluates the suggestions. The length of the discussion for each of the ideas varies substantially. For example, the idea about rating suppliers on three criteria might precipitate a 30-minute discussion. The discussion about retaining the plant manager's political connections might last only 5 minutes.

6. The meeting ends with a silent, independent rating of the alternatives. The final group decision is the pooled outcome of the individual votes. The team members are instructed to rate each alternative on a 1 to 10 scale, with 10 being the most favorable rating. The ratings that follow are the pooled ratings (the sum of the individual ratings) received for each alternative. The maximum score is 50 (10 points $\times$ 5 raters).

Alternative A, price alone: 35

Alternative B, quality-award record: 30

Alternative C, good service: 39

Alternative D, plant manager's favorites: 14

Alternative E, combination of quality, price, and service: 44

Team leader Ortiz agrees with the group's preference for choosing the 4 suppliers with the best combination of quality, price, and service. He schedules a meeting to decide which suppliers meet these standards. Ortiz brings the team's recommendations to the plant manager, and they are accepted. Although the team is empowered to make the decision, it is still brought to management for final approval. To practice the NGT, do Skill-Building Exercise 6-5.

The Job-Oriented Interpersonal Skills in Action box describes how a highly successful inventor believes in the creative problem-solving ability of teams using one or more of the techniques described so far.

SKILL-BUILDING EXERCISE 6-5

The NGT

With a clear understanding of the mechanics of the NGT as described in the text, the technique can be demonstrated in about 30 minutes. The class is divided into groups of about seven. One person plays the role of the team leader, who can also assume the responsibility of the office assistant (recording information on flip charts or a computer).

You are the key member of a motion picture and television film production company. You have a contract to produce a series of four films. The problem you face is which North American (United States, Canadian, or Mexican) city to choose as the film site. The president has ruled out Hollywood because expenses are too high. Solve this problem using the NGT, and make a decision about which city to choose for your film site.

World-Class Inventor Believes in the Creativity of Teams

A Xerox Corp. researcher moved into lofty company in April a few years ago. Santokh S. Badesha, who joined Xerox in 1980, received his 150th U.S. patent. Basdesha is just the second Xerox scientist to reach the milestone. Badesha's latest patent is titled "Amino-functional siloxane copolymer release agents for fuser members." It covers the fuser oil material composition and its use for color fusing, especially in Xerox's iGen3 digital press.

The company also said Badesha was to receive an honorary doctorate from Clarkson University in Potsdam. "Either event would be a fantastic achievement, so to have both happening simultaneously is really quite extraordinary," said Sophie Vandebroek, Xerox chief technology officer and president of the company's innovation group.

And he's not done. Badesha has about 35 other applications pending at the patent office and planned to file about 10 within eight months. Badesha said he never thought of himself as someone who comes across "real breakthrough inventions." He said he enjoys solving problems with a team. "When you get the right people in a team and present them with a real problem, they can be very creative, particularly when they take a fresh approach to the problem," he said.

Questions

1. Why is what a physical scientist has to say about the creativity of groups relevant to business and other fields?
2. Which of the group problem-solving methods described in this chapter do you think is or are well-suited to creating inventions?

Source: Excerpted with permission from David Tyler, "150 Patents, and Still Going Strong," *Rochester Democrat and Chronicle*, April 4, 2007, p. 8D.

USING STANDUP MEETINGS TO FACILITATE PROBLEM SOLVING

LEARNING OBJECTIVE 5

Problem solving and decision making can sometimes be improved by conducting meetings while standing up instead of sitting down. The general idea is that participants standing up in the problem-solving group are likely to be more alert and will come to a decision more quickly. Some people solve problems better when standing because they literally "think well on their feet." Few people would be willing to stand for several hours, so they reach a decision quickly.

Many meeting leaders who use standup meetings are pleased with the results in terms of reaching high-quality decisions rapidly. At UPS, every morning and several times a day, managers assemble workers for a required standup meeting that lasts precisely three minutes. Among the topics covered are local information, traffic conditions, or customer complaints. Each meeting ends with a safety tip. The 180-second limit helps enforce punctuality throughout UPS.[11]

A team of researchers investigated the effectiveness of standup meetings.[12] Study participants were 555 students in an introduction to management course who were offered extra credit for participating in the study. The students were randomly assigned to five-person groups, producing 111 groups. They were divided almost equally into standup and sit-down groups.

All groups were assigned the Lost on the Moon exercise, which presents a scenario involving a crash on the moon. Participants were asked to rank 15 pieces of equipment that survived the crash in terms of their importance for survival. Correct answers to the problem were the ranking of the equipment given by NASA astronauts and scientists. The major results of the experiment were as follows:

1. Sit-down meetings lasted about 34 percent longer than the standup meetings (788 seconds vs. 589 seconds).
2. Sit-down and standup meetings made decisions of equal quality.
3. More suggestions about task accomplishment were used by groups in the sit-down meetings than in the standup meetings.
4. Participants in the sit-down meetings were more satisfied than participants in the standup meetings.

One implication for this study is that people make decisions more quickly when standing up, without sacrificing decision quality. However, people prefer to sit down. In general, if you think that a task can be performed in 30 minutes or less, a standup meeting is likely to be effective.

> " The meeting is part training, part operations, part philosophy—all conducted with drill-like efficiency. We work in a 7-days-a-week, 24-hours-a-day business, and our customers are diverse. Employees need to know how to think on their feet to solve a problem. "
>
> —Horst Schulze, president and COO of the Ritz-Carlton hotel chain, talking about standup meetings

Indeed, the rocket scientists and other workers at the Jet Propulsion Lab use standup meetings to make major decisions. At one standup meeting, Graf challenged the group to come up with an alternative method for covering the spacecraft deck so they could avoid potential heat loss while operating the radar antenna. The current plan could cost the orbiter to lose 15 watts of power as wasted heat, and every watt of power and every ounce of heat counts in space. So the group thrashed out a complicated solution to the problem of a minor heat loss.

USING E-MAIL AND GROUPWARE TO FACILITATE GROUP DECISION MAKING

The presence of so many teams in the workplace means that people must work collectively and that they must make decisions together. Collective effort usually translates into meetings. Without any meetings, people are working primarily on their own and thus are not benefiting from working in teams. Yet with too many meetings it is difficult to accomplish individual work such as dealing with e-mail, making telephone calls, analyzing information, and preparing reports.

Appropriate use of e-mail and groupware can facilitate interaction among team members and group decision making, while at the same time minimizing the number of physical meetings. Such use of e-mail and other electronic tools makes possible the virtual teams described in the previous chapter.

Using E-Mail to Facilitate Meetings

By using e-mail, team members can feed important information to all other members of the team without the ritual of entering a meeting and passing around handouts.[13] Using e-mail, many small details can be taken care of in advance of the meeting. During the meeting, major items can be tackled. The typical use of e-mail is to send brief memos to people on a distribution list. A more advanced use of e-mail is to distribute word processing documents as well as spreadsheets and graphics, including photographs, as attachments.

Think back to the decision reached by the team using the NGT. As a follow-up to the meeting, the team was to get together to rate all 12 suppliers on quality, price, and service. Using e-mail, the group could cut down substantially on the amount of time they would have to spend in a group meeting. They might even be able to eliminate a group meeting. Pedro Ortiz might instruct the team members to send their ratings and explanations to each other within 10 working days.

Each team member would then rate all 12 suppliers on quality, service, and price. The ratings would then be sent to all other team members by e-mail. Ortiz could tally the results and report the final tally to each team member by e-mail. Since all team members could have performed the same calculation themselves, there would be no claims of a biased decision. A team meeting could be called to discuss the final results if Ortiz or the other team members thought it was necessary.

Pushing the use of e-mail too far can inhibit rather than enhance group decision making and teamwork. If people communicate with each other almost exclusively by e-mail, the warmth of human interaction and facial expressions is lost. Piggybacking of ideas is possible by reading each other's ideas on a computer monitor. Nevertheless, the wink of an eye, the shared laughter, and the encouraging smiles that take place in a traditional meeting make an important contribution to team effort, including group problem solving. Also, face-to-face interaction facilitates creativity as people exchange ideas.

Using Groupware to Facilitate Group Problem Solving

The application of e-mail just described can be considered part of groupware because e-mail was used to facilitate work in groups.

At its best, groupware offers certain advantages over single-user systems. Some of the most common reasons people use groupware are as follows[14]:

- To facilitate communication by making it faster, clearer, and more persuasive
- To communicate when it would not otherwise be possible
- To enable telecommuting (working from home)
- To reduce travel costs
- To bring together multiple perspectives and expertise
- To assemble groups with common interests where it would not be possible to gather a sufficient number of people face-to-face
- To facilitate group problem solving

Another example of groupware is a *shared whiteboard* that allows two or more people to view and draw on a common drawing surface even when they are at a distance. The link to group decision making is that drawing sketches and diagrams might be an important part of the decision making. An example would be a sales team suggesting ways of dividing a geographic territory for selling.

Despite all these potential applications and benefits of groupware, the system will break down unless almost all the parties involved use the software successfully. For example, all members of the virtual team must be willing to get online at the same time to have a successful meeting.

SUGGESTIONS FOR BEING AN EFFECTIVE MEETING PARTICIPANT

LEARNING OBJECTIVE 6

Except for virtual meetings such as those made possible by groupware, group problem solving takes place within the context of a face-to-face meeting. A major problem with most meetings is that they frustrate the participants, particularly those who are accomplishment oriented. Steven G. Rogelberg and his associates conducted an online survey of 980 participants from the United States, Australia, and the United Kingdom. The more meetings the accomplishment-oriented workers attended, the worse they felt about their job and the lower their feelings of well-being. The meetings appeared to have been perceived as an interruption to the tasks these ambitious people set out to accomplish.[15]

Meetings are not likely to be eliminated despite their unpopularity with accomplishment-oriented workers. A possible solution is for meeting participants to conduct themselves in a professional, task-oriented manner. In this way, meetings will most likely be shorter and more productive. A few key suggestions for being an effective meeting participant follow[16]:

- Arrive at the meeting prepared, such as having studied the support material and agenda, thought through your potential contribution, and taken care of some details by e-mail beforehand.
- Arrive on time, and stay until the meeting is completed. The meeting leader will often wait for the last participant before getting down to business. Leaving early distracts other participants.
- Do not hog the meeting or sit silently. Meetings are much more effective when the participants make balanced contributions.
- Use constructive nonverbal communication rather than slouching, yawning, looking bored and frustrated, leaving the room frequently, chewing gum, checking your cell phone or laptop computer, or engaging in similar negative behaviors.
- Converse with others in the meeting only when someone else is not speaking. Some executives will oust from a meeting those who engage in *sidebar conversations*.
- Be prepared to offer compromise solutions when other meeting participants and the meeting leader are haggling about a conflict of opinion.
- When possible, have data ready to support your position, such as estimating from industry data how much money your suggestion will save the company.

From studying these suggestions, you will observe that conducting yourself productively and professionally in a meeting is yet another job-oriented, interpersonal skill.

SELF-ASSESSMENT QUIZ IN OVERVIEW

Self-Assessment Quiz 6-1 provided an indication of your tendencies toward being interested in group problem solving, and is much like the quiz you took in the previous chapter in terms of attitude toward teamwork. You will most likely perform better in group decision making if you enjoy the activity. Learning about techniques of group problem solving will most likely be of more interest to you if you have a positive attitude toward the process.

Concept Review and Reinforcement

Key Terms

Group decision making, 111
rational decision-making model, 111

political decision-making model, 111
brainstorming, 116

brainwriting, 117
nominal group technique (NGT), 118

Summary of Key Concepts

An important aspect of interpersonal relations in organizations is that groups solve many key problems. Group problem solvers and decision makers often use the rational model or the political model. The rational decision-making model is the traditional, logical approach to decision making based on the scientific method. The model assumes that each alternative is evaluated in terms of how well it contributes to reaching the goals involved in making the decision.

The political decision-making model assumes that people bring preconceived notions and biases into the decision-making situation. Because the decision makers are politically motivated, the individuals often do not make the most rational choice. Instead, the decision makers attempt to satisfy their own needs.

General problem-solving groups are likely to arrive at better decisions when they follow standard steps or guidelines for group problem solving. The steps are as follows: (1) identify the problem, (2) clarify the problem, (3) analyze the cause, (4) search for alternative solutions, (5) select alternatives, (6) plan for implementation, (7) clarify the contract, (8) develop an action plan, and (9) provide for evaluation and accountability.

Disagreements about group decisions can be managed by giving dissenters the freedom to express doubt, and expressing doubts collaboratively rather than contentiously. Group decision making is more productive when group members are involved in inquiry, or looking for the best alternative. Advocacy, or fighting for one position, leads to poorer decisions. Research indicates that teams are more likely to make optimal decisions when they take the time to debate the issues and thoughtfully discuss alternative solutions.

When the organization is seeking a large number of alternatives to problems, brainstorming is often the tech-

nique of choice. Brainstorming is used as a method of finding alternatives to real-life problems and as a creativity-training program. Using the technique, group members spontaneously call out alternative solutions to the problem. Members build on the ideas of each other, and ideas are not screened or evaluated until a later stage. The right physical environment, such as sunlight, facilitates brainstorming. Brainstorming by working alone, or brainwriting, is also effective in generating alternative solutions.

The nominal group technique (NGT) is recommended for a situation in which a leader needs to know what alternatives are available and how people will react to them. In the NGT, a small group of people contributes written solutions to the problem. Other members respond to their ideas later. Members rate each other's ideas numerically, and the final group decision is the sum of the pooled individual votes.

Problem solving and decision making can sometimes be improved by conducting meetings while standing up instead of sitting down. The general idea is that participants who are standing up are more likely to be alert and come to a decision quickly. An experiment with management students indicated that standup groups made decisions more quickly, but that decision makers who sat down were more satisfied.

Electronic mail can be used to facilitate group decision making because members can feed information to each other without having to meet as a group. Memos, spreadsheet analyses, and graphics can be distributed through the network. Too much emphasis on e-mail, however, results in losing the value of face-to-face human interaction.

Various types of groupware, including e-mail, can facilitate group decision making. Also, a shared whiteboard allows two or more people to view and draw on a common drawing surface even when they are at a distance.

To help avoid the frustration of many accomplishment-oriented people in meetings, participants should conduct themselves in a professional, task-oriented manner. The suggestions presented here include arrive prepared, arrive on time and stay for the full meeting, do not hog the meeting or sit silently, use constructive nonverbal communication, avoid sidebar conversations, offer compromise solutions to conflict, and use data to support your position.

Check Your Understanding

1. Why are group decisions more likely to lead to commitment than decisions made by a manager acting alone?

2. Based on any experience you have had at school or at work, what process or method is usually followed in making group decisions?

3. Which personality characteristics described in Chapter 2 do you think would help a person be naturally effective in group problem solving?

4. Identify several problems on or off the job for which you think brainstorming would be effective.

5. What is your opinion of the importance of the physical setting (such as sunlight and refreshments) for stimulating creative thinking during brainstorming?

6. Identify two work-related problems for which the NGT is particularly well suited.

7. If you were a UPS manager, how would you deal with the situation of an employee who was consistently one-minute late for the three-minute meetings?

8. How can a team leader apply groupware to help the group become more productive?

9. What annoys you the most about how some people conduct themselves in problem-solving meetings of any type? What changes in their behavior would you recommend?

10. Which group decision-making technique described in this chapter do you think members of a professional sports team are the most likely to use? Why?

The Web Corner

http://www.thinksmart.com/
(Group problem solving and creativity. Go to Work Out Your Creativity.)

http://www.nova-mind.com/
(Mind mapping for group and individual problem solving. See the demonstration.)

Internet Skill Builder: Where Did I Put That Great Idea I Had?

Many people involved in group brainstorming hit upon useful ideas when away from the brainstorming session, then forget the idea by the time they get to the session. So during the session, the person fails to make an outstanding contribution. Search the Internet for some cool ideas for recording your ideas. An example would be sending yourself an e-mail or voice-mail message if you come upon a useful idea while hiking. One superior Web site for your search is *http://www.innovationtools.com*. However, you are encouraged to look widely for a few concrete suggestions for filing your creative ideas right on the spot. Remember that fresh ideas are the building block for all types of group as well as individual problem solving.

Developing Your Human Relations Skills

Interpersonal Relations Case 6.1

Struggling to Make a Decision at BMI

Building Maintenance, Inc. (BMI), a firm of 325 full- and part-time employees, is engaged in the cleaning and general maintenance of offices and shopping plazas. Bud Nyrod founded BMI as "one man and one van" 10 years ago. The four other members of the executive team also have a financial stake in the business.

BMI is headquartered in an old office building scheduled for demolition. The pending demolition has forced the firm to face a relocation decision. Bud called a 10 A.M. meeting of the executive team to address the problem. As he entered the conference room, Karen, Liz, Marty, and Nick were already seated.

Bud: Good to see the whole team here. I assume that you've already given some thought to our relocation decision. Let me review the alternatives I see. Either we can relocate to some decent space in one of the newly refurbished downtown buildings, or we can get some slightly better space in a suburban park. Karen, as our financial officer, you must have some relevant facts and figures.

Karen: As you requested a few weeks ago, Bud, I have looked into a variety of possibilities. We can get some decent downtown space at about $35 per square foot. And, we can get first-rate accommodations in a suburban office park for about $38 per square foot. Relocation costs would be about the same.

Marty: Customers are influenced by image. So long as we have a good image, I think the customers will be satisfied. By the way, we're doing something that is negatively affecting our image. Our customer service representatives are just too rude over the phone. I think these folks should have proper training before we turn them loose on the customer phone. Lots of other companies have good brooms, vacuum cleaners, and power-cleaning equipment. Our only edge is the good service we offer customers.

Bud: Liz, what's your position on this relocation decision?

Liz: As employment director, I have a lot to say about relocation. I agree with Marty that customer service should receive top weight in any decision we make about relocation. Customer service, of course, is a direct result of having an efficient crew of maintenance employees. A suburban office park may sound glamorous, but it could be a disaster in terms of recruiting staff. Maintenance workers can afford to get downtown. The majority of them live in the city, and they are dependent on mass transit to get to work.

You typically need private transportation to get to an office park. Most of our permanent and temporary employees do not own cars or trucks. And many of them who do own vehicles usually can't afford to keep them in good repair. Many of the temporary help can put gas in their cars only on payday.

So if we relocate to a suburban park, we'll have to rent a small employment office downtown anyway.

Bud: So you're telling us that maybe we should choose both alternatives. We should open an employment office downtown and move the executive office to a suburban office park.

Liz: Now you're introducing a third alternative. We would have two offices downtown: one for the executive and clerical staff and one for hiring maintenance workers.

Bud: Nick, what do you think? Which location would be best for you as director of maintenance operations?

Nick: I'm not in the office too much. I spend most of my time in the field overseeing our supervisors and their crews. Most of our help never see the office after they are hired unless they have a major problem. They report directly to the site. To them their place of work is the building or shopping plaza where they are assigned. Other things are more important than the location of company headquarters.

One of the most important things we should be considering is a big holiday party for this year. I think a year-end party is a real morale builder. It's cost effective in terms of how much turnover it reduces. Some of the maintenance staff will stay on an extra month just to attend the party.

Marty: It looks like you folks have got the major issues out on the table. I really don't care where we locate so long as the needs of our customers come first. I'm eager to know what you people decide. But right now I have to run. I have a luncheon appointment on the other side of town that could mean a big shopping-plaza contract for us.

Bud: Good luck with the sales call, Marty. However, I think you could've scheduled that luncheon for another day. This is a pretty important issue. I'd like you to stay for five more minutes.

Nick: It seems that it's premature for us to reach a decision on this important matter today. Maybe we should call in an office location consultant to help us decide what to do. In the meantime, let's talk some more about the office party. I kind of like that idea.

Case Questions

1. How effective is the BMI team as a problem-solving group?
2. What recommendations can you make to the BMI team to better solve the problem it is facing?
3. How might the team have used the NGT to help solve the problem of office relocation?

Interpersonal Relations Case 6.2

The Picnic Committee Brainstorms

The picnic committee surveyed a sample of the workforce about what type of picnic they wanted. The most popular request was for a themed event (not just the same old sitting around eating sandwiches). The committee knew the constraints: limited cost and distance. The chairperson asked the works manager to facilitate a brainstorming session so he could join the group.

The meeting started with the facilitator introducing himself and the recorder (his administrative assistant), and laying down the ground rules. The problem, "Theme for a company picnic," was pinned to a wall and two flip charts were set up to record ideas where everyone could see them. The meeting started:

Facilitator: Mike, you start.
Mike: How about Country and Western?
Facilitator: Fine. Jane, you're next in line...
Jane: Cowboys and Indians.
John: No, we did that a couple of years ago...
Facilitator: Sorry, John, can we stick to the rules? No criticism of any kind, no matter what.
John: Sorry, Jane. Ok...horse racing.
Celia: Dog racing!
<later>

Jane: Green.
Sandra: (laughing) Sky-blue pink with purple dots!
John: Yes! Airplanes! We could hold it at the local airfield, and have plane rides...
Facilitator: Sounds good, John, but let's discuss details later. Ken, you look like you're thinking about something . . .
<later>

Facilitator: Ok, we seem to have a good set of ideas. Now it's time to find the best ones. Can you all come up and put three crosses against your favorite idea, two against the next one, and one each against three "runners up"?

<a little later>

Facilitator: Right. The top three, airplanes, clowns, and hats, are clearly more popular than any of the others. Let's take a little time to discuss them. Jane, could you tell us why airplanes would be a good theme? **[Jane did not vote for the airplanes.]**

<later>

Celia: We could have a funny plane theme, or an airplane hat competition.
Mike: Mmm. Fun in the air could include things like kite flying.
<later>

Facilitator: The suggested theme is "Clowning around in the air." Are we all agreed, then, that is the joint recommendation of this group?

Case Questions

1. How would you evaluate the effectiveness of the facilitator in this brainstorming session?
2. In what way was the picnic theme chosen a synthesis of a straight suggestion with an idea that was sparked by humor?
3. What technique did the facilitator use that resembled the NGT?
4. What is your guess as to the success of the picnic?

Source: "Brainstorming: Examples," *http://syque.com/ quality_tools/toolbook/Brainstorm/example.htm*

CHAPTER 7

....

Cross-Cultural Relations and Diversity

Getting a day off from work for Martin Luther King Jr. Day is certainly nice, but to Jennifer Lee, a black employee at Horizon Blue Cross Blue Shield of New Jersey's Wall office, the company commitment to diversity comes through in more subtle ways.

Lee's managers take her seriously when she suggests ways to work more effectively. They don't dole out special favors to some workers and not others. And they offer workers full support when they spend time organizing charitable events, she said.

"Diversity is not something I'm looking for," said Lee, a 41-year-old claims policy specialist. "Being treated equal is more of my concern. I don't want to be treated any different. Just the same."

More than one half of the Horizon Blue Cross Blue Shield located in Newark, N.J. is minority, but that's not the end of the story. The company asks frontline employees with leadership skills to participate in a mentoring program that ultimately trains them to be managers. Those classes include women and minorities who might be left behind by corporations not attuned to diversity issues, said Eugene Tucker, the company's chief diversity leader.[1]

The story about the health insurance company illustrates how some business firms and not-for-profit organizations value cultural diversity in the workforce by treating people equally, yet at the same time create opportunities for all people who demonstrate leadership skills to advance.

Learning Objectives

After reading and studying this chapter and doing the exercises, you should be able to

1. Recognize who fits under the diversity umbrella.
2. Describe the major values accounting for cultural differences.
3. Overcome many cross-cultural communication barriers.
4. Improve your cross-cultural relations.

Top management at business firms continues to recognize the importance of a diverse workforce as well as diverse customers. Not only is the workforce becoming more diverse, but business has also become increasingly international. Small- and medium-size firms, as well as corporate giants, are increasingly dependent on trade with other countries. An estimated 10 to 15 percent of jobs in the United States depends on imports or exports. Furthermore, most manufactured goods contain components from more than one country. Also, more and more work, such as call centers and manufacturing, is subcontracted to companies in other countries.

All this workplace diversity has an important implication for the career-minded individual. To succeed in today's workplace, a person must be able to relate effectively to people from different cultural groups from within and outside his or her country. Being able to relate to a culturally diverse customer base is also necessary for success.

This chapter presents concepts and techniques you can use to sharpen your ability to work effectively with people from diverse backgrounds. To get you started thinking about your readiness to work in a culturally diverse environment, take Self-Assessment Quiz 7-1.

THE DIVERSITY UMBRELLA

Improving cross-cultural relations includes understanding the true meaning of appreciating diversity. To appreciate diversity, a person must go beyond tolerating and treating people from different racial and ethnic groups fairly. The true meaning of valuing diversity is to respect and enjoy a wide range of cultural and individual differences. Appreciating these differences is often referred to as *inclusion* to emphasize unity rather than diversity. To be diverse is to be different in some measurable way, even if what is measurable is not visible (such as religion or sexual orientation).

To be highly skilled in interpersonal relations, one must recognize and appreciate individual and demographic (group or category) differences, as well as cultural differences. People from the same demographic group often come from many different cultures. For example, the Hispanic or Latino demographic group is composed of many different cultures. Some people are more visibly diverse than others because of physical features or disabilities. Yet the diversity umbrella is supposed to include everybody in an organization. To value diversity is therefore to appreciate individual differences among people.

Cross-Cultural Skills and Attitudes

Directions: Listed below are skills and attitudes that various employers and cross-cultural experts think are important for relating effectively to coworkers in a culturally diverse environment. For each of the statements, check *applies to me now* or *not there yet.*

	Applies to me now	Not there yet
1. I have spent some time in another country.	_____	_____
2. At least one of my friends is deaf, is blind, or uses a wheelchair.	_____	_____
3. Currency from other countries is as real as the currency from my own country.	_____	_____
4. I can read in a language other than my own.	_____	_____
5. I can speak in a language other than my own.	_____	_____
6. I can write in a language other than my own.	_____	_____
7. I can understand people speaking in a language other than my own.	_____	_____
8. I use my second language regularly.	_____	_____
9. My friends include people of races different from my own.	_____	_____
10. My friends include people of different ages.	_____	_____
11. I feel (or would feel) comfortable having a friend with a sexual orientation different from mine.	_____	_____
12. My attitude is that although another culture may be very different from mine, that culture is equally good.	_____	_____
13. I am willing to eat (or have eaten) food from other countries that are not served in my own country.	_____	_____
14. I would accept (or have already accepted) a work assignment of more than several months in another country.	_____	_____
15. I have a passport.	_____	_____
16. I know the approximate difference in value between the U.S. dollar and the euro.	_____	_____

Interpretation: If you answered *applies to me now* to 11 or more of the preceding questions, you most likely function well in a multicultural work environment. If you answered *not there yet* to 11 or more of the questions, you need to develop more cross-cultural awareness and skills to work effectively in a multicultural work environment. You will notice that being bilingual gives you at least five points on this quiz.

Sources: Several ideas for statements on this quiz are derived from Ruthann Dirks and Janet Buzzard, "What CEOs Expect of Employees Hired for International Work," *Business Education Forum,* April 1997, pp. 3–7; and Gunnar Beeth, "Multicultural Managers Wanted," *Management Review*, May 1997, pp. 17–21.

Appreciating cultural diversity in organizations was originally aimed at assisting women and minorities. The diversity umbrella continues to include more people as the workforce encompasses a greater variety of people. For example, in recent years much attention has been paid to the rights of employees included in the group GLBT (gay, lesbian, bisexual, and transsexual). The rights of members of diverse religious groups are also receiving attention. One such group is a Christian employee network that opposes rights for people of nontraditional sexual orientation.[2] The goal of a diverse organization is for persons of all cultural backgrounds to achieve their full potential, not restrained by group identities such as gender, nationality, or race. Another important goal is for these groups to work together harmoniously.

Figure 7-1 presents a broad sampling of the ways in which workplace associates can differ from one another. Studying this list can help you anticipate the types of differences to understand and appreciate in a diverse workplace. The differences include

FIGURE 7-1 Diversity Umbrella

- Race
- Sex (or gender)
- Religion
- Age (young, middle-age, and old)
- Ethnicity (country of origin)
- Education
- Abilities
- Mental disabilities (including attention deficit disorder)
- Physical disabilities (including hearing status, visual status, able-bodied, wheelchair user)
- Values and motivation
- Sexual orientation (heterosexual, homosexual, bisexual, transsexual)
- Marital status (married, single, cohabitating, widow, widower)
- Family status (children, no children, two-parent family, single parent, grandparent)
- Personality traits
- Functional background (area of specialization)
- Technology interest (high-tech, low-tech, technophobe)
- Weight status (average, obese, underweight, anorexic)
- Hair status (full head of hair, bald, wild hair, tame hair, long hair, short hair)
- Tobacco status (smoker versus nonsmoker, chewer versus nonchewer)
- Styles of clothing and appearance (dress up, dress down, professional appearance, casual appearance)

cultural as well as individual factors. Individual factors are also important because people can be discriminated against for personal characteristics as well as group factors. Many people, for example, believe they are held back from promotion because of their weight-to-height ratio.

UNDERSTANDING CULTURAL DIFFERENCES

The groundwork for developing effective cross-cultural relations is to understand cultural differences. The information about different communication patterns between men and women presented in Chapter 4 is relevant here. Some researchers think that men and women represent different cultures! One cultural difference between the two groups is that women tend to speak indirectly and soften criticism. Men, in contrast, tend to be more direct in giving criticism. Here we discuss six aspects of understanding cultural differences: (1) cultural sensitivity including political correctness, (2) cultural intelligence, (3) respect for all workers, (4) cultural fluency, (5) dimensions of differences in cultural dimensions, and (6) avoidance of cultural bloopers. To work smoothly with people from other cultures, it is important to become competent in all six areas.

LEARNING OBJECTIVE 2

Cultural Sensitivity and Political Correctness

To relate well to someone from a foreign country, a person must be alert to possible cultural differences. When working in another country, a person must be willing to acquire knowledge about local customs and learn how to speak the native language at least passably.

When working with people from different cultures, even from his or her own country, the person must be patient, adaptable, flexible, and willing to listen and learn. The characteristics just mentioned are part of **cultural sensitivity**, an awareness of and willingness to investigate the reasons why individuals of another culture act as they do.[3] A person with cultural sensitivity will recognize certain nuances in customs that will help build better relationships with those from cultural backgrounds other than his or her own.

Another aspect of cultural sensitivity is **political correctness**—being careful not to offend or slight anyone, and being extra civil and respectful.[4] An effective use of political correctness would be to say, "We need a ladder in our department because we have workers of different heights who need access to the top shelves." It would be politically incorrect to say, "We need ladders because we have some short workers who cannot reach the top shelves." Carried too far, political correctness can push a person in the direction of being too bland and imprecise in language. The ultra-politically correct person, for example, will almost never mention a person's race, sex, ethnicity, or health status when referring to another worker. For example, the ultra-politically correct person would not make a statement like "Sadie is German, so she was a natural to be our liaison with the manufacturing group." (The cultural stereotype here is that Germans are quite interested in manufacturing technology and think precisely.) Ultra-political correctness also involves using supposedly correct terms to describe people even if a given individual rejects the label. For example, many black people are correctly referred to as "black" rather than "African American" because they might be citizens of Africa, Haiti, England, and so on. Also, the same people do not consider themselves to be African American.

Empathy is a major trait and skill that facilitates cultural sensitivity and political correctness. You have to place yourself in the other person's perspective, and ask yourself questions such as "How would I like it if somebody snarled and said an ugly word when he or she looked at my favorite food?" Kim Oliver and Sylvester Baugh offer this insight into developing the type of empathy helpful in building cross-cultural relations in the workplace: "We want to try to develop an understanding for the majority about what it might be like to be the minority, and help the minority understand what it's like to be the majority."[5]

Cultural Intelligence

An advanced aspect of cultural sensitivity is to be able to fit in comfortably with people of another culture by observing the subtle cues they give about how a person should act in their presence. **Cultural intelligence (CQ)** is an outsider's ability to interpret someone's unfamiliar and ambiguous behavior the same way that person's compatriots would. With high cultural intelligence, a person would be able to figure out what behavior would be true of all people and all groups, such as rapid shaking of a clenched fist to communicate anger. Also, the person with high cultural intelligence could determine what is peculiar to this group, as well as those aspects of behavior that are neither universal nor peculiar to the group. These ideas are so abstract that an example will help clarify.

> *An American expatriate manager served on a design team that included two German engineers. As other team members floated their ideas, the engineers condemned them as incomplete or underdeveloped. The manager concluded that the Germans in general are rude and aggressive.*
>
> *With average cultural intelligence the American would have realized he was mistakenly equating the merit of an idea with the merit of the person presenting it. The Germans, however, were able to make a sharp distinction between the two. A manager with more advanced cultural intelligence might have tried to figure out how much of the two Germans' behavior was typically German and how much was explained by the fact that they were engineers.*[6]

Similar to emotional intelligence, cultural intelligence encompasses several different aspects of behavior. The three sources of cultural intelligence relate to the cognitive,

---

cultural sensitivity

An awareness of and willingness to investigate the reasons why people of another culture act as they do.

political correctness

Being careful not to offend or slight anyone, and being extra civil and respectful

cultural intelligence (CQ)

An outsider's ability to interpret someone's unfamiliar and ambiguous behavior the same way that person's compatriots would.

FIGURE 7-2 The Components of Cultural Intelligence

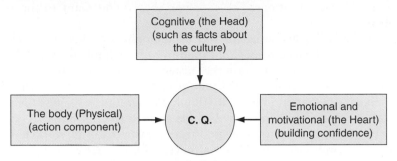

```
                   ┌──────────────────┐
                   │ Cognitive (the Head) │
                   │ (such as facts about │
                   │   the culture)       │
                   └──────────────────┘
                            │
                            ▼
┌──────────────────┐    ╭──────╮    ┌──────────────────────┐
│ The body (Physical) │──▶│ C. Q. │◀──│ Emotional and         │
│ (action component)  │   ╰──────╯    │ motivational (the Heart) │
└──────────────────┘               │ (building confidence)  │
                                   └──────────────────────┘
```

emotional/motivational, and the physical, are shown in Figure 7-2, and explained as follows:[7]

1. **Cognitive (the Head).** The cognitive part of CQ refers to what a person knows and how he or she can acquire new knowledge. Here you acquire facts about people from another culture such as their passion for football (soccer in North America), their business practices, and their promptness in paying bills. Another aspect of this source of cultural intelligence is figuring out how you can learn more about the other culture.

2. **Emotional/Motivational (the Heart).** The emotional/motivational aspect of CQ refers to energizing one's actions and building personal confidence. You need both confidence and motivation to adapt to another culture. A man on a business trip to Africa might say to himself, "When I greet a work associate in a restaurant, can I really pull off kissing him on both cheeks? What if he thinks I'm weird?" With strong motivation, the same person might say, "I'll give it a try. I kind of greet my grandfather the same way back in the United States."

3. **The Body (Physical).** The body aspect of CQ is the action component. The body is the element for translating intentions into actions and desires. Kissing the same-sex African work associates on both cheeks is the *physical* aspect just mentioned. We often have an idea of what we should do, but implementation is not so easy. You might know, for example, that when entering an Asian person's home you should take off your shoes, yet you might not actually remove them— thereby offending your Asian work associate (or personal friend).

To practice high cultural intelligence, the mind, heart, and body have to work together. You need to determine how to act with people from another culture; you need motivation and confidence to change; and you have to translate your knowledge and motivation into action. So when you are on a business trip to London, go ahead and hold your fork in your left hand!

Respect for All Workers and Cultures

An effective strategy for achieving cross-cultural understanding is to simply respect all others in the workplace, including their cultures. An important component of respect is to believe that although another person's culture is different from yours, it is equally good. Respect comes from valuing differences. Respecting other people's customs can translate into specific attitudes, such as respecting one coworker for wearing a yarmulke on Friday or another for wearing African clothing to celebrate Kwanzaa. Another way of being respectful would be to listen carefully to the opinion of a senior worker who says the company should never have converted to voice mail in place of assistants answering the phone (even though you disagree).

An aspect of respecting all workers that achieves current attention is the importance of respecting the rights of majorities, particularly white males. Many of these men want to be involved in—not excluded from—bringing about cultural diversity in organizations. For example, they might want to mentor minority group members.

Company policies that encourage respect for the rights of others are likely to create a positive influence on tolerance throughout the firm. An example is that many employers have taken steps to recognize and affirm the existence of gay and lesbian workers. Among these steps are publishing formal statements of nondiscrimination and the inclusion of issues about sexual orientation in diversity training programs. A major policy change has been to grant same-sex couples the same benefits granted to opposite-sex couples.

employee network (or affinity) groups.

A group composed of employees throughout the company who affiliate on the basis of group characteristics such as race, ethnicity, gender, sexual orientation, or physical ability status.

Another formal (official) way of demonstrating respect for all workers is to provide for the presence of **employee network (or affinity) groups.** Such a group is composed of employees throughout the company who affiliate on the basis of group characteristics such as race, ethnicity, gender, sexual orientation, or physical ability status. The network group provides members of the same demographic or cultural group an avenue for sharing ideas with management. Employee network groups at McDonald's, for example, include the African-American Council, the Hispanic Employee Network, the Asian Employee Network, and the Gays, Lesbians and Allies at McDonald's.[8] A study of 537 gay and lesbian employees working for a variety of organizations demonstrated that the more prevalent policies dealing with respect, the more equitably sexual minorities are likely to be treated at work. More equitable treatment, in turn, was associated with gays and lesbians being more satisfied and less likely to leave the firm.[9]

BACK TO THE OPENING CASE

Management at Blue Cross Blue Shield of New Jersey continues to be successful in building a culturally diverse workforce. Management's most important approach to accomplishing this end is to show respect for all workers by treating them equally. Employees with good ideas are listened to, and both majority group members and minority group members who appear to have leadership skills have an equal shot at being part of the management training program.

Cultural Fluency

cultural fluency

The ability to conduct business in a diverse, international environment.

A high-level goal in understanding cultural differences is to achieve **cultural fluency,** the ability to conduct business in a diverse, international environment.[10] Achieving cultural fluency includes a variety of skills, such as relating well to people from different cultures and knowing a second language. Cultural fluency also includes knowledge of the international business environment, such as how the exchange rate can affect profits. Having high CQ would contribute to cultural fluency because such intelligence makes it easier to work well with people from other cultures.

Skill-Building Exercise 7-1 is a warm-up activity for achieving cultural sensitivity and perhaps respect for all workers.

SKILL-BUILDING EXERCISE 7-1

Developing Cultural Sensitivity

Carefully observe products and services such as tennis shoes, notebooks, bicycles, and banking services, and attempt to find out how they are marketed and sold in other countries. For a convenient reference source, interview foreign students and foreigners outside class about these products and services. Your digging for information might uncover such nuggets as the following:

- In India, cricket champions are celebrities comparable to U.S. basketball stars who endorse soft drinks like Coca-Cola and Pepsi.

- In Hungary, peanut butter is considered a luxury food item.

- In some countries in warm climates, meat is freshly killed and hung on hooks for sale—without refrigeration or freezing.

  After conducting these product and service interviews, arrive at some kind of interpretation or conclusion. Share your insights with other class members.

Source: "Teaching International Business," *Keying In,* January 1999, p. 1. National Business Education Association. Reprinted with permission.

Dimensions of Differences in Cultural Values

One way to understand how national cultures differ is to examine their values or cultural dimensions. The formulation presented here is based on the worldwide research in 62 societal cultures and builds on previous analyses of cultural dimensions.[11] The cultural dimensions presented here are those most directly related to interpersonal skills. Keep in mind that these cultural dimensions are stereotypes that apply to a representative person from a particular culture, and are not meant to insult anybody. As with gender stereotypes in communication, individual differences are substantial. For example, many Americans are not assertive, and many French are willing to work 70 hours per week.

1. **Performance orientation** is the degree to which a society encourages (or should encourage) and rewards group members for performance improvement and excellence. Countries high on this dimension are the United States and Singapore, whereas those low on this dimension are Russia and Greece.

2. **Assertiveness** is the degree to which individuals are (and should be) assertive, confrontational, and aggressive in their relationships with one another. Countries scoring high on this dimension are the United States and Austria, whereas those low on this dimension are Sweden and New Zealand. Assertive people enjoy competition in business, in contrast to less assertive cultural groups who prefer harmony, loyalty, and solidarity.

3. **Time orientation** is the importance nations and individuals attach to time. People with an urgent time orientation perceive time as a scarce resource and tend to be impatient. People with a casual time orientation view time as an unlimited and unending resource and tend to be patient. Americans are noted for their urgent time orientation. They frequently impose deadlines and are eager to get started doing business. Asians, Mexicans, and Middle Easterners, in contrast, are patient negotiators.

4. **Humane orientation** is the degree to which a society encourages and rewards, and should encourage and reward, individuals for being fair, altruistic, caring, and to others. Egypt and Malaysia rank high on this cultural dimension, and France and Germany rank low.

5. **In-group collectivism** is the degree to which individuals express, and should express, pride, loyalty, and cohesiveness in their organizations and families. Asian societies emphasize collectivism, as do Egypt and Russia. One consequence of collectivism is taking pride in family members and the organizations that employ them.

6. **Gender egalitarianism** is the degree to which a culture minimizes, and should minimize, gender inequality. European countries emphasize gender egalitarianism, and so do the United States and Canada. South Korea is an example of a country that is low on gender egalitarianism and is male dominated.

7. **Acceptance of power and authority** is the degree to which members of a society expect, and should expect, power to be distributed unequally. Individuals who accept power and authority expect the boss to make the major decisions. These same individuals are more formal; however, being formal toward people in positions of authority has decreases substantially throughout the world in recent years. Examples of societies that score high on acceptance of power and authority are Thailand, Brazil, France, and Japan.

8. **Work orientation** is the number of hours per week and weeks per year people expect to invest in work versus leisure, or other non-work activities. American corporate professionals typically work about 55 hours per week, take 45-minute lunch breaks, and two weeks of vacation. Americans tend to have a stronger work orientation than Europeans but a weaker one than Asians. U.S. employees average 1,804 hours of work per year, compared with 1,407

for Norwegian workers and 1,564 for the French. Workers in seven Asian countries including South Korea, Bangladesh, and China worked 2,200 hours per year.[12]

How might a person use information about cultural differences to improve his or her interpersonal relations on the job? A starting point would be to recognize that a person's national values might influence his or her behavior. Assume that you wanted to establish a good working relationship with a person from a high humane orientation culture. An effective starting point would be to emphasize care and concern when communicating with that individual.

Attitudes toward acceptance of power and authority can make a difference in establishing working relationships. A worker who values deference to age, gender, or title might shy away from offering suggestions to an elder or manager to avoid appearing disrespectful. This worker would need considerable encouragement to collaborate in decision making.[13] A *time orientation* may create a conflict if you are committed to making deadlines and a team member has a laid-back attitude toward time. You might explain that although you respect his attitudes toward time, the company insists on getting the project completed on time.

Self-Assessment Quiz 7-2 will help you think about how cultural dimensions might be influencing your interpersonal relations in the workplace.

Cultural Bloopers

An effective way of being culturally sensitive is to minimize actions that are likely to offend people from another culture based on their values. Cultural bloopers are most likely to take place when you are visiting another country. The same bloopers, however, can also be committed with people from a different culture within your own country. To avoid these bloopers, you must carefully observe persons from another culture. Studying another culture through reading is also helpful.

E-commerce and other forms of Internet communication have created new opportunities for creating cultural bloopers. The Web site developers and workers responsible for adding content must have good cross-cultural literacy, including an awareness of how the information might be misinterpreted.

- Numerical date formats can be readily misinterpreted. To an American, 4/9/11 would be interpreted as April 9, 2011 (or 1911!). However, many Europeans would interpret the same numerical expression as September 4, 2011.
- Colors on Web sites must be chosen carefully. For example, in some cultures purple is the color of royalty, whereas in Brazil purple is associated with death.
- Be careful of metaphors that may not make sense to a person for whom your language is a second language. Examples include "We've encountered an ethical meltdown" and "Our biggest competitor is over the hill."

English has become the language of business and science throughout the world, yet communicating in a customer's native tongue has its advantages. Being able to communicate your message directly in your customer's mother tongue provides a competitive advantage. Bilingualism also has career implications. Some telemarketing, banking, engineering, and financial service companies are searching for workers with bilingual skills. The two major contributing factors are the growing immigrant population in the United States, and companies engaging in more international business.[14] Furthermore, according to the research firm IDC, consumers are four times more likely to purchase a product online if the Web site is in their preferred language.[15] The translator, of course, must have good knowledge of the subtleties of the language to avoid a blooper. An English-to-French translator used the verb *baiser* instead of *baisser* to describe a program of lowering prices. *Baisser* is the French verb "to lower," whereas *baiser* is the verb "to kiss." Worse, in slang, *baiser* is a verb that refers to having intimate physical relationships!

Keep two key facts in mind when attempting to avoid cultural mistakes. One is that members of any cultural group show individual differences. What one member of the group might regard as an insensitive act, another might welcome. Recognize also that one or two cultural mistakes will not peg you permanently as a boor. Skill-Building Exercise 7-2 will help you minimize certain cultural bloopers.

> " The Fortune 100 companies I deal with are asking more frequently for managers who speak Spanish, Portuguese, Mandarin Chinese and other languages. And when it's not mandatory for some jobs, being bilingual is icing on the cake. "
>
> —Dayna Romanick, a national recruiter for Manpower Professional[16]

OVERCOMING CROSS-CULTURAL COMMUNICATION BARRIERS

We have already discussed the importance of overcoming communication barriers in Chapter 4. Cultural differences create additional barriers. Here are some guidelines for overcoming cross-cultural communication barriers.

LEARNING OBJECTIVE 3

1. **Be sensitive to the fact that cross-cultural communication barriers exist.** If you are aware of these potential barriers, you will be ready to deal with them. When you are dealing with a person in the workplace with a different cultural background than yours, solicit feedback to minimize cross-cultural barriers to communication. Being aware of these potential barriers will help you develop cultural sensitivity.

2. **Show respect for all workers.** The same behavior that promotes good cross-cultural relations in general helps overcome communication barriers. A widely used comment that implies disrespect is to say to another person from another culture, "You have a funny accent." Should you be transposed to that person's culture, you, too, might have a "funny accent."

Cultural Mistakes to Avoid with Selected Cultural Groups

EUROPE

Great Britain
- Asking personal questions. The British protect their privacy.
- Thinking that a businessperson from England is unenthusiastic when he or she says, "Not bad at all." English people understate their positive emotion.
- Gossiping about royalty.

France
- Expecting to complete work during the French two-hour lunch.
- Attempting to conduct significant business during August—*les vacances* (vacation time).
- Greeting a French person for the first time and not using a title such as "sir," or "madam," or "miss" (*monsieur, madame,* or *mademoiselle*).

Italy
- Eating too much pasta, as it is not the main course.
- Handing out business cards freely. Italians use them infrequently.

Spain
- Expecting punctuality. Your appointments will usually arrive 20 to 30 minutes late.
- Making the American sign for "OK" with your thumb and forefinger. In Spain (and many other countries) this is vulgar.

Scandinavia (Denmark, Sweden, Norway)
- Being overly rank conscious. Scandinavians pay relatively little attention to a person's rank in the hierarchy.

ASIA

All Asian countries
- Pressuring an Asian job applicant or employee to brag about his or her accomplishments. Asians feel self-conscious when boasting about individual accomplishments; they prefer to let the record speak for itself. In addition, they prefer to talk about group rather than individual accomplishment.

Japan
- Shaking hands or hugging Japanese (as well as other Asians) in public. Japanese consider these practices to be offensive.
- Not interpreting "We'll consider it" as a no when spoken by a Japanese businessperson.

Japanese negotiators mean no when they say "We'll consider it."
- Not giving small gifts to Japanese when conducting business. Japanese are offended by not receiving these gifts.
- Giving your business card to a Japanese businessperson more than once. Japanese prefer to give and receive business cards only once.

China
- Using black borders on stationery and business cards, because black is associated with death.
- Giving small gifts to Chinese when conducting business. Chinese are offended by these gifts.
- Making cold calls on Chinese business executives. An appropriate introduction is required for a first-time meeting with a Chinese official.

Korea
- Saying no. Koreans feel it is important to have visitors leave with good feelings.

India
- Telling Indians you prefer not to eat with your hands. If the Indians are not using cutlery when eating, they expect you to do likewise.

MEXICO AND LATIN AMERICA

Mexico
- Flying into a Mexican city in the morning and expecting to close a deal by lunch. Mexicans build business relationships slowly.

Brazil
- Attempting to impress Brazilians by speaking a few words of Spanish. Portuguese is the official language of Brazil.

Most Latin American countries
- Wearing elegant and expensive jewelry during a business meeting. Latin Americans think people should appear more conservative during a business meeting.

Note: A cultural mistake for Americans to avoid when conducting business in most countries outside the United States and Canada is to insist on getting down to business quickly. North Americans in small towns also like to build a relationship before getting down to business. The preceding suggestions will lead to cross-cultural skill development if practiced in the right setting. During the next 30 days, look for an opportunity to relate to a person from another culture in the way described in these suggestions. Observe the reaction of the other person for feedback on your cross-cultural effectiveness.

3. **Use straightforward language and speak slowly and clearly.** When working with people who do not speak your language fluently, speak in an easy-to-understand manner. Minimize the use of idioms and analogies specific to your language. A computer analyst from Greece left confused after a discussion about a software problem with her manager. The manager said, "Let's talk about this another time because *I can't seem to get to first base with you.*" (The manager was referring to the fact that the conversation was headed nowhere because he couldn't come to an agreement with the analyst.) The computer analyst did not ask for clarification because she did not want to appear uninformed.

4. **Observe cultural differences in etiquette.** Violating rules of etiquette without explanation can erect immediate communication barriers. A major rule of etiquette

in many countries is that people address superiors by their last name unless they have worked together for a long time. Or, the superior might encourage being on a first-name basis with him or her. Be aware that an increasing number of cultures are moving toward addressing each other and customers by using the first name only. Yet, it is best to error on the side of formality.

5. **Be sensitive to differences in nonverbal communication.** Stay alert to the possibility that a person from another culture may misinterpret your nonverbal signal. Hand signals of various types, such as a thumb up or the OK sign to indicate acceptance, are the most liable to misinterpretation. Another key area of cross-cultural differences in nonverbal communication is the handshake. In some cultures, a woman is expected to extend her hand first to shake with a man. In other cultures, people hug, embrace, or bow instead of shaking hands.[17] (With good cultural sensitivity and cultural intelligence, you can determine what to do when meeting another person.)

6. **Do not be diverted by style, accent, grammar, or personal appearance.** Although these superficial factors are all related to business success, they are difficult to interpret when judging a person from another culture. It is therefore better to judge the merits of the statement or behavior.[18] A brilliant individual from another culture may still be learning your language and thus make basic mistakes in speaking your language. Also, he or she might not yet have developed a sensitivity to dress style in your culture.

7. **Be attentive to individual differences in appearance.** A major cross-cultural insult is to confuse the identity of people because they are members of the same race or ethnic group. An older economics professor reared in China and teaching in the United States had difficulty communicating with students because he was unable to learn their names. The professor's defense was that "So many of these Americans look alike to me." Research suggests that people have difficulty seeing individual differences among people of another race because they code race first, such as thinking, "He has the nose of an African American." However, people can learn to search for more distinguishing features, such as a dimple or eye color.[19] In this way, individual differences are recognized.

TECHNIQUES FOR IMPROVING CROSS-CULTURAL RELATIONS

LEARNING OBJECTIVE 4

Many training programs have been developed to improve cross-cultural relations and to help workers value diversity. All of the information presented so far in this chapter is likely to be included in such programs. In this section we describe programs for improving cross-cultural relations, including cultural training, cultural intelligence training, language training, diversity training, and cross-cultural mentoring.

Cultural Training

For many years, companies and government agencies have prepared their workers for overseas assignments. The method most frequently chosen is **cultural training**, a set of learning experiences designed to help employees understand the customs, traditions, and beliefs of another culture. In today's diverse business environment and international marketplace, learning about individuals raised in different cultural backgrounds has become more important. Many industries therefore train employees in cross-cultural relations.

cultural training

A set of learning experiences designed to help employees understand the customs, traditions, and beliefs of another culture.

Cultural training is also important for helping people of one culture understand their customers from another culture in particular, such as Chinese people learning to deal more effectively with their American customers. For example, in one training program Chinese businesspeople are taught how to sprinkle their e-mail with English phrases like "How are you?" "It was great to hear from you" and "Can we work together?"[20]

The Job-Oriented Interpersonal Skills in Action Box describes how cultural training can improve the effectiveness of establishing call centers overseas.

To practice improving your cross-cultural relations, do Skill-Building Exercise 7-3.

Cross-Cultural Relations Role-Play

One student plays the role of Ritu, a call center representative in New Delhi, India. Her specialty is helping customers with cell phone problems. Another student plays the role of Todd, an irate American. His problem is that he cannot get his camera-equipped cell phone to transmit his photos over e-mail. He is scheduled to attend a party in two hours, and wants to take loads of photos with his cell phone. Todd is impatient, and in the eyes of Ritu, somewhat overbearing. Ritu is good-natured and pleasant, but feels she must help Todd solve his problem without being bullied by him. Because Ritu is instructed to spend the minimum time necessary to resolve the problem, she spends about five minutes on this problem.

The observers should make note of how well Ritu has made the necessary cross-cultural adaptations.

Cultural Intelligence Training

A new development in assisting people work more effectively with workers in other cultures is *cultural intelligence training*, a program based on the principles of cultural intelligence described earlier in this chapter. A key part of the training is to learn the three contributors to CQ—head, heart, and body. Instead of learning a few simple guidelines for working effectively with people from another culture, the trainee is taught strategies for sizing up the environment to determine which course of action is best. The culturally intelligent overseas worker would learn how to determine how much humor to interject into meetings, what kind of handshake is most appropriate, and so forth. The following excerpt will give you a sense for what is involved in cultural intelligence training:

> *A Canadian manager is attempting to interpret a "Thai smile." First, she needs to observe the various cues provided in addition to the smile gesture itself (e.g., other facial or body gestures, significance of others who may be in proximity, the source of the original smile gesture) and to assemble them into a meaningful whole and make sense of what is really experienced by the Thai employee. Second, she must have the requisite motivation (directed effort and self-confidence) to persist in the face of confusion, challenge, or apparently mixed signals. Third, she must choose, generate, and execute the right actions to respond appropriately.*
>
> *If any of these elements is deficient, she is likely to be ineffective in dealing with the Thai employee. A high CQ manager has the capability with all three facets as they action in unison.* [21]

JOB-ORIENTED INTERPERSONAL SKILLS IN ACTION

Indian Call Center Workers Learn to Think and Act Like Americans

In a sleek new office building, two dozen young Indians are studying the customs of a place none of them have ever seen. One by one, the students present their conclusions about this fabled land. "Americans eat a lot of junk food. Table manners are very casual," says Ritu Khanna. "People are self-centered. The average American has 13 credit cards," says Nerissa Dcosata.

The Indians, who range in age from 20 to 27, have been hired to take calls from cranky or distraught Americans whose computers have gone haywire. To do this, they need to communicate in a language that is familiar but a culture that is foreign. "We're not saying India is better or America is better," says their trainer, Alefiya Rangsala. "We just want to be culturally sensitive so there's no disconnect when someone phones for tech support."

Call centers took root in India during the 2001 recession, when U.S. companies were struggling to reduce expenses. At first, training was simple. The centers gave employees names that were acceptable to American ears, with *Arjun* becoming *Aaron* and *Sangita* becoming *Susan*. The new hires were instructed to watch American television shows to get an idea of American folkways.

But whether Aaron and Susan were repairing computers, selling long-distance service, or fulfilling orders for diet tapes, problems immediately cropped up. The American callers often wanted a better deal or an impossibly swift resolution, and were aggressive and sometimes abrasive about saying so. The Indians responded according to their deepest natures: They were silent when they didn't understand, and they often committed to more than their employers could deliver. They would tell the Americans that someone would get back to them tomorrow to check on their problems, and no one would.

Customer satisfaction plummeted. The U.S. clients grew alarmed. Some even returned their business to U.S. call centers. Realizing that the multibillion-dollar industry with 150,000 employees was at risk, Indian call centers have recently embarked on more comprehensive training. New hires are taught how to express empathy, strategies to successfully open and close conversations, and above all how to be assertive, however unnatural it might feel.

Khanna, Dcosata, and their new colleagues work for Sutherland Global Services, an upstate New York firm that is one of the larger outsourcing companies in India. They've been put through a three-week training session where they research hot-button issues, and pretend they are American anchors reporting the latest news, and imitate celebrities.

On the students' last day of cultural and voice training, Rangsala warns them that at least half a dozen are still speaking incomprehensibly and might wash out. As they slip away one by one to make a short recording that will test their pronunciation skills, K. S. Kumar, Sutherland's director of operations for India, gives a little graduation speech. "You're shortchanging yourself if you don't stick with this." (The shift work and difficult work goals contribute to high turnover.)

Originally, the ever-agreeable Indian agents had a hard time getting people to pay bills that were six months overdue. Too often, says trainer Deepa Nagraj, the calls would go like this:

"Hi," the Indian would say. "I'd like to set up a payment to get your account current. Can I help you do that?"

"No," the American responds.

"OK, let me know if you change your mind," the Indian says and hangs up.

Now, says Nagraj, the agents take no excuses.

Like Sutherland, Mphasis is basing a lot of its hopes on training. Indrandiel Ghosh, an Mphasis trainer, gives refresher courses to reps who handle customer service accounts for a big credit-card company. One rep says he recently was helping a customer change his card data because his wife left him. When the rep expressed sympathy, the man cut him short, saying he hadn't really liked his wife.

"In case you empathize and then you see they don't want your empathy, move on," Ghosh advises. "This is someone from another culture. That increases the complexity tenfold."

Questions

1. What do you see as a major cultural difference between Indians and Americans that makes the call center job so challenging for Indians?
2. Some of the call center representatives in India are instructed to identify themselves as students in Salt Lake City, in addition to giving them American first names. What is your take on the ethics of these disguises?

Source: From David Streitfeld, "A Crash Course on Irate Calls," *Los Angeles Times,* August 2, 2004. Reprinted with permission.

As the example illustrates, to be culturally intelligent you need to apply cognitive skills, have the right motivation, and then put your knowledge and confidence into action. Armed with such skills you would know, for example, whether to greet a Mexican worker on a business trip to Texas with a handshake, a hug, or a kiss on both cheeks.

Language Training

Learning a foreign language is often part of cultural training, yet it can also be a separate activity. Knowledge of a second language is important because it builds better connections with people from other cultures than does relying on a translator. Building connections with people is still important even if English has become the international language of business. Many workers, aside from international business specialists, also choose to develop skills in a target language. Speaking another language can help build rapport with customers and employees who speak that language. As mentioned earlier, it is easier to sell to customers when using their native language.

Almost all language training has elements similar to taking a course in another language or self-study. Companies invest heavily in helping employees learn a target language because it facilitates conducting business in other countries. For this reason, companies that offer language training and translation services are currently experiencing a boom. Medical specialists, police officers, and firefighters also find second language skills to be quite helpful because clients under stress, such as an injured person, are likely to revert to their native tongue. Learning a second language is particularly important when many of your customers and employees do not speak your country's official language. For example, Casa Rio, in San Antonio, Texas, found that its English-speaking managers were unable to communicate with Spanish-speaking employees regarding benefits and other issues.[22]

Skill-Building Exercise 7-4 presents a low-cost, pleasant method of enhancing your foreign language and cross-cultural skills.

As with any other skill training, investments in language training can pay off only if the trainee is willing to work hard at developing the new skill outside the training sessions. Allowing even 10 days to pass without practicing your target language will result in a sharp decline in your ability to use that language.

Using the Internet to Help Develop Foreign Language Skills

A useful way of developing skills in another language, and learning more about another culture, is to create a computer "bookmark," "favorite," or home page written in your target language. In this way, each time you go to the Internet on your own computer, your home page will contain fresh information in the language you want to develop.

Enter a search word or phrase such as *Italian newspaper* or *Spanish language newspaper* in the search engine. After you find a suitable choice, enter the function for "Favorites" or "Bookmarks" and insert that newspaper as your home page.

For example, imagine that French is your target language and culture. The search engine might have brought you to the site http://www.france2.fr. This Web site keeps you abreast of French and international news, sports, and cultural events—written in French. Every time you access the Internet you can spend five minutes on your second language, thereby becoming multicultural. You can save a lot of travel costs and time using the Internet to help you become multicultural, including developing proficiency in another language.

Diversity Training

diversity training

Training that attempts to bring about workplace harmony by teaching people how to get along better with diverse work associates.

The general purpose of cultural training is to help workers understand people from other cultures. Understanding can lead to dealing more effectively with them as work associates or customers. **Diversity training** has a slightly different purpose. It attempts to bring about workplace harmony by teaching people how to get along better with diverse work associates. Quite often the program is aimed at minimizing open expressions of racism and sexism. Diversity training takes a number of forms. Nevertheless, all center on increasing awareness of and empathy for people who are different in some noticeable way from oneself.

Training sessions in appreciating cultural diversity focus on the ways that men and women or people of different races reflect different values, attitudes, and cultural backgrounds. These sessions can vary from several hours to several days. Training sessions can also be held over a long period of time. Sometimes the program is confrontational, sometimes not.

An essential part of relating more effectively to diverse groups is to empathize with their points of view. To help training participants develop empathy, representatives of various groups explain their feelings related to workplace issues, including how they have felt different in a way that made them feel uncomfortable. A representative segment of a training program designed to enhance empathy took the following format. A minority group member was seated at the middle of a circle. First, the coworkers listened to a Vietnamese woman explain how she felt excluded from the in-group composed of whites and African Americans in her department. "I feel like you just tolerate me. You do not make me feel that I am somebody important." The next person to sit in the middle of the circle was a Muslim. He complained about people wishing him Merry Christmas. "I would much prefer that my coworkers stop to think that I do not celebrate Christian holidays. I respect your religion, but it is not my religion."

Another form of diversity training is cross-generational diversity, or relating effectively to workers much older or younger than you. Wendy's International, Inc., with the help of a consultant, has developed training programs that raise awareness of generational issues. Allen Larson, director of management resources, says, "Since generational cohorts help form people's attitudes toward work, employees of different generations who must work together may find that their work styles conflict with those of coworkers."[24]

Cross-generational awareness training is one component in the corporate training program. The premise behind the program is that after acquiring cognitive knowledge, engaging in dialogue, and role-playing, employees will learn to accept people's differences, some of which are age driven. For example, younger employees might feel less guilty than would seniors when calling in sick just to have a day's vacation.

Skill-Building Exercise 7-5 provides you an opportunity to simulate an empathy-building experience in a diversity training program. Diversity training has frequently improved cross-cultural relationships in the workplace. Yet such programs can also create ill will and waste time. One problem is that participants are sometimes encouraged to be too confrontational and express too much hostility. Companies have found that when

Developing Empathy for Differences

Class members come up to the front of the room one by one and give a brief presentation (perhaps even three minutes) of any way in which they have been perceived as different, and how they felt about this perception. Sometimes this exercise is referred to as "When I Felt Different." The difference refers to feeling different from the majority.[23] The difference can be of any kind, relating to characteristics such as ethnicity, race, choice of major, physical appearance, height, weight, hair color, or body piercing. After each member of the class (perhaps even the instructor) has presented, class members discuss what they learned from the exercise. It is also important to discuss how this exercise can improve relationships on the job.

employees are too blunt during these sessions, it may be difficult to patch up interpersonal relations in the work group later on.

A negative consequence of diversity training is that it sometimes results in perpetuating stereotypes about groups, such as people from Latin America not placing much value on promptness for meetings. A related problem is that diversity training might focus too much on differences instead of similarities.[25] For example, even if people are raised with different cultural values they must all work harmoniously together to accomplish work. Although a worker believes that relationships are more important than profits, he or she must still produce enough to be a good investment for the company.

Cross-Cultural and Cross-Gender Mentoring Programs

An advanced method of improving cross-cultural relations is mentoring members of targeted minority groups. The mentoring demonstrates the company's interest in enhancing cross-cultural relations, and simultaneously enhances the minority group member's opportunities for advancement. To achieve cross-culture and cross-gender mentoring, companies often assign the member of the minority group a mentor who is typically an experienced manager. For example, a 24-year-old African American woman might be mentored by a 45-year-old Caucasian middle manager. Or, a minority group member could be the mentor, such as a 45-year-old African American woman mentoring a 24-year-old Indian man.

As described in Chapter 11, mentors might help the person being mentored in such ways as making the right contacts and learning useful professional skills. A challenge noted with cross-cultural and cross-gender mentoring is a shortage of mentors with the right knowledge and interpersonal skills.

Sprint started a trial mentoring program with 50 employees at company headquarters. Although open to all employees, the program targeted minority groups. Soon the program had 500 participants. "The demand was overwhelming," says Tammy Edwards, director of inclusion and diversity, who became a mentor to several employees. She adds that the mentee (person who is mentored) numbers became so large that each mentor had to be paired with up to five mentees.[26]

As with all other diversity programs, a major business case or justification for these mentoring programs is the increased purchasing power of various ethnic groups in the United States and the potential for new markets within these cultures. One study showed an estimated 423 percent increase in Latino buying power in the United States from 1990 to 2010.[27]

SELF-ASSESSMENT QUIZZES IN OVERVIEW

Self-Assessment Quiz 7-1 provides a reminder of your cross-cultural skills and attitudes mostly based on previous experiences. As you develop more exposure to cross-cultural relations, your score is likely to increase. The weight given to knowing a second language is an alert to its importance in the modern world even though English has become the official language of business and science. Self-Assessment Quiz 7-2 asks you to assess a finer point about cross-cultural relations—where you stand on eight key cross-cultural dimensions. A subtle point here is that people from the same culture often vary widely on these dimensions despite stereotypes of the average person from that culture. For example, many Mexicans have an urgent time orientation and many Americans have a casual time orientation.

Concept Review and Reinforcement

Key Terms

cultural sensitivity, 134
political correctness, 134
cultural intelligence (CQ), 134

employee network (or affinity)
  groups, 136
cultural fluency, 136

cultural training, 141
diversity training, 144

Summary of Key Concepts

Today's workplace has become more culturally diverse, and business has become increasingly international. As a result, to succeed one must be able to relate effectively to people from different cultural groups from within and outside one's country. The true meaning of valuing diversity is to respect and enjoy a wide range of cultural and individual differences. The diversity umbrella continues to include more people as the workforce encompasses a greater variety of people.

The groundwork for developing effective cross-cultural relations is to understand cultural differences. Six key aspects of understanding cultural differences are (1) cultural sensitivity, including political correctness; (2) cultural intelligence; (3) respect for all workers and all cultures; (4) cultural fluency—the ability to conduct business in a diverse, international environment; (5) differences in cultural dimensions; and (6) avoidance of cultural bloopers. Cultural intelligence is based on cognitive, emotional/motivational, and physical (taking action) factors.

Countries differ in their national values or cultural dimensions, leading to differences in how most people from a given country will react to situations. The dimensions studied here are (1) performance orientation, (2) assertiveness, (3) time orientation, (4) human orientation, (5) ingroup collectivism, (6) gender egalitarianism, (7) acceptance of power and authority, and (8) work orientation.

An effective way of being culturally sensitive is to minimize actions that are likely to offend people from another culture based on their values. These cultural bloopers can take place when working in another country or when dealing with foreigners in one's own country. Studying potential cultural bloopers is helpful, but recognize also that individual differences may be of significance.

Communication barriers created by cultural differences can often be overcome by the following: (1) be sensitive to the fact that these barriers exist; (2) show respect for all workers; (3) use straightforward language and speak slowly and clearly; (4) observe cultural differences in etiquette; (5) be sensitive to differences in nonverbal communication; (6) do not be diverted by style, accent, grammar, or personal appearance; and (7) be attentive to individual differences in appearance.

Cultural training is a set of learning experiences designed to help employees understand the customs, traditions, and beliefs of another culture. In today's diverse business environment and international marketplace, learning about individuals raised in different cultural backgrounds has become more important. Cultural intelligence training includes developing strategies for sizing up the environment to determine which course of action is best. Learning a foreign language is often part of cultural training, yet it can also be a separate activity.

Diversity training attempts to bring about workplace harmony by teaching people how to get along better with diverse work associates. Most forms of diversity training center on increasing awareness of and empathy for people who are different in some noticeable way from yourself. Cross-cultural and cross-gender mentoring are advanced methods of improving cross-cultural relations. The minority-group member or woman is assigned a mentor who helps the person advance in his or her career.

A business case for improving cross-cultural relations is that ethnic groups in the United States, such as Hispanics, are growing rapidly in purchasing power.

Check Your Understanding

1. How can a person demonstrate to others on the job that he or she is culturally fluent (gets along well with people from other cultures)?

2. What can you do this week to sharpen your cross-cultural skills?

3. Some companies, such as Singapore Airlines, make a deliberate effort for customer-contact personnel to all be of the same ethnic group (Singapore natives). How justified is this practice in an era of cultural diversity and valuing differences?

4. Provide an example of cultural insensitivity of any kind that you have seen, read about, or could imagine.

5. Why is knowing the language of the other person more important when selling to rather than buying from that person?

6. How could you use the information comparing U.S. values to those of other countries to help you succeed in business?

7. How useful is the adage, "When in Rome, do as the Romans do" for someone who wants to work in another country for a while?

8. If you were a supervisor, how would you deal with a group member who had a very low acceptance of power and authority?

9. The cultural bloopers presented in Skill-Building Exercise 7-2 all deal with errors people make about people who are not American. Give an example of a cultural blooper a person from another country might make in the United States.

10. Many people speak loudly to other people who are deaf, blind, and those who speak a different language. Based on the information presented in this chapter, what mistakes are these people making?

The Web Corner

http://www.DiversityInc.com
(Extensive information about cultural diversity in organizations.)

http://www.berlitz.com
(Information about language training and cultural training in countries throughout the world. Investigate in your second language to enhance the cross-cultural experience.)

Internet Skill Builder: Avoiding Cultural Insensitivity

One of the most effective ways of hampering relationships with people of another culture is to be grossly insensitive. If you can avoid these gross errors, you will be on your way toward at least acceptable relationships with people from another domestic or foreign culture. Two examples of cultural insensitivity uncovered on the Internet follow: (1) In Alberta, Canada, a sign in the window of a large chain restaurant read, "No drunken Indians allowed." (2) Wal-Mart performed poorly in Germany because it did not recognize the cultural fact that Germans do not like to spend a lot of time shopping by walking through a giant store and waiting on line.

Search the Internet for examples of cultural insensitivity. You may have to dig hard to find these nuggets of insensitivity, but the activity will help you become more culturally sensitive and aware.

Developing Your Human Relations Skills

The Multicultural Dealership

Manuel Ortiz is the owner and operator of Futura Motors, a large automobile and small-truck dealership in Brooklyn, New York. The dealership represents several Japanese and Korean vehicle manufacturers. For more than a decade, Ortiz and his management team have invested time, effort, and money into building a culturally diverse sales and service staffs to better serve the many ethnic, cultural, and racial groups that make up the dealership's customer base. Ortiz brags that in total his sales staff speaks 13 different languages. "In this way, we can communicate in the native tongue of almost any customer or sales prospect who shows up on the floor," says Ortiz. (A *sales prospect* is anyone who visits Futura without the full intention of purchasing a vehicle from the dealership, including the people who are "just looking.")

The culturally diverse sales and service staffs apparently have contributed to the growth and profitability of Futura, although such an assertion would be difficult to prove. For example, Ortiz has not been able to compare the dollar volume of Futura to a comparably sized foreign dealership in Brooklyn that has a more homogeneous workforce.

Penny Shakelford, the office manager at Futura, has recently brought a potential problem to Ortiz's attention that has caused him some concern about how well he and his staff are managing diversity. According to Shakelford, the multi-cultural sales staff appears to be well accepted by most customers and prospects, yet some problems are surfacing. Based on direct concerns expressed by both customers and prospects, Shakelford believes that they are being patronized on the basis of their demographic group. She explains:

"My impression is that some customers think we are bending over backwards to make them feel at home. If a person who walks on the floor appears to be an African American, immediately an African American sales rep walks up to him or her. The same goes for several other visible ethnic or racial groups. Two different Asiatic Indians wrote down on customer service survey cards that they thought it was too obvious that an Indian rushed out on the floor as soon as they appeared.

"A Mexican American woman said she thought it was a little bit much that three minutes after she and her husband walked into the dealership, a young sales rep introduced himself in Spanish. The customer said she was in Brooklyn, not Mexico City, and wanted to be treated like an American."

Ortiz said that it appears that the majority of customers and prospects find no problem with the dealership's attempt to make a direct appeal to their racial or ethnic group, but that maybe some adjustment needs to be made.

"We need to give this problem some thought. We don't want to insult anybody, but neither do we want to lose our competitive edge of having a multicultural workforce."

Case Questions

1. What is your opinion of the merits of a vehicle dealership attempting to match the demographic group of a customer with a sales rep of the same demographic group?
2. What do you recommend Ortiz and his management team do about the several complaints the Futura dealership has received?
3. To help you analyze this case, get the input from a few people in your network about how they would feel about having a person from their demographic group approach them when they visited a dealership. (Perhaps a few classmates representing different ethnic groups can provide useful input.)

Interpersonal Relations Case 7.2

Akiak Wants to Fit in

Akiak Nori was raised in Noorvik, Alaska, and then attended a career school in Juneau, Alaska, majoring in electronic technology. Approaching graduation, Akiak sorted out dozens of job offers he had obtained, several of which did not even require an in-person interview.

Akiak accepted a position with a construction company in International Falls, Minnesota, because of the job opportunities and the long brisk winters that would be natural and comfortable for him. Akiak was assigned to a construction team for new buildings. He was also assigned maintenance work for existing electronic systems in office buildings, factories, and mills.

Akiak's goal from the first day on the job was to perform well and fit in with his coworkers. He recognized that fitting in with a non-Eskimo group would require some patience on his part. Akiak had been counseled by several teachers that patience was not one of his strong points.

During employee orientation, two other new employees asked Akiak if his name meant kayak in Eskimo language. With a smile, Akiak replied, "No, it means 'brave.' I guess my parents thought I would have to be brave to grow up in Noorvik, where you have to be tough to survive."

Later that morning, Akiak was asked if ice fishing and seal hunting were his two favorite sports. "Not at all," said Akiak, "We had a first-rate hockey rink in town, so I got to love hockey. And, I'm a Minnesota Viking [professional football team] fan. That's why I took a job in Minnesota." (Said with a smile.)

During lunch, Mary, another new employee asked Akiak, "Tell me, Akiak, are you an Eskimo? Or are you an Inuit? I don't want to make a mistake."

Akiak responded, "It's no mistake to call me an Eskimo. It's no mistake to call me an Inuit. Some people think that the term *Eskimo* is wrong, and that we should be called *Inuit*. It doesn't matter to me or to my friends and family. We like both terms.

"Yet, Mary, the mistake you are making is not thinking of me as just another American. Alaska is one of the 50 states. We vote. We pay and receive Social Security. And, we learn English in school and we eat at McDonalds."

"I'm sorry," said Mary. "I was just trying to be friendly."

Ned, the supervisor of the orientation program, said to the group, "I think we have asked Akiak enough about his cultural heritage for now. Yet, I have just one favor to ask Akiak. I wish he would show us how he positions his arm, head, and body to spear a big fish."

Akiak said with a sarcastic tone, "Time out. I'm taking a break from this orientation right now. I have to go back to my igloo and chew on some frozen fish."

Case Questions

1. What does this case tell us about cultural sensitivity?
2. How might have Akiak's coworkers related better to him during the orientation?
3. How might have Akiak done a better job of relating to his new coworkers?
4. Does Akiak have an "attitude" (meaning negative attitude problem)?

Interpersonal Skills Role-Play 7.1

Building a Relationship with an Eskimo Electronic Technician

Several class members play the role of new workers at the company in International Falls, Minnesota, as described in Interpersonal Relations Case 7.2. One of the other new workers is Akiak Nori. You want to welcome him and help him feel part of the group. At the same time, you believe that recognizing his Eskimo heritage would be part of showing respect for his culture. Yet, you do not want to be patronizing or make Akiak feel that he is a curiosity. Another student plays the role of Akiak, who regards himself an American, yet is also proud of his Eskimo heritage.

Run the role-play for about seven minutes. Other students will provide feedback about the cross-cultural sensitivity of the workers attempting to build a relationship with Akiak. Also provide feedback about Akiak's interpersonal skills.

CHAPTER 8

Resolving Conflicts with Others

It was a perfect case of shooting the messenger, even if it seemed to Elliott Gordon like a protracted mugging. Last year, the former sales associate watched the fallout after one of his colleagues made a big sale that faltered. The salesman was assured that the goods would be shipped from a supplier, but only half of the inventory arrived.

A receiving clerk had to tell the salesman, who responded to the bad news by vowing to the clerk, "I will ruin your life," and then throwing him against the wall. He then kicked his own cubicle wall, "which in turn collapsed on his neighbor's cubicle wall and thus started a domino effect of wrecking everyone's office in the row," Gordon recalls.

The salesman then threw the clerk on top of the collapsed wall and used his phone receiver to smash his own computer screen, which popped like a blown light bulb. "I just sat, staring at my computer screen with the cubicle wall to my right tented over my head," says Gordon.[1]

This bizarre and unfortunate incident between the salesman and the receiving clerk illustrates the importance of being able to resolve conflict constructively. The sales rep became so furious about a delayed shipment that ruined his big sale that he struck out in revenge against the messenger of the bad news. Although the sales rep was probably emotionally unstable long before the incident, he still might have profited from developing conflict resolution skills.

Learning Objectives

After reading and studying this chapter and doing the exercises, you should be able to

1. Specify why so much interpersonal conflict exists in organizations.
2. Recognize your typical method of resolving conflict.
3. Identify the five styles of handling conflict.
4. Acquire effective techniques for resolving conflict and negotiating.
5. Understand how to combat sexual harassment in the workplace.

This chapter will help you improve your ability to resolve conflicts with people at work. The same techniques are also useful in personal life. To improve your understanding of how to resolve conflict, this chapter presents specific techniques and explains why so much conflict exists. To start relating the topic of conflict to yourself, take Self-Assessment Quiz 8-1.

SOURCES OF INTERPERSONAL CONFLICT IN ORGANIZATIONS

A **conflict** is a situation in which two or more goals, values, or events are incompatible or mutually exclusive. A conflict is also a strife, quarrel, or battle, such as the unstable sales rep battling with the receiving clerk over a partial shipment of the goods he needed to close a sale.

LEARNING OBJECTIVE 1

conflict
A situation in which two or more goals, values, or events are incompatible or mutually exclusive.

Conflict between and among people has many sources, or causes. In this section, I describe six of the leading sources. If you understand the cause of a conflict, it can help you resolve the conflict and help prevent a similar recurrence. For example, if you learn that much conflict on the job is caused by people being uncivil toward each other, you might remind yourself to behave civilly. You can also learn how to deal with uncivil coworkers so they treat you less rudely. Although specific sources of conflict can be identified, keep in mind an important fact. All conflict includes the underlying theme of incompatibility between your goals, values, or events and those of another person.

Competition for Limited Resources

An underlying source of job conflict is that few people can get all the resources they want. These resources include money, material, and human resources. Conflicts arise when two or more people squabble over who should get the resources. Even in a prosperous organization, resources have to be divided in such a manner that not everybody gets what he or she wants.

Assume that you believe you need to have a photocopier immediately accessible the entire workday. Yet the company has decided that three people must share one photocopier. As a result, you are likely to enter into conflict with the two others sharing the photocopier. The conflict will be intense if your two coworkers also think they need full-time access to a photocopier.

Role Conflict

role conflict

The situation that occurs when a person has to choose between two competing demands or expectations.

A major source of conflict (and stress) on the job relates to being placed in a predicament. **Role conflict** stems from having to choose between two competing demands or expectations. If you comply with one aspect of a role, compliance with the other is difficult or impossible. An important example would be receiving contradictory orders from two people above you in your company. If you comply with the wishes of one person, you will antagonize the other. A higher-ranking manager might encourage as many employees as possible to work from home a few days per week. In contrast, your own manager demands that you be on the work premises full time.

LEARNING OBJECTIVE 2

SELF-ASSESSMENT QUIZ 8-1

Styles of Conflict Management

Directions: Check the alternative that best fits your typical reaction to the situation described.

Part I: The Quiz

1. When someone is overly hostile toward me, I usually:
   - _____ A. respond in kind
   - _____ B. persuade him or her to cool down
   - _____ C. hear the person out
   - _____ D. walk away

2. When I walk in on a heated argument, I'm likely to:
   - _____ A. jump in and take sides
   - _____ B. mediate
   - _____ C. keep quiet and observe
   - _____ D. leave the scene

3. When I suspect that another person is taking advantage of me, I:
   - _____ A. try to get the person to stop
   - _____ B. rely on persuasion and facts
   - _____ C. change how I relate to the person
   - _____ D. accept the situation

4. When I don't see eye to eye with someone, I typically:
   - _____ A. try to get him or her to see things my way
   - _____ B. consider the problem logically
   - _____ C. search for a workable compromise
   - _____ D. let the problem work itself out

5. After a run-in with someone I care about a great deal, I:
   - _____ A. try to make him or her see it my way
   - _____ B. try to work out our differences
   - _____ C. wait before renewing contact
   - _____ D. let it lie

6. When I see conflict developing between two people I care about, I usually:
   - _____ A. express disappointment
   - _____ B. try to mediate
   - _____ C. watch to see what develops
   - _____ D. leave the scene

7. When I see conflict developing between two people who are relatively unimportant to me, I usually:
   - _____ A. express disappointment
   - _____ B. try to mediate
   - _____ C. watch to see what develops
   - _____ D. leave the scene

8. The feedback people give me indicates that I:

   _____ A. push hard to get what I want

   _____ B. try to work out differences

   _____ C. take a conciliatory stance

   _____ D. sidestep conflict

9. When having serious disagreements, I:

   _____ A. talk until I've made my point

   _____ B. talk a little more than I listen

   _____ C. listen and make sure I understand

   _____ D. listen passively

10. When someone does something that angers me, I generally:

   _____ A. use strong, direct language

   _____ B. try to persuade him or her to stop

   _____ C. go easy, explaining how I feel

   _____ D. say and do nothing

Part II: Score Analysis

When you've completed the questions, add all the As, Bs, Cs, and Ds to find where you collected the most responses. Then consider these profiles:

A. Competitive. If you picked mostly "A" responses, you feel best when you're able to direct and control others. Taken to extremes, you can be intimidating and judgmental. You are generally contemptuous of people who don't stand up for themselves, and you feel frustrated when you can't get through to someone.

B. Collaborative. If you scored high in this category, you may be from the "use your head to win" school of conflict management—strong-willed and ambitious, but not overbearing. You'll use persuasion, not intimidation, and are willing to compromise to end long-running conflicts.

C. Sharing. People who score high here do not get fired up. They listen to the opponent's point of view, analyze situations, and make a factual pitch for their case. But in the end, they will defer to opponents in the interest of harmony.

D. Accommodative. A high score suggests that you avoid conflict and confrontation at all costs and suppress your feelings—strong as they may be—to keep peace.

Observation: No one style of conflict management is better than another. Most people use all four, depending on the situation. But if you rely too much on one, start shifting your approach.

Source: "Quiz on Styles of Conflict Management," *National Institute of Business Management*, February 20, 1990, p. 6. Reprinted with permission.

Role conflict can take various forms. You might be asked to accomplish two objectives that are in apparent conflict. If your boss asked you to hurry up and finish your work but also to decrease your mistakes, you would experience the conflict of incompatible demands (plus, perhaps, a headache!). Another problem occurs when two or more people give you incompatible directions. Your immediate supervisor may want you to complete a crash project on time, but company policy temporarily prohibits authorizing overtime payments to clerical help or hiring office temporaries.

Role conflict also results when two different roles that you play are in conflict. Your company may expect you to travel 50 percent of the time, whereas your spouse threatens a divorce if you travel over 25 percent of the time. To complete the picture, **role-person conflict** takes place when the role(s) your organization expects you to occupy is in conflict with your basic values. Your company may ask you to fire the bottom 10 percent of performers, but this could be in conflict with your humanistic values.

role-person conflict

A situation that takes place when the role(s) your organization expects you to occupy is in conflict with your basic values.

Competing Work and Family Demands

Balancing the demands of career and family life has become a major role conflict facing today's workforce. Caring about work and family responsibilities is more likely to intensify work–family conflict. The challenge is particularly intense for employees who are part

work–family conflict

A state that occurs when an individual's roles of worker and active participant in social and family life compete with each other.

of a family with two wage earners. **Work–family conflict** occurs when an individual's roles of worker and active participant in social and family life compete with one another. This type of conflict is frequent because the multiple roles are often incompatible. Imagine having planned to attend your child's solo recital and then being ordered at the last minute to be present at an after-hours meeting. Work–family conflict can lead to interpersonal conflict because your boss or coworkers might think that you are asking them to cover for you while you attend to personal matters.

Work–family conflict can be viewed from two perspectives, with both leading to conflict and stress. A person's work can interfere with family responsibilities, or family responsibilities can interfere with work. In the example just mentioned, the person might say, "This is terrible. The meeting called for at the last minute will block me from attending my child's solo recital." Or the same person might say, "This is terrible. My child's solo recital is going to block me from attending an important last-minute meeting."

Work–family conflict can be a major stressor and can lead to emotional disorders, as revealed by a study of 2,700 employed adults. Two types of work–family conflict were studied: family life creating problems at work and work creating problems at home. Emotional problems were measured by diagnostic interviews. Both types of conflict were associated with having mood disorders, disturbing levels of anxiety, and substance abuse. Also, employees who reported work–family conflict were much more likely to have a clinically significant mental health problem.[2]

A later analysis of practically all available scientific studies on the subject found again that work demands can create some stress and low satisfaction at home, and that personal demands can create some stress and low satisfaction on the job.[3] Have you ever noticed that problems at work or school can negatively influence personal life? And also that problems in personal life can negatively influence work or school?

Another study investigated the effect of work–family conflict on the emotions of guilt and hostility among employed adults. The study also explored how work–family conflict, guilt, and hostility affected job satisfaction and marital satisfaction. It was found that work-to-family conflict and family-to-work conflict led to guilt and hostility at work and at home, respectively. A sidelight finding of interest to the study of human relations is that hostile people suffer even more conflict at home and on the job.[4]

Companies can often avoid or minimize serious work–family conflict among employees by implementing equitable time-off policies. The underlying company attitude is that all employees need a work–life balance. Encouraging such an atmosphere of goodwill among coworkers can help prevent conflicts and resentments when one employee leaves early to take care of family responsibility.[5]

Many companies offer flexible working hours to a majority of their employees. In this way, a worker might be able to meet family demands that take place during typical working hours. An example would be taking off the morning to care for an ill parent and working later that same evening to make up the time. People who are exceptionally good at organizing their time and efforts will often experience less work–family conflict, by such behaviors as staying on top of work to minimize periods of time when they are completely work-centered.[6]

The accompanying Job-Oriented Interpersonal Skills in Action provides an extreme example of a company helping workers minimize work–family conflict.

Personality Clashes

personality clash

An antagonistic relationship between two people based on differences in personal attributes, preferences, interests, values, and styles.

Many workplace disagreements arise because people simply dislike each other. A **personality clash** is thus an antagonistic relationship between two people based on differences in personal attributes, preferences, interests, values, and styles. A personality clash reflects negative chemistry between two people, while personal differences are based more specifically on a value clash. According to the research of psychologist Judith Sills, the most commonly reported office problem is the personality conflict. One of the most frequent conflicts is between the sweeping "big-picture" person and the cautious, detail-oriented person.[7] The big-picture concert manager might say, "Give me a general idea of ticket sales for the Dixie Chicks" expecting a response like "We might have a full house with luck." Instead, the detail-oriented person says, "Last time I checked, we had 37,431 tickets sold."

Reducing Work–Family Conflict at Guerra DeBerry Coody

Employers often claim they treat employees like family. But few embrace family-friendliness to the degree of Guerra DeBerry Coody, a San Antonio advertising and public relations firm.

The company provides its employees on-site, subsidized child care, and encourages parent employees to spend time with their kids throughout the workday—much as if they worked at home. Many employees eat lunch with their children in the family kitchen, put them down for afternoon naps, and join play time. Michele Autenrieth Brown, the company's director of promotions and loyalty, says she frequently eats breakfast with her 2-year-old daughter at work in the mornings and plays with her on the on-site playground. "I know a lot of traditional day-care centers don't like parents checking in," she says. But "with our group, that's not the case."

The center, which is 85 percent subsidized by the company, charges $20 a day per child. It has an average of one child-care professional for every two kids, and about 11 kids attend on a given day.

Though child care is available only until kids enter kindergarten, employees say the company endorses family involvement in many ways. For instance, kids often join their parents at the office after school. Patti Tanner, a senior account supervisor, says her 13-year-old daughter and her 14-year-old son join her occa-sionally in the office after school to hang out or do homework. "I don't even have any angst about having them here because I know it's completely and totally accepted," she says.

There are other family-oriented benefits as well. Employees facing a financial crisis are eligible for interest-free loads from the company, a perk about 10 employees have used so far. And the company offers telecommuting and flexible work schedules so employees can be at home when they need to be.

The company pays $100 of health-care coverage for all employees, though employees must pay premiums of $125 to $200 to cover dependents. And the company automatically contributes an amount equal to 3% of employees' salaries into their 401(k) plans each year.

Questions

1. In what specific ways is this advertising and public relations firms helping prevent work–family conflict?
2. How do the insurance and 401(k) retirement contributions help prevent work–family conflict?
3. What kind of conflict might the family-friendly policies create with respect to employees who do not have children?

Source: Kelly R. Spors, "What Makes a Great Workplace? Guerrra DeBerry Coody," *The Wall Street Journal*, October 1, 2007, p. R4.

People involved in a personality clash often have difficulty specifying why they dislike each other. The result, however, is that they cannot maintain an amiable work relationship. A peculiarity about personality clashes is that people who get along well may begin to clash after working together for a number of years. A contributing factor is that as both people change and as the situation changes, the two people may no longer be compatible.

Aggressive Personalities, Including Bullies

Coworkers naturally disagree about topics, issues, and ideas. Yet some people convert disagreement into an attack that puts down other people and damages their self-esteem. As a result, conflict surfaces. An **aggressive personalitiy** is a person who verbally, and sometimes physically, attacks others frequently. Verbal aggression takes the form of insults, teasing, ridicule, and profanity. The aggression may also be expressed as attacks on the victim's character, competence, background, and physical appearance.[8]

aggressive personality

A person who verbally, and sometimes physically, attacks others frequently.

An aggressive personality frequently engages in bullying others. Among the typical behaviors of bullies are interrupting others, ranting in a loud voice, and making threats. A typical attitude of a bullying boss is "My way or the highway," sending the message that the employee's suggestions are unwelcome. Bullied workers complain of a range of psychological and physical ailments such as anxiety, sleeplessness, panic attacks, and low self-esteem.

Aggressiveness can also take extreme forms, such as the shooting or knifing of a former boss or colleague by a mentally unstable worker recently dismissed from the company. Violence has become so widespread that homicide is the fourth leading cause of workplace deaths, with about 600 workers murdered each year in the United States. According to the Bureau of Labor Statistics Census of Fatal Occupations, homicides account about 10 percent of all fatal workplace injuries.[9] Most workplace deaths result from a robbery or commercial crime. Many of these killings, however, are perpetrated by a disgruntled worker or former employee harboring an unresolved conflict. As companies have continued to reduce their workforce despite being profitable, these incidents have increased in frequency.

Incivility and Rudeness

incivility

In human relations, employees' lack of regard for each other.

A milder form of aggressiveness in the workplace is being rude or uncivil toward work associates. **Incivility** (or employees' lack of regard for one another) has gained attention as a cause of workplace conflict. What constitutes being uncivil or rude depends upon a person's perceptions and values.

> *Imagine two people having a business lunch together. One of them answers his cell phone during lunch, and while still eating engages the caller in conversation. To some people this everyday incident would be interpreted as double rudeness—interrupting lunch with a cell phone call and eating while talking. Another person might perceive the cell phone incident to be standard behavior in a multitasking world. Rudeness also includes swearing at coworkers, a cubicle dweller shouting loudly on the phone while making a personal call, and performing other work at a meeting. Typical forms of "other work" are sorting through paper mail or surfing the Internet on a notebook computer.*

A study conducted by Lisa Penney found that 69 percent of 300 workers she surveyed reported experiencing condescending behavior and put-downs in the workplace. In addition, those who reported incivility on the job were more likely to engage in counterproductive behaviors including bad-mouthing their company, missing deadlines, and being rude to customers or clients. "Even though civility may not seem like a very serious thing," says Penney, "it is related to behaviors that have more serious consequences" that can affect profits.[10] An investigation using many forms of data collection with 2,400 people found that being treated in an uncivil manner leads employees to decrease work effort, time on the job, and productivity. When incivility is not curtailed, job satisfaction and loyalty to the company also diminish.[11]

To place rudeness and incivility in perspective, it may be simply part of modern life where self-expression counts for everything and manners nothing. Rudeness in the workplace is therefore just a natural extension of rudeness occurring in everyday life.[12] Yet, a person who has good manners and behaves civilly can capitalize on these behaviors in his or her career.

CONFLICT-MANAGEMENT STYLES

LEARNING OBJECTIVE 3

The information presented so far is designed to help you understand the nature of conflict. Such background information is useful for resolving conflict because it helps you understand what is happening in a conflict situation. The next two sections offer more specific information about managing and resolving conflict. Before describing specific methods of resolving conflict, it is useful to present more details about five general styles, or modes, of handling conflict. You received preliminary information on four of these five styles when you completed Self-Assessment Quiz 8-1.

As shown in Figure 8-1, Kenneth Thomas identified five major styles of conflict management. Each style is based on a combination of satisfying one's own concerns (assertiveness) and satisfying the concerns of others (cooperativeness).[13]

Competitive Style

The competitive style is a desire to win one's own concerns at the expense of the other party, or to dominate. A person with a competitive orientation is likely to engage in power struggles in which one side wins and the other loses (an approach referred to as win–lose). "My way or the highway" is a win–lose strategy. Workplace bullies prefer the competitive style of conflict management. The competitive style works best when quick, decisive action is essential, such as in an emergency.

Accommodative Style

The accommodative style favors appeasement, or satisfying the other's concerns without taking care of one's own. People with this orientation may be generous or self-sacrificing just to maintain a relationship. An irate customer might be accommodated with a full

FIGURE 8-1 Conflict-Handling Styles According to Degree of Cooperation and Assertiveness

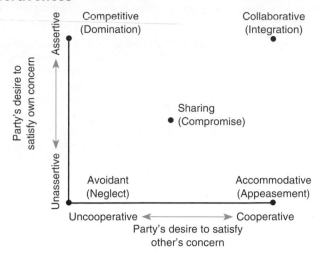

refund, just to calm down the person. The intent of such accommodation might also be to retain the customer's loyalty. Accommodation sounds harmless, but, according to Sidney Simon, when it runs unchecked at the expense of what somebody really wants it can lead to debilitating resentment, sickness, or even violence.[14] The problem is that the suppressed feelings create inner conflict and stress.

Accommodation works best when you are wrong, or when the issues are more important to the other side. For example, an automobile sales associate might say yes to a last-minute demand for another $25 concession, rather than continue to haggle.

Sharing Style

The sharing style is halfway between domination and appeasement. Sharers prefer moderate but incomplete satisfaction for both parties, which results in a compromise. The phrase *splitting the difference* reflects this orientation and is commonly used in such activities as purchasing a house or car. The sharing (or compromising) style is well suited to a situation in which both sides have equal power, yet are committed to mutually exclusive goals such as the buyer and seller of the house wanting to maximize financial gain.

Collaborative Style

In contrast to the other styles, the collaborative style reflects a desire to fully satisfy the desires of both parties. It is based on an underlying philosophy of **win–win**, the belief that after conflict has been resolved, both sides should gain something of value. The use of a win–win approach is aimed at arriving at a settlement that meets the needs of both parties, or at least does not badly damage the welfare of the other side. The option chosen results in a mutual gain. When collaborative approaches to resolving conflict are used, the relationships among the parties are built on and improved. The following example uses a win–win approach to resolve conflict.

win–win

The belief that after conflict has been resolved both sides should gain something of value.

Bruce is an office assistant in a company that supplies food to restaurants, hospitals, and nursing homes. According to his budget

Win–Win Conflict Resolution

The class organizes into small problem-solving groups. Each group spends about 10 minutes finding a win–win solution to one of the following conflict situations:

1. Two coworkers want you to go to lunch with them more regularly, but you believe that you are too busy to go out to lunch regularly.

2. William, an accountant, wants workmates to call him "William." Yet several people in the office persist in calling him "Bill" or "Will."

3. You are offered a transfer within your company to an exciting job that you want strongly. Your manager says he cannot let you go because you are too valuable.

4. A group of workers at a small business would like a giant-screen, high-definition television set placed in the employee lounge to enhance their enjoyment of breaks. The business owner wants to keep employees satisfied but concludes that investing about $4,000 in a television set for the lounge is too big an investment.

After the groups have found their solutions for mutual gains, specify carefully what gain each side attained. Share your solutions with other class members to obtain their feedback about the effectiveness of the mutual gains.

---

analysis, Bruce needed a 5 percent salary increase to meet his monthly expenses. The company owner explained that there was no money in the budget for a salary increase. A cordial discussion about the issue led to an option for mutual gain. Bruce would receive the 5 percent salary increase as long as he increased his productivity enough to cover the increase. His target was to increase his productivity to the point that the company could decrease the hours worked by an office temporary. The amount of the decrease covered the 5 percent salary increase.

Wireless phone companies in search of antenna sites have led to win–win conflict resolution between companies and communities. Many of these companies have integrated antennas into church steeples, high-rise buildings, and other tall structures without defacing them. A wireless telephone company has sometimes constructed a new church steeple that harbors a giant antenna. The company wins by having an antenna to provide cell telephone service, and community groups do not object to the sight of a freestanding antenna. At the same time, the church wins by having a new steeple.

Collaborating is particularly important when both sides must be committed to the solution, such as the situation with the hidden cell antennae. Divorcing parents also need collaboration in their division of assets because they need to work together long-term for the good of the children.

Finding win–win solutions to problems (or options for mutual gain) is one of the most important conflict-resolution skills. To obtain practice in this skill, do Skill-Building Exercise 8-1.

Avoidant Style

The avoider is a combination of a person who is uncooperative and unassertive. He or she is indifferent to the concerns of either party. The person may actually be withdrawing from the conflict to rely upon fate. Avoiding works well when an issue is trivial, or there are more pressing issues to worry about. For example, a supervisor might not bother reprimanding workers who are a few minutes late because the supervisor is flooded with other work.

In the following description of specific techniques for resolving conflict, attempt to relate most of them to these five key styles. For example, you will observe that the confrontation and problem-solving technique reflects the collaborative style.

GUIDELINES AND TECHNIQUES FOR RESOLVING CONFLICTS

LEARNING OBJECTIVE 4

Interpersonal conflict in organizations is inevitable. A career-minded person must therefore learn effective ways of resolving conflict. This section describes methods of conflict resolution that you can use on your own. All are based somewhat on the underlying model of win–win, or integrating the interests of both parties. Integrating both interests focuses on resolving the underlying concerns of the parties in conflict. By dealing with these concerns, it is more worthwhile for both sides to resolve the conflict than it is to have no agreement.

Suppose a man named Bill Budweiser wanted to open a beer brewery and name his beer Budweiser. The company lawyers from Anheuser-Busch, which own the rights to the brand name Budweiser, would attempt to block him from using the same brand name—even if his family name is Budweiser. Bill Budweiser would hire his own lawyer to fight back. Two key concerns must be addressed. Mr. Budweiser's underlying concern is that he feels his civil liberties have been violated because he cannot name a business after himself. And Bill Budweiser must deal with Anheuser-Busch's concern about a smaller company capitalizing on its well-known name (brand equity).

Later in the chapter you are be asked to resolve the beer company conflict. The following paragraphs describe four methods of conflict resolution.

Confrontation and Problem Solving

The ideal approach to resolving any conflict is to confront the real issue and then solve the problem. **Confrontation** means taking a problem-solving approach to differences and identifying the underlying facts, logic, or emotions that account for them. When conflicts are resolved through confronting and understanding their causes, people feel responsible for finding the soundest answer.[15]

Confrontation can proceed gently, in a way that preserves a good working relationship, as shown by this example. Assume that Mary, the person working at the desk next to you, loudly cracks chewing gum while she works. You find the gum chewing both distracting and nauseating. If you don't bring the problem to Mary's attention, it will probably grow in proportion with time. Yet you are hesitant to enter into an argument about something that a person might regard as a civil liberty (the right to chew gum in public places).

A psychologically sound alternative is for you to approach her directly in this manner:

You: Mary, there is something bothering me that I would like to discuss with you.

She: Go ahead, I don't mind listening to other people's problems.

You: My problem concerns something you are doing that makes it difficult for me to concentrate on my work. When you chew gum, you make loud cracking noises that grate on my nerves. It may be my problem, but the noise does bother me.

She: I guess I could stop chewing gum when you're working next to me. It's probably just a nervous habit.

When resolving conflict through confrontation and problem solving, as well as other methods of conflict resolution, it is helpful to bring closure by shaking hands, repeating your individual commitments, and then saying, "Thank you." Following through on your commitments is also essential for effective conflict resolution.[16]

Constructive Handling of Criticism

Learning to profit from criticism is an effective way of benefiting from conflict. People who benefit from criticism are able to stand outside themselves while being criticized. It is as if they are watching the criticism from a distance and looking for its possible merits. People who take criticism personally anguish when receiving negative feedback. The following are several specific suggestions for dealing with criticism, including two methods that will often get the other party on your side.[17]

1. **See yourself at a distance.** Place an imaginary Plexiglas shield between you and the person giving the criticism. Attempt to be a detached observer looking for useful information.

2. **Ask for clarification and specifics.** Ask politely for more details about the negative behavior in question so you can change if change is warranted. If your boss is criticizing you for being rude to customers, you might respond, "I certainly

confrontation

Taking a problem-solving approach to differences and identifying the under lying facts, logic, or emotions that account for them.

don't want to be rude. Can you give me a couple of examples of how I was rude? I need your help in working on this problem." After asking questions, you can better determine whether the criticism is valid.

3. **Decide on a response.** An important part of learning from criticism is to respond appropriately to the critic. Let the criticizer know what you agree with. Apologize for the undesirable behavior, such as saying, "I apologize for being rude to customers. I know what I can do differently now. I'll be more patient so as not to appear rude." Apology is a highly effective method of getting the criticizer on your side. Without an apology, the attack is likely to continue.

4. **Look for a pattern in terms of other criticism.** Is the criticism you are receiving something you have heard several times before from different people? The more times you have heard the same criticism, the more likely it is to be valid. If three different supervisors have told you that you do not follow through with your promises to get work done, the criticism is most likely valid.

5. **Disarm the opposition.** As an extension of the point just made, you will often decide to agree with the criticizer because the person has a legitimate complaint about you. If you deny the reality of that person's complaint, he or she will continue to harp on that point and the issue will remain unresolved. By agreeing with the criticism of you, you may set the stage for a true resolution of the problem.

Agreeing with criticism made by a person with formal authority over you is effective because by doing so you are then in a position to ask for his or her help in improving the situation. Rational managers realize that it is their responsibility to help group members overcome problems, not merely to criticize them. Imagine that you have been chronically late with reports during the last six months. It is time for a performance evaluation, and you know that you will be reprimanded for your tardiness. You also hope that your manager will not downgrade all other aspects of your performance because of your tardy reports. Here is how disarming the opposition would work in this situation:

Your manager: Have a seat. It's time for your performance evaluation, and we have a lot to talk about. I'm concerned about some things.

You: So am I. It appears that I'm having a difficult time getting my reports in on time. I wonder if I'm being a perfectionist. Do you have any suggestions?

Your manager: Well, I like your attitude. Maybe you're trying to make your reports too perfect before you turn them in. I think you can improve in getting your reports in on time. Try not to figure out everything to three decimal places. We need thoroughness around here, but we can't overdo it.

Disarming is effective because it takes the wind out of the other person's sails and has a calming effect. The other person is often waiting to clobber you if you deny guilt. If you admit guilt, you are more difficult to clobber. Skill-Building Exercise 8-2 gives you an opportunity to practice disarming the opposition.

SKILL-BUILDING EXERCISE 8-2

Disarming the Opposition

In each of these two scenarios, one person plays the role of the person with more power in the situation. The other person plays the role of the individual attempting to disarm the criticizer.

1. A representative from a credit agency telephones you at work to inform you that you are 60 days behind schedule on your car payment. The agent wants a settlement as soon as possible. Unfortunately, the credit agent is correct. Run this happy scenario for about five minutes.

2. Your manager calls you into his office to discuss the 10-page report you just submitted. The boss says in a harsh tone,

"Your report is a piece of trash. I counted 25 word-use mistakes such as writing *whether* for *weather* and *seen* for *scene*. (Your spell checker couldn't catch these errors.) Besides that, I can't follow many of your sentences, and you left out the table of statistics. I'm wondering if you're qualified for this job."

Observers of the role-play will judge how effective the person being criticized is in reducing some of the anger directed against him or her. Look also for any changes in attitude on the part of the criticizer.

Reframing

Another useful approach to resolving conflict is to reexamine or *reframe* the conflict situation by looking at in a different light. What follows are two practical approaches to reframing, one by searching for the positives in the situation, and the other by asking questions.

Reframing through Cognitive Restructuring An indirect way of resolving interpersonal conflict is to lessen the conflicting elements in a situation by viewing them more positively. According to the technique of **cognitive restructuring**, you mentally convert negative aspects into positive ones by looking for the positive elements in a situation. How you frame or choose your thoughts can determine the outcome of a conflict situation. Your thoughts influence your actions. If you search for the beneficial elements in the situation, there will be less area for dispute. Although this technique might sound like a mind game to you, it can work effectively.

Imagine that a coworker of yours, Jeff, has been asking you repeated questions about how to carry out a work procedure. You are about ready to tell Jeff, "Go bother somebody else; I'm not paid to be a trainer." Instead, you look for the positive elements in the situation. You say to yourself, "Jeff has been asking me a lot of questions. This does take time, but answering these questions is valuable experience. If I want to become a manager, I'll have to help group members with problems."

After having completed this cognitive restructuring, you can then deal with the conflict situation more positively. You might say to Jeff, "I welcome the opportunity to help you, but we need to find a mutually convenient time. In that way, I can better concentrate on my own work." To get started with cognitive restructuring, do Skill-Building Exercise 8-3.

Reframing by Asking Questions Another way to use reframing is to ask step back, take a deep breath, and then ask the following questions about the conflict situation that arises within the work group:

- Do I fully understand the situation?
- Am I sure what my coworker is really saying?
- Is the person really angry at me or just worried and anxious?
- Have I missed something important?
- Do I have all the facts?
- What is the real issue here?
- How do I want to react in this situation?
- How would I want to be treated if the situation were reversed?

By taking such an approach, you are more likely to communicate effectively and constructively with each your coworkers when conflict situations arise. You carefully talk through the issues rather than becoming explosive, defensive, and argumentative. A useful scenario for reframing through questioning would be when a coworker accuses you of not carrying your fair share of the workload.[18]

SKILL-BUILDING EXERCISE 8-3

Reframing Through Cognitive Restructuring

The following are examples of negative statements about others in the workplace. In the space provided, cognitively restructure (reframe) each comment in a positive way.

Negative: Nancy is getting on my nerves. It takes her two weeks longer than anyone else on the team to complete her input.

Positive:

Negative: Rob is so obsessed with sports he is hurting my productivity. Where does it say in the employee handbook that I have to spend 30 minutes on Monday listening to Rob's comments on his team's weekend performance? Doesn't he know that I have a job to do and that I just don't care about his team?

Positive:

Negative: My boss is driving me crazy. He's forever telling me what I did wrong and making suggestions for improvement. He makes me feel like I'm in elementary school.

Positive:

Negotiating and Bargaining

negotiating

Conferring with another person to resolve a problem.

Conflicts can be considered situations calling for **negotiating**, or conferring with another person to resolve a problem. When you are negotiating a fair salary for yourself, you are trying to resolve a conflict. At first the demands of the two parties may seem incompatible, but through negotiation, a salary figure may emerge that satisfies both.

A new perspective on negotiation is that people are not just negotiating for the economic value of the negotiation. They are also negotiating for intangibles, such as feeling good about the negotiation process, the other party, and themselves.[19] For example, after the negotiation is complete, the individual might want to be perceived as an honest, sincere, professional, and not a dishonest person out to maximize gain.

Managers and staff specialists must negotiate both internally (e.g., with subordinates, managers, and team leaders) and externally (e.g., with customers, suppliers, and government agencies). Considerable negotiation also takes place among coworkers. Team members, for example, sometimes negotiate among themselves about work assignments. One might say to the other, "I'm willing to be note taker this year if there's some way I can cut back on the amount of plant visits I make this year." Six useful negotiating tactics are presented here. Before studying them, do Self-Assessment Quiz 8-2.

Understand the Other Party's Perspective

As in being a good listener, empathy can be an important part of negotiation. Deepak Malhotra and Max H. Bazeman observe that negotiators often channel too much effort into pushing their own position and too little into understanding the other side's perspective.[20] To obtain a good deal, or sometimes any deal at all, negotiators have to dig for information about *why* the other side wants what it demands. Inaccurate assumptions about the other side's motives can lead negotiators to propose solutions to the wrong problems, waste money, or kill a deal. How about a personal life example for dog lovers?

> You have wanted a Great Dane puppy for a long time. You enter into negotiations with the owner of the puppy and his mother. The owner is asking $800, and is adamant about her demands. If you are low on empathy you will raise such negotiating points as how much the little Great Dane is costing the owner in food; that you will pay cash; and that the little fellow is ugly and therefore is only worth $400. (You might get invited off the premises in a hurry.) In contrast, with high empathy and a detective-like mind, you recognize that the owner wants the puppy to go to a wonderful home. So, if she asks for a lot of money, the potential owner is likely to be really interested in finding someone who truly wants the dog, and would therefore probably take good care of the puppy.
>
> With this negotiating point in mind, you point out what great care you will give the Great Dane, what a spacious yard you have, how you would take him jogging every day, and how he would be your dream dog. The owner is happy because one of her key motives is for the pup to have a wonderful home. She is touched and agrees to your offer of $500.

Another key part of understanding the other party's perspective is that you look for common ground. Your talk of care and concern about the dog's health indicates that both you and the owner share a humanitarian attitude toward dogs.

To understand the other party's perspective, you often have to prepare in advance. Obtain as much information as you can about the other party's side before the negotiation session. A basic example is that many prospective car buyers first research the fair value of a vehicle before making an offer. Knowing how long the vehicle has been sitting on the lot or in the showroom is also useful advance information because dealers often borrow money to build inventory.

Focus on Interests, Not Positions   Rather than clinging to specific negotiating points, keep your overall interests in mind and try to satisfy them. Remember that the true object of negotiation is to satisfy the underlying interests on both sides, as in the case of Bill Budweiser. Part of focusing on interests is to carefully study the other side's comments for clues to the type of agreement that will satisfy both of you.

The Negotiator Quiz

Directions: The following quiz is designed to give you tentative insight into your tendencies toward being an effective negotiator. Check whether each statement is *mostly true* or *mostly false* as it applies to you.

		Mostly True	Mostly False
1.	Settling differences of opinion is a lot of fun.	_____	_____
2.	I try to avoid conflict and confrontation with others as much as possible.	_____	_____
3.	I am self-conscious asking people for favors they have not offered me spontaneously.	_____	_____
4.	I am generally unwilling to compromise.	_____	_____
5.	How the other side feels about the results of our negotiation is of little consequence to me.	_____	_____
6.	I think very well under pressure.	_____	_____
7.	People say that I am tactful and diplomatic.	_____	_____
8.	I have heard that I express my viewpoint clearly.	_____	_____
9.	Very few things in life are not negotiable.	_____	_____
10.	I always (or would always) accept whatever salary increase is offered me.	_____	_____
11.	A person's facial expression often reveals as much as what the person actually says.	_____	_____
12.	I wouldn't mind taking a few short-term losses to win a long-term battle.	_____	_____
13.	I'm willing to work long and hard to win a small advantage.	_____	_____
14.	I'm usually too busy talking to do much listening.	_____	_____
15.	It's fun to haggle over price when buying a car.	_____	_____
16.	I almost always prepare in advance for a negotiating session.	_____	_____
17.	When there is something I need from another person, I usually get it.	_____	_____
18.	It would make me feel cheap if I offered somebody only two-thirds of his or her asking price.	_____	_____
19.	People are usually paid what they are worth, so there's no use haggling over starting salaries.	_____	_____
20.	I rarely take what people say at face value.	_____	_____
21.	It's easy for me to smile when involved in a serious discussion.	_____	_____
22.	For one side to win in negotiation, the other side has to lose.	_____	_____
23.	Once you start making concessions, the other side is bound to get more than you.	_____	_____
24.	A good negotiating session gets my competitive urges flowing.	_____	_____
25.	When negotiations are completed, both sides should walk way with something valuable.	_____	_____
	Total Score	_____	_____

Scoring and Interpretation: Score yourself 1 for each of your answers that agrees with the scoring key. The higher your score, the more likely it is that you currently have good negotiating skills, providing your self-assessment is accurate. It might prove useful to also have somebody who has observed you negotiate on several occasions to answer the Negotiator Quiz for you. Scores of 7 or lower and 20 or higher are probably the most indicative of weak or strong negotiating potential. Here is the scoring key:

1. Mostly True	8. Mostly False	15. Mostly False	22. Mostly True
2. Mostly False	9. Mostly False	16. Mostly False	23. Mostly False
3. Mostly False	10. Mostly False	17. Mostly False	24. Mostly False
4. Mostly True	11. Mostly True	18. Mostly False	25. Mostly True
5. Mostly True	12. Mostly False	19. Mostly False	
6. Mostly True	13. Mostly False	20. Mostly False	
7. Mostly False	14. Mostly True	21. Mostly True	

Careful listening will help you uncover the negotiating partner's specific interests and motivations. (This is another application of understanding the other party's perspective.) Here is how this strategy works:

You are considering accepting a job offer that will enable you to work on the type of problems you prefer and also develop your professional skills. You have a starting salary in mind that would make you very happy—10 percent higher than you are currently making. Your negotiating position is thus your present salary plus 10 percent. However, your true interests are probably to have more discretionary income than at present. (You want to make more purchases and invest more.) You will therefore be better off negotiating for a work situation that spreads your money further. You can now accept the offer by negotiating other points in addition to a 10 percent higher salary, including (1) working in a geographic area with a lower cost of living, (2) having a better opportunity for earning a bonus, or (3) receiving a generous expense account. During the negotiations you may discover that the other party is looking for a talented employee at a salary and benefits the company can afford.

compromise

Settlement of differences by mutual concessions.

Compromise   The most widely used negotiating tactic is **compromise**, settlement of differences by mutual concessions. One party agrees to do something if the other party agrees to do something else. Compromise is a realistic approach to resolving conflict. Most labor–management disputes are settled by compromise. For instance, labor may agree to accept a smaller salary increase if management will subcontract less work to other countries.

Some people argue that compromise is not a win–win tactic. The problem is that the two parties may wind up with a solution that pacifies both but does not solve the problem. One example would be purchasing for two team leaders half the new equipment each one needs. As a result, neither department really shows a productivity gain. Nevertheless, compromise is both inevitable and useful.

Begin with a Plausible Demand or Offer, Yet Allow Room for Negotiation   The commonsense approach to negotiation suggests that you begin with an extreme, almost fanciful demand or offer. The final compromise will therefore be closer to your true demand or offer than if you opened the negotiations more realistically. However, a plausible demand is useful because it shows you are bargaining in good faith. Also, if a third party has to resolve a conflict, a plausible demand or offer will receive more sympathy than an implausible one will. An example would be an arbitrator giving only a minimum settlement to an investor who wanted $10 million in damages for having received bad advice from an investment broker. (The arbitrator thinks that a $10 million settlement would be ridiculous.)

Although it is advisable to begin with a plausible demand, one must still allow room for negotiation. A basic strategy of negotiation is to begin with a demand that allows room for compromise and concession. If you think you need $5,000 in new software for your department, you might begin negotiations by asking for a $7,000 package. Your boss offers you $4,000 as a starting point. After negotiation, you may wind up with the $5,000 you need.

Make Small Concessions Gradually   Making steady concessions leads to more mutually satisfactory agreements in most situations. Gradually, you concede little things to the other side. The hard-line approach to bargaining is to make your concession early in the negotiation and then grant no further concession. The tactic of making small concessions is well suited to purchasing a new car. To reach a price you consider acceptable, you might grant concessions such as agreeing to finance the car through the dealer or purchasing a service contract.

Know Your Best Alternative to a Negotiated Agreement (BATNA)   The reason you would probably negotiate would be to produce something better than the result obtainable without negotiating. The goal of negotiating is thus not just to agree, but to obtain more valuable results than would otherwise have occurred. Being aware of your BATNA sets a floor to the agreement you are willing to accept. Your BATNA becomes the standard that can protect both parties from accepting terms that are too unfavorable. It also keeps you from walking away from terms that would be beneficial for you to accept.

What might a BATNA look like in practice? Suppose you are negotiating a starting salary for a full-time, professional position. The figure you have in mind is $40,000 per year. Your BATNA is $34,500 because this is the salary your future in-laws will pay you to enter the family business. You will therefore walk away from any offer of less than $35,000—just taking salary into account.

Knowing the other side's BATNA is also important because it helps define the other participant's bargaining zone. Understanding each other's bargaining zones makes it possible to arrive at mutually profitable trade-offs. In the preceding salary negotiations, the company's BATNA might be to hire a less well-educated job candidate at $29,500 and then upgrade his or her knowledge on the job.

Use Anger to Your Advantage Master negotiators make selective use of anger as a negotiating and bargaining tool. When a person becomes genuinely angry, the anger can energize him or her to be more resourceful and creative while bargaining. If you are angry about an issue or a negotiating point, the other side may be willing to submit to your demand rather than receive more of your anger. The director of a company wellness program might say with an angry look toward top management, "Why is there money in the budget for all kinds of frills like corporate jets, when a program that is preventing millions of dollars in lost productivity has to grovel for a decent budget?"

The downside of anger is that it can degenerate into incivility and personal insults. A touch of anger can be effective, but overdone it becomes self-defeating. You have to size up how far you can push people before damaging a work relationship—or being fired. To make effective use of anger during negotiation, it has to be used at the right time, with the right tone, and in the right amount.[21] A person who is always angry will often not be taken seriously.

> " In ordinary life, we classify anger as an emotion—a catalytic and cathartic one that provokes comment, discussion and often backlash. At the bargaining table, however, anger is better viewed as nothing more than a tactic. "
>
> —Marc Diener, a speaker and attorney in Los Angeles

BACK TO THE OPENING CASE

A major part of the sales representative's problem is that he could not manage his anger effectively, most likely in part because he scores high on neuroticism (refer back to Chapter 2). A constructive use of his anger would have been for the sales representative to have been stimulated to figure out how to salvage the current sale, or prevent a partial shipment from ruining a sale in the future. The rep's explosive approach cost him his job, and ruined his reputation as a professional sales representative. You can imagine what a negative employment reference he received from the company.

Effective negotiation, as with any other form of conflict resolution, requires extensive practice and knowledge of basic principles and techniques. As a starting point, you might take one of the negotiating tactics just described and practice it where the stakes are not so high. You might attempt to negotiate the price of a consumer electronics device, or negotiate for getting a particular Friday afternoon off from work.

A major theme running through the various approaches to conflict resolution, including negotiating and bargaining, is that cooperating with the other side is usually preferable to competing. A study with 61 self-managing teams with 489 employees supports this idea of the superiority of cooperation over competition in successful conflict resolution. The style of conflict resolution was measured through questionnaires. For example, a question geared toward cooperative behavior was, "We seek a solution that will be good for the whole team." Conflict efficacy was measured by a questionnaire indicating that the extent to which team members believed that they could successfully measure different conflict situations. Group effectiveness was measured by the ratings of supervisor and team leaders on productivity, quality, and cost savings—central reasons why self-directed teams are formed.

Negotiating a Starting Salary

A scenario for negotiation for many people is asking for a starting salary. In large organizations with many written rules and regulations, there is less opportunity for negotiating compensation (except for high-level executive positions) than in smaller firms. In the negotiating scenarios listed below, assume that you are applying for work with a small-size or medium-size firm. Assume also that you (a) have about three years of experience in the position in question, (b) have a good reputation including high job performance and a clean record, and (c) strongly want the position. Five positions are listed below with along with a plausible starting salary that you are seeking. The sixth position allows for your unique situation.

1. Accountant, $48,500
2. Computer support specialist, $39,500
3. Telemarketer, $18,000
4. Fitness trainer, $29,500
5. Personal financial advisor, $56,500
6. Your field, your salary demands

The other person involved in the role play is the hiring manager who has a general idea of what he or she would like to pay as a starting salary. The hiring manager is impressed with you, yet still wants to economize on the starting salary. Do not simply start debating a starting salary. Both sides should use at least two of the negotiation tactics described in this chapter.

Several different duos might try this negotiating activity in front of the class for approximately eight minutes. Observers should attempt to identify (a) how well the negotiation went, and (b) which specific negotiating tactics were used.

The study found that the cooperative approach to conflict was positively related to conflict efficacy. In contrast, the competitive approach to conflict was negatively related to conflict efficacy. Equally important, conflict efficacy was strongly associated with supervisory and team leader ratings of team effectiveness.[22]

Skill-Building Exercise 8-4 provides you the opportunity to practice negotiating in a scenario that most people encounter at least once in their career.

LEARNING OBJECTIVE 5

COMBATING SEXUAL HARASSMENT: A SPECIAL TYPE OF CONFLICT

sexual harassment

Unwanted sexually oriented behavior in the workplace that results in discomfort or interference with the job.

Many employees face conflict because a supervisor, coworker, or customer sexually harasses them. **Sexual harassment** is generally defined as unwanted sexually oriented behavior in the workplace that results in discomfort or interference with the job. It can include an action as violent as rape or as subtle as a sexually oriented comment about a person's body or appearance. Harassment creates conflict because the harassed person has to make a choice between two incompatible motives. One motive is to get ahead, keep the job, or have an unthreatening work environment. But to satisfy this motive, the person is forced to sacrifice the motive of holding on to his or her moral value or preferences. Here we focus on the types and frequency of sexual harassment, the effects of harassment, and guidelines for dealing with the problem.

Types and Frequency of Harassment

The courts recognize two types of sexual harassment. In *quid pro quo* sexual harassment, the individual suffers job loss, or threatened loss of a job benefit, because of his or her responses to a request for sexual favors. The demands of a harasser can be explicit or implied. An example of quid pro quo harassment would be a manager promising an employee a promotion in exchange for sexual favors and then not promoting the employee because the employee refused.

The other form of sexual harassment is *hostile environment*. It occurs when someone in the workplace creates an intimidating, hostile, or offensive working environment. An employee who is subjected to sexually suggestive comments, lewd jokes, or advances is a victim of hostile environment harassment. No tangible loss has to be suffered in this form of sexual harassment.

An analysis of many studies indicated that women perceive a broader range of social–sexual behaviors as harassing. The analysis also found that the female–male difference was larger for behaviors associated with hostile work environment harassment, derogatory attitudes toward women, dating pressure, or physical sexual contact. Men and women, however, agree closely that various types of sexual coercion, such as encounters that are made a condition of promotion, can be classified as quid pro quo harassment.[23]

Sexual harassment is also regarded as an expression of power by one individual over another because the harasser has more formal power than the harassed. The harasser, following this logic, is a power abuser as well as a legal offender. Sexual harassment is widespread in the U.S. workplace as well as in the workplaces of other countries. According to one large-scale study, when conclusions are based on more scientific studies, 58 percent of women report having experienced potential harassment behaviors, and 24 percent report having experienced sexual harassment on the job.[24] Recent data suggest that sexual harassment directed at professional women by clients and customers is more frequent than harassment within the company. Sexist hostility, such putting a person down because of his or her sex, was the most frequently noted type of harassment.[25] Women in nontraditional jobs (such as welder or pressroom supervisor) are especially likely to be harassed. Similarly, a study found that women in male-dominated manufacturing plants are harassed more than women in female-dominated community service centers.[26] A possible reason is that in a male-dominated organization men may feel they have more power over women. An earlier study in the same organizations just mentioned indicated that minority women are the most likely to be harassed, perhaps because of sex and race discrimination.[27]

The Adverse Effects of Sexual Harassment

Aside from being unethical, immoral, and illegal, sexual harassment is widely thought to have adverse consequences. The harassed person may experience job stress, lowered morale, severe conflict, and lowered productivity. Table 8-1 summarizes the results of a synthesis of many studies about the adverse effects of sexual harassment. The studies indicate that harassment negatively effects job performance, loyalty to the firm, and personal well-being. Note also that some women suffered post-traumatic stress disorder, almost as if they had been involved in a serious accident.[28]

TABLE 8.1 Consequences of Sexual Harassment

Job-Related Outcomes	Number of Responses to the Question about the Problem	Direction of Change
Coworker satisfaction	34,221	Decreased
Supervisor satisfaction	34,450	Decreased
Work satisfaction	33, 486	Decreased
Global job satisfaction	14,455	Decreased
Organizational commitment	31,194	Decreased
Job withdrawal	6,201	Increased
Work withdrawal	4,940	Increased
Workgroup productivity	27,425	Decreased
Health and Well-Being Outcomes	*Number of Responses to the Question about the Problem*	*Direction of Change*
Mental health	45,880	Decreased
Physical health	32,121	Decreased
PTSD (post-traumatic stress disorder)	4,076	Increased number of cases
Life satisfaction	4,545	Decreased

Source: Portion of a table adapted from Chelsea R. Willness, Piers Steel, and Kibeom Lee, "A Meta-Analysis of the Antecedents and Consequences of Workplace Sexual Harassment," *Personnel Psychology,* Spring 2007, p. 141.

Guidelines for Preventing and Dealing with Sexual Harassment

A starting point in dealing with sexual harassment is to develop an awareness of the types of behaviors considered sexual harassment. Often the difference is subtle. Suppose, for example, you placed copies of two nudes painted by Renoir, the French painter, on a coworker's desk. Your coworker might call that harassment. Yet if you took that coworker to a museum to see the originals of the same nude prints, your behavior usually would not be classified as harassment. What follows is a sampling of behaviors that will often be interpreted as environmental harassment.[29] Awareness of these behaviors is important because many harassers have no desire to offend, or knowledge that they are offending others. Such individuals are insensitive, and often ill-informed.[30] If people refrain from doing these acts, many instances of sexual harassment will be avoided.

1. **Inappropriate remarks and sexual implications.** Coworkers, subordinates, customers, and suppliers should not be referred to as sexual beings, and their appearance should not be referred to in a sexual manner. Telling a coworker she has gorgeous feet, or he has fabulous biceps, is out of place at work.

2. **Terms of endearment.** Refrain from calling others in the workplace by names such as "cutie," "sweetie pie," "honey," "dear," or "hunk." One might argue that these terms are simply sexist (different roles for men and women) and not sexual harassment. However, this argument is losing ground because any behavior that puts people down based on their gender can be interpreted as harassment from a legal perspective. Keep in mind also that some people find terms of endearment to have a sexual connotation. If you felt no physical attraction toward another adult, would you call that person "cutie" or "hunk"?

3. **Suggestive compliments.** It is acceptable to tell another person he or she looks nice, but avoid sexually tinged comments such as mentioning that the person's clothing shows off his or her body to advantage.

4. **Physical touching.** To avoid any appearance of sexual harassment, it is best to restrict physical touching to handshakes and an occasional sideways hug. Hugging a long-term work associate is much more acceptable than hugging a new hire. Minimize such behaviors as adjusting a coworker's earring, touching hair, and tweaking a person's chin.

5. **Work-related kissing.** It is best to avoid all kissing in a work context—except, perhaps, a light kiss at an office party. It is much more professional to greet a work associate with a warm, sincere handshake. Cultural differences must be taken into account here, as many Europeans and Africans greeting work associates with a peck on both sides of the face.

Company management also plays a major role in preventing and dealing with sexual harassment. Based on the observations of dozens of human resource specialists and employment law attorneys, several actions by management are critical.[31] The cornerstone of control of sexual harassment is creating and widely disseminating a policy about harassment. The policy should carefully define harassment and state that the company has zero tolerance for such behavior. Company officials designated for hearing complaints should be specified. In addition, the company should have an *open-door policy* about harassment. Such a policy means that any employee with a concern about being harassed is able to go directly to a senior manager without worrying about his or her supervisor taking revenge.

Brief company training programs covering the type of information presented in this chapter are also part of a serious program to prevent and deal with sexual harassment. However, a one-time presentation of a 15-minute videotape about sexual harassment is not sufficient. Periodic discussion about the topic is recommended.

After sexual harassment has taken place, the victim will usually want to resolve the conflict. Two key strategies are either to use a formal complaint procedure or to resolve the conflict on one's own. If the victim chooses the latter course, he or she will save the time of going through a lengthy investigation procedure. Figure 8-2 presents details about the two key strategies for dealing with sexual harassment. Skill-Building Exercise 8-5 offers you an opportunity to simulate the control of sexual harassment.

FIGURE 8-2 How to Deal with Sexual Harassment

The potential or actual victim of sexual harassment is advised to use the following methods and tactics to deal with the problem.

Formal Complaint Procedure. Whenever an employee believes that he or she has encountered sexual harassment, or if an employee is suspected to be the perpetrator of sexual harassment, the complainant should report the incident to his or her immediate supervisor (if that person is not the harasser) or to the next higher level of management if the supervisor is the harasser. The supervisor contacted is responsible for contacting a designated company official immediately regarding each complaint. The officer will explain the investigative procedures to the complainant and any supervisor involved. All matters will be kept strictly confidential, including private conversations with all parties.

Dealing with the Problem on Your Own. The easiest way to deal with sexual harassment is to speak up before it becomes serious. The first time it happens, respond with a statement such as: "I won't tolerate this kind of talk," "I dislike sexually oriented jokes," or "Keep your hands off me."

SKILL-BUILDING EXERCISE 8-5

Combating Sexual Harassment

The two role-plays in this exercise provide practice in applying the recommended techniques for combating sexual harassment. The activities have an implied sexual content, and they are for educational purposes only. Any students offended by these role-plays should exclude themselves from participating.

Scenario 1: The Offensive Jester. One student plays the role of Max, a man who delights in telling sexually oriented jokes and anecdotes in the office. He often brings a tabloid newspaper to the office to read sexually oriented passages to coworkers, both male and female. Another student assumes the role of Maxine, a woman in the office who takes offense to Max's humor. She wants to convince Max that he is committing sexual harassment with his sexually oriented humor. Max does not see himself as committing sexual harassment.

Scenario 2: The Flirtatious Office Manager. One student assumes the role of Bertha, an office manager who is single. Another student plays the role of Bert, a married man who recently joined the company as an office assistant. Bert reports to Bertha, and she finds him physically attractive. Bertha visits Bert at his desk and makes such comments as "It looks like you have great quadriceps. I wonder what you look like in running

shorts." Bert wants to be on good terms with Bertha, but he feels uncomfortable with her advances. He also wants to behave professionally in the office.

Run both role-plays in front of the class for about eight minutes. Other students in the class will observe the role-plays and then provide feedback about how well Maxine and Bert were able to prevent or stop sexual harassment.

A major recommendation for documenting acts of sexual harassment is to keep a running diary of incidents against you. A log of the incidents is impressive to company officials, lawyers, and judges (should a lawsuit ultimately be involved). Examples of log entries—one from a woman, and one a man—follow:

- January 17, 2009: Jim Quattrone, the manager of accounts payable, asked me to have dinner with him for the sixth time, and I turned him down again. I said no, no, no.

- March 13, 2009: Meg Evans, my supervisor, said that I would receive a much better performance evaluation if I could come over to her house for dinner. She said her husband would be out of town, so I could stay overnight if I wanted to. I felt so uncomfortable and pressured. I made up an excuse about having an exclusive relationship.

SELF-ASSESSMENT QUIZZES IN OVERVIEW

Self-Assessment Quiz 8-1, Styles of Conflict Management, provides some tentative insights into your style of managing conflict. A possible clue to personal development stemming from this quiz is whether you are able to use different style of conflict resolution to adapt to a situation. Sue might be the assistant manager at a fashion boutique. A customer might be raising a big fuss about wanting to return shoes that she says are uncomfortable. Although the customer has passed the limit for returns, Sue accommodates the customer by giving her a complete merchandise exchange just to "shut her up." At other times, Sue might be more collaborative in resolving conflict.

Self-Assessment Quiz 8-2 measures your negotiating skills as reflected in your attitudes toward negotiating. These attitudes must be backed up with good communication skills to translate into effective negotiating. The two quizzes are related because negotiation is a major part of resolving conflict, such as attaining a compromise or collaborating with the other side.

Concept Review and Reinforcement

Key Terms

conflict 153
role conflict 154
role–person conflict 155
work–family conflict 156
personality clash 156

aggressive personality 157
incivility 158
win–win 159
confrontation 161
cognitive restructuring 163

negotiating 164
compromise 166
sexual harassment 168

Summary of Key Concepts

A conflict is a situation in which two or more goals, values, or events are incompatible or mutually exclusive. Interpersonal conflicts have many sources or causes. An underlying source of job conflict is that people compete for limited resources. Another leading cause of incompatibility is role conflict, having to choose between two competing demands or expectations. Competing work and family demands represent a major role conflict. Other key sources of conflict are personality clashes, aggressive personalities including bullies, and incivility and rudeness.

Five major styles of conflict management have been identified: competitive, accommodative, sharing, collaborative (win–win), and avoidant. Each style is based on a combination of satisfying one's own concerns (assertiveness) and satisfying the concerns of others (cooperativeness).

Confrontation and problem solving is the ideal method for resolving conflict. Learning to benefit from criticism is an effective way of benefiting from conflict. People who benefit from criticism are able to stand outside themselves while being criticized. Another way to deal with criticism is to disarm the opposition by agreeing with his or her criticism. Reframing a situation can be helpful in resolving conflict. Reframing through cognitive restructuring lessens conflict by the person looking for the positive elements in a situation. Asking questions, such as, "How would I want to be treated if the situation were reversed" is another type or reframing.

Negotiating and bargaining is a major approach to resolving conflict. People negotiate for economic value and for intangibles such as feeling good. Negotiation tactics include understanding the other party's perspective, focusing on interests rather than positions, compromising, beginning with a plausible demand or offer yet allowing room for negotiation, and making small concessions gradually. It is also important to know your BATNA (best alternative to a negotiated agreement). Using anger to your advantage can sometimes work.

Sexual harassment is a form of interpersonal conflict with legal implications. The two forms of sexual harassment are (1) demanding sex in exchange for favors and (2) creating a hostile environment. Sexual harassment is widespread in the workplace. Research has pinpointed adverse mental and physical consequences of sexual harassment.

A starting point in dealing with sexual harassment is to develop an awareness of the types of behaviors it encompasses. Company policies and complaint procedures about harassment are a major part of dealing with the problem. To deal directly with harassment, the harassed person can file a formal complaint or confront the harasser when the behavior first begins. Keeping a diary of harassing events is strongly recommended.

Check Your Understanding

1. Several large companies dismiss each year the 5 percent of their workforce receiving the lowest performance evaluations. What kind of conflicts do you think this practice leads to?

2. Why is being able to resolve conflict well such an important skill for career success?

3. What are the disadvantages of having an accommodative style of handling conflict?

4. Remember the hypothetical conflict between Bill Budweiser and Anheuser-Busch? What solution do you propose to satisfy the underlying interests of both parties?

5. Several school systems in recent years have requested that teachers correct student work with a purple marker rather than a red one because the color red is associated with harsh criticism. What is your opinion of the merits of a shift from red markers to purple?

6. Have you ever attempted to disarm the opposition? How effective was the tactic?

7. How might a student use cognitive restructuring to get over the anger of having received a low grade in a course?

8. Visualize yourself buying a vehicle of your choice. Which negotiating technique (or techniques) would you be most likely to use?

9. Studies have shown that women working in male-dominated positions, such as a female construction supervisor or bulldozer operator, are more likely to experience sexual harassment than women in other fields. What explanation can you offer for this finding?

10. Imagine yourself as a human resources professional who wants to alert top-level management to the importance of developing a policy against sexual harassment. What interpretations could you make of Table 8-1 on page 169 to help you emphasize the importance of developing such a policy?

The Web Corner

http://www.mediate.com
(Resolving workplace conflict.)

http://www.karrass.com
(Negotiating ideas for managers and corporate professionals.)

Internet Skill Builder: The Seven Steps to Conflict Resolution

The Web site http://www.teambuildinginc.com includes a section titled, "The 7 Steps to Conflict Resolution." You can get to it through their search function. Among the seven steps are (1) Develop an attitude of resolution, (5) Listen actively and with empathy, and (7) Test for satisfaction. As you go through the Teambuilding, Inc., program of resolving conflict, look for similarities between the information presented on the Web site and in this chapter.

Developing Your Human Relations Skills

Interpersonal Relations Case 8.1

The Refrigerator Caper*

Two e-mail messages were sent at a technology company in northern Virginia, covering the same topic:

From: Nestor, Jenna
Sent: Tuesday, August 7, 12:50 P.M.
To: All employees on 3rd, 4th, and 8th floors
Subject: Re: Refrigerator Etiquette
Importance: High

To the person who ate my lunch:

I would like to thank you for completely taking it upon yourself to deny me sustenance this afternoon. It is completely inappropriate to take things that are not yours. Are we in the 1st grade?

Please read Diana's e-mail that I have copied below. I would be happy to read it out loud and explain it to you if it is too hard to understand.

Jenna
A Very Angry Victim

P.S.: In case you were wondering what that extra flavor was, each and every day I take the time to spit in my lunch. I hope you enjoyed it.

From: Sanders, Diana
Sent: Monday, July 30, 4:32 P.M.

To: All employees on 3rd, 4th, and 8th floors
Subject: Refrigerator Etiquette

Over the last month, a number of employees have been disappointed when they went to grab their lunch out of the refrigerator. Unfortunately, they found that someone had either taken part of their lunch out of their lunch bag and or the entire lunch was missing.

Please be respectful of others and do not eat anything from the fridge that is not your personal property. If you bring your lunch, please label it with your name and date. Thank you for your immediate cooperation and consideration of coworkers.

Diana Sanders
Director of Administration

Case Questions

1. What is the exact conflict in this situation? What is the source of the conflict?
2. What is your evaluation of Jenna Nestor's method of resolving the conflict over her stolen lunch?
3. How can professional adults really act in this manner?

*The company involved in this incident chose to remain anonymous.

Interpersonal Relations Case 8.2

Caught in a Squeeze

Heather Lopez is a product development specialist at a telecommunications company. For the last seven months she has worked as a member of a product development team composed of people from five different departments within the company. Heather previously worked full time in the marketing department. Her primary responsibilities were to research the market potential of an idea for a new product. The product development team is now working on a product that will integrate a company's printers and copiers.

Heather's previous position in the marketing department was a satisfactory fit for her lifestyle. Heather thought that she was able to take care of her family responsibilities and

her job without sacrificing one for the other. As Heather explains, "I worked about 45 predictable hours in my other job. My hours were essentially 8:30 A.M. to 4:30 P.M. with a little work at night and on Saturdays. But I could do the work at night and on Saturdays at home.

"Brad, my husband, and I had a smooth working arrangement for sharing the responsibility for getting our son Christopher off to school and picking him up from the after-school child-care center. Brad is a devoted accountant, so he understands the importance of giving high priority to a career yet still being a good family person."

In her new position as a member of the product development team, Heather is encountering some unanticipated demands. Three weeks ago, at 3 P.M. on a Tuesday, Tyler Watson, Heather's team leader, announced an emergency meeting to discuss a budget problem with the new product. The meeting would start at 4, and end at about 6:30. "Don't worry folks," said the team leader, "if it looks like we're going past 6:30 we'll order in some Chinese food." With a look of panic on her face, Heather responded to Tyler, "I can't make the meeting. Christopher will be expecting me at about 5 at the child-care center. My husband is out of town, and the center closes at 6 sharp. So count me out of today's meeting."

Tyler replied, "I said that this is an emergency meeting, and that we need input from all the members. You need to organize your personal life better to be a contributing member to this team. But do what you have to do, at least this once."

Heather chose to leave the office at 4:30 so she could pick up Christopher. The next day, Tyler did not comment on her absence. However, he gave her a copy of the minutes and asked for her input. The budget problem surfaced again one week later. Top-level management asked the group to reduce the cost of the new product and its initial marketing costs by 15 percent.

Tyler said to the team on a Friday morning, "We have until Monday morning to arrive at a reduced cost structure on our product development. I am dividing up the project into segments. If we meet as a team Saturday morning at 8, we should get the job done by 6. Get a good night's rest, so we can start fresh tomorrow morning. Breakfast and lunch will be on the company."

Heather could feel stress overwhelming her body, as she thought to herself, "Christopher is playing in the finals of his little league soccer match tomorrow morning at 10. Brad has made dinner reservations for 6, so we can make it to the *Phantom of the Opera* at 8 P.M. Should I tell Tyler he is being unreasonable? Should I quit? Should I tell Christopher and Brad that our special occasions together are less important than a Saturday business meeting?"

Case Questions

1. What type of conflict is Heather facing?
2. What should Heather do to resolve her conflicts with respect to family and work responsibilities?
3. What should the company do to help deal with the type of conflict Heather is facing? Or, should the company not consider Heather's dilemma to be its problem?

Interpersonal Skills Role-Play 8.1

Conflict Resolution Role-Play

Imagine that Heather, in the case just presented, decides that her job is taking too big a toll on her personal life. However, she still values her job and does not want to quit. She decides to discuss her problem with her team leader, Tyler. From Tyler's standpoint, a professional person must stand ready to meet unusual job demands, and cannot expect an entirely predictable work schedule. One person plays the role of Heather, another plays the role of Tyler, as they attempt to resolve this incident of work–family conflict.

CHAPTER 9

Becoming an Effective Leader

Mary DiSalvo is the director of operations of a printing company that specializes in printing shrink-wrapped labels for food and consumer products including bottled water, orange juice, and packaged meat. Company CEO Bruce Denton observed that over a six-year period, DiSalvo's group had the highest productivity and lowest employee turnover at the company. Denton had a hunch that DiSalvo's passion for people and her love of printing had something to do with her outstanding record. However, he wanted more insight into what made for superb leadership at his company. So with Mary's permission, an outside human relations specialist interviewed several people about their experiences working in the company, and what they thought of Mary's leadership.

Cheryl, a shipping supervisor, described DiSalvo's leadership in these terms: "Mary is so gung ho about labels and production efficiency that her excitement rubs off on you. She makes us feel that we are on a crusade to produce the best labels in the business. At the same time, she really cares about everybody who works at the company. I remember when she personally went to help out a production worker whose house was severely damaged by a tree falling on it."

Jeff, a quality technician, expressed these ideas to the human relations interviewer: "I don't have too much direct contact with Mary because she is two levels up the ladder from me. But I feel her impact almost every day. Mary is committed to quality, and her e-mails to the company about quality make me

Learning Objectives

After reading and studying this chapter and doing the exercises, you should be able to

1. Identify key leadership traits for personal development.
2. Develop several attitudes and behaviors that will help you appear charismatic.
3. Develop your team leadership skills.
4. Understand how you can develop your leadership potential.

feel that my work is very important. Mary is the hardest worker in the plant, so she sets a good example for us. She also has a great warm smile and a cheerful attitude that makes you want to do your best."[1]

As in the story just presented, effective leaders have a combination of admirable qualities, including expertise, a passion to succeed, high energy, and the ability to inspire others. In working toward improving your leadership ability, the following definition is a goal to strive for. **Leadership** is the ability to inspire support and confidence among the people who are needed to achieve company goals. A company president might have to inspire thousands of people, while a team leader is concerned with inspiring about six people. Both of these leaders nonetheless play an important role.

Leadership has also been defined in many other ways. Bill Bradley, former U.S. senator and professional basketball player, uses a definition of leadership that points to what a leader actually accomplishes. Bradley perceives leadership as getting people to think, believe, see, and do what they might not have without your presence.[2] In other words, the leader makes a difference.

Becoming a leader does not necessarily mean that the company has to put you in charge of others (or assign you a formal leadership position). You can also rise to leadership when people come to respect your opinion and personal characteristics and are thus influenced by you. Leadership is thought by many to exist at all levels with people anywhere in the organization being able to influence others if they have the right skills or know the right work procedures.[3] Your greatest opportunity for exerting leadership will come about from a combination of holding a formal position and exerting personal influence. An individual with appealing personal characteristics and expertise who is placed in a position of authority will find it relatively easy to exert leadership.

The purpose of this chapter is twofold. One is to make you aware of the basic concepts you need to become a leader. The other purpose is to point you toward developing skills necessary for leadership effectiveness.

leadership
The ability to inspire support and confidence among the people who are needed to achieve common goals.

KEY LEADERSHIP TRAITS TO DEVELOP

An important part of being an effective leader is to have the *right stuff*. This section and the following one about charisma describe personal attributes that help a person lead others in many situations. Recognize, however, that radically different situations require a different set of leadership characteristics. For example, a leader might have to be more assertive with group members performing distasteful work than with those whose work is enjoyable.

Each of the nine leadership traits described next, and shown in Figure 9-1, can be developed. For such development to take place, you need to be aware of the importance of the personal characteristic, and then monitor your own behavior to make progress. To assist you with such development, the description of each trait is accompanied by a suggestion for improvement.

Self-Confidence

In virtually every leadership setting, it is important for the leader to be realistically self-confident. A leader who is self-assured without being bombastic or overbearing instills confidence in group members. Self-confidence was among the first leadership traits researchers identified. Current research with leaders in many situations has continued to underscore the importance of this trait. A series of research studies have shown that increased self-confidence can bring about improvement in performance, including helping a group attain its goals.[4] In addition to being self-confident, the leader must project that self-confidence to the group.[5] Self-confidence is not only a personality trait. It also refers to the behavior a person exhibits in a number of situations. It is similar to being cool under pressure. We can conclude that a person is a self-confident leader when he or she retains composure during a crisis, such as when the company suffers flood damage during a busy season.

You can appear more self-confident to the group by using definitive wording, maintaining good posture, and making appropriate gestures such as pointing an index finger outward. Developing self-confidence is a lifelong process of performing well in a variety of situations. You need a series of easy victories to establish self-confidence. Further development of your self-confidence requires performing well in challenging circumstances.

FIGURE 9-1 Nine Key Leadership Traits

People who possess the traits listed in this figure are usually well suited to being an effective leader. However, many other traits and behaviors are also important contributors to effective leadership.

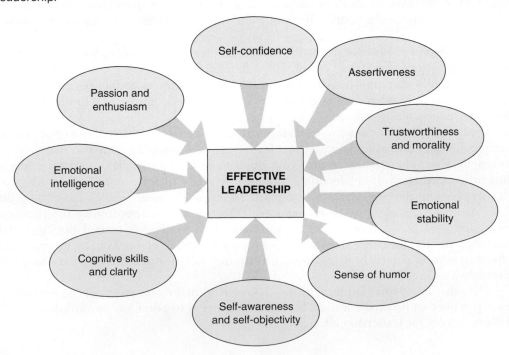

Taking risks, such as volunteering to work on an unfamiliar project, contributes to self-confidence when the risk proves to be worthwhile.

Assertiveness

A widely recognized leadership trait is **assertiveness**, being forthright in expressing demands, opinions, feelings, and attitudes. If you are self-confident, it is easier to be assertive with people. An assertive team leader might say, "I know that the ice storm put us out of business for 4 days, but we can make up the time by working smart and pulling together. Within 30 days, we will have met or surpassed our goals for the quarter." This statement reflects self-confidence in her leadership capabilities and assertiveness in expressing exactly what she thinks.

Assertiveness helps leaders perform many tasks and achieve goals. Among them are confronting group members about their mistakes, demanding higher performance, and setting high expectations. An assertive leader will also make legitimate demands on higher management, such as asking for equipment needed by the group.

To be assertive differs significantly from being aggressive or passive (or nonassertive). Aggressive people express their demands in an overly pushy, obnoxious, and abrasive manner. Passive people suppress their own ideas, attitudes, feelings, and thoughts as if they were likely to be perceived as controversial. Nonassertive people are also too accommodating. A series of three studies with a variety of workers indicated that leaders with moderate assertiveness were considered more effective than leaders low (passive) or high (aggressive) in this trait.[6]

Developing assertiveness is much like attempting to become less shy. You must force yourself to take the opportunity to express your feelings and demands. For example, if something a teammate does annoys you, make the statement, "I enjoy working with you in general, but what you are doing now annoys me." You can also practice expressing positive emotion, such as telling a coworker, "I'm happy that you and I are working on this project together, because I like your approach to work."

Expressing demands is easier for most people to practice than expressing feelings. People who do start expressing their demands are often surprised at the result. For example, if you are contemplating the purchase of an item that is beyond your budget, try this statement: "I like this product very much. Yet all I have to spend is $75 below your asking price. Can we do business?" For a reading on your own level of assertiveness, do Self-Assessment Quiz 9-1.

assertiveness

Being forthright in expressing demands, opinions, feelings, and attitudes.

SELF-ASSESSMENT QUIZ 9-1

The Assertiveness Scale

Directions: Check whether each of the following statements is *mostly true* or *mostly false* as it applies to you. If in doubt about your reaction to a particular statement, think of how you would generally respond.

	Mostly true	Mostly false
1. It is extremely difficult for me to turn down a sales representative if he or she is a nice person.	_____	_____
2. I express criticism freely.	_____	_____
3. If another person were being very unfair, I would bring it to his or her attention.	_____	_____
4. Work is no place to let your feelings show.	_____	_____
5. There's no use in asking for favors; people get what they deserve.	_____	_____
6. Business is not the place for tact; say what you think.	_____	_____
7. If a person looked as if he or she were in a hurry, I would let that person in front of me in a supermarket line.	_____	_____
8. A weakness of mine is that I'm too nice a person.	_____	_____
9. I usually give other people what they want rather than do what I think is best, just to avoid an argument.	_____	_____

(Continued)

10. If the mood strikes me, I will laugh out loud in public. _____ _____

11. People would describe me as too outspoken. _____ _____

12. I am quite willing to return merchandise that I find has even a minor blemish. _____ _____

13. I dread having to express anger toward a coworker. _____ _____

14. People often say that I'm too reserved and emotionally controlled. _____ _____

15. Nice guys and gals finish last in business. _____ _____

16. I fight for my rights down to the last detail. _____ _____

17. I have no misgivings about returning an overcoat to the store if it doesn't fit me right. _____ _____

18. After I have an argument with a person, I try to avoid him or her. _____ _____

19. I insist on my spouse (or roommate or partner) doing his or her fair share of undesirable chores. _____ _____

20. It is difficult for me to look directly at another person when the two of us are in disagreement. _____ _____

21. I have cried among friends more than once. _____ _____

22. If someone near me at a movie kept up a conversation with another person, I would ask him or her to stop. _____ _____

23. I am able to turn down social engagements with people I do not particularly care for. _____ _____

24. It is in poor taste to express what you really feel about another individual. _____ _____

25. I sometimes show my anger by swearing at or belittling another person. _____ _____

26. I am reluctant to speak up at a meeting. _____ _____

27. I find it relatively easy to ask friends for small favors such as giving me a ride to work while my car is being repaired. _____ _____

28. If another person were talking very loudly in a restaurant and it bothered me, I would inform that person. _____ _____

29. I often finish other people's sentences for them. _____ _____

30. It is relatively easy for me to express love and affection toward another person. _____ _____

Total Score _____ _____

Scoring and Interpretation: The answers for determining your assertiveness are as follows:

1. Mostly false	9. Mostly false	17. Mostly true	25. Mostly true
2. Mostly true	10. Mostly true	18. Mostly false	26. Mostly false
3. Mostly true	11. Mostly true	19. Mostly true	27. Mostly true
4. Mostly false	12. Mostly true	20. Mostly false	28. Mostly true
5. Mostly false	13. Mostly false	21. Mostly true	29. Mostly true
6. Mostly true	14. Mostly false	22. Mostly true	30. Mostly true
7. Mostly false	15. Mostly true	23. Mostly true	
8. Mostly false	16. Mostly true	24. Mostly false	

Score yourself a +1 for each of your answers that agrees with the scoring key. If your score is 15 or less, it is probable that you are currently nonassertive. A score of 16 through 24 suggests that you are assertive. A score of 25 or higher suggests that you are aggressive. Retake this quiz about 30 days from now to give yourself some indication of the stability of your answers. You might also discuss your answers with a close friend to determine whether that person has a similar perception of your assertiveness.

Trustworthiness and Morality

Group members consistently believe that leaders must display honesty, integrity, and credibility—and therefore must be trustworthy. Right Management Consultants conducted a survey of 570 employees in which they found that the white-collar workers value honesty and integrity in a manager more than any other trait. When asked, "What is the most important trait or attribute that the leader of your company should possess?" 24 percent of the survey participants cited honesty and 16 percent named integrity/morals, or ethics.[7] Leaders themselves believe that honesty makes a difference in their effectiveness.

Being honest with team members helps build trust, which in turn leads to good cooperation and team spirit. In recent years, trust in business leaders has been damaged by financial scandals in well-known companies. Executives in those companies enriched themselves by selling company stock just before the time they correctly forecast that the stock price would tumble. At the same time, the executives encouraged employees to not sell their stock, or to purchase more. Also, records were falsified to enhance the value of stock purchases by executives.

To trust group members, the leader has to be willing to give up some control over them, such as letting group members make more decisions and not challenging their expense accounts. The following anecdote, told by Fred Smith, the founder of FedEx, illustrates what trust can mean in an organization:

> A blizzard shut down a radio relay located on top of a mountain, cutting phone service to several FedEx offices. The phone company said it would take five days to repair the problem. On his own, a FedEx telecommunications expert named Hal chartered a helicopter to get to the site. The pilot was unable to land, but he got close enough to the ground for Hal to jump safely. Hal slogged through the deep snow and fixed the problem.

According to Smith, Hal went to such great lengths to keep the organization going because there was mutual trust between employer and employee. Hal knew he would not be reprimanded for going to such expense to fix the telephone problem.[8]

Being moral is closely linked to trustworthiness because a moral leader is more likely to be trusted. A leader with high morality would perceive that he or she had an ethical responsibility to group members, as well as outsiders.[9] The moral leader would therefore not give preferential treatment to workers with whom he had an friendship outside of work. At the same time, the moral leader would not try to fool customers or make up false excuses for not paying bills on time to suppliers.

Chapter 14, about ethical behavior, provides details about honesty on the job. Being honest is an effective way of getting others to trust you. A starting point in developing a strong sense of honesty and morality is to follow a variation of the Golden Rule: Be as honest with others as you want them to be with you.

Emotional Stability

Anyone who has ever worked for an unstable supervisor will attest to the importance of emotional stability as a leadership trait. (As described in Chapter 2, emotional stability is equivalent to scoring low on neuroticism in the Five-Factor Model.) Emotional stability is important for a leader because group members expect and need consistency in the way they are treated.

Kenneth Chenault, the chief executive officer of American Express—and the first African American man to be the top executive of a Fortune 500 company—is known for his even temperament. Although an assertive and tough executive, he is calm and in control. A survey of Chenault's former and present colleagues found that his personality is free of the rough edges that usually accompany fierce ambition. Nobody questioned could recall Chenault losing his temper or even raising his voice. Chenault's emotional stability was also demonstrated by how well he led AmEx cope with the difficult times following the terrorist attacks of 9/11. Part of his recovery plan was to shift the company from primarily an offline business to one that was mostly online. Chenault emphasizes that having the right values (such as caring for people) gives stability to a person's career.[10]

Emotional stability is difficult to develop, but people can learn to control many of their emotional outbursts. People who cannot control their emotions, yet still want to become leaders, should seek assistance from a mental health professional.

Sense of Humor

A sense of humor is on the borderline between being a trait and a behavior. However you classify it, the effective use of humor is considered an important part of a leader's role. Humor serves such functions in the workplace as relieving tension and boredom and defusing hostility. Because humor helps the leader dissolve tension and defuse conflict, it helps him or her exert power over the group. A study conducted in a large financial institution indicated that leaders who made frequent use of humor had higher-performing units. (Another interpretation is that it's easier to laugh when the group is performing well!) Among the forms of humor used by the managers were "[using] humor to take the edge off during stressful periods" and "[making] us laugh at ourselves when we are too serious."[11]

Self-effacing humor is the choice of comedians and organizational leaders alike. When you are self-effacing, nobody else is insulted or slighted, yet a point can be made. A marketing executive at Gateway (now part of Acer Computer) said a few years ago to a subcontractor, "I want you people to design photo software so uncomplicated that even managers at my level could learn how to use it."

Creativity is required for humor. Just as creativity can be enhanced with practice, so can a sense of humor. To gather some experience in making humorous comments in the workplace, do Skill-Building Exercise 9-1.

Self-Awareness and Self-Objectivity

Effective leaders are aware of their strengths and limitations. This awareness enables them to capitalize upon their strengths and overcome their weaknesses. A leader, for example, might realize that he or she is naturally distrustful of others. Awareness of this problem cautions the leader to not distrust people without good evidence. Another leader might realize that he or she is adept at counseling team members. This leader might then emphasize that activity in an effort to improve performance. Self-objectivity refers to being detached or nonsubjective about your perceived strengths and limitations.

Another way in which self-awareness and self-objectivity contribute to leadership effectiveness is that these traits help a person become an authentic leader. Such a leader demonstrates passion for his or her pupose, practices values consistently, and leads with the heart as well as the head. Instead of being a phony, or acting out of character, the person is genuine. Authenticity helps the leader be perceived as trustworthy.[12] "Being yourself" thus

---

SKILL-BUILDING EXERCISE 9-1

The Witty Leader

Students gather in problem-solving groups of about five to invent humorous comments a leader might make in the following scenarios. After the problem-solving groups have formulated their witty comments, the comments can be shared and compared. Groups also have the option of deciding that a particular scenario is too grim for humor.

Scenario 1: A store manager wants to communicate to employees how bad business has been lately. Sales have declined about 20 percent for three consecutive weeks.

Scenario 2: A leader has to communicate to the group that salaries have been frozen for another year because of limited business. The leader knows that group members have been eagerly awaiting news about the salary increase.

Scenario 3: Owing to an unprecedented surge in orders, all salaried personnel will be required to work about 65 hours per week for the next 10 weeks. Furthermore, the office and factory must be staffed on Saturdays and Sundays.

Scenario 4: A consulting firm that specializes in helping companies downsize their workforce has seen the demand for its services decline substantially in recent months. The company must therefore downsize itself. The company founder has to announce the layoff decision to the company.

Observers might rate the attempts at humor on a 1 (low) to 10 (high) scale. Observe also if any of the role players made you laugh.

contributes to leadership effectiveness assuming that you have personal qualities, such as those presented in this chapter, that facilitate leadership. Mary DiSalvo, the leader described in the chapter opener, appears to be an authentic leader.

You can enhance your self-awareness and self-objectivity by regularly asking for feedback from others. You then compare the feedback to your self-perception of your standing on the same factor. You might, for example, think that you communicate in colorful, interesting terms. In speaking to others about your communication style, you might discover that others agree. You can then conclude that your self-awareness about your communication skills is accurate.

Another technique for improving self-awareness and self-objectivity is to take several self-examination exercises such as those found in this text. Even if they do not describe you exactly, they stimulate you to reflect on your characteristics and behaviors.

Cognitive Skills and Clarity

Mental ability, as well as personality, is important for leadership success. To inspire people, bring about constructive changes, and solve problems creatively, leaders need to be mentally sharp. Problem-solving and intellectual skills are referred to collectively as **cognitive factors**. The term *cognition* refers to the mental process or faculty by which knowledge is gathered.

A major reason that cognitive skills have increased in importance for leadership is that they enable the leader to acquire knowledge. The processing of knowledge is now considered to be the *core competence* (key ability) of organizations. The leader's role is to both originate useful ideas and collect them from smart people throughout the organization.[13] Two cognitive skills were discussed in Chapter 2: mental ability and the personal factor of openness to experience. Another cognitive skill of major importance is *knowledge of the business,* or technical skill. An effective leader

cognitive factors

The collective terms for problem-solving and intellectual skills.

has to be technically or professionally competent in some discipline, particularly when leading a group of specialists. It is difficult for the leader to establish rapport with group members when he or she does not know what they are doing. A related damper on leadership effectiveness is when the group does not respect the leader's technical skill.

High intelligence is particularly important for leaders, when they have the opportunity to make decisions by themselves and provide direction (such as giving technical instructions) to group members.[14] Problem-solving ability is less important when the leader delegates most of his or her responsibilities to others (or empowers them). High intelligence is important for three major aspects of the leader's job. One aspect is dealing with tasks such as developing ideas for cost cutting. A second aspect is working with and through other people, or the human relations focus. The third is judging oneself and adapting one's behavior accordingly as in self-awareness and self-objectivity.[15]

Closely related to cognitive skills is the leader's ability to be clear about what needs to be accomplished to build a better future, even if the future is next week. Based on his study of some of the world's most successful business leaders, Marcus Buckingham concludes that the leader should define the future in vivid terms so people can see where they are headed. The leader also has to be clear about such matters as who the group is trying to serve.[16] For example, when Deborah Wahl Meyer was appointed as chief marketing officer for Chrysler, he reasoned that her main challenge would be crafting a clear identity for the Chrysler brand. She noted that the Jeep and Dodge nameplates "have a lot of strength and equity in the market."[17] Meyer had in mind serving the consumer group of those who purchase vehicles. A beauty salon operator could provide clarity to her hairstylists with a statement such as, "Our real purpose here is to boost our customers' self-esteem. Every customer who leaves our salon should feel a little better about himself or herself."

Increasing one's mental ability, or raw intelligence, may not be easy to accomplish. Yet people can develop their cognitive skills by continuous study and by working on challenging problems. The mere act of keeping up with developments in your field can keep you mentally sharp. For a leader to provide clarity, the leader would have to think through clearly what it is that he or she is really attempting to accomplish.

Emotional Intelligence

Emotional intelligence, as described in Chapter 2, refers to the ability to recognize your emotions and those of people around you. Emotional intelligence also refers to being able to work effectively with the emotions of others to resolve problems, including listening and empathizing. As such, emotional intelligence is a blend of psychological skills that enable the leader to relate effectively to people. Research conducted by Daniel Goleman in many different firms suggests that superb leaders all have one trait in common: superb emotional intelligence.[19] A specific example is that an effective manager or leader can often recognize the motives behind an employee's actions.

> *Visualize yourself as a team leader. Vanessa, one of the team members, says to you, "I'm worried about Rick. I think he needs help. He looks like he has a drinking problem." If you have good emotional intelligence, you might think to yourself, "I wonder why Vanessa is telling me this. Is she simply being helpful? Or is she out to backstab Rick?" Therefore, you would seek some tangible evidence about Rick's alleged problem before acting. You would also seek to spend more time with Vanessa so you can better understand her motives.*
>
> *With much less emotional intelligence, you would immediately get in touch with Rick, accuse him of having a drinking problem, and tell him to get help or get fired.*

Emotional intelligence is also reflected in a leader who incorporates the human touch into business activities, such as building personal relationships with employees and customers. Several years ago Robert A. Eckert was recruited from Kraft Foods to become chair and CEO of toy maker Mattel. At the time Mattel was in deep financial trouble, and key managers were leaving the company. Eckert moved quickly to bring the famous toy manufacturer back to health. The first steps he took were to share meals with employees in the company cafeteria at every opportunity. During these lunches he engaged in candid dialogue with employees chosen at random. He reassured employees that their personal growth and development were integral to his plans for rebuilding Mattel. Eckert notes, "In this case the emotional intelligence I'd developed over the years was even more important to my success than my traditional, analytical management skills were."[20]

Leaders with emotional intelligence are in tune with the thoughts and emotions of their own and those of other people. The emotionally intelligent leader recognizes that emotions are contagious, such as optimists making other workers optimistic, and pessimists making other workers pessimistic. At the same time, these leaders know that their own emotions are powerful drivers of their group member's moods, and ultimately performance.[21]

Emotional intelligence can be developed through working on some of its components, as described in Chapter 2. It is also important to develop the habit of looking to understand the feelings and emotions of people around you. Ask yourself, "How do I feel about what's going on here?" When you have a hunch about people's motives, look for feedback in the future to see if you were right. For example, a little investigation might indicate that Vanessa and Rick are indeed rivals and have a personality clash.

Passion and Enthusiasm

A prominent characteristic of effective leaders is the passion and enthusiasm they have for their work, much like the same quality in creative people. The passion reflects itself in such ways as an intense liking for the business, the customers, and employees. Passion is also reflected in a relentless drive to get work accomplished and an obsession for achieving company goals. Passion for their work is especially evident in entrepreneurial leaders and small business owners who are preoccupied with growing their businesses. Many leaders use the term *love* to describe their passion for their work, business, and employees.

To display passion and enthusiasm for your work, you must first find work that creates an inner spark. The work that you choose should be equally or more exciting than your favorite pastime. If not everything about your job excites you, search for its most satisfying or intrinsically motivating elements. For example, the Mattel executive described previously is so excited about the interpersonal aspects of his work that his passion inspires employees.

SUGGESTIONS FOR DEVELOPING CHARISMA

LEARNING OBJECTIVE 2

The study of leadership in recent years has emphasized the importance of inspirational leaders who guide others toward great heights of achievement. Such leaders are said to possess **charisma**, a special quality of leaders whose purposes, powers, and extraordinary determination differentiate them from others.[22] Being charismatic can make a leader's job easier, because leaders have to energize group members.[23]

An important fact about charisma is that it reflects a subjective perception on the part of the person being influenced. Many people regard a leader such as Steve Jobs of Apple Corp. as being powerful and inspirational. Yet he is also disliked by many people who consider him to be arrogant, prone to throwing tamper tantrums, and a control freak.

charisma

A special quality of leaders whose purposes, powers, and extraordinary determination differentiate them from others. (However, people besides leaders can be charismatic.)

The term *charisma* is most frequently used in association with nationally and internationally known leaders. Yet first-level supervisors, team leaders, and minor sports coaches can also be charismatic. Possessing a naturally dynamic personality is a major contributor to charisma, but a person can engage in many tangible actions that also contribute to charisma. What follows are a number of suggestions for behaving charismatically, all based on characteristics and behaviors often found among charismatic leaders. If you are not currently a leader, remember that being perceived as charismatic will help you become one.

1. **Communicate a vision.** A charismatic leader offers an exciting image of where the organization is headed and how to get there. A vision is more than a forecast because it describes an ideal version of the future of an entire organization or an organizational unit such as a department. Richard Branson, the colorful British entrepreneur, has inspired hundreds of employees with his vision of the Virgin brand being a leader in dozens of fields. Among his accomplishments to reach this vision are the Virgin Atlantic airline, Virgin Megastores, and Virgin Cinema. The supervisor of paralegal services might communicate a vision such as, "Our paralegal group will become known as the most professional and helpful paralegal group in Arizona." A visionary leader should also have the courage to communicate the vision to others, and to help implement the vision.[24] For the paralegal supervisor, part of implementing the vision might be teaching new technology skills to the paralegals.

Skill-Building Exercise 9-2 will give you a chance to develop visioning skills (a buzzword in business).

2. **Make frequent use of metaphors and analogies.** To inspire people, the charismatic leader uses colorful language and exciting

Creating a Vision

The class organizes into small problem-solving groups. Each group constructs a vision for a unit of an organization or for a total organization of its choosing. Students can choose a well-known business firm, government agency, or an organization with which they are familiar. The vision should be approximately 25 words long and depict a glorious future. A vision is not simply a straight-forward goal, such as, "In 2010 our firm will gross $10 million in sales." Remember, the vision statement drawn should inspire people throughout the organization.

If class time permits, volunteers can share their visions with other class members who will provide feedback on the clarity and inspirational qualities of the visions presented.

BACK TO THE OPENING CASE

Several of Mary DiSalvo's leadership qualities were mentioned in the opening case. She also is a leader with vision. She says, "As food-product safety becomes more of an issue in our world, the importance of secure labeling and packaging will multiply, and our company will be at the forefront."

metaphors and analogies. Develop metaphors to inspire people around you. A metaphor commonly used after a group has suffered a setback is, "Like the phoenix, we will rise from the ashes of defeat." To pick up the spirits of her maintenance group, a maintenance supervisor told the group, "We're a lot like the heating and cooling system in a house. A lot of people don't give us much thought, but without us their lives would be very uncomfortable."

3. **Inspire trust and confidence.** Make your deeds consistent with your promises. As mentioned earlier in this chapter, being trustworthy is a key leadership trait. Get people to believe in your competence by making your accomplishments known in a polite, tactful way. The *socialized charismatic* is likely to inspire trust and confidence because such a leader is ethical and wants to accomplish activities that help others rather than pursuing personal ends such as glory and power.[25]

4. **Be highly energetic and goal oriented.** Impress others with your energy and resourcefulness. To increase your energy supply, exercise frequently, eat well, and get ample rest. Closely related to being goal oriented is being optimistic about what you and the group can accomplish. People also associate optimism with energy. Being grumpy is often associated with being low on energy. You can add to an image of energy by raising and lowering your voice frequently, and avoiding a slow pace.

5. **Be emotionally expressive and warm.** A key characteristic of charismatic leaders is the ability to express feelings openly. Assertiveness is therefore an important component of charisma. In dealing with team members, refer to your feelings at the time, such as, "I'm excited because I know we are going to hit our year-end target by mid-October." Nonverbal emotional expressiveness, such as warm gestures and occasional touching (nonsexual) of group members, also exhibits charisma. Remember, however, that many people resent being touched when at work. Frequent smiling is another way of being emotionally expressive. Also, a warm smile seems to indicate a confident, caring person, which contributes to a perception of charisma.

6. **Make ample use of true stories.** An excellent way of building rapport is to tell stories that deliver a message. People like to hear stories about how a department or company went through hard times when it started, such as how Dell Computer began in a dormitory room at the University of Texas. Telling positive

stories has become a widely accepted technique for building relationships with employees. Storytelling adds a touch of warmth to the teller and helps build connections among people who become familiar with the same story.

7. **Be candid and direct.** Practice being direct in saying what you want, rather than being indirect and evasive. If you want someone to help you, don't ask, "Are you busy?" Instead, ask, "Can you help me with a problem I'm having right now?"

8. **Make everybody you meet feel that he or she is important.** For example, at a company social gathering, shake the hand of every person you meet. Also, thank people frequently both orally and by written notes.

9. **Multiply the effectiveness of your handshake.** Shake firmly without creating pain, and make enough eye contact to notice the color of the other person's eyes. When you take that much trouble, you project care and concern.[26]

10. **Stand up straight and use other nonverbal signals of self-confidence.** Practice good posture. Minimize fidgeting, scratching, foot tapping, and speaking in a monotone. Walk at a rapid pace without appearing to be panicked. Dress fashionably without going to the extreme that people notice your clothes more than they notice you.

11. **Be willing to take personal risks.** Charismatic leaders are typically risk takers, and risk taking adds to their charisma. Risks you might take would include extending additional credit to a start-up business, suggesting a bright but costly idea, and recommending that a former felon be given a chance in your firm.

12. **Be self-promotional.** Charismatic leaders are not shy. Instead, they toot their own horns and allow others to know how important they are. Without appearing self-absorbed, you, too, might let others know of your tangible accomplishments. Explain to others the key role that you played on your team or how you achieved a few tough goals.

Despite the importance of developing charisma, being excessively and flamboyantly charismatic can backfire because others may perceive you as self-serving. Therefore, the idea is to sprinkle your charisma with humility, such as admitting when you make a mistake. Also, in recent years top level management at some companies have replaced highly charismatic, rock-star-like leaders with those who concentrate more on running the business instead of gathering publicity for themselves.

DEVELOPING TEAM LEADERSHIP SKILLS

LEARNING OBJECTIVE 3

As organizations rely heavily on teams, some of the best opportunities for practicing leadership occur as a team leader. A team leader typically reports to a higher-level manager. The team leader is not a boss in the old-fashioned sense, but a facilitator or coach who shares decision making with team members. (A facilitator is a person who helps make things happen without taking control.) A team leader practices **participative leadership,** or sharing authority with the group. Being a participative leader does not mean that the leader just stays out of the way and provides no guidance or encouragement to team members. Recent research conducted with Norwegian companies supports the belief that danger lurks in the hands of leaders who turn over all responsibility to the group. Employees who received almost no direction from their boss suffered from role ambiguity—confusion about what needs to be done. As a result, these employees suffered from stress, and often found themselves in conflict with each other, including bullying.[27] (The conflict and bullying may have stemmed from workers in dispute over who should do what.)

participative leadership

Sharing authority with the group.

Self-Assessment Quiz 9-2 gives you an opportunity to gauge your attitudes toward being a participative leader. We next discuss tentechniques that would contribute to your effectiveness as a team leader, as outlined in Figure 9-2.

What Style of Leader Are You or Would You Be?

Directions: Check whether each of the following questions is *mostly true* or *mostly false*, keeping in mind what you have done, or think you would do, in the scenarios and attitudes described.

	Mostly true	Mostly false
1. I am more likely to take care of a high-impact assignment myself than turn it over to a group member.	_____	_____
2. I would prefer the analytical aspects of a manager's job rather than working directly with group members.	_____	_____
3. An important part of my approach to managing a group is to keep the members informed almost daily of any information that could affect their work.	_____	_____
4. It's a good idea to give two people in the group the same problem, and then choose what appears to be the best solution.	_____	_____
5. It makes good sense for the leader or manager to stay somewhat aloof from the group, so he or she can make a tough decision when necessary.	_____	_____
6. I look for opportunities to obtain group input before making a decision, even on straightforward issues.	_____	_____
7. I would reverse a decision if several of the group members presented evidence that I was wrong.	_____	_____
8. Differences of opinion in the work group are healthy.	_____	_____
9. I think that activities to build team spirit, like the team fixing up a low-income family's house on a Saturday, are an excellent investment of time.	_____	_____
10. If my group were hiring a new member, I would like the person to be interviewed by the entire group.	_____	_____
11. An effective team leader today uses e-mail for about 98 percent of communication with team members.	_____	_____
12. Some of the best ideas are likely to come from the group members rather than the manager.	_____	_____
13. If our group were going to have a banquet, I would get input from each member on what type of food should be served.	_____	_____
14. I have never seen a statue of a committee in a museum or park, so why bother making decisions by a committee if you want to be recognized?	_____	_____
15. I dislike it intensely when a group member challenges my position on an issue.	_____	_____
16. I typically explain to group members what method they should use to accomplish an assigned task.	_____	_____
17. If I were out of the office for a week, most of the important work in the department would get accomplished anyway.	_____	_____
18. Delegation of important tasks is something that would be (or is) very difficult for me.	_____	_____
19. When a group member comes to me with a problem, I tend to jump right in with a proposed solution.	_____	_____
20. When a group member comes to me with a problem, I typically ask that person something like, "What alternative solutions have you thought of so far?"	_____	_____
Total Score	_____	_____

Scoring and Interpretation: The answers for determining what style of leader you are (or would be) are as follows:

1. Mostly false	4. Mostly false	7. Mostly true	10. Mostly true
2. Mostly false	5. Mostly false	8. Mostly true	11. Mostly false
3. Mostly true	6. Mostly true	9. Mostly true	12. Mostly true

Build a Mission Statement

A starting point in developing teamwork is to specify the team's mission. The mission should contain a specific goal and purpose, and it should be optimistic and uplifting. Here is an example from a service team at a Cadillac dealership:

To plan and implement a level of automobile service and repair of the highest quality, at a competitive price, that will delight customers and retain their loyalty.

The leader can help develop the mission statement when the team is first formed or at any other time. Developing a mission statement for a long-standing team breathes new life into its activities. Being committed to a mission improves teamwork, as does the process of formulating a mission statement. Skill-Building Exercise 9-3 gives you practice in developing a mission statement for a team.

Show Your Team Members That They Are Trusted

An effective leader is perceived as honest and trustworthy, and he or she trusts team members. The leader should recognize and reward ethical behavior, particularly when there is a temptation to be dishonest—such as not reporting a quality defect to a customer or cheating on tax returns. Raise expectations of honesty by telling group members you are confident they will act in ways that bring credit to the organization.[28]

FIGURE 9-2 Developing Teamwork

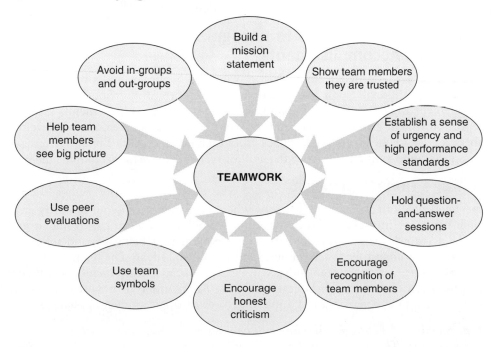

Developing a Team Mission Statement

The class organizes into teams of about six people and appoints a team leader. Each team plays the role of a specific team within a company, government agency, or hospital. An example would be the customer service team at a utility company. The task is to develop a mission statement approximating the type described in the text. The team leader might also take notes for the group.

Remember that a mission statement contains a goal and a purpose, and it is uplifting and optimistic. Allow about 15 minutes for preparing the mission statements. The groups then compare mission statements. One representative from each group presents the mission statements to the rest of the class.

micromanager

One who closely monitors most aspects of group members' activities, sometimes to the point of being a control freak.

A practical way of demonstrating trust in group members is to avoid closely monitoring their work and second-guessing their decisions about minor matters such as the best type of border for a report. A **micromanager** is one who closely monitors most aspects of group members' activities, sometimes to the point of being a control freak. As a result, the group members do not feel that the leader or manager trusts them to make even the smallest decisions. One manager checked travel Web sites himself for the best deal after a team member booked plans for a business trip. As a result, team members felt that they were not trusted to care about the financial welfare of the company.

Establish a Sense of Urgency and High Performance Standards

To build teamwork, members need to believe that the team has urgent, constructive purposes. A demanding performance challenge helps create and sustain the team. Team members also want to know exactly what is expected of them. The more urgent and relevant the rationale, the more likely it is that the team will perform well.[29] Based on this information, as a team leader you might project a sense of urgency and encourage setting high goals.

Hold Question-and-Answer Sessions with the Team

An effective way of demonstrating participative or team leadership is to hold question-and-answer sessions with team members. Both leader and members ask and answer questions, such as, "How can we make an even bigger contribution to the company?" The Quality Department at Delta Dental Plan of California used question-and-answer sessions with success. The process not only boosted morale and made managers more accessible to employees, but also yielded more than 1,000 employee suggestions in the first year. The department head said, "This program totally revolutionized the company. Now employees from other divisions are eager to work in our department."[30]

Encourage Team Members to Recognize Each Other's Accomplishments

Members of a high-spirited team look for ways to encourage and praise each other, including the traditional "high five" signifying an important contribution to the team. Encouragement and praise from the team leader is important, but team members also play an important role in giving positive reinforcement to each other. Team spirit develops as members receive frequent positive feedback from each other.[31] Skill-Building Exercise 9-4 gives you the opportunity to practice the skill of recognizing team accomplishments.

Encourage Honest Criticism

A superficial type of camaraderie develops when team members avoid honestly criticizing each other for the sake of group harmony. Avoiding criticism can result in groupthink. As a team leader, you should therefore explain that being a good team player includes offering honest feedback on mistakes and flawed ideas. The team benefits from mutual criticism. A stronger team spirit will develop because team members realize they are helping each other through honest feedback. An example of honest criticism took place in the shipping department of a manufacturer of small kitchen appliances:

One member of a customer service team had designed a satisfaction survey to mail to customers. The purpose of the survey was to investigate whether the packing

Recognizing Team Accomplishments

The class organizes into teams of about six, ideally into teams or groups that already worked with each other during the course. If you have not worked with each other, you will have to rely on any impressions you have made of the other members of the team during the course. Team members will be equipped with about six 3 × 5 index cards. However, any other small-size piece of paper will work. Each member of the team thinks carefully about what other members of the team have accomplished during the course, including contribution to team problem solving, class participation, or perhaps some accomplishment outside of class.

Assume you have six members on the team. Prepare a card for each member by jotting down whatever accomplishments you have observed of the other team members. Each person therefore prepares five cards that will be handed to the person whose name is on the card and then given to that person. Each team member will receive five "accomplishment cards," one from the other five members. Each member studies his or her accomplishment cards,

consisting of statements of accomplishments and perhaps a couple of words of praise. Here are two examples:

"I like the way you showed up on time for our study group, and were prepared for action. Nice job, Ben."

"A few times you came up with great ideas in our problem-solving groups. Shauna, you are a really nice team player."

After all cards have been read carefully, discuss your feelings about their cards and their potential contribution to teamwork. Include observations such as the following:

- How much closer to the group do you feel now?
- How much have your efforts in being a team player paid off?
- How useful a technique would this technique of accomplishment recognition be for a workplace team?
- What potential disadvantages do you see to the technique?

---

materials were of satisfactory quality. Another member said, "Are you sure you want to do this? Would we just annoy our customers by asking about packing ingredients? Why waste more paper? We've never had a complaint about packing materials."

The person whose idea was challenged was miffed at first, but then expressed appreciation. She said, "I guess I went a little overboard on trying to measure customer satisfaction. Maybe we should save our survey dollars for a more important issue."

Use Team Symbols

Teamwork on the athletic field is enhanced by team symbols such as uniforms and nicknames. The term *Lady Vols*, for example, deserves some credit for contributing to the mystique of the University of Tennessee women's basketball team. Symbols can also be an effective team builder in business. Trademarks, logos, mottoes, and other indicators of products both advertise the company and signify a joint effort. Company jackets, caps, T-shirts, mugs, ballpoint pens, and business cards can be modified to symbolize a work unit. As a team leader, you might therefore invest part of your team's budget in an appropriate symbol. Use the opportunity to practice participative leadership. Conduct a group problem-solving session to develop a team logo to place on a T-shirt or cap.

Use Peer Evaluations

In the traditional performance-evaluation system, the manager evaluates group members at regular intervals. With peer-evaluation systems, the team members contribute to the evaluation by submitting evaluations of each other. The evaluations might consist of filling out rating forms about each other's performance. Sometimes brief essays are written about each other and then synthesized by the team leader.

Peer evaluations contribute to teamwork because team members realize that helping each other becomes as important as helping the boss. Similarly, team members recognize that pleasing each other counts as much as pleasing the boss. A potential disadvantage of peer evaluations, however, is that the group members will agree to give each other outstanding evaluations, or to get even with coworkers they do not like.

As a team leader, you might not have the authority to initiate a peer-evaluation system without first checking with your manager. Making a recommendation for peer input into evaluations might demonstrate that you are committed to participative leadership.

Help Team Members See the Big Picture

The team is likely to work together more smoothly when members have a clear understanding of how their work contributes to the company. Communicating the mission as described earlier is a good starting point. Showing the team its specific contribution to the overall organization is equally important. As the team leader, you might create a flow-chart that tracks an order from the time it is taken to when it is delivered. Show the team its role at each step. The team members may be aware how they contribute to the team, but not how the team contributes to the success of the organization.[32] The team leader of a shipping department at a distribution center explains to his team regularly, "Let's keep this clearly in mind. A big factor in determining whether a customer stays with us is whether the goods arrive on time and in good shape."

Minimize Formation of In-Groups and Out-Groups

leader-member exchange model

A theory explaining that group leaders establish unique working relationships with group members, thereby creating in-groups and out-groups.

An established leadership theory, the **leader–member exchange model**, provides useful information for the aspiring team leader. According to this theory, leaders establish unique working relationships with group members. By so doing, they create in-groups and out-groups. The in-groups become part of a smoothly functioning team headed by the leader. Out-group members are less likely to experience good teamwork.[33] Figure 9-3 depicts the major concept of the leader–member exchange model.

The in-group may come about because the leader prefers certain group members and therefore is motivated to form good working relationships with them. Conversely, the leader may neglect to form good relationships with people with whom he or she has limited rapport. First impressions count heavily when the leader decides on who is "in" and who is "out." Team leaders should therefore guard against the formation of out-groups just because they are not fond of a few team members, or because a given team member gives a poor first impression.

The leader–member exchange model does not mean that the team leader should avoid forming unique relationships with team members. What should be avoided is forming an out-group. A study investigated the relationships a group of female sales managers established with both men and women members of their sales groups. Treating members differently based on their needs contributed to leadership effectiveness, such as producing good results.[34] An example of a unique relationship would be to give more recognition to a sales representative who craved recognition.

LEARNING OBJECTIVE 3

DEVELOPING YOUR LEADERSHIP POTENTIAL

Much of this book deals directly and indirectly with information that could improve your leadership effectiveness. Chapter 4, on communications, is a case in point. Improving your communications effectiveness would be one way to enhance your ability to lead people.

FIGURE 9-3 The Leader–Member Exchange Model

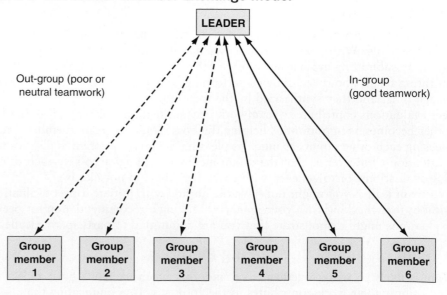

My Personal Leadership Journal

A potentially important assist in your development as a leader is to maintain a journal or diary of your leadership experiences. Make a journal entry within 24 hours after you have carried out a leadership action of any kind, or failed to do so when the opportunity arose. You will therefore have entries dealing with leadership opportunities both capitalized upon and missed. An example would be as follows: "A few of my neighbors were complaining about trash flying around the neighborhood on trash pick-up days, particularly when the wind was strong. I took the initiative to send e-mails and flyers to neighborhood residents discussing what could be done about the problem. I suggested that people pack their recycling boxes more tightly. I also suggested ever-so-politely that people should pick up their own flying trash. Soon the problem just about disappeared."

Also include in your journal such entries as feedback you receive on your leadership ability, leadership traits that you appear to be developing, and leadership ideas you learn about. Also, keep a list of leadership articles and books you intend to read. You might also want to record observations about significant acts of leadership or leadership blunders that you have observed in others, either firsthand or through the media.

Review your journal monthly, and make note of any progress you think you have made in developing your leadership skills. Also consider preparing a graph of your progress in developing leadership skills. The vertical axis can represent skill level on a 1–100 scale, and the horizontal axis might be divided into time intervals, such as calendar quarters.

SELF-ASSESSMENT QUIZZES IN OVERVIEW

Self-Assessment Quiz 9-1, The Assertiveness Scale, gave you an opportunity to measure your degree of assertiveness, a key personality trait that is important for leadership as well as many other interpersonal activities such as resolving conflict, volunteering for assignments, getting noticed by your manager, and finding companionship. Self-Assessment Quiz 9-2, What Style of Leader Are You or Would You Be?, takes you more specifically into the basics of leadership. For many situations it will be helpful to emphasize participative or team leadership because organizations have become more democratic. For example, imagine yourself as the supervisor of a credit and collection group. It would probably be to your advantage to ask the credit specialists in your group what they think would be a few good ways to collect more payments on time. Yet in crises, it may be more helpful to be more directive and tell people what to do without emphasizing group participation. For example, if you were the supervisor of credit and collections, the company might ask you to bring in some money fast to help fend off bankruptcy.

Formal education and leadership development programs also contribute to enhancing leadership potential. (Many such programs include some of the activities found in this chapter.) Here we describe six strategies for developing your leadership potential, in addition to studying and participating in formal programs.

Our approach to developing leadership potential is based on the assumption that leaders are both born and made.[35] You need some basic cognitive and personality characteristics to have the potential to be a leader, yet you need to develop these characteristics through experience and practice. A person who has good problem-solving ability and is charismatic, still needs to assume leadership responsibility and engage in certain actions to become an effective leader. Among these dozens of activities would be recognizing the accomplishments of others. Skill-Building Exercise 9-5, about maintaining a personal leadership journal, provides a start in practicing and refining leadership skills.

First-level supervisory jobs are an invaluable starting point for developing your leadership potential. It takes considerable skill to manage a rapid-service (fast-food) restaurant or direct a public playground during the summer. First-level supervisors frequently face situations in which group members are poorly trained, poorly paid, and not well motivated to achieve company objectives. Motivating and inspiring entry-level workers is one of the major challenges facing organizations. One of the lessons from the U.S. Marines is that if you want to fire up the frontline, you must use discipline to develop pride. The point is that entry-level workers often take pride in being able to abide by tough rules.[36]

1. **Acquire broad experience.** Because leadership varies somewhat with the situation, a sound approach to improving leadership effectiveness is to attempt to gain supervisory experience in different settings. A person who wants to become an

executive is well advised to gain supervisory experience in at least two different organizational functions, such as marketing and operations.

2. **Model effective leaders.** Another strategy for leadership development is to observe capable leaders in action and then model some of their approaches. You may not want to copy a particular leader entirely, but you can incorporate a few of the behavior patterns into your own leadership style. For instance, most inexperienced leaders have difficulty confronting others. Observe how a skilled confronter handles the situation, and try that person's approach the next time you have unfavorable news to communicate to another person.

3. **Self-develop leadership traits and behaviors.** Study the leadership traits and behaviors described earlier in this chapter. As a starting point, identify several attributes you think you could strengthen within yourself, given some determination and perhaps combined with the right training program. For example, you might decide that with some effort you could improve your sense of humor. You might also believe that you could remember to encourage honest criticism within the team. It is also helpful to obtain feedback from valid sources (such as a trusted manager) about which traits and behaviors you particularly need to develop.

4. **Become an integrated human being.** A philosophical approach to leadership suggests that the model leader is first and foremost a fully functioning person. According to William D. Hitt, mastering the art of leadership comes with self-mastery. Leadership development is the process of self-development. As a result, the process of becoming a leader is similar to the process of becoming an integrated human being. For example, you need to develop values that guide your behavior before you can adequately guide the behavior of others.

   The model (or ideal) leader, according to Hitt, must possess six character traits: identity (know thyself), independence, authenticity, responsibility, courage, and integrity.[37] A more recent analysis of leadership development suggests that self-understanding is a major vehicle for improvement. After attaining self-insight, you can move forward with leadership development.[38] Suppose you discover that you feel intimidated by people who are older and more experienced than you. Armed with this self-insight you can gradually overcome the problem and feel more comfortable leading workers who are older and more experienced than you. All of the traits Hitt mentions have everyday meanings, but they can also have personal meanings. Part of becoming an integrated person is to answer such questions as, "What do I mean when I say I have integrity?"

   Another approach to becoming an integrated human being, and therefore a more effective leader, is to figure out how you perceive the world. For example, if you perceive yourself as inferior to most people, you will forever be in competition with others to impress them. You will even compete rather than work collaboratively with team members.[39]

5. **Practice a little leadership.** An effective way to develop your leadership skills is to look for opportunities to exert a small amount of helpful leadership in contrast to waiting for opportunities to accomplish extraordinary deeds. The "little leadership" might involve such behaviors as mentoring a struggling team member, coaching somebody about how to use a new high-tech dSevice, or making a suggestion about improving a product. In the words of Michael E. McGill and John W. Slocum, Jr., "For those who want to stand atop the dugout, dance with the elephants, fly with the buffaloes, soar with eagles, or perform other mystical and heroic acts of large leadership, our little leadership may seem all too managerial, too modest, and too mundane."[40]

6. **Help your leader lead.** According to Michael Useem, leaders need your assistance so they can do a good job. "If people are afraid to help their leaders lead, their leaders will fail."[41] A group member is often closer to the market and closer to how the product is used. Therefore, he or she can provide useful information to the person in the formal leadership position. When you help the people above you avoid a mistake or capitalize upon an opportunity, you help the entire company. At the same time, you are developing your ability to take the initiative and lead.

Concept Review and Reinforcement

Key Terms

leadership, 177
assertiveness, 179
cognitive factors, 183

charisma, 185
participative leadership, 187

micromanager, 190
leader–member exchange model, 192

Summary of Key Concepts

Effective leadership depends on having the right personal characteristics and taking the appropriate actions. Leadership is the ability to inspire support and confidence among the people who are needed to achieve company goals. People can exercise leadership whether or not they occupy a formal leadership position.

Certain traits contribute heavily to leadership effectiveness. Among them are self-confidence, assertiveness, trustworthiness and morality, emotional stability, sense of humor, self-awareness and self-objectivity, cognitive skills and clarity, emotional intelligence, and passion and enthusiasm.

Possessing a naturally dynamic personality is a major contributor to charisma, but a person can engage in many tangible actions that contribute to charisma. Suggestions for behaving charismatically include the following:

1. Communicate a vision.
2. Make frequent use of metaphors and analogies.
3. Inspire trust and confidence.
4. Be highly energetic and goal oriented.
5. Be emotionally expressive and warm.
6. Make ample use of true stories.
7. Be candid and direct.
8. Make everyone you meet feel that he or she is important.
9. Multiply the effectiveness of your handshake.
10. Stand up straight and use other nonverbal signals of self-confidence.
11. Be willing to take personal risks.
12. Be self-promotional.

A team leader acts as a facilitator or coach who shares decision making with team members, thus practicing participative leadership. The following are some techniques for effective team leadership:

1. Build a mission statement.
2. Show your team members that they are trusted.
3. Establish a sense of urgency and high performance standards.
4. Hold question-and-answer sessions with the team.
5. Encourage team members to recognize each other's accomplishments.
6. Encourage honest criticism.
7. Use team symbols.
8. Use peer evaluations.
9. Help team members see the big picture.
10. Minimize formation of in-groups and out-groups.

In addition to participating in formal leadership-development programs, six strategies for developing leadership potential are to (1) acquire broad experience, (2) model effective leaders, (3) self-develop leadership traits and behaviors, (4) become an integrated human being (a fully functioning person), (5) practice a little leadership, and (6) help your leader lead.

Check Your Understanding

1. Informal observation suggests that people who were voted "most likely to succeed" in high school are frequently found in leadership positions later in life. What explanation can you offer for these predictions about success so often being true?

2. What is your reaction to Rudy Giuliani's statement that the leader should tell people what is right, rather than the people telling him or her what is right and then the leader telling them what they want to hear?

3. What does it mean to say that a person has the "right stuff" for being a leader?

4. How can a person demonstrate to others in the company that he or she is trustworthy enough to be considered for a leadership position?

5. Why does a leader need good emotional intelligence? Shouldn't a leader be a take-charge person focused on obtaining results like making money or winning ball games?

6. What does the term *self-objectivity* mean to you, and why is it important for leadership?

7. What can you do this week to increase your charisma?

8. What kind of *clarity* could your instructor provide for you in his or her role as the leader of this course?

9. In what ways do the concepts of charismatic leadership and participative leadership differ substantially from each other?

10. Assume that a student obtains a part-time job as an assistant store manager. What can this person do to capitalize on this position for leadership experience?

The Web Corner

http://www.ccl.org
(Center for Creative Leadership.)

http://www.core-edge.com
(Attaining power and charisma.)

http://www.SelfGrowth.com
(Developing your charisma.)

Internet Skill Builder: Developing Your Charisma

You have already received in this chapter suggestions for developing your charisma. Visit http://www.core-edge.com to search for additional ideas for charisma development. Go to the section on *charismatology*, and read a couple of the case histories to uncover ideas you might try to enhance your charisma. After digging through core-edge.com, list two concrete ideas you might implement to enhance your charisma.

Developing Your Human Relations Skills

Interpersonal Relations Case 9.1

Jim Press Wants to Steer Chrysler in the Right Direction

His hiring from Toyota Motor Corp. rocked the auto industry, but James Press didn't join Chrysler LLC to be its savior. Instead, the 60-year-old veteran had a pretty simple view of his role as vice chairman and chief product strategist for Chrysler: "My role is to be the voice of the consumer and to represent the needs of the dealers in the marketplace," he said. "That's my passion."

Press's departure after 37 years with Toyota was one of the most dramatic personnel moves in the recent history of Detroit's Big Three automakers. As Toyota's top North American executive, Press enjoyed a stellar reputation as perhaps the savviest sales and marketing executive in the business. Next, he turned his talents to reviving the product lineup and invigorating sales at Chrysler, which had recently been acquired by the investment group Cerberus Capital Management.

In one of his first interviews since joining Chrysler, Press said he saw great opportunities and some challenges in the automaker's product portfolio. "There are some products that may go away, and there are probably some products that we need to add," he said. "We need a more strategic product portfolio going forward that is customer-driven."

Press's role in the new management team at Chrysler was to take a hard look at Chrysler's place in the brutally competitive U.S. market. He saw Chrysler as a company with strong heritage, capable people, and a chance for quick improvement.

He gave other executives a taste of his vision during a product review of the new Jeep Grand Cherokee. As members of the executive product committee looked on, Press meticulously critiqued the design of the SUV, all the way down to the placement of its cup holders. Afterward, chief executive Bob Nardelli said, "That's why we hired him."

Chrysler dealers welcomed Press into the fold, but were realistic about his ability to improve sales in the short term. "Jim is a great listener and knows the business," said Martin "Hoot" McInerney, a longtime Chrysler and Toyota dealer. "But all the Jim Presses in the world won't help if you don't have a good product."

The president of an automobile consulting firm said about Press, "The dealers loved him. He is very approachable, and very smart. He asks good questions and he's very engaged with the product."

Over time, Press said that he will push to empower engineers and designers to have freedom of expression and more influence on products, and give dealers a bigger say in Chrysler's overall direction. "I brought no Toyota secrets along with me," said Press. "But the company I came from definitely proves the strength of bottom-up management."

Case Questions

1. What leadership qualities and traits does Press appear to demonstrate?
2. What does the cup holder incident tell you about Press's approach to leadership?
3. To what extent does Press appear to believe in participative leadership and empowerment?
4. How trustworthy can Press be if he would jump ship from Toyota to work for a rival?
5. What suggestions can you offer James Press to help him move Chrysler forward?

Source: Bill Vlasic, "Chrysler Executive Sees Vehicle Tuneup," *Detroit News* (detnews.com), October 2, 2007.

Interpersonal Relations Case 9.2

So Is This How You Learn Leadership?

Len Olsen, age 23, was proud to be selected as part of the leader's program at a national chain of family restaurants. Workers selected for the leadership program are considered to be in line for running individual restaurants and as potential candidates in the long run for leadership positions in corporate headquarters. Before entering the key phase of the leadership program, all candidates must first work a minimum of one year as a server or bartender at one of the company stores (restaurants).

Olsen worked one year as a server in a downtown Chicago restaurant, and then was assigned to another Chicago restaurant to begin his formal leadership training as an assistant manager. Olsen's assignments as an assistant manager included scheduling the wait staff, conducting preliminary screen interviews of job applicants, and resolving problems with customers. After three months on the job, Olsen was asked by a member of the corporate human resources staff how his leadership training program was going. Olsen replied, "I'm a little bit skeptical. I don't think I'm learning much about leadership."

When asked why he didn't think he was learning much about leadership, Olsen listed what he considered three recent examples of the type of responsibilities he faced regularly:

- "At 11 yesterday morning, I received a phone call from Annie, one of the servers. She told me she wouldn't be to work that afternoon because her Labrador retriever had become quite ill and she had to take the Lab to the vet. I told Annie that we desperately needed her that afternoon because of a large luncheon party. Annie told me her dog was more important to her than the job."

- "Two weeks ago, Gus, one of our salad chefs, showed up to work absolutely drunk. I told him that working while drunk was absolutely against company rules. He got a little belligerent, but I did get him to take a taxi home at company expense."

- "Two days ago a customer in the restaurant spilled a cup of hot coffee on herself while answering a call on her cell phone. She told me that the coffee was too hot and that she was going to sue the restaurant. I explained to her tactfully that unless she was truly burned, she had no claim. I offered to have the restaurant pay for her dry cleaning, and then she calmed down."

Olsen then said to the human resources manager, "What has stuff like this got to do with leadership? I mean, I'm not creating great visions or inspiring hordes of people. In what way am I becoming a leader?"

Case Questions

1. What is your opinion of the contribution of Olsen's representative experiences to his development as a leader?
2. What else can the restaurant chain do to help Olsen, and others in the leadership program, develop as leaders?

CHAPTER 10

Motivating Others

The Commercial Division of the Toro Company supplies mowing, utility, and turf cultivation products to domestic and international golf courses. For many years, Toro has engaged Maritz Travel to design and execute group travel incentive programs as part of their commitment to superior customer care, and recognition of their top sales performers. Over the past 10 years, Toro distributor teams have competed for the chance to win luxury trips to destinations ranging from Munich to Australia to Kauai.

In addition to reaching sales goals, top performers demonstrated improved product knowledge and customer satisfaction scores. Still, in reviewing overall costs, senior management raised questions about the impact of the travel incentive programs, wondering if the dollars spent were cost-effective. Toro engaged a third-party researcher to evaluate the effects that the Maritz travel programs had on their business. The research compared the growth of the Commercial Division over 11 years, including both promotional and non-promotional years. (A promotion year is one in which the luxury trip incentives were available.)

The research clearly showed the positive impact of the group travel incentive programs: (1) Sales growth averaged 19% in promotion years versus 12% in non-promotion years. (2) Increased gross profits (after program costs) amounted to millions of dollars over the 10-year period. (3) Winning distributors tended to have high customer satisfaction scores.[1]

The case history about Toro demonstrates that by rewarding workers for good performance, they will often increase their performance. You may not be in a position to offer a trip to Australia to a coworker who does what you want, but the principle of being systematic about motivating others remains the same. **Motivation** has two meanings: (1) an internal state that

After reading and studying this chapter and doing the exercises, you should be able to

1. Motivate people by responding to their self-interests.
2. Make effective use of positive reinforcement to motivate people in many situations.
3. Make effective use of recognition to motivate others.
4. Apply expectancy theory as a comprehensive way of motivating others.
5. Diagnose situations to analyze the strength of motivation present.

leads to effort expended toward objectives, and (2) an activity performed by one person to get another to accomplish work. We often think of a manager or leader as the one attempting to motivate group members. Yet many people in the workplace have a need to motivate others. To accomplish their work, people must motivate individuals who report to them, coworkers, supervisors, or customers. Developing motivational skills will therefore help you accomplish more work than you would if you relied strictly on the good nature and team spirit of others.

This chapter describes how to develop motivational skills based on four related explanations of motivation. We progress from the simplest to the most complex explanation. As a starting point in thinking through how to motivate others, do Self-Assessment Quiz 10-1.

motivation

An internal state that leads to effort expended toward objectives; an activity performed by one person to get another to accomplish work.

SELF-ASSESSMENT QUIZ 10-1

My Approach to Motivating Others

Directions: Describe how often you act or think in the way indicated by the following statements when you are attempting to motivate another person. Circle the appropriate number for each statement using the following scale: Very infrequently (VI); Infrequently (I); Sometimes (S); Frequently (F); Very frequently (VF).

	VI	I	S	F	VF
1. I ask the other person what he or she is hoping to achieve in the situation.	1	2	3	4	5
2. I attempt to figure out whether the person has the ability to do what I need done.	1	2	3	4	5
3. When another person is heel-dragging, it usually means he or she is lazy.	5	4	3	2	1
4. I explain exactly what I want to the person I'm trying to motivate.	1	2	3	4	5

(Continued)

5. I like to give the other person a reward up front so he or she will be motivated.	5	4	3	2	1
6. I give lots of feedback when another person is performing a task for me.	1	2	3	4	5
7. I like to belittle another person enough so that he or she will be intimidated into doing what I need done.	5	4	3	2	1
8. I make sure that the other person feels treated fairly.	1	2	3	4	5
9. I figure that if I smile nicely I can get the other person to work as hard as I need.	5	4	3	2	1
10. I attempt to get what I need done by instilling fear in the other person.	5	4	3	2	1
11. I specify exactly what needs to be accomplished.	1	2	3	4	5
12. I generously praise people who help me get my work accomplished.	1	2	3	4	5
13. A job well done is its own reward. I therefore keep praise to a minimum.	5	4	3	2	1
14. I make sure I let people know how well they have done in meeting my expectations on a task.	1	2	3	4	5
15. To be fair, I attempt to reward people similarly no matter how well they have performed.	5	4	3	2	1
16. When somebody doing work for me performs well, I recognize his or her accomplishments promptly.	1	2	3	4	5
17. Before giving somebody a reward, I attempt to find out what would appeal to that person.	1	2	3	4	5
18. I make it a policy not to thank somebody for doing a job he or she is paid to do.	5	4	3	2	1
19. If people do not know how to perform a task, motivation will suffer.	1	2	3	4	5
20. If properly laid out, many jobs can be self-rewarding.	1	2	3	4	5

Total Score _____

Scoring and Interpretation: Add the circled numbers to obtain your total score.

90–100 You have advanced knowledge and skill with respect to motivating others in a work environment. Continue to build on the solid base you have established.

50–89 You have average knowledge and skill with respect to motivating others. With additional study and experience, you will probably develop advanced motivational skills.

20–49 To effectively motivate others in a work environment, you will need to greatly expand your knowledge of motivation theory and techniques.

Source: The idea for this quiz, and a few items, are from David A. Whetton and Kim S. Cameron, *Developing Management Skills,* 5th ed. (Upper Saddle River, NJ: Prentice Hall, 2002), pp. 302–303.

LEARNING OBJECTIVE 1

MOTIVATION SKILL BASED ON THE PRINCIPLE OF "WHAT'S IN IT FOR ME?"

The most fundamental principle of human motivation is that people are motivated by self-interest. This principle is referred to as "What's in it for me?" or WIIFM (pronounced wiff'em). Reflect on your own experience. Before working hard to accomplish a task, you probably want to know how you will benefit. If your manager asks you to work extra hours to take care of an emergency, you will most likely oblige. Yet underneath you might be thinking, "If I work these extra hours, my boss will think highly of me. As a result, I will probably receive a good performance evaluation and maybe a better-than-average salary increase."

If your instructor asks you to prepare a lengthy research paper, you might be motivated to work to the best of your ability. But before getting down to the task, it is likely that questions have raced through your mind, such as, "Will this paper elevate my grade?" or, "Will I pick up information that will help me in my career?"

A perplexing issue is how the WIIFM principle explains why people are motivated to help others. Why would a company CEO donate gift baskets of food to homeless people? Why hire a virtually unemployable person for a nonproductive job in the mailroom? People who perform acts of social good receive the reward of feeling better about themselves. In psychological terms, they satisfy their needs to nurture (take care of) others. More cynically, helping those less fortunate leads to recognition for being a Good Samaritan.

To use the WIIFM principle in motivating others, you have to be aware of the intensity of the person's desire.[2] A person can be highly motivated, mildly motivated, or only slightly motivated, depending on the intensity of his or her WIIFM principle. A company might offer outstanding performers the opportunity to work at home one day per week. Employees who are intensely motivated to work at home will work virtually up to capacity to achieve a rating of outstanding performer.

Applying the WIIFM principle irequires you to find out what needs, desires, or motives a person is attempting to satisfy. A need acts as an internal energy force. In simple language, responding to the needs of people is referred to as touching their hot buttons. You find out what these needs are by asking people what they want or by observing what interests them. For instance, the way a manager might motivate a recognition-hungry group member is to tell that person, "If you perform 10 percent above quota for six consecutive months, we will get you a plaque signifying your achievement to hang on the wall."

One of the reasons needs are so important in understanding motivation is that needs lead to behavior, or what people actually do. A person might be extraverted because of a need to affiliate with others, so that person might be motivated by the opportunity to work closely with others. Another person might be conscientious partly because of a need for achievement. This individual might be motivated by the opportunity to accomplish useful work.[3]

Employee needs have been classified in many ways, yet most of these lists overlap. According to a representative classification, 99 percent of employees are motivated by one or more of the following seven needs:

1. **The need for achievement.** Employees with strong achievement needs seek the satisfaction of completing projects successfully. They want to apply their talents to attain success, and they find joy in accomplishment for its own sake.

2. **The need for power.** Employees with a strong power need derive satisfaction from influencing and controlling others, and they aspire to become executives. These employees like to lead and persuade and be in charge of resources such as budgets.

3. **The need for affiliation.** Employees with a strong need for affiliation derive satisfaction from interacting with others, being part of a work group, and forming friendships. The same employees are motivated to avoid working alone for long periods of time.

4. **The need for autonomy.** Employees with a strong need for autonomy seek freedom and independence, such as having almost complete responsibility for a project. The same employees are motivated to avoid working in a team effort for long periods of time. Many industrial sales representatives (those who sell to companies) have a strong need for autonomy.

5. **The need for esteem.** Employees with a strong need for esteem want to feel good about themselves, and they judge their worth largely based on how much recognition and praise they receive.

6. **The need for safety and security.** Employees with strong needs for safety and security seek job security, steady income, ample medical and dental insurance, and a hazard-free work environment.

7. **The need for equity.** Employees with a strong need for equity seek fair treatment. They often compare working hours, job responsibilities, salary, and privileges to those of coworkers, and they will become discouraged if coworkers are receiving better treatment.[4]

Recognizing such needs, as well as other needs and interests, helps you apply the WIIFM principle. Skill-Building Exercise 10-1 gives you the opportunity to do the preliminary work needed for applying the WIIFM principle.

LEARNING OBJECTIVE 2

USING POSITIVE REINFORCEMENT TO MOTIVATE OTHERS

behavior modification

An attempt to change behavior by manipulating rewards and punishments.

law of effect

Behavior that leads to a positive consequence for the individual tends to be repeated, whereas behavior that leads to a negative consequence tends not to be repeated.

positive reinforcement

Increasing the probability that behavior will be repeated by rewarding people for making the desired response.

The most widely used formal method of motivating people in the workplace is **behavior modification,** an attempt to change behavior by manipulating rewards and punishments. Behavior modification is based on a fundamental principle of human behavior: the law of effect. According to the **law of effect,** behavior that leads to a positive consequence for the individual tends to be repeated, whereas behavior that leads to a negative consequence tends not to be repeated.

The focus of behavior modification on the job is to reward employees for behaving in ways that support what the organization is attempting to accomplish, such as improved productivity. Our approach to skill development in behavior modification is to emphasize positive reinforcement because this is the modification strategy most widely used in the workplace. **Positive reinforcement** means increasing the probability that behavior will be repeated by rewarding people for making the desired response. The phrase *increasing the probability* means that positive reinforcement improves learning and motivation, but is not 100 percent effective. The phrase *making the desired response* is also noteworthy. To use positive reinforcement properly, a reward must be contingent upon doing something right. Simply paying somebody a compliment or giving the person something of value is not positive reinforcement. Behavior modification involves linking consequences to what the person has or has not accomplished.

Positive reinforcement is easy to visualize with well-structured jobs such as data entry or producing parts. Yet positive reinforcement is also used to encourage desired behavior in highly paid, complex jobs. An accountant who developed a new method for the company getting paid faster might be rewarded with two extra days of vacation.

Negative reinforcement (or **avoidance motivation**) means rewarding people by taking away an uncomfortable consequence of their behavior. Negative reinforcement is a reward because a disliked consequence is avoided or withdrawn. You are subject to negative reinforcement when you are told, "Your insurance rate will go down if you receive no traffic violations for 12 months." The uncomfortable consequence removed is a high insurance premium. Removing the undesirable consequence is contingent upon your making the right response—driving within the law.

negative reinforcement (avoidance motivation)

Rewarding people by taking away an uncomfortable consequence of their behavior.

Be careful not to make the common mistake of confusing negative reinforcement with punishment. Negative reinforcement is the opposite of punishment. It involves rewarding someone by removing a punishment or uncomfortable situation.

To use positive reinforcement effectively, certain rules and procedures must be followed, as outlined in Figure 10-1. Although using rewards to motivate people seems straightforward, behavior modification requires a systematic approach. The rules are specified from the standpoint of the person trying to motivate another individual, such as a group member, coworker, supervisor, or customer.

Rule 1: State Clearly What Behavior Will Lead to a Reward. The nature of good performance, or the goals, must be agreed upon by the manager and group member. Clarification might take this form: "We need to decrease by 40 percent the number of new credit card customers who have delinquent accounts of 60 days or more."

Rule 2: Choose an Appropriate Reward. An appropriate reward is effective in motivating a given person and feasible from the standpoint of the individual or the company. If one reward does not motivate the person, try another. The importance of choosing the right reward underscores the fact that not all rewards are reinforcers. A reward is something of perceived value by the person giving the reward. However, if the reward does not lead to strengthening a desired response (such as wearing safety goggles), it is not a true reinforcer.[5]

Figure 10-2 lists the factors that employees indicated would satisfy them on the job. At the same time, these factors can be translated into potential rewards for employees. For example, if employees value bonuses, a high-performing employee might be given some assurance of receiving a bonus for above-average employment. Because all of these factors are ranked as *important* job factors by employees, all of them are potentially appropriate rewards.

Rule 3: Supply Ample Feedback. Positive reinforcement cannot work without frequent feedback to individuals. Feedback can take the form of simply telling people they have done something right or wrong. Brief e-mail messages or handwritten notes are other forms of feedback. Many effective motivators, including Jack Welch, the legendary former CEO of General Electric, made extensive use of handwritten thank-you notes. Negative feedback by e-mail should be written tactfully to avoid resentment.

> " The real opportunity for growth comes in utilizing your strengths. Great managers catch people doing the right things. "
> —Curt Coffman of the Gallup Organization

FIGURE 10-1 Rules and Procedures for Positive Reinforcement

1. State clearly what behavior will lead to a reward.
2. Choose an appropriate reward.
3. Supply ample feedback.
4. Schedule rewards intermittently.
5. Make the reward follow the observed behavior closely in time.
6. Make the reward fit the behavior.
7. Make the reward visible.
8. Change the reward periodically.
9. Reward the group or team also.

FIGURE 10-2 What Workers Want from Their Jobs and Their Employers

1. Competitive salary
2. 100 percent of health care coverage paid by employers
3. Company-matched 401(k) investments
4. Bonus programs
5. Flexible schedules
6. Compressed workweek
7. Good relationship with the boss
8. Being treated with respect

Note: Although only factors 1, 2, and 3 are in rank order, factors 4 through 8 are also considered important for job satisfaction.

Source: Table prepared from survey of 1,051 workers presented in "Listen up Employers: Employees Know What They Want This Labor Day," http://www.kronos.com, August 2, 2006, p. 1. The survey was conducted by Harris Interactive® and sponsored by Kronos® Incorporated.

intermittent rewards

Rewards given for good performance occasionally, but not always.

Rule 4: Schedule Rewards Intermittently. Rewards should not be given on every occasion of good performance. **Intermittent rewards** sustain desired behaviors longer and slow down the process of behaviors fading away when they are not rewarded. If each correct performance results in a reward, the behavior will stop shortly after a performance in which the reward is not received. Another problem is that a reward given continuously may lose its impact. Also, automatic rewards for doing the right thing become perceived as entitlements. As the reward becomes almost guaranteed, the employee feels entitled to it, and the reward loses its motivational effectiveness, much like a weekly paycheck. A practical value of intermittent reinforcement is that it saves time. Few managers or team leaders have enough time to dispense rewards for every correct action by group members.

Rule 5: Make the Reward Follow the Observed Behavior Closely in Time. For maximum effectiveness, people should be rewarded soon after doing something right. A built-in, or intrinsic, feedback system, such as software working or not working, capitalizes on this principle. If you are administering rewards and punishments, strive to administer them the same day they are earned. Suppose a coworker feeds you exactly the information you need to make a PowerPoint presentation for the group. Send your coworker an e-mail or text message of appreciation that very day. Or, be old-fashioned and thank him or her in person.

Rule 6: Make the Reward Fit the Behavior. People who are inexperienced in applying positive reinforcement often overdo the intensity of spoken rewards. When an employee does something of an ordinary nature correctly, simple praise such as "Good job" is preferable to "Fantastic performance." A related idea is that the magnitude of the reward should vary with the magnitude of the accomplishment.

Rule 7: Make the Reward Visible. Another important characteristic of an effective reward is the extent to which it is visible, or noticeable, to other employees. When other workers notice the reward, its impact multiplies because other people observe what kind of behavior is rewarded.[6] Assume that you are being informed about a coworker having received an exciting assignment because of high performance. You might strive to accomplish the same level of performance. Rewards should also be visible, or noticeable, to the employee. A reward of $10 per week added to a person's paycheck might be hardly noticeable, after payroll deductions. However, a bonus check for $300 might be very noticeable.

Rule 8: Change the Reward Periodically. Rewards do not retain their effectiveness indefinitely. Employees and customers lose interest in striving for a reward they have received many times in the past. This is particularly true of a repetitive statement such as "Nice job" or "Congratulations." It is helpful for the person giving out the rewards to study the list of potential rewards and try different ones from time to time. A general approach relating to the previous rules is to look for creative ways to apply behavior modification. The creativity might be in the selection of the reward, or how the reward is administered. Several illustrative ideas include:

- *Applause*: Choose an especially effective employee, and at the end of the week or month have coworkers gather and clap for the person.
- *Giraffe award*: Give a certificate saying, "Thanks for sticking your neck out." The name of the reward and the certificate reward risk taking.
- *Safety jackpot*: Managers give five "lottery" cards to employees who follow safety practices. Workers scratch off the cards to learn how many points they have won. Points are then redeemed via a gift catalog or Web site.[7]

Rule 9: Reward the Group or Team Also. Positive reinforcement applies to groups as well as individuals in the sense that individuals within the group can be rewarded collectively. An obvious rule is that the group should receive a reward commensurate with its accomplishment. However, several of the other eight rules also apply. An example of a team reward is to implement a "Team of the Month" program.[8]

Perform Skill-Building Exercise 10-2 to practice several of these rules for using positive reinforcement.

USING RECOGNITION TO MOTIVATE OTHERS

LEARNING OBJECTIVE 3

Motivating others by giving them recognition and praise can be considered a direct application of positive reinforcement. Nevertheless, recognition is such a potentially powerful motivator that it merits separate attention. Also, recognition programs to reward and motivate employees are standard practice in business and nonprofit firms. Examples would be rewarding high-performing employees with a crystal vase (company logo inscribed) or designating them "employee of the month." Outstanding Mary Kay sales representatives ("beauty consultants") receive recognition and rewards in the form of pink cell phones, pink Buicks, and pink Cadillacs—in the United States, as well as in China and other countries.[9] The pink, however, is just a tinge of pink to give it a modern look. In keeping with the theme of this book, the emphasis is on individual, rather than organizational, use of recognition to motivate.

Recognition is a strong motivator because it is a normal human need to crave recognition. At the same time, recognition is effective because most workers feel they do not receive enough notice. Several studies conducted over a 50-year time span have indicated that employees welcome praise for a job well done as much as a regular pay-

check. Furthermore, according to one estimate, 79 percent of employees who quit their job point to lack of appreciation as a key factor for leaving. This finding should not be interpreted to mean that praise is an adequate substitute for salary. Employees tend to regard compensation as an entitlement, whereas recognition is perceived as a gift.[10] Workers, including your coworkers, want to know that their output is useful to somebody. To appeal to the recognition need of others, identify a meritorious behavior and then recognize that behavior with an oral, written, or material reward. E-mail, instant messaging, and text messaging are useful vehicles for providing quick recognition when in-person appreciation is not feasible. Also, sometimes people like to print a copy of the recognition they receive. The rules for the use of positive reinforcement are directly applicable. An additional suggestion relates closely to making rewards visible: Time your praise for when it will do the most good. Praise delivered during a staff meeting, for example, can be a potent form of recognition.[11] The recognition award should help the employee feel appreciated for having made a contribution. The economic value of the award, such as engraved metal bowl, is much less important.

Some specific examples of using recognition to sustain desired behavior (a key aspect of motivation) follow:

- A coworker shows you how to more effectively perform an important task on the Internet. Three days later, you send her an e-mail message with a copy to the boss: "Hi, Jessica. Your suggestion about copying company logos was dynamite. I've used it five times with success since you showed me what to do." (You are reinforcing Jessica's helpful and cooperative behavior.)

- As the team leader, you receive a glowing letter from a customer about how Kent, one of your team members, solved his or her problem. You have the letter laminated and present it as a gift to Kent. (The behavior you are reinforcing is good customer service.)

- One member of your department, Jason, is a mechanical engineer. While at a department lunch taking place during National Engineers Week, you stand up and say, "I want to toast Jason in celebration of National Engineers Week. I certainly wouldn't want to be sitting in this office building today if a mechanical engineer hadn't assisted in its construction." (Here the only behavior you are reinforcing is the goodwill of Jason, so your motivational approach is general rather than specific.)

As you might have inferred from the examples presented, statements of recognition tend to be more effective when they are expressed in specific, rather than general, terms. "You're doing a great job" is an example of a general recognition statement. Here are a few more specific recognition statements:

"You really made a difference by . . ."
"You're right on the mark with . . ."
"We couldn't have done it without your . . ."[12]

An outstanding advantage of recognition, including praise, as a motivator is that it is no cost or low cost, yet powerful. Recognition thus provides an enormous return on investment in comparison to a cash bonus. A challenge in using recognition effectively is that not everyone responds well to the same form of recognition. A good example is that highly technical people tend not to like general praise such as "Great job" or "Awesome." Instead, they prefer a laid-back, factual statement of how their output made a contribution. Furthermore, women are slightly more responsive to praise than are men, as revealed in a study of working adults.[13]

Giving recognition to others as a motivational tactic is more likely to be effective if a culture of recognition exists within the company. This is true because the person giving the recognition will feel that what he or she is doing fits what top management thinks is appropriate behavior. At the same time, the recipient of the recognition is likely to take it seriously.

USING EXPECTANCY THEORY TO MOTIVATE OTHERS

LEARNING OBJECTIVE 4

So far, we have described motivating others through applying the principle of WIIFM and behavior modification, including recognition. We now shift to expectancy theory, a more comprehensive explanation of motivation that includes elements of the two other approaches. Expectancy theory is given special attention here for these reasons. First, expectancy theory can help you diagnose motivational problems. Second, it is comprehensive because it incorporates many different aspects of motivating others. Third, it gives the person attempting to motivate others many guidelines for triggering and sustaining constructive effort from group members.

Capsule Overview of Expectancy Theory

The **expectancy theory** of motivation is based on the premise that how much effort people expend depends on the reward they expect to receive in return. (Notice the similarity to WIIFM?) Expectancy theory assumes that people are rational and logical, and the process resembles rational gambling. In any given situation, they want to maximize gain and minimize loss. The theory assumes that people choose among alternatives by selecting the one they think they have the best chance of attaining. Furthermore, they choose the alternative that appears to have the biggest personal payoff. How intensely they want that alternative is also an important consideration. Given a choice, people select an assignment they think they can handle and that will benefit them the most.

An example will help clarify the central thesis of expectancy theory. Hector, a 27-year-old credit analyst at a machine tool company, recognizes that he needs to increase his income by about $500 per month to cover his expenses. After carefully reviewing his options, Hector narrows his alternatives to the following three choices:

1. Work as a dining-room server one night a week and on most weekends, with a variable income of somewhere between $600 and $850 per month.
2. Work for an income tax preparation service about four months per year for 20 hours per week, yielding an annual income of about $7,000.
3. Work extra hard at his regular job, including taking a course in corporate finance, to improve his chances of receiving a promotion and a salary increase of $700 per month.

Hector rejects the first choice. Although he knows he can do the work, he anticipates several negative outcomes. He would much prefer to engage in extra work related to his field of expertise. The unpredictable income associated with being a dining-room server is also a concern. Hector sees merit in the second alternative because income tax preparation work relates to his accounting background. Furthermore, the outcome (amount of pay) is relatively certain. But Hector also has some concerns that working so many extra hours for four months a year could hurt his performance on his day job.

Hector decides to take a chance with the third alternative of going all out to position himself for promotion. He is confident he can elevate his performance, but he is much less certain that hard work will lead to promotion. Yet Hector attaches such high value to being promoted and upgrading his professional credentials that he is willing to gamble.

Basic Components of Expectancy Theory

All versions of expectancy theory have the following three major components: effort-to-performance expectancy, performance-to-outcome expectancy, and valence.[14] Figure 10-3 presents a glimpse of expectancy theory.

Effort-to-Performance Expectancy. **Effort-to-performance expectancy** is the probability assigned by the individual that effort will lead to performing the task correctly. An important question rational people ask themselves before putting forth effort to accomplish a task is this: "If I put in all this work, will I really get the job done properly?" Each behavior is associated in the individual's mind with a certain expectancy, or subjective hunch of the probability of success.

expectancy theory

A motivation theory based on the premise that the effort people expend depends on the reward they expect to receive in return.

effort-to-performance expectancy

The probability assigned by the individual that effort will lead to performing the task correctly.

FIGURE 10-3 A Basic Version of Expectancy Theory

Person will be motivated under these conditions
$\Big\{$
A. Effort-to-performance expectancy is high: Person believes he or she can perform the task.
B. Performance-to-outcome expectancy is high: Person believes that performance will lead to certain outcomes.
C. Valence is high: Person highly values the outcomes.

Expectancies range from 0 to 1.0. The expectancy would be 0 if the person thought that there was no chance of performing the task correctly. An expectancy of 1.0 would signify absolute faith in being able to perform the task properly. Expectancies thus influence whether you will even strive to earn a reward. Self-confident people have higher expectancies than do those with low self-confidence. Being well trained will also increase your subjective hunch that you can perform the task.

The importance of having high expectancies for motivation meshes well with a thrust in work motivation that emphasizes the contribution of **self-efficacy**, the confidence in your ability to carry out a specific task. If you have high self-efficacy about the task, your motivation will be high. Low self-efficacy leads to low motivation.[15] Some people are poorly motivated to skydive because they doubt they will be able to pull the ripcord while free-falling at 120 mph.

self-efficacy

The confidence in your ability to carry out a specific task.

performance-to-outcome expectancy

The probability assigned by the individual that performance will lead to outcomes or rewards.

Performance-to-Outcome Expectancy. **Performance-to-outcome expectancy** is the probability assigned by the individual that performance will lead to certain outcomes or rewards. When people engage in a particular behavior, they do so with the intention of achieving a desired outcome or reward. Performance-to-outcome expectancies also range from 0 to 1.0. If you believe there is no chance of receiving the desired reward, the assigned probability is 0. If you believe the reward is certain to follow from performing correctly, the assigned probability is 1.0; for example: "I know for sure that if I show up for work every day this month, I will receive my paycheck."

valence

The value, worth, or attractiveness of an outcome.

Valence. A **valence** is the value, worth, or attractiveness of an outcome. It signifies how intensely you want something (as described in WIIFM). In each work situation there are multiple outcomes, each with a valence of its own. Remember Hector, the credit analyst? The potential outcomes of working part time as an income tax preparer would include extra income, new experience, and interference with his day job.

In the version of expectancy theory presented here, valences range from -100 to $+100$. A valence of $+100$ means that you desire an outcome strongly. A valence of -100 means that you are strongly motivated to avoid an outcome, such as being fired. A valence of 0 means that you are indifferent toward an outcome, and it is therefore no use as a motivator. An outcome with a probable valence of 0 would be as follows: To gain the cooperation of coworkers, you promise them gold stars as a reward (or outcome).

Skill-Building Exercise 10-3 will help sensitize you to the importance of estimating valences when attempting to motivate others. A major problem faced by managers and others who attempt to motivate others is that they have limited knowledge about the valences of their motivators (or rewards).

How Moods Influence Expectancy Theory

Expectancy theory emphasizes the rational side of people, yet emotions still play a key role in determining the impact of expectancies, instrumentalities, and valences. Moods are relatively long-lasting emotional states that do not appear tied to a clear source of the emotion. For example, a person might be in a good mood despite experiencing

Estimating Valences for Applying Expectancy Theory

Directions: Listed here are rewards and punishments (outcomes) stemming from job scenarios. Also included is a space for rating the reward or punishment on a scale of −100 to +100. Work with about six teammates, with each person rating all the rewards and punishments. Compute the mean (average) rating for each reward and punishment.

Potential Outcome	Rating (−100 to +100)
1. A 20-percent salary increase	_____
2. Profit-sharing plan in successful company	_____
3. Stock ownership in company	_____
4. Fully paid three-day leave	_____
5. A $8,000 performance bonus	_____
6. A $400 gift certificate	_____
7. Outstanding performance review	_____
8. Above-average performance review	_____
9. One-step promotion	_____
10. Two-step promotion	_____
11. Flexible working hours	_____
12. Chance to work at home one day per week	_____
13. Chance to do more of preferred task	_____
14. Take over for supervisor when supervisor is away	_____
15. Fancy job title without change in pay	_____
16. Bigger cubicle	_____
17. Private office	_____
18. Company-paid cell phone	_____
19. Wall plaque indicating accomplishment	_____
20. Employee-of-the-month designation	_____
21. Warm smile and word of appreciation	_____
22. Compliment in front of others	_____
23. Threat of being suspended for a month	_____
24. One-month suspension without pay	_____
25. Demotion to undesirable job	_____
26. Being fired	_____
27. Being fired combined with promise of negative references	_____
28. Being placed on probation	_____
29. Being ridiculed in front of others	_____
30. A 30-percent pay reduction	_____

After completing the ratings, discuss the following topics:

1. Which outcomes received the most variable ratings?
2. Which outcomes received the most similar ratings?
3. Which are the three most desirable rewards?
4. Which are the three most undesirable punishments?

Another analytical approach would be to compute the class mean for all 30 outcomes. Each student could then compare his or her rating with the class average.

To apply this technique to the job, modify the preceding outcomes to fit the outcomes available in your work situation. Explain to team members that you are attempting to do a better job of rewarding and disciplining and that you need their input. The ratings made by team members will give strong clues to which rewards and punishments would be the most effective in motivating them.

a negative situation such as an automobile breaking down. Also, people may feel glum despite good news such as having won a prize.

Several studies have shown that moods shape people's perceptions of expectancies and valence in expectancy theory. A positive mood increases the perceived connection between effort and performance (E → P expectancy), between performance and desired outcome (P → O expectancy), and in the valence attached to those outcomes. When we are in a good mood, we are more likely to believe that we can accomplish a task, so we have more of a "can do" attitude. We are also more optimistic about the outcomes (rewards) of our effort, and the outcomes look even better to us.[16] The opposite might also be true—when we are in a bad mood we feel less capable of task accomplishment, we are more pessimistic about getting the reward, and the reward appears less enticing.

Diagnosing Motivation with Expectancy Theory

LEARNING OBJECTIVE 5

An important potential contribution of expectancy theory to interpersonal relations is that it helps a person diagnose whether motivation is present and the intensity of the motivation. In performing your diagnosis, seek answers to the following questions:

1. Does the person I am attempting to motivate have the skills and self-efficacy to do the job? If the person feels ill-equipped to perform, he or she will be discouraged and show very little motivation.

2. What assurance does the person have that if he or she performs the work, the promised reward will be forthcoming? Does the company have a decent reputation

for following through on promises? What about me? Have I established my credibility as a person who follows through on promises? (If you or the company is not trusted, motivation could be reduced to zero.)

3. How badly does the person want the reward being offered in the situation? Am I offering a reward that will make it worthwhile for the person to do what I need done? If the sum of the valences of the outcomes in the situation is close to 0 (some positive, some negative), motivation will be absent.

4. Are there any zeroes in response to the first three questions? If there are, motivation will be absent, because the expectancy theory equation is Motivation = (effort-to-performance expectancies) × (performance-to-outcome expectancies) × (the sum of the valences for all the outcomes). Remember what happens when you multiply by 0 in an equation.

5. Is the person in a reasonably good mood? Perhaps the person is poorly motivated today because of being in a bad mood.

BACK TO THE OPENING CASE

Management at the Commercial Division of Toro correctly diagnosed the motivation of its sales force. Although these industrial sales representatives take considerable pride in their work, they still respond well to external incentives. The opportunity to win expense-paid vacations to exotic locales gave them a motivational boost strong enough to boost sales growth by 7 percent—a substantial amount of revenue for Toro.

Guidelines for Applying Expectancy Theory

The information about expectancy theory presented so far provides ideas for motivating others. Here we discuss several additional specific guidelines to improve your skill in motivating others.

1. **Train and encourage people.** If you are a manager, you should give employees the necessary training and encouragement to be confident that they can perform the required tasks. Some employees who appear poorly motivated simply lack the right skills and self-efficacy.

2. **Make explicit the link between rewards and performance.** Employees should be reassured that if they perform the job up to standard, they will receive the promised reward. It is sometimes helpful for employees to speak to coworkers about whether they received promised rewards.

3. **Make sure the rewards are large enough.** Some rewards fail to motivate people because, although they are the right kind, they are not in the right amount. The promise of a large salary increase might be motivational, but a 1 percent increase will probably have little motivational thrust for most workers.

4. **Understand individual differences in valences.** To motivate others in the workplace effectively, you must discover individual differences in preferences for rewards. An attempt should be made to offer a worker rewards to which he or she attaches a high valence. For instance, one employee might value a high-adventure assignment; another might attach a high valence to a routine, tranquil assignment. Also keep individual differences in mind when attempting to motivate customers. One customer might attach a high valence to a volume discount, while another might favor follow-up service.

5. **Use the Pygmalion effect to increase effort-to-performance expectancies.** The **Pygmalion effect** refers to the phenomenon that people will rise (or fall) to the expectations another person has of them. Even if these expectations are not communicated explicitly, the other person will catch on to the nonverbal language. As the levels of expectation increase, so will performance. The high expectations thus become a self-fulfilling prophecy.

Pygmalion effect

The phenomenon that people will rise (or fall) to the expectations that another person has of them.

SKILL-BUILDING EXERCISE 10-4

Applying Expectancy Theory

One student plays the role of the manager of a telemarketing firm (selling over the telephone). Another student plays the role of Terry, a telemarketing specialist who has been with the company for three months. Terry is 40 percent below target in selling magazine renewals. The manager calls Terry into the office for a discussion of the problem.

Terry goes on at length to explain how confusing the job has become. Terry makes comments such as, "I don't even know if I have the right kind of voice for this job. People I reach on the phone think I'm just a kid." Terry also wonders what kind of money he can make in this job and whether it is a dead-end job. (The student who plays the role of Terry can improvise about more of these kinds of problems.)

The manager will apply expectancy theory to motivate Terry to achieve satisfactory performance. Other class members should jot down statements the manager makes that indicate the use of expectancy theory. Also, observe whether it appears that Terry is being helped.

SKILL-BUILDING EXERCISE 10-5

Working on My Own Motivators

The focus of this chapter has been the skill of motivating others. Yet, if you neglect motivating yourself, you (a) might not gain a formal position in which you can motivate others, and (b) you will not be able to motivate others by leading through example. Apply some of the concepts in this chapter to help work through this exercise.

What Motivates Me?

Think back on what situations, and factors within a situation, have prompted you to put forth your best effort and work the hardest—on the job, at community work, at school, in sports, or in other recreational activities such as being a band member. Which needs were you attempting to satisfy? Which tangible or intangible rewards were you pursuing? Here is a portion of a sample answer:

"I was lucky enough to be entered in Domino's national speed contest for making a store-usable pizza. I jumped into the situation like somebody obsessed. Here I was at 20 years old with a chance to win a national contest and be lifted up over the head of my buddies. I would have been King Pizza for a day. I didn't win, but I came close.

"Now I know that competition and recognition get my adrenalin flowing. I think that's why I will be successful in industrial sales. I need that big carrot dangling out in front of me."

What Can I Do to Capitalize on My Motivators?

It is helpful to know what motivates you, but it is even more helpful to follow up by placing yourself in situations in which you will be highly motivated. The Pizza King aspirant provides us a good example. Attempt to manage your career by placing yourself in highly motivational situations. For example, if the opportunity to work alone without supervision and the opportunity to schedule your own time motivates you, strive to work at home in the near future.

Now write down the type of situations that will most likely enable you to work at your motivated best.

It is difficult to keep all the points made about expectancy theory in your head at the same time. Nevertheless, with practice and by referring to this book and your notes, you can apply many of the ideas. Skill-Building Exercise 10-4 will help you get started applying expectancy theory. Skill-Building Exercise 10-5 will help you apply the information in this chapter to self-motivation.

SELF-ASSESSMENT QUIZ IN OVERVIEW

Self-Assessment Quiz 10-1 is different from the other quizzes presented in this text because it emphasizes cognitive knowledge about the subject (in this case motivation). Nevertheless, your attitudes toward people often become translated into knowledge about motivation. For example, if you are warm and supportive toward people, you would likely respond "very frequently" to Statement 8, "I make sure that the other person feels treated fairly." And, if you were essentially hostile toward people, you would respond "very frequently" to Statement 3, "When another person is heel-dragging, it usually means he or she is lazy."

Concept Review and Reinforcement

Key Terms

motivation, 201
behavior modification, 204
law of effect, 204
positive reinforcement, 204
negative reinforcement
(avoidance motivation), 205

intermittent rewards, 206
expectancy theory, 209
effort-to-performance
expectancy, 209
self-efficacy, 210

performance-to-outcome
expectancy, 210
valence, 210
Pygmalion effect, 212

Summary of Key Concepts

Motivation refers to an internal state that leads to effort expended toward objectives and to an activity performed by one person to get another person to work. Managers, as well as people working by themselves, often need to motivate others.

The most fundamental principle of human motivation is that people are motivated by self-interest, referred to as "What's in it for me?" (WIIFM). Even those who help others are simultaneously helping themselves by feeling good. In using the WIIFM principle, be aware of the intensity of a person's desire for a reward.

Behavior modification is an attempt to change behavior by manipulating rewards and punishments. Its key principle is the law of effect—behavior that leads to a positive effect tends to be repeated, while the opposite is also true. Negative reinforcement, or avoidance motivation, can be used to supplement positive reinforcement. Rules for the effective use of positive reinforcement include the following:

1. State clearly what behavior will lead to a reward.
2. Choose an appropriate reward.
3. Supply ample feedback.
4. Schedule rewards intermittently.
5. Make the reward follow the observed behavior closely in time.
6. Make the reward fit the behavior.
7. Make the reward visible.
8. Change the reward periodically.
9. Reward the group or team also.

A general approach to applying these rules is to look for creative ways to apply positive reinforcement.

Motivating others by giving them recognition and praise is a direct application of positive reinforcement. Recognition is a strong motivator because it is a normal human need to crave recognition, and most workers feel they do not get enough recognition. Choosing when to deliver recognition can be important. Statements of recognition tend to be more effective when they are specific. Recognition and praise are low-cost, powerful motivators. Recognition is more likely to be an effective motivator in a culture of recognition.

The expectancy theory of motivation assumes that people are decision makers who choose among alternatives by selecting the one that appears to have the biggest personal payoff at the time. Expectancy theory has three major components: expectancies about being able to perform, expectancies about performance leading to certain outcomes, and valence (the value attached to the reward). A positive mood state can enhance the components of expectancy theory.

Expectancy theory is useful in diagnosing whether motivation is present by examining the strength of the expectancies and the valences of the rewards. If any element is 0, motivation will not be present. Expectancy theory provides important ideas for motivating others, including the following:

1. Train and encourage people.
2. Make explicit the link between rewards and performance.
3. Make sure the rewards are large enough.
4. Understand individual differences in valences.
5. Use the Pygmalion effect to increase effort-to-performance expectancies.

Check Your Understanding

1. Explain whether the ability to motivate others is a soft skill or a hard skill.
2. A recent Google search identified 68,600,600 listings for the subject of "work motivation." With all this information available, why is motivating workers still such a hassle for so many managers?
3. For what purpose would someone need to motivate his or her supervisor?
4. If people really live by the WIIFM principle, how can a leader still achieve teamwork?
5. What evidence can you suggest that some people prefer exciting and interesting work over exceptional financial rewards?
6. Identify several factors in Figure 10-1 that you think would be particularly effective in motivating managers and professional-level workers. Explain your reasoning.
7. Answer Question 6 for entry-level service workers, such as supermarket cashiers.
8. How do individual differences show themselves in attempting to motivate others?
9. How might you use expectancy theory to improve your own level of work motivation?
10. How might cultural differences affect the valence ratings in Skill-Building Exercise 10-3?

The Web Corner

http://www.awards.com
(One-stop supersite for rewards and recognition.)

http://www.ZeroMillion.com
(Go to Positive Reinforcement in the Workplace.)

http://www.Entrepreneur.com
(Go to "Think Positive," which deals with positive reinforcement in the workplace.)

Internet Skill Builder: Motivating Other People

Visit *http://www.nelson-motivation.com* to watch a five-minute video clip of one of Bob Nelson's talks. After watching the video, answer the following questions: (1) What have I learned that I could translate into a skill motivating other people as well as employees? (2) Which theory, or approach, to motivation does Nelson emphasize in his presentation?

Developing Your Human Relations Skills

Interpersonal Relations Case 10.1

Motivating the Kitchen Staff at the Blue Gardenia

Jimmy Gomez aspires to someday be the manager of a large hotel. To help work toward that goal, he is working part-time on a degree in hospitality administration. He attends classes at various times to fit his demanding full-time position as the kitchen staff supervisor at the Blue Gardenia, a well-established downtown hotel. Gomez supervises a staff of about 45 kitchen workers, including food preparers, butchers, bakers, and cooks. The highly paid chefs report to the restaurant manager, Sonya Rosato, who is also Gomez's manager.

The average wage is $9.50 per hour for the kitchen staff reporting to Gomez. Half of these workers work part-time and receive almost no benefits. Full-time staff members receive a few modest benefits, such as vacation, a $25,000 life insurance policy, and medical insurance. Blue Gardenia management believes strongly that the company pays competitive wages for kitchen staff and that paying them much more would eat into profits too much.

During a goal-setting conference with Rosato, Gomez agreed that an important area for improvement in his operation would be to reduce turnover and increase productivity among the kitchen staff. Rosato pointed out that although the turnover rate for Gomez's employees was about average for kitchen staff in the geographic area (75 percent per year), it was still too high. If the turnover rate could be trimmed down to about 45 percent, it would save the hotel thousands of dollars in hiring and training costs. Also, less food would be wasted because trainees make so many mistakes in food preparation. Skilled workers also drop fewer dishes and glasses.

Rosato and Gomez also agreed that lower turnover would mean more kitchen staff would have good job skills and therefore would be able to produce more. For example, a skilled salad maker can make twice as many salads as a beginner. Another concern Rosato expressed was that many of the kitchen staff seemed lazy.

During the week following the meeting with his boss, Gomez kept thinking about the problem. He decided tentatively that he was really dealing with a motivational issue. He reasoned that if the staff were better motivated, they would stay with the job longer and obviously should not appear lazy. As a starting point in attempting to better motivate the kitchen staff, Gomez conducted a few informal interviews with them during breaks and toward the end of the workday. He asked 12 of the kitchen workers what Blue Gardenia management could do to keep kitchen staff on the job longer and working harder. A few of the comments Gomez collected were as follows:

- "What do you expect for $9.50 an hour? Some kind of superman? I work as hard as a factory worker, but I don't get paid like a factory worker in a union plant."
- "This is like a dead-end job. If I could find a job with a better future, I'd be out of here in no time."
- "I like this job fine. But just like a few of the other guys here, I've got a problem. My wife and I are expecting a child. If I stay in this job, I won't be able to support my child. My wife wants to drop out of work for a year to care for the baby."
- "Not me, but I think some of the workers here think management doesn't care much about them. So if they can find another job that pays even 50¢ more per hour, they're gone."
- "I like this kind of work. I mean, we're really doing some good. People like nice entertainment, and eating good food is a form of entertainment. Also, we're keeping people healthy and helping them live longer. Our food is made with the best ingredients. Even the beef we prepare is lean and healthy."
- "My gripe is not with the work, but that we don't get enough respect. The chef gets the glory, but we do a lot of the real work. I think I'm doing important work, but nobody tells me I am. Sometimes I think I'm treated like just another piece of kitchen equipment. A few of the other guys and gals feel the same way about how they're treated."

After the interviews were completed, Gomez thought to himself that he had a lot of information. Yet he wondered how he could translate all this information into an action plan that would reduce turnover and keep the kitchen staff working harder.

Case Questions

1. How effective do you think it was for Jimmy Gomez to interview members of the kitchen staff to investigate possible motivational problems?
2. What does the information revealed by the kitchen staff tell you about their valences?
3. Which needs among the people interviewed are not being satisfied?
4. What recommendations can you make to Blue Gardenia management about decreasing the turnover and increasing the productivity of the kitchen staff?

Interpersonal Relations Case 10.2

On Time at Prime Time

Prime Time Furniture is a manufacturer and distributor of inexpensive, ready-to-assemble furniture for the home and small business, including home-based businesses. Among their products are bookcases, television stands, computer workstations, and kitchen tables. Some of the higher-end products are manufactured at the Wisconsin factory and distribution center. The vast majority of products, however, are imported from Malaysia and then placed in the distribution center until sold.

Demand for ready-to-assemble furniture has increased steadily as more people are looking for ways to reduce household expenses. To meet the increased demand, more companies have entered the field, making the business more competitive and therefore reducing prices.

Eton Westin, the distribution center manager, searches continuously for ways to make the center more efficient. During a two-hour productivity meeting with supervisors, Westin learned that employee lateness is costing Prime Time a lot of money. Ashley Novak explained the problem in these terms:

"We are short-handed as it is. When an employee is late, it makes it more difficult to ship on time. We have learned the hard way that when we do not ship on time, we lose some business. A big part of our business now comes from online sales through Amazon and other resellers. These outfits promise rapid delivery, and when we don't ship on time, we get heat from both the resellers and the end customers." (The resellers inform the end customer that Prime Time Furniture is the source of the furniture.)

Jimmy Gerber, the director of administration and human resources, said he had an idea for improving punctuality that has worked in other companies. The program is set up by a company specializing in performance improvement. Gerber then outlined the basics of the program.

"We run a punctuality race, with each department being represented by a horse, assigned a name by the department. The consulting company sets up the race with its own software, and we visit our race Web site any time we want. The setup looks like a video game. You can see graphically the relative positions of the horses as they run the 'punctuality race.'

"Every time a worker arrives on time, that fact is entered into the database, and the department's horse gets two points. Every time a worker is late, the department's horse is penalized two points. Coming back from breaks on time earns one point, and coming back late is a one-point penalty. Leaving work, or leaving early, also follows the same one-point value.

"At the end of each month, the points are totaled. The team with the winning horse can then convert the points into gifts from a catalog or gift certificates to a few selected restaurants."

Westin asked the group for their opinion on the horse race to improve punctuality. "I'm a little concerned," he said. "Isn't this too child-like? I mean, running a horse race for coming to work on time. Let's get real."

"In all respect, Eton," said Liz Lopez, the shipping supervisor. "Adults are motivated by games and small prizes. We are all children at heart, even Prime Time employees."

Case Questions

1. What do you predict will be the outcome of the horse-race motivation program if implemented?
2. Which approach, or approaches, to motivating people does this horse-race program represent?
3. What other program for improving punctuality might you recommend?

CHAPTER 11

Helping Others Develop and Grow

Behind almost every accomplished project manager stands a wise and generous adviser who sets an example, helps define goals, lends an ear or simply provides a much-needed dose of reality. (A project manager manages a major task, like sending a spaceship to Mars.) Of course, finding that wise and generous adviser is often a project itself.

Over the course of his 36-year career at the National Aeronautics and Space Administration (NASA), Robert J. Shaw, Ph.D., has managed to develop relationships with several great mentors. Now chief of the New Business and Partnership Office at Glenn Research Center in Cleveland, Ohio, USA, he says it was through their insights that he recognized the human element of good project management. He also learned how to navigate the sometimes murky waters of office dynamics. "You can take the requisite courses and learn various tools or techniques, but management goes beyond numbers and charts," Dr. Shaw says. "That's where mentors come in."[1]

As shown in Shaw's case, receiving the right advice and encouragement from the right person can help a person grow and develop, as well as learn interpersonal skills. This chapter describes the major ways in which employees help each other, and lays the groundwork for skill development in these vital activities. Learning to take the initiative to help others is particularly important because there is a natural tendency for people to be embarrassed or fearful of asking for help. The concern is that the person asking for help will be seen as deficient in some important way. Despite these concerns, a company is at an advantage when workers help each other.[2]

Among the key helping roles are nurturing others, mentoring, coaching and training, and helping difficult people become more cooperative. A study of how new employees are developed, involving 378 recent graduates, underscores the importance of workers helping each other. Among the findings relevant in the study were that (1) buddying with a coworker was the

Learning Objectives

After reading and studying this chapter and doing the exercises, you should be able to

1. Understand how being a nurturing, positive person can influence the development of coworkers.
2. Specify the behaviors and skills helpful for being a mentor and role model.
3. Acquire beginning skills in coaching and training.
4. Deal with difficult people on the job.

most helpful developmental method, and (2) the company did not provide enough mentoring despite its importance.[3]

Do Self-Assessment Quiz 11-1 to gain preliminary insight into your attitudes toward helping others in the workplace.

BEING A NURTURING, POSITIVE PERSON

LEARNING OBJECTIVE 1

A major strategy for helping others grow and develop is to be a nourishing, positive person. A **nurturing person** promotes the growth of others. Nurturing people are positive and supportive and typically look for the good qualities in others. A **toxic person** stands in contrast to a nourishing person, because he or she dwells on the negative. Visualize the following scenario to appreciate the difference between a nurturing person and a toxic one.

nurturing person
One who promotes the growth of others.

toxic person
One who negatively affects others.

> Randy, a purchasing specialist, enters the office where two coworkers are talking. One person is nurturing, the other is toxic. With a look of panic, Randy says, "I'm sorry to barge in like this, but can anybody help me? I've been working for three hours preparing a spreadsheet on the computer, and it seems to have vanished. Maybe one of you can help me retrieve it."
>
> Margot, the nourishing person, says, "I'm no computer expert, but since I'm not the one who lost the document, I can be calm enough to help. Let's go right now." Ralph, the toxic person, whispers to Margot: "Tell Randy to use his software manual. If you help him now, you'll only find him on your doorstep every time he needs help."

If you listen to toxic people long enough, you are likely to feel listless, depressed, and drained. Toxic people have been described as energy vampires because they suck all the positive energy out of you.[4] Nurturing people, in contrast, are positive, enthusiastic, and supportive. The guideline for skill development here is to engage in thoughts and actions every day that will be interpreted by others as nourishing. Three actions and attitudes that support being a nourishing person are as follows.

1. **Recognize that most people have growth needs.** Almost everybody has a need for self-fulfillment, although people vary widely in the extent of this need. If

Attitudes Toward Helping Others

Directions: Describe how well you agree with the following statements by circling the appropriate letter after each statement: disagree (D); neutral (N); agree (A).

1. If I see a coworker make a mistake, I do not inform him or her of the mistake.	D	N	A
2. It should be part of everybody's job to share skills and ideas with coworkers.	D	N	A
3. The manager should have exclusive responsibility for coaching people within the work unit.	D	N	A
4. I can think of many instances in my life when somebody thanked me for showing him or her how to do something.	D	N	A
5. I have very little patience with coworkers who do not give me their full cooperation.	D	N	A
6. To save time, I will do a task for another person rather than invest the time needed to show him or her how to do it.	D	N	A
7. I would take the initiative to put an inexperienced worker under my wing.	D	N	A
8. As a child, I often took the time to show younger children how to do things.	D	N	A
9. Rather than ask a coworker for help, I will wait until the manager is available to help me.	D	N	A
10. It is best not to share key information with a coworker, because that person could then perform as well as or better than me.	D	N	A

Total Score_____

Scoring and Interpretation: Use the following score key to obtain your score for each answer, and then calculate your total score.

1. D = 3, N = 2, A = 1	5. D = 3, N = 2, A = 1	8. D = 1, N = 2, A = 3
2. D = 1, N = 2, A = 3	6. D = 3, N = 2, A = 1	9. D = 3, N = 2, A = 1
3. D = 3, N = 2, A = 1	7. D = 1, N = 2, A = 3	10. D = 3, N = 2, A = 1
4. D = 1, N = 2, A = 3		

25–30 You have very positive attitudes toward helping, developing, and training others in the workplace. Such attitudes reflect strong teamwork and a compassion for the growth needs of others.

16–24 You have mixed positive and negative attitudes toward helping, developing, and training others in the workplace. You may need to develop more sensitivity to the growth needs of others to be considered a strong team player.

10–15 You have negative attitudes toward helping, developing, and training others in the workplace. Guard against being so self-centered that it will be held against you.

Being a nurturing, positive person is a lifelong process rather than a tactic that can be used at will. Nevertheless, making a conscious attempt to be nurturing and positive can help you develop the right mind-set. For example, today you might encourage a coworker or friend who is facing a work or personal problem. Skill-Building Exercise 11-1 provides an opportunity to practice being a positive person.

you recognize this need, it may propel you toward helping people satisfy the need. You might engage in interactions with coworkers such as sharing new skills with them, clipping or forwarding relevant news articles, or telling them about an important new Web site you have discovered. You might also tell them about an exciting course you have taken that has enhanced your self-confidence.

2. **Team up with a coworker inside or outside your department so the two of you can form a buddy system.** The buddy system is used during war com-

bat and with children in a swimming program. You and a friend can use the same system to keep each other informed of decisions and events that could affect your careers. You might nurture your buddy by telling that person about growth opportunities in the company he or she might not have heard about. Your buddy would reciprocate. One person told her buddy about expanding opportunities for company employees who were fluent in both English and Spanish. The two buddies, who already knew some Spanish, worked together to become fluent.

3. **Be a role model for others.** An indirect way of being a nurturing, positive person is to conduct yourself in such a way that others will model your behavior. By serving as a role model, you help another person develop. How to become a role model for coworkers is as comprehensive a topic as learning to be successful. Among the many factors that make you role-model material are a strong work ethic, job expertise, personal warmth, good speaking ability, a professional appearance, and great ethics. Do you qualify yet, or do you need some more work?

SKILL-BUILDING EXERCISE 11-1

The Nurturing, Positive Person

One student plays the role of Pat, a worker who is experiencing difficulty on the job and in personal life. Pat approaches a coworker during lunch in the company cafeteria and says, "What a day. I just received a rotten performance review. If my work doesn't improve within a month, the company may let me go. To add to my woes, my fiancé has threatened to break off the engagement if I don't get a big raise or a promotion. I feel like my whole world is collapsing." The other person plays the role of Leslie, who attempts to be nurturing and positive in order to help get Pat out of the doldrums. Run the role-play for about 10 minutes.

The rest of the class provides feedback on Leslie's skill in being nurturing and helpful. Jot down specific behaviors you think are nurturing and helpful. Also be on the alert for any toxic behaviors.

BEING A MENTOR TO COWORKERS

In Homer's tale the *Odyssey*, Mentor was a wise and trusted friend as well as a counselor and adviser. The term *mentor* has become a buzzword in the workplace, as well as in the community. A **mentor** is an individual with advanced experience and knowledge who is committed to giving support and career advice to a less experienced person. The less experienced person is the **protégé** (from the French word for "protected").

A mentor usually outranks the protégé and is much older. For the present purpose, however, be aware that one coworker can be a mentor to another. As long as you are more experienced and wiser than a coworker in some important aspect of the job, you can be a mentor. A person who is not a manager can also be a mentor in another important way. He or she can select an entry-level person in the firm and serve as the inexperienced person's coach and adviser. Even when a person has a high-ranking person as a mentor, you can also be his or her mentor. The reason is that having more than one mentor improves a person's chances for developing job and career skills.[5]

BACK TO THE OPENING CASE

Robert J. Shaw believes he was fortunate to be in the right place at the right time to receive the type of mentoring he did. NASA now has a formal mentoring program and he finds himself on other side of the relationship, as the sage mentor offering advice.

He says, "It's not just telling someone to do something. It's telling them [him or her] what you did it and exposing them [him or her] to a repository of knowledge."[6]

Mentoring is more important than ever because it supports the modern, team-based organization. Also, after years of downsizing, many organizations have fewer managers available to mentor employees. Coworkers often have to fill this void. More people work together as equals, and they are expected to train and develop each other. Mentoring facilitates such learning and supports the current emphasis on continuous learning.

Mentoring often takes the form of the mentor and protégé communicating by e-mail, referred to as *virtual* (or *online*) *mentoring*. Many companies have established electronic matching programs that enable employees to receive mentoring from workers who are geographically distant from them. The virtual mentoring can include Web sites for matching mentors and protégés, following the model of online dating sites. Companies making extensive use of virtual mentoring include Intel and KPMG LLP, the tax and audit firm.[7]

As the time of corporate professionals and managers has become scarcer, virtual mentoring increases in practicality. Also, online mentoring gives the protégé an opportunity to be mentored by a geographically distant mentor, who may even be overseas. The person being mentored might send a quick e-mail, instant message, or text message to the mentor explaining that he just received an outstanding performance review. The mentor might reply with an encouraging message. When asked about a problem facing the protégé, the mentor might reply with advice quickly. Answers by the mentor within 48 hours are recommended to communicate an attitude of concern.[8]

Mentoring coworkers can take place in one of two ways. With informal mentoring, the mentor and protégé come together naturally, in the same way that friendships develop. The formal approach is for the company to assign you somebody to mentor. Several studies have shown that mentoring is likely to be more effective when both the mentor and protégé have some input into the matching.[9] Measures of mentoring effectiveness include rate of promotions, salary increases, and job satisfaction. Being mentored is also a career-advancement tactic, and will be discussed in Chapter 16.

Serving as a mentor is an excellent way of helping others on the job. Mentoring is also gaining acceptance off the job. Many communities have developed programs whereby working adults volunteer to serve as mentors to youths. Mentoring in these programs is designed to help the adolescents and teenagers succeed at school and avoid a life of crime and substance abuse. To be a mentor, a person engages in a wide range of helping behaviors, all related to being a trusted friend, coach, and teacher. To prepare you for mentoring a less experienced person, a list of specific mentoring behaviors follows[10]:

- **Sponsoring.** A mentor actively nominates somebody else for promotions and desirable positions. In some situations, one person is asked to nominate a coworker for a promotion to supervisor or team leader or for a special assignment.
- **Coaching.** A mentor gives on-the-spot advice to the protégé to help her or him improve skills. Coaching is such an important part of helping others that it receives separate mention in this chapter.
- **Protecting.** A mentor might shield a junior person from potentially harmful situations or from the boss. For example, the mentor might tell her protégé, "In your meeting today with the boss, make sure you are well prepared and have all your facts at hand. He is in an ugly mood and will attack any weakness."
- **Sharing challenging assignments.** One member of the team does not ordinarily give assignments to another, yet in some situations you can request that your protégé help you with a difficult task. You would then offer feedback on your protégé's performance. The purpose of these high demands is to help the protégé develop more quickly than if he or she were brought along too slowly.
- **Acting as a referral agent.** The mentor sometimes refers the protégé to resources inside and outside the company to help with a particular problem. For example, the protégé might want to know how one goes about getting the employee benefits package modified.

- **Role modeling.** An important part of being a mentor is to give the protégé a pattern of values and behaviors to emulate. Several of the specific behaviors included under being a role model were described earlier in connection with being a positive, nurturing person.
- **Giving support and encouragement.** A mentor can be helpful just by giving support and encouragement. In turn, the protégé is supposed to support the mentor by offering compliments and defending the mentor's ideas. In a team meeting, for example, the protégé might make a statement such as, "I think John's ideas will work wonders. We should give them a try."
- **Counseling.** A mentor listens to the protégé's problems and offers advice. Given that counseling plays such a central role in helping others, it, too, receives separate mention in this chapter.
- **Providing friendship.** A mentor is, above all, a trusted friend, and the friendship extends two ways. "Trusted" means that the mentor will not pass on confidential information or stab you in the back. (It is also possible to mentor someone who is not a friend, providing that person is interested primarily in learning business or technical skills from you.)
- **Encouraging problem solving.** Mentors help their protégés solve problems by themselves and make their own discoveries. A comment frequently made to mentors is "I'm glad you made me think through the problem. You triggered my thinking."
- **Explaining the ropes.** A general-purpose function of the mentor is to help the protégé learn the ropes, which translates into explaining the values and do's and don'ts of the organization.
- **Teaching the right skills.** The original role of the mentor in teaching skills (such as a master teaching an apprentice) is highly relevant today. Among the many skills a mentor can help the protégé develop are those dealing with information technology, customer service, corporate finance, and achieving high quality.
- **Encouraging of continuous learning.** A major role for the modern mentor is to encourage the protégé to keep learning. Part of encouraging lifelong learning is to emphasize that formal education and an occasional workshop are not sufficient for maintaining expertise in today's fast-changing workplace. The individual has to stay abreast of new developments through courses and self-study. A specific way in which the mentor can encourage continuous learning is to ask the protégé questions about new developments in the field.

As implied by the preceding list, mentoring is a complex activity that involves a variety of helping behaviors. To develop mentoring skills, you need to offer help to several people for at least six months. Skill-Building Exercise 11-2 is a good starting point in mentoring. In preparation for more advanced mentoring, it is helpful to think of the type of person you would prefer to have as a protégé. Skill-Building Exercise 11-3 is designed to help you think through this issue. Be prepared for a potential protégé seeking you out because many people serious about advancing their careers search for potential mentors with whom they have rapport. Similarly, if you are looking for a mentor, take the initiative to establish contact with someone you like and whom you think could help you.

Mentoring is designed to help another individual grow and develop, yet mentoring can also help your employer at the same time. An important way in which the company benefits from coworker mentoring is that the mentor passes along, or transfers, valuable knowledge to the protégé.[11] For example, the mentor might share with the protégé a few good tricks for collecting money from a delinquent debtor. Workers who receive mentoring are likely to feel more satisfied about their jobs and stay with the organization longer. A study with over 1,300 U.S. Army officers showed that officers who were mentored felt more emotionally committed to the Army than did their nonmentored counterparts. Furthermore, mentored officers felt more likely to stay in the Army and were less likely to leave the military voluntarily.[12]

Getting Started Mentoring

If you choose to do this skill-building exercise, it will take time outside of class, and the exercise could turn into an ongoing activity. Successful mentoring requires experience, and all mentors need to start somewhere. The task is to find somebody to mentor, and then become his or her mentor. For starters, it is usually easier to find a protégé among people younger and less experienced than you in some domain, such as math, information technology, reading, or a sport. A source of a protégé might be a community center, a park and recreational center, a school, a church, or temple. It is conceivable that you could find a source of people wanting mentoring in your community through an Internet search engine.

Identify the ways in which you might be able to function as a mentor, such as imparting knowledge, providing emotional sup-

port, or being a Big Brother or Big Sister. Be prepared to be subjected to a background check before being selected as a mentor.

After finding a protégé, keep a diary of your activities, including any observations about how your protégé is being helped. Identify mentoring roles that you have carried out. Record also how you are enjoying the experience. An example, "Today I was mostly a friend to Teddy. He was bummed out because the coach gave him only two minutes of playing time in Friday night's game. He was also complaining that he was the only kid on the team without an iPod. I listened carefully, and then explained that patience in life is important. Teddy felt a little better and smiled. I felt wonderful for having been helpful."

Observe any mentoring skills you need to work on to become more effective as a mentor. Also evaluate whether the mentoring appears to be having a positive impact on the life of your protégé.

Selecting a Protégé

To be a successful mentor it is necessary to select protégés who will respond well to your advice and coaching. Because the mentor–protégé relationship is personal, much like any friendship, you must choose protégés carefully. In about 50 words (in the space provided), describe the type of person you would like for a protégé. Include cognitive, personality, and demographic factors in your description (refer to Chapter 2 for ideas). Indicate why you think the characteristics you chose are important.

My Ideal Protégé

As many class members as time allows can present their descriptions to the rest of the class. Look for agreement on characteristics of an ideal protégé.

As business has become highly internationalized, mentoring people from different cultures has become more frequent. In general, to engage in cross-cultural mentoring effectively, you need to follow the principles described in Chapter 7 about cross-cultural relations. The accompanying Job-Oriented Skills in Action provides a few specific insights about mentoring somebody from another culture.

JOB-ORIENTED INTERPERSONAL SKILLS IN ACTION

Consultant Alexandre Rodrigues Mentors Across the Globe

Alexandre Rodrigues, Ph.D., PMO Consulting, has mentored project managers from Australia, Mozambique, the United Kingdom and at the international headquarters of the North Atlantic Treaty Organization (NATO) in Brussels, Belgium.

Although global mentoring relationships will undoubtedly have their benefits, it can be quite easy to send the wrong signals when dealing with someone from another culture. Dr. Rodrigues recommends mentors make an effort to learn and recognize differences in attitudes toward uncertainty, time, emotions, and even humor in working relationships. For example, in areas that aren't as driven by the clock, project managers may need to be trained to build extra time into the schedule.

Perceptions of power can also vary around the world. Rodrigues says, "In some cultures, the way advice is delivered can be mistaken as exerting power over the other. The person being mentored can either perceive the mentor as being directive or as being too soft and unsure. In some cultures, if you say, 'Perhaps you can try this,' it can be interpreted as the mentor not really knowing. They may expect you to say, '*This* is how it works.'"

Questions

1. Identify a culture in which you think a mentor should be more directive (or assertive). Why?
2. Identify a culture in which you think a mentor should be more indirect and less assertive. Why?

Source: Elisa Ludwig, "Trade Secrets," *PM Network*, July 2007, p. 38.

COACHING AND TRAINING OTHERS

Two direct approaches to helping others in the workplace are coaching and training. In the traditional organization, managers have most of the responsibility for coaching and training, with some assistance from the human resources department. In the new workplace, team members share responsibility for coaching and training. High-tech companies, such as Google and Microsoft, heavily emphasize workers sharing knowledge with each other. Open workspaces, including the presence of whiteboards, are used to facilitate workers exchanging ideas and passing along information. Although coaching and training are described separately in the following subsections, recognize that the two processes are closely related.

Coaching Skills and Techniques

Most readers probably have some experience in coaching whether or not the activity was given a formal label. If you have helped somebody improve his or her performance on the job, on the athletic field, in a musical band, or on the dance floor, you have some coaching experience. In the workplace, **coaching** is a method of helping workers grow and improve their job competence by providing suggestions and encouragement. The suggestions for coaching are generally easier to implement if you have formal authority over the person being coached. Nevertheless, with a positive, helpful attitude on your part, coworkers are likely to accept your coaching.

coaching
A method of helping workers grow, develop, and improve their job competence by providing suggestions and encouragement.

Coaching other employees requires skill. One way of acquiring this skill is to study basic principles and then practice them on the job. Another way is to coach under simulated conditions such as role-playing and modeling an effective coach. Here are 11 suggestions for effective coaching, as outlined in Figure 11-1. For the best results, combine them with the suggestions for effective listening presented in Chapter 4.

1. **Build relationships.** A starting point in being an effective coach is to build relationships with coworkers before coaching them. Having established rapport with coworkers or subordinates facilitates entering into coaching relationships with them. The suggestions that follow about giving encouragement and support are part of relationship building. Another vital aspect of relationship building to be trusted by the people you coach.[13] For example, the person being coached has to believe that the coach is trying to help rather than undermine him or her.

FIGURE 11-1 Coaching Skills and Techniques

1. Build relationships.
2. Provide specific feedback.
3. Make criticism pain free and positive.
4. Encourage the person you are coaching to talk.
5. Ask powerful questions.
6. Give emotional support.
7. Give some constructive advice.
8. Coach with "could," not "should."
9. Interpret what is happening.
10. Allow for modeling of the desired performance and behaviors.
11. Applaud good results.

2. **Provide specific feedback.** Instead of making generalities about an improvement area for another person, pinpoint areas of concern. A generality might be, "You just don't seem as if you're interested in this job." A specific on the same problem might be, "You neglect to call in on days that you are going to be out ill. In this way, you are letting down the team." Sometimes it can be effective to make a generalization (such as not being "interested in the job") after you first produce several concrete examples. Closely related to minimizing generalizations is to avoid exaggerating, for example, by saying such things as "You're always letting down the team." Specific feedback is sometimes referred to as **behavioral feedback** because it pinpoints behavior rather than personal characteristics or attitudes. "Neglecting to call in" pinpoints behavior, whereas "not into the job" focuses more on an attitude.

3. **Make criticism pain free and positive.** To be an effective coach, you will inevitably have to point out something negative the person you coach has done, or is planning to do. It is helpful to come right to the point about your criticism, such as, "In our department meeting this morning, you acted so angry and hostile that you alienated the rest of the group. I know that you are generally a positive person, so I was surprised. My recommendation is that you keep your bad days to yourself when in a meeting." The positive aspect is important because you want to maintain good communications with the person you coach, whether you are the person's supervisor or coworker.[14]

4. **Encourage the person you are coaching to talk.** Part of being a good listener is encouraging the person being coached to talk. Ask the person you are coaching open-ended questions. Closed questions do not provide the same opportunity for self-expression, and they often elicit short, uninformative answers. Assume you are coaching a coworker on how to use the e-mail system properly. An effective open-ended question might be, "Where are you having the biggest problems using e-mail?" A closed question covering the same topic might be, "Do you understand how to use e-mail?" The latter question would not provide good clues to specific problem areas faced by your coworker. A useful technique is to begin each coaching session with a question to spark the other person's thinking.[15] An example is to ask, "What new ideas do you have for decreasing turnover among our teenage cashiers?"

5. **Ask powerful questions.** A major role for the coach is to ask *powerful* or *tough* questions that help the protégé think through the strengths and weaknesses of what he or she is doing or thinking. The powerful question is confrontational in a helpful way. The person being coached might be thinking of selling management on a program of distributing free ginkgo baloba (a food supplement believed to stimulate mental energy) to every employee to enhance productive thinking. Your powerful question might be, "What kind of figures are you going to use to support your expensive idea?"

6. **Give emotional support.** By being helpful and constructive, you provide much-needed emotional support to the person who needs help in improving job performance. A coaching session should not be an interrogation. An effective way of providing emotional support is to use positive rather than negative motivators. For example, as a team leader you might say to a team member, "If you learn how to analyze manufacturing costs, you will be eligible for an outstanding performance review." A negative motivator on the same topic might be, "If you don't learn how to analyze manufacturing costs, you're going to get zapped on your performance review."

    Workers who are performing well can also profit from praise and encouragement, often so they can perform even better. In addition, even the best performers have flaws that might be preventing them from elevating their performance.[16] As a team leader or coworker, you can therefore make a contribution by giving emotional support to a star performer.

7. **Give some constructive advice.** Too much advice-giving interferes with two-way communication, yet some advice can lead to improved performance. Assist the

person being coached to answer the question, "What can I do about the problem?" Advice in the form of a question or suppositional statement is often effective. One example is, "Could the root of your problem be that you have not studied the user manual?"

8. **Coach with "could," not "should."** When instructing somebody else to improve, tell the person he or she *could* do something rather than he or she *should* do it. *Should* implies the person is doing something morally wrong, such as, "You should recycle the empty laser cartridges." *Could* leaves the person with a choice to make: to accept or reject your input and weigh the consequences.[17]

9. **Interpret what is happening.** An interpretation given by the person doing the coaching is an explanation of why the person being coached is acting in a particular manner. The interpretation is designed to give the person being coached insight into the nature of the problem. For instance, a food service manager might be listening to the problems of a cafeteria manager with regard to cafeteria cleanliness. After a while the food service manager might say, "You're angry and upset with your employees because they don't keep a careful eye on cleanliness. So you avoid dealing with them, and it only makes problems worse." If the manager's diagnosis is correct, an interpretation can be extremely helpful.

10. **Allow for modeling of the desired performance and behaviors.** An effective coaching technique is to show the person being coached an example of what constitutes the desired behavior. A customer service representative was harsh with customers when facing heavy pressure. One way the supervisor coached the service representative was by taking over the manager's desk during a busy period. The representative then watched the supervisor deal tactfully with demanding customers.

11. **Applaud good results.** Effective coaches on the playing field and in the workplace are cheerleaders. They give positive reinforcement by applauding desired results. Some effective coaches shout in joy when the person coached achieves outstanding results; others give high fives or clap their hands in applause.[18]

Many people are concerned that if they offer too much coaching and feedback to others, they will be perceived as interfering with their work, or being a micromanager. In reality, the majority of workers believe that they do not receive enough coaching and guidance on the job. RainmakerThinking, Inc., has conducted long-term research suggesting that the undermanaged worker struggles because his or her supervisor is not sufficiently engaged to provide the needed direction and support.[19]

One implication of the coaching suggestions just presented is that some people are more adept at coaching than others. Self-Assessment Quiz 11-2 provides insight into the right stuff for being an effective coach. After doing that exercise and reading the suggestions, you will be prepared for Skill-Building Exercise 11-4 about coaching.

Training Others

A direct way of helping others in the workplace is to train them. **Training** is the process of helping others acquire a job-related skill. Supervisors and trainers are responsible for much of the training in organizations. Yet as organizations operate with fewer managers, coworkers have more responsibility to train each other. Coworker training is part of the process of knowledge transfer mentioned already. While training others, keep in mind certain time-tested principles that facilitate learning—and therefore training. Applying these principles consistently will increase the chances that the people you are training will acquire new skills.

training

The process of helping others acquire a job-related skill.

1. **Encourage concentration.** Not much learning takes place unless the trainee concentrates carefully on what is being learned. Concentration improves the ability to do both mental and physical tasks. In short, encourage the person you are training to concentrate.

Characteristics of an Effective Coach

Directions: What follows is a list of traits, attitudes, and behaviors of effective coaches. Indicate under each trait, attitude, or behavior whether you need to improve on it (for example, "Yes, patience toward people"). Then in the right column prepare an action plan for improving each trait, attitude, or behavior that you need to develop. Sample action plans are provided.

Trait, attitude, or behavior	Action plan for improvement
Empathy	*Sample:* Will listen until I understand the person's point of view. *Your own:*
Listening skill	*Sample:* Will concentrate extra hard to listen. *Your own:*
Ability to size up people	*Sample:* Will jot down observations about people upon first meeting, then verify in the future. *Your own:*
Diplomacy and tact	*Sample:* Will study a book of etiquette. *Your own:*
Patience toward people	*Sample:* Will practice staying calm when someone makes a mistake. *Your own:*
Concern for welfare	*Sample:* When interacting with another person, will ask self, of others, "How can this person's interests best be served?" *Your own:*
Self-confidence	*Sample:* Will attempt to have at least one personal success each week. *Your own:*
Noncompetitiveness	*Sample:* Will keep reminding myself that all boats with team members rise with the same tide. *Your own:*
Enthusiasm for people	*Sample:* Will search for the good in each person. *Your own:*
Work on my personal development, thereby leading by example	*Sample:* Overcome projecting the attitude that people who disagree with me are really stupid. *Your own:*
Develops trust and respect[19]	*Sample:* Consistently tells the truth to people. *Your own:*

Coaching a Good Performer

Visualize a team of five people working at a Sir Speedy print shop. The shop provides such services as photocopying, desktop publishing, and printing. One student plays the role of the team leader and owner of this Sir Speedy franchise. Another student plays the role of Chris, a team member who is a standout performer. However, the impatience Chris displays toward teammates when taking care of a good customer is a problem. When Chris is taking care of a large job, he expects others on the team to drop every-thing to help with that customer. "When I'm serving a customer, that customer's needs come first," says Chris.

The team leader and Chris get together for a coaching session initiated by the team leader. Chris is convinced that he is right to place customer needs over those of team members. Students not actively participating in this role-play will observe the two role-players. Be alert for indicators of both good and poor coaching by the team leader.

2. **Use motivated interest.** People learn best when they are interested in the problem facing them. Explain to the trainee how the skill being taught will enhance his or her value as an employee, or relate the skill to the person's professional goals. Trainees can be encouraged to look for some relationship between the information at hand and their personal welfare. With this relationship in mind, the person will have a stronger intention to learn.

3. **Remind learners to intend to remember.** We often fail to remember something because we do not intend to commit it to memory. Many executives are particularly effective at remembering the names of employees and customers. When one executive was asked how she could commit so many names to memory, she replied, "I look at the person, listen to the name, and try hard to remember." An example of reminding a protégé to remember would be to advise him or her to memorize the company mission statement.

4. **Ensure the meaningfulness of material.** The material to be learned should be organized in a meaningful manner. Each successive experience should build on the other. In training another person how to process a customer order, you might teach the skill in terms of the flow of activities from customer inquiry to product delivery.

5. **Give feedback on progress.** As a person's training progresses, motivation may be maintained and enhanced by providing knowledge on his or her progress. To measure progress it may be necessary to ask the trainee questions or ask for a job sample. For example, you might ask the person being trained on invoices to prepare a sample invoice.

6. **Ask the trainee to reflect on what he or she has learned.** Research indicates that if you think carefully about what you have learned, your retention of the information increases. The idea is to step back from the experience to ponder carefully and persistently its meaning to you.[20] After participating in a team development exercise involving white-water rafting, a person might reflect, "What did I really learn about being a better team player? How was I perceived by my teammates in the rubber raft? Did they even notice my contribution? Or did they think I was an important part of the team success?"

7. **Deal with trainee defensiveness.** Training is sometimes retarded because the person being trained is defensive about information or skills that clash with his or her beliefs and practices. The person might have so much emotional energy invested in the status quo that he or she resists the training. For example, a sales representative might resist learning how to use e-commerce because she believes that her warm smile and interpersonal skills have made her an excellent communicator. She is concerned that if she communicates with customers exclusively through e-mail or a company Web site, her human touch will be lost. Sensing this defensiveness, the trainer is advised to talk about e-commerce as being a supplement to, but not a substitute for, in-person communication. (However, the sales rep might also be worried that her position will be eliminated.)

8. **Take into account learning style.** Another key factor that influences training is **learning style,** the way in which a person best learns new information. An example of a learning style is passive learning. People who learn best through passive learning quickly acquire information by studying texts, manuals, magazine articles, and Web sites. They can juggle images in their mind as they read about abstract concepts such as supply and demand, cultural diversity, or customer service. Others learn best by doing rather than studying—for example, learning about customer service by dealing with customers in many situations.

learning style

The way in which a person best learns new information.

Another key dimension of learning styles is whether a person learns best by working alone or cooperatively in a study group. Learning by oneself may allow for more intense concentration, and one can proceed at one's own pace. Learning in groups through classroom discussion allows people to exchange viewpoints and perspectives.

Designing a Training Program

The class organizes into training design teams of approximately six people. Each team sketches the design of a training program to teach an interpersonal skill to employees, such as being polite to customers or interviewing job candidates. The teams are not responsible for selecting the exact content of the training program they choose. Instead, they are responsible for designing a training program based on the principles of learning. Two examples here would be (a) how to encourage the trainees to concentrate, and (b) developing a mechanism to provide feedback to the trainee.

The activity should take about 15 minutes and can therefore be done inside or outside the class. After the teams have designed their programs, they can compare the various versions.

Because of differences in learning styles, you may decide to design training to fit these differences. For example, if your trainees prefer cooperative learning you could combine learning from reading books, articles, and online information with discussions in a conference room.

To start applying these principles of learning to a training situation, do Skill-Building Exercise 11-5.

LEARNING OBJECTIVE 4

HELPING DIFFICULT PEOPLE

A challenge we all face from time to time is dealing constructively with workers who appear intent on creating problems. For a variety of reasons, these difficult or counter-productive people perform poorly themselves or interfere with the job performance of others. A **difficult person** is an individual who creates problems for others, yet has the skill and mental ability to do otherwise. The difficult person may meet or exceed attendance and performance standards, yet has a toxic personality.[21] Here we briefly discuss various types of difficult people, and then emphasize methods for helping them behave more productively. To pretest your skill in dealing with and helping difficult people, do Self-Assessment Quiz 11-3.

difficult person

An individual who creates problems for others, even though he or she has the skill and mental ability to do otherwise.

SELF-ASSESSMENT QUIZ 11-3

Helping Difficult People

Directions: For each of the following scenarios, circle the letter of what you think is the most effective way to handle the situation. There may be more than one correct method listed.

1. A coworker in the cubicle next to you is talking loudly on the telephone about the fabulous weekend she and a few friends enjoyed. You are attempting to deal with a challenging work problem. To deal with this situation, you
   a. get up from your chair, stand close to her, and say loudly, "Shut up, you jerk! I'm trying to do my work."
   b. slip her a handwritten note that says, "I'm happy that you had a great weekend, but I have problems concentrating on my work when you are talking so loudly. Thanks for your help."
   c. get the boss on the phone and ask that she please do something about the problem.
   d. wait until lunch and then say to her, "I'm happy that you had a great weekend, but I have problems concentrating on my work when you are talking so loudly. Thanks for your help."

2. One of your coworkers, Olaf, rarely carries his fair load of the work. He forever has a good reason for not having the time to do an assignment. This morning he has approached you to load some new software onto his personal computer. You deal with this situation by
   a. carefully explaining that you will help him, providing he will take over a certain specified task for you.
   b. telling him that you absolutely refuse to help a person as lazy as he is.

c. counseling him about fair play and reciprocity.
   d. reviewing with him a list of five times when he has asked other people to help him. You then ask if he thinks this is a good way to treat coworkers.

3. In your role as supervisor, you have noticed that Diane, one of the group members, spends far too much work time laughing and joking. You schedule a meeting with her. As the meeting opens, you
   a. joke and laugh with her to establish rapport.
   b. explain to Diane that you have called this meeting to discuss her too-frequent laughing and joking.
   c. talk for a few moments about the good things Diane has done for the department, then confront the real issue.
   d. explain to Diane that she is on the verge of losing her job if she doesn't act more maturely.

4. As a team member, you have become increasingly annoyed with Jerry's ethnic, racist, and sexist jokes. One day during a team meeting, he tells a joke you believe is particularly offensive. To deal with the situation, you
   a. meet privately with the team leader to discuss Jerry's offensive behavior.
   b. catch up with Jerry later when he is alone, and tell him how uncomfortable his joke made you feel.
   c. confront Jerry on the spot and say, "Hold on Jerry. I find your joke offensive."
   d. tell the group an even more offensive joke to illustrate how Jerry's behavior can get out of hand.

5. You have been placed on a task force to look for ways to save the company money, including making recommendations for eliminating jobs. You interview a supervisor about the efficiency of her department. She suddenly becomes rude and defensive. In response, you
   a. politely point out how her behavior is coming across to you.
   b. get your revenge by recommending that three jobs be eliminated from her department.
   c. explain that you have used up enough of her time for today and ask for another meeting later in the week.
   d. tell her that unless she becomes more cooperative this interview cannot continue.

Scoring and Interpretation: Use the following key to obtain your score:

1. a. 1	2. a. 4	3. a. 1	4. a. 2	5. a. 4
b. 4	b. 1	b. 4	b. 4	b. 1
c. 2	c. 3	c. 3	c. 3	c. 2
d. 3	d. 2	d. 2	d. 1	d. 3

18–20 You have good intuition about helping difficult people.

10–17 You have average intuition about helping difficult people.

5–9 You need to improve your sensitivity about helping difficult people.

Types of Difficult People

Dozens of types of difficult people have been identified, with considerable overlap among the types. For example, one method of classifying difficult people might identify the dictator, while another method might identify the bully. For our purposes, here I list a sampling of the many types of difficult people found in the workplace and as customers. As you read the following list, look for familiar types[22]:

- *Know-it-alls* believe they are experts on everything. They have opinions on every issue, yet when they are wrong they pass the buck or become defensive.
- *Blamers* are workers who never solve their own problems. When faced with a challenge or a hitch, they think the problem belongs to the supervisor or a group member.
- *Gossips* spread negative rumors about others and attempt to set people against each other.
- *Bullies* cajole and intimidate others. They are blunt to the point of being insulting, and will sometimes use harsh, vulgar language to attain their goals. Bullies constantly make demands on workmates.

- *Repulsives* are people whose poor personal hygiene, eating habits, appearance, or foul language disrupt the tranquility of others.
- *Yes-people* agree to any commitment, promise any deadline, but rarely deliver. Although sorry about being late, they cannot be trusted to deliver as promised.
- *No-people* are negative, pessimistic, and quick to point out why something will not work. They also are inflexible, resist change, and complain frequently.
- *Jekyll and Hydes* have a split personality. When dealing with supervisors, customers, or clients, they are pleasant, engaging people; yet, when carrying out the role of supervisors, they become tyrannical.
- *Whiners* gripe about people, processes, and company regulations. They complain about being overworked and underpaid, or not receiving assignments up to their true capabilities.
- *Backstabbers* pretend to befriend you and encourage you to talk freely about problems or personality clashes you face. Later, the backstabber reports the information—often in exaggerated form—to the person you mentioned in a negative light. Or the backstabber simply says negative things about you behind your back to discredit you to others.
- *High-maintenance* types require considerable attention from others in such forms as demanding much of the supervisor's time, making unusual requests to the human resources department, and taking the maximum number of sick days and personal days allowable. High-maintenance types are often a combination of several of the previous types described above.
- *Clods* are master procrastinators who can find plenty of excuses as to why a project has not been started. When the clod finally gets started on a project, the work proceeds so slowly that other people who need the clod's input fall behind schedule and become stressed.
- *Minimalists* are apathetic and low-performing, and do just enough work to avoid being fired. They do the bare minimum, and thrive on being mediocre.
- *Office cheats* take claim for the ideas of other people, and benefit from these ideas, leaving the originator of the idea without deserved credit and feeling frustrated because of the stolen ideas.

Tactics for Dealing with Difficult People

How one deals most effectively with a difficult person depends to some extent on the person's type. For example, you might need more time to get through to a passive person than to a bully. Figure 11-2 presents specific ideas for dealing with a bully. (You will recall that bullying was described in Chapter 8 as a source of workplace conflict.) The following techniques have wide applicability for helping difficult people change to a more constructive behavior pattern. This general approach should prove more helpful than being concerned with specific tactics for each type of difficult person you encounter.

The problems that difficult people (sometimes referred to collectively as *office jerks*) create have received considerable attention in recent years from managers. The precise definition of an office jerk is someone who consistently leaves people feeling demeaned, belittled, and deenergized. In addition, the office jerk typically targets people of lesser power than he or she possesses.[23] (Despite the frequent use of the term, labeling people as *jerks* tends to exclude constructive thinking about dealing with the problem, and is not good human relations practice.)

Such companies as Google, Mozilla, and Southwest Airlines have taken many of the steps described next to minimize the negative impact difficult people have on productivity and job satisfaction. Another problem is some positive contributors will quit when forced to work permanently with a difficult person. Many difficult people are also being fired instead of counseled because of the problems they create.[24]

FIGURE 11-2 How to Be a Bully Buster

Christine Pearson, a management professor at the University of North Carolina at Chapel Hill, says that employees can take steps to keep uncivil behavior out of the workplace.[25]

- The first step is to admit to yourself that you are being bullied and that the bullying is unfair and unjustified.

- If the bully is affecting you physically, see your doctor.

- Stand up for yourself and be confident.

- Check out your body language. If you stoop, hang your head, or hunch over, you may be giving off victim signals.

- Try not to show that the bully has upset you; the bully may get bored and leave you alone.

- Don't suffer in silence; tell someone you trust.

- Find out about your rights, consider using any complaints procedure available in your company, and if necessary, consult a lawyer.

Give Ample Feedback   The primary technique for dealing with counterproductive behavior is to feed back to the difficult person how his or her behavior affects you. As in other forms of feedback, be clear about what you want. Focus on the person's behavior rather than on characteristics or values. If a *repulsive type* is annoying you by constantly eating when you are working together, say something to this effect: "I have difficulty concentrating on the work when you are eating." Such a statement will engender less resentment than saying, "I find you repulsive, and it annoys me." As in coaching, it is better to avoid *should* statements because they often create defensiveness instead of triggering positive behavior. Instead of saying, "You shouldn't be eating when you are working," you might try, "Could you find another place to eat when we are working together?"

Feedback will sometimes take the form of confrontation, and it is important not to lose emotional control during the confrontation. If the difficult person has criticized you unjustly in your eyes, attempt not to be defensive. Ask the difficult person exactly what he or she is upset about rather than argue. In this way the burden of responsibility is now back on the antagonist. For example, if a bully was swearing at you during a meeting, later ask for the reason behind the outburst. Following the technique of disarming the opposition described in Chapter 8, you might agree with at least one of the bully's points. This will help establish rapport.[26] An example here would be "Yes, I should have consulted you before making the final report. I apologize for the oversight."

Criticize Constructively   Feedback sets the stage for criticism. It is best to criticize in private and to begin with mild criticism. Base your criticism on objective facts rather than subjective impressions. Point out, for example, that the yes-person's lack of follow-through resulted in $10,000 in lost sales. Express your criticism in terms of a common goal. For example, "We can get the report done quickly if you'll firm up the statistical data while I edit the text." When you criticize a coworker, avoid acting as if you have formal authority over the person.

Help the Difficult Person Feel More Confident   Many counterproductive employees are simply low in self-confidence and self-efficacy. They use stalling and evasive tactics because they are afraid to fail. Working with your manager or team leader, you might be able to arrange a project or task in which you know the difficult person will succeed. With a small dose of self-confidence and self-efficacy, the person may begin to complain less. With additional successes, the person may soon become less difficult.[27] Self-confidence building takes time. However, self-efficacy can build more quickly as the person learns a new skill.

Use Tact and Diplomacy   Tactful actions on your part can sometimes take care of annoying behavior by coworkers without having to confront the problem. Close your door, for example, if noisy coworkers are gathered outside. When subtlety does not work, it may be necessary to proceed to a confrontation style of feedback.

Tact and diplomacy can still be incorporated into confrontation. In addition to confronting the person, you might also point out one of the individual's strengths. In dealing with a know-it-all you might say, "I realize you are creative and filled with good ideas. However, I wish you would give me an opportunity to express my opinion."

Use Nonhostile Humor   Nonhostile humor can often be used to help a difficult person understand how his or her behavior is blocking others. Also, the humor will help you defuse the conflict between you and that person. The humor should point to the person's unacceptable behavior, yet not belittle him or her. Assume that you and a coworker are working jointly on a report. For each idea that you submit, your coworker gets into the know-it-all mode and informs you of important facts you neglected. An example of nonhostile humor that might jolt the coworker into realizing that his or her approach is annoying is as follows:

> If there is ever a contest to choose the human being with a brain that can compete against a Zip file, I will nominate you. But even though my brain is limited to human capacity, I still think I can supply a few facts for our report.

Your humor may help the other person recognize that he or she is attempting to overwhelm you with facts at his or her disposal. You are being self-effacing and thereby drawing criticism away from your coworker. Self-effacement is a proven humor tactic.

Work Out a Deal   A direct approach to dealing with problems created by a difficult person is to work out a deal or a negotiated solution. Workers who do not carry their load are successful in getting others to do their work. The next time such a worker wants you to carry out a task, agree to it if he or she will reciprocate by performing a task that will benefit you. For working out a deal to be effective, you must be specific about the terms of the deal. The worker may at first complain about your demands for reciprocity, so it is important to be firm.

Reinforce Civil Behavior and Good Moods   In the spirit of positive reinforcement, when a generally difficult person is behaving acceptably, recognize the behavior in some way. Reinforcing statements would include "It's fun working with you today" and "I appreciate your professional attitude."

Ask the Difficult Person to THINK Before Speaking   Human relations specialist John Maxwell suggests that you ask the difficult person to THINK before he or she speaks, with "THINK" referring to the acronym[28]:

T   Is it true?
H   Is it helpful?
I   Is it inspiring?
N   Is it necessary?
K   Is it kind?

Although Maxwell's suggestion is aimed at difficult people, is would be a helpful rule of thumb for building relationships with people in many situations.

Have a Job Description That Disallows Difficult Behavior   When difficult behavior is prohibited by the job description, the difficult person can be reminded that his or her behavior is out-of-bounds. A legalistic approach like this must be executed tactfully.

Employment law specialist David Wimmer encourages employers to add something similar to the following to job descriptions:

> *Employee must be able to relate to other people beyond giving and receiving instructions: (a) can get along with coworkers without exhibiting behavior extremes; (b) perform work activities requiring negotiating, instruction, supervising, persuading or speaking with others; and (c) respond appropriately to criticisms from a superior.*[29]

Using this legalistic approach, you might say to a coworker who keeps swearing at teammates and telling them to shut up when he or she disagrees with them, "You are getting your work done, and that pleases me. Yet, I think your behavior is not in line with the complete job description that we all have to work by."

The tactics for dealing with the difficult people just described require practice to be effective. When you next encounter a difficult person, try one of the tactics that seems to fit the occasion. Role-plays, such as those presented in Skill-Building Exercise 11-6, are a good starting point for implementing tactics in dealing with difficult people.

SELF-ASSESSMENT QUIZZES IN OVERVIEW

Self-Assessment Quiz 11-1, Attitudes toward Helping Others, deals with perhaps the most humanistic topic in the book. If you truly believe in helping others, you will be a better coworker, team leader, supervisor, manager, coach, or mentor. If your attitudes toward helping others are not so positive, perhaps this might be an area for improvement so you can be more effective in the various roles just mentioned. Self-Assessment Quiz 11-2, Characteristics of an Effective Coach, takes you one step further into self-reflection in relation to helping others. You will notice that the characteristics of an effective coach are similar to good interpersonal skills in general, such as using diplomacy and tact and being enthusiastic. Self-Assessment Quiz 11-3 is different from the other self-assessment quizzes in this text because it provides you various scenarios to solve. At the same time, you are given the opportunity to check your intuition about an important aspect of human behavior.

Concept Review and Reinforcement

Key Terms

nurturing person, 219
toxic person, 219
mentor, 221

protégé, 222
coaching, 225
behavioral feedback, 226

training, 227
learning style, 229
difficult person, 230

Summary of Key Concepts

Workers have a responsibility to help each other learn, grow, and develop. A major strategy for helping others grow and develop is to be a nurturing, positive person. A toxic person stands in contrast to a nurturing person because he or she dwells on the negative. Nurturing people are positive, enthusiastic, and supportive. Three actions and attitudes that support being a nurturing person are to (1) recognize growth needs in others, (2) use the buddy system, and (3) be a role model.

Being a mentor is another way to help others. To be a mentor, a person engages in a wide range of helping behaviors. Among them are sponsoring, coaching, protecting, sharing challenging assignments, and being a referral agent. Mentors also help protégés solve problems and learn the ropes of an organization. Mentoring can sometimes help the organization by helping workers become more committed to the firm.

Coaching and training are direct helping roles. Coaching is a method of helping workers grow and develop by providing suggestions and encouragement. Suggestions for effective coaching include the following:

1. Build relationships.
2. Provide specific feedback.
3. Make criticism pain free and positive.
4. Encourage the person you are coaching to talk.
5. Ask powerful questions.
6. Give emotional support.
7. Give some constructive advice.
8. Coach with "could," not "should."
9. Interpret what is happening.
10. Allow for modeling of the desired performance and behaviors.
11. Applaud good results.

Training involves helping people acquire job skills. To facilitate training, apply principles of learning such as the following: (1) encourage concentration, (2) use motivated interest, (3) remind learners to intend to remember, (4) ensure the meaningfulness of material, (5) give feedback on progress, (6) ask the trainee to reflect on what he or she has learned, (7) deal with trainee defensiveness, and (8) take into account learning style.

Dealing with difficult people is a major challenge in helping others. The many types of difficult people include know-it-alls, blamers, gossips, bullies, repulsives, yes-people, no-people, Jekyll and Hydes, whiners, backstabbers, high-maintenance types, and office cheats. Companies are concerned about the damage difficult people create, and sometimes fire them. Tactics for dealing with them include the following: (1) give ample feedback (including confrontation), (2) criticize constructively, (3) help the difficult person feel more confident, (4) use tact and diplomacy, (5) use humor, (6) work out a deal, (7) reinforce civil behavior and good moods, (8) ask the person to THINK before speaking, and (9) have a job description that disallows difficult behavior.

Check Your Understanding

1. Explain your position on whether workers have a responsibility to help each other grow and develop.

2. What is your opinion of the potential effectiveness of the buddy system in your career?

3. Visualize yourself in a full-time professional job working for a company that believes strongly in mentoring. Explain whether you would prefer to find a mentor for yourself, or be assigned a mentor by the company.

4. In what way does a coach in the workplace function much like an athletic coach?

5. Describe any constructive advice you have received from anybody who has coached you. What was the impact of this advice?

6. Many career-minded workers today hire their own coach, much like a personal trainer for solving job problems and advancing. Explain whether you would be willing to invest money to hire a "business coach" for yourself.

7. Do you think trainee defensiveness is a bigger problem in teaching technical or interpersonal skills? Explain.

8. How would you know if people perceive you as a *difficult person?*

9. How might humor help you deal with the repulsive type of difficult person? Supply an example of a witty comment you might use.

10. What did the project manager in the opening case mean by his statement that "management goes beyond numbers and charts"?

The Web Corner

http://www.jobshadow.org
(Job shadowing as a form of mentoring.)

http://www.BlueSuitMom.com/career/management/difficultpeople.html
(Strategies for dealing with difficult people.)

http://www.newtrainingideas.com/coaching-mentoring.html
(Advantages of coaching and mentoring.)

Internet Skill Builder: Mentoring Online

As mentioned in the chapter, many mentors stay in touch with the people they mentor primarily through e-mail and Web sites, including company and social-networking Web sites. Such virtual networking has advantages and disadvantages. Search the Internet for three useful ideas about how to mentor effectively online. Try the search terms *virtual mentoring* and *online mentoring* as well as other terms you think might work. Think through which of these ideas you would use as an online mentor.

Developing Your Human Relations Skills

Interpersonal Relations Case 11.1

The Demanding Protégé

Dawn Albright is a sales representative for an office-supply company. She has five years of successful experience selling furnishings and interior designs to business firms in her area. Dawn worked her way up from taking telephone orders for small supplies such as computer paper, print cartridges, pencils, ballpoint pens, and pencils. By the fifth year of her employment, Dawn became the highest producer in the office. Later she was placed in charge of orders received on the company's Web site.

One day Dawn's manager, Jim Bastian, requested a favor: "Dawn, would you be willing to take Marilyn Lake under your wing? Marilyn is the newest member of the sales staff. I think she could benefit from the guidance of a real pro like you." Dawn enthusiastically agreed to assume responsibility for becoming Marilyn's mentor. She told Jim, "I sure could have used help myself when I was getting started."

Jim explained to Dawn that Marilyn might need a lot of help. He pointed out that the company was taking a chance on placing Marilyn in a sales position. Jim's reasoning was that although Marilyn had a professional appearance, she didn't appear to have much self-confidence. When Dawn asked Jim to give her a few specifics, he commented, "A lot of little things have given me the impression that Marilyn needs more self-confidence. When I interviewed her, Marilyn could not give me any examples of how she had ever been a leader in anything. Also, when I ask her opinion about almost anything, she says, 'I'm really not sure' or 'I don't have an informed opinion.'"

Dawn later met with Marilyn to explain that although she was not her boss she had volunteered to spend time showing her the ropes. Marilyn expressed appreciation and acknowledged that she had a lot to learn about the business.

Dawn began working with Marilyn by taking her along on visits to a few of her best accounts. Dawn even allowed Marilyn to receive credit for the sale of a few desks, chairs, and coffee tables because she assisted in the sales. Over the next several months, Dawn would discuss Marilyn's sales progress with her from time to time. The two would discuss Marilyn's tactics and the plans she formulated to develop each account. Marilyn listened attentively and followed Dawn's advice carefully.

Toward the end of the sixth month of their working relationship, Dawn received a telephone call from Marilyn late one night. Marilyn pleaded with Dawn to accompany her on a sales call to a potentially big account. "I know that if you are present at this meeting, between the two of us we will close the sale," said Marilyn.

Dawn's first thought was that Marilyn needed the experience of closing a big sale herself, yet she obliged. "Marilyn has a point," thought Dawn to herself. "Experience is a big factor in closing such a large account. And our firm could sure use the business."

As the months rolled by Marilyn made an increasing number of requests for Dawn's advice on sales tactics. Twice more she pressured Dawn into helping her close big sales. Dawn hinted that Marilyn should close the sale herself, but Marilyn insisted that she needed help just one more time.

Soon Marilyn began to seek Dawn's advice on matters outside work. One day Marilyn asked if Dawn would help her choose a dress for an engagement shower. Another time Marilyn sought Dawn's advice on how she should handle her parents' negative reaction to her latest boyfriend. Soon Marilyn was telephoning Dawn at least twice a weekend, asking to discuss questions about both work and her personal life. Marilyn would also send regular e-mail messages to Dawn, asking her opinion on many small matters such as, "How much should I thank a customer for a small order?"

One day Dawn thought to herself, "My being a mentor to Marilyn has gone too far. I'm her confidante, her big sister, and her sales consultant. At times I also feel I'm her mother. This relationship is draining me."

Case Questions

1. How effective is Dawn as Marilyn's mentor?
2. In what way might Dawn be hindering her protégée's development?
3. What should Dawn do about her relationship with Marilyn?
4. What underlying issue might Dawn be neglecting in dealing with Marilyn?

Interpersonal Relations Case 11.2

What to Do About Brian?

Brian is one of 10 home mortgage refinance specialists working in his department of Cypress Finance, a substantially sized financial services firm. Most of the customer contact work of the mortgage refinance department is conducted over the telephone (using a toll-free number), even when potential customers initiate their inquiry through the company Web site. Each refinance specialist does considerable individual work—including interacting with customers and potential customers and evaluating the mortgage applicant's credit worthiness. Credit checks are made with computerized databases, but occasionally clarifying information is sought.

Refinance specialists have to cooperate with each other on complex cases. The cooperation often takes the form of asking a teammate's opinion on the creditworthiness of the risk. A member of management, however, gives final approval to all but the most routine refinance applications.

At times, the supervisor of the group, Nina, makes assignments to balance the workload among the specialists. However, the work piles up so quickly that the specialists are supposed to look for ways to spread the work out evenly among themselves to prevent delays in processing refinance applications.

Nina perceives Brian to be a superior performer. His most recent performance evaluation stated that he was an outstanding refinance specialist with potential for promotion to a supervisory position in the future. Nina also rated Brian's sales performance to be outstanding. A "sale" means that an inquiry over the telephone or Web site is converted into an application to refinance that becomes approved. Despite his outstanding performance, Nina did mention that Brian could strengthen his teamwork skills. She specifically mentioned that Brian was sometimes so busy with his individual cases that he neglected to help other team members.

During a recent team meeting, Nina told the group, "Once again I am pleased to announce that Brian has been the outstanding producer in the department. I know that we work together as a team yet still have our individual goals. Brian is great at closing applicants with good credit risks, and he still contributes his share as a team player."

Kenny, one of the other refinance specialists, gave a gentle nudge with his elbow to Cindy, a specialist seated to his right. Kenny murmured, "What a kiss-up this guy is. Nina should know what an annoyance Brian is in the office."

After the meeting, Kenny, Cindy, and Lindsay, a third specialist, were standing together near the elevator. Lindsay said while giggling, "Did you see the look on Brian's face? All smiles, like he was voted the MVP [Most Valuable Player] of the Super Bowl. Brian sometimes forgets that we help him with his trickiest applications, and then he grabs the glory. But ask Brian for a little help, and he'll say something to the effect that he's too busy closing a major deal. You'd think he was refinancing the Sears Tower in Chicago." Kenny, Cindy, and Lindsay giggled simultaneously.

The next workday at Cypress was one of the busiest ever. Newspaper and television reports throughout the country announced that mortgage rates were expected to climb by one and one-half percent the following month. The number of applicants for refinancing doubled, as many homeowners were eager to lock in the present low rates for refinancing. The refinance specialists were asked to put in 60-hour weeks until the workload drifted back to normal.

During the lunch break on one of the peak-load days, Brian approached the three other specialists taking the break at the same time as he with this proposition. "As everyone in this office knows, I am really talented at closing deals. And the more deals we close as a group, the bigger will be the group bonus at the end of the year. So I'm suggesting that when I have a couple of big deals on the hook, I send my minnows over to you. [Minnows refer to small deals.] Also, I'd like your cooperation in doing some of the detail work, such as a lengthy credit inquiry for a major deal. My time is better invested in reeling in the big deals."

One of the specialists said, "Sounds good to me." Cindy took an opposite approach, as she told Brian, "Happy fishing, but you're not my boss. Why should I volunteer to help you when you never volunteer to help me?"

Brian retorted, "Cindy, you may be a nice person, but I think you're a rotten team player. We have to divide up responsibilities for the good of the team."

Later that day, Cindy chatted with Kenny and Lindsay about the incident during the lunch break. She said, "We've got to do something about Brian, but I don't know what. It's tough when you have to do battle with the boss's pet."

Questions

1. Is Brian a *difficult person?* Explain.
2. What steps should the refinance specialists objecting to Brian's work style take?
3. How might a system of peer evaluation (workers contributing to the evaluation of each other) help Nina in her supervision of the department?
3. Do you think Cindy is being a rotten team player?

CHAPTER 12

Positive Political Skills

Todd Madison, age 26, was working successfully as a heating and air-conditioning technician for a large firm in Atlanta, Georgia. With technicians in his field in high demand in Atlanta, Todd was earning more money than he anticipated when he graduated from technical school several years ago. Madison and his wife, a licensed practical nurse, were looking toward purchasing a condominium.

A close friend of Madison's, Jerry Weaver, age 27, was also in the heating and air-conditioning field. Weaver, however, was a little more advanced in his career, working as a manager in the largest firm of its kind in Atlanta. Madison and Weaver were friends in a number of ways. Their families entertained each other at home occasionally, the two men fished and played golf together from time to time, and sometimes they watched Atlanta Falcons games together.

During one golf outing together, Weaver surprised Madison with an offer to become an area supervisor in his firm, reporting directly to Weaver. After careful reflection about the prospects of having a close buddy as a boss, Madison accepted the position as a heating and air-conditioning supervisor, with 12 technicians reporting to him. As he settled into the job, Madison began to wonder how he was going to deal with any charges of favoritism, and how he would handle any disagreements with Weaver. At the same time, Weaver began to worry how he would discipline Madison if necessary, and how he should avoid any possible favoritism in terms of performance evaluations and recommended salary increases.

One implication of the anecdote about the two friends is that to prosper in the workplace you have to be aware of the political factors that could damage a working relationship. At the same time, the proper use of positive political tactics helps build good interpersonal relationships. In turn, these good relationships can facilitate achieving career goals. Recognize, however, that being competent in your job is still the most effective method of achieving career success. After skill come hard work and luck as

Learning Objectives

After reading and studying this chapter and doing the exercises, you should be able to

1. Explain the importance of political skill and social intelligence for becoming skilled at using positive political tactics.
2. Manage effectively the impression you give, including developing an awareness of the rules of business etiquette.
3. Implement political techniques for building relationships with managers and other key people.
4. Implement political techniques for building relationships with coworkers and other worker associates.
5. Avoid committing political blunders.

important success factors. A fourth ingredient is also important for success—positive political skills.

Few people can achieve success for themselves or their group without having some awareness of the political forces around them and how to use them to advantage. It may be necessary for the career-minded person to take the offensive in using positive and ethical political tactics. As used here, **organizational politics** refers to gaining power through any means other than merit or luck. (Luck, of course, is what happens when preparation meets opportunity.) Politics are played to achieve power, either directly or indirectly. **Power** refers to the ability or potential to control anything of value and to influence decisions. The results of such power may take diverse forms like being promoted, being transferred, receiving a salary increase, or avoiding an uncomfortable assignment. As you study this chapter, it will become evident that communication skills and team player skills are necessary for being skilled at politics. Figure 12-1 depicts the relationship among politics, power, and control and influence. Political tactics, such as developing contacts with key people, lead to power, which enables one to control and influence others.

In this chapter we approach skill development in organizational (or office) politics from several standpoints. Information is presented about such topics as managing your impression, using political tactics to improve interpersonal relationships, and avoiding hazardous political mistakes. In addition, you have the opportunity to take two quizzes about political tactics and engage in skill-building exercises. To measure your current tendencies toward playing politics, do Self-Assessment Quiz 12-1.

organizational politics

Gaining power through any means other than merit or luck.

power

The ability or potential to control anything of value and to influence decisions.

FIGURE 12-1 Relationship among Politics, Power and Influence, and Political Tactics, such as developing contacts with key people, lead to power, which enables one to control and influence others.

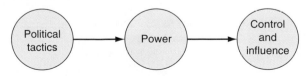

Organizational Politics Questionnaire

Directions: For each of the following statements, check whether you *mostly agree* or *mostly disagree*, even if it is difficult for you to decide which alternative best describes your opinion.

	Mostly agree	Mostly disagree
1. The boss or team leader is always right.	_____	_____
2. It is wise to flatter important people.	_____	_____
3. If you do somebody a favor, remember to cash in on it.	_____	_____
4. Given the opportunity, I would go out of my way to develop friendships with powerful people.	_____	_____
5. I would be willing to say nice things about a rival to get that person transferred from my department.	_____	_____
6. If it would help me get ahead, I would take credit for someone else's work.	_____	_____
7. Given the chance, I would offer to help my boss fix something in his or her home.	_____	_____
8. I laugh heartily at my boss's humor, even if I do not think it is funny.	_____	_____
9. Dressing to create a favorable appearance is foolish. At the office, wear clothing that you find to be the most comfortable.	_____	_____
10. Never waste lunchtime by eating with somebody who can't help you solve a problem or gain advantage.	_____	_____
11. I think using e-mail to zap somebody for his or her mistake, and sending copies to key people, is a good idea.	_____	_____
12. If somebody higher up in the organization offends you, look for ways to get even with him or her.	_____	_____
13. Being candid is the best policy even if it means insulting somebody.	_____	_____
14. Obtaining power for its own sake would make me feel wonderful.	_____	_____
15. If I had a legitimate gripe against my employer, I would express my views publicly (such as distributing my comments over the Internet).	_____	_____
16. I would invite my boss or team leader to a party at my home even if I didn't like him or her.	_____	_____
17. An effective way to impress people is to tell them what they want to hear.	_____	_____
18. Having a school, college, or skyscraper named after me would be an incredible thrill.	_____	_____
19. Hard work and good performance are usually sufficient for career success.	_____	_____
20. Even if I made only a minor contribution to a project, I would get my name listed as being associated with it.	_____	_____
21. I would never publicly correct mistakes made by my supervisor or team leader.	_____	_____
22. I would never use my personal contacts to gain a promotion.	_____	_____
23. If you happen to dislike a person who receives a big promotion in your firm, don't bother sending that person a congratulatory note.	_____	_____
24. I would never openly criticize a powerful executive in my organization.	_____	_____
25. I would stay late in the office just to impress my supervisor or team leader.	_____	_____
Total Score	_____	_____

(Continued)

POLITICAL SKILL AND SOCIAL INTELLIGENCE

LEARNING OBJECTIVE 1

Political skill does not stand alone, separated from other human relations skills. For starters, being sensitive to your surroundings and to other people helps make you politically aware. Imagine that you are applying for a position at Google doing exactly the kind of work you want. You have seen photos of Google employees, and you have visited their headquarters before your interview just to see what the company looks like. No Google worker including the founders are ever seen in a business suit, yet this fact escapes you. You show up for your interview wearing a business suit and leather shoes as if you were applying for a position as an investment banker trainee at a Wall Street firm. Zap, you are done. The Google employees wearing jeans, casual shirts or blouses, and running shoes think you would be a poor cultural fit despite your intelligence and talent. You were not sensitive enough to the environment to choose the appropriate attire for you interview.

social intelligence

An understanding of how relationships with bosses and colleagues, family and friends, shape our brains and affect our bodies.

Political skill also relates to emotional intelligence because you need to be able to read the emotions of others to establish rapport with them. For example, a person with good emotional intelligence would ask for a raise when the boss appeared to be in a good mood. Also, the person would avoid asking for a raise when the boss was upset, preoccupied, and in an ugly mood.

Political skill is also directly related to **social intelligence**, an understanding of how relationships with bosses and colleagues, family, and friends shape our brains and affect our bodies. Social intelligence is a book-length subject, yet we can take away a couple of basic lessons that are linked to positive political skill.[1]

Social intelligence tells us that good relationships act like vitamins, energizing us to perform well. In contrast, bad relationships are like poison that undermines our cognitive efficiency and creativity. The person with good social intelligence would work at having positive relationships with others on the job, so he or she could concentrate on the task and perform well.

Another aspect of having social intelligence would be to recognize that being arrogant or derisive toward others can cause emotional distress

Political Skill Inventory

Instructions: Using the following 7-point scale, write in each box the number that best describes how much you agree with the statement. 1 = strongly disagree; 2 = disagree; 3 = slightly agree; 4 = neutral; 5 = slightly agree; 6 = agree; 7 = strongly agree.

1. I spend a lot of time and effort networking with others. ☐
2. I am able to make most people feel comfortable and at ease around me. ☐
3. I am able to communicate easily and effectively with others. ☐
4. It is easy for me to develop good rapport with most people. ☐
5. I understand people very well. ☐
6. I am good at building relationships with influential people at work (or at school). ☐
7. I am particularly good at sensing the motivations and hidden agendas of others. ☐
8. When communicating with others, I try to be genuine in what I say and do. ☐
9. I have developed a large network of colleagues and associates at work (or school) who I can call on for support when I really need to get things done. ☐
10. At work (or at school), I know a lot of important people and I am well connected. ☐
11. I spend a lot of time at work (or at school) developing connections with others. ☐
12. I am good at getting people to like me. ☐
13. It is important that people believe I am sincere in what I do and say. ☐
14. I try to show a genuine interest in other people. ☐
15. I am good at using my connections and network to make things happen at work (or at school). ☐
16. I have good intuition and I [am] savvy about how to present myself to others. ☐
17. I always seem to instinctively know the right things to say or do to influence others. ☐
18. I pay close attention to people's facial expressions. ☐

Total = ☐   Total ÷ 18 = ☐

Scoring and Interpretation: Compute your overall score by adding together your response scores on all the questions and dividing the total by 18. You will have an overall political score between 1 and 7. Larger scores identify people who have higher political skill, and smaller scores identify people who have lower political skill.

Source: Adapted from Gerald R. Ferris et al., "Development and Validation of the Political Skill Inventory," *Journal of Management*, vol. 31, 2005, pp. 126–152.

that impairs the brain's ability to learn and think clearly. So a good team player or a manager would relate more positively toward others to help attain a productive workplace.

CEO Steve Bennett of Intuit exemplifies a manager who deliberately practices social intelligence. For instance, he gives constructive criticism but avoid angry attacks. During one meeting he criticized a senior manager who was dominating a meeting even though the subject was not his field of expertise. Bennett attempted to criticize him in a joking way rather than being hostile.[2]

In short, political skill is closely related to social intelligence, as well as other human relations skills. Self-Assessment Quiz 12-2 gives you an opportunity to measure your political skill with a questionnaire that has been used in dozens of research studies.

IMPRESSION MANAGEMENT AND ETIQUETTE

LEARNING OBJECTIVE 2

impression management

A set of behaviors directed at enhancing one's image by drawing attention to oneself.

Being an effective, responsible contributor is not always sufficient to gain the attention you deserve. It may also be necessary to make others aware of your capability. **Impression management** is a set of behaviors directed at enhancing one's image by drawing attention to one's self. Often the attention is directed toward superficial aspects of the self, such as clothing and appearance. Impression management also includes telling people about your accomplishments and appearing self-confident. The following subsections list specific tactics of impression management and discuss business etiquette. We discuss etiquette here because how you behave in certain situations shapes your image.

Tactics of Impression Management

Managing the impression you create encompasses dozens of specific tactics, limited only by your imagination of what will impress others. Part of your power in the organization stems not only from your formal position, but also from how you are perceived by others. Creating the right image is the practice of impression management.[3]

Although impression management can be used in a variety of relationships, it is most commonly found in the attempt of a worker to please the manager. For example, impression management is frequently used during performance evaluation to impress the manager with the worker's accomplishments. Five positive tactics of impression management are described next.

Build Trust and Confidence   A key strategy for creating a positive impression with your immediate superior and higher-ranking managers is to build trust and confidence. Project the authentic impression of a person who can be trusted to carry out responsibilities faithfully and ethi cally. Rather than take action without permission (e.g., spending beyond budget), know the bounds of your authority and work within those bounds. Be aware that your boss has other responsibilities, so do not take more than your fair share of his or her time. You will generate an impression of confidence if you suggest alternative solutions to the problems you bring to your manager.[4]

Be Visible and Create a Strong Presence   An essential part of impression management is to be perceived as a valuable contributor on the job. Visibility is attained in many ways such as regular attendance at meetings and company social events, being assigned to important projects, and doing volunteer work in the community. Helping in the launch of a new product or redesigning work methods are other ways of attaining visibility and creating a strong presence. Face-to-face visibility is perhaps the best, but electronic visibility can also be effective. This includes making intelligent contributions to company intranets and blogs, and sending e-mail messages of substance to the right people. Terry Bragg observes that many employees are shocked to learn that they lost their jobs during a downsizing because upper management did not know that they were valuable contributors.[5]

Admit Mistakes   Many people believe that to create a good impression, it is best to deny or cover up mistakes. In this way, you will not appear vulnerable. A higher level of political skill is to admit mistakes, thereby appearing more forthright and trustworthy. The simple statement, "I goofed," will often gain you sympathy and support whereas an attempted cover up will decrease your social capital. For purposes of impression management, the bottom line of being wrong is to (a) admit the error; (b) request guidance; (c), step up, repair; and (d) learn from it.[6] Requesting guidance is important because it conveys the impression that you have humility and that you trust the advice and counsel of others. Here is an example of this tactic in action:

> *Cindy, a call-center operator, is listening on the phone to a woman rant and rave about a $5.87 charge on her credit card that seems unwarranted. Thinking that she has the telephone receiver covered, Cindy says in a sigh of exasperation to a coworker, "I'm about to scream. I'm talking to the biggest jerk of year right now." Unfortunately, "the biggest jerk of the year" heard the comment and reported it to Cindy's supervisor.*
>
> *During a review of the incident with her supervisor, Cindy said, yes, indeed she made the comment, and then asked how to deal with the pressures of such an overreacting customer. Cindy offered to send a written apology from the customer. So far, Cindy has learned from her error and has not repeated the incident.*

Minimize Being a Yes-Person   A conventional view of organizational politics suggests that being a yes-person is an excellent way of developing a good relationship with higher-ups, and generating the impression of a loyal and supportive subordinate. The yes-person operates by the principle, "the boss is always right." Often the boss cultivates yes-person behavior among subordinates by being intimidating, and unapproachable.[7]

When working for an emotionally secure and competent manager, you are likely to create a better impression by not agreeing with all the boss's ideas and plans. Instead, express constructive disagreement by explaining how the boss's plan might be enhanced, or how an error be avoided.

> *Assume that you work in the marketing department of Jitterbug, a simplified cell phone that focuses on the senior market. Your boss suggests an advertising theme demonstrating that even people with arthritis and who are technically challenged can easily operate a Jitterbug. Your intuition tells you this theme would be a humiliating insult to seniors. So, you respond to your boss, "I know that Jitterbug targets seniors, but I suggest that we tone down the terms* arthritis *and* technically challenged. *Why not be positive and state that the keys are easy to manipulate, and that the Jitterbug is as easy to operate as a land-line phone?"*

Create a Healthy Image   A superficial yet important part of impression management is to project, a healthy, physically fit appearance. Appearing physically fit in the workplace has gained in importance as many business firms offer workers rewards for being physically fit and avoiding smoking and obesity. Among the rewards offered by employers are electronic gadgets, discounted health insurance, and cash bonuses. At IBM, employees get as much as $300 annually for exercising regularly, quitting smoking, or logging on to the company's preventive-care Web site.[8] Microsoft has a wellness program directed specifically at combating obesity with such features as a personal trainer, custom nutritional plan, and health spa facilities.[9] From an impression-management perspective, being obese at health-conscious companies would be a negative.

Projecting an image of emotional fitness also contributes to a healthy image. *Emotional fitness* would include such behaviors as appearing relaxed, appropriate laughing and smiling, and a minimum of nervous mannerisms and gestures. Being physically fit helps project emotional fitness.

When managing the impression you create, be mindful of the advice offered by William L. Gardner III. He urges that you be yourself. When selecting an image, do not attempt to be somebody you are not because people will see through this facade. Gardner concludes, "Make every effort to put your best foot forward—but never at the cost of your identity or integrity!"[10] Impression management is geared toward looking good, but not creating a false impression.

Another important aspect of effectively managing your impression is that you need good political skills to be effective at impression management. *Political skill* in this context refers to the type of behaviors indicated in Self-Assessment Quiz 12-2. A study of 204 employees working on environmental issues indicated that employees with good political skill use impression-management tactics are likely to receive higher job performance ratings from their supervisor. In contrast, individuals low in political skill who engage in impression management tend to be seen less positively by their supervisors.[11] In other words, you need a little finesse and sensitivity to people to be good at office politics.

Another essential part of impression management is to avoid creating a negative impression through such behaviors as being absent or late frequently, speaking poorly, or talking in a meeting while the presenter is speaking. The discussion of etiquette helps guide a person away from behaviors that would bring negative attention to one's self.

Skill-Building Exercise 12-1 gives you an opportunity to try out a highly practical application of impression management.

Business Etiquette

business etiquette

A special code of behavior required in work situations.

A major component of managing your impression is practicing good etiquette. **Business etiquette** is a special code of behavior required in work situations. The term *manners* has an equivalent meaning. Both *manners* and *etiquette* generally refer to behaving in a refined and acceptable manner. Jim Rucker and Jean Anna Sellers explain that business etiquette is much more than knowing how to use the correct utensil or how to dress in a given situation. Businesspeople today must know how to be at ease with strangers and with groups, be able to offer congratulations smoothly, know how to make introductions, and know how to conduct themselves at company social functions.[12] Studying etiquette is important because knowing and using proper business etiquette contributes to individual and business success.[13] People who are considerate of the feelings of others, and companies that are courteous toward customers, are more likely to succeed than are their rude counterparts. Another perspective on etiquette is that it is a way of presenting yourself with the kind of polish that shows you can be taken seriously. So many people are rude and uncivil today that practicing good etiquette will often give you a competitive advantage.[14]

Business etiquette includes many aspects of interpersonal relations in organizations, as described in the following discussion.[15] What is considered proper etiquette and manners in the workplace changes over time and may vary with the situation. At one time, addressing one's superior by his or her first name was considered brash. Today it is commonplace behavior. A sampling of etiquette guidelines is nevertheless helpful. A general principle of being considerate of the feelings of work associates is more important than any one act of etiquette or courtesy. Keep in mind, also, that you will find a few contradictory statements in writings about etiquette.

Etiquette for Work Behavior and Clothing   Work behavior etiquette includes all aspects of performing in the work environment, such as completing work on time, punctuality, being a good team player, listening to others, and following through. For instance, having the courtesy to complete a project when it is due demonstrates good manners and respect for the work of others.

Clothing might be considered part of general work behavior. The casual standards in the information technology field, along with dress-down days, have created confusion about proper office attire. A general rule is that *casual* should not be interpreted as sloppy, such as torn jeans or a stained sweatshirt. Many companies have moved back toward emphasizing traditional business attire, such as suits for men and women. In many work situations, dressing more formally may constitute proper etiquette.

Introductions   The basic rule for introductions is to present the lower-ranking person to the higher-ranking person regardless of age or sex. "Ms. Barker (the CEO), I would like you to meet my new coworker, Reggie Taylor." (Observe that the higher-ranking person's name is mentioned first.) If the two people being introduced are of equal rank, mention the older one first. Providing a little information about the person being introduced is considered good manners. When introducing one person to the group, present the group to the individual. "Sid Foster, this is our accounts receivable team." When being introduced to a person, concentrate on the name and repeat it soon, thus enhancing learning. A fundamental display of good manners is to remember people's names and to pronounce them correctly. When dealing with people senior to you or of higher rank, call them by their last name and title until told otherwise. (Maybe Ms. Barker, above, will tell you, "Please call me Kathy.")

It is good manners and good etiquette to remember the names of work associates to whom you are introduced, even if you see them only occasionally. If you forget the name of a person, it is better to admit this than to guess and come up with the wrong name. Just say, "I apologize, but I have forgotten your name. Tell me once more, and I will not forget your name again."

Both men and women are expected to extend their right hand when being introduced. Give a firm, but not overpowering, handshake, and establish eye contact with the person you are greeting. However, some people are concerned about handshakes being unhygienic, so be willing to use the modern fist-to-fist light touch often used in social life. If the other person extends the fist, you do the same.

Relationships Between Men and Women and Between People of Different Ages   Social etiquette is based on chivalry and the gender of the person, whereas business etiquette is based on generally equal treatment for all. Women should no longer be treated differently when approaching a door, riding in an elevator, or walking in the street. According to the new rules, the person in the lead (no matter the gender or age) should proceed first and hold the door for the others following. However, a man should still follow a woman when using an escalator. When using stairs, a man usually follows a woman going up and precedes her going down. Men no longer have to walk next to the street when walking with one or two women. Elders should still be respected, but not in such ways as holding doors open for them, helping them off with their overcoats, or getting coffee for them.

Unless you are good friends who typically hug when meeting, it is best to avoid touching others of the same or opposite sex except for a handshake. Some people believe that nonsexual touching is part of being charming and warm, yet many workers are offended when touched by another worker. The subject is controversial because public figures often drape their arms around others, and physical touching is part of the ritual of offering congratulations in sports. Of note, many athletic coaches have switched to fist-to-fist touching to say hello or offer congratulations to teenagers and young children to avoid being charged with sexually suggestive contact.

Use of Wire and Cell Telephones   Despite the prominence of voice mail and text messaging, most business communication over the phone requires live interaction between people. Guidelines for proper telephone usage include the following:

- Answer the phone by the third ring.
- Identify your company, your department, and yourself.
- Say "good morning," "good afternoon," or "good evening."
- Always end the call on a pleasant note and say "goodbye." Never say "bye-bye" (except for social calls).
- If possible, avoid call waiting and other forms of putting people on hold. Putting people on hold after the conversation has begun is a low point in rudeness.

Cell telephones have created substantial challenges in etiquette, going beyond the points just mentioned. The general point is not to annoy or irritate others with your cell phone, particularly by being loud and interrupting or disturbing the tranquility of others. Among the cell phone behaviors likely to be interpreted as rude (at least by some people) are making personal calls while in your cubicle, using your cell phone in meetings, and talking loudly into your cell phone while in public space such as hallways, dining areas, and break rooms. Above all, do not answer the cell phone while talking to customers or your manager face-to-face.

Dining Etiquette surrounding meals involves planning for the meeting, making seating arrangements, bill paying, tipping, using proper table manners, and appropriate drinking of alcoholic beverages. We all know not to slurp spaghetti one strand at a time, pour ketchup over sauce, or leave a 50¢ tip. The key point is not to draw negative attention to you. Less obvious are the following guidelines:

- Arrange seating for meal meetings in advance.
- Establish with the server who will be paying the check.
- Place your napkin on your lap immediately after being seated.
- Bread should not be used to push food onto a fork or spoon.
- Attempt to pace your eating to those of others at the table.
- The wait staff, not the diners, should be responsible for moving plates around the table.
- Circulate rolls and bread to the right, not the left.
- Order an alcoholic beverage only when invited to do so by the person sponsoring the meal, and then only if he or she does. Do not get drunk or even high.

E-Mail, Instant Messaging, and Text-by-Phone Correspondence Many people believe that formality and careful use of language can be neglected when sending messages by e-mail, instant messaging, and when sending text messages. Remember, however, that the way in which any message is sent tells something about the sender. E-mail messages should be proofread, should be sent only when necessary, and generally should be no longer than one screen—not including attachments. Although many e-mail users rely on a strikingly formal and casual writing style, such informality for business correspondence is poor etiquette. For example, avoid confirming a meeting with your CEO in these words: "C U later, 4 sure." Overloading the company system with attachments containing space-consuming graphics is often considered rude. Text messaging, because of its limited space, can be more casual than other electronic messages.

An e-mail etiquette problem with legal implications is that company e-mail messages are the property of the company, not the sender. So avoid sending through e-mail insulting, vulgar, or inflammatory comments because even deleted e-mail messages can be retrieved. Be careful not to forward an e-mail message that has negative comments about the recipient. For example, a customer service representative sent an e-mail to a customer attempting to resolve a complaint. However, instead of beginning with a fresh e-mail, the representative included an e-mail from her boss that said, "Give this idiot what she wants to get her off our back." The customer later sued the company, and then agreed to a small financial settlement.

Instant messaging has created new challenges for e-mail etiquette. Because instant messaging (IM) allows you to intrude on coworkers anytime—and them to drop in on you—the opportunities to be rude multiply. Managers should not intrude upon workers through IM unless it is urgent. Think before you send, and make sure the message has real value to the recipient. Suggest politely to "buddies" who are taking up too much of your time with messages that they contact you after work.

Use of Electronic Devices Other than Phones Electronic devices such as Internet access devices, personal digital assistants, or PDAs, such as the BlackBerry, and photocopiers create opportunities for good and poor etiquette. Violations of etiquette surrounding the Internet include receiving nonwork-related material on your monitor in the presence of others and surfing the Internet on company time. A growing etiquette problem is workers at meetings using their notebook computers to do other work. Yet in some companies such multitasking may be regarded as acceptable behavior. Displaying pornographic or sports sites on an office computer is taboo. An open pornographic site might lead to charges of sexual harassment. The BlackBerry can be a great boost to productivity, but has created a culture of rudeness of its own as managers and professionals consult their BlackBerrys while talking to others, playing golf, and even skiing. Many children have begun to rebel at parents consulting their BlackBerry during family dinners and while helping children with their homework.

Key violations of photocopier etiquette include hogging the machine, jumping in ahead of others, and leaving the machine at a setting only you require. A generally accepted guideline is that if you are using the photocopier for a large job and somebody approaches with a small job, let that person go first.

Working in a Cubicle   Workplace cubicles were invented by fine-arts professor Bob Probst in the 1960s, and they have been praised and condemned ever since. The praise generally relates to saving the company money on office space and having more open communication. The condemnation usually relates to lack of privacy, and therefore ties in directly with workplace etiquette. Cubicles represent a major etiquette challenge because a variety of coworkers and superiors can observe your everyday work behavior.[16] Among the many etiquette challenges for the cubicle dweller are as follows: (a) speaking low enough into a wired phone so as not to annoy others or reveal confidential information; (b) not allowing a personal cell phone ring during the workday; (c) not displaying material on the computer that others might find offensive, unless the subject is business related; (d) not wearing a sports cap indoors unless an acceptable part of the company culture; and (e) not taking care of personal hygiene such as dental flossing, hair spraying, or nail clipping.

Cross-Cultural Relations   What constitutes proper etiquette may differ from culture to culture. Be alert to differences in etiquette in areas such as gift giving, dining, drinking alcoholic beverages, and when and where to discuss business. A culture must be studied carefully, including asking questions, to understand what constitutes proper etiquette. Many of these differences in customs were described in Chapter 7. Violating these customs is poor etiquette. For example, using the index finger to point is considered rude in most Asian and Middle Eastern countries. Also, people in Middle Eastern countries tend to stand as close as two or three inches from the person with whom they are talking. To back away is interpreted as an insult. An American visitor to China nearly lost a major sale because after receiving a business card from the Chinese company representative, he stuffed it in his pocket without first carefully reading the card. Proper etiquette in China is to carefully read the giver's business card, and perhaps holding it with both hands out of respect. We emphasize again that stereotypes such as those just mentioned refer to typical behavior and are accurate perhaps only about 70 percent of the time.

Suppose you are in doubt about the proper etiquette for any situation and you do not have a handbook of etiquette readily available. As a substitute, observe how your host or a successful person in the group behaves.

Interaction with People with Disabilities   Many able-bodied people are puzzled by what is proper etiquette in working with people with disabilities. Be as natural and open as you can. In addition, consider these guidelines for displaying good manners when dealing with a physical disability:

- Speak directly to a person with a disability, not to the person's companion.
- Don't assume that a person with a disability needs help. If someone is struggling, ask for permission to assist.
- When talking to a person in a wheelchair, place yourself at that person's eye level.
- When speaking to a person with impaired vision, identify yourself and anyone who may be with you. Do not shout when speaking to a blind person.
- To get the attention of a deaf person, tap the person's shoulder or wave your hand.
- Treat a person with a disability as you would anyone else except for the differences noted in this list.[17]

As shown in Figure 12-2, impression management combined with managing relationships and avoiding political blunders contributes to being a more polished and successful professional worker. Skill-Building Exercise 12-2 gives you an opportunity to practice appropriate etiquette in several situations.

FIGURE 12-2 Relationship between Positive Political Behaviors and Individual Success

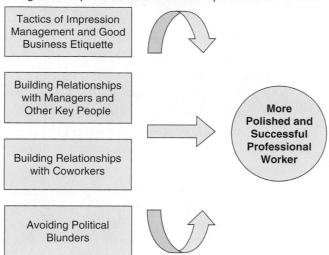

Impression management, building relationships with influential people, and avoiding political blunders all contribute to being a more polished and successful professional worker.

- Tactics of Impression Management and Good Business Etiquette
- Building Relationships with Managers and Other Key People
- Building Relationships with Coworkers
- Avoiding Political Blunders

→ More Polished and Successful Professional Worker

BUILDING RELATIONSHIPS WITH MANAGERS AND OTHER KEY PEOPLE

The political purpose of building good relationships with managers is to gain power through such means as being recommended for promotion and key assignments. A good relationship with the boss is also important for the basic purpose of receiving a good performance evaluation. Building these good relationships is also important because it helps create a positive, supportive work environment for you. Good relationships can also be established with managers for the nonpolitical purpose of trying to get the job accomplished. The strategies and tactics described next are outlined in Figure 12-3.

Network with Influential People

A basic success strategy is developing contacts, or **networking**, with influential people. In addition to making contacts, networking involves gaining the trust and confidence of the influential people. Before you can network with influential people, you must identify who those power players are.[18] You might make observations of your own, such as

networking

Developing contacts with influential people, including gaining their trust and confidence. Also, contacting friends and acquaintances and building systematically on these relationships to create a still wider set of contacts that might lead to employment.

SKILL-BUILDING EXERCISE 12-2

Business Etiquette

An effective way of improving business etiquette is by using your best manners in real-life situations. Role-playing etiquette scenarios can also help you develop the right mental set for using good etiquette.

Scenario 1: Dining Etiquette. A small group of students plan to conduct a high-etiquette meal at a local family restaurant during nonpeak hours. Pretend the stainless-steel utensils are fine silver and that the glasses are crystal. Each class member uses his or her best etiquette. At the same time, each group member carefully observes the etiquette displayed by the other members.

At the conclusion of the meal, critique each other's etiquette. If you were courteous enough to invite your instructor to your high-etiquette meal, get his or her feedback.

Scenario 2: Telephone Etiquette. Two people using cell phones are separated by about six feet. Several pairs of students might conduct phone conversations covering such matters as discussing customer complaints, inquiring about a job, or asking about product availability. (*Note:* The students merely *pretend* they are using the phone, rather than waste phone minutes.) Students not making the calls will carefully observe the callers. Look for examples of good and poor telephone etiquette. Feedback will be provided after the phone conversations are completed.

FIGURE 12-3 Strategies and Tactics for Building Relationships with Managers and Other Key People

1. Network with influential people.
2. Help your manager succeed.
3. Understanding unwritten boundaries.
4. Volunteer for assignments.
5. Flatter influential people sensibly.
6. Use information power.
7. Appear cool under pressure.
8. Laugh at your manager's humor.
9. Express constructive disagreement.

listening for whose names are mentioned frequently by people in the company. Asking the opinions of others about which people influence decision making can be illuminating. Sometimes a person without a fancy job title might be a highly influential person. An example is an administrative assistant who heavily influences the decisions of his or her boss.

Networking also takes place with people inside and outside the organization who are not your managers. Developing contacts with influential people is likely to pay big career dividends. Jack Welch, the legendary former CEO of General Electric and business author, believes that networking skills are essential for success. During a presentation at MIT, he said that networking is the most important skill to learn in business school.[19] (Welch, as you might guess, is prone to exaggeration.)

A standard procedure is to create a card or computer file of the people in your network and update it frequently. To keep your network effective, it is necessary to contact people on your list periodically.

Developing a network of influential people requires alertness and planning. You have to identify influential people and then think of a sensible reason to contact them. Here are a few possibilities:

- Send an e-mail message to a high-ranking manager, offering a money-saving or revenue-producing suggestion. A related tactic is to inform the person of something of significance you did that might lie directly in his or her area of interest. As social networking on the Internet grows in popularity, sites such as Facebook and Linkedin can be used for networking with influential people. An influential person who joins such a site is usually open to making new contacts.

- Do a standout job as a member of a task force or committee that includes a high-ranking official.

- Discuss your career plans with a neighbor who has an outstanding position.

- Take the initiative to develop a friendship with an influential person who is a member of your athletic club, YMCA, YWCA, or place of worship.

Networking is so often used—and abused—that suggestions and guidelines for networking etiquette have emerged. A starting point is to be clear, concise, and specific when making requests of networking contacts.[20] Explain, for example, that you want to become an industry specialist and would like to acquire specific information. Be frank about the amount of time you would want from the network member, such as 15 minutes per month of e-mail and telephone contact.

After making contact with a potential network member, explain the benefit this person is likely to derive from his or her association with you. Provide a *benefit statement* for interacting with you and helping you with you career.[21] Indicate specifically how this person might benefit from you being in his or her network. (If a person is in your network, you are also in that person's network.) If the potential network member is more powerful than you are, it is still possible to think of what benefit you might be able to provide. Two examples follow:

- I would like to contact you a few times a year about career concerns. In return, I would be happy to help you prepare PowerPoint slides for any presentation you might be making.
- In return for my receiving career advice from you from time to time, I would be happy to collect information for you about how people in my area perceive one of your products. I have lots of useful contacts in my community.

Avoid being a pest. Many influential people are bombarded with requests to be part of someone's network, so ask for a modest amount of time and assistance. Good networking etiquette is to request a collaborative relationship in which you give as much as you get. The benefit statement just mentioned will place you in a collaborative relationship with the influential person.

Help Your Manager Succeed

The primary reason you are hired is to help your manager achieve the results necessary to succeed. Avoid an adversarial relationship with your manager. Also figure out both obvious and subtle ways of ensuring the manager's success. One subtle way of increasing your manager's chances for success is to help that person when he or she is under attack from another department. One example would be to supply information to support your manager's position on a controversial issue. Also keep in mind the cornerstone tactic of performing your job superbly. Your manager will then share in your success.

BACK TO THE OPENING CASE

The major approach Madison and Weaver took to avoiding conflict and awkwardness in their relationship was to talk about their expectations and roles at the heating and air-conditioning firm. The two men agreed that their relationship in the office and in the field should be kept separate from their relationship outside work.

Also, Madison and Weaver made a pact that during social activities they would not talk about their work relationship, nor about salary and work assignments.

Understand Unwritten Boundaries

A person skilled at positive organizational politics is able to read unwritten rules about who has the authority to do what. According to psychologist Judith Sills, there exist **unwritten boundaries,** or dividing lines, of behavior appropriate to different roles. Many workers struggle with office problems that are boundary issues in disguise. Sills observes that boundaries for office interactions are like the rope lanes in a swimming pool. The purpose of the ropes is to enhance safety, but they can be budged or even removed depending on need, skill, and circumstance.

Unwritten boundaries deal with such issues as when it is appropriate to correct your boss, how much anger to display, which influential people you can invite to a social engagement, and whose speech or appearance can you criticize. A person with an exaggerated sense of his or her worth may have trouble perceiving that a boundary exists at all, such as one woman who felt free to protest angrily when her boss changed something in her report.[22] Two other examples of unacceptable boundary crossing are (a) a man who told a vice president that his hairpiece looked phony, and (b) a woman who told her boss that she needed to upgrade her information technology skills to be a credible leader.

An example of successful boundary crossing took place when an accounts receivable specialist sent an unsolicited e-mail to the director of marketing. The young worker said that he grew up in Mexico and would be happy to provide input for the company's plans to penetrate the Mexican market. Although the accounts receivable worker was from outside of the marketing department, he was invited to participate in a focus group about expanding into the Mexican market.

unwritten boundaries

Dividing lines of behavior appropriate to different roles.

Look for indicators as to whether boundaries can be crossed in your company. First, count the layers in your company's organization structure. The more layers (or more hierarchical) the company, the less welcome boundary crossing is likely to be. Look for established border crossings. Observe where people of different rank in the company mix. Among the possibilities are the fitness center, the cafeteria, and after-hours drinks. Make your first attempts at border crossing at those places.[23]

Volunteer for Assignments

An easily implemented method of winning the approval of superiors is to become a "hand raiser." By volunteering to take on assignments that do not fit neatly into your job description, you display the kind of initiative valued by employers. Among the many possible activities to volunteer for are fund-raising campaigns assigned to your company, project membership, and working overtime when most people prefer not to (for example, on a Saturday in July). Task force and committee assignments are also useful for being noticed by key people in the organization. Offer to help coordinate a charity campaign such as the United Way. As a team member, volunteer to assume any leadership responsibility you think you can handle. If your team offers rotating leadership assignments, express an interest in taking your turn.

Flatter Influential People Sensibly

One of the most effective relationship builders is to flatter people sensibly and credibly. Despite the risk of being called obsequious or a cheap office politician, the flatterer wins. A study on how to advance in big business pointed out that a company's top employees tend to be equal in performance. Advancing was based on image (30 percent) and contact time with the manager (50 percent). Flattery can play a big role in both.[24] A recent study indicates that even at the highest positions in business, flattery helps a person get ahead. Specifically, ingratiating yourself to the CEO, including flattery, was a major factor in receiving an appointment as a board of director at major companies. Not carefully monitoring (carefully scrutinizing) the CEO's activities also worked in a person's favor for obtaining a board appointment.[25] You might interpret not finding fault with a CEO to be a subtle form of flattery.

Flattery is likely to be effective because most people want to receive accolades, even if they are not completely warranted. People who pay us compliments are likely to be treated kindly in turn.[26] Remember, however, the discussion about recognition in Chapter 10 suggesting that less technically oriented people are often the most receptive to praise and flattery. Flattery geared toward the more technically oriented person might have to be more concrete and tied to specific accomplishments. Recent evidence supports the idea that constructive compliments are not overblown. Descriptions of what went right are more effective than evaluative phrases such as "magnificent," or "extraordinary." An effective, general-purpose piece of flattery is to tell another person that you are impressed by something he or she accomplished. Rather than telling an influential person that he or she is a genius, you might say to a manager after a meeting,[27] "Everyone in the meeting was listening so attentively when you gave your report. And the industry statistics you found really drove home the point."

Another way of flattering somebody is to listen attentively. If you actively listen to the other person, he or she will feel flattered. The person might think, "What I have to say is valuable. This person really cares about what I have to offer." Flattery can also take the form of quoting another person, or referring to something he or she said to you earlier.

During the next two weeks, try flattering an influential person. In the interim, do Skill-Building Exercise 12-3.

Use Information Power

Power accrues to those who control vital information. At the same time, being a source of useful information will help you build constructive working relationships with managers. You will be relied on as an important contributor. Controlling vital information includes knowing how to gain access to useful information that others do not know how to retrieve. Many workers are aware of the mechanics of using the Internet, but fewer have the skills to use the Internet to retrieve commercially useful information. During a tight labor market, for example, human resource specialists can acquire power if they know how to use the Internet to find talented people who might want to join the company. These specialists have knowledge beyond using commercially available Internet recruiting services.

Information power is closely related to *expert power*, which refers to having valuable expertise. If your expertise or skill is in high demand at the moment, power will flow in your direction. Currently, an important type of expert power is being able to use social networking sites to gain publicity for products and to recruit employees. .

Appear Cool under Pressure

Showing signs of panic generally hurts your reputation with influential people. In contrast, appearing to be in emotional control when things around you are falling apart helps convey the impression that you are worthy of additional responsibility. Being cool under pressure is part of emotional stability, and it is a key leadership characteristic. An example of coolness under pressure follows.

A snow-making-machine technician was rushed to a Vermont ski resort three days before the start of the holiday season. The problem was that the equipment was not spraying water with enough pressure for the water to convert to snow. When the technician arrived at the ski resort, a snarling owner said that if the equipment was not working within 24 hours, his company would be sued for $5 million. Despite all the mental pressure, the technician fixed the water pressure problem within four hours. Several weeks later, he was promoted to field maintenance supervisor.

Laugh at Your Manager's Humor

When you indicate by your laughter that you appreciate your manager's sense of humor, it helps establish rapport between the two of you. An indicator of good two-way communication between people is that the two parties comprehend each other's subtle points. Most humor in the workplace deals with subtle meanings about work-related topics. To implement the tactic of laughing at your manager's jokes, do not worry excessively about having heard the joke before.

Express Constructive Disagreement

At one time the office politician thought an effective way of pleasing the boss was to be a "yes-person," as mentioned earlier A more intelligent tactic in the modern business world is to be ready to disagree in a constructive manner when you sincerely believe the boss is wrong. In the long run you will probably earn more respect than if you agree with the boss just to please him or her. Constructive disagreement is based on a careful analysis of the situation and is tactful.

The right way to disagree means not putting your manager in a corner or embarrassing your manager by confronting him or her loudly or in public. If you disagree with your boss, use carefully worded, inoffensive statements. In this way, you minimize the chances of a confrontation or hostile reaction. Remember the smart mattress mentioned in Skill-Building Exercise 12-3? Suppose the marketing vice president claims that the mattress is geared exclusively toward the senior citizen market, and you disagree. You might say, "I think that marketing our smart mattress to seniors is a breakthrough. Yet I also see some other possibilities. There are loads of cold-sensitive young people who wanted a heated mattress. Also, a lot of young people with athletic injuries or orthopedic problems would welcome an adjustable mattress. Does my thinking make any sense?"

The reason constructive disagreement helps you build a good relationship with most managers is that the boss comes to respect your job knowledge and your integrity. However, if you are working with a very insecure boss, he or she may be taken aback by disagreement. In that case, you have to be extra tactful in expressing disagreement.

BUILDING RELATIONSHIPS WITH COWORKERS AND OTHER WORK ASSOCIATES

LEARNING OBJECTIVE 4

Another strategy for increasing your power is to form alliances with coworkers and other work associates. You need the support of these people to get your work accomplished. In addition, when you are being considered for promotion, coworkers and other work associates may be asked their opinion of you. Under a peer-evaluation system, the opinion of coworkers about your performance counts heavily. Long-term research conducted by Tom Rath of the Gallup Organization with many thousands of employees emphasizes the contribution of friendships and alliances in the workplace. Rath's concludes that employees who have a best friend in the office are more productive, more likely to have positive interactions with customers, share ideas, and stay longer on the job. Also, many workers succeed or fail based on the support and involvement of best friends.[28] (The term *best* appears to imply that the contact is not simply an acquaintance or someone on your contact list on a social networking Web site.)

Figure 12-4 lists eight strategies and techniques for developing good interpersonal relationships at or below your level. The information about developing teamwork skills presented in Chapter 5 is also relevant here. To examine your self-perception of your coworker relations skills, do Self-Assessment Quiz 12-3.

"If you want to be happier and more engaged at work, considering developing a few strong friendships at the office, maybe even one with your boss. "
—Tom Rath, head of the Gallup Organization's Workplace Research and Leadership Consulting, and author of *Vital Friends*[29]

Maintain Honest and Open Relationships

Although being honest may appear to contradict organizational politics, it is representative of the nature of positive politics. Giving coworkers frank but tactful answers to their requests for your opinion is one useful way of developing open relationships. Assume that a coworker asks your opinion of an e-mail he intends to send to his supervisor. As you read it, you find it somewhat incoherent and filled with spelling and grammatical errors.

FIGURE 12-4 Strategies and Tactics for Developing Relationships with Coworkers and Other Work Associates

> 1. Maintain honest and open relationships.
> 2. Make others feel important.
> 3. Be diplomatic.
> 4. Exchange favors.
> 5. Ask for advice.
> 6. Share constructive gossip.
> 7. Minimize microinequities.
> 8. Follow group norms.

An honest response to this message might be: "I think your idea is a good one. But I think your e-mail needs more work before that idea comes across clearly."

Accurately expressing your feelings, whether positive or negative, also leads to constructive relationships. If you have been singled out for good performance, let other team members know that you are happy and proud. If you arrive at work upset over a personal problem and appearing obviously fatigued, you can expect some reaction. A coworker might say, "What seems to be the problem? Is everything all right?" A dishonest reply would be "Everything is fine." In addition to making an obviously untrue statement, you would also be perceived as rejecting the person who asked the question. If you prefer not to discuss your problem, an honest response would be, "Thanks for your interest. I am facing some problems today. But I think things will work out."

Make Others Feel Important

A fundamental principle of fostering good relationships with coworkers and others is to make them feel important. Visualize that everyone in the workplace is wearing a small sign around the neck that says, "Please make me feel important."[30] Although the leader has the primary responsibility for satisfying this recognition need, coworkers also play a key role. One approach to making a coworker feel important would be to bring a notable accomplishment of his or hers to the attention of the group. Investing a small amount of time in recognizing a coworker can pay large dividends in terms of cultivating an ally. Expressing an interest in the work of others helps them feel important. A basic way to accomplish this end is to ask other employees questions that express an interest in their work, such as the following:

- How is your work going?
- How does the company use output from your department?
- How did you establish all the contacts you did to be so successful in sales?
- How did you develop the skills to do your job?

Expressing an interest in the work of others is also an effective tactic because so many people are self-centered. They are eager to talk about their own work, but rarely pause to express a genuine interest in others. Expressing an interest in the work of others is also effective because it is a form of recognition.

Self-Assessment Quiz 12-3 gives you an opportunity to think about your tendencies toward making others feel important.

Be Diplomatic

Despite all that has been said about the importance of openness and honesty in building relationships, most people fail to be convinced. Their egos are too tender to accept the raw truth when faced with disapproval of their thoughts or actions. Diplomacy is still an essential part of governmental and office politics. Translated into action, diplomacy often means finding the right phrase to convey disapproval, disagreement, or discontent. Here is an example of a delicate situation and the diplomatic phrase used to handle it.

During a staff meeting, a coworker suggests that the entire group schedule a weekend retreat to formulate a strategic plan for the department. The boss looks around the room to gauge the reactions of others to the proposal. You want to say: "What a stupid idea. Who needs to ruin an entire weekend to do something we could easily accomplish on a workday afternoon?" The diplomatic response is: "I've heard that retreats sometimes work. But would spending that much time on the strategic plan be cost-effective? Maybe we could work on the plan during one long meeting. If we don't get the planning accomplished in that time frame, we could then consider the off-site."

Exchange Favors

An important part of human interaction on and off the job is to reciprocate with others. Exchanging favors with others can make it easier for people to accomplish their work

How Important Do I Make People Feel?

Directions: Indicate on a one-to-five scale how frequently you act (or would act if the situation presented itself) in the ways indicated below: very infrequently (VI); infrequently (I); sometimes (S); frequently (F); very frequently (VF). Circle the number underneath the column that best fits your answer.

	VI	I	S	F	VF
1. I do my best to correctly pronounce a coworker's name.	1	2	3	4	5
2. I avoid letting other people's egos get too big.	5	4	3	2	1
3. I brag to others about the accomplishments of my coworkers.	1	2	3	4	5
4. I recognize the birthdays of friends in a tangible way.	1	2	3	4	5
5. It makes me anxious to listen to others brag about their accomplishments.	5	4	3	2	1
6. After hearing that a friend has done something outstanding, I shake his or her hand.	1	2	3	4	5
7. If a friend or coworker recently received a degree or certificate, I would offer my congratulations.	1	2	3	4	5
8. If a friend or coworker finished second in a contest, I would inquire why he or she did not finish first.	5	4	3	2	1
9. If a coworker showed me how to do something, I would compliment that person's skill.	1	2	3	4	5
10. When a coworker starts bragging about a family member's accomplishments, I do not respond.	5	4	3	2	1

Total Score _____

Scoring and Interpretation: Total the numbers corresponding to your answers. Scoring 40 to 50 points suggests that you typically make people feel important; 16 to 39 points suggests that you have a moderate tendency toward making others feel important; 10 to 15 points suggests that you need to develop skill in making others feel important. Study this chapter carefully.

because they are able to call on assistance when needed. The adept political player performs a favor for another employee without asking a favor in return. The favor is then cashed in when a favor is needed. Several examples of workday exchanges are as follows:

- A paralegal agrees to help another overburdened paralegal in the same law office, knowing that the other paralegal will reciprocate if needed in the future.
- A credit manager agrees to expedite a credit application for a sales representative. In reciprocation, the sales rep agrees to not commit the company to a delivery date on the next sale until the customer's credit has been evaluated.
- An assistant restaurant manager agrees to substitute for another assistant manager on New Year's Eve. A month later, the first person asks the second to take over her shift so she can get away for the weekend.

Ask for Advice

Asking advice on technical and professional topics is a good way of building relationships with other employees. Asking for advice from another person—someone whose job does not require giving it—will usually be perceived as a compliment. Asking advice transmits the message, "I trust your judgment enough to ask your opinion on something important to me." You are also saying, "I trust you enough to think that the advice you give me will be in my best interest." Asking advice is also a subtle form of flattery because it shows that you value the person's judgment.

To avoid hard feelings, inform the person whose advice you are seeking that his or her opinion will not necessarily be binding. A request for advice might be prefaced with a comment such as, "I would like your opinion on a problem facing me. But I can't guarantee that I'll be in a position to act on it." As with any other political tactic, asking for advice must be done in moderation. Too much advice asking can make you appear to indecisive or a pest.

Share Constructive Gossip

An effective way of building workplace relationships is to share constructive gossip with others. Gossip has been defined in many ways, but as used here refers to talk about other people, usually assumed to be based on fact.[31] Gossip serves as a socializing force because it is a mode of intimate relationships for many employees. Workers get close to each other through the vehicle of gossip. It also serves as the lifeblood of personal relationships on the job. If you are the person supplying the gossip, people will develop positive attitudes toward you. **Constructive gossip** is unofficial information that supports others, is based on truth, and respects confidential information. Given these restrictions, here are two examples of positive gossip:

- "I heard that business is really picking up. If this week is any example, the company's profits for the quarter will far exceed expectations."
- "I heard yesterday that the director of public relations just got engaged to a cool guy she met on a cruise."

Constructive gossip
Unofficial information that supports others, is based on truth, and respects confidential information.

Minimize Microinequities

A potent way of alienating coworkers is to snub them, or put them down, in a small way without being aware of your behavior. A **microinequity** is a small, semiconscious message we send with a powerful impact on the receiver. A microinequity might also be considered a subtle slight. The inequity might take the form of ignoring another person, a snub, or a sarcastic comment. Understanding microinequities can lead to changes in one-on-one relationships that may profoundly irritate others.[32]

Imagine that you are in line in the company cafeteria with three coworkers. You turn around and notice an old friend from school who is visiting the company. Next, you introduce your old friend to two of the coworkers with you, but not the third. That coworker is likely to feel crushed and irritated, and it will take you awhile to patch your relationship. Looking at a microinequity from the standpoint of the receiver, a work associate might say to you, "Some computer illiterate sent me an e-mail this morning without the attachment he said was there." You respond, "Excuse me, but that *computer illiterate* was me."

To overcome giving microinequities, it is important to think through the consequences of what you are doing and saying before taking action. In the cafeteria situation above, you might say to yourself, "Here comes time for an introduction, and this is not easy for me. I will remember to introduce everybody to my old friend."

microinequity
A small, semiconscious message we send with a powerful impact on the receiver.

group norms
The unwritten set of expectations for group members.

Follow Group Norms

A summary principle to follow in getting along with other employees is to heed **group norms**, the unwritten set of expectations for group members. Group norms also take the form of social cues about how to act, and therefore contribute to the organizational culture. Representative group norms include the following: (1) help coworkers with problems if you have the right expertise; (2) do not wear formal business attire on casual dress days; (3) have lunch with your coworkers at least once a week; (4) do not complain to the boss about a coworker unless his or her negative behavior is outrageously bad; (5) do not take a sick day unless you are really sick; (6) take your turn in bringing snacks to a meeting at least once a month; and (7) side with your coworkers rather than management when there is a dispute between the two groups.

If you do not deviate too far from these norms, the group will accept much of your behavior. If you do deviate too far,

Getting Along With Coworkers

An inventory auditor in a department store chain decides to take action aimed at getting along better with coworkers. In each of the following two scenarios, one person plays the role of the inventory auditor. Another person plays the role of an employee whom the auditor is attempting to cultivate.

Scenario1: Exchanging Favors. The auditor decides to strike a bargain with a store associate. (The role-player decides what this exchange of favors should be.) Unknown to the auditor, the store associate is concerned about an inventory audit because he or she is worried about being accused of stealing merchandise.

Scenario2: Expressing an Interest in Their Work. The auditor decides to express an interest in a tech fixer because he or she can be a valuable ally when conducting an inventory audit. The inventory audit is computerized, and the appropriate software is confusing and crashes frequently. The tech fixer has a heavy workload and is not prone toward small talk, but he or she does get excited talking about information technology.

After these scenarios have been completed, the class might discuss favors they have exchanged on the job that helped build relationships. Strive for at least five students to present examples of exchanges that enhanced their working relationships.

you will be subject to much rejection and therefore lose some of your power base. Yet if you conform too closely to group norms, higher-level management may perceive you as unable to identify with management. Employees are sometimes blocked from moving up the ladder because they are regarded as "one of the gang."

Some of the relationship building described in the eight strategies and tactics mentioned in this section is now being done on company social networking sites. These sites are being used to connect employees who have limited opportunity to meet face-to-face, or who simply prefer the Internet for most of their social interactions. Often the company social networking sites are supplemented with Web sites such as Facebook and MySpace because so many employees from the same firm might be members. For many workers, social networks provide a desirable way of communicating because they include photos, videos, and personal information like hobbies and music preferences—all of which are good for relationship building. Julio Fernandez, a global marketing manager in south Florida, rarely has face-to-face contact with coworkers from around the world. However, he regularly converses with them on a social networking site.[33]

Skill-Building Exercise 12-4 provides an opportunity to practice several of the techniques for building interpersonal relationships with coworkers and other work associates.

AVOIDING POLITICAL BLUNDERS

LEARNING OBJECTIVE 5

A strategy for not losing whatever power you have accumulated is to refrain from making power-eroding blunders. Committing these politically insensitive acts can also prevent you from attaining power. Self-Assessment Quiz 12-4 will get you started thinking about blunders. Several leading blunders are described in the quiz.

1. **Criticizing your manager in a public forum.** The oldest saw in human relations is to "praise in public and criticize in private." Yet in the passion of the moment, you may still surrender to the irresistible impulse to criticize your manager publicly. As a result, the manager will harbor resentment toward you and perhaps block your chances for advancement.

2. **Bypassing the manager.** Many people believe that because most organizations are more democratic today, it is not important to respect the layers of authority (the chain of command). In reality, following etiquette is highly valued in most firms. Going around the manager to resolve a problem is therefore hazardous. You might be able to accomplish the bypass, but your career could be damaged and your recourses limited. It is much better to work out differences with your manager using standard methods of resolving conflict.

3. **Displaying disloyalty.** Being disloyal to your organization is a basic political blunder. Making it known that you are looking for a position elsewhere is the best-known form of disloyalty. Criticizing your company in public settings, praising the high quality of competitors' products, and writing angry internal e-mail

The Blunder Quiz

Directions: Check whether you *agree* or *disagree* with the following statements.

	Agree	Disagree
1. It's fine to criticize your manager in a meeting as long as the criticism is valid.	_____	_____
2. If I objected to a decision made by top management, I would send a companywide e-mail explaining my objection.	_____	_____
3. I am willing to insult any coworker if the insult is deserved.	_____	_____
4. I see no problem in using competitors' products or services and letting my superiors know about it.	_____	_____
5. If I thought the CEO of my company were way overpaid, I would send him or her an e-mail making my opinion known.	_____	_____
6. Never bother with company-sponsored social events, such as holiday parties, unless you are really interested.	_____	_____
7. I would not attend a company social function if I had the chance to attend another social activity of more interest to me.	_____	_____
8. I am very open about passing along confidential information.	_____	_____
9. I openly criticize most new ventures my company or department is contemplating.	_____	_____
10. I avoid any deliberate attempt to please or impress coworkers or superiors.	_____	_____

Scoring and Interpretation: The greater the number of statements you agree with, the more prone you are to political blunders that can damage your interpersonal relationships and your career. You need to raise your awareness level of blunders on the job.

messages about your company are others. You may not get fired, but overt signs of disloyalty may place you in permanent disfavor.

4. **Being a pest.** Common wisdom suggests that diligently pressing for one's demands is the path to success. This may be true up to a point, but when assertiveness is used too often it becomes annoying to many people. The overpersistent person comes to be perceived as a pest, and this constitutes a serious political blunder. An example of being a pest would be asking your manager every month when you are going to receive the raise you deserve.

5. **Being (or being perceived as) a poor team player.** An employee is expected to be a good team player in almost all organizations because cooperation makes collective effort possible. If you are a poor team player, or are perceived as such, your chances for promotion will diminish because you will be recognized as having poor interpersonal skills. Among the ways to be perceived as a poor team player are to engage in social loafing, miss many department meetings, take too much credit for group accomplishments, and minimize your interactions with coworkers. In short, if you ignore all the advice about team play presented in Chapter 5, you will be committing a political blunder.

6. **Burning your bridges.** A potent political blunder is to create ill will among former employers or people who have helped you in the past. The most common form of bridge burning occurs when a person departs from an organization. A person who leaves involuntarily is especially apt to express anger toward those responsible for the dismissal. Venting your anger may give a temporary boost to your emotional well-being, but it can be detrimental in the long run.

7. **Indiscreet behavior in private life.** Employees are representatives of the company, so their behavior off the job is considered to contribute to their performance—particularly for managers, supervisors, and professionals with visible jobs. Embarrassing the company will often lead to dismissal, combined with a

negative reputation that will be difficult to shake for purposes of future employment. Indiscreet behavior in private life that can lead to dismissal includes being caught shoplifting, a citation for drunk driving, being arrested for a drug offense, charges of sexual harassment or rape, and assault and battery. Several years ago, top-level managers at Time-Warner asked Chris Albrecht, the CEO of its Home Box Office unit, and a high performer, to resign after he was accused of assaulting his girlfriend in a hotel parking lot in Las Vegas.[34]

If you want to overcome having committed a blunder, avoid defensiveness. Demonstrate that you are more interested in recovering from the blunder than in trying to share the blame for what happened. Focus on solutions to the problem rather than faultfinding. Suppose you have been too critical of your team leader in a recent team meeting. Explain that your attempts to be constructively critical backfired and that you will choose your words more carefully in the future.

Another way to patch up a blunder is to stay poised. Admit that you made the mistake and apologize, but do not act or feel inferior. Mistakes are inevitable in a competitive work environment. Avoid looking sad and distraught. Instead, maintain eye contact with people when you describe your blunder.

SELF-ASSESSMENT QUIZZES IN OVERVIEW

Four self-assessment quizzes are presented in this chapter. Collectively, they should heighten your awareness of the importance of positive politics and point you toward developing political skills. Self-Assessment Quiz 12-1 measures your tendency toward engaging in political behavior on the job, whereas Self-Assessment Quiz 12-2 is designed to measure political skill or ability. Self-Assessment Quiz 12-3 measures your tendency toward a key aspect of relationship building—making others feel important. Self-Assessment 12-4 measures your tendency to suffer from "foot-in-the-mouth disease," or committing political blunders.

Concept Review and Reinforcement

Key Terms

organizational politics, 243
power, 243
social intelligence, 245
impression management, 246

business etiquette, 248
networking, 253
unwritten boundaries, 255
constructive gossip, 261

microinequity, 261
group norms, 261

Summary of Key Concepts

Positive political tactics help build good interpersonal relationships. Organizational politics refers to gaining power through any means other than merit or luck. Power refers to the ability or potential to control anything of value and influence decisions. Impression management is one aspect of organizational politics. Managing the impression you create encompasses a wide range of behaviors designed to create a positive influence on work associates, including the following: build trust and confidence, be visible and create a strong presence, minimize being a yes-person, and create a healthy image. Also, attempt to be authentic and avoid creating a negative impression.

A major component of managing the impression you create is business etiquette. The general principle of etiquette is to be considerate of the feelings of work associates. Areas of business etiquette include the following: work behavior and clothing; introductions; relationships between men and women and between people of different ages; use of wire and cell telephones;dining; e-mail, instant messaging, and text-by-phone correspondence; use of electronic devices other than phones; working in a cubicle; cross-cultural relations; and interaction with people with disabilities.

Political strategies and tactics for building relationships with managers and other key people include networking with influential people, helping your manager succeed, understanding unwritten boundaries, volunteering for assignments, flattering influential people sensibly, using information power, admitting mistakes, appearing cool under pressure, laughing at your manager's humor, and expressing constructive disagreement.

Political strategies and tactics for developing relationships with coworkers and other work associates include maintaining honest and open relationships, making others feel important, being diplomatic, exchanging favors, asking for advice, sharing constructive gossip, minimizing microinequities, and following group norms.

A strategy for not losing whatever power you have accumulated is to refrain from making political blunders. Political blunders can also prevent you from attaining power. Representative blunders include criticizing your manager publicly, bypassing your manager, displaying disloyalty, being a pest, being a poor team player, burning your bridges, and indiscreet behavior in private life. If you want to make up for a blunder, avoid defensiveness and stay poised.

Check Your Understanding

1. To what extent are office politics skills important for a person who is technically competent and hard-working?

2. Many people have said that a major reason for wanting to work out of their home is to avoid office politics. What type of behaviors are they really trying to avoid?

3. Identify three jobs in which you think practicing good business etiquette would be extremely important.

4. Etiquette training for people in high-level business positions is more popular than ever. How would you explain the popularity of such training?

5. A physically able man encounters his vice president, a frail woman, as they are both entering an airport. From an etiquette perspective, should the man ask to carry the woman's bags to the check-in counter? (The man does not have a suitcase with him.)

6. It has been said that although most businesspeople can see through flattery, the technique still works. How would you explain this observation?

7. How ethical is it to ask a person for advice with a problem even if you already know which solution you will use?

8. Describe how e-mail and instant messaging can be used to play positive office politics, as well as for unethical purposes.

9. In what way might being politically incorrect be a political blunder?

10. Why might the study of organizational politics seem more relevant to people with at least several years of work experience than to career beginners?

The Web Corner

http://www.politicalsavvy.com/docs/quiz.html
(Test your political savvy IQ.)

http://lovequizzes.netfirms.com/boss.html
(Quiz about your relationship with your boss.)

http://www.ExecutivePlanet.com
(Guide to international business culture and etiquette in over 35 countries.)

Internet Skill Builder: Sharpening Your Compliments

An important part of being a skilled office politician, as well as a government one, is to compliment people effectively. The information about flattery contained in the chapter gives you some ideas about how to use compliments effectively. Search the Internet for a few more useful suggestions for giving compliments to others. A good starting point for this assignment is *http://www.lifehacker. com* because it provides intelligent, research-based suggestions about giving compliments. This week try out the best idea you find in this skill-building assignment. Observe the results of your compliment so you can refine your technique.

Developing Your Human Relations Skills

Interpersonal Relations Case 12.1

What Do My Table Manners Have to Do with the Job?

Suzanne Chavez was mentally set for a wonderful day. She was returning to AutoPay, Inc., for her third job interview for a position as a human resources representative. As an HR rep, Suzanne would have a variety of responsibilities including answering employee questions about benefits, organizing company parties and picnics, and conducting exit interviews with employees who quit the firm.

Suzanne reasoned that the third interview should be mostly to confirm the opinion of AutoPay managers that she was an excellent candidate for the position. Suzanne admired how AutoPay had grown into one of the largest payroll processing companies in the region, managing payroll and other human resource functions for hundreds of small employers. She also admired the professional appearance and behavior of almost all the AutoPay workers she met.

Two hours before leaving for the job interview, Suzanne received an e-mail message from her prospective boss, Steve Adams. The message indicated that there would be a slight change of schedule. Instead of her arriving at 10 A.M., Adams wanted Suzanne to arrive at 11:30 A.M. Adams and a few other company representatives decided they wanted to take her to lunch. The setting for the lunch would be Silo's, an upscale restaurant that emphasized Italian specialties.

On company premises, Suzanne met briefly with three company representatives and exchanged a few pleasantries. At this point, Suzanne knew that any heavy questions would be asked over lunch. The inevitable question about Suzanne's motives for entering human resources came up before the group even ordered: "Why do you want to work in human resources?" Suzanne knew to avoid the stereotypical answer, "Because I like people."

Instead, Suzanne explained that she enjoyed working with the complexity of people, and that she believed strongly that taking care of human resources translates directly into profits. Adams blurted out, "Great answer Suzanne."

The server came to the table and asked for drink orders. Two people ordered a glass of club soda, one person ordered tonic water, and Suzanne asked for a Coors Light. "And, don't forget," she added, "I would like another one during the meal."

Suzanne ordered clams over linguini for an entrée. When the server asked what the diners wanted for dessert, only Suzanne said yes. Her choice was Neapolitan ice cream.

Conversation flowed freely during the lunch, and Suzanne was feeling confident that she would receive a job offer. After lunch, Adams took her aside, thanked her for joining the group for lunch, and said that she would be hearing from them soon.

A week passed without hearing from Adams or another company representative. Suzanne sent an e-mail thanking the company for the three interviews, and pointed out that she was still enthused about the prospects of working for AutoPay. Two days later a letter arrived in the mail explaining that the company had decided to offer the job to another candidate. A little bit shocked and disappointed, Suzanne telephoned Adams and asked if she could please be told exactly why she was turned down for a job, when she seemed so qualified and the company seemed so interested.

"We all thought you were a strong candidate, Suzanne," answered Adams. "But my boss said we could not hire a person with such poor manners."

"Poor manners? What are you talking about?" inquired Suzanne.

"My boss and I noticed three faux pas. First, you were the only person to order an alcoholic beverage, and you ordered two. Second, you sucked in a strand of linguini more than once. Third, you were the only person to order dessert. I am very sorry."

Disappointed and angry, Suzanne asked, "What do my table manners have to do with the job? I didn't get drunk, and I wasn't a slob."

Case Questions

1. How justified were the company managers in turning down Suzanne based on their perception of her table manners?
2. Should Steve Adams have warned Suzanne Chavez that her table manners would be a factor in evaluating her job qualifications?
3. How might Suzanne benefit from the time she invested in her interviews with AutoPay?

Interpersonal Relations Case 12.2

Lunch 2.0 for Free

A few months after Google Inc. fired Mark Jen for blogging about work, he slipped into one of the company's cafeterias to score a free lunch with friends. He had no idea that he was also helping to launch a nationwide phenomenon. "We thought this was a great way to check out different companies and also get a free lunch," said Jen, now a 24-year old programming manager at Tagged Inc., a San Francisco-based online social network.

That lunch went so well, the group decided to make it a regular event: They began meeting at corporate cafeterias around the Bay Area in an effort to rub elbows with employees at other technology companies—and share some of the free food that many tech companies provide. They posted their lunch schedule on a blog, and opened the meetings to anyone interested. "We are in Silicon Valley, which has a lot of tech companies," says Jen. But he says that employees "don't really branch out and meet other people from other companies."

The concept—dubbed Lunch 2.0 by its founders—has grown into a social networking phenomenon that now draws hundreds of engineers, venture capitalists, and even summer interns to various companies for free meals and conversations. It used to be that the group, which initially consisted of fewer than 10 people, practically had to sneak through company doors. Some attendees would get in with friends who were employees, while others sneaked by security. (Google, where it all started, allows employees to bring guests to the company cafeteria. Jen got in with a friend who worked there.)

But now, as the lunches have begun to draw larger crowds, companies are inviting in the Lunch 2.0-goers as a way to woo potential hires and push their products to influence bloggers who attend. Employers ranging from social-networking company Facebook Inc. to Microsoft Corp. have hosted Lunch 2.0 events.

And the idea is spreading. Similar lunch groups have already sprouted in Seattle and Germany, followed by chapters in Bangalore and Los Angeles. The Lunch 2.0 founders have received inquiries from employees who want to start chapters in New York, Atlanta, and Singapore.

"Lunch 2.0 builds positive brand associations both for those who attend and those who hear about it later in conversation, posted photos, and blog entries," says Paul C. Jeffries, a consultant to start-ups in Silicon Valley. Although the events are now hosted by companies, they still have a "guerrilla feel, like the tech community is crashing the gate and taking over the company."

Other than nametags, the events are unstructured—and hardly swanky. For one thing, everyone shows up in jeans, typical of the Bay Area culture. One time, about 300 people showed up at a Plaxo lunch in Mountain View, California to eat Popeye's chicken. "We went for the comfort food," says John McCrea, the vice president of marketing, adding that a couple of employees decided to deejay the event.

Lunch 2.0 attendees aren't necessarily looking for a job. Some show up just to talk shop. Others simply crave a free meal outside their own cafeterias. "It's a perfect applicant pool because they are gainfully employed people who are geared toward passively looking for a job," says Tey Scott, recruiting manager at Time Warner Inc.'s AOL. A recent lunch at AOL drew about 200 people into the company's Mountain View office for pizza. The company had set up a table with information for prospective hires.

Attendees say the casual atmosphere makes it easy to interact with higher-ups at a company while getting a glimpse of the networking environment. For instance, Mike Miller, a former senior staff engineer at Sun Microsystems Inc., met both a senior recruiter and Linkedin Chief Executive Dan Nye at the company's Lunch 2.0 event.

"I though it was really cool," says Miller, who says he enjoyed playing Wii, and took home a ball for his kids. "It was a high energy atmosphere." After the lunch, the recruiter contacted him for an interview. Miller was hired as a principal software engineer in July.

Recently representatives of employee recruiting firms have started to attend Lunch 2.0 lunches. Also, vendors of recruiting services have . . . been noticed at the events.

Case Questions

1. How might you use Lunch 2.0 events to assist your career? (Note that these lunches have expanded to other occupations as well as IT workers.)
2. What do you think of the ethics of people who attend a Lunch 2.0 gathering just to get a free lunch?

3. If you were your company's organizer of Lunch 2.0, what steps would you take to keep recruiting firms and recruiting vendors off the premises?

Source: Anjali Athavaley, "The Power Lunch, Cafeteria-Style," *The Wall Street Journal*, August 29, 2007, pp. D1, D8. Permission obtained through the Copyright Clearance Center.

CHAPTER 13

Customer Satisfaction Skills

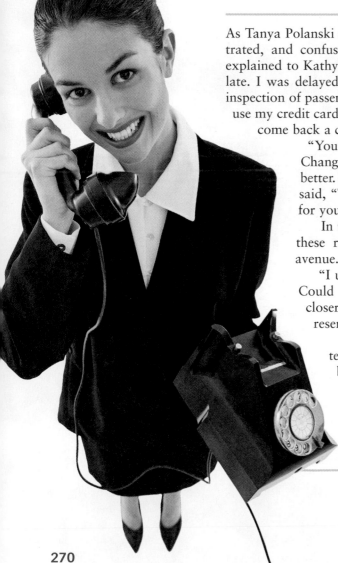

As Tanya Polanski approached the receptionist counter at the hotel, she was tired, frustrated, and confused. "Everything has gone wrong for me the last two days," she explained to Kathy Chang, the receptionist. "My flight from Moscow arrived 10 hours late. I was delayed at customs for an hour. The man said they were doing a random inspection of passengers, even though I didn't look or act like a terrorist. When I tried to use my credit card at the airport, they told me the computer wasn't working so I had to come back a couple of hours later."

"You certainly have had a difficult couple of days, Ms. Polanski," said Chang. "After you are settled in your room, you will start to feel much better. Let me access your reservations." After checking her computer, Chang said, "There seems to be a little problem here. We do not have reservations for you."

In tears, Polanski said, "Has everything gone crazy in America? I made these reservations three months ago for the Holiday Inn right on this avenue."

"I understand why you are upset. Let's work out this problem together. Could it be that you made reservations at our other Holiday Inn, a little closer to downtown? It's on the same street. I will check into our worldwide reservation system right now."

"You're in luck, Ms. Polanski," said Chang after a few minutes at the terminal. "Your reservations are at our other Holiday Inn, just five blocks away. I will have our van take you there right away, and I will phone ahead to make sure you get to the front of the line as soon as possible. Enjoy your stay in the United States, and we look forward to seeing you again."

"Thank you, thank you, you have saved my day," replied Polanski.

Learning Objectives

After reading and studying this chapter and doing the exercises, you should be able to

1. Explain the three components of customer experience (or service).
2. Enhance your ability to satisfy customers by using general principles of customer satisfaction.
3. Create bonds with present or future customers.
4. Have a plan for dealing effectively with customer dissatisfaction.

Maybe the hotel receptionist in question is naturally gifted in interpersonal skills, or maybe she combined the right personality traits with the right training to become a compassionate and helpful hotel receptionist. Either way, she has a lesson for workers at all levels in many different types of jobs. Outstanding customer service enhances a company's reputation and leads to repeat business. This chapter presents information and exercises that can enhance your ability to satisfy both external and internal customers at a high level.

External customers fit the traditional definition and include clients, guests, and patients. External customers can be classified as retail or industrial. The latter represents one company buying from another, such as purchasing steel or a gross of printer cartridges. *Internal customers* are the people you serve within the organization or those who use the output from your job. Also, everyone you depend upon is an internal customer. The emphasis in this chapter is on satisfying external customers. Much of the rest of the book deals with better serving internal customers, because improved interpersonal relationships enhance the satisfaction of work associates.

Customer satisfaction skills are necessary for all workers in contact with customers, including sales representatives, customer service representatives (those who back up sales and take care of customer problems), and store associates. Workers in a wide variety of jobs need good customer satisfaction skills. The founder of a technology consulting firm observes, "Ninety percent of the time when a client has an issue with a consultant, it's related to soft skills."[1] Another way of understanding the importance of customer satisfaction skills is to recognize that employees who can satisfy customers contribute heavily to profits. The chief executive of a firm that surveys approximately 20 million customers a year for retail and restaurant chains concludes, "A good employee or a good sales associate might be worth five or 10 times an average one. We've seen that. It's unreal."[2]

Various aspects of developing customer satisfaction skills are divided into three parts in this chapter: following the general principles of customer satisfaction, bonding with customers, and dealing with customer dissatisfaction. As you work through this chapter, you will observe that to implement its suggestions you need many of the interpersonal skills you have been acquiring such as communication, teamwork, motivation, and conflict resolution. To reflect on your attitudes toward satisfying customers, do Self-Assessment Quiz 13-1.

The Customer Orientation Quiz

Directions: Answer each of the following statements about dealing with customers as *mostly true* or *mostly false*. The statements relate to your attitudes, even if you lack direct experience in dealing with customers. Your experiences as a customer will also be helpful in responding to the statements.

	Mostly true	Mostly false
1. All work in a company should be geared toward pleasing customers.	_____	_____
2. The real boss in any business is the customer.	_____	_____
3. Smiling at customers improves the chances of making a sale.	_____	_____
4. I would rather find a new customer than attempt to satisfy one who is difficult to please.	_____	_____
5. Dealing with customers is as (or more) rewarding than dealing with coworkers.	_____	_____
6. I enjoy (or would enjoy) helping a customer solve a problem related to the use of my product or service.	_____	_____
7. The best way to get repeat business is to offer steep discounts.	_____	_____
8. In business, your customer is your partner.	_____	_____
9. Dealing directly with customers is (or would be) the most boring part of most jobs.	_____	_____
10. If you have the brand and model the customer wants, being nice to the customer is not so important.	_____	_____
11. A good customer is like a good friend.	_____	_____
12. If you are too friendly with a customer, he or she will take advantage of you.	_____	_____
13. Now that individual consumers and companies can shop online, the personal touch in business is losing importance.	_____	_____
14. Addressing a customer by his or her name helps build a relationship with that customer.	_____	_____
15. Satisfying a customer is fun whether or not it leads to a commission.	_____	_____

Scoring and Interpretation: Give yourself a +1, for each of the following statements receiving a response of "mostly true": 1, 2, 3, 5, 6, 8, 11, 14, and 15. Give yourself a +1 for each of the following statements receiving a response of "mostly false": 4, 7, 9, 10, 12, and 13.

13–15 points: You have a strong orientation toward providing excellent customer service.

8–12 points: You have an average customer service orientation.

1–7 points: You have a below-average orientation toward providing excellent customer service.

THE THREE COMPONENTS OF CUSTOMER EXPERIENCE (SERVICE)

A useful starting point in becoming skilled at satisfying customers is to understand how customers form impressions of their experience. The term *experience* is often used as to replace *service* because customer service is often perceived as getting help from a call center or returning merchandise in a retail store. According to the research of marketing professors Leonard L. Berry, Eileen A. Wall, and Lewis P. Carbone, customers form three clues about the service experience based on their presence or absence. A clue is anything the customer can see, hear, taste, or smell. It is often small clues that influence a customer's overall perception of an experience, such as a customer service rep yawning while taking care of the person's problem.[3]

The key point is that customers form perceptions based on three components of the experience. First are functional clues derived from the technical performance of the service, such as the technician from the call center enabling you to get your new

FIGURE 13-1 Clue Influences on Customer Perceptions

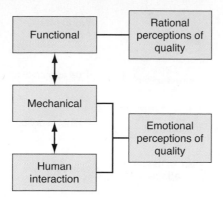

Source: Adapted from Leonard L. Berry, Eileen A. Wall, and Lewis P. Carbone, "Service Clues and Customer Assessment of the Service Experience: Lessons from Marketing," *Academy of Management Perspectives*, May 2006, p. 46.

printer up and running. Second are mechanical clues stemming from the sensory presentation of the service, including sights, smells, sounds, tastes, and textures. At Target stores, the mechanical clues include the red color scheme, the wide isles, and the numerous checkout counters. Third are the human interaction clues detected from the behavior and appearance of service providers. Such clues include the service provider's choice of words, tone of voice, enthusiasm, body language, and dress. Much of this chapter deals with the human-touch component of the customer experience.

Human interaction in the service experience offers the biggest opportunity to deepen customers' emotional connection to the company and the service provider. For example, many customers return to a given restaurant because the server is so polite, friendly, and helpful—assuming the food and décor are also satisfactory.

Figure 13-1 presents an overview of the three components of or clues about customer experience. Notice that only the functional clues are based mostly on rational perceptions of quality of service. If the call center technician gets your printer working, you are not so concerned about his or her lack of warmth and enthusiasm. In contrast, the mechanical and human interaction clues are based mostly on emotional perceptions of the quality of service. For example, you might return to a hotel mostly because of the view of the bay and the soothing beige colors in the room. For the customer service to be truly outstanding, all three clues should be positive.

FOLLOWING THE GENERAL PRINCIPLES OF CUSTOMER SATISFACTION

Knowing how to satisfy customers is a subset of effective interpersonal relations in organizations. Nevertheless, there are certain general principles that will sharpen your ability to satisfy customers and thereby improve customer retention. This section presents eight key principles for satisfying customers. Remember, however, that satisfaction is considered a minimum expectation. If you do an outstanding job of satisfying customers, they will experience delight, as shown in Figure 13-2.

Customer satisfaction is important for several reasons. To begin with, without satisfying customers, a business would cease to exist. The slogan of Tops Markets, Inc., a supermarket chain, is "Customer satisfaction is our only business." Satisfied customers are likely to tell friends and acquaintances about their satisfactory experiences, helping a firm grow its business. In contrast, dissatisfied customers—especially those with an unresolved problem—are likely to tell many people about their dissatisfaction, thus dissuading a large number of people from becoming new customers. Studies indicate that an upset or angry customer tells an average of between 10 and 20 other people about an unhappy

FIGURE 13-2 Levels of Customer Satisfaction

experience.[4] Customer satisfaction is also highly valued because it breeds customer loyalty, which in turn is very profitable. Repeat business is a success factor in both retail and industrial companies.

Another reason for satisfying customers is the humanitarian aspect. Satisfying people enhances their physical and mental health, whereas dissatisfaction creates negative stress. Have you ever been so angry at poor service that you experienced stress?

Be Satisfied So You Can Provide Better Customer Service

Employees who are happy with their jobs are the most likely to satisfy customers. As stated by Frank DeRiso, a local president of the United Food and Commercial Workers union, "The employees are your No. 1 asset. You don't have a customer base without employees."[5] Treating employees well puts them in a better frame of mind to treat their customers well and provide better service, especially in the human interaction aspect of service. According to consumer behavior specialist James Hazen, good service comes down to creating a positive and memorable customer experience. For example, Starbucks can command a premium price for its coffee beverages not simply because of the quality of its beans and its stylish cardboard cups, but because of the overall experience. And the employees—particularly the baristas—are part of that experience.[6]

Acting alone, you cannot improve company conditions that contribute to job satisfaction. What you can control to some extent, however, is your own attitudes that are related to job satisfaction. A checklist of attitudes and beliefs related to job satisfaction, and over which you can exert some control, follows:

- **Interest in the work itself.** Job satisfaction stems directly from being interested in what you are doing. People who love their work experience high job satisfaction and are therefore in the right frame of mind to satisfy customers.
- **A feeling of self-esteem.** If you have high self-esteem you are more likely to experience high job satisfaction. High-status occupations contribute more to self-esteem than do those of low status. Feelings of self-esteem also stem from doing work the individual sees as worthwhile. This perception is less influenced by external standards than it is the status associated with a particular job or occupation.
- **Optimism and flexibility.** An optimistic and flexible person is predisposed to be a satisfied employee. A pessimistic and rigid person will most likely be a dissatisfied employee. Every company has its share of "pills" who always find something to complain about. Some evidence suggests that a tendency toward optimism versus pessimism is inherited.[7] If you have a predisposition toward pessimism, you can still become more optimistic with self-discipline. For example, you can look for the positive aspects of a generally unpleasant situation.
- **Positive self-image.** People possessing a positive self-image are generally more satisfied with their jobs than are those possessing a negative self-image. One explanation

is that the people who view themselves negatively tend to view most things negatively. You have to like yourself before you can like your job.

- **Positive expectations about the job.** People with positive expectations about their jobs are frequently more satisfied than are those with low expectations. These expectations illustrate a self-fulfilling prophecy. If you expect to like your job, you will behave in such a way that those expectations will be met. Similarly, if you expect your job not to satisfy your needs, you will do things to make your expectations come true. Assume that a worker expects to earn low commissions in a sales job. The person's negativism may come through to customers and prospective customers, thereby ensuring low customer satisfaction and low commissions.

- **Effective handling of abuse from customers.** Customer service workers are often verbally abused by customers over such matters as products not working, merchandise returns not being acceptable, and the customer having been charged a late fee. Automated telephone-answering systems often force callers to hack through a thicket of prompts before reaching a human being. By the time a live person is reached, the customer is angry and ready to lash out at the customer service representative.[8] To prevent these oral tirades from damaging one's job satisfaction, it is essential to use effective techniques of dealing with criticism and resolving conflict as described in Chapter 8. The section on dealing with dissatisfied customers presented later in this chapter is also important. Combating sexual harassment by customers is also important for retaining emotional equilibrium.

High job satisfaction contributes to good customer service in another important way. Employees who are satisfied with their jobs are more likely to engage in service-oriented organizational citizenship behavior. As you will recall, *organizational citizenship behavior* relates to going beyond one's ordinary job description to help other workers and the company. A customer service worker with high organizational citizenship behavior will go beyond ordinary expectations to find ways to solve a customer problem.[9] A member of the tech support staff in a consumer electronics store volunteered to drop by a customer's house to help him install a programmable DVD, even though such home visits were not required. As a result of the technician's kindness, the man purchased a $6,000 plasma screen TV receiver from the store.

Receive Emotional Support from Coworkers and Management to Give Better Customer Service

Closely related to the idea that satisfied workers can better satisfy customers is the finding that the emotional support of coworkers often leads to providing better customer service. According to a research study, the support of coworkers is even more important than supervisory support. The participants in the study were 354 customer service workers employed in service-based facilities. Customer satisfaction surveys were collected from 269 customers. The major finding was that employees who perceived their coworkers to be supportive had a higher level of commitment to their customers.

The researchers concluded that it is important to have a supportive group of coworkers by your side to help you perform service-related duties. In this study, supervisory support was less important than coworker support in terms of bringing about a strong customer orientation. (A *customer service orientation* includes a desire to help customers and a willingness to act in ways that would satisfy a customer. The hotel receptionist portrayed in the chapter opener exemplifies a service worker with a strong customer orientation.) Another important conclusion drawn from the study was that customer satisfaction was positively associated with the strength of the service worker's customer orientation.[10]

Research also supports the idea that the type of leadership sales representatives receive influences the type of relationships the reps build with customers. The study in question involved 300 pairs of sales managers and 1,400 salespeople reporting directly to them. Sales managers who were charismatic and good at setting visions strongly affected the use of customer-oriented selling behaviors, such as building good relationships. Other key factors related to building good relationships with customers were the level of support the sales workers received from the organization and how much cohesiveness (closeness) they felt with coworkers.[11] A similar study conducted in Taiwan with 450 hairstylists and 112 store managers found that charismatic and visionary leaders enhanced employee service. In turn, better service was associated with customers coming back to the salon.[12] You probably already knew that if your hairstylist gives good service, you will return—but now there is a quantitative study to support your belief.

The major point here is that the organization plays an important role in how well your ability or willingness to build relationships with customers. A thought to take away is that if you perceive your manager to be charismatic, you are more likely to provide better customer service.

Understand Customer Needs and Put Them First

The most basic principle of selling is to identify and satisfy customer needs. One challenge is that many customers may not be able to express their needs clearly. To help identify customer needs, you may have to probe for information. For example, the associate in a camera and video store might ask, "What uses do you have in mind for a video camera?" Knowing such information will help the associate identify which camcorder will satisfy the customer's needs.

The concept of adding value for customers is widely accepted as a measure of satisfying customer needs. If you satisfy customer needs, you are adding value for them. A person might be willing to pay $10 more per ticket to watch an athletic event if the extra $10 brought a better view and a chair instead of a backless bench. (The better view and more comfortable back add value for the spectator.)   After customer needs have been identified, the focus must be on satisfying those needs rather than the needs of oneself or the company. Assume that the customer says, "The only convenient time for me to receive delivery this week would be Thursday or Friday afternoon." The sales associate should not respond, "On Thursday and Friday our truckers prefer to make morning deliveries." Instead, the associate should respond, "I'll do whatever is possible to accommodate your request."

A major contributor to identifying customer needs is to listen actively to customers. Listening can take place during conversations with customers, and "listening" can mean absorbing information sent by e-mail and written letters. A policy at Southwest Airlines is that if a customer (or employee) has an idea, a manager must respond instantaneously.[13] For example, Southwest obliged the customer suggestion that more reservation agents be Spanish speaking.

Focus on Solving Problems, Not Just Taking Orders

Effective selling entails sales representatives to not only take orders but to solve problems as well. An example is the approach taken by sales representatives for Xerox Corporation. Instead of focusing on the sale of photocopiers, printers, and related equipment, the sales reps look to help customers solve their information-flow problems. The solution could involve selling machines, but it might also involve selling consulting services.

The focus on problem solving enables sales reps to become partners in the success of their customers' businesses. By helping the customer solve problems, the sales rep enhances the value of the supplier–customer relationship to the customer. The customer is receiving consulting services in addition to the merchandise or service being offered. In some situations, a store associate can capitalize on the same principle. If the customer appears unsure about a purchase, ask him or her which problem the product should solve. The following scenario in a computer store illustrates this point:

> **Customer:** I think I would like to buy this computer. I'm pretty sure it's the one I want. But I don't know too much about computers other than how to use them for word processing, e-mail, sending photos, and basic Web search.
>
> **Store Associate:** I'm happy you would like to purchase a computer. But could you tell me what problems you're facing that you want a computer to help you solve?
>
> **Customer:**   Right now I feel I'm not capitalizing on the Internet revolution. I want to do more online and get into digital photography so I can send cool photos to

friends all over. I also want to purchase music online, so I can walk around with an MP3 player like my friends do.

Store Associate: To solve your problem you'll need a more powerful computer than the one you're looking at. I'd like you to consider another model that is about the same price as the one you have chosen. The difference is that it has the memory you need to e-mail photos and download music from a subscription service.

Respond Positively to Moments of Truth

An effective customer contact person performs well during situations in which a customer comes in contact with the company and forms an impression of its service. Such situations are referred to as **moments of truth**. If the customer experiences satisfaction or delight during a moment of truth, the customer is likely to return when the need for service arises again. A person who is frustrated or angered during a moment of truth will often not be a repeat customer. A moment of truth is an important part of customer service because what really matters in a service encounter is the customer's perception of what occurred.[14] Visualize a couple who has just dined at an expensive restaurant as part of celebrating their anniversary. The food, wine, and music might have been magnificent, but the couple perceives the service as poor because one of them slipped on ice in the restaurant parking lot.

You can probably visualize many moments of truth in your experiences with service. Reflect on how a store associate treated you when you asked for assistance, the instructions you received when an airplane flight was canceled, or how you were treated when you inquired about financial aid. Each business transaction has its own moment of truth, yet they all follow the same theme of a key interaction between a customer and a company employee.

One way you can track moments of truth is to prepare a cycle-of-service chart, as shown in Figure 13-3. The **cycle-of-service chart** summarizes the moments of truth encountered by a customer during the delivery of a service.[15] To gain insight into these charts, do Skill-Building Exercise 13-1.

Be Ready to Accept Empowerment

A major strategy for improving customer service is to empower customer contact employees to resolve problems. **Empowerment** refers to managers transferring, or sharing, power with lower-ranking employees. In terms of customer relations, it means pushing decision making and complaint resolution downward to employees who are in direct contact with customers. The traditional method of dealing with all but the most routine customer

moments of truth
Situations in which a customer comes in contact with a company and forms an impression of its service.

cycle-of-service chart
A method of tracking the moments of truth with respect to customer service.

empowerment
The process of managers transferring, or sharing, power with lower-ranking employees.

FIGURE 13-3 A Cycle-of-Service Chart for Obtaining a Car Loan at a Bank

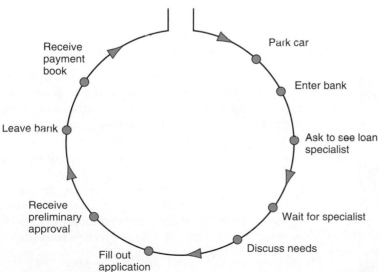

Moments of Truth

The class organizes into small groups to discuss what can go right versus what can go wrong during customer moments of truth. First refer to the cycle-of-service chart shown in Figure 13-3. Discuss what can go right or wrong at each moment of truth.

Second, have the team develop its own cycle-of-service chart for another service, using its own experiences and imagination. After making the two analyses, discuss the usefulness of a cycle-of-service chart for improving customer satisfaction.

problems is for the customer contact worker to refer them to the manager. Many manufacturing firms and service firms now authorize customer contact workers to take care of customer problems within limits. For example, at the Hampton Inn, any worker can offer a guest a free night of lodging to compensate for a service problem.

Empowerment is not giving away the store, especially because limits are established to the customer contact worker's authority. Empowerment does involve taking a reasonable risk based on company principles to provide meaningful customer service. For empowerment to work, the company must grant decision-making latitude to employees. The employees, in turn, must be willing to accept empowerment (or decision-making authority).[16] Imagine yourself in a customer contact position. For empowerment to work effectively, you should be able to answer the following statements in the affirmative:

- I would bewilling to arrive at a quick decision as to whether the company or the customer is right.
- I would be willing to admit to a customer that the company has made a mistake.
- I would be willing to take the risk that at times I will lose money for the company on a given transaction.
- I would be comfortable making an out-of-the-ordinary decision about a customer problem without consulting a manager.

For additional practice in identifying the three components of customer of service, label each moment of truth in one of three perceptions: functional, mechanical, or human interaction. For example, you might have observed that the retail store had a nice scent (a perception of mechanics).

Enhance Customer Service through IT

Much has been said and written about how IT has depersonalized customer service, such as having customers select from a long menu of choices on a telephone. IT, however, also plays an important role in recording customer preferences and individualizing service. A major contribution of IT to enhancing customer service is to develop individualized appeals to customers. With the right software in place, you can make a direct appeal to customer preferences based on past purchases and the habits of customers with similar preferences. If you have purchased online at a major e-tailer like Amazon.com or Buy.com, you may be familiar with this technology. Two examples follow:

1. Computerized information tells you immediately what the customer on the phone or online has bought in the past, so you may ask a question such as, "Two years ago you installed a centralized vacuum cleaning system. Do you need another set of bags by now?"

2. Speaking to the person, or sending an e-mail message to the customer, you might say, "Last year you purchased a heated doghouse for your Yorkshire terrier. Our information suggests that people who own a heated doghouse are also interested in dog sweaters. Please take a moment to look at our new line of dog sweaters for the canines who appreciate warmth."

Developing individualized appeals to customers is likely to be included in customer relationship management (CRM) software. The complex software is used to implement a strategy of interacting with your customers to bring them more value and more profits to your firm. One of its basic purposes is to make the company easier for customers to do business with, including facilitating placing orders over the Internet.[17] As such, the individual customer service worker would not have the authority to install such a system. Yet the individual worker can always look for ways to apply the CRM system (such as that provided by Salesforce.com, or SAP) in a way that best serves the customer.

A major challenge in providing good customer service when using IT is to preserve the human touch. Here are some hints for adding a personal touch to your electronic communications to help build customer loyalty.

Using voice mail

1. Vary your voice tone and inflection when leaving messages and in your greeting to avoid sounding bored or uninterested in your job and the company.

2. Smile while leaving your message—somehow a smile gets transmitted over the telephone wires or optic fibers!

3. Use voice mail to minimize "telephone tag" rather than to increase it. If your greeting specifies when you will return, callers can choose to call again or to leave a message. When you leave a message, suggest a good time to return your call. Another way to minimize telephone tag is to assure the person you are calling that you will keep trying.

4. Place an informative and friendly greeting (outgoing message) on your voice mail. Used effectively, a voice-mail greeting will minimize the number of people irritated by not talking to a person.

5. When you respond to a voice-mail outgoing message, leave specific, relevant information. As in the suggestions for minimizing telephone tag, be specific about why you are calling and what you want from the person called. The probability of receiving a return call increases when you leave honest and useful information. If you are selling something or asking for a favor, be honest about your intent.

6. When leaving your message, avoid the most common voice-mail error by stating your name and telephone number clearly enough to be understood. Most recipients of a message dislike intensely listening to it several times to pick up identifying information.

Using e-mail

1. Use the customer's name. Begin the greeting, "Hello, Lisa King." Many companies now greet customers by their first name only, but some customers consider this practice to be rude. However, few people are likely to be offended when you use both their first and last names.

2. Choose a human e-mail address. Marysmith@kaset.com feels more personal than an odd sequence of numbers, letters, and dashes. To enhance your credibility and professional stature, avoid cool electronic addresses such as Steelabs@aol.com or Angellady42@gmail.com.

3. Be conversational. Mention events you have shared, such as, "I enjoyed seeing you at the company meeting."

4. Sign your name. Don't neglect your signature. "Best regards, Jim Woods."[18]

Avoid Rudeness and Hostility toward Customers

I have reserved the most frequently violated principle of good customer service for last: Avoid being rude or hostile to customers. Although rudeness to customers is obviously a poor business practice, the problem is widespread. Rudeness by customer contact personnel is a major problem from the employer's standpoint. A widely practiced form of rudeness is for two store associates to converse with each other about nonwork matters while a customer waits for attention. Or, how about a store associate making a personal phone call while waiting on you?

Rude treatment creates more lost business than does poor product quality or high prices. Several years ago McDonald's franchises were facing a downturn in sales. Surveys indicated that one of the problems facing McDonald's Corporation was the indifferent and rude behavior by many frontline workers. McDonald's then increased the training of store employees and upgraded the menu to achieve a substantial rebound in sales.

Rudeness is sometimes a form of hostility because rudeness, such as grimacing at a customer, stems from anger. Being outright hostile toward customers can be a bigger problem than rudeness, which is more subtle. The impact of service provider hostility on customer satisfaction was explored by studying 142 naturally occurring service interactions at a telephone service center of a bank. A typical interaction would be a customer phoning the bank to inquire about an account balance. Service interactions usually lasted about two minutes. Customers were later contacted to complete a quality survey about their transaction. Hostility was measured through raters' judgment of the tone of the service providers' voices.

A major finding of the study was that when the technical performance (for example, providing the information needed) was low, hostility by the service provider lowered customer satisfaction considerably. When the technical performance of the service provider was good, hostility had a less negative impact on service quality.[19] When you get the information you need from a service provider, you are willing to put up with a few angry tones! The overall message supports a human relations perspective: Being hostile toward customers lowers their perception of the quality of service.

To elevate your awareness level about rudeness among customer contact personnel, do Self-Assessment Quiz 13-2.

SELF-ASSESSMENT QUIZ 13-2

Am I Being Rude?

Directions: The following is a list of behaviors that would be interpreted as rude by many customers. Check *Yes* if you have engaged in such behavior in your dealings with customers or if you would be *likely* to do so if your job involved customer contact, and *No* if you would not engage in such behavior.

	Yes	No
1. I talk to a coworker while serving a customer.	_____	_____
2. I conduct a telephone conversation with someone else while serving a customer.	_____	_____
3. I address customers by their first names without having their permission.	_____	_____
4. I address customers as "You guys."	_____	_____
5. I chew gum or eat candy while dealing with a customer.	_____	_____
6. I laugh when customers describe an agonizing problem they are having with one of our company's products or services.	_____	_____
7. I minimize eye contact with customers.	_____	_____
8. I say the same thing to every customer, such as "Have a nice day," in a monotone.	_____	_____
9. I accuse customers of attempting to cheat the company before carefully investigating the situation.	_____	_____
10. I hurry customers when my breaktime approaches.	_____	_____
11. I comment on an attractive customer's appearance in a flirtatious, sexually oriented way.	_____	_____
12. I sometimes complain about or make fun of other customers when I am serving a customer.	_____	_____
13. I sometimes look and act impatient if a customer fumbles around trying to locate his or her credit card, debit card, or cash.	_____	_____

Interpretation: The more of these behaviors you have engaged in, the ruder you are and the more likely it is that you are losing potential business for your company. If you have not engaged in any of these behaviors, even when faced with a rude customer, you are an asset to your employer. You are also tolerant.

CREATING A BOND WITH YOUR CUSTOMER

Another key perspective on achieving customer satisfaction and delight is to create a bond—or emotional relationship—with customers. The rationale is that if you form warm, constructive relationships with your customers, they will keep buying. Staying focused on the importance of customers will help provide the motivation for forming such a bond. The willingness to form a bond with the customer is part of having a **strong customer orientation**, defined as "a set of basic individual predispositions and an inclination to provide service, to be courteous and helpful in dealing with customers and associates."[20] You may recall Self-Assessment Quiz 13-1 about customer orientation at the outset of the chapter. Service-oriented organizational citizenship behavior relates to the same idea of focusing on customer needs.

Creating a bond is aimed at increasing sales, but it also enhances service. If the customer relies on and trusts the sales representative, the customer will perceive the service to be of high quality. Similarly, people perceive medical and legal services to be of high quality if they trust the physician or lawyer. Virtually all of the principles and techniques presented in this chapter will help form a bond with customers. However, six key principles are as follows:

1. Create a welcoming attitude, including a smile.
2. Provide exceptional service.
3. Show care and concern.
4. Make the buyer feel good.
5. Build a personal relationship.
6. Invite the customer back.

Create a Welcoming Attitude, Including a Smile

An effective starting point in creating a customer bond is to use enthusiastic expressions, including a smile, when greeting customers. Attempt to show a sincere, positive attitude that conveys to customers and prospects, "I'm here to make you happy."[21] In addition to being an effective greeting, smiling is also a natural relationship builder and can help you bond with your customer. Smile several times at each customer meeting, even if your customer is angry at your product or service. A camcorder is a useful device for getting feedback on the quality of your smile. Practicing your smile in a mirror might feel a little less natural, but it is still helpful. Smiling at customers has a potential disadvantage, despite its general effectiveness. If your smile is too friendly and inviting, the customer might think that you want to get to know him or her outside the business relationship.

Smiling is such a key part of bonding with customers that the smiles of customer service workers have been the subject of scientific study. Twenty pairs of first-year college students who were trained as coders for the experiment observed 220 employee–consumer encounters in food–coffee services. Customers were later asked to report their mood, appraisal of service quality, and encounter satisfaction. Several of the findings were as follows: Even in brief encounters, substantial smiling by employees made customers smile in return. Smiling employees were perceived as providing quality service, and the customers felt overall satisfaction with their encounters. Smiling somehow did not affect customer mood after the encounter. One interpretation of the study is that service employees should keep smiling, but not the point that they lack authenticity.[22] Phony smiles backfire in work and personal life.

Provide Exceptional Service (or Customer Experience)

The best-accepted axiom about keeping customers is to provide exceptional service or experience. Many successful companies contend that their competitive advantage is good service. An important part of the comeback of Burger King in 2005 was a subtle way of providing top service to the company's most profitable demographic group, males between

strong customer orientation
A set of individual predispositions and an inclination to provide service, to be courteous and helpful in dealing with customers and associates.

❝ It's definitely a profitable strategy. When a customer comes in and the person behind the counter says hello, and maybe greets you by name, you feel a connection you don't find with most retailers anymore. It makes you feel welcome, and it makes you want to come back. ❞

—Dave Pace, Starbucks executive vice president of partner resources, quoted in *Workforce Management*, February 2005, p. 30

the ages of 18 and 34 who visit the stores three to four times a week. These "Super Fans" want indulgent, fat-laden, high-caloric, tasty food. So Burger King served up the Enormous Omelet Sandwich. CEO Greg Brenneman says he gives his customers what they want, not what others (such as nutritionists and physicians) think they should have.[23]

Exceptional service includes dozens of customer transactions, including prompt delivery, a fair-returns policy, accurate billing, and prompt attention to a customer's presence. Exceptional service also includes giving customers good advice about using the product or service. As shown in Figure 13-1, providing exceptional service leads to customer delight. An interesting perspective on providing customer service is that some industries are more successful than others in receiving high customer satisfaction scores. As shown in Figure 13-4, the highest customer satisfaction ratings are attained in express delivery and Internet retail. The lowest ratings are received by airlines, by cable or satellite TV, and by newspapers. One interpretation is that less can go wrong when packages are delivered to your door. An implication for customer service skills is that if you work in an industry that typically receives lower customer service ratings, you and your coworkers have to be extra diligent in serving customers.

Show Care and Concern

During contacts with the customer, the sales representative should show concern for the customer's welfare. The rep should ask questions, such as, "How have you enjoyed the optical scanner you bought a while back?" "How much time and money have you saved since you installed the new system?" After asking the questions, the sales rep should project a genuine interest in the answer. Microsoft is one of many companies that ask about the quality of their service, and their inquiries are pointed and specific rather than canned. For example, a small business owner responded to an inquiry about service Microsoft provided, and he complimented "Jocelyn" for pointing him in the right direction. A team manager at Microsoft wrote back: "Thank you for taking the time to commend Jocelyn on a Job Well Done. Our primary goal at Microsoft is that our customers are very satisfied with the support they receive. I am pleased to read that we have met that goal in your case."

Make the Buyer Feel Good

A fundamental way of keeping a relationship going is to make the buyer feel good about himself or herself. In addition, the customer should be made to feel good because of having bought from the representative. Offer compliments about the customer's appearance or about a report that specified vendor requirements clearly. In retail, an effective feel-good line is to point out how well the product fits the customer, such as, "It looks like Toro made that riding mower just for you." An effective feel-good line is: "I enjoy doing business with you."

Build a Personal Relationship through Interaction with Customers

Interacting with customers in a personal way often enhances the customer experience, leading to repeat business. Interaction with pleasant staff members gives customers a temporary feeling of friendship that many of them value. Executives at Staybridge Suites recognize how human interaction contributes to profitability, and use this principle as a guide for making investments in customer service. Staybridge, similar to other extended-stay hotels, provides limited services and is sparsely staffed to reduce costs. Rooms are fully cleaned only once a week and the front desk is usually staffed by only one or two people.

Instead of providing loads of amenities, Staybridge concentrates its customer service on staff members interacting with guests. "A lot of our guests really want that personal interaction—the thing they get from home that they'd like to get from a hotel," says Rob Radomski, the vice president for brand management for Staybridge Suites. "There are conversations between guests and staff about projects they're working on, and their family back home, . . . the kid, the dog." Staybridge also offers "Sundowner receptions" on Tuesday, Wednesday, and Thursday evening in the lobby. General managers are required to attend the receptions in which guests are given a free meal and an opportunity to socialize.

FIGURE 13-4 Customer Satisfaction Scores for Service Industry

Rank for 2006	Industry	Customer satisfaction 2006	2007
1	Express delivery	83	81
2	Internet retail	81	
3	Internet search engines	79	75
4	Internet auctions Property/Casualty insurance	78 78	
6	Internet travel Limited service restaurants	77 77	 77
8	Health/personal-care stores Internet brokerage Internet portals	76 	 75
11	Commercial banking Department/discount stores Hotels Life insurance	75 75 75 75	 74 71
15	Hospitals Specialty retails stores Supermarkets	74 74 74	77
18	Internet news/information	73	75
19	Energy/utilities	72	73
20	U.S. postal service	71	73
21	Fixed-line telephone services	70	70
22	Gasoline stations	69	
23	Health insurance	68	
24	Wireless telephone service	66	68
25	Airlines	65	63
26	Cable/satellite TV Newspapers	63 	62 66

Note: Scores are on a scale of 0 to 100.

Source: University of Michigan, Customer Satisfaction Index. Data are from 2006, and from 2007 in categories where the newer data are available. *www.theacsi.org*, 2006, 2007. Reprinted from Kemba J. Dunham, "Beyond Satisfaction: What Is Customer Satisfaction Anyway? And How Do You Measure It? *The Wall Street Journal*, October 30, 2006, p. R4.

Radomski believes the meals are cost-effective in terms of developing customer loyalty.[24]

A high-tech way of building relationships with large numbers of customers is to interact with them through company *blogs,* or Web logs. The company representative is authorized to chat with hundreds of customers and potential customers by placing informal comments on the Web log in a manner similar to a personal diary. The worker lets out tidbits of information to customers without betraying company confidences or making defamatory statements about the company. However, the blog entries are not usually as positive as advertisements, which help form bonds with the customers. Many customers post replies and swap ideas with the company rep. Company-approved blogs are widely used as customers demand information presented in a more unvarnished way. A major advantage of blogs is that they humanize large organizations, such as the company representative mentioning a favorite recipe as well as chatting about a new product.[25]

BACK TO THE OPENING CASE

The hotel receptionist appears to be doing everything right in terms of satisfying this frazzled guest. She shows care and concern for the customer's problem, and then engages in mutual problem solving.

Invite the Customer Back

The southern U.S. expression "Y'all come back, now!" is well suited for bonding with customers. Specific invitations to return may help increase repeat business. The more focused and individualized the invitation, the more likely it will have an impact on customer behavior. ("Y'all come back, now!" is sometimes used too indiscriminately to be effective.) Pointing out why you enjoyed doing business with the customer, and what future problems you could help with, is an effective technique. An industrial cleaning company supervisor might say, "Our crew enjoyed cleaning such a fancy office. Keep us in mind when you would like your windows to sparkle."

Whoever observes the scenarios can look for the specific behaviors called for in the two role-plays, such as "make the buyer feel good." In addition, stay alert to other aspects of customer satisfaction skills. Provide feedback on what you observed to the role players.

Despite the importance of forming a bond with your customer, getting too personal can backfire. Most customers want a business relationship with the company, and are not looking for a personal relationship with a company representative. As Daniel Askt observes, "Most customers want value and service without contending that a salesman who insists that he wants to be like family to you. Chances are you've already got a family, and for most of us, one is enough."[26]

Skill-Building Exercise 13-2 gives you an opportunity to practice techniques for bonding with customers.

SKILL-BUILDING EXERCISE 13-2

Bonding with Customers

Role-players in this exercise will demonstrate two related techniques for bonding with customers: show care and concern and make the buyer feel good.

Scenario 1: Show Care and Concern.

A sales representative meets with two company representatives to talk about installing a new information system for employee benefits. One of the company reps is from the human resources department and the other is from the information systems department. The sales rep will attempt to show care and concern for both company representatives during the same meeting.

Scenario 2: Make the Buyer Feel Good.

A couple, played by two role-players, enters a new-car showroom to examine a model they have seen advertised on television. Although they are not in urgent need of a new car, they are strongly interested. The sales representative is behind quota for the month and would like to close a sale today. The rep decides to use the tactic "make the buyer feel good" to help form a bond.

DEALING WITH CUSTOMER DISSATISFACTION

Most companies put honest effort into preventing customer dissatisfaction. In addition to employing many of the principles and techniques already cited, many companies routinely survey customers to detect problem areas that could lead to dissatisfaction. A representative survey used by a successful company in its field is shown in Figure 13-5. Despite all these efforts to achieve total customer satisfaction, some customer dissatisfaction is inevitable. One reason is that mistakes in serving customers are almost inevitable; for example, a piece of equipment may have a faulty component unknown to the seller. A second reason is that some customers have a predisposition to complain. They will find something to complain about with respect to any product or service. Visualize the billions of transactions that take place every year between Wal-Mart service personnel and customers. Inevitably, some customer, somewhere, is going to rant and rave about poor service no matter how hard Wal-Mart managers and store associates try to please.

Dealing openly with dissatisfaction and complaints can improve both customer retention and sales. One study found that 63 percent of dissatisfied customers who fail to complain will not buy from the company again. Given a chance to complain and have their problem resolved, 90 percent will remain loyal customers.[27]

FIGURE 13-5 A Retail Store Customer Satisfaction Survey

How are we doing?
Dick's Clothing & Sporting Goods

Name (optional)   Address

Phone number   City

Date and time of visit   Name of associate who helped you

	Excellent	Good	Average	Needs improvement	Poor
Prompt and courteous greeting	☐	☐	☐	☐	☐
Knowledgeable salespeople	☐	☐	☐	☐	☐
Store cleanliness	☐	☐	☐	☐	☐
Store displays	☐	☐	☐	☐	☐
Prices	☐	☐	☐	☐	☐
Speedy checkouts	☐	☐	☐	☐	☐
How do you rate us overall?	☐	☐	☐	☐	☐

	Newspaper	TV	Radio	Other
What brought you to Dick's?	☐	☐	☐	☐

Did you make a purchase? _____

Items you wanted that we did not have? _____

_____

General comments: _____

_____

Source: Dick's Clothing and Sporting Goods. Customer satisfaction survey. Reprinted with permission.

An important point to remember in dealing with dissatisfied customers is that the negative personality traits of customers can bring down your level of customer service. For example, a study conducted in two major fast-food chains in Singapore found that customers who scored high on the trait of agreeableness, tended to bring out positive emotion by the service personnel. In contrast, customers who scored high on negative affectivity (being disagreeable) brought out negative emotion among customer service personnel.[28] A service worker cannot change the personality traits of customers, yet a little self-management of emotion is in order. The service worker might say to himself or herself, "I won't let this nasty customer get me down. I'll do my best to do my job without overreacting." Be careful not to fake your emotion too frequently because it can create stress. Instead, be assertive with a comment like, "I want to help you, but might you tell me what you want in a more positive way?"

The following subsections describe three approaches to handling customer dissatisfaction: dealing with complaints and anger, involving the customer in working out a problem, and handling an unreasonable request.

Deal Constructively with Customer Complaints and Anger

In an era when customer satisfaction is so highly valued, both retail and industrial customers are likely to be vocal in their demands. When faced with an angry customer, use one or more of the following techniques recommended by customer satisfaction specialists.[29]

1. **Acknowledge the customer's point of view.** Make statements such as "I understand," "I agree," and "I'm sorry." Assume, for example, a customer says, "The accounts payable department made a $1,000 overcharge on my account last month. I want this fixed right away." You might respond, "I understand how annoying this must be for you. I'll work on the problem right away."

2. **Avoid placing blame on the customer.** Suggesting that the customer is responsible for the problem intensifies the conflict. With the customer who claims to have been overcharged, refrain from saying, "Customers who keep careful account of their orders never have this problem."

3. **Use six magic words to defuse anger.** The magic words are *I understand* [that this is a problem], *I agree* [that it needs to be solved], and *I'm sorry* [that this happened to you].

4. **Apologize for the problems created by you or your company.** To recover from a breakdown in customer service, it is best to acknowledge an error immediately. Apologies are most effective when stated in the first person (such as, "I created the problem"). The corporate "we're sorry" sounds less sincere than when one specific person accepts responsibility for what went wrong. Professional workers at the Kaiser Permanente HMO receive training in how to apologize to patients for medical errors. It has been found that sincere apologies can significantly reduce the cost of settling lawsuits, and may even convince unhappy patients not to sue at all. A sincere apology includes a statement of what the apologizer is going to do to fix the problem.[30]

5. **Take responsibility, act fast, and be thorough.** This technique is a simplified framework for managing customer dissatisfaction. As illustrated by Mark Delp, the manager of a fleet maintenance service, "Suppose a customer calls about an oil leak after Fleet Response services a car. I have the car immediately picked up from his office and clean any oil spots that may have been left on the driveway. I make sure there are no further leaks. Furthermore, I apologize and accept full responsibility, even if the problem is not our fault, such as when a part fails."[31]

6. **Tell the difficult customers how much you value them.** Quite often customers with problems feel unappreciated. Just before resolving the problem of a difficult customer, explain how important he or she is to your firm. You might say, "We value your business, so I want to correct this for you quickly."[32] (Of course, you would value the customer even more after he or she becomes less difficult.)

7. **Follow up on the problem resolution.** Following up to see whether the resolution to the problem is satisfactory brings closure to the incident. The follow-up also helps the service deliverer know that he or she can rebound from an episode of customer dissatisfaction. One useful form of follow-up is to telephone or send an e-mail to the customer whose problem was solved. For example, a representative from the service department of an automobile dealership might telephone a customer whose new car required substantial warranty repairs. "Hello, this is Jill Gordon from Oak Automotive. We replaced your original transmission last month. How is the new transmission working?" The Microsoft example presented earlier in the chapter illustrates the use of e-mail for follow-up on problem resolution.

A less personal, and usually less effective, form of follow-up is to send a customer satisfaction questionnaire to the person with the problem. The questionnaire will often be interpreted as a company procedure that does not reflect specific concern about the individual's problem.

Involve the Customer in Working Out the Problem

Mistakes and problems in serving customers are inevitable regardless of how hard service workers strive for perfection. To minimize the perception of poor service, the customer must be involved in deciding what should be done about the problem. By being involved in the solution to the problem, the customer is more likely to accept a deviation from the service promised originally. The ideal condition is for the customer service representative and dissatisfied customer to work as partners in resolving the problem. The following case history illustrates the technique of customer involvement and partnering.

> *Seth Bradbury is a sales promotion specialist at an advertising agency. A furniture store hired the agency to prepare and mail 3,000 postcards advertising a new line of furniture. One side of the postcard contained a photograph of the furniture, and the other side contained product details and space for addressing and stamping the card. After the cards were mailed, Seth received an urgent call from the client. "The photograph of the furniture is printed vertically. It looks horrible. We agreed on a horizontal shot. This means 3,000 cards have been mailed with a mistake."*
>
> *After allowing the client to finish his complaint, Seth responded, "You're right, it is a vertical shot. Perhaps we misinterpreted your directions. However, I think your furniture still looks beautiful. The extra white space that the vertical shot provides creates an interesting effect. It's unfortunate that the cards have already been mailed. What would you like us to do? It's important that you are satisfied."*
>
> *The client responded, "I guess there's nothing we can do to change the photograph. Would you be willing to give us a discount off the price we agreed on?"*

Anticipate How to Handle an Unreasonable Request

No matter how hard the customer contact worker attempts to provide outstanding customer service, at some point a customer comes along with an unreasonable request—or the customer may raise an unfair objection. Speak to any experienced store associate to obtain a case history of a "customer from Hell." For example, a small-business owner demanded that a store associate grant him exchange credit for six printer cartridges. The cartridges were purchased four years previously and were now obsolete.

Recognize that the customer who makes an unreasonable demand is usually aware of the unreasonableness. The customer may not expect to be fully granted the request. Instead, the customer is bargaining by beginning with an unreasonable demand. The small-business owner who brought in the cartridges was probably looking to salvage whatever he could.

Sales representatives and other customer contact workers who stand their ground with dignity and courtesy generally will not lose customers with unreasonable requests.

Dealing with Difficult Customers

The following scenarios require one person to play the role of the customer contact worker and another person to play the difficult customer. As usual, the role-players project their feelings into the role-play by imagining how they would behave in the situation.

Scenario 1: One person is a store associate in a high-fashion women's clothing store. A woman who bought a $2000 gown the previous week brings back the gown today. She claims that she is returning the gown because it doesn't fit comfortably. The store associate strongly suspects the woman bought the gown originally with the intent of wearing it for a special occasion and then returning it.

Scenario 2: One person plays the role of a customer service representative in a consumer-electronics store. Another person plays the role of a customer who purchased a $3,500 giant-screen television receiver three months ago. He comes up to the service rep's counter ranting about the store's ineptitude. The customer claims that the TV has broken down three times. After the first repair, the TV worked for two weeks and then broke down again. The second repair lasted two weeks, only for the TV to break down during a Super Bowl party at his house. The customer is red in the face and shouting loudly. The service rep wants to resolve the customer's problem and prevent him from bad-mouthing the store.

These suggestions will help you deal with unreasonable demands while retaining the customer's business.[33]

- Let your customers retain their dignity by stating your position politely and reasonably.
- Avoid arguing with an upset customer. As the adage says, "You never win an argument with a customer."
- Appeal to your customer's sense of fair play and integrity. Explain that your intention is to do what is right and fair.
- Be firm by repeating the facts of the situation, but keep your temper under control.
- Accept responsibility for your decision rather than blaming company policy or your manager. Making somebody else the villain may intensify the problem.
- Be willing to say no to a customer when it is justifiable. Saying yes to an outrageous demand opens the door for a series of outrageous demands.

Maintain a Realistic Customer Retention Attitude

Some customers are too unreasonable, and therefore may not be worth keeping.[34] A realistic goal is to retain as many profitable customers as possible. An extreme example of a customer not worth keeping is the airline passenger who engages in *air rage*. Symptoms of air rage include (1) insisting on being served more alcoholic beverages than permissible by airline regulations, (2) sexually harassing or physically attacking flight attendants or other passengers, (3) refusing to fasten his or her seat belts, (4) using electronic gear such as cell phones and laptop computers when not allowed by regulations, (5) smoking in the lavatory, and (6) using the aisles for a lavatory.

It is best to set limits for unruly customers and see if their behavior changes. If the customer insists on creating disturbances, it is best to suggest the customer never return. Another problem is that some customers require so much service, or demand such high discounts, that they are unprofitable to retain. Good service to these customers means there is less time available to respond to the needs of profitable customers.

Dealing diplomatically and effectively with difficult customers requires an awareness of the types of tactics described in the previous several pages. Practice on the firing line is indispensable. The type of experience provided by Skill-Building Exercise 13-3 is helpful.

SELF-ASSESSMENT QUIZZES IN OVERVIEW

Two self-assessment quizzes were presented in this chapter, and the two quizzes support each other. Self-Assessment Quiz 13-1 is designed to measure your orientation toward serving customers well. A high service orientation is obviously a plus for dealing with customers. Self-Assessment Quiz 13-2 measures tendencies toward being rude toward customers. A low rudeness score is certainly a plus, and it contributes to having a strong service orientation.

Concept Review and Reinforcement

Key Terms

moments of truth, 277
cycle-of-service chart, 277

empowerment, 277

strong customer orientation, 281

Summary of Key Concepts

Many companies today emphasize total customer satisfaction because it leads to goodwill, repeat business, and referrals. Customer satisfaction skills are necessary for all workers in contact with customers. Internal customers must also be taken into consideration.

Customers form three clues about the service experience. Functional clues are derived from the technical performance of the service. Mechanical clues stem from the sensory presentation of the service, including sights, smells, sounds, tastes, and textures. Human interaction clues are detected from the behavior and appearance of the service provider.

Eight key principles for satisfying and delighting customers are as follows:

1. Be satisfied so you can provide better customer service. (Some of your own attitudes, such as optimism and flexibility, influence your job satisfaction.)
2. Receive emotional support from coworkers and management so you can give better customer service.
3. Understand customer needs and put them first.
4. Focus on solving problems, not just taking orders.
5. Respond positively to moments of truth (points at which the customer forms an impression of company service).
6. Be ready to accept empowerment. (Being empowered enables you to solve customer problems.)
7. Enhance customer service through IT.
8. Avoid rudeness and hostility toward customers. (Rude and hostile treatment of customers creates lost business.)

Another key perspective on achieving customer satisfaction and delight is to create a bond—or emotional relationship—with customers. Almost any act of good customer service helps create a bond, but six principles are highlighted here:

1. Create a welcoming attitude, including a smile.
2. Provide exceptional service (or customer experience).
3. Show care and concern.
4. Make the buyer feel good.
5. Build a personal relationship through interaction with customers.
6. Invite the customer back.

Despite the best efforts on the company's part, some customer dissatisfaction is inevitable. One approach to dealing with customer dissatisfaction is to deal constructively with customer complaints and anger. Tactics for achieving this end include the following:

1. Acknowledge the customer's point of view.
2. Avoid placing blame on the customer.
3. Use six magic words to defuse anger.
4. Apologize for the problem created by you or your company.
5. Take responsibility, act fast, and be thorough.
6. Tell the difficult customers how much you value them.
7. Follow up on the problem resolution.

Another approach to dealing with customer dissatisfaction is to involve the customer in working out the problem. The customer contact worker must sometimes deal with an unreasonable request. Remember that the customer probably recognizes that he or she is being unreasonable. Do not argue with an unreasonable customer, but at times you must say no. Maintain a realistic customer retention attitude, meaning that as hard as you try to please, some customers are not worth keeping.

Check Your Understanding

1. Assume that you find it necessary to telephone a call center to help you with a technical problem with your cell phone or computer. Identify the functional, mechanical, and human-interaction clues that you are likely to encounter in the resolution of your problem.

2. For what reason is a satisfied employee more likely to provide better customer service?

3. A couple walks into an automobile showroom and says they want a big safe vehicle for themselves and their three children, yet they are unsure about what vehicle they should purchase. Describe how you might identify customer needs in this situation.

4. Describe several customer moments of truth you have experienced this week. What made you classify them as moments of truth?

5. Visualize yourself as an executive at Target. Develop a policy to empower customer service desk associates to resolve customer problems, including the limits to their empowerment.

6. What is your opinion of the impact of IT on customer service? Offer at least two specifics in your answer.

7. Can you identify any ways in which a customer contact worker has made you feel good? If so, provide the details.

8. Have you ever smiled at a customer? What effect, if any, did this have on his or her behavior toward you?

9. How effective is the principle "the customer is always right" when dealing with dissatisfied customers?

10. A few weeks after renewing a subscription, a customer received a postcard that included the following: "We appreciate your prompt payment for your magazine subscription. However, our records indicate that you overpaid and are due a balance of $0.10. We will extend your subscription for 1 additional issue(s). Or, if you would prefer a refund check for the balance, please contact our customer service department at 1-800-.... " What is your evaluation of this interaction in terms of the customer experience?

The Web Corner

http://www.csmassociation.org
(Customer Satisfaction Measurement Association.)

http://www.customersatisfaction.com
(Improving customer satisfaction and retention.)

http://www.customer-service.com
(Improving your customer service.)

Internet Skill Builder: Building Customer Relationships

An axiom of business is that customer relationships are essential. Direct your Internet search for this assignment toward finding customer-relationship building suggestions that can be converted into specific interpersonal skills, such as making a phone call to see how things are going. An example of a Web site that offers concrete suggestions for building customer relationships related to interpersonal skills is http://www.sideroad.com. Walk away from this exercise with a couple of ideas you might put into practice in dealing with customers.

Developing Your Human Relations Skills

Interpersonal Skills Case 13.1

Making Nice at Home Depot

John Parsons of Shreveport, La., owns a 50-year-old house that needs constant repair, and for years he was a regular customer of a nearby Home Depot store. About a year ago, he switched to a Lowe's Co. home-improvement store, even though it is farther from his house, because he received better service there. "The people at Home Depot don't want to talk to you," he said. "They hide or they say they're busy."

Home Depot Inc. grew to become the world's largest home-improvement chain largely on the strength of its skilled workers, many of whom were former plumbers, electricians, and carpenters who were eager to impart their knowledge to do-it-yourselfers. They took pride in helping customers find just the right shade of latex paint or an elusive-size screw.

But service began to slip during the six years preceding 2007. In order to cut costs, the company started hiring more part-timers and added a salary cap that drove off the more seasoned workers. The retailer also moved about 40% of workers to overnight stocking positions, ostensibly to clear the aisles of clutter. But it left customers searching in vain for someone in an orange apron to ask about picking out the proper power tool.

In 2007 as it attempted to ignite sluggish sales under new chief executive Frank Blake, Home Depot was trying to reverse a reputation for shoddy service. Under former Chief Executive Robert Nardelli, Home Depot management focused on measuring all aspects of the stores' productivity and too often ignored shoppers. "We were busy writing reports instead of taking care of the customer," says Shane Moore, manager of a Home Depot store in Mesquite, Texas.

Before he was forced to resign, Nardelli moved to improve the shopping experience. The retailer spiffed up displays, added workers and rewarded stores for improved customer service. A customer-satisfaction survey published by the University of Michigan in 2007 indicated that Home Depot narrowed the gap with Lowe's. But Home Depot executives said they still had a long way to go.

A few summers ago, James McAvoy of Ophelia, Va., hired Home Depot to install glass sliding doors in a room in his house overlooking Chesapeake Bay. It turned into a nightmare. The subcontractor Home Depot hired installed the doors incorrectly and the room flooded, ruining the carpet. Furniture was strewn throughout the house, as the family waited for the problem to be resolved. "Home Depot just got too big, too fast and took their eye off the ball," McAvoy says.

CEO Blake has made restoring Home Depot's once vaunted customer service his No. 1 priority. Blake has repeatedly told managers that stores will be liberated from many of the time-consuming, mind-numbing tasks the home office required them to do in the six previous years. Under Nardelli, stores had to measure everything from how many pallets were removed from a truck per hour to how many extended warranties each employee sold per week.

"They are trying to get as many aprons on the floor as possible," says Moore, the manager of the Texas store. "We are not going to let a customer go untouched."

As sales finally slowed down under Nardelli's regime, he appointed a chief customer officer inside headquarters to improve customer service. Each week, a team of Home Depot staffers scour up to 250,000 customer surveys rating dozens of store qualities—from the attentiveness of the sales help to the cleanliness of the aisles.

Bruce Wing, a private chef and handyman from Missouri City, Texas, says "Home Depot needs to bring back knowledgeable salespeople who had been in the trades, instead of an inexperienced staff who don't know anything about the company's products or how to use them."

Case Questions

1. What do you recommended Home Depot do to restrengthen its reputation for high-quality customer service?
2. Identify the three components of customer experience (functional, mechanic, and human interaction) as they apply to a customer shopping for a replacement kitchen sink at Home Depot. (If the kitchen sink does not interest you, substitute another product.)
3. What is your evaluation of customer Wing's (the chef and handyman) suggestion for improving the customer experience at Home Depot?
4. How good is customer service at Home Depot these days? Base your evaluation on input from people in your network or an in-person visit to a Home Depot.

Source: Ann Zimmerman, "Home Depot Tries to Make Nice to Customers," *The Wall Street Journal*, February 20, 2007, pp. D1, D2.

Interpersonal Relations Case 13.2

Repeat Business at Whopper Wash

Jim McNamara worked for 25 years in a variety of sales and marketing positions for a large company. In his last position he was the manager of direct marketing (selling products directly to customers rather than through stores or other intermediaries). As part of a company downsizing, McNamara's position was consolidated with another department's and he was laid off.

McNamara said he was disappointed to lose a good job, but he recognized that dealing with drastic changes in one's life is part of the modern world. He also recognized that at age 50, he was still young enough to pursue a new career and a new lifestyle. McNamara and his wife, Gwen, discussed the situation for many days, and decided to work as partners in a franchise business. Gwen worked part-time as a home health aid, so she could find time to help with the business. Many of the best-known franchises seemed out of reach for the McNamaras because of start-up prices as high as $500,000.

After several weeks of research, the McNamaras decided to purchase a power washing franchise, Whopper Wash, for a start-up fee of $10,000. The company provided the training, including advice on marketing the program. Typical services for power washing would include cleaning house siding, swimming pools, and the sidewalks of small businesses. Jim and Gwen would do the work themselves, including climbing on high ladders to wash the second level of a house.

The McNamaras opened their business officially on June 1 one year later. They placed ads in local newspapers, and had a Web site of their own, http://www.JimandGwenWhopperWash.com. Their first 10 orders for power washes were from friends and relatives, with the average price of the wash being $300. The newspaper ads were the most effective in drawing new customers, with the Web site also attracting some customers.

The business grew slowly. In a typical scenario, the McNamaras would show up at the site, get the job done in about two hours, and then receive payment. When Gwen had a conflict in the schedule, Jim would do the job himself. The customer would typically thank them for the service, and then say goodbye. Given the opportunity, either Jim or Gwen would attempt to engage the customer in light conversation. Gwen developed a standard joke to suggest repeat business. If she noticed that a dog was on the premises, she asked, "Can we power wash your dog next?" Not all pet owners laughed at her comment.

As the McNamaras reviewed their business results after six months, they observed a shortcoming. After completing a job, they would typically recommend that the service be repeated in two years. However, two years is a long time between repeat calls to a customer, the couple thought.

Jim remarked, "We don't have any good way of getting repeat business. I could see that our business could dry up quickly after we take care of most people who want their home or small business power washed. What do you think we can say to customers to get more repeat business?"

Case Questions

1. In what way is this case about customer satisfaction?
2. How might the McNamaras form better bonds with their customers?
3. What can this Whooper Wash couple do to get more repeat business?

CHAPTER 14

Enhancing Ethical Behavior

For Tina Byles Williams hiring ethical employees is doing the smart thing as much as doing the right thing. The pension funds and other institutions that pay her 10-year-old firm, FIS Group Inc., for investment advice and management naturally expect that none of her 16 employees will make off with their funds. They also expect no conflicts of interest or other improprieties—a matter brought into high relief three years ago when a former employee's activities made Williams consider measures to prevent unethical employee behavior.

Since the incident, the $6 million company has re-examined its process for hiring, evaluating, and retaining ethical employees. Williams, 45, how regards hiring ethical employees to be a core mission: "If part of what we're selling is trust, it's critical to hire people of integrity and high ethics."

Williams pays for background checks on job applicants, and notices how cheerfully employees complete reports on personal investments, which detect conflicts of interest. [As described later in the chapter, a conflict of interest occurs when you are not in position to be entirely objective about an issue.] Williams says, "I think people are fundamentally good. But you need to establish a framework of expectations and monitoring."[1]

The scenario just described illustrates that ethical issues in the workplace are not just about big business and corporate executives. People performing all types of work need a good sense of ethics (and etiquette) to be successful. Also, you often need to have an ethical reputation to get the job you want. *Ethics* refers to what is good and bad, right and wrong, just and unjust, and what people should do. Ethics is the vehicle for turning values into action. If you value fair play, you will do such things as giving honest performance evaluations to members of your group.

We study ethics here because a person's ethical code has a significant impact on his or her interpersonal relationships. This chapter's approach will emphasize the importance of ethics, common ethical problems, and guidelines for behaving ethically. Self-Assessment Quiz 14-1 gives you the opportunity to examine your ethical beliefs and attitudes.

Learning Objectives

After reading and studying this chapter and doing the exercises, you should be able to

1. Recognize the importance of ethical behavior for establishing good interpersonal relationships in organizations.

2. Describe why the character trait of virtuousness contributes to being ethical in the workplace.

3. Identify job situations that often present ethical dilemmas.

4. Use a systematic method for making ethical decisions and behaving ethically.

SELF-ASSESSMENT QUIZ 14-1

The Ethical Reasoning Inventory

Directions: Describe how well you agree with each of the following statements, using the following scale: disagree strongly (DS); disagree (D); neutral (N); agree (A); agree strongly (AS). Circle the number in the appropriate column.

	DS	D	N	A	AS
1. When applying for a job, I would cover up the fact that I had been fired from my most recent job.	5	4	3	2	1
2. Cheating just a few dollars in one's favor on an expense account is okay if a person needs the money.	5	4	3	2	1
3. Employees should report on each other for wrongdoing.	1	2	3	4	5
4. It is acceptable to give approximate figures for expense account items when one does not have all the receipts.	5	4	3	2	1
5. I see no problem with conducting a little personal business on company time.	5	4	3	2	1
6. Just to make a sale, I would stretch the truth about a delivery date.	5	4	3	2	1
7. I would fix up a purchasing agent with a date just to close a sale.	5	4	3	2	1
8. I would flirt with my boss just to get a bigger salary increase.	5	4	3	2	1
9. If I received $400 for doing some odd jobs, I would report it on my income tax return.	1	2	3	4	5
10. I see no harm in taking home a few office supplies.	5	4	3	2	1
11. It is acceptable to read the e-mail messages and faxes of coworkers, even when not invited to do so.	5	4	3	2	1
12. It is unacceptable to call in sick to take a day off, even if only done once or twice a year.	1	2	3	4	5
13. I would accept a permanent, full-time job even if I knew I wanted the job for only six months.	5	4	3	2	1

(Continued)

14. I would first check company policy before accepting an expensive gift from a supplier.	1	2	3	4	5
15. To be successful in business, a person usually has to ignore ethics.	5	4	3	2	1
16. If I felt physically attracted toward a job candidate, I would hire that person over a more qualified candidate.	5	4	3	2	1
17. On the job, I tell the truth all the time.	1	2	3	4	5
18. If a student were very pressed for time, it would be acceptable to either have a friend write the paper or purchase one.	5	4	3	2	1
19. I would be willing to put a hazardous chemical in a consumer product if the product made a good profit for the company.	5	4	3	2	1
20. I would never accept credit for a coworker's ideas.	1	2	3	4	5

Total Score _____

Scoring and Interpretation: Add the numbers you have circled to obtain your total score.

90–100 You are a strongly ethical person who may take a little ribbing from coworkers for being too straitlaced.

60–89 You show an average degree of ethical awareness, and therefore should become more sensitive to ethical issues.

41–59 Your ethics are underdeveloped, but you at least have some awareness of ethical issues. You need to raise your level of awareness of ethical issues.

20–40 Your ethical values are far below contemporary standards in business. Begin a serious study of business ethics.

LEARNING OBJECTIVE 1

WHY BE CONCERNED ABOUT BUSINESS ETHICS?

When asked why ethics is important, most people would respond with something to the effect that "Ethics is important because it's the right thing to do. You behave decently in the workplace because your family and religious values have taught you what is right and wrong." All this is true, but the justification for behaving ethically is more complex, as described next.[2]

A major justification for behaving ethically on the job is to recognize that people are motivated by both self-interest and moral commitments. Most people want to maximize gain for themselves (remember the expectancy theory of motivation?). At the same time, most people are motivated to do something morally right. As one of many examples, vast numbers of people donate money to charity, although keeping that amount of money for themselves would provide more personal gain.

Many business executives want employees to behave ethically because a good reputation can enhance business. A favorable corporate reputation may enable firms to charge premium prices and attract better job applicants. A favorable reputation also helps attract investors, such as mutual fund managers who purchase stock in companies. Certain mutual funds, for example, invest only in companies that are environmentally friendly. Managers want employees to behave ethically because unethical behavior—for example, employee theft, lost production time, and lawsuits—is costly.

Behaving ethically is also important because many unethical acts are illegal as well, which can lead to financial loss and imprisonment. According to one estimate, the cost of unethical and fraudulent acts committed by U.S. employees totals $400 billion per year. A company that knowingly allows workers to engage in unsafe practices might be fined and the executives may be held personally liable. Furthermore, unsafe practices can kill people. In recent history, two employees burned to death in a fire they could not escape in a chicken processing plant. Management had blocked the back doors to prevent employees from sneaking chicken parts out of the plant. Low ethics have also resulted in financial hardship for employees as company executives raid pension funds of other companies they purchase, sharply reducing or eliminating the retirement funds of many workers.

A subtle reason for behaving ethically is that high ethics increases the quality of work life. Ethics provides a set of guidelines that specify what makes for acceptable behavior. Being ethical will point you toward actions that make life more satisfying for work associates. A company code of ethics specifies what constitutes ethical versus unethical behavior. When employees follow this code, the quality of work life improves. Several sample clauses from ethical codes are as follows:

- Demonstrate courtesy, respect, honesty, and fairness.
- Do not use abusive language.
- Do not bring firearms or knives to work.
- Do not offer bribes.
- Maintain confidentiality of records.
- Do not harass (sexually, racially, ethnically, or physically) subordinates, superiors, coworkers, customers, or suppliers.

To the extent that all members of the organization abide by this ethical code, the quality of work life will improve. At the same time, interpersonal relations in organizations will be strengthened.

WHY WE HAVE SO MANY ETHICAL PROBLEMS

LEARNING OBJECTIVE 2

To become more skilled at behaving ethically, it is important to familiarize yourself with common ethical problems in organizations. Whether or not a given situation presents an ethical problem for a person depends to some extent on its **moral intensity**, or how deeply others might be affected.[3] A worker might face a strong ethical conflict about dumping mercury into a water supply but would be less concerned about dumping cleaning fluid. Yet both acts would be considered unethical and illegal. Here we first look at why being ethical is not as easy as it sounds. We then look at some data about the frequency of ethical problems and an analysis of predictable ethical temptations, and examine the subtle ethical dilemma of choosing between rights.

moral intensity

In ethical decision making, how deeply others might be affected by the decision.

Why Being Ethical Isn't Easy

As analyzed by Linda Klebe Treviño and Michael E. Brown, behaving ethically in business is more complex than it seems on the surface for a variety of reasons.[4] To begin with, ethical decisions are complex. For example, someone might argue that hiring children for factory jobs in overseas countries is unethical. Yet if these children lose their jobs, many would starve or turn to crime to survive. Second, people do not always recognize the moral issues involved in a decision. The home-maintenance worker who finds a butcher knife under the bed might not think that he has a role to play in perhaps preventing murder. Sometimes language hides the moral issue involved, such as when the term *file sharing* music replaces *stealing* music.

Another complexity in making ethical decisions is that people have different levels of moral development. At one end of the scale, some people behavior morally just to escape punishment. At the other end of the scale, some people are morally developed to the point that they are guided by principles of justice and want to help as many people as possible. The environment in which we work also influences whether we behave ethically. Suppose a restaurant owner encourages such practices as serving customers food that was accidentally dropped on the kitchen floor. An individual server is more likely to engage in such behavior to obey the demands of the owner—even though the server knows that dangerous bacteria may have attached to the food.

utilitarian predisposition

A belief that the value of an act's outcomes should determine whether it is moral.

A fundamental reason that being unethical is not always easy is that some people have a predisposition to be unethical. The predisposition works almost like a personality trait, compelling certain people to be devious. A person with a **utilitarian predisposition** believes that the value of an act's outcomes should determine whether it is moral.[5] A server with this predisposition might be willing to serve food that dropped on the floor as long as no customer became sick or sued the restaurant. A small business owner with a utilitarian predisposition might be willing to sell fake luxury goods on the Internet as long as nobody complained and he or she was not caught. When asked about why he sold imitation watches, one vendor said, "What's the difference? My watches look like the real thing, and they tell time."

A Survey of the Extent of Ethical Problems

The ethical misdeeds of executives have received substantial publicity in recent years. However, recent surveys show that ethical violations by rank-and-file employees are widespread, particularly with respect to lying. According to two separate surveys, more than one-third of U.S. workers admit to having fabricated about their need for sick days. More employees are stretching the reasons for taking time off. Job applicants reporting false or embellished academic credentials have hit a three-year high.[6]

Figure 14-1 presents data about unethical behavior noticed by employees. Notice that the type of bullying behavior described in Chapter 11 is perceived to be unethical. As found in other surveys, lying is another widespread ethical problem in the workplace. Although these findings might suggest that unethical behavior is on the increase, another explanation is possible. Workers today might be more observant of ethical problems and more willing to note them on a survey.

Frequent Ethical Dilemmas

Certain ethical mistakes, including illegal actions, recur in the workplace. Familiarizing oneself can be helpful in monitoring one's own behavior. The following subsections describe a number of common ethical problems faced by business executives as well as workers at lower job levels.[7] Figure 14-2 outlines these problems.

Illegally Copying Software   A rampant ethical problem is whether or not to illegally copy computer software. According to the Business Software Alliance, approximately 35 percent of applications used in business are illegal.[8] Figure 14-3 offers details about and insight into this widespread ethical dilemma.

Treating People Unfairly   Being fair to people means equity, reciprocity, and impartiality. Fairness revolves around the issue of giving people equal rewards for accomplishing

FIGURE 14-1 Questionable Workplace Behavior as Reported by Employees

Despite a heightened emphasis on business ethics following scandals earlier this decade, a significant number of employees say they still witness questionable workplace behavior. Here is the percentage of employees who say they observed certain behaviors in the previous year, according to a survey of 3,015 workers by the Ethics Resource Center.

Abusive or intimidating behavior toward employees	21%
Lying to employees, customers, vendors, or public	19%
Violations of safety regulations	16%
Misreporting of actual time worked	16%
Race, sex, or other discrimination	12%
Theft	11%
Sexual harassment	9%

Source: Ethics Resource Center as reported in Erin White, "What Would You Do? Ethics Courses Get Context," *The Wall Street Journal*, June 12, 2006, p. B3.

FIGURE 14-2 Frequent Ethical Dilemmas

Many ethical temptations face the individual on the job, forcing him or her to think through ethical issues practically every workday.

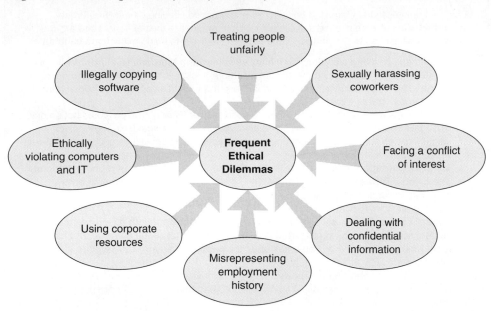

equal amounts of work. The goal of human resource legislation is to make decisions about people based on their qualifications and performance—not on the basis of demographic factors such as gender, race, or age. A fair working environment is where performance is the only factor that counts (equity). Employer–employee expectations must be understood and met (reciprocity). Prejudice and bias must be eliminated (impartiality).

Treating people fairly—and therefore ethically—requires a deemphasis on political factors, or favoritism. Yet this ethical doctrine is not always easy to implement. It is human nature to want to give bigger rewards (such as fatter raises or bigger orders) to people we like.

A major contributor to treating people unfairly is cronyism, or giving jobs to people who have done personal favors for you. Often the unqualified friend is given a position when competent and qualified candidates are available. Cronyism is often practiced in government, where heads of government agencies are sometimes appointed mostly because they are a supporter and friend of the person in power. Earl E. Devaney, the Interior Department's inspector general, said at a hearing, "Simply stated, short of a crime, anything goes at the highest levels of the Department of the Interior." Among the ethical charges were cronyism and cover-ups of incompetence.[9] Cronyism is also sometimes found in business, with buddies, relatives, and lovers often being chosen over more qualified workers for a variety of positions.

Sexually Harassing Coworkers   In Chapter 8 we looked at sexual harassment as a source of conflict and an illegal act. Sexual harassment is also an ethical issue because it is morally wrong and unfair. All acts of sexual harassment flunk an ethics test. Before sexually harassing another person, the potential harasser should ask, "Would I want a loved one to be treated this way?"

Facing a Conflict of Interest   Part of being ethical is making business judgments only on the basis of the merits or facts in a situation. Imagine that you are a supervisor who is romantically involved with a worker within the group. When it comes time to assign raises, it will be difficult for you to be objective. A **conflict of interest** occurs when your judgment or objectivity is compromised. Conflicts of interest often take place in the sales end of business. If a company representative accepts a large gift from a sales representative, it may be difficult to make objective judgments about buying from the rep. Yet being taken to dinner by a vendor would not ordinarily cloud one's judgment. Another common

> " Follow the *Platinum Rule:* Treat people the way they wish to be treated. "
>
> —Eric Harvey and Scott Airitam, authors of *Ethics 4 Everyone*

conflict of interest

A situation that occurs when a person's judgment or objectivity is compromised.

FIGURE 14-3 The Top Ten Reasons for Illegally Copying Software (and Why None of Them Are Good Enough)

A flagrant unethical and **illegal** job behavior is unauthorized copying of software. When confronted with software pirating, people are quick to rationalize their actions. Here are the top ten defenses of software pirates. (None of them are likely to hold up if you are caught.)

1. **I'm allowed to make a backup disk in case something happens to the original, so it must be okay to use it on another machine.** A backup is strictly a backup to be used on the same computer. The original should be safely locked away, and the copy should be stored away only as a backup.

2. **I didn't copy it—a friend gave it to me.** Technically you are right. You would not be guilty of illegally copying software in this case, although your friend would. However, since illegally copied software is regarded as stolen property, you are just as guilty as you would be for stealing it in the first place.

3. **My boss (or department head, or instructor) told me to. It's that person's problem.** The defense "I was just following orders" is a weak one. Complying with your boss's demands to commit an illegal act does not get you off the hook. You could be fired for obeying an order to commit a crime.

4. **I bought the software; shouldn't I be able to do what I want with it?** Software is seldom ever sold to individuals. What is sold is a license to use the software, not full rights to do what you want. When you break open the package, the law assumes that you have agreed to abide by those terms.

5. **It's not like I'm robbing somebody.** Software is intellectual property just like a song, a book, an article, or a trademark. You are taking bread from the table of software engineers when you copy their work.

6. **It's OK if you're using the software for educational purposes.** If education were a justification for theft, driving instructors would be able to steal cars with impunity. There is a doctrine of **fair use** that allows some limited use of written materials in classrooms without permission from the copyright holder.

7. **I needed it, but the price was unreasonably high. If I had to actually pay for it, there is no way I could ever afford it.** Software prices are high for the same reason the price of houses is high: both require a lot of highly skilled labor to create. You cannot steal a DVD player just because you cannot afford one.

8. **I didn't know it was illegal.** Unauthorized duplication of software is a felony in many states and provinces. State and federal laws provide for civil and criminal penalties if you are convicted. It would be difficult to convince a judge or jury that you had no idea that unauthorized copying was illegal.

9. **It's only illegal if you get caught.** Criminal behavior is illegal whether or not you are caught. If you do get caught illegally copying software, you could face fines, imprisonment, and/or civil penalties. Some educational institutions take disciplinary action against software pirates, including suspension.

10. **Oh, come on, everyone is doing it.** This excuse has been used to justify everything from speeding to lynching. The popularity of a criminal act does not make it legal.

Source: The Top Ten Reasons for Illegally Copying Software (and Why None of Them Are Good Enough). Rochester Institute of Technology. Reprinted with permission.

example of a conflict of interest is making a hiring decision about a friend who badly needs a job, but is not well qualified for the position.

Conflicts of interest have been behind some of the major business scandals in recent times, such as Enron Corporation auditors giving the company a favorable rating. The accounting and consulting firm Arthur Andersen had earned $25 million in auditing fees and $27 million for consulting prior to the company's collapse. The conflict of interest was that if the Arthur Andersen auditors were too critical of Enron, the firm might not have received such lucrative consulting contracts.[10] Some financial research analysts give glowing public reports about the fiscal condition of a company when that company is a client of the analyst's own firm. The analyst's firm sells services for issuing new stock and assisting with corporate mergers and acquisitions.

Dealing with Confidential Information   An ethical person can be trusted by others not to divulge confidential information unless the welfare of others is at stake. Suppose a coworker tells you in confidence that she is upset with the company and is therefore looking for another job. Behaving ethically, you do not pass along this information to your supervisor even though it would help your supervisor plan for a replacement. Now suppose the scenario changes slightly. Your coworker tells you she is looking for another job because she is upset. She tells you she is so upset that she plans to destroy company computer files on her last day. If your friend does find another job, you might warn the company about her contemplated activities.

The challenge of dealing with confidential information arises in many areas of business, many of which affect interpersonal relations. If you learned that a coworker was indicted for a crime, charged with sexual harassment, or facing bankruptcy, there would be a temptation to gossip about the person. A highly ethical person would not pass along information about the personal difficulties of another person.

Misrepresenting Employment History   Many people are tempted to distort in a positive direction information about their employment history on their job résumé, on job application form, and during the interview. Distortion, or lying, of this type is considered unethical and can lead to immediate dismissal if discovered. A well-known case in point is George O'Leary, who was dismissed after five days on the job as head coach of the Notre Dame Football team. After his résumé distortions were uncovered, O'Leary resigned and admitted he falsified his academic and athletic credentials for decades. He had falsely claimed to have a master's degree in education and to have played college football for three years.[11] Shortly thereafter, O'Leary made good use of his network of professional contacts and was hired by the Minnesota Vikings professional football team in a coaching position. Despite being disgraced nationally, O'Leary's political skills provided him with a safety net. O'Leary later became the head football coach at the University of Central Florida, showing that people can recover from a single ethical lapse.

Using Corporate Resources   A corporate resource is anything the company owns, including its name and reputation. If Jake Petro worked for Ford Motor Company, for example, it would be unethical for him to establish a body shop and put on his letterhead and Web site, "Jake Petro, Manufacturing Technician, Ford Motor Company." (The card and Web site would imply that the Ford Motor Co. supports this venture.) Other uses of corporate resources fall more into the gray area. It might be quite ethical to borrow a laptop computer for the weekend from your employer to conduct work at home. But it would be less ethical to borrow the laptop computer to prepare income taxes. In the latter case, you might be accused of using corporate resources for personal purposes. Loading personal software on company computers so you can access your bank account and so forth also can be considered an ethical violation.

FIGURE 14-4 Eleven Commandments for Computer Ethics

1. Do not use a computer to harm other people. Avoid all obscene, defamatory, threatening, or otherwise harassing messages. Take precautions against others developing repetitive motion disorders.
2. Do not interfere with other people's computer work. (This includes intentionally spreading computer viruses.)
3. Do not snoop around in other people's files.
4. Do not use a computer to steal.
5. Do not use a computer to bear false witness.
6. Do not use or copy software for which you have not paid (see Figure 14-1).
7. Do not use other people's resources without authorization.
8. Do not appropriate other people's intellectual output.
9. Do not use the employer's computer for the personal promotion of commercial goods or services, unless granted permission by the employer.
10. Do think about the social consequences of the program you write.
11. Do use a computer in ways that show consideration and respect.

Source: Adapted and updated from Arlene H. Rinaldi and Florida Atlantic University, rinaldi@acc.fau.edu; "Code of Conduct for Computer and Network Use," *http://www.rit.edu/computerconduct.*

The Ethics Game

Many companies teach ethics by asking small teams of employees to confront difficult scenarios such as those that follow. Discuss these ethical problems in teams. As you discuss the scenarios, identify the ethical issues involved.

Scenario 1: One of your assignments is to find a contractor to conduct building maintenance for your company headquarters. You invite bids for the job. High-Performance Cleaners, a firm staffed largely by teenagers from troubled families who have criminal records, bids on the job.

Many of these teenagers also have severe learning disabilities and cannot readily find employment. High-Performance Cleaners proves to be the second-highest bidder. You:

A. advise High-Performance Cleaners that its bid is too high for consideration and that your company is not a social agency.
B. award the bid to High-Performance Cleaners and justify your actions with a letter to top management by talking about social responsibility.
C. falsify the other bids in your report to management, making High-Performance Cleaners the low bidder—and thus the contract winner.
D. explain to High-Performance Cleaners that it lost the bid, but you will award the company a piece of the contract because of its sterling work with teenagers in need.

Scenario 2: You live in Texas and your company sends you on a three-day trip to New York City. Your business dealings in the Big Apple will keep you there Wednesday, Thursday, and Friday morning. You have several friends and relatives in New York, so you decide to stay there until Sunday afternoon. Besides, you want to engage in tourist activities such as taking a boat tour around Manhattan and visiting Radio City Music Hall. When preparing your expense report for your trip, you request payment for all your business-related costs up through Friday afternoon, plus:

A. your return trip on Sunday.
B. the return trip and the room cost for Friday and Saturday nights.
C. the return trip, one-half of your weekend food expenses, and two extra nights in the hotel.
D. the return trip and your food costs for the weekend (which you justify because you ate at fast-food restaurants on Wednesday, Thursday, and Friday).

Scenario 3: You are the leader of a self-managing work team in a financial services company. The work of your team has expanded to the point where you are authorized to hire another team member. The team busily interviews a number of candidates from inside and outside the company. The other team members agree that one of the candidates (Pat) has truly outstanding credentials. You agree that Pat is a strong candidate, yet you don't want Pat on the team because the two of you were emotionally involved for about a year. You think that working with Pat would disrupt your concentration and bring back hurtful memories. You decide to:

A. tell the group that you have some negative information about Pat's past that would disqualify Pat for the job.
B. telephone Pat and beg that Pat find employment elsewhere.
C. tell the group that you agree Pat is qualified, but explain your concerns about the disruption in concentration and emotional hurt.
D. tell the group that you agree Pat is right for the position, and mention nothing about the past relationship.

Scoring and Observation: Scenario 1, about High-Performance Cleaners, raises dozens of ethical questions, including whether humanitarian considerations can outweigh profit concerns. Teams that chose "a" receive 0 points; "b," 20 points; "c," −10 points; "d," 10 points. (Answer "d" is best here because it would not be fair to give the bid to the second-highest bidder. However, you are still finding a way to reward the High-Performance Cleaners for its meritorious work in the community. Answer "c" is the worst because you would be outright lying.)

Scenario 2 raises ethical issues about using company resources. Teams that chose "a" receive 20 points; "b," −10 points; "c," −15 points; "d," 0 points. (Answer "a" is fairest because the company would expect to reimburse you for your roundtrip plus the expenses up through Friday afternoon. Answer "c" is the worst because it would be unjustified for you to be reimbursed for your vacation in New York.)

Scenario 3 raises issues about fairness in making selection decisions. Teams that chose "a" receive −20 points; "b," −10 points; "c," 15 points; "d," 0 points. (Answer "c" is the most ethical because you are being honest with the group about the reason you do not wish to hire Pat. Answer "a" is the most unethical because you are telling lies about Pat. Furthermore, you might be committing the illegal act of libel.)

Ethically Violating Computers and IT As computers dominate the workplace, many ethical issues have arisen in addition to pirating software. One ethical dilemma that surfaces frequently is the fairness of tracking the Web sites a person visits and those he or she buys from. Should this information be sold, like a mailing list? The scams that appear on e-mail everyday are another prime example of the unethical use of information technology. Another issue is the fairness of having an employee work at a keyboard for 60 hours in one week when such behavior frequently leads to repetitive motion disorder. Figure 14-4 lists some major ethical issues involved in computer use.

You may have observed that these common ethical problems are not always clear-cut. Aside from obvious matters such as prohibitions against stealing, lying, cheating, and intimidating, subjectivity enters into ethical decision making. Skill-Building Exercise 14-1 provides an opportunity to try out your ethical reasoning.

Choosing between Two Rights: Dealing with Defining Moments

Ethical decision making usually involves choosing between two options: one we perceive to be right and one we perceive to be wrong. A challenging twist to ethical decision making is to sort through your values when you have to choose between two rights, or two morally sound choices. Joseph L. Badaracco, Jr., uses the term **defining moment** to describe choosing between two or more ideals in which we deeply believe.[12] If you can learn to work through defining moments, your ethical skills will be enhanced. Let's first take a nonwork example to illustrate a defining moment.

> *Imagine yourself as a basketball referee in a league for boys 10 years old and younger. Luis, the smallest boy on the team, has a self-confidence problem in general, and he has not scored a basket yet this season. This is the final game of the season. The other team is ahead by 10 points with one minute to go. Luis lets fly with a shot that goes into the basket, but his right heel is on the line. If the goal is allowed, Luis will experience one of the happiest moments in his life, and his self-confidence might increase. You strongly believe in helping people grow and develop. Yet you also strongly believe in following the rules of sports. What should you do?*

You may have recognized that a defining moment is a role conflict in which you have to choose between competing values. A CEO might deeply believe that she has an obligation to the stockholders to make a profit, and at the same time believe in being generous and fair toward employees. However, to make a profit this year she will be forced to lay off several good employees with long seniority. The CEO now faces a moment of truth. Badaracco suggests that the individual can work through a defining moment by discovering "Who am I?" You discover who you are by soul searching answers to three questions:

1. What feelings and intuitions are coming into conflict in this situation?
2. Which of the values that are in conflict are the most deeply rooted in my life?
3. What combinations of expediency and shrewdness, coupled with imagination and boldness, will help me implement my personal understanding of what is right?

Skill-Building Exercise 14-2 gives you an opportunity to deal with defining moments. The three questions just asked could help you find answers, but do not be constrained by these questions.

SKILL-BUILDING EXERCISE 14-2

Dealing with Defining Moments

The toughest ethical choices for many people occur when they have to choose between two rights. The result is a defining moment, because we are challenged to think in a deeper way by choosing between two or more ideals. Working individually or in teams, deal with the two following defining moments. Explain why these scenarios could require choosing between two rights, and explain the reasoning behind your decisions.

Scenario 1: You are the manager of a department in a business firm that assigns each department a fixed amount of money for salary increases each year. An average-performing member of the department asks you in advance for an above-average increase. He explains that his mother has developed multiple sclerosis and requires the services of a paid helper from time to time. You are concerned that if you give this man an above-average increase,

somebody else in the department will have to receive a below-average increase.

Scenario 2: You are the team leader of an e-tailing (retail selling over the Internet) group. In recent months each team member has been working about 60 hours per week, with little prospect of the workload decreasing in the future. Because the e-tailing project is still losing money, higher management insists that one person be dropped from the team. One member of the team, Mildred, is willing to work only 45 hours per week because she spends considerable time volunteering with autistic children. Mildred's work is satisfactory, but her output is the lowest in the group because of her shorter number of working hours. You must make a decision about whether to recommend that Mildred be dismissed.

GUIDELINES FOR BEHAVING ETHICALLY

Following guidelines for ethical behavior is the heart of being ethical. Although many people behave ethically without studying ethical guidelines, they are usually following guidelines programmed into their minds early in life. The Golden Rule exemplifies a guideline taught by parents, grandparents, and kindergarten teachers. In this section, we approach ethical guidelines from five perspectives: (1) developing virtuousness, (2) following a guide to ethical decision making, (3) developing strong relationships with work associates, (4) using corporate ethics programs, and (5) following an applicable professional code of conduct.

Developing Virtuousness

A deep-rooted approach to behaving ethically is to have strong moral and ethical principles, or to be virtuous. A person of high virtue has good character, and genuine motivation and intentions. A major problem in becoming virtuous is to agree on what values constitute virtuousness. Management professor Edwin A. Locke has prepared a modern analysis of what values constitute virtue in a business environment.[13] Here we highlight his findings because they are representative of what constitutes virtuousness. Other observers might have a different list of virtuous values.

1. *Rationality* is a principle that leads to being virtuousness. Being rational includes taking reality (facts) seriously, thinking hard, thinking long-range, and thinking of the consequences of one's actions. A rational parachute technician would not ship a defective parachute just because it was close to quitting time and he did not want to work late. And we hope that the manager is rational (and therefore ethical) when writing performance evaluations.

2. *Honesty*, the refusal to fake reality, is a value that contributes directly to ethical behavior. Being dishonest can also be illegal, such as when a company lies to the Internal Revenue Service about expenses it incurred or hides revenue when preparing a tax report. Dishonesty in terms of making false statements about the financial health of an enterprise has been one of the most frequent business frauds. Being caught lying can lead to dismissal at many employers. An example of such a lie would be blaming someone else for a mistake of your own. *Integrity* means loyalty to one's rational convictions, or sticking with one's principles. If you believe that favoritism is immoral, then you would not recommend that the company hire a friend of yours who you know to be unqualified.

3. *Independence* refers to the responsibility of using your own rational judgment rather than relying too heavily on the thinking of others. In personal life being independent means not relying too heavily on others for permanent support. A worker with a strong value of independence would not readily go along with the thinking of the group if he or she had a better idea.

4. *Productivity* means creating, or obtaining through trade, the materials values your life requires. You are therefore virtuous if are productive on the job and contribute enough to be worth of your compensation. *Justice* refers to looking at the facts of the character and achievements of others and judging them objectively. To be just is to be fair, such as willing to pay somebody what he or she are worth, or pay a fair price for merchandise. When a big company executive "squeezes" a supplier to the point that the supplier can barely make a profit, the executive is not practicing justice.

5. Forgiveness is a virtue providing the breach of morality was not too severe, such as forgiving an employee who ate a sandwich without paying when eating food without paying was not authorized.

6. Pride in the context of virtues refers to working to perfect one's moral character. You would thus be proud because you are virtuous.

These values that contribute to being virtuousness are useful in the study of human relations because they all translate into interpersonal skills, such as knowing how to be productive and treat people justly.

Following a Guide to Ethical Decision Making

A powerful strategy for behaving ethically is to follow a guide for ethical decision making. Such a guide for making contemplated decisions includes testing ethics. **Ethical screening** refers to running a contemplated decision or action through an ethics test. Such screening makes the most sense when the contemplated action or decision is not clearly ethical or unethical. If a sales representative were to take a favorite customer to Pizza Hut for lunch, an ethical screen would not be necessary. Nobody would interpret a "veggie super" to be a serious bribe. Assume, instead, that the sales rep offered to give the customer an under-the-table gift of $1000 for placing a large offer with the rep's firm. The sales representative's behavior would be so blatantly unethical that conducting an ethical screen would be unnecessary.

Several useful ethical screens, or guides, to ethical decision making have been developed. A guide developed by Treviño and Nelson is presented here because it incorporates the basic ideas in other ethical tests.[14] After studying this guide, you will be asked to ethically screen three different scenarios. The eight steps to sound ethical decision making follow.

LEARNING OBJECTIVE 4

ethical screening

Running a contemplated decision or action through an ethics test.

1. **Gather the facts.** When making an important decision in business, it is necessary to gather relevant facts. Ask yourself the following questions: "Are there any legal issues involved here?" "Is there precedent in our firm with respect to this type of decision?" "Do I have the authority to make this decision?" "Are there company rules and regulations governing such a decision?"

   The manager of a child-care center needed to hire an additional child-care specialist. One of the applicants was a 55-year-old male with experience as a father and grandfather. The manager judged him to be qualified, yet she knew that many parents would not want their preschool children to be cared for by a middle-age male. Many people perceive that a younger woman is better qualified for child care than an older man. The manager therefore had to gather considerable facts about the situation, including facts about job discrimination and precedents in hiring males as child-care specialists.

   Gathering facts is influenced by emotion, with the result that ethical decision making is not an entirely rational process.[15] We tend to interpret facts based upon our biases and preconceived notions. For example, if the child-care center manager has heard negative information about middle-age men who want to engage in child care, the manager might look hard for indicators that this candidate should be disqualified.

2. **Define the ethical issues.** The ethical issues in a given decision are often more complicated than a first glance suggests. When faced with a complex decision, it may be helpful to talk over the ethical issues with another person. The ethical issues might involve character traits such as being kind and caring and treating others with respect. Or the ethical issues might relate to some of the common ethical problems described earlier in the chapter. Among them are facing conflict of interest, dealing with confidential information, and using corporate resources.

   The manager of the child-care center is facing such ethical issues as fairness, job discrimination, and meeting the demands of customers at the expense of job applicants. The manager is also facing a diversity issue: Should the workforce in a child-care center be culturally diverse, or do we hire only young women?

3. **Identify the affected parties.** When faced with a complex ethical decision, it is important to identify all the affected parties. Major corporate decisions can affect thousands of people. If a company decides to shut down a plant and outsource the manufacturing to a low-wage country, thousands of individuals and many different parties are affected. Workers lose their jobs, suppliers lose their customers, the local government loses out on tax revenues, and local merchants lose many of their customers. You may need to brainstorm with a few others to think of all the parties affected by a given decision.

   The parties affected by the decision about hiring or not hiring the 55-year-old male include the applicant himself, the children, the parents, and the board of directors of the child-care center. The government might also be involved if the man were rejected and filed charges of age and sex discrimination.

4. **Identify the consequences.** After you have identified the parties affected by a decision, the next step is to predict the consequences for each party. It may not be necessary to identify every consequence, yet it is important to identify the consequences with the highest probability of occurring and those with the most negative outcomes. The problem is that many people can be harmed by an unethical decision, such as not fully describing the possible side effects of a diet program.

Both short-term and long-term consequences should be specified. A company closing a plant might create considerable short-term turmoil, but in the long-term the company might be healthier. People participating in a diet program might achieve their short-term objective of losing weight. Yet in the long-term, their health might be adversely affected because the diet is not nutritionally balanced.

The symbolic consequences of an action are important. Every action and decision sends a message (the decision is a symbol of something). If a company moves manufacturing out of a community to save on labor costs, it means that the short-term welfare of domestic employees is less important than profit or perhaps the company surviving.

We return to the child-care manager and the job applicant. If the applicant does not get the job, his welfare will be adversely affected. He has been laid off by a large employer and cannot find work in his regular field. His family will also suffer because he will not be able to make a financial contribution to the family. Yet if the man is hired, the child-care center may suffer. Many traditionally minded parents will say, "Absolutely not. I do not want my child cared for by a middle-age man. He could be a child molester." (It may be unethical for people to have vicious stereotypes, yet they still exist.) If the child-care center does hire the man, the act will symbolize that the owners of the center value diversity.

5. **Identify the obligations.** Identify the obligations and the reasons for each obligation when making a complex decision. The manufacturer of automotive brakes has an obligation to produce and sell only brakes that meet high safety standards. The obligation is to the auto manufacturer who purchases the brakes and, more importantly, to the ultimate consumer whose safety depends on effective brakes. The reason for the obligation to make safe brakes is that lives are at stake. The child-care center owner has an obligation to provide for the safety and health of the children at the center. She must also provide for the peace of mind of the parents and be a good citizen of the community in which the center is located. The decision about hiring the candidate in question must be balanced against all these obligations.

6. **Consider your character and integrity.** A core consideration when faced with an ethical dilemma is how relevant people would judge your character and integrity. What would your family, friends, significant others, teachers, and coworkers think of your actions? To refine this thinking even further, how would you feel if your actions were publicly disclosed in the local newspaper or over e-mail? Would you want the world to know that you gave an under-the-table kickback or that you sexually harassed a frightened teenager working for you? If you would be proud for others to know what decision you made when you faced an ethical dilemma, you are probably making the right decision.

The child-care center manager might ponder how she would feel if the following information were released in the local newspaper or on the Internet:

> The manager of Good Times Child Care recently rejected the application of a 55-year-old man for a child-care specialist position. She said that although Mr. _____ was well qualified from an experience and personality standpoint, she couldn't hire him. She said that Good Times would lose too much business because many parents would fear that Mr. _____ was a child molester or pedophile.

7. **Think creatively about potential actions.** When faced with an ethical dilemma, put yourself in a creative-thinking mode. Stretch your imagination to invent

several options rather than thinking you have only two choices—to do or not do something. Creative thinking may point toward a third, and even fourth, alternative. Imagine this ethical dilemma: A purchasing agent is told that if her firm awards a contract to the sales representative's firm, she will find a leather jacket of her choice delivered to her door. The purchasing agent says to herself, "I think we should award the contract to the firm, but I cannot accept the gift. Yet if I turn down the gift, I will be forfeiting a valuable possession that the company simply regards as a cost of doing business."

The purchasing agent can search for another alternative. She may say to the sales rep, "We will give the contract to your firm because your products fit our requirements. I thank you for the offer of the leather jacket, but instead I would like you to give the jacket to the Salvation Army."

A creative alternative for the child-care manager might be to offer the applicant the next position that opened for an office manager or maintenance person in the center. In this way she would be offering a qualified applicant a job, but placing him in a position more acceptable to parents. Or do you feel this is a cop-out?

8. **Check your intuition.** So far we have emphasized the rational side of ethical decision making. Another effective way of conducting an ethical screen is to rely on your intuition. How does the contemplated decision feel? Would you be proud of yourself or would you hate yourself if you made the decision? Imagine how you would feel if you took money from the handbag of a woman sleeping in the park. Would you feel the same way if you took a kickback, sold somebody a defective product, or sold an 80-year-old man an insurance policy he didn't need? How will the manager of the child-care center feel if she turns down the man for the child-care specialist position? In general, experienced workers rely more heavily on intuition when making ethical choices. The reason is that intuition is based largely on experience.[16] Rules for ethical behavior are important, yet often we have to follow our hunches. Experience and rules are not wasted because intuition includes both experience and the study of rules.

You are encouraged to use the guide for ethical decision making when you next face an ethical dilemma of consequence. Skill-Building Exercise 14-3 gives you an opportunity to practice using the eight steps for ethical decision making.

Developing Strong Relationships with Work Associates

A provocative explanation of the causes of unethical behavior emphasizes the strength of relationships among people.[17] Assume that two people have close professional ties to each other, such as having worked together for a long time or knowing each other both on and off the job. As a consequence, they are likely to behave ethically toward one another on the job. In contrast, if a weak professional relationship exists between two individuals, either party is more likely to engage in an unethical relationship. The owner of an auto service center is more likely to behave unethically toward a stranger passing through town than toward a long-time customer. (The section in Chapter 12 about building relationships with coworkers and work associates provides suggestions for developing strong relationships.) The opportunity for unethical behavior between strangers is often minimized because individuals typically do not trust strangers with sensitive information or valuables.

The ethical skill-building consequence of information about personal relationships is that building stronger relationships with people is likely to enhance ethical behavior. If you build strong relationships with work associates, you are likely to behave more ethically toward them. Similarly, your work associates are likely to behave more ethically toward you. The work associates I refer to are all your contacts, both internal and external customers.

Ethical Decision Making

Working in small groups, take one or more of the following ethical dilemmas through the eight steps for screening contemplated decisions. If more than one group chooses the same scenario, compare your answers for the various steps.

Scenario 1: To Recycle or Not. Your group is the top management team at a large insurance company. Despite the movement toward digitizing all records, your firm still generates tons of paper each month. Customer payments alone account for truckloads of envelopes each year. The paper recyclers in your area claim they can hardly find a market any longer for used paper, so they will be charging you just to accept your paper for recycling. Your group is wondering whether to recycle.

Scenario 2: The Hole in the Résumé. Emily has been working for the family business as an office manager for five years. Because the family business is being sold, Emily has started a job hunt. She also welcomes the opportunity to work in a larger company so she could learn more about how a big company operates. As she begins preparing her job résumé, she ponders how to classify the year of unemployment prior to working at the family business. During that year she worked a total of 10 weeks in entry-level jobs at three fast-food restaurants. Otherwise she filled her time with such activities as walking in the park, watching daytime television shows, surfing the Internet, playing video games, and pursuing her hobby of visiting graveyards. Emily finally decides to tack that year onto the five years in the family business. She indicates on her résumé that she has been working *six* years at the family business. As Emily says, "It's a tight job market for office managers, and I don't want to raise any red flags." Evaluate the ethics of Emily's decision to fill in the year off from work, and perhaps offer her some advice.

Scenario 3: The High-Profit Toys. You are a toy company executive starting to plan your holiday season line. You anticipate that the season's hottest item will be Robo-Woman, a battery-operated crime fighter and superheroine. Robo-Woman should wholesale for $25 and retail for $45. Your company figures to earn $15 per unit. You receive a sales call from a manufacturing broker who says he can produce any toy you want for one-third of your present manufacturing cost. He admits that the manufacturer he represents uses prison labor in China, but insists that his business arrangement violates no law. You estimate you can earn $20 per unit if you do business with the manufacturing broker. Your decision is whether to do business with him.

Using Corporate Ethics Programs

Many organizations have various programs and procedures for promoting ethical behavior. Among them are committees that monitor ethical behavior, training programs in ethics, and vehicles for reporting ethical violations. The presence of these programs is designed to create an atmosphere in which unethical behavior is discouraged and reporting on unethical behavior is encouraged.

Ethics hotlines are one of the best-established programs to help individuals avoid unethical behavior. Should a person be faced with an ethical dilemma, the person calls a toll-free line to speak to a counselor about the dilemma. Sometimes employees ask questions to help interpret a policy, such as, "Is it okay to ask my boss for a date?" or "Are we supposed to give senior citizen discounts to customers who qualify but do not ask for one?" At other times, a more pressing ethical issue might be addressed, such as, "Is it ethical to lay off a worker just five months short of his qualifying for a full pension?"

Human resource professionals contend that no amount of training will ensure that employees will act ethically in every situation, particularly because ethics deals with subtle matters rather than strictly right or wrong. However, Deborah Haliczer, director of employee relations at Northern Illinois University, explains that training is valuable in starting a useful dialogue about right and wrong behavior that employees could remember in murky situations.[18]

Sears Holding Corp. has an ethics hotline the company refers to as an "Assist Line" because very few of the 15,000 calls it receives per year represent crises. Often the six full-time ethics specialists who handle the calls just listen; at other times they intervene to help resolve the problem. The Assist Line is designed to help with the following kinds of calls: guidance about company policy, company code of conduct issues, workplace harassment and discrimination, selling practices, theft, and human resource issues. Employees and managers are able to access information and guidance without feeling they are facing a crisis. The Assist Line is thus a cross between "911" and "411" calls. At times an ethical problem of such high moral intensity is presented that employee confidentiality cannot be maintained. However, the Ethics Office handles the inquiries in as confidential a manner as practical and assigns them case identification numbers for follow-up.[19]

Wells Fargo & Co., a mammoth bank, emphasizes both a code of conduct and ethics training. Its Code of Ethics and Business Conduct specifies policies and standards for employees, covering a variety of topics from maintaining accurate records to participating in civic activities. Each year, employees also participate in ethics training. Any Wells Fargo employee may ask questions or report ethical breaches anonymously using an ethics hotline or dedicated e-mail address. The company will fire violators, dismissing about 100 people a year for misconduct ranging from conflicts of interest to cheating on incentive plans.

Patricia Callahan, executive vice president and director of human resources at the bank, says, "I'm the biggest soft touch in the world. But when someone lies or cheats, you can't have people like that representing us to our customers, whose trust is all we have."[20] The link between the programs just described and individual ethical skills is that these programs assist a worker's skill development. For example, if you become comfortable in asking about ethical issues, or turning in ethical violators, you have become more ethically skilled.

BACK TO THE OPENING CASE

Careful background screening of job candidates continues to pay off for FIS Group Inc. The company's client satisfaction is high, and no complaints by clients about ethical behavior have been received .

Being Environmentally Conscious

Another ethical skill is to be *green* or to do your job in helping sustain the physical environment. (*Green* derives from the idea that green vegetation such as trees and forests are a plus for the environment.) The reasoning behind this statement is that it is morally responsible to protect the environment. Do not be concerned with taking sides on the issue of global warming. Whether or not humans and the carbon dioxide emissions they create have contributed to global warming, the physical environment needs your help.

The skill of being environmentally conscious has two major components. The first is to take as many steps as you can individually to help preserve the environment even in such small steps as carrying a reusable cloth bag to the grocery store and not throwing a plastic bottle on a lawn. The second is to be an advocate for the environment by mentioning its importance at work. You might, for example, present data to management about how solar heating can save the company money in the long-run, and how benches and walkways made from recycled tires and plastics are attractive and economical. Figure 14-5 gives you a starting point for contributing to a sustainable environment. You might want to add to this list with suggestions of your own, or those you find in the media and scientific articles.

You may need to use your persuasive communication skills to make an impact on the environment. You will also need to use your positive political skills so you will not be perceived as an environmental, tree-hugging pest.

Following an Applicable Professional Code of Conduct

Professional codes of conduct are prescribed for many occupational groups including physicians, nurses, lawyers, paralegals, purchasing managers and agents, and real estate salespeople. A useful ethics guide for members of these groups is to follow the code of conduct for their profession. If the profession or trade is licensed by the state or province, a worker can be punished for deviating from the code of conduct specified by the state. The code of conduct developed by the profession or trade is separate from the legal code, but usually supports the same principles and practices. Some of these codes of conduct developed by the professional associations are 50 and 60 pages long, yet all are guided by the kind of ethical principles implied in the ethical decision-making guide described earlier. Figure 14-6 presents a sampling of provisions from these codes of conduct.

FIGURE 14-5 Representative Suggestions for Helping a Company Contribute to a Sustainable Environment

1. Conserve energy by adjusting thermostats to keep working areas cooler during cold months and warmer during warm months.

2. Place a lawn on the roof, which can reduce its surface temperature by 70° F and internal temperatures by 15° F.

3. Carpool to work with at least three coworkers, and provide preferred parking spaces for carpoolers and hybrid or electric cars.

4. Encourage employee use of mass transportation, and provide company shuttle buses from locations convenient to where employees live.

4. Offer employees at least $2,000 toward the purchase of a hybrid vehicle or electric car.

4. Turn off electronic machines when not in use unless starting and stopping them frequently uses more energy than leaving the machines turned on during working hours. Encourage the replacement of incandescent bulbs with fluorescent ones (providing the replacement bulb gives enough light for the purpose).

5. Recycle as many packages as possible and purchase products, such as office furniture and driveways, made from recycled products including vehicle tires. When possible, use old newspapers for packing material instead of new paper and plastic.

6. Use mugs instead of Styrofoam and set up bins to recycle aluminum cans and plastic bottles.

7. When constructing a new building, seek Leadership in Energy and Environmental Design (LEED) certification from the U.S. Green Building Council.

8. Provide bicycle racks and shows that enable employees to bike to work.

9. Construct a system that captures rainwater to be reused for irrigation.

10. Grow as much vegetation on company premises as feasible, including celebrating special events by planting another tree. Use plants that are native to the region because native vegetation does not require as much maintenance, fertilizer, chemical sprays, or water.

11. Drink as much tap water as possible to minimize the use of bottled water, or filter tap water to one's specifications.

12. Combat litter and clutter in your work area and on company premises to help attain a pleasant, environmentally friendly atmosphere. Take such actions as alerting the company to exposed, rusted pipes, broken concrete in the parking lot, peeling paint, and broken fences.

13. Alert influential people to energy-saving and money-saving solar heating systems, such as solar buildings that provide solar hot water and solar heating.

14. Encourage people in your network not to drive at high speeds or sit in an idling vehicle while making phone calls. Encourage safe driving in general because vehicular accidents consume enormous amounts of energy including tow trucks, salvage operations, and life-sustaining hospital stays. Also encourage them to walk to errands instead of driving, whenever feasible.

15. Your own suggestions.

Source: Several of the ideas are from Michael Barbaro, "At Wal-Mart, Lessons in Self-Help," *The New York Times* (*nytimes.com*), April 5, 2007; Matthew Haggan, "Staples to Build Its First 'Green' Store in Miami," *MiamiHerald.com*, September 29, 2007; Kathryn Tyler, "Going Green," *HR Magazine*, October 2006, pp. 99–104; Charles Lockwood, "Building the Green Way," *Harvard Business Review*, June 2006, pp. 129–137.

FIGURE 14-6 Excerpts from Professional Codes of Conduct

Professional Organization	Sample of Ethical Guidelines and Regulations
Institute of Management Accountants	1. Maintain an appropriate level of professional competence by ongoing development of their knowledge and skills. 2. Refrain from disclosing confidential information acquired in the course of their work and monitor their activities to assure the maintenance of that confidentiality. 3. Actual or apparent conflicts of interest and advise all appropriate parties of any potential conflict.
National Association of Legal Assistants	1. A legal assistant (paralegal) must not perform any of the duties that attorneys only may perform nor take any actions that attorneys may not take. 2. A legal assistant may perform any task which is properly delegated and supervised by an attorney, as long as the attorney is ultimately responsible to the client, maintains a direct relationship with the client, and assumes professional responsibility for the work product. 3. A legal assistant must protect the confidences of a client and must not violate any rule or statute now in effect or hereafter enacted controlling the doctrine of privileged communications between a client and an attorney.
National Association of Purchasing Management	1. Avoid the intent and appearance of unethical or compromising practice in relationships, actions, and communications. 2. Refrain from any private business or professional activity that would create a conflict between personal interests and the interest of the employer. 3. Refrain from soliciting or accepting money, loans, credits, or prejudicial discounts, and the acceptance of gifts, entertainment, favors, or services from present or potential suppliers which might influence, or appear to influence purchasing decisions.

Sources: Institute of Management Accountants Code of Ethics; National Association of Legal Assistants Professional Standards; National Association of Purchasing Management Principles and Standards of Purchasing Practice.

Be Ready to Exert Upward Leadership

A politically delicate situation can arise when a worker wants to behave ethically, yet he or she works for an unethical manager. He or she might worry that being ethical will lead to being reprimanded or job loss. The ethical person working for an unethical boss might feel that his or her values are being compromised, such as a virtuous credit-card specialist being told to approve credit cards for people who will probably wind up paying many late fees. **Upward ethical leadership** is leadership displayed by individuals who take action to maintain ethical standards although higher-ups engage in questionable moral behaviors.[21]

> **upward ethical leadership**
>
> Leadership displayed by individuals who take action to maintain ethical standards although higher-ups engage in questionable behavior.

At the extreme, an employee might blow the whistle on the boss and report the unethical behavior to top management or a government agency. An example would be telling the Consumer Protection Agency that your company was selling cribs with too much lead paint, after your boss refused to accept your complaint.

The upward leadership approach would be to attempt to resolve the problem before going to the extreme of whistle-blowing. The employee who spots the immoral or unethical behavior would use problem-solving and communication skills, along with conflict-resolution skills. For example, the employee who spotted the lead-paint problem might say to the boss, "I have a problem and I would like to discuss it with you." The employee would therefore be engaging the boss in helping solve the problem. Recognizing that you

Confronting the Unethical Boss

One student plays the role of Fred, a manager who makes frequent business trips by airplanes. Fred also likes to fly frequently on vacation, and appreciates accumulating frequent-flyer miles. Company policy allows employees to keep the frequent-flyer miles they accumulate for work, so Fred will often take indirect trips to a destination to accumulate more air miles. For example, to fly to San Francisco, he will fly from Boston to Atlanta, and then to San Francisco. In this instance, he could have made a shorter trip by flying directly from Boston to San Francisco, or from Boston to Chicago to San Francisco. In general, the longer, indirect flights are more expensive.

Another person plays the role of Kelly, the office administrative assistant who sometimes helps Fred prepare his travel vouchers.

Kelly, who has good knowledge of geography, notices this strange pattern of Fred taking indirect flights. She is also aware of company policy that permits employees to accumulate frequent-flyer miles that are earned on business trips. Kelly is disturbed about what she perceives to be an inappropriate use of company resources—and therefore an ethical violation.

Kelly decides to discuss this most likely ethical violation with Fred. The role-play takes place in Fred's cubicle, and you can imagine how defensive Fred is going to be.

Observers look to see if Kelly can preserve her sense of ethics while not doing too much damage to her relationship with her boss, Fred.

have less power than your boss does, you would have to be diplomatic and nonaccusatory. It would be important to point to the problem (high levels of lead paint) rather than accusing the boss of being unethical or immoral.

Skill-Building Exercise 14-4 gives you an opportunity to practice upward leadership skills for correcting unethical behavior.

SELF-ASSESSMENT QUIZ IN OVERVIEW

One self-assessment quiz was presented in this chapter, The Ethical Reasoning Inventory. Use the quiz as an alert to keep your ethical values in mind whenever faced with an ethical dilemma. Although you may study ethics, and learn to use a guide to ethical decision making, your values will continue to exert a strong influence on your behavior. For example, if a person values the environment, he or she will not empty a car ashtray of cigarette butts onto a parking lot pavement. If you know that your ethical values are in the low range, you will have to work extra hard to be ethical in work and personal life.

Concept Review and Reinforcement

Key Terms

moral intensity, 297
utilitarian predisposition, 298

conflict of interest, 299
defining moment, 303

ethical screening, 305
upward ethical leadership, 311

Summary of Key Concepts

Ethics refers to what is good and bad, right and wrong, just and unjust, and what people should do. Ethics turn values into action. A person's ethical code has a significant impact on his or her interpersonal relationships.

Understanding ethics is important for a variety of reasons. First, people are motivated by self-interest and a desire to be morally right. Second, good ethics can enhance business and avoid illegal acts. Third, having high ethics improves the quality of work life.

Being ethical is not always easy for several reasons, including the complexity of ethical decisions, lack of recognition of the moral issues, poor moral development, and pressures from the work environment. Ethical violations in the form of lying are widespread in the workplace. Another problem is that some people have a utilitarian predisposition that tends toward unethical behavior.

Commonly faced ethical dilemmas include illegally copying software; treating people unfairly, including cronyism; sexually harassing coworkers; facing a conflict of interest; dealing with confidential information; misrepresenting employment history; using corporate resources; and ethically violating computers and IT.

A challenging twist to ethical decision making is to sort through your values when you have to choose between two morally sound choices. A defining moment is when you have to choose between two or more ideals in which you deeply believe.

One strategy for behaving ethically is to develop virtuousness, which includes rationality, honesty, independence, productivity, forgiveness and pride. A key strategy for behaving ethically is to follow the eight steps in making a contemplated decision:

1. Gather the facts.
2. Define the ethical issues.
3. Identify the affected parties.
4. Identify the consequences.
5. Identify the obligations (such as to customers and society).
6. Consider your character and integrity.
7. Think creatively about potential actions.
8. Check your intuition.

Another way to raise the level of ethical behavior is to form strong professional relationships with work associates. This is true because people tend to behave more ethically toward people who are close to them. At times using a corporate program such as an ethics hotline can help a person resolve ethical dilemmas. Being environmentally conscious contributes to ethical behavior. Following an applicable code of professional conduct, such as that for accountants, paralegals, and purchasing specialists, is another guide to behaving ethically. Upward leadership behavior can help you deal with the situation of maintaining ethical standards when the boss engages in questionable moral behavior.

Check Your Understanding

1. The business owner described in the chapter opener contends that people are fundamentally good. What is your opinion about people being fundamentally good?

2. How can behaving ethically improve a person's interpersonal relationships on the job?

3. What would most likely be some of the specific behaviors of a manager who scored 20 points on the ethical reasoning inventory?

4. An animal advocacy group turned up coats with fur from domesticated dogs and from raccoon dogs from Asia. The fur was labeled as "faux" (false or synthetic). What is your opinion of the ethics of these coat manufacturers who used dog fur labeled as faux fur?

5. Give an example from your own experiences or the media in which a business executive did something of significance that was morally right.

6. Provide an example of an action in business that might be unethical but not illegal.

7. Virtually all accountants have studied ethics as part of their education, yet many business scandals involve accountants. What's their problem?

8. Based on your knowledge of human behavior, why do professional codes of conduct—such as those for doctors, paralegals, and realtors—not prevent all unethical behavior on the part of members?

9. Check out the Web site of a couple of major business corporations such as GE and Ford Motor Company. What conclusion do you reach about whether an environmentally conscious (or green) person would fit in those companies?

10. What decision of ethical consequence have you made in the last year that you would not mind having publicly disclosed?

The Web Corner

http://www.ethics.org
(Ethics Resource Center.)

http://trade.gov/index.asp
(Business ethics and anticorruption as presented by the International Trade Administration of the U.S. Department of Commerce.)

http://globalethicsuniversity.com
(An examination of many phases of business ethics.)

Internet Skill-Builder: Learning from Ethical Role Models

One of the many ways of learning ethical skills is to get good ideas from ethical role models. For example, you might observe a professor who takes the initiative to change a grade upward because she later discovered a calculation error. This Internet skill-builder is more abstract than some others, so you might find it a little frustrating. Search for a few specific ways in which you can learn from an ethical role model. To illustrate, you might learn from a business executive, sports figure, or public servant you admire.

Developing Your Human Relations Skills

Interpersonal Relations Case 14.1

"Where Does My Loyalty Lie?"

As HR (human resources) director, Lauren had fiduciary responsibility for the company's defined contribution retirement plan. (Under this type of plan, the company agrees on how much it will contribute to the pension fund, not how much it will pay.) After the small nonprofit hired a new president, Lauren was instructed to enroll him in the plan immediately and to waive the mandatory one-year waiting period in effect for new employees. She also was ordered to keep quiet about employees who were wrongly classified as exempt (from overtime regulation)—an effort to avoid paying them overtime. When she protested that these actions were illegal and would expose her and the company to liability, an attorney acting for the firm informed her that "you will do what you're told."

But Lauren viewed her duties as an HR professional as "the antithesis of just doing what you are told." She enjoyed using her analytical skills. With a master's degree in business communication and certification in professional human resource management, she had served as president of her local HR organization and had become a "go-to" person for other HR professionals. She also taught HR at the university level.

"I believe HR is the conscience of the organization," says Lauren, so she was "rocked to my core," by the behavior of senior management at her company. "Where does my loyalty lie," she asked herself, "to my company or to my personal and professional ethics? I always felt I walked a tightrope in HR between 'crazy management ideas' and being an advocate for employees."

Following her conscience, Lauren resigned and began a search for a new job. Because Lauren lives in a very small community, job opportunities are scarce. She did eventually find another HR position 75 miles from her home, but the grueling commute became too difficult and she left that job. In addition, says Lauren, she realized that "they hired me because they could pay me $38,000 in an area where the going rate was $90,000." She feels she lost out on other job openings because "I was thought of as a problem" after she explained her reason for leaving her previous employer.

Today, Lauren works part time as a secretary. "I didn't sell out my integrity, and I can hold my head up," she says. But there's a trade-off: "I basically decided to give up my career. My husband and I adjusted our lifestyle downward," she says, "I'm pretty sure my HR days are over."

Even now with the benefit of hindsight, she doesn't see a different course she could have taken. "I have racked by brain for seven years, and I just don't see what else I could have done," says Lauren.

Case Questions

1. What do you think Lauren could have done to save her career and preserve her sense of ethics at the same time?
2. Does Lauren have a useful message for you and others in your network? Or, is she just a loser who we can forget about?
3. To what extent does it surprise you that a lawyer would ask someone to act unethically?

Source: Ann Pomeroy, "The Ethics Squeeze," *HR Magazine*, March 2006, pp. 51–52, 55.

Interpersonal Relations Case 14.2

The Highly Rated but Expendable Marsha

Department manager Nicholas had thought for a long time that Marsha, one of his financial analysts, created too many problems. Although Marsha performed her job in a satisfactory manner, she required a lot of supervisory time and attention. She frequently asked for time off when her presence was needed the most because of a heavy workload in the department. Marsha sent Nicholas many long and complicated e-mail messages that required substantial time to read and respond. When Nicholas responded to Marsha's e-mail message, she would typically send another e-mail back asking for clarification.

Marsha's behavior during department meetings irritated Nicholas. She would demand more time than any other participant to explain her point of view on a variety of issues. At a recent meeting she took 10 minutes explaining how the company should be doing more to help the homeless and invest in the development of inner cities.

Nicholas coached Marsha frequently about the problems she was creating, but Marsha strongly disagreed with his criticism and concerns. At one time, Nicholas told Marsha that she was a high-maintenance employee. Yet Marsha perceived herself as a major contributor to the department. She commented once, "Could it be, Nick, that you have a problem with an assertive woman working in your department?"

Nicholas developed a tactic to get Marsha out of the department. He would give her outstanding performance evaluations, emphasizing her creativity and persistence. Marsha would then be entered into the company database as an outstanding employee, thereby making her a strong candidate for transfer or promotion. Within six months, a manager in a new division of the company took the bait. She requested that Marsha be recruited into her department as a senior financial analyst. Nicholas said to the recruiting manager, "I hate to lose a valuable contributor like Marsha, but I do not want to block her career progress."

Two months later, Marsha's new manager telephoned Nicholas, and asked, "What's the problem with Marsha? She's kind of a pill to have working with us. I thought she was an outstanding employee."

Nicholas responded, "Give Marsha some time. She may be having a few problems adjusting to a new environment. Just give her a little constructive feedback. You'll find out what a dynamo she can be."

Case Questions

1. How ethical was Nicholas in giving Marsha a high performance evaluation for the purposes of attracting her to other departments?
2. What should the manager do who was hooked by Nicholas's bait of the high performance evaluation?
3. What might the company do to prevent more incidents of inflated performance evaluations for the purpose of transferring an unwanted employee?

Interpersonal Skills Role-Play 14.1

Confronting the Ethical Deviant

One student plays the role of the manager who transferred Marsha into his or her department. The new manager has become suspicious that Nicholas might have manipulated Marsha's performance evaluations to make her appear like a strong candidate for transfer or promotion. In fact, the new manager thinks she (or he, if a man plays the role) may have caught an ethical deviant. Another student plays the role of Nicholas who wants to defend his reputation as an ethical manager. During the role-play, pay some attention to ethical issues. As usual, other students will provide feedback on the effectiveness of the interaction they observed.

CHAPTER 15

Stress Management and Personal Productivity

Karen Behnke is CEO of Juice Beauty, a San Rafael, California, organic beauty products firm with approximately $10 million in annual sales. "Our top line is doubling, our EBITDA (earnings before interest, taxes, depreciation, and amortization) is doubling," says Behnke, 49. "We're doing very well."

But like the rest of us, Behnke has days when life gets in the way. She recalls one chaotic workday when her husband, Howard Luria, an interventional cardiologist, was away and she needed to make an hour-long drive to Napa where her dad, who is battling a brain tumor, had gotten worse.

To add to the stress, Behnke was between babysitters and didn't have anyone to watch her son and daughter, ages 9 and 7, until she got back. She made hasty child-care arrangements with another mom and began making her way over the winding roads to Napa with her phone ringing nonstop. One minute, her 83-year-old mother was calling; the next minute, she was talking to a scheduled client call or speaking with one of Juice Beauty's 30 employees. Then there was the emotion involved in checking her dad into the hospital.

It was 9 P.M. when Behnke finally got home and put the kids to bed, but it wasn't lights out for her yet: She opened her laptop to find 120 e-mails waiting for her. "Those are the days that you think, 'Oh, my God: How am I going to do this?'" she says. "When something lands on top of my schedule, that's when it just kind of falls apart."[1]

Learning Objectives

After reading and studying this chapter and doing the exercises, you should be able to

1. Explain many of the symptoms and consequences of stress, including burnout.
2. Describe personality factors and job factors that contribute to stress.
3. Manage your own stress effectively.
4. Reduce any tendencies you might have toward procrastination.
5. Identify attitudes and values that will enhance your productivity.
6. Identify work habits and skills that will enhance your productivity.
7. Pinpoint potential time wasters that drain your productivity.

The small business owner just described is attempting to manage stress and juggle her schedule at the same time. In the process she is engaging in dangerous (and often against the law) multitasking as she talks on her phone while navigating a busy California highway. The urgency of the topics makes the calls even more distracting. Although this book is primarily about interpersonal skills, information about managing stress and enhancing personal productivity is relevant. Having your work under control and not being stressed out enables you to focus better on interpersonal relationships.

The first half of this chapter deals with the nature of stress and how it can be managed, whereas the second half describes various approaches to improving personal productivity. The two topics are as closely related as nutrition and health. When you effectively manage stress, you can be more productive. And when your work is under control, you avoid the heavy stress of feeling overwhelmed. A useful thought to keep in mind is that many readers of this book will become or are already **corporate athletes**, workers who engage in high-level performance for sustained periods.[2] To be a corporate athlete, you have to manage your energy and stress well, in addition to having good work habits and time management.

corporate athletes

Workers who engage in high-level performance for sustained periods.

UNDERSTANDING AND MANAGING STRESS

A major challenge facing any worker who wants to stay healthy and have good interpersonal relationships is to manage stress effectively. A recent survey conducted by the American Psychological Association indicates that work is America's No. 1 source of stress. A full 74 percent of respondents reported that work is their top stressor.[3] Although *stress* is an everyday term, a scientific definition helps clarify its meaning. **Stress** is an adaptive response that is the consequence of any action, situation, or event that places special demands on a person. Note that stress, as used here, refers to a reaction to the situation, not the situation or force itself. A **stressor** is the external or internal force that brings about the stress.

Individual differences in the perception of an event play a key role in determining what events are stressful. Giving a presentation to management, for example, is stressful for some people but not for others. Some people perceive a presentation as a threatening

stress

An adaptive response that is the consequence of any action, situation, or event that places special demands on a person.

stressor

The external or internal force that brings about stress.

and uncomfortable experience, while others might perceive the same event to be an invigorating challenge.

The term *special demands* is also critical because minor adjustments, such as a pencil point that breaks, are usually not perceived as stressful. Yet piling on of minor adjustments, such as having 10 small things go wrong in one day, is stressful. This is true because stress is additive: A series of small doses of stress can create a major stress problem.

This textbook's approach to understanding stress centers on its symptoms and consequences, personality and job factors that contribute to stress, and methods and techniques for stress management. Managing stress receives more emphasis because the same techniques can be used to combat a variety of stressors.

Symptoms and Consequences of Stress

LEARNING OBJECTIVE 1

The physiological changes that take place within the body in response to stress are responsible for most stress symptoms. These physiological changes are almost identical for both positive and negative stressors. Ski racing, romantic attraction, and being downsized can make you feel about the same physically. The experience of stress helps activate hormones that prepare the body to run or fight when faced with a challenge. This battle against the stressor is referred to as the **fight-or-flight response**. It helps you deal with emergencies.

A modern explanation of the fight-or-flight response theory explains that, when faced with stress, the brain acts much like a thermostat. The brain is the organ that decides whether a situation is stressful and produces the behavioral and physiological responses. Yet, the brain's response is based on personal experience and culture. Eating seal meat would rarely be stressful for an Eskimo, yet might be for a Floridian. When outside conditions deviate from an ideal point, the thermostat sends a signal to the furnace to increase heat or air-conditioning. The brain senses stress as damage to well-being and therefore sends out a signal to the body to cope. The purpose of coping is to modify the discrepancy between the ideal (low-stress) and actual (high-stress) conditions.[4] The brain is thus a self-regulating system that helps us cope with stressors.

Physiological Reactions The activation of hormones when the body has to cope with a stressor produces a short-term physiological reaction. Among the most familiar reactions is an increase in heart rate, blood pressure, blood glucose, and blood clotting. The stress hormone cortisol and other chemical responses to a stress can increase the cardiovascular function and the immune system in the short-term. To help you recognize these symptoms, try to recall your internal bodily sensations the last time you were almost in an automobile accident or heard some wonderful news. Less familiar changes are a redirection of the blood flow toward the brain and large muscle groups and a release of stored fluids from places throughout the body into the bloodstream.

If stress is continuous and accompanied by these short-term physiological changes, annoying and life-threatening conditions can occur. Damage occurs when stress levels rarely subside. Eventually the immune system is suppressed, and memory is impaired. When the immune system is impaired, the severity of many diseases and disorders increases. For example, people whose stress level is high recover more slowly from colds and injuries, and they are more susceptible to sexually transmitted diseases.[5]

A stressful life event usually leads to a high cholesterol level (of the unhealthy type) and high blood pressure. Other conditions associated with stress are cardiac disease, migraine headaches, ulcers, allergies, skin disorders, irritable bowel syndrome, and cancer. People under continuous negative stress, such as having severe family problems or having a life out of control, also age more quickly partially because of cell damage.[6] (Have you ever observed that stressed-out friends of yours appear older looking than their chronological age?) A study of 812 Swedish workers conducted over a 25-year period found that work stress doubles the risk of dying from a heart attack. Seventy-three of the workers died from cardiac disease during the study. The major type of stress studied was having high work demands with little control over the work, combined with being underpaid.[7]

Stress symptoms vary considerably from one person to another. A general behavioral symptom of intense stress is for people to exaggerate their weakest tendencies. For instance,

---

fight-or-flight response

The body's physiological and chemical battle against a stressor in which the person tries to cope with the adversity head-on or tries to flee from the scene.

FIGURE 15-1 A Variety of Stress Symptoms

Mostly Physical and Physiological	
Shaking or trembling	Mouth dryness
Dizziness	Upper and lower back pain
Heart palpitations	Frequent headaches
Difficulty breathing	Low energy and stamina
Chronic fatigue	Stomach problems
Unexplained chest pains	Constant craving for sweets
Frequent teeth grinding	Increased alcohol or cigarette consumption
Frequent nausea	Frequent need to eliminate
Mostly Emotional and Behavioral	
Difficulty concentrating	Anxiety or depression
Nervousness	Forgetfulness
Crying	Restlessness
Anorexia	Frequent arguments with others
Declining interest in sex	Feeling high strung much of the time
Frequent nail biting or hair tugging	

Note: Anxiety is a general sense of dread, fear, or worry not linked to a specific event, such as being anxious about your future.

a person with a strong temper who usually keeps cool under pressure may throw a tantrum under intense pressure. Some common stress symptoms are listed in Figure 15-1.

Job Performance Consequences   Stress has both negative and positive consequences. **Hindrance stressors** are those stressful events and thoughts that have a negative effect on motivation and performance. Many of these have already been mentioned. In contrast, **challenge stressors** have a positive direct effect on motivation and performance.[8] The right amount of stress prepares us for meeting difficult challenges and spurs us on to peak intellectual and physical performance. An optimum level of stress exists for most people and most tasks. In general, performance tends to be best under moderate amounts of stress. If the stress is too great, people become temporarily ineffective; they may freeze or choke. Under too little stress, people may become lethargic and inattentive. Figure 15-2 depicts the relationship between stress and job performance. An exception to this relationship is that certain negative forms of stress are likely to lower performance even if the stress is moderate. For example, the stress created by an intimidating supervisor or worrying about radiation poisoning—even in moderate amounts—will not improve performance.

hindrance stressors

Those stressful events and thoughts that have a negative effect on motivation and performance.

challenge stressors

Those stressful events and thoughts that have a positive direct effect on motivation and performance.

FIGURE 15-2 Relationship between Stress and Job Performance

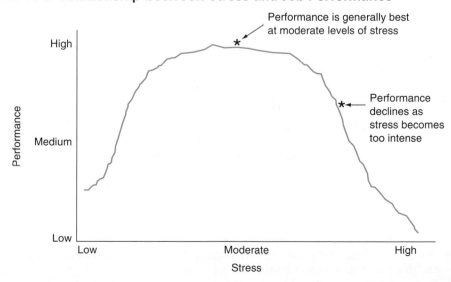

Job stress can also lower job performance indirectly because distressed workers are more likely to be absent from the job, thereby not accomplishing as much work. A study of 323 health service workers in the United Kingdom found that job-related psychological distress, particularly depression, was associated with more days absent and a greater number of times absent.[9] (That is, one worker could be absent only twice and miss a total of 20 days, while another worker could be absent 10 times yet miss a total of 10 days.)

The optimum amount of stress is a positive force that is the equivalent of finding excitement and challenge. Your ability to solve problems and deal with challenge is enhanced when the right amount of adrenaline flows in your blood to guide you toward peak performance. In fact, highly productive people are sometimes said to be hooked on adrenaline.

Burnout and Stress   One of the major problems of prolonged stress is that it may lead to **burnout**, a condition of emotional, mental, and physical exhaustion in response to long-term stressors. Burnout is also referred to as work exhaustion because fatigue is usually involved. Burned-out people are often cynical. Two other examples of burnout symptoms are irritability and impatience.

Burnout is a complex phenomenon, but it often occurs when people feel out of control. Other critical factors that contribute to burnout are insufficient recognition and reward, a lack of emotional support in the workplace, or an absence of fairness. Christina Maslach observes, "When the workplace does not recognize the human side of work, then the risk of burnout grows, carrying with it a high price and hurting all the parties involved."[10]

The key feature of burnout is the distancing that occurs in response to work overload. Burnout sufferers shift into a mode of doing the minimum as a way of protecting themselves. They start leaving work early and dehumanizing their clients, patients, or customers. People experiencing burnout may do their jobs, but their heart is not in it anymore.[11]

A synthesis of dozens of studies shows that burnout often damages the physical health of workers. Partly because burnout is a consequence of stress, burnout increases the risk for cardiovascular disease as much as well-known risk factors such as smoking, an elevated body mass index, and too much bad cholesterol. Other potential links between burnout and health problems include poor health behaviors and sleep disorder.[12]

Figure 15-3 provides more insight into how job stress affects the attitudes and job performance of workers. Note that stress leads to increased absenteeism and decreased job performance.

LEARNING OBJECTIVE 2

Personality and Job Factors Contributing to Stress

Workers experience stress for many different reasons, including personal predispositions, factors stemming from the job, or the combined influence of both. If a person with an

---

burnout

A condition of emotional, mental, and physical exhaustion in response to long-term stressors.

FIGURE 15-3 Job Stress Takes a Toll

1. Survey research shows that stress is a major issue for many employees.

2. **51%** of employees say they have "high levels of stress, with extreme fatigue/feeling out of control."

3. **50%** of employees miss one to two days of work per year due to stress.

4. **46%** of employees surveyed say they come to work one to four days a year when they are too stressed to be effective.

Source: EAP provider ComPsych's first half of 2006 StressPulse Survey, as reported in Kathryn Tyler, "Stress Management," *HR Magazine*, September 2006, p. 81.

extreme negative predisposition has to deal with irate customers, he or she is most likely to experience substantial stress. Here we describe a sampling of important individual and organizational factors that contribute to job stress.

Personality Factors Predisposing People toward Stress Individuals vary considerably in their susceptibility to job stress based on their personality traits and characteristics. Four such factors are described next.

Low Perceived Control. A key factor in determining whether workers experience stress is how much they believe they can control a given adverse circumstance. **Perceived control** is the belief that an individual has at his or her disposal a response that can control the negative aspects of an event. A survey of over 100 studies indicated that people with a high level of perceived control had low levels of physical and psychological symptoms of stress. Conversely, people with low perceived control are more likely to experience work stress.[13]

perceived control

The belief that an individual has at his or her disposal a response that can control the negative aspects of an event.

Low Self-Efficacy. Self-efficacy, like perceived control, is another personal factor that influences susceptibility to stress. (Note that because self-efficacy is tied to a specific situation, it is not strictly a personality trait.) When workers have both low perceived control and low self-efficacy, the stress consequences may be much worse. However, having high self-efficacy softens the stress consequences of demanding jobs.[14]

Two studies with about 2,300 U.S. Army soldiers each showed that respondents with strong self-efficacy were less stressed out mentally and physically by long work hours and work overload. A key conclusion of the studies is that high levels of self-efficacy may help employees cope more effectively with job stressors.[15] To illustrate, an active coping method would be to reorganize an overwhelming workload so it can be performed more efficiently.

Type A Behavior and Hostility. A person with **Type A behavior** is demanding, impatient, and overstriving, and is therefore prone to negative stress. Type A behavior has two main components. One is the tendency to try to accomplish too many things in too little time. This leads the Type A individual to be impatient and demanding. The other component is free-floating hostility. Because of this sense of urgency and hostility, trivial things irritate these people. People with Type A behavior are aggressive and hardworking.

Type A behavior

A behavior pattern in which the individual is demanding, impatient, and overstriving, and therefore prone to negative stress.

Type A personalities frequently have cardiac diseases, such as heart attacks and strokes, at an early age, but only certain features of the Type A personality pattern may be related to coronary heart disease. The heart attack triggers are hostility, anger, cynicism, and suspiciousness, as contrasted to impatience, ambition, and being work driven. In fact, hostility is more strongly associated with coronary heart disease in men than smoking, drinking, overeating, or high levels of bad (LDL) cholesterol.[16] A recent review of studies confirms that there is no significant association between Type A personalities and heart disease. However, there is a strong association between hostility and coronary heart disease. Hostility of the sort seen in habitual angry driving is also a heart disease risk factor.[17] Note that the heart attack triggers also make for strained interpersonal relationships.

Negative Affectivity. A major contributor to being stress prone is **negative affectivity**, a tendency to experience aversive emotional states. In more detail, negative affectivity is a pervasive disposition to experience emotional stress that includes feelings of nervousness, tension, and worry. The same disposition also includes such emotional states as anger, scorn, revulsion, guilt, self-dissatisfaction, and sadness.[18] Such negative personalities seem to search for important discrepancies between what they would like and what exists. Poor interpersonal relationships often result from the frequent complaining of people with negative affectivity.

negative affectivity

A tendency to experience aversive emotional states.

Job Sources of Stress Almost any job situation can act as a stressor for some employees, but not necessarily for others. As just described, certain personality factors make it more likely that a person will experience job stress. Furthermore, other personal life stressors may spill over into the workplace, making it more likely that a person will experience job stress. Five frequently encountered job stressors are outlined in Figure 15-4 and described in the following.

FIGURE 15-4 Five Significant Sources of Job Stress

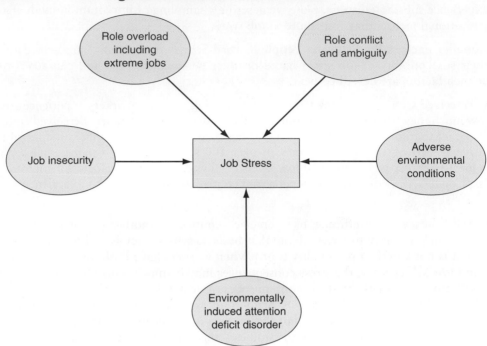

role overload

Having too much work to do.

Role Overload, Including Extreme Jobs. Having too much work to do, **role overload**, can create negative stress in two ways. First, the person may become fatigued and thus be less able to tolerate annoyances and irritations. Second, a person subject to unreasonable work demands may feel perpetually behind schedule, a situation that is itself a powerful stressor. Downsizing often creates overload because fewer people are left to handle the same workload as before. (If work is carefully streamlined, role overload is minimized.)

According to a Families and Work Institute survey, one in three American workers feels chronically overworked. People were found to be working longer and harder, yet nowadays younger workers in particular are finding ways to balance the demands by dividing their focus between the job and personal life. Many employers were found to be more flexible in helping workers achieve this balance, such as allowing flexible working hours.[19]

Work overload often takes the form of an **extreme job** in which the incumbent works at least 60 hours per week in a position that usually requires tight deadlines and heavy travel. Many of these jobs with long hours are found in IT and financial services fields, yet many business owners work comparable hours. The availability of work associates across the globe in different time zones facilitates extreme jobs. One financial analyst who immigrated to the United States from India reportedly works 120 hours per week, leaving only 48 hours for nonwork activities, including sleep. Although many extreme job holders experience considerable job stress, many are exalted by the excitement and the high income.[20]

extreme job

A situation in which the incumbent works at least 60 hours per week in a position that usually requires tight deadlines and heavy travel.

role ambiguity

A condition in which the job holder receives confusing or poorly defined expectations.

Role Conflict and Role Ambiguity. Role conflict, described in Chapter 8 as an important workplace conflict, is also a major workplace stressor. People experience stress when they have to choose between two sets of expectations. Suppose an accountant is asked by her manager to state company earnings in a way that conflicts with the professional norms of accountants. If she complies with her manager, she will feel that she is betraying her profession. If she does not comply with her manager, she will enter into dispute with the manager. The woman is likely to experience job stress.

Role ambiguity is a condition in which the jobholder receives confusing or poorly defined expectations. Workers in many organizations are placed in situations in which they are unsure of their true responsibilities. Some workers who are placed on a self-managing work team experience role ambiguity because they are asked to solve many problems by themselves. It is less ambiguous to have the manager tell you what to do. Many people experience stress symptoms when faced with role ambiguity.

Adverse Environmental Conditions.   A variety of adverse organizational conditions are stressors, as identified by the National Institute for Occupational Safety and Health (NIOSH). Among these adverse organizational conditions are unpleasant or dangerous physical conditions, such as crowding, noise, air pollution, or ergonomic problems. Enough polluted air within an office building can create a sick building in which a diverse range of airborne particles, vapors, molds, and gases pollute the indoor environment. The result can be headaches, nausea, and respiratory infections as well as the stress created by being physically ill.[21]

Ergonomic problems refer to a poor fit between the physical and human requirements of a job. The demands of the modern workplace contribute to the development of musculoskeletal disorders. Working at a computer monitor for prolonged periods of time can lead to adverse physical and psychological reactions. The symptoms include headaches and fatigue, along with eye problems. According to the Vision Syndrome Information Center, about 90 percent of people working on computers more than three hours a day have vision problems, with some 10 million a year seeking treatment. Common visual problems are dry eyes and blurred or double vision. Another vision-related problem is that people lean forward to scan the monitor, leading to physical problems such as back strain.

The repetitive-motion disorder most frequently associated with keyboarding and the use of optical scanners is **carpal tunnel syndrome**. The syndrome occurs when repetitive flexing and extension of the wrist causes the tendons to swell, thus trapping and pinching the median nerve. Carpal tunnel syndrome creates stress because of the pain and misery. About one in five computer users will suffer from carpal tunnel syndrome at some point.[22] The thoughts of having to permanently leave a job requiring keyboarding is another potential stressor. If ergonomic principles, such as erect posture, are incorporated into computer usage, these stress symptoms diminish.

carpal tunnel syndrome
A condition that occurs when repetitive flexing and extension of the wrist causes the tendons to swell, thus trapping and pinching the median nerve.

Commuting to and from work is a major stressor for many people that could be classified as an adverse environmental condition. We emphasize *for many people* because individual differences again come into play. Some people enjoy driving, or being on a train or bus, for such reasons as the opportunity to listen to the radio or read. A study with New Jersey–to–New York commuters found that train rides of over one hour are particularly stressful for commuters. Longer commutes were associated with elevated cortisol (a stress hormone), poorer performance on a proofreading task given the study participants, and high levels of perceived commuting stress. The researcher also observed that for many workers commuting is the most stressful aspect of work.[23]

To avoid the stress of commuting in rush hour traffic, some workers leave home several hours before work, and then use the early arrival time to have breakfast, read the newspaper, or visit an athletic club near the work site.[24] Furthermore, a major reason many people work from home is to avoid the stresses associated with commuting.

Environmentally Induced Attention Deficit Disorder.   According to psychiatrist Edward Hallowell, many people suffer from an attention deficit disorder brought on by technology and activity overload. This problem appears to be a combination of the environment and the individual who chooses to overuse IT devices. The symptoms of environmentally induced attention deficit disorder include frequently feeling rushed and impatient, being easily distracted, forgetfulness, and having little time for creative thought. In short, the person feels frazzled. A major cause of this type of attention deficit disorder is attempting to do more in less time.[25] Many of the suggestions about work habits and time management described later are useful in coping with environmentally induced attention deficit disorder.

Job Insecurity.   Worrying about losing your job is a major stressor. Even when jobs are plentiful, having to search for another job and facing the prospect of geographic relocation are stressors for many people. Downsizing and corporate mergers (which usually result in downsizing) have contributed to job insecurity. The anticipation of layoffs among employees can increase negative stress and lower job performance. In addition, the survivors of a downsizing often experience pressure from the fear of future cuts, loss of friends, and worry about a sudden increase in workload.[26]

Methods and Techniques for Stress Management

Unless stress is managed properly, it may lead to harmful long-term consequences, including disabling physical illness and career retardation. Managing stress refers to controlling stress by making it a constructive force in your life. Managing thus refers to both preventing and reducing stress. However, the distinction between methods of preventing and reducing stress is not clear-cut. For example, physical exercise not only reduces stress, it also contributes to a relaxed lifestyle that helps you prevent stress.

A key principle about managing stress is that you are less likely to experience distress from stressors if you have the right resources. Having the right personality characteristics, such as high perceived control, high self-efficacy, and not being hostile, helps ward off stress. External resources to help ward off negative stress include having a network of friends who provide support, an encouraging manager, and programs for helping distressed employees.[27] Assume for example that a worker is heavily stressed from by a long rush hour commute. If the company provides flexible working hours that help decrease commuting during rush hour, the worker can experience less of a hindrance stressor.

Coping with, or managing, stress includes hundreds of activities, with substantial individual differences in which technique is effective. Running is a case in point. For many people running or jogging is an excellent method of stress reduction. Others find that running creates new stressors, such as aching knees, shin splints, dizziness from breathing in vehicle exhausts, and worrying about being hit by vehicles. In general, coping efforts involve cognitions and behaviors aimed at managing the stressor and its associated emotions. For example, you might have to decrease the troublesome elements in your job (such as role overload) and deal with the tension generated by overwork. The following subsections describe eight methods for managing stress, including a list of everyday stress busters.

Eliminate or Modify the Stressor   The most potent method of managing stress is to eliminate or modify the stressor giving you trouble. One value of relaxation techniques and tranquilizing medication is that they calm a person enough so that he or she can deal constructively with the stressor. A helpful way to attack the cause of stress is to follow the steps in problem solving and decision making. You clarify the problem, identify the alternatives, weigh the alternatives, and select one alternative. One difficulty, however, is that your evaluation of the real problem may be inaccurate. There is always a limit to self-analysis. For example, a person might think that work overload is the stressor when the true stressor is low self-efficacy.

Get Appropriate Physical Exercise   A moderate amount of physical exercise is a cornerstone of managing stress and achieving wellness. To manage stress, it is important to select an exercise program that is physically challenging but does not lead to overexertion and muscle and bone injury. Competitive sports, if taken too seriously, can actually increase stress. Aerobic exercises are most beneficial because they make you breathe faster and raise your heart rate. Walking is highly recommended as a stress reducer because it is inherently relaxing, and offers many of the benefits of other forms of exercise with a minimum risk of physical danger. Doing housework, yard work, and waxing a vehicle are examples of everyday forms of gentle exercise that offer the side benefits of getting tasks accomplished. A major mental and emotional benefit of physical exercise stems from endorphins produced in the thalamus portion of the brain. The endorphins are associated with a state of euphoria referred to as "runner's high." Endorphins also work like painkillers, adding to their stress-reduction value.

Millions of people seek to reduce and prevent stress through yoga, which is both physical exercise and a way of developing mental attitudes that calm the body and mind. One of yoga's many worthwhile goals is to solder a union between the mind and body, thereby achieving harmony and tranquility. Another benefit of yoga is that it helps people place aside negative thoughts that act as stressors.[28]

A caution about yoga is that too much bending too soon can lead to injured hamstring muscles and torn blood vessels.

Rest Sufficiently   Rest offers benefits similar to those of exercise, such as stress reduction, improved concentration, improved energy, and better tolerance for frustration. Achieving proper rest is closely linked to getting proper exercise. The current interest in adult napping reflects the awareness that proper rest makes a person less stress prone and enhances productivity. A study was conducted of 23,681 healthy Greek adults over a six-year period, many of whom napped for about 30 minutes three times a week. Study participants who napped had a 37 percent lower risk of dying from a heart attack than the people who did not. A criticism offered of this study is that the people who napped may also take better care of their bodies and mind in general.[29] The connection of this study to stress management is that many heart attacks are stress induced.

A growing number of firms have napping facilities for workers, and many workers nap at their desks or in their parked vehicles during lunch breaks. Naps of about 15 minutes' duration taken during the workday are used both as energizers and as stress reducers. Napping can help a worker become more less stressed as well as more productive. A rested brain is a more effective brain. To keep the effectiveness of workday napping in perspective, workers who achieve sufficient rest during normal sleeping hours have less need for a nap during working hours.[30]

Maintain a Healthy Diet   Another practical method of stress reduction and prevention is to maintain a well-balanced, and therefore healthy, diet. Nutritious food is valuable for physical and mental health, making it easier to cope with frustrations that are potential stressors. Some non-nutritious foods, such as those laden with caffeine or sugar, tend to enhance a person's level of stress. According to the Dietary Guidelines of the United States Department of Agriculture, a healthy diet is one that

- Emphasizes fruits, vegetables, whole grains, and fat-free or low-fat milk and milk products
- Includes lean meats, poultry, fish, beans, eggs, and nuts
- Is low in saturated fats, *trans* fats, cholesterol, salt (sodium), and added sugars

These recommendations are for the general public over two years of age. Using MyPyramid, the government personalizes a recommended diet, taking into account our age, sex, and amount of physical exercise. Consult *http://www.mypyramid.gov,* as shown in Figure 15-5.

Build a Support Network   A **support network** is a group of people who can listen to your problems and provide emotional support. These people, or even one person, can

support network

A group of people who can listen to your problems and provide emotional support.

FIGURE 15-5 Dietary Guidelines for Americans, developed by the U.S. Department of Agriculture. Access the pyramid to receive your personalized set of recommendations for a healthy diet.

The Food Groups

Grains

Vegetables

Fruits

Milk

Meat & Beans

Oils

Source: U.S. Department of Agriculture, *http://www.mypyramid.gov.*

Visualization for Stress Reduction

A standard, easy-to-use method for reducing stress symptoms is to visualize a pleasant and calm experience. You need to concentrate carefully on your object or scene, otherwise stress reduction is unlikely to take place. If you are experiencing stress right now, try the technique. Otherwise, wait until the next time you perceive your body to be experiencing stress. In this context, visualization means to picture yourself doing something that you would like to do. Whatever fantasy suits your fancy will work, according to the advocates of this relaxation technique. Visualizations that work for some people include smiling at a loved one, floating on a cloud, caressing a baby, petting a kitten or puppy, and walking in the woods. Notice that all of these scenes are relaxing rather than exciting. What visualization would work for you?

To implement the technique, close your eyes and bring the pleasant image into focus in your mind. Think of nothing else at the moment (as in meditation). Imagine that a DVD of the pleasant experience is playing on the television screen in your brain. Breathe softly and savor the experience. Slowly return to reality, refreshed, relaxed, and ready to tackle the challenges of the day.

help you through your difficult episodes. Members of your network can provide you with a sense of closeness, warmth, and acceptance that will reduce your stress. Also, the simple expedient of putting your feelings into words can be a healing experience. The way to develop this support network is to become a good listener so that the other person will reciprocate. A support network is therefore a method of stress management based squarely on effective interpersonal skills.

Practice Visualization and Meditation   Perhaps the most effortless and enjoyable relaxation technique for managing stress is to visualize a pleasant experience, as explained in Skill-Building Exercise 15-1. Visualization, like so many stress-reduction techniques, including meditation, requires concentration. Concentrating helps slow down basic physiological processes such as the heartbeat and dissipates stress. Forcing yourself to concentrate is also valuable because a key stress symptom is difficulty in concentrating.

Meditation is a relaxation technique used to quiet the mind, as well as to relieve stress, and is more complicated than simple visualization. A typical mediation technique proceeds as follows: Hold your back straight, and relax the body. Take three gentle breaths, breathing in and out through the nostrils. Let the respiration follow its natural flow. Your body breathes as if it was fast asleep, yet you remain vigilant. If you become distracted, simply let go of the thought and return to the breath. It is helpful to count each inhale up to 21. Each time your mind wanders, return back to one. Practice meditating about 20 minutes a day, and meditate on the spot after a stressful event or thought.[31] The breathing part of meditation is so important that is an everyday method of stress reduction itself.

Meditation is practiced by many corporate athletes (mentioned at the outset of the chapter). A. G. Lafley, the top executive at Procter & Gamble says, "I've tried to teach myself to meditate. When I travel, which is 60% of the time, I find that meditating for five, ten, or 15 minutes in a hotel room at night can be as good as a workout. Generally, I think I know myself so much better than I used to. And that has helped me stay calm and cool under fire."[32]

Practice Everyday Methods of Stress Reduction   The simple expedient of learning how to relax is an important method of reducing the tension and anxiety brought about by both positive and negative stress. Visualization of a pleasant experience is one such method. A sample of everyday suggestions for relaxation and other methods of stress reduction are presented in Figure 15-6. If you can accomplish these, you are less likely to need tranquilizing medication to keep you calm and in control. Your stress symptoms will ordinarily return, however, if you do not eliminate and modify the stressor. If the stress is an emotional conflict you do not see or understand, assistance from a mental health professional is recommended.

Now that you have studied various methods of managing stress, reinforce your thinking by doing Skill-Building Exercise 15-2.

FIGURE 15-6 Stress Busters

- Take a deep breath and exhale slowly. Inhale and your heart beats faster. Exhale and your heart beats more slowly, and slow down the cardiac muscle.[31]
- Give in to your emotions. If you are angry, disgusted, or confused, admit your feelings. Suppressing your emotions adds to stress.
- Take a brief break from the stressful situation and do something small and constructive, such as washing your car, emptying a wastebasket, or getting a haircut.
- Get a massage, because it can loosen tight muscles, improve your blood circulation, and calm you down.
- Get help with your stressful task from a coworker, supervisor, or friend.
- Concentrate intensely on reading, surfing the Internet, a sport, or a hobby. Contrary to common sense, concentration is at the heart of stress reduction.
- Have a quiet place at home and have a brief idle period there every day.
- Take a leisurely day off from your routine.
- Finish something you have started, however small. Accomplishing almost anything reduces some stress.
- Stop to smell the flowers, make friends with a young child or elderly person, or play with a kitten or puppy.
- Strive to do a good job, but not a perfect job.
- Work with your hands, doing a pleasant task.
- Find somebody or something that makes you laugh, and have a good laugh.
- Minimize drinking caffeinated or alcoholic beverages, and drink fruit juice or water instead. Grab a piece of fruit rather than a can of beer.
- Help somebody less fortunate than you. The flood of good feelings will act like endorphins.

SKILL-BUILDING EXERCISE 15-2

Personal Stress-Management Action Plan

Most people face a few powerful stressors in their work and personal life, but few people take the time to clearly identify these stressors or develop an action plan for remedial action. The purpose of this exercise is to make you an exception. Here is an opportunity to inventory your stressors, think through the problems they may be causing you, and develop action plans you might take to remedy the situation. Use the form below or create one with a word processing table or a spreadsheet.

Work or School Stressor	Symptoms This Stressor Is Creating for Me	My Action Plan to Manage This Stressor
1.		
2.		
3.		
Personal Life Stressor	Symptoms This Stressor Is Creating for Me	My Action Plan to Manage This Stressor
1.		
2.		
3.		

Seven days after preparing this work sheet, observe if any of your stress symptoms have diminished. Also, identify those stressors for which only a long-term solution is possible. One student reported that a major work stressor he faced is that he wanted to work in international business, particularly business with Italian fashion companies. Yet he was experiencing stress because he had almost zero knowledge of the Italian language or culture. (By the way, can you offer this man any suggestions?)

LEARNING OBJECTIVE 4

personal productivity

The amount of resources, including time, you consume to achieve a certain level of output.

procrastination

Delaying action for no good reason.

IMPROVING PERSONAL PRODUCTIVITY

Achieving personal productivity is more in vogue than ever. Companies strive to operate with smaller staffs than in the past by pushing workers to achieve higher productivity. At the same time, there is a movement toward simplifying personal life by reducing clutter and cutting back on tasks that do not add much to the quality of life. **Personal productivity** refers to the amount of resources, including time, you consume to achieve a certain level of output. We approach productivity improvement from four perspectives: (1) dealing with procrastination, (2) attitudes and values that enhance personal productivity, (3) work habits and skills that enhance personal productivity, and (4) overcoming time wasters.

Dealing with Procrastination

The person who procrastinates delays action on tasks that need to de done for no good reason. **Procrastination** lowers productivity because it wastes time and many important tasks never get done. Another serious problem is that undone tasks rumble around in the back of your consciousness, thereby decreasing your concentration. Chronic procrastination can even lead to debt, divorce, and job loss.[33] Even productive people sometimes procrastinate. If these people did not procrastinate, they would be even more productive.

Many people regard procrastination as a laughable weakness, particularly because procrastinators themselves joke about the problem. Yet procrastination has been evaluated as a profound, debilitating problem, with about 20 percent of working adults identifying themselves as chronic procrastinators.[34]

Approximately 90 percent of college students report problems with overdue papers and delayed studying. About 25 percent are chronic procrastinators, and many of them drop out of school.[35] The enormity of the procrastination problem makes it worthwhile to examine methods for bringing it under control. Do Self-Assessment Quiz 15-1 to think through your own tendencies toward procrastination—and don't wait until tomorrow.

SELF-ASSESSMENT QUIZ 15-1

Procrastination Tendencies

Directions: Circle yes or no for each item.

1. I usually do my best work under the pressure of deadlines.	Yes	No
2. Before starting a project, I go through such rituals as sharpening every pencil, straightening up my desk more than once, and reading and responding to all possible e-mail.	Yes	No
3. I crave the excitement of the "last-minute rush," such as researching and writing a paper right before the deadline.	Yes	No
4. I often think that if I delay something, it will go away, or the person who asked for it will forget about it.	Yes	No
5. I extensively research something before taking action, such as obtaining three different estimates before getting the brakes repaired on my car.	Yes	No
6. I have a great deal of difficulty getting started on most projects, even those I enjoy.	Yes	No
7. I keep waiting for the right time to do something, such as getting started on an important report.	Yes	No
8. I often underestimate the time needed to do a project, and say to myself, "I can do this quickly, so I'll wait until next week."	Yes	No
9. It is difficult for me to finish most projects or activities.	Yes	No
10. I have several favorite diversions or distractions that I use to keep me from doing something unpleasant, such as a difficult homework assignment.	Yes	No

Total Yes Responses_____

Scoring and Interpretation: The greater the number of "yes" responses, the more likely it is that you have a serious procrastination problem. A score of 8, 9, or 10 strongly suggests that your procrastination is lowering your productivity.

Choose from among the following suggestions for controlling procrastination, based on those that appear to best fit your type of procrastination. A combination of techniques is likely to be the most effective.

1. **Commit to what you want in life.** According to psychology professor Timothy Psychl, if you are not committed to something you want in life, you are likely to be chronic procrastinator. The reason is that it is difficult to prioritize and take action. (See the later discussion about a personal mission and work habits.)[36]

2. **Calculate the cost of procrastination.** You can reduce procrastination by calculating its cost. You might lose out on obtaining a high-paying job you really want by not having your résumé and cover letter ready on time. Your cost of procrastination would include the difference in compensation between the job you do find and the one you really wanted. Another cost would be the loss of potential job satisfaction.

3. **Follow the WIFO principle, which stands for "worst in, first out."** [37] If you tackle the worst task on your list first, doing the other tasks may function like a small reward. You get to do what you dislike the least by doing first what you dislike the most. WIFO is particularly effective when faced with a number of tasks simultaneously.

4. **Break the task into manageable chunks.** To reduce procrastination, cut down a task that seems overwhelming into smaller projects that seem less formidable. If your job calls for preparing an enormous database, begin by assembling some readily available information. Then take the next step by assembling another small segment of the database—perhaps all customers whose last names begin with Z. Think of your task as pulling together a series of small databases that will fit into a master database.

5. **Make a commitment to other people.** Try to make it imperative that you get something done on time by making it a commitment to one or more other people. You might announce to coworkers that you are going to get something accomplished by a certain date. If you fail to meet this date, you are likely to feel embarrassed.

6. **Remove some clutter from your mind.** Procrastination escalates when people have many unfinished projects in the back of their mind, draining their concentration. Too much to do can freeze us into inaction. Just eliminating a few trivial items from your to-do list can give you enough mental energy to overcome procrastination on a few major tasks. Notice carefully that this approach to overcoming procrastination requires that you apply enough self-discipline to take the first step. Notice the unfortunate cycle: procrastination leads to poor concentration (as described above), and procrastination hampers concentration.

7. **Satisfy your stimulation quota in constructive ways.** If you procrastinate because you enjoy the rush of scrambling to make deadlines, find a more constructive way of using busyness to keep you humming. If you need a high level of stimulation, enrich your life with extra projects and learning new skills. The fullness of your schedule will provide you the stimulation you had been receiving from squeezing yourself to make deadlines and reach appointments on time.[38]

8. **Eliminate tangible rewards you are giving yourself for procrastinating.** If you are procrastinating through socializing with coworkers, taking a walk to obtain a beverage, surfing the Internet, or any other pleasant experience—stop rewarding yourself. Just sit alone in your work area doing nothing while procrastinating. If you remove the pleasant activities from your stalling routine, you may be able to reduce procrastination.

Enhancing Personal Productivity through Attitudes and Values
LEARNING OBJECTIVE 5

Developing good work habits and time-management practices is often a matter of developing the right attitudes toward your work and toward time. If, for example, you think that your schoolwork or job is important and that time is a precious resource, you will be on your way toward developing good work habits. In this section, we describe a group of attitudes, values, and beliefs that can help a person become more productive through better use of time and improved work habits.

Begin with a Mission and Goals   A mission, or general purpose, propels you toward being productive. Assume that a person says, "My mission is to be an outstanding professional in my field and a loving, constructive spouse and parent." The mission serves as a compass to direct your activities, such as being well organized in order to accomplish more work and be highly valued by your employer. Goals are more specific than mission statements; they support the mission statement, but the effect is the same. Being committed to a goal also propels you toward good use of time. If you know that you can obtain the position in international business that you really want by mastering a second language, you are likely to work diligently on learning that language. Skill-Building Exercise 15-3 gives you the opportunity to establish a mission statement and supporting goals.

Play the Inner Game of Work   Timothy Gallwey developed the inner game of tennis to help tennis players focus better on their game. Over time the inner game spread to skiing, other sports, life in general, and work. The key concept is that by removing inner obstacles such as self-criticism, you can dramatically improve your ability to focus, learn, and perform. According to Gallwey, two selves exist inside each person. Self 1 is the critical, fearful, self-doubting voice that sends out messages like, "You have almost solved this tough problem for the customer. Don't blow it now." Intimidating comments like these hinder Self 2 from getting the job done. Self 2 encompasses all the inner resources—both actual and potential—of the individual.

Self 1 must be suppressed so Self 2 can accomplish its task and learn effectively without being lectured. The process required to move Self 1 aside is to focus your attention on a critical variable related to performance rather than on the performance you are attempting to achieve. An example would be for a customer service representative to focus on the amount of tension in a caller's voice.[39] Or, you might focus on the facial expressions of your manager as you attempt to sell him or her on an idea for improving productivity.

Work Smarter, Not Harder   People caught up in trying to accomplish a job often wind up working hard, but not in an imaginative way that leads to good results. Much time and energy are therefore wasted. A working-smart approach also requires that you spend a few minutes carefully planning how to implement your task. An example of working smarter, not harder is to invest a few minutes of critical thinking before conducting a tele-

---

SKILL-BUILDING EXERCISE 15-3

Using a Mission Statement and Goals to Power Work Habits

People with a well-defined mission statement and supporting goals tend to have better work habits and time management than those who do not. The following exercise is designed to help you establish a mission statement and goals so you will be energized to be more productive.

A. Mission Statement: To help develop your mission statement, or general purpose in life, ask yourself, "What are my five biggest wishes in life?" These wishes give you a hint to your purpose because they point toward an ideal purpose in life. Feel free to think big, because mission statements tend toward being idealistic.

B. Long-Range Goals to Support Mission Statement: Now write down what long-range goals would support your mission statement. Suppose your mission statement related to "creating a better life for people who are disadvantaged." Your long-range goals might include establishing a foundation that would fund your efforts. You would also need to be successful enough in your career to get the foundation started.

C. Intermediate-Range Goals to Support Long-Range Goals: Write down the intermediate-range goals needed to support the long-range goals. You will probably need to complete your education, obtain broad experience, and identify a lucrative form of self-employment.

D. Weekly Goals to Support Intermediate-Range Goals: Write down what you have to do this week to help you complete your education, such as researching and writing a paper for a particular course, registering for courses for next term, and inquiring about career opportunities in your field.

E. Today's Goals to Support Weekly Goals (My To-Do List): Here's where your lofty purpose in life gets translated into reality. What do you have to do today to get that paper written? Do you need to get your car battery replaced so you can get to the library so you can write your paper, so you can graduate, so you can become rich, so you can ultimately help all those people who are disadvantaged? Get going.

marketing campaign for home replacement windows. Develop a list of homeowners of houses of at least 15 years old. People with relatively new homes are poor prospects for replacing their windows.

A new perspective on working smarter, not harder is to keep perfecting your skills through **deliberate practice**—strong effort to improve target performance over time. Practice alone does not lead to nearly as much improvement as thinking through what you have done to look for areas for improvement.[40] Feedback from others is also helpful. Assume that a loan officer at a bank signs off on loans to small business owners. She engages in deliberate practice by following the history of these loans to evaluate which business owners proved to be good risks, and those that proved to be poor risks. She frequently asks herself, "What did I miss here? What did I do right here?" In this way, the loan officer is working smarter by honing her risk-evaluation skills.

Value Orderliness and Cleanliness   An orderly desk, work area, briefcase, hard drive, or storage drive does not inevitably indicate an orderly mind. Yet it does help most people become more productive because they can better focus their mind. Being surrounded by a collection of small, unfinished tasks interferes with your ability to focus on major tasks. Also, less time is wasted and less energy is expended if you do not have to hunt for information that you thought you had on hand. The central message of the best-seller, *Getting Things Done* by David Allen is that to achieve maximum efficiency and relaxation is to clear clutter both outside and inside your mind.[41] If you are orderly, you clear clutter.

According to time-management consultant Barbara Hemphill, the average person spends 150 hours per year searching for misplaced information. Hemphill says, "Your ability to accomplish any task or goal is directly related to your ability to find the right information at the right time."[42] Knowing where information is and what information you have available is a way of being in control of your job. When your job gets out of control, you are probably working at less than peak efficiency. Valuing cleanliness improves productivity in several ways. According to the Japanese system, cleanliness is the bedrock of quality. Also, after you have thoroughly cleaned your work area, you will usually attain a fresh outlook.

As with any suggestions about human behavior, individual differences exist with respect to the impact of clutter on productivity. Internet guru, Esther Dyson, has a work area so cluttered she resembles a caricature of a person needing help from a personal productivity consultant. It has also been argued that focusing too much on tidiness might detract from creative thinking, and that many messy people, such as Albert Einstein, believe that a messy work area facilitates their creative thinking. To quote the great man, "If a cluttered desk is a sign of a cluttered mind, of what then, is an empty desk?"[43]

Value Good Attendance and Punctuality   Good attendance and punctuality are expected of both experienced and inexperienced employees. You cannot be productive unless you are physically present in your work area. The same principle applies whether you work on company premises or at home. One exception is that some people can work through solutions to job problems while engaged in recreation. Keep in mind, too, that being late for or absent from meetings sends the silent message that you do not regard the meeting as being important.

The relationship of lateness to absenteeism and work performance has been researched. Based on 30 studies and over 9,000 workers, it was found that employees who were late also tended to have high absenteeism records. In addition, employees who were late tended to have poorer work performance than workers who were prompt, but the relationship was not strong.[44] Despite this weak association, being late must still be regarded as a productivity drain.

Attain a Balance in Life and Avoid Being a Workaholic   A productive attitude to maintain is that overwork can lead to negative stress and burnout. Proper physical rest and relaxation can contribute to mental alertness and an improved ability to cope with frustration. Many people do not achieve enough rest and relaxation, as inferred from the fact that more than one half of American workers fail to take all their vacation days.[45] The environmentally induced attention deficit disorder and extreme jobs described earlier represent a life out of balance. A strategy for preventing overwork is to strive for a balance in which you derive satisfaction from various spheres of life. Major spheres in addition to work include family life, romance, sports, the arts and music, faith, and intellectual growth.

A strongly recommended technique for attaining balance between work and other spheres of life is to learn how to say no diplomatically to your boss and family members.[46] For example, your boss might ask you to take on a project when you are already overloaded. It would be necessary to *occasionally* explain that you are so overloaded that you could not do a good job with the new assignment. And, you might have to *occasionally* turn down your family's or friend's request to take a weekend vacation when you face heavy work demands.

Neglecting the normal need for rest and relaxation can lead to **workaholism**, an addiction to work in which not working is an uncomfortable experience. Some types of workaholics are perfectionists who are never satisfied with their work and therefore find it difficult to leave work behind, and have no real hobbies outside of the office. In addition, the perfectionist-type workaholic may become heavily focused on control of people and information, leading to rigid behavior and strained interpersonal relationships. Many workaholics take laptops to bed, and leave their cell phones on during the night to catch any potential calls from distant time zones. However, some people who work long and hard are classified as achievement-oriented workaholics who thrive on hard work and are usually highly productive.[47] For example, a person with strong family values might nevertheless work 65 hours per week for one year while establishing a new business. In contrast, giving up on the income and status you are striving for to avoid working long hours may not be a good idea.

Increase Your Energy   According to Tony Schwartz, the founder of the Energy Project in New York City, increasing your energy is the best way to get more done faster and better. Becoming more energetic leads to more productivity gains than merely working longer hours. Schwartz believes that energy has four wellsprings—the body, emotions, mind, and spirit. Rituals can be established to build energy in the four areas, highlighted as follows:

1. *Body*. Increasing bodily energy closely follows some of the guidelines for stress management described earlier. Proper nutrition, moderate physical exercise, adequate rest, and taking brief breaks from work all enhance a person's energy level.

2. *Emotions*. Positive emotions bring us much more energy than do negative ones. Being in the fight-or-flight mode too frequently lowers emotional energy. Deep abdominal breathing can help ward off negative emotion. A powerful ritual that helps generate positive emotion is to express appreciation to others, following the suggestions for giving recognition presented in Chapter 10. Overcoming the idea that you are a victim can also bring about positive energy.

3. *Mind*. To enhance mental energy, it is particularly important to minimize distractions that lead to constant multitasking. Switching to another task increases the amount of time required to complete the primary tasks by up to 25 percent, a phenomenon know as *switching time*. Dan Cluna, a vice president at Wachovia, designed two rituals to enhance his mental energy by focusing his attention: (1) he leaves his desk to go to a conference room, away from phones and e-mail, when he has a task that requires concentration; (2) during meetings he lets his phone calls go to voice mail so he can focus completely on the person in front of him.

We recognize, however, that you still have to live in a modern world. If you are preparing a report and your boss sends you an urgent IM, or your sick parent or child calls you on your cell phone, it is natural to be distracted away from your primary task. The sensible strategy is to minimize distractions not eliminate them completely.

4. *Spirit*. Participating in activities that give you a sense of meaning and purpose, such as coaching and mentoring others, boosts the energy of the spirit. Being attentive to your deeper needs, such as being concerned about human or animal welfare, can boost your effectiveness and satisfaction on the job.[48]

You may have observed that this energy program for business executives is quite similar to what you have been studying in relation to developing interpersonal skills.

Enhancing Personal Productivity through Work Habits and Skills

Overcoming procrastination and developing the right attitudes contribute to personal productivity. Effective work habits and skills are also essential for high productivity. Six key work habits and skills are described next. They represent a mixture of traditional productivity boosters and those geared toward information technology.

Prepare a To-Do List and Set Priorities   At the heart of every time-management system is list making, whether the list is placed on an index card, in a leather-bound planner, or in a personal digital assistant such as the BlackBerry. As already described, the to-do list is the basic tool for achieving your daily goals, which in turn helps you achieve bigger goals and your mission. Almost every successful person in any field composes a list of important and less important tasks that need to be done. Before you compose a useful list, you need to set aside a few minutes of quiet time every day to sort out the tasks at hand. This is the most basic aspect of planning.

As is well known, it is helpful to set priorities for items on the to-do list. A typical system is to use A to signify critical or essential items, B to signify important items, and C for the least important ones. Although an item might be regarded as a C (for example, emptying the wood shavings from the electronic pencil sharpener), it still makes a contribution to your management of time and sense of well-being. Accomplishing anything reduces some stress. Also, many people obtain satisfaction from crossing off an item on their list, however trivial. If you are at all conscientious, small, unaccomplished items will come back to interfere with your concentration.

To-do lists contribute enormously to productivity, yet a to-do list may have to be revamped to meet the changing demands of the day. Marissa Mayer, vice president of Search Products and User Experience at Google, explains that she keeps a task list in a text file. She uses the list as high-priority things to focus on. "But at Google things can change pretty fast. This morning I had my list of what I thought I was going to do today, but now I'm doing entirely different things," says Mayer.[49] As a result, she quickly prepares a new to-do list.

Time-management consultant Harold Taylor warns that preparing to-do lists should not become an end in itself, with so much time devoted to list making that accomplishing some of the tasks get neglected.[50] Another danger is filling the to-do list with items you would have to accomplish anyway, such as "check e-mail." The to-do list can become so long that it becomes an overwhelming task.

BACK TO THE OPENING CASE

Is Behnke's life crazy? Absolutely. Would she have it any other way? Absolutely not. She says, "When I see an opportunity, I have to go after it." Apparently this small business owner places high priority on both work and personal life. Behnke out- sources her housekeeping and she schedules her occasional out-of-town trips for the seven consecutive days every month that her husband is at home.[51]

Streamline Your Work and Emphasize Important Tasks   As companies continue to operate with fewer workers than in the past despite prosperity, more unproductive work must be eliminated. Getting rid of unproductive work is part of *business process improvement* in which work processes are radically redesigned and simplified. Every employee is expected to get rid of work that does not contribute to productivity or help customers. In general, to streamline your work, look for duplication of effort and waste. An example of duplication of effort would be to routinely send people e-mail and voice mail messages covering the same topic. An example of waste would be to call a meeting for disseminating information that could easily be communicated by e-mail.

Emphasizing important tasks means that you make sure to take care of A items on your to-do list. It also implies that you seek to accomplish a few work activities that, if done well, would make a big difference in your job performance. Although important tasks may take less time to accomplish than many routine tasks, they can represent the difference between success and failure. Five minutes of telephone conversation with a major customer might do more good for your company than three hours of arranging obsolete inventory in the warehouse.

Concentrate on One Important Task at a Time Instead of Multitasking   While working on important tasks, concentrate on what you are doing. Effective executives and professionals have a well-developed capacity to concentrate on the problem or person facing them, however surrounded they are with other obligations. Intense concentration leads to crisper judgment and analysis and also minimizes major errors. Another useful by-product of concentration is that it helps reduce absentmindedness. If you really concentrate on what you are doing, the chances diminish that you will forget what you intended to do.

As you are concentrating on an important task, such as performing analytical work or writing a report, avoid multitasking, or performing more than one activity simultaneously. Common forms of multitasking include surfing the Internet or reading e-mail while engaged in a phone conversation with a coworker or customer. Both experimental evidence and opinion has accumulated that multitasking while performing important tasks leads to problems in concentration, along with significant errors—for most people. The information about mental energy described earlier applies here. Multitasking on routine tasks has less negative consequences, and can sometimes be a legitimate time saver.

David E. Meyer, the director of the Brain, Cognition and Action Laboratory at the University of Michigan, notes that when people attempt to perform two or more related tasks at the same time or alternating rapidly—instead of doing them sequentially—two negative consequences occur. Errors increase substantially, and the amount of time to perform the task may double.[52] Also, according to new research about the brain, few people can concentrate on more than four tasks at once.[53]

Personal finance advisor and television personality Suze Orman is a strong advocate of avoiding multitasking when doing serious work. She prides herself on her ability to focus on one thing at a time and adhere to her agenda. She says, "The people who multitask, I think, do everything to mediocrity at best. While they are getting a lot done, they are getting it done in such an inefficient way that they usually have to do it over again."[54]

Place the potential dangers of multitasking on a personal level. Would you want a cardiac surgeon to operate on a loved one while she was receiving personal calls on her cell phone? Would you want your commercial airline pilot to be sending text messages to "friends" on a social network while he was flying through a storm?

Stay in Control of Paperwork and Electronic Work   Although it is fashionable to complain about paperwork in responsible jobs, the effective career person does not neglect paperwork. (Paperwork includes electronic work such as electronic mail and voice mail.) Paperwork involves taking care of administrative details such as correspondence, invoices, human resource reports, expense reports, and inventory forms. A considerable amount of electronic work results in paperwork because many e-mail messages and attachments wind up being printed. Unless paperwork and electronic work are attended to, a person's job may get out of control. A small amount of time should be invested in paperwork every day. Nonprime time (when you are at less than your peak of efficiency but not overfatigued) is the best time to take care of paperwork.

An effective technique is to respond quickly to high-priority e-mail messages, and permanently delete those you will most likely not need to refer to again. Print and file only those e-mail messages of high importance to avoid being overwhelmed with piles of old messages.

Communicating by e-mail or telephone with coworkers in distant time zones creates special challenges in terms of staying in control of electronic work. Assume that Pedro working in Washington, DC, has clients in London who want to have telephone conferences at 9 A.M. their time. Pedro has to be on the phone at 3 A.M. his time, so it is best to make all his 3 A.M. calls one morning per week rather than having a life out of control because he has to be on the phone many days at 3 A.M.

Work Productively from Your Home Office or Virtual Office   A growing segment of the workforce works either full- or part-time from home or from a **virtual office**. Estimates vary considerably, but it appears that about 4 percent of corporate employees work primarily from the home. Such an office is a place of work without a fixed physical location from which the worker or workers communicate their output electronically. A virtual office might be in a car, train, airplane, or hotel room; on a park bench; or wherever the worker happens to be at the time. Many people adapt well to working at home and from virtual offices because they are self-starters and self-disciplined. Many other workers lack the self-discipline and effective work habits necessary to be productive outside of a traditional office. The following is a list of representative suggestions for being productive while working independently.[55]

virtual office

A place of work without a fixed physical location, where the output is communicated electronically.

- Act as if you work in a traditional office. Set specific working hours, get dressed, go outside the house for a few minutes, then return and get to work. Also, close your office at home or virtual office at some regular time. Otherwise, you are open for business all the time. If you work at home, establish a clear workspace and let your family and friends know when you cannot be disturbed.

- Stay in touch with teammates to enhance your team player skills and not lose out on important information that could lower your effectiveness (such as missing an appointment at the traditional office). Stay in touch with other workers also, such as visiting an office supply store or attending networking meetings. In this way you will feel less isolated from the workforce—assuming feeling isolated is a problem for you.

- Minimize conducting your personal life at the same time as working (for example, working while watching television, talking to neighbors, or shopping over the Internet).

- Schedule regular times for meals and snacks; otherwise, you will lose many minutes and gain many pounds taking food and beverage breaks.

The practice of working at home or from virtual offices is increasing rapidly, so these suggestions merit careful consideration. Several of the productivity ideas also fit the conventional office.

Enhance Your Internet Search Skills   An important job skill is searching the Internet for a variety of information. It follows that if you develop your Internet search skills, you will be more productive by obtaining the results you need within a reasonable time. First, it is helpful to rely on several search engines to seek needed information. Several meta-search engines claim to be so comprehensive that no other engine is required. Such claims are exaggerated, because the same search word entered into several different comprehensive engines will reveal a different list of sources.

Second, give careful thought to the search word or phrase you use. The more specific you are, the better. Assume that you want to find software to enhance your productivity, and that you enter the word *software* into a search engine. You will probably receive a message indicating that 115 million entries have been located in response to your personal inquiry. You are better advised to use the search phrase *software for increasing personal productivity*.

Third, for many searches, framing the query as a phrase by enclosing it in quotation marks refines the number of hits (or sites) returned. Place quotation marks before and after the search word, such as "software for improving work habits." Fourth, if you don't find what you want in your initial search, reframe your question in another way or change the terms. How about *"software for time management"* or *"computer programs for increasing personal efficiency"*? Skill-Building Exercise 15-4 will help you make better use of the Internet to enhance your personal productivity.

Overcoming Time Wasters

Another basic thrust to improve personal productivity is to minimize wasting time. The average worker wastes 1.7 hours of a typical 8.5-hour workday, according to an informal survey by Salary.com.[56] Many of the techniques already described in this chapter help save time, such as eliminating nonessential work. Whether or not an activity is a time

Productivity Boosting Through Work Habits

The chapter has already given you ideas about using work habits to increase productivity. Here is a chance to make some personal applications of your own. Gather into small teams or work individually to identify 10 ways in which good work habits, as well as using the Internet, can increase personal productivity either on the job or at home. To supplement your own thinking, you might search the Internet for ideas on how the Internet is supposed to boost productivity.

waster depends on the purpose of the activity. Suppose you play computer solitaire for 10 minutes to reduce stress and then return to work refreshed. In contrast, another worker who spends 10 minutes playing solitaire just for fun is wasting time.

Figure 15-7 presents a list of common time wasters. Being aware of time wasters will help sensitize you to the importance of minimizing them. Even if you saved just 10 minutes per workday, the productivity gain over a year could be enormous.

FIGURE 15-7 Ways to Prevent and Overcome Time Wasting

1. Use a time log for two weeks to track time wasters. (See Skill-Building Exercise 15-5.)

2. Minimize daydreaming on the job by forcing yourself to concentrate.

3. Avoid the computer as a diversion from work, such as sending jokes back and forth to work members, playing video games, and checking out recreational Web sites during working hours.

4. Cluster together tasks such as returning phone calls or responding to e-mail messages. For example, in most jobs it is possible to be polite and productive by reserving two or three 15-minute periods per day for taking care of e-mail correspondence.

5. Socialize on the job just enough to build your network. Chatting with coworkers is a major productivity drain.

6. Be prepared for meetings by, for example, having a clear agenda and sorting through the documents you will be referring to. Make sure electronic equipment is in working order before attempting to use it during the meeting.

7. Keep track of important names, places, and things to avoid wasting time searching for them.

8. Set a time limit for tasks after you have done them once or twice.

9. Prepare a computer template for letters and computer documents that you send frequently. (The template is essentially a form letter, especially with respect to the salutation and return address.)

10. When you arrive at work, be ready to get started working immediately. Greet people quickly, avoid checking your personal e-mail, and shut off your cell phone.

11. Take care of as much e-mail correspondence as you can after you have finished your other work, unless a key part of your job is dealing with e-mail. It consumes substantial time.

12. Avoid perfectionism, which leads you to keep redoing a project. Let go and move on to another project.

13. Make use of bits of time—for instance, five minutes between appointments. Invest those five minutes in sending a work-related e-mail message or revising your to-do list.

14. Minimize procrastination, the number one time waster for most people.

15. Avoid spreading yourself too thin by doing too many things at once, such as having one project too many to handle. When you are overloaded, time can be wasted because of too many errors.

16. Manage interruptions by letting coworkers know when you are available for consultation, and when you need to work independently—except for emergencies. Respond to instant messages only if your job requires responding immediately. Batch your instant messages just as you would other e-mails.

Sources: Suggestions 4, 5, and 6 are based on Stephen R. Covey with Hyrum Smith, "What If You Could Chop an Hour from Your Day for Things That Matter Most?" *USA Weekend,* January 22–24, 1999, pp. 4–5; Suggestion 10 is from Anita Bruzzese, "Tips to Avoid Wasting Time," Gannet News Service, August 9, 2004. Support for suggestion 13 is found in Vince Thompson, "Make the Most of Your White Space," jobs@UpLadder. com, October 3, 2007. Data about the productivity drain of interruptions are analyzed in Quintus R. Jett and Jennifer M. George, "Work Interrupted: A Closer Look at the Role of Interruptions in Organizational Life," *Academy of Management Review,* July 2003, pp. 494–507.

Maintaining a Time Log

An effective starting point to avoid wasting time is to identify how you spend the 168 hours you have each week (24 hours × 7 days). For two weeks, catalog all the time you spend, down to as much detail as you can tolerate. Include the large obvious items, as well as the small items that are easy to forget. Keep track of any activity that requires at least five minutes. Major items would include working, attending class, studying, reading, watching television, sleeping, eating, going places, time with loved ones and friends (hanging out). Small items would include visiting the coffee shop or vending machine, purchasing gum, and clipping your nails. If you multitask, such as walking and listening to music, do not double-count the time.

When your time logs have been completed, search for complete wastes of time, or activities that could be shortened. You might find, for example, that you spend about 45 minutes per day in the pursuit and consumption of coffee. If you reduced that time to 30 minutes you would have an additional 15 minutes per day that you could invest in your career. However, if coffee time includes forming alliances with people or maintaining relationships, maybe the 45-minute-per-day investment is worthwhile.

To analyze whether you might be wasting time, do Skill-Building Exercise 15-5. Self-Assessment Quiz 15-2 gives you an opportunity to think through your tendencies toward a subtle type of time wasting.

Tendencies toward Perfectionism

Directions: Many perfectionists hold some of the behaviors and attitudes described below. To help understand your tendencies toward perfectionism, rate how strongly you agree with each of the statements below on a scale of 0 to 4 by circling the appropriate number. 0 means disagree, 4 means agree.

1. Many people have told me that I am a perfectionist.	0	1	2	3	4
2. I often correct the speech of others.	0	1	2	3	4
3. It takes me a long time to write an e-mail because I keep checking and rechecking my writing.	0	1	2	3	4
4. I often criticize the color combinations my friends are wearing.	0	1	2	3	4
5. When I purchase food at a supermarket, I usually look at the expiration date so I can purchase the freshest.	0	1	2	3	4
6. I can't stand when people use the term *remote* instead of *remote control*, or *cell* instead of *cell phone*.	0	1	2	3	4
7. If a company representative asked me, "What is your *social*?" I would reply with something like, "Do you mean my *social security number*?"	0	1	2	3	4
8. I hate to see dust on furniture.	0	1	2	3	4
9. I like the Martha Stewart idea of having every decoration in the home just right.	0	1	2	3	4
10. I never put a map back in the glove compartment until it is folded just right.	0	1	2	3	4
11. Once an eraser on a pencil of mine becomes hard and useless, I throw away the pencil.	0	1	2	3	4
12. I adjust all my watches and clocks so they show exactly the same time.	0	1	2	3	4
13. It bothers me that clocks on personal computers are often wrong by a few minutes.	0	1	2	3	4
14. I clean the keyboard on my computer at least every other day.	0	1	2	3	4
15. I organize my e-mail messages and computer documents into many different, clearly labeled files.	0	1	2	3	4
16. You won't find old coffee cups or soft drink containers on my desk.	0	1	2	3	4
17. I rarely start a new project or assignment until I have completed my present project or assignment.	0	1	2	3	4
18. It is very difficult for me to concentrate when my work area is disorganized.	0	1	2	3	4

(Continued)

19. Cobwebs in chandeliers and other lighting fixtures bother me.	0	1	2	3	4
20. It takes me a long time to make a purchase such as a digital camera because I keep studying the features on various models.	0	1	2	3	4
21. When I balance my checkbook, it usually comes out right within a few dollars.	0	1	2	3	4
22. I carry enough small coins and dollar bills with me so when I shop I can pay the exact amount without requiring change back.	0	1	2	3	4
23. I throw out any underwear or T-shirts that have even the smallest holes or tears.	0	1	2	3	4
24. I become upset with myself if I make a mistake.	0	1	2	3	4
25. When a fingernail of mine is broken or chipped, I fix it as soon as possible.	0	1	2	3	4
26. I am carefully groomed whenever I leave my home.	0	1	2	3	4
27. When I notice packaged goods or cans on the floor in a supermarket, I will often place them back on the shelf.	0	1	2	3	4
28. I think that carrying around antibacterial cleaner for the hands is an excellent idea.	0	1	2	3	4
29. If I am with a friend, and he or she has a loose hair on the shoulder, I will remove it without asking.	0	1	2	3	4
30. I am a perfectionist.	0	1	2	3	4

Total Score: _____

Scoring and Interpretation: Add the numbers you circled to obtain your total score.

91 or over: You have strong perfectionist tendencies to the point that it could interfere with your taking quick action when necessary. Also, you may annoy many people with your perfectionism.

61–90: You have a moderate degree of perfectionism that could lead you to produce high-quality work and be a dependable person.

31–60: You have a mild degree of perfectionism. You might be a perfectionist in some situations quite important to you, but not in others.

0–30: You are not a perfectionist. You might be too casual about getting things done right,

SELF-ASSESSMENT QUIZZES IN OVERVIEW

Self-Assessment Quiz 15-1 measures tendencies toward procrastination. Thinking about the extent of your procrastination, and overcoming excessive amounts, can help you develop career thrust. You might be able to get by procrastinating small tasks, but delaying the completion of large, complex tasks like preparing a budget or developing a report about customer service will eventually result in low performance. Self-Assessment Quiz 15-2 measures perfectionism, which in large doses can lead to procrastination and not getting things done. However, like fat in the diet, a healthy dose of perfectionism is an asset because it can lead to high levels of performance. Oprah Winfrey and Donald Trump are both perfectionists without being obsessed over details.

Concept Review and Reinforcement

Key Terms

corporate athletes, 319
stress, 319
stressor, 319
fight-or-flight response, 320
hindrance stressors, 321
challenge stressors, 321
burnout, 322

perceived control, 323
Type A behavior, 323
negative affectivity, 323
role overload, 324
extreme job, 324
role ambiguity, 324
carpal tunnel syndrome, 325

support network, 327
personal productivity, 330
procrastination, 330
deliberate practice, 333
workaholism, 334
virtual office, 337

Summary of Key Concepts

A major challenge facing any worker who wants to stay healthy and have good interpersonal relationships is to manage stress effectively. Individual differences play a big role in determining whether an event will lead to stress. The physiological changes that take place within the body in response to stress are responsible for most of the stress symptoms. The fight-or-flight response is the battle against the stressor.

The activation of hormones, such as cortisol, when the body has to cope with a stressor produces short-term physiological reactions, including an increase in heart rate and blood pressure. When stress levels rarely subside, the physiological changes create damage. People under continual negative stress age quickly. However, the right amount of stress (challenge stressors) prepares us for meeting difficult challenges and improves performance. An optimum level of stress exists for most people and most tasks. In general, performance tends to be best under moderate amounts of stress.

One of the major problems of prolonged stress is that it may lead to burnout, a condition of emotional, mental, and physical exhaustion in response to long-term stressors. Burnout also creates cynicism and a distancing from tasks and people. Workers who perceive the cause of burnout to be external are more likely to become less committed to the firm and more cynical. Burnout also damages the physical health of workers.

Four personality factors predisposing people toward stress are low perceived control, low self-efficacy, Type A behavior and hostility, and negative affectivity. The heart attack triggers associated with Type A behavior are hostility, anger, cynicism, and suspiciousness, with hostility having the biggest impact. Four frequently encountered job stressors are role overload, role conflict and ambiguity, adverse environmental conditions including carpal tunnel syndrome and long commutes, environmentally induced attention deficit disorder, and job insecurity.

Managing stress refers to controlling stress by making it become a constructive force in your life. Coping with, or managing, stress includes hundreds of activities, with substantial individual differences in which technique is effective. Eight representative stress-management methods are to eliminate or modify the stressor, get appropriate physical exercise, rest sufficiently, maintain a healthy diet, build a support network, practice visualization and meditation, and practice everyday methods of stress reduction.

Achieving high personal productivity on the job is more in demand than ever. A starting point in improving productivity is to minimize procrastination, an enormous problem for many people that can be approached as follows: Commit to what you want in life; calculate the cost of procrastination; follow the worst in, first out (WIFO) principle; break the task into manageable chunks; make a commitment to other people; remove some clutter from your mind; satisfy your stimulation quota in constructive ways; and eliminate rewards for procrastinating.

Developing good work habits and time-management practices is often a matter of developing the right attitudes toward your work and toward time, as follows: (1) begin with a mission and goals; (2) play the inner game of work, (3) work smarter, not harder including the use of deliberate practice (4) value orderliness and cleanliness; (5) value good attendance and punctuality; (6) attain a balance in life and avoid being a workaholic, and increase your energy (body, emotions, mind, and spirit).

Effective work habits and skills are essential for high productivity, including the following: (1) Prepare a to-do list and set priorities; (2) streamline your work and emphasize important tasks; (3) concentrate on one important task at a time instead of multitasking; (4) stay in control of paperwork and electronic work; (5) work productively from your home office or virtual office; and (6) enhance your Internet search skills.

Another basic thrust to improved personal productivity is to minimize time wasting. Whether or not an activity is a time waster depends on its purpose. Being aware of time wasters such as those presented in Figure 15-6 will sensitize you to the importance of minimizing them.

Check Your Understanding

1. Why might it be true that people who love their work live much longer than people who retire early because they dislike working?

2. Why might having your stress under control improve your interpersonal relationships?

3. What would be the advantages and disadvantages of an *extreme job* for you?

4. Interview a person in a high-pressure job in any field. Find out whether the person experiences significant stress and what method he or she uses to cope with it.

5. Provide an example from your own or somebody else's life of how having a major goal in life can help a person be better organized.

6. Executives at Toyota, among many other Japanese companies, emphasize that clean work areas in the factory enhance productivity. What might explain this relationship between cleanliness and productivity?

7. Describe any way in which you have used IT to make you more productive.

8. Use information in this chapter to explain how a person might be well organized yet still not get very far in his or her career.

9. For many young corporate professionals, a date often consists of the two people getting together in his or her place to spend three hours doing office work on their laptop computers, followed by a take-out meal. What is your evaluation of this approach to boosting personal productivity?

10. Ask an experienced high-level worker to identify his or her most effective method of time management. How effective do you think this technique would be for you?

The Web Corner

http://www.theinnergame.com
(The inner game of work, sports, and team building.)

http://www.stress.org
(Institute for Stress Management.)

http://stress.about.com
(Considerable information about stress plus several self-quizzes.)

http://ub-counseling.buffalo.edu/stressprocrast. shtml
(Overcoming procrastination for students.)

Internet Skill Builder: Getting Personal Help from Your Employer

Use your favorite search engines to learn about Employee Assistance Programs (EAPs). After visiting several sites, answer these questions: (1) What type of help can an employee expect to receive from an EAP? (2) How does an EAP help with stress management? (3) Does the EAP counselor typically tell the company the nature of the problem facing the employee who sought assistance? (4) What benefits do companies expect from offering an EAP to employees? (5) What would I tell the company if I needed help with problems that are causing me severe stress?

Internet Skill Builder: What Are You Doing with Your Time?

Go to *http://www.getmoredone.com/tabulator.html* to find the Pace Productivity Tabulator. This interactive module enables you to enter the time you spend on 11 major activities (such as employment, eating, sleeping, and television watching) and compare your profile to others. You are also able to enter your ideal profile to see where you would like to be. You just follow the straightforward instructions. After arriving at your personal pie chart, ask yourself, "What have I learned that will enhance my personal productivity?"

Developing Your
Human Relations Skills

Interpersonal Relations Case 15.1

Rachel Runs the Treadmill

At 6:30 Tuesday morning, 38-year-old Rachel Mendez hops out of her bed while her husband Ben Mendez is still sleeping. Rachel's first stop is to wake up her nine-year-old daughter, and encourage her to start getting ready to meet the school bus on time. By 8 A.M. Rachel is in her car and on her way to her job as a business development specialist for a human resource outsourcing company. Her primary responsibility is to entice small- and medium-size companies to turn over most of their human resource functions to her firm.

Just as Rachel begins to manage her e-mail and plan her agenda for the day, she places her right hand about three inches to the right of her heart. Rachel can feel the tightness next to her heart, and in her left arm. She thinks to herself, "This feels like I'm going to have a heart attack, but it doesn't make sense for a woman my age to be a heart attack victim. But I'm happy that I have an appointment at the cardiology center on Thursday."

At the North Side Cardiology Center, Rachel is first interviewed by nurse practitioner Janet Trudeau before her interview with Dr. Harry Ching, the cardiologist. Trudeau first took a brief medical history, followed by an interview. Parts of the interview with Trudeau went as follows:

Trudeau: So tell me in more detail why you came to visit our cardiology center.

Mendez: I have these annoying chest pains next to my heart and in my left arm. The pains usually start when I am extremely aggravated and frustrated. I have the pains about once a day.

Trudeau: Do you ever faint or become light-headed during the pains?

Mendez: No, my problem is just the pains. I keep doing whatever I'm doing when the pain hits.

Trudeau: Tell me about the situations you find so aggravating and frustrating.

Mendez: I'm really stressing out. I have a ton of aggravations and worries. To begin, my nine-year-old daughter Samantha has seizures. She is under treatment but the problem remains, and it's worrisome. I worry every day that Samantha will have a seizure and strike her head or get involved in an accident.

My work is also quite worrisome. I work mostly on commission selling human resource services. Our business has grown rapidly in the last few years, but we have kind of dried up the territory. I have to travel more to find new clients. My earnings are taking a turn downward despite the extra travel.

Trudeau: Are you the sole breadwinner in the family?

Mendez: No, my husband Alex is an assistant manager at a Ruby Tuesday restaurant, and he makes a modest living. But talking about aggravation, my husband is a decent guy but he gives me chest pains. I think he cares much more about professional sports, especially the NFL and the NHL, than he does about Samantha and me. If he's watching a game, I can forget about talking about something serious.

And then, of course, Alex works the hours of a restaurant manager, which means that he's often working when I am not working, like on Saturdays and Sundays.

Trudeau: Any other major aggravations in your life?

Mendez: Yes, commuting on busy highways. I can feel my chest pains starting when I think of sitting still for 15 minutes during rush-hour traffic.

Trudeau: Thank you, Rachel. I will be studying this information before your interview with Dr. Ching. Have a seat in the waiting room. He will be with you in about 10 minutes.

Later that day, Mendez had an extensive cardiology exam, including an electrocardiogram. Dr. Ching informed her that despite the muscle tension she was experiencing, her heart was in excellent condition.

Case Questions

1. What sources of stress does Rachel Mendez appear to be facing?
2. What do you recommend Mendez do about the stressors she is facing?
3. Given that Mendez does not have a heart problem, should she be concerned about the stressors in her life? Explain your answer.

The Extreme Job Firefighter

Jim Blaesi brings a strange mix to the world of work—he's an entrepreneur and a civil servant, a risk taker with a good pension and benefits package. But Blaesi, 32, a full-time Rochester, New York firefighter who owns an automotive repair shop on Hudson Avenue in the inner city, just sees himself as a guy who gets to do what he loves—even if it requires 80 to 100 hours a week.

"I kissed my wife goodbye yesterday and said 'I'll see you Friday,'" Blaesi said Tuesday. "But, you know, my accountant told me, 'The majority of people in life don't get to chase one of their dreams. You get to chase both of yours.'"

The son, grandson, and nephew of firefighters who developed an interest in mechanics at a young age, Blaesi opened Blaesi Automotive in 2000 when he was actively seeking a job as a city firefighter. He was hired in 2002, eight years after his submitted his first application.

It's not unusual for firefighters to own small businesses or hold second jobs because half their shifts are at night and the weekly rotation creates three and four-day "weekends" that often fall on weekdays. "It's a combination of a schedule that allows you to concentrate hours with a career that attracts high energy people," said Fire Capt. Dan McBride.

Blaesi, who has two full-time employees, works at his shop on his days off or when he's on the night shift. When he works days, he puts in a few hours of shop time in the later afternoon before taking his paperwork home for the night.

He works at a firehouse located hear the shop, so he often goes days at a time without seeing his suburban home. He and his wife Gina don't have children yet, and she has a full-time job as a tax specialist at Paychex, a national payroll and human resource services firm. "I love her to death because we're just getting to know each other," Blaesi said of his wife of four years.

Blaesi said he started working as a mechanic's apprentice for a friend's car dealership when he was 14. In high school he worked for oil-change and tune-up franchises and advanced to auto dealerships and a truck-rental company.

He started exploring the option of owning his own shop in the late 1990s and discovered a two-lift garage for sale on Hudson Avenue. Located in a part of the city known for high rates of crime and poverty, Blaesi remembers how his friends told him he was crazy to buy the shop. But at a price of $120,000 for more than 9,000 square feet, Blaesi saw an opportunity that other locations didn't offer. "It would cost you two, two and one-half million dollars in a suburb," he said. In the years since he opened the shop, Blaesi has paid off the original loan and invested about $400,000 to expand the job to seven lifts.

Blaesi said he's making a profit with a strong client base that includes the fleets of several government agencies. Because he and his wife have good-paying jobs, he's been able to invest all the profit from his shop back into the business. Upgrades have also included a striking red-and-silver façade that stands out in an area with many vacant storefronts and rundown buildings. Blaesi designed the exterior himself, using the look of firehouses as an influence.

Blaesi, who said he may soon hire two more employees, is content to move slowly for now. He might soon buy more property in the neighborhood to build a parking lot large enough to open a towing service. He's also thinking of other real estate ventures. And of course, plans are in the works with his wife to grow a family.

"I'm always looking for the next adventure," he said.

Case Questions

1. What advice can you offer Jim Blaesi about achieving balance in his life?
2. In what way does it appear that Blaesi might be making good use of contacts?
3. What is your evaluation of Blaesi's personal productivity?
4. Why might Blaesi's work be considered an *extreme job*?
5. What advice might you offer Blaesi's wife?

Source: Adapted from Patrick Flanigan, "Risk Taker Builds Business with Patience, Planning," *Rochester Democrat and Chronicle*, November 8, 2007, pp. 8D, 9D

CHAPTER 16

Job Search and Career Management Skills

Ellis Rowe, Group President, Mars Drinks Group and Mars Developing Pet Care, at age 54, was interviewed by *Black Enterprise*, about his career. A portion of the interview follows:

BE: You've been in a manufacturing role, moved into information systems, then finance. You were responsible for all pet care and snack foods factories in North America, held a corporate staff officer role in finance, were general manager of the confectionary business, and held a corporate HR role. You attribute your varied career in almost 30 years at Mars Inc., where you've had more than 20 staff and line jobs crossing many function areas, to your internal network. [Staff jobs are support positions, whereas line jobs deal with the primary purpose of the business, such as manufacturing.]

ER: An internal network allows you to connect with individuals who can influence your career as well as guide you through opportunities that you might not otherwise be aware of. Internal networking is building a wall brick by brick. You can start on the foundation level, and if you're with the business for a while, you just keep adding bricks until one day you have a wall.

BE: How can executives build internal networks?

ER: They need to identify where they want their careers to go and the people who can help them get there. If you want something, you have to move toward it. To do that, you have to find a way to add value, whether it's exchanging information or identifying what you can do to help that person—be it a colleague or someone senior to you. We work in teams in our business, and if you help your team and individuals on the team succeed, they can support you in building your career.

After reading and studying this chapter and doing the exercises, you should be able to

1. Acquire new insights into conducting a job search, including writing an impressive cover letter, preparing a résumé, and being interviewed.

2. Describe the difference between a vertical and a horizontal career path.

3. Identify a handful of career-enhancing strategies and tactics you intend to use.

You become a senior person in business not because of time but because you've built relationships with individuals of influence who recognize that value you can add. In your career, there'll be opportunities that you'll want to be considered for. The best way is to not have to interview for those jobs but to be considered by people who want you on their team.[1]

As the experience of the business executive just described suggests, being systematic about advancing your career can pay big dividends. In this case, the person effectively capitalized on internal networks. This final chapter of the book focuses on career success, including a description of strategies and tactics that will help you gain advantage.

Our approach to achieving career success is divided into three major segments: conducting a job campaign, understanding two major types of career paths, and using career advancement strategies and tactics. The previous 15 chapters also deal with topics and skills that facilitate success. However, the information presented in this chapter is more specifically about managing your career.

CONDUCTING A JOB SEARCH

The vast majority of workers have to conduct a job search at various times in their careers. Job searches are conducted to find employment in a firm the job seeker is not already working for, or sometimes to find a new position within one's own firm. When job openings are on short supply, job search skills are especially important. Even during the most prosperous of times, when jobs are in ample supply, learning more about conducting a job search is useful. It can help you land an excellent position. Included in the job search are job-hunting tactics and preparing a résumé and cover letter.

LEARNING OBJECTIVE 1

Job-Hunting Tactics

Most people already have usable knowledge about how to find a job. Some of the ideas discussed next will therefore be familiar; some will be unfamiliar. We recommend using this list of tactics as a checklist to ensure that you have not neglected something important. Also, it is important to search for employment systematically. It is easy to overlook the obvious when job hunting because your emotions may cloud your sense of logic.

Identify Your Job Objectives An effective job search begins with a clear perception of what kind of position (or positions) you want. If you express indecision about the type of work you seek, the prospective employer will typically ask in a critical tone, "What kind of work are you looking for?" Your chances of finding suitable employment increase when several different types of positions will satisfy your job objectives. Assume that one person who majored in business administration is only willing to accept a position as an office manager in a corporation. Another person with the same major is seeking a position as (1) an office manager; (2) a management trainee in a corporation; (3) an assistant manager in a retail store, restaurant, or hotel; (4) a sales representative; (5) an assistant purchasing agent; or (6) a management analyst. The second person has a much better chance of finding a suitable position.

Be Aware of Qualifications Sought by Employers What you are looking for in an employer must be matched against what an employer is looking for in an employee. If you are aware of what employers are seeking, you can emphasize those aspects of yourself when applying for a position. For example, applicants for almost any type of position should emphasize their IT skills. Job interviewers and hiring managers do not all agree on the qualifications they seek in employees. Nevertheless, a number of traits, characteristics, skills, and accomplishments are important to many employers. Self-Assessment Quiz 16-1 summarizes these qualifications in a way that you can apply to yourself as you think about your job hunt.

SELF-ASSESSMENT QUIZ 16-1

Qualifications Sought by Employers

Directions: The following is a list of qualifications widely sought by prospective employers. After reading each qualification, rate yourself on a 1 to 5 scale by circling the appropriate number: 1 = very low, 2 = low, 3 = average, 4 = high, 5 = very high.

1. Appropriate education for the position under consideration and satisfactory grades	1	2	3	4	5
2. Relevant work experience	1	2	3	4	5
3. Communication and other interpersonal skills	1	2	3	4	5
4. Motivation and energy	1	2	3	4	5
5. Problem-solving ability (intelligence) and creativity	1	2	3	4	5
6. Judgment and common sense	1	2	3	4	5
7. Adaptability to change	1	2	3	4	5
8. Emotional maturity (acting professionally and responsibly)	1	2	3	4	5
9. Teamwork (ability and interest in working in a team effort)	1	2	3	4	5
10. Positive attitude (enthusiasm about work and initiative)	1	2	3	4	5
11. Emotional intelligence (ability to deal with own feelings and those of others)	1	2	3	4	5
12. Customer service orientation (wanting to meet customer needs)	1	2	3	4	5
13. Information technology skills	1	2	3	4	5
14. Willingness to continue to study and learn about the job, company, and industry	1	2	3	4	5
15. Likableness and sense of humor	1	2	3	4	5
16. Dependability, responsibility, and conscientiousness (including good work habits and time management)	1	2	3	4	5
17. Willingness and ability to work well with coworkers and customers from different cultures	1	2	3	4	5
18. Behaves ethically toward customers and company employees and obeys laws and regulations	1	2	3	4	5

Interpretation: Consider engaging in some serious self-development, training, and education for items on which you rated yourself low or very low. If you accurately rated yourself as 4 or 5 on all the dimensions, you are an exceptional job candidate.

Identify Your Skills and Potential Contribution The job market has been skill based for some time. Employers typically seek out job candidates with tangible skills (including interpersonal skills) that can be put to immediate use in accomplishing work. Job-relevant skills you might identify include IT skills, written communication skills, oral communication skills, math skills, and listening skills. The cornerstone of a job search should be a thorough list of assets and accomplishments, because they point to useful skills and abilities you can use to help the employer.

A successful candidate for a customer service position at a telecommunications company told the interviewer, "I know I can help your customers with their software and hardware problems. I worked at the technical support center at college, and my friends and family members are forever coming to me with their computer problems. I even get long-distance calls for help. Give me a chance to help your customers." (Notice that the candidate implied that he or she had good listening skills.)

Develop a Comprehensive Marketing Strategy A vital job-finding strategy is to use multiple approaches to reach the right prospective employer. This is particularly true when the position you seek is in short supply. Among the many approaches employers use to recruit candidates are employee referrals, newspaper ads, job boards, employer Web sites, social networking Web sites, college and professional school recruitment, job fairs, temporary help firms, walk-ins, unsolicited résumés and phone calls, and government employment services.

Use Networking to Reach Company Insiders The majority of successful job campaigns stem from personal contacts. Employers rely heavily on referrals from employees to fill positions, even though many good positions are also announced publicly, such as through Web sites and classified ads. In regard to job hunting, networking is contacting friends and acquaintances and building systematically on these relationships to create a still wider set of contacts that might lead to employment. Formal mechanisms to develop network contacts have been introduced in recent years, such as bar parties in metropolitan areas devoted just to making job contacts.

Figure 16-1 presents a list of potential network contacts. In addition, a skill-building exercise about networking as a method of career advancement, including a job search, is presented toward the end of this chapter.

The networking technique is so well known today that it suffers from overuse. It is therefore important to use a tactful, low-key approach with a contact. For example, instead of asking a person in your network to furnish you a job lead, ask that person how someone with qualifications similar to yours might find a job. In addition, guard against taking up a large portion of a busy person's workday, for instance, by insisting on a luncheon meeting.

FIGURE 16-1 Potential Sources of Network Contacts

- Coworkers and previous employers
- Friends and neighbors
- Faculty and staff
- Graduates of any schools you have attended
- Former employers
- Present employers (assuming you hold a temporary position)
- Professional workers such as bankers, brokers, and clergy
- Political leaders at the local level
- Members of your club or athletic team
- Community groups, churches, temples, and mosques
- Trade and professional associations
- Student professional associations
- Career fairs
- People met in airports and on airplanes
- People met in aerobic classes and health clubs
- People you get to know through Internet social networks

Another way of reaching company insiders is to write dozens of e-mail messages or hard-copy letters to potential employers. A surprisingly large number of people find jobs by contacting employers directly. Most large company Web sites have a section allocated to inviting job inquiries as part of the employee recruitment program. Prepare a prospective employer list, including the names of executives to contact in each firm. The people who receive your letters and e-mail messages become part of your network. A variation of this approach is to develop a 30-second telephone presentation of your background. After you have researched firms that may have opportunities for you, call them and make your pitch. However, voice-mail systems usually make it difficult to speak directly to your target person.

Use Multiple Online Approaches The Internet is a standard avenue for job hunting, even for middle-management and executive positions. Sources of job leads on the Internet include general job boards, specialty job boards, company Web sites, and social networking Web sites.

With a job board (or job search site), the job seeker can post a résumé or scroll through hundreds of job opportunities. A number of job board Web sites are résumé database services because they give employers access to résumés submitted by job hunters. Many position announcements on the Internet require the job seeker to send a résumé by attached file. A few position announcements still request that the résumé be sent by fax or paper mail. Figure 16-2 lists some of the leading job boards, and dozens of others can be found quickly with an Internet job search. Job boards post positions by both field and geographic region. Specialty job boards, such as those listed in Figure 16-2, are preferred by some job seekers and employers because these boards are less flooded with positions and applicants. An Internet search will quickly reveal any specialty job site in your field.

Many managers prefer the employment section of their Web site over commercial job boards. Some of the more advanced company job sites, such as GE, present possible career paths for people who enter the company in the position sought.

A growing number of employers believe that the best way to find good job candidates is to advertise on Web sites where these candidates are likely to be spending considerable time, such as MySpace or Linkedin. Job boards also have a presence on social networking sites, as do recruiting firms. HotJobs has an application form on the social networking site Facebook. The potential applicant can send an e-mail or instant message to a particular posting. Another example of using social networking sites to find applicants is that recruiting companies have set up shop on Second Life. Job possibilities on this site on found on the job board, SLJobFinder.com.[2] Hundreds of people every day land jobs they first learned about through a job board or company Web site, so this approach offers some promise. A caution is that job hunting on the Internet can lead to a false sense of security. Using the Internet, a résumé is cast over a wide net, and hundreds of job postings can be explored. As a consequence, the job seeker may think that he or she can sit back and wait for a job offer to come through e-mail. In reality, the Internet is just one source of leads that should be used in conjunction with other job-finding methods, especially personal contacts that might lead to an interview. Employers still extensively use print ads in news-

FIGURE 16-2 General and Specialty Job Boards

1. *Leading General Job-Search Web Sites*
   www.CareerBuilder.com
   www.Monster.com
   www.HotJobs.Yahoo.com
   www.Job.com
   www.Indeed.com

2. *Examples of Specialized Job-Search Web Sites*
   www.Dice.com (technology positions)
   www.SalesAnimals.com (sales positions)
   www.Healthcaresource.com (health-care positions)
   www.cruisejobfinder.com (cruise and hospitality positions)

Job Hunting on the Internet

Job hunting on the Internet can be a rewarding or frustrating experience, depending on your skill in navigating job search Web sites and the availability of positions for a person with your qualifications. Use several job boards to locate a position opening for the following three persons:

Position 1: You.

Find a position listed on the Internet that would appear to be an excellent fit for you at this time in your career.

Position 2: Sales Representative, Fluent in English and Chinese.

Attempt to find an opening for an industrial sales representative or retail sales position that requires the applicant to be fluent in English and Chinese.

Position 3: Sports Administrator.

Attempt to find an opening for a sports administrator, typically a person who does administrative work for a professional sports team. Set a time limit for your surfing, perhaps 60 minutes. If you are working in a team, each team member can search for one position. Share with each other your approaches and job boards that appear to achieve the best results.

papers to recruit employees. Remember also that thousands of other job seekers can access the same job opening, and many of the positions listed have already been filled.

Skill-Building Exercise 16-1 will give you an opportunity to learn firsthand about job hunting on the Internet.

Establishing your own Web site or blog, with résumé included, will sometimes attract an employer who conducts an Internet search for potential candidates. For example, Ryan Loken, a Wal-Mart Stores, Inc., recruitment manager, says he spends a couple hours per week scanning blogs for new talent or additional information about candidates already interviewed.[3] A blog is most likely to attract a recruiter's attention if it relates to work in your contemplated field, such as explaining how you helped your employer save energy.

Smile at Network Members and Interviewers and Be Enthusiastic Assuming that you have the right qualifications, the simple act of smiling can be an effective job-hunting technique. One reason that smiling is effective at any stage of the job search is that it helps build a relationship, however brief. If you use a Webcam or video as part of your job search, smile on camera. Closely related to smiling is to display enthusiasm and excitement when speaking to people who can help you land a position. Conducted properly, a job search should be exciting and invigorating, and you should express these emotions to your contacts.[4] The excitement and invigoration stem from each small step you take leading to your goal of finding suitable employment.

Smooth Out Rough Spots in Your Background About 95 percent of employers routinely conduct background investigations of prospective employees. A background investigation by a firm hired for the purpose could include speaking to neighbors and coworkers about your reputation. In addition, the investigator may delve into your driving record, check for criminal charges or convictions, survey your credit record, and find out whether you have had disputes with the government about taxes. The information just mentioned is used to supplement reference checks because so many employers are hesitant to say anything negative about past employees. The information uncovered through the background check is often compared to the information presented on your résumé. A discrepancy between the two sends up an immediate red flag.

A job seeker's credit history has gained importance as part of a background investigation. Rightfully or wrongfully, many otherwise qualified candidates are rejected because of a poor credit history. Whether or not the law is usually followed, U.S. law requires companies to get permission from applicants to run credit checks. Applicants should also be given the opportunity to respond.[5] Concerns about hiring someone with a poor credit record include (a) worries that finances will interfere with his or her concentration, (b) the person is unreliable in general, or (c) that being in dire need of money, he or she might steal from the company. Under ideal circumstances an employer would give the applicant a chance to explain a poor credit history. For example, many reliable people have poor credit records because their medical bills went into collection while they waited for an insurance company to pay, or were victims of identity theft.[6]

Any job seeker who has severe negative factors in his or her background cannot readily change the past. Yet the job seeker can receive copies of a credit bureau report to make sure it is fair and accurate. If inaccuracies exist, or certain credit problems have been resolved, the credit report might be changed in the applicant's favor. Or, bring up the negative credit rating during an interview to present your side of the story. Perhaps you had cosigned a loan for a friend who fell behind on his or her payments. It might also be possible to obtain a more favorable reference from an employer by making a polite request. A third step can be to request a copy of the consumer report, which is a report of your reputation based on interviews with coworkers, neighbors, and others. A person might be able to negotiate a deletion of damaging information that is incorrect or exaggerated.[7]

Another way to learn about what public information exists about you is to place your own name into a couple of search engines. Sometimes another person with the same name as yours—particularly if many people have the same name as you—might have been involved in criminal activity, so be prepared to defend yourself! "Googling" candidates has become standard practice to uncover both positive and negative information about job applicants. Going one step further, many employers search social Web sites like MySpace to see if the candidate has engaged in outrageous behavior such as swimming in a public fountain while under the influence of alcohol—and then bragged about the episode on the social Web site.

Concerns about having negative information about one self somewhere on the Internet have prompted several entrepreneurs to help job seekers, as well as others, help buy negative or embarrassing postings on other people's Web sites. Reputation Defender, Inc., is one such firm.[8]

The Job Résumé and Cover Letter

A résumé is usually an essential part of the job hunt. Yet you can sometimes join a family business for a friend's enterprise without submitting a résumé. In some instances you will be asked to complete a job application form instead of, or in addition to, a résumé. Résumés are also important for job hunting within your own firm. You may need one to be considered for a transfer with a large firm, or to be assigned to a team or project.

Résumé Purpose Regard your résumé as a marketing tool for selling your skills and potential to handle new responsibilities. The most specific purpose of a résumé is to help you obtain an interview that can lead to a job. Your résumé, whether electronic, paper, or video, must therefore attract enough attention for an employer to invite you for an interview. A poorly prepared résumé often leads to an immediate rejection of the candidate. Recognize that you are competing against many carefully prepared résumés, some of which have been prepared with assistance from others. If the demand for your skills is high enough, it is conceivable that you will be hired without an interview.

Résumé Length and Format Opinions vary about the desirable length for a résumé. For a recent graduate with limited work experience, a one-page résumé may be acceptable. One page might seem too short for more experienced workers. Employers today demand considerable detail in résumés, particularly about the candidate's skills, accomplishments, and teamwork and leadership experience. Nevertheless, a three-page or longer résumé may irritate an impatient reader. Two pages are therefore recommended for early stages in your career. Professors and scientists often use a CV (curriculum vitae) instead of a résumé. The CV goes into considerable detail about their research activities and publications, and might take about seven pages. To add to the confusion of terms, Europeans and Canadians are more likely to use the term *curriculum vitae* rather than *résumé*.

A general-purpose résumé is presented in Figures 16-3 and 16-4. Recognize that hiring managers and human resource professionals have widely different perceptions of what constitutes an effective résumé. Both résumés include job duties performed as well as a chronological history, and could therefore be referred to as *chronological* résumés. A résumé that focuses on work performed rather than a job chronology is referred to

FIGURE 16-3 A General Purpose Résumé

Scott Wayland
170 Glenview Drive
Dallas, Texas 75243
Phone/Fax (312) 555-3986
swayland@gmail.com
http://www.scottwayland.com

Qualification Summary	Experience in selling industrial machinery. Education in business administration, combined with apprenticeship in tool and die making. In one year sold $500,000 worth of excess machine inventory. Received letter of commendation from CEO.
Job Objective	Industrial sales, handling large, complex machinery. Willing to work largely on commission basis. Want to use my skill and contacts to help employer gain market share.
Job Experience 2009–present	Industrial account representative, Bainbridge Corporation, Dallas, Texas. Sell line of tool and die equipment to companies in Southwest. Responsibilities include servicing established accounts and canvassing new ones.
2007–2009	Inside sales representative, Bainbridge Corporation. Answered customer inquiries through e-mail, Web site, and telephone. Filled orders for replacement parts. Trained for outside sales position. Served as sales team representative on company productivity-improvement team.
2003–2007	Tool and die maker apprentice, Texas Metals, Inc., Dallas. Assisted senior tool and die makers during four-year training program. Worked on milling machines, jigs, punch presses, computer-assisted manufacturing, computer-assisted design (CAD/CAM).
Formal Education 2003–2009	Madagascar College, Dallas. Associate Degree in Business Administration; graduated with 3.16 grade point average. Courses in marketing, sales techniques, consumer behavior, accounting, and statistics. President of Commuter's Club.
1999–2003	Big Horn High, Dallas. Honors student; academic major with vocational elective. Played varsity football and basketball. Earned part of living by selling magazine subscriptions.
Job-Related Skills	Professional sales representative. Able to size up customer manufacturing problem and make recommendations for appropriate machinery. Precise in preparing call reports and expense accounts. Good skill in gathering input from the field for market research purposes.
Personal Interests and Hobbies	Information technology enthusiast (developed and installed own Web site), scuba diving, recreational golf player, read trade and business magazines. Auto enthusiast, including restoring a 1976 Corvette.
References	On file with placement office at Madagascar College.

as a *functional* résumé. This type of résumé can be helpful in directing attention toward skills and away from employment gaps.[9] Check at least two résumé guides before preparing a final version of your résumé. Microsoft Word includes several templates for job résumés. A study conducted with 64 business professionals provides some useful information about which résumé characteristics are perceived positively enough to invite a job candidate for an interview. The business professionals reviewed résumés for new business graduates. The following résumé characteristics were more likely to lead to first choices for an interview: One page in contrast to two pages, a specific objective statement in comparison to a general objective statement, relevant coursework better than no coursework listed, GPAs of 3.0 in contrast to no GPA

FIGURE 16-4 A Job Résumé for a Recent Business Graduate

Jennifer A. Koster

700 Anderson St., Apt. B ∞ Fairfax, VA 22033 ∞ (703) 555-2121 ∞ Email: jakerwin@yahoo.com

Objective	Sales management trainee position, leading eventually to becoming a sales manager
Education	**B.A. Business Administration, Marketing Major, Advertising Minor, December 2010** George Mason University, Fairfax, VA GPA: In-major, 3.4/4.0 Overall, 2.7/4.0 Earned 40% of educational expenses

Accomplishments and skills

Marketing / Sales / Promotion
- Grossed $16,000 in three months with summer landscaping business
- Raised $75,000 in advertising space for environmental club folder project
- Raised $50,000 for sorority sponsored car show
- Cold canvassed community for potential clients
- Created informational brochure for apartment leasing company
- Developed advertising campaign for class project

Mangement / Training / Organizational Ability
- Managed daily activities of own landscaping business including renting/purchasing equipment and supplies, hiring assistants, budgeting, payroll
- Arranged client contracts for landscaping business
- Coordinated sales presentation strategy for sorority car show and trained others in sales techniques
- Trained new fast-service restaurant employees
- Aided in refurbishing and renovating a restaurant
- Performed restaurant duties ranging from server to night manager

Communications / Language / Creative Projects
- Created multimedia presentation using slides, music, and narration to brief incoming George Mason students during orientation
- Developed sales presentations and assisted with advertising campaigns including radio spots, newspaper ads, billboards, posters, brochures
- Designed and distributed flyers for landscaping business
- Conversational Spanish skills; write reasonably well in Spanish

Work Experience	**Self-Employed,** (Partnership) Whole Earth Landscaping, Reston, VA, Summer 2008 **Waiter,** Rainbow's of Washington, Washington, DC, Summers 2007, 2008, 2009
Activities	**Theater Arts,** George Mason, several roles in dramas and musicals. Regularly participate in clothing and fund drives for homeless people in Washington, DC

listed, GPAs of 3.50 in contrast to GPAs of 2.75, and accomplishment statements in contrast to no accomplishment statement.[10] In support of these findings, a résumé that does not list the candidate's skills and accomplishments is considered insufficient today.

In writing your résumé, keep in mind that certain key words attract the attention of managers and specialists who scan job résumés manually or with software. Among these key words are *languages, wireless, WiFi, global outsourcing, hands-on, flexible, results-driven, communication skills, e-commerce, cultural diversity,* and *sustainable environment.* The attention-grabbing words and terms are often referred to as *Google-optimized key words* because they show up frequently in an Internet search. You can find the key words that apply to your field by studying relevant ads. Key words are particularly important for online submission of your credentials because software is used by human resource departments of large companies to reduce a large stack of candidates into a manageable list of finalists.[11]

When submitting your résumé and cover letter electronically, make it easy for the employer to access, such as using an attached Word file. Many employers will refuse to open a link to your Web site or a PowerPoint presentation. Furthermore, concerns about computer viruses have prompted some employers to refuse to open any attached file. So you might send an attached word processing file, plus insert your résumé on the e-mail message. Make sure the formatting is not lost when cutting and pasting your document into e-mail. Send your cover letter and résumé to yourself to check for lost formatting.

Although an up-to-date job search may require online submission, recognize that you may be subject to identify theft. In one scam, the job seeker is sent an e-mail claiming to be from a recruiter representing a company seeking personal details for a pre-employment background check. Your identifying information is then used for identity theft. Sometimes you are asked for bank account information so your prospective new employer can make direct deposits to your account.[12]

Also, you may receive phony job offers requiring you to engage in such tasks as sending packages to an overseas country. The packages are usually stolen merchandise, and you never receive payment for your work. Another frequent scam is paying you a commission to transfer money overseas. You are sent a phony check, and then asked to send your own check overseas for perhaps 80 percent of the value of the check.

Video Résumés and Creative Formats A rapidly growing approach to résumé construction is the online video résumé. Turning the camcorder or Webcam on yourself, you present much of the basic information that would be found on a written résumé. The video approach is good for capturing your appearance, personality, and oral communication skills. Some job seekers place their video on their Web site or on YouTube, or simply as an attachment.

Unless you are highly skilled at video presentation, it is best to get professional help in constructing your video résumé. Careful editing might be needed to eliminate vocalized pauses and inadvertent distracting expressions. Another potential problem with the video résumé is that it focuses too much attention on soft skills for a candidate who wants to emphasize hard skills. Because some employers do not wish to spend the time watching a video, it is a good human relations tactic is also include a more conventional résumé. If an employer uses a video on its job site, the climate is probably right for you to submit a video résumé.

Another alternative to developing a distinctive résumé is to create an unusual format in factors such as color, size, and layout, including presenting the résumé in the form of a marketing brochure. If aesthetically pleasing, the offbeat résumé could suggest that you are creative and courageous. Allan Zander, a vice president of SolaCom Technologies in Quebec, receives up to 300 résumés when he has a position open, with fewer than 5 percent having creative designs. Among the more appealing ones, Zander says, are those that display corporate logos representing an applicant's current and past employers. (A school logo might also be eye appealing.) Another design element Zander admires is the pull-out quote—a short amount of text displayed in large type.[13] An example would be, "Have quickly developed a reputation as a finisher."

Whatever type of résumé you choose, and whatever mode of transmission, honesty is important. Many managers believe that a person who lies on a résumé might also behave unethically once on the job. ResumeDoctor.com, a résumé-preparation business, discovered that of 1,000 résumés checked for truthfulness, 43 percent contain significant inaccuracies. A background screening company found that 14 percent of U.S. job applicants lie about education on their résumés.[14]

The Cover Letter A résumé should be accompanied by a cover letter explaining who you are and why you are applying for a particular position. The cover letter customizes your approach to a particular employer, whereas the résumé is a more general approach. Sometimes it is helpful to prepare an attention-getting cover letter in which you make an assertive statement about how you intend to help the employer deal with an important problem. A person applying for a credit manager position might state, "Let me help you improve your cash flow by using the latest methods for getting customers to pay on time, or even early."

Career advisor Jim Pawlak suggests that the cover letter should take no longer than one minute to read, and should focus on the skills and background you'll bring to the job. Follow this with a brief bulleted list of your accomplishments. A useful alternative to the bulleted list is a two-column table that compares the requirements stated by the employer with your qualifications.[15] An example follows:

Your Requirements	My Qualifications
Sales experience	Four years of part-time selling including working a newspaper subscription and renewal kiosk at a shopping mall.
Ability to resolve conflict	Worked three seasons as lifeguard, and frequently had to stop rule violators and people in fights. Worked as Little League baseball coach, and resolved many conflicts between parents and myself, or between parents and the umpires.

If possible, mention a company insider in your network, and then close the cover letter with appreciation for any consideration your qualifications might be given. Figure 16-5 presents a traditional, yet quite brief, cover letter. Use this approach if you are concerned about being too bold in your cover letter, or if you are applying to a highly traditional business firm.

Performing Well in a Job Interview

After a prospective employer has reacted favorably to your cover letter and résumé, the next step is a telephone screening interview or a more comprehensive job interview. The purpose of the telephone screening interview is generally to obtain some indication of the candidate's oral communication skill. Such an interview is most likely when one applies for a customer contact position or one that requires knowledge of a second language. Having passed the screening interview, the candidate is invited for an in-person job interview.

FIGURE 16-5 A Traditional Cover Letter

27 Running Brook Road
Baton Rouge, Louisiana 70801
(507) 825-6742
swooden@aol.com

Ms. Melissa Flowers
Director of Human Resources
Medical Supplies Corporation
7385 South Clinton Avenue
New Orleans, Louisiana 70130

Dear Ms. Flowers:

Please accept my application for the position of purchasing assistant, posted on your company Web Site and also in the *Times Picayune*, March 27.
My company, Wentworth Industries, is currently sending its manufacturing operations to Malaysia, and my position will be terminated April 30. I am strongly interested in being considered a candidate for the position of purchasing assistant. As shown in my job resume, I have the following key qualifications:

- ∞ Two years of experience in a purchasing department, including one year as an office assistant and one year as a purchasing assistant
- ∞ An appropriate academic background with a major in business administration
- ∞ Courses in purchasing and inventory management, and computer applications

Thank you for considering my application.
Cordially,
Sara Wooden

Some job candidates overlook the fact that the phone interview is a serious contact with their employer, and do not differentiate between a social interview and a professional one. Outrageously wrong behaviors during the screening interview include having a television set turned on, letting a dog bark, using call waiting, and conducting the interview while washing dishes. When asked by a phone interviewer, why he could hear water splashing, one candidate replied, "I'm taking a bath, that's the way I relax." It is preferable to use a landline, nonportable phone for a screen interview because you will be less likely to be distracted if you are stationary.

Another type of screening interview is to respond to computerized questions, including a sample job problem. Your answers are printed for the interviewer to review. Candidates who get through the computer-assisted interview get to be interviewed by a company representative.

Typically one person at a time interviews the job candidate, yet team interviews are becoming more commonplace. In this format, members of the team or department with whom you would be working take turns asking you questions. One justification for team interviews is to observe how the candidate fits in with the team. Another variation on the traditional interview is that you meet for a brief interview with a series of interviewers. The process is referred to as *speed interview*, because of its similarity to speed dating in which the relationship-seeker meets briefly with a series of prospective dates or mates at a planned event. Busy employers like speed interviews because they can quickly screen several candidates for the same position.[16]

A general guide for performing well in the job interview is to present a positive but accurate picture of you. Your chances of performing well in a job increase if you are suited for the job. Tricking a prospective employer into hiring you when you are not qualified is therefore self-defeating in terms of your career. What follows is a list of some key points to keep in mind when being interviewed for a job you want:

1. **Be prepared, look relaxed, and make the interviewer feel comfortable.** Coming to the interview fully prepared to discuss yourself and your background and knowing key facts about the prospective employer will help you look relaxed. Use the company Web sites to gather background information about the prospective employer. Check out stories found on the Web about the employer. Many middle-age job hunters take Botox treatments to appear relaxed (rather than frowning) during the job interview, and after being hired as well.

2. **Avoid talking too much during the interview.** It is natural to think that during a job interview, you will be expected to talk. However, talking too much, including the presentation of your thoughts in a rambling, disorganized manner, will be perceived quite negatively by experienced interviewers. Being perceived as a compulsive talker will often lead to immediate rejection. Display effective communication skills by presenting your ideas in depth, yet concisely. A facilities administrator ruined her chances of employment at an accounting firm in this manner: When asked to describe her strengths, she delivered a long-winded reply focused on how she cleaned every cabinet in her home. "She probably went on for three to four minutes," recalls the human resources director. "I doubted she could get the job done in an eight-hour day." Rehearsing answers to typical interview questions beforehand, such as those presented in Figure 16-6, can help you present your ideas more concisely. Also, if the interviewer looks bored, you may be rambling.[17]

3. **Establish a link between you and the prospective employer.** A good way to build rapport between you and the prospective employer is to mention some plausible link you have with that firm. To illustrate, if being interviewed for a position at a Sears store, one might say, "It's fun to visit the office part of Sears. Our family has been shopping here for years. In fact, I bought a DVD player here last month. It works great."

4. **Ask perceptive questions.** The best questions are sincere ones that reflect an interest in the content of the job (intrinsic motivators) and job performance, rather than benefits and social activities. A good question to ask is, "What would you

FIGURE 16-6 Questions Frequently Asked of Job Candidates

An effective way of preparing for job interviews is to rehearse answers to the types of questions you will most likely be asked by the interviewer. The following questions are a sampling of the types found in most employment interviews. Rehearse answers to them prior to going out on job interviews. One good rehearsal method is to role-play the employment interview with a friend who asks these typical questions or to videotape yourself.

1. What would be your ideal job?
2. What are your career goals?
3. What are your salary requirements?
4. What new job skills would you like to acquire in the next few years?
5. Give me an example of how you displayed good teamwork.
6. Describe how you have shown leadership on the job or off the job.
7. What are your strengths (or good points)?
8. What are your weaknesses (or areas for needed improvement)?
9. What would a former boss say about you?
10. How well do you work under pressure?
11. What positions with other companies are you applying for?
12. What makes you think you will be successful in business?
13. What do you know about our company?
14. Here is a sample job problem. How would you handle it?
15. How would you use the Internet to perform better in this job?
16. What questions do you have for me?

Source: Questions 1 and 9 are from "Questions Job Interviewers Are Asking Most," http://www.csmonitor.com/2003/0317/pl5s01-wmno.html, April 20, 2003.

consider to be outstanding performance in this job?" If the issue of compensation is not introduced by the interviewer, ask about such matters after first discussing the job and your qualifications.

5. **Be prepared to discuss your strengths and developmental opportunities.** Most interviewers will ask you to discuss your strengths and developmental opportunities. (These and other frequently asked questions are presented in Figure 16-6.) Knowledge of strengths hints at how good your potential job performance will be. If you deny having areas for improvement, you will appear uninsightful or defensive. Some candidates describe developmental opportunities that could be interpreted as strengths. A case in point: "I have been criticized for expecting too much from myself and others." Do you think this approach is unethical?

6. **Be prepared to respond to behavioral interview questions.** A behavioral interview asks questions directly about the candidate's behavior in relation to an important job activity. The job candidate is expected to give samples of important job behaviors. The behavioral interview is therefore more applicable to candidates with substantial work experience. Two behavioral inquiries are "Tell me about a time in which your ability to work well on a team contributed to the success of a project" and "Give me an example of a creative suggestion you made that was actually implemented. In what way did it help the company?" Instruction 6 and Question 14 in Figure 16-6 are also behavioral interview questions. To prepare for such questions, think of some examples of how you handled a few difficult job challenges. The idea is to document specific actions you took or behaviors you engaged in that contributed to a favorable outcome.

" Share your achievements and qualifications with confidence, but not arrogance."

—Marie Artim, assistant vice president for recruiting, Enterprise Rent-A-Car, quoted in *Business Week*, September 24, 2007, p. 54

7. **Show how you can help the employer.** A prospective employer wants to know whether you will be able to perform the job well. Direct much of your conversation toward how you intend to help the company solve problems and get important work accomplished. Whatever the question, think about what details of your skills and experiences will be useful to the employer. Joe Hodowanes, a career strategy advisor, recommends that before your interview, think of an answer to "What value do I bring to a company and why should they hire me?" As you think of your key selling points, write them down.[18]

8. **Use body language that projects confidence and decisiveness.** A job interviewer will often carefully observe the candidate's body language. Monitor your body language to appear confident and decisive. A case in point: An executive coach helped a manager hone his nonverbal communication skills. The manager was concerned because he came close to getting three job offers but did not get hired. The coach showed the manager how his relaxed posture and habit of picking up anything in reach made him appear indecisive. Therefore, the manager practiced sitting upright and keeping his hands at his sides. Soon thereafter the manager was hired into a position he wanted.[19] Being carefully groomed, looking crisp and fresh, and having clean, unbroken nails also help project self-confidence.

9. **Practice good etiquette during the interview, including during a meal.** Under the pressures of applying for a job, it is easy to let etiquette slip. To display poor etiquette and manners, however, could lead to a candidate being rejected from consideration. Most of the suggestions made about etiquette in Chapter 12 apply to the job interview, but be particularly sensitive to allowing company officials to talk without interrupting them, and practicing good table manners. Even interviewers who are rude themselves, such as taking phone calls while interviewing you, expect *you* not to do the same.

10. **Send a follow-up letter.** As part of displaying good manners, mail a courteous follow-up letter or send an e-mail message several days after the interview, particularly if you want the job. A follow-up letter is a tip-off that you are truly interested in the position. You should state your attitudes toward the position, the team, and the company and summarize any conclusions reached about your discussion.

Now do Skill-Building Exercise 16-2 to practice the job interview.

SKILL-BUILDING EXERCISE 16-2

The Job Interview

As described in Figure 16-6, a good way to prepare for a job interview is to rehearse answers to frequently asked questions. In this role-play, one student will be the interviewer and one will be the interviewee (job applicant). The job in question is that of property manager for a large apartment complex in Phoenix, Arizona. Assume that the applicant really wants the job. The interviewer, having taken a course in human resource management, will ask many of the questions in Figure 16-3.

In addition, the interviewer will ask at least one behavioral question, perhaps about teamwork. The interviewer might also have other questions, such as, "Why do you want to live in Phoenix?"

Before proceeding with the role-play, both people should review the information in this chapter about the job interview and in Chapter 4 about listening.

THE VERTICAL AND HORIZONTAL CAREER PATHS

Career planning can begin at any point, including a kindergarten child saying, "I want to be an astronaut." Many other people think about developing their career after they have worked in a full-time professional position for several years. Planning and developing your career involves some form of goal setting. If your goals are laid out systematically to lead to your ultimate career goal, you have established a **career path**, a sequence of positions necessary to achieve a goal. Here we look at the more traditional career path

LEARNING OBJECTIVE 2

career path
A sequence of positions necessary to achieve a goal.

with an emphasis on moving upward, along with the more contemporary path that emphasizes acquiring new skills and knowledge.

The Vertical (Traditional) Career Path

The vertical, or traditional, career path is based on the idea that a person continues to grow in responsibility with the aim of reaching a target position, such as becoming a top-level manager. The vertical career path is synonymous with "climbing the corporate ladder." The same path is based somewhat on the unwritten contract that a good performer will have the opportunity to work for one firm for a long time and receive many promotions in the process. However, a vertical career path can be spread out over several employers.

A career path should be related to the present and future demands of one firm or the industry. If you aspire toward a high-level manufacturing position, it would be vital to know the future of manufacturing in that firm and in the industry. Many U.S. firms, for example, outsource much of their manufacturing to China and Mexico. If you were really determined, you might study the appropriate language and ready yourself for a foreign position.

While laying out a career path, it is also helpful to list your personal goals. They should mesh with your work plans to avoid major conflicts in your life. Some lifestyles, for example, are incompatible with some career paths. It would be difficult to develop a stable home life (spouse, children, friends, community activities, sports team, and garden) if a person aspired toward holding field positions in international marketing. Contingency ("what if") plans should also be incorporated into a well-designed career path. For instance, "If I am not promoted within two years, I will pursue an advanced degree."

Mary Gonzalez, an ambitious 20-year-old, formulated the career path shown in Figure 16-7 prior to receiving an associate degree in business management. After she presented her tentative career path to her classmates, several exclaimed that Mary was aiming too high. Mary's career goals are high, but she has established contingency plans.

FIGURE 16-7 A Vertical (or Traditional) Career Path

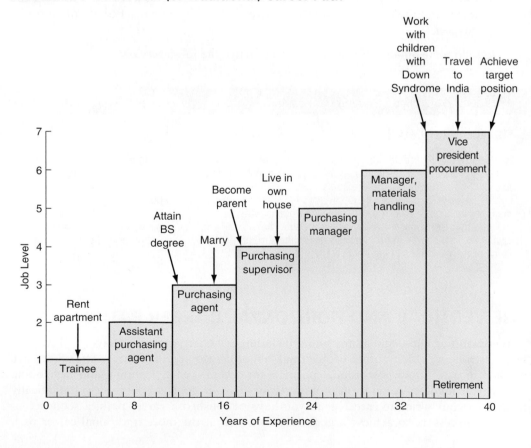

Developing a Career Path

1. Each class member will develop a tentative career path, perhaps as an outside assignment. About six volunteers will then share their paths with the rest of the class. Feedback of any type will be welcomed. Class members studying the career paths of others should keep in mind such issues as the following:

   a. How logical does it appear?

   b. Is this something the person really wants, or is it simply an exercise in putting down on paper what the ambitious person is supposed to want?

   c. How well do the individual's work plans mesh with personal plans?

2. Each class member will interview an experienced working person outside of class about his or her career path. Most of the people interviewed will have already completed a portion of their path. They will therefore have less flexibility (and perhaps less idealism) than people who are just getting started in their careers. The conclusions reached about these interviews will make a fruitful class discussion. Among the issues raised might be the following:

   a. How familiar were these people with the idea of a career path?

   b. How willing were they to talk about themselves?

   c. Were many actual "paths" discovered, or did a series of jobs simply come about by luck or "fate"?

A career path laid out in chart form gives a person a clear perception of climbing steps toward his or her target position. As each position is attained, the corresponding step can be shaded in color or cross-hatched. The steps, or goals, include a time element, which is helpful for sound career management even in work environments that are less predictable than they used to be. Your long-range goal might be clearly established in your mind (such as to become regional manager of a hotel chain). At the same time, you must establish short-range (get any kind of job in a hotel) and intermediate-range (be manager of a hotel by age 27) goals. Goals set too far in the future that are not supported with more immediate goals may lose their motivational value.

Skill-Building Exercise 16-3 gives you the opportunity to practice building a career path—an activity that could have an enormous impact on your professional and personal life.

The Horizontal Career Path

In many organizations, the hope of staying for a long time and receiving a long series of promotions has vanished. Instead of climbing the ladder, the person makes a series of horizontal moves, as illustrated in Figure 16-8. A significant feature of the horizontal career path is that people are more likely to advance by moving sideways than by moving up. Or, at least people who get ahead will spend a considerable part of their career

FIGURE 16-8 A Horizontal Career Path

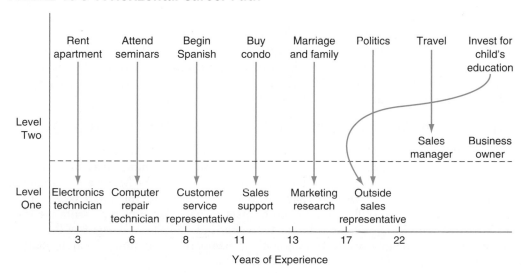

working in different positions at or nearly at the same level. In addition, they may occasionally move to a lower-level position to gain valuable experience. With a horizontal career path, the major reward is no longer promotion, but the opportunity to gain more experience and increase job skills. Organizations that reward people for good work, rather than simply because they have high rank, is another force encouraging the horizontal career path.[20]

The horizontal career path is closely linked to the contemporary employment contract that offers shared responsibility for career growth. The old employment contract was lifetime employment in exchange for corporate loyalty. Instead, today employees get a chance to develop new technical and professional skills. Rather than being offered job security, they become more employable because of the diversity of skills they acquire. The company provides the environment for learning, and the employees are responsible for developing their skills. Another justification for the horizontal career path is that many employees want the option of decelerated rather than accelerated career progress—they want to take their time in developing their career.

Furthermore, they would rather have a work–life balance rather than aim for promotions that could mean long work weeks and work overload, including considerable business travel and time away from home.[21]

Despite this trend, many employers are reverting to the traditional promises of an opportunity to climb the organizational ladder. Furthermore, it is not unusual for workers to aspire toward holding higher level, higher-paying positions, or a corner office or corner cubicle.

A horizontal career path, as well as a traditional (or vertical) career path, does not necessarily mean the person stays with the same firm. For example, a worker might spend three years in one company as an electronics technician, three years in another as a sales representative, and then three years as a customer service specialist in a third company. All three positions would be approximately at the same level. The third company then promotes the individual to a much-deserved position as the marketing team leader. Figure 16-8 illustrates a horizontal career path for Larry Chang, a career school graduate who did attempt to make long-range predictions about his career. Notice that all the positions through Year 17 are at the first level, and the positions for Year 22 and beyond are at the second level. Chang's career contingency plans are as follows:

(1) If I cannot obtain experience as a market research analyst, customer service rep, or sales rep, I will continue to develop as an electronics technician. (2) If I cannot find employment as a sales manager, I will attempt to become supervisor of electronic technicians. (3) If I do not raise sufficient funds for starting my own business, I will continue in a corporate job until retirement.

LEARNING OBJECTIVE 3

CAREER ADVANCEMENT STRATEGIES AND TACTICS

The many ways of improving interpersonal relationships described in this book can help advance and enhance a person's career. People who enhance their relationships with others are laying a foundation for career advancement. The following section discusses 14 other key strategies and tactics for career advancement, whether the advancement be vertical, horizontal, or a combination of the two. The first 8 of the methods described deal more with controlling your own characteristics and behaviors, whereas the remaining 6 deal more with interacting with the environment.

Capitalize on Your Strengths and Build Your Personal Brand

A long-established principle of getting ahead in your career, as well as managing others, is to capitalize on strengths rather than focus solely on overcoming areas for improvement. A recent bestselling book, *Go Put Your Strengths to Work* by Marcus Buckingham, elaborates on this idea.[22] Visualize Sam, who has excellent interpersonal skills, but is mediocre in quantitative skills. Sam will go far as a manager or sales representative if he continues to hone his interpersonal skills. Yet as hard as he tries to strengthen his quantitative skills, he probably would become only a mediocre accountant, research analyst, or actuary.

One key point made by Buckingham is that you should forget the myth that fixing one's weaknesses is the path to success. Another key point is that you should identify your strengths in realms in which you have delivered near-perfect performance. One flaw in Buckingham's thinking is that some weaknesses need to be patched reasonably well before you can capitalize on your strengths over time. For example, you might be masterful at composing pop-up ads that people click on and then make a purchase. However, if you cannot overcome your urge to steal from the company and sexually harass coworkers, you won't last long in your position.

Understanding your basket of strengths forms the basis for developing your **personal brand** (or, the *brand called you*). Your personal brand makes you unique, thereby distinguishing you from the competition. Perhaps your brand will not reach the recognition of Nike or Rolex, but it will help develop your reputation. Your personal brand also helps you attract employers and perhaps potential clients. Your identity as shown on the Internet including social networking sites such as Facebook is also part of your personal brand. Here is an example of a brand identity developed for a 25-year old college graduate, Rob Borden:

> *The branding consultants learned that Borden had opened a landscaping business in college, captained an NCAA-championship lacrosse team and was deeply interested in land development and conservation. They drafted a marketing plan around five qualities: a passion for commercial real estate, strong business experience, leadership abilities, and a sparkling wit when not nervous. In job interviews, Borden hammered away at those key points and, after meeting with about eight companies land a job that he loves in commercial real estate.*[23]

Your personal brand will be more effective if it is authentic in the sense of accurately reflecting who you are. You might add a little drama to your strengths, but the strengths should still be true. For example, if Lisa regularly volunteers time to feed homeless people, she might describe herself as having "enduring humanitarian values." Yet it would be a stretch for her to say that she "is committed to ending world hunger." As business advisors Jack and Suzy Welch suggest, "The most powerful thing you can do to get a head is, well, be real. As in not phony. As in authentic."[24]

Be Passionate about and Proud of Your Work

Successful people in all fields are passionate about their work. Without passion, you rely too heavily on external rewards to sustain effort. Passion contributes to both your career growth and company productivity. Effective leaders and business owners are usually passionate about their work, and group members expect their leader to be passionate.[25] For example, a joyous small-business owner is so excited about a product or service that it makes a difference. Bob Werts, the owner of Waxman Candles, says, "I love coming in in the morning and pouring wax."[26] Being passionate is also important because it is linked to developing expertise and high job performance. Taking pride in your work stems naturally from passion. If you invest the emotional energy into having passion, you are likely to be proud of your work.

The surest path to career success is to identify your area of expertise and then build a career around it. The more passionate and proud you are about your area of expertise, the better. Becoming wealthy and achieving recognition are by-products of making effective use of your talents. Expertise combined with passion helps you attain high job performance. Consistently good job performance is the foundation on which you build your career. Job competence is still the major success ingredient in all but the most political organizations (those where favoritism outweighs merit).

Develop a Code of Professional Ethics

Another solid foundation for developing a career is to establish a personal ethical code. An ethical code determines what behavior is right or wrong, good or bad, based on values. The values stem from cultural upbringing, religious teachings, peer influences, and professional or industry standards. As implied in Chapter 14, a code of professional ethics helps a worker deal with such issues as accepting bribes, backstabbing coworkers, and sexually harassing a work associate.

personal brand
The qualities based on your basket of strengths that make you unique, thereby distinguishing you from the competition

Develop a Proactive Personality

If you are an active agent in taking control of the forces around you, you stand a better chance of capitalizing on opportunities. Also, you will seek out opportunities such as seeing problems that need fixing. A **proactive personality** is a person who is relatively unconstrained by situational forces and who brings about environmental change. The proactive personality has high perceived control over situations. Self-Assessment Quiz 16-2 offers you an opportunity to learn about your tendencies toward having a proactive personality.

People who are highly proactive identify opportunities and act on them, show initiative, and keep trying until they bring about meaningful change. A health and safety specialist with a proactive personality might identify a health hazard others had missed. She would identify the nature of the problem and urge management to supply funding to control the problem. Ultimately, her efforts in preventing major health problems would be recognized. The proactive employee can also be regarded as displaying organizational citizenship behavior because he or she is a good citizen who will step outside the job description to be helpful. For example, he or she might take the initiative to help a coworker without being asked, or report a leaking faucet to the maintenance department.

Two studies conducted with close to 700 male and female workers in diverse occupations examined the relationship between career success and a proactive personality. Proactive personality, as measured by a test, was related to salary, promotions, taking the initiative in one's career, and career satisfaction.[27] Another reason that being proactive facilitates career success is that employees are expected to be self-managing more so than in the past. The proactive employee will identify and resolve many problems without being directed to do so by the manager. A more recent study indicated that a proactive personality influenced job search success among 180 graduating college students. The students took the test of proactive personality presented here. Search success was measured in terms of being offered follow-up interviews and receiving offers.[28] It may not be easy to develop a proactive personality, but a person can get started by taking more initiative to fix problems and attempt to be self-starting. Asking for permission to

SELF-ASSESSMENT QUIZ 16-2

Proactive Personality Scale

Indicate on a 1-to-7 scale how much you agree with the following statements: 1 = *strongly disagree*, 2 = *disagree*, 3 = *disagree somewhat*, 4 = *neutral*, 5 = *agree somewhat*, 6 = *agree*, 7 = *strongly agree*.

No.	Statement about Proactive Behavior	Answer (1–7)
1.	I am constantly on the lookout for new ways to improve my life.	
2.	Wherever I have been, I have been a powerful force for constructive change.	
3.	Nothing is more exciting than seeing my ideas turn into reality.	
4.	If I see something I don't like, I fix it.	
5.	No matter what the odds, if I believe in something, I will make it happen.	
6.	I love being a champion for my ideas, even against the opposition of others.	
7.	I excel at identifying opportunities.	
8.	I am always looking for better ways to do things.	
9.	If I believe in an idea, no obstacles will prevent me from making it happen.	
10.	I can spot a good opportunity long before others can.	

Total Score _____

assume responsibility for a project that needs doing is also helpful. Many newcomers to an organization have enhanced their reputation by asking for permission to organize the current year's office party.

Keep Growing through Continuous Learning and Self-Development

Given that continuous learning is part of the new employment contract, engaging in regular learning can take many forms, including formal schooling, attending training programs and seminars, and self-study. An everyday method of continuous learning is to ask intelligent questions about processes or procedures that will help you understand the business. For example, a manager might say that she checks out the competition every week by going to the Internet. You might ask, "Specifically, how do you get the information? Where do you look? The process sounds fascinating."

It is particularly important to engage in new learning in areas of interest to the company, such as developing proficiency in a second language if the company has customers and employees in other countries. Many companies support continuous learning because they perceive themselves to be *learning organizations*. It may therefore be easy for you to implement the tactic of growth through continuous learning.

Document Your Accomplishments

An accurate record of what you have accomplished in your career can be valuable when being considered for reassignment, promotion, or a position outside your company. The same log of accomplishments is useful for résumé preparation and to bring to a performance review. Sending e-mail updates to your manager about your noteworthy accomplishments is effective if not done to the point of being an annoyance. It is preferable to point to tangible, quantifiable accomplishments than to another person's subjective impression of your performance. Let's assume that a retail store manager, Kelly, reduced inventory shrinkage by 30 percent in one year. It would be better to state that fact than to record a statement from her manager saying, "Kelly shows outstanding ability to reduce inventory shrinkage."

Career coach Peggy Klaus recommends that you weave your accomplishments into an interesting story to tell other people.[29] The story approach has more appeal than a straightforward list of your accomplishments. Here is a fragment of a story that a man who worked for a food supplier to restaurants, schools, and hospitals used to document his accomplishments:

> *Our area was hit with a vicious lightning storm last March 12. Our computer and telephone systems went haywire because of power outages. We had to be in touch with our customers. I rounded up 10 people in the company who had cell phones with them. Using all the battery power we had left in our phones, we were able to contact all our customers. My manager said my cell phone rescue effort saved the day.*

Documenting your accomplishments in a business field is similar to a person in the arts such as a photographer, interior designer, or architect developing a portfolio of work. When the person applies for a job or assignment, he or she carries along the portfolio of representative work.

Documentation enables you to promote yourself in a dignified, tactful way. When discussing work with key people in the company, let them know of your good deeds without taking too much credit for team accomplishments. If you distinguish yourself in the community, for example, by fund-raising for a shelter for homeless people, let your manager know of your activities. The rationale is that most companies want their workers to be responsible community members.

Project a Professional Image

Your clothing, desk and work area, speech, and general knowledge should project the image of a professional, responsible person if you seek career advancement. A positive scent also contributes to a person's professional image, with light perfume, toilet water, or cologne *often* contributing to a positive image. Good grammar and sentence structure can give you the edge because so many people use highly informal patterns of speech. Being a knowledgeable person is important because today's professional businessperson is supposed to be aware of the external environment. Also, as noted by a human relations specialist, projecting a professional image hastens the development of trust and rapport in business relationships.[30]

A subtle part of projecting a professional image is to have a positive attitude. Assume that things are not going well in the office, such as the CEO announcing that no year-end bonuses will be forthcoming this year. Instead of joining the complainers, you might say to your coworkers, "A bonus would be wonderful, but I am happy to know that by not giving bonuses there will be no layoffs." Joining in the negativity makes you appear unprofessional. Yet offering constructive criticisms can be quite professional.

A challenge in projecting a professional image is to figure out what constitutes a professional image in your particular environment. Less restrictive dress codes have made it more confusing to select clothing that will create a favorable appearance. For the last several years, business formal attire for both men and women has been making a strong comeback. Yet, the IT field in Silicon Valley is still extremely informal. A programmer who wore a tank top and running shoes and brought a parrot to the office might be considered to project a professional image. Yet a marketing specialist for a health insurance provider behaving in the same way in Boston would be perceived as unprofessional.

Hairstyle is a superficial part of appearance that the career-minded person must ponder, whether or not standards for coiffeur border on being discriminatory. Some employers prefer that men in customer contact positions do not wear shoulder-length hair. The short-hair stereotype is also pronounced for women. Research suggests that both sexes perceive women with short, highlighted hairstyles as smart and confident, but not sexy, finds Marianne LaFrance, a psychologist at Yale University. "More hair equals more femininity, but also less intelligence," she says.[31]

A general guideline is to dress somewhat like the successful people in your firm or the customer's firm. It might pay to contact a company you plan to visit in advance and inquire about the dress standards for key people in the company. Skill-Building Exercise 16-4 is designed to sensitize you to what constitutes a professional image in a specific environment.

Perceive Yourself as a Provider of Services

A useful perspective for upgrading your professional self-image and enhancing your feelings of job security is to perceive yourself as something other than a traditional employee. According to career specialist John A. Thomson, each person should see him- or herself as a personal service business entity. Basically you are a business, offering the company (also your client from this perspective) a valuable service. You keep offering the service so long as the company keeps you on the payroll and you enjoy the work. Note the similarity to a high-level professional such as a dentist or IT consultant. You are offering a service that many people need. Part of the same perception is that you own your skills, and that these are the service your business (you) offers to others.[32]

The Professional Image Investigation

Find out what constitutes a *professional image* in a specific job environment, either where you work or at another employer. Ask a handful of people, "What makes for a professional image here?" Speak to or correspond by e-mail with a top-level manager, as well as a few workers without managerial responsibility. Another approach to this assignment is to make some observations directly in a retail establishment like Safeway, Albertson's, Target, or Nordstrom. How do the people in supervisory positions appear to dress, behave, and talk? Maybe you can conduct a one-minute interview with a service worker or two.

Share your observations with classmates, and see what conclusions can be drawn. For example, how does the type of company influence what constitutes a professional image? Are there different standards for men and women?

Another way of perceiving yourself as different from a traditional employee is to think of yourself as a professional-level temporary employee. Sometimes you will have a long stay with one employer, acting like a permanent temporary employee. At other times, you will move on to another company where your skills are more in need.

Develop Depth and Breadth

A continuing concern about career management is whether to acquire substantial depth in a specialty or to obtain broader experience. Is it better to be a specialist or a generalist? Typically it pays to have good depth in one area of expertise, yet also to acquire broad experience. A distribution specialist who helped set up shipping systems in an automobile supply company, an office supply company, and a hospital supply company would have excellent credentials. Yet some career specialists would argue that knowing one industry well has its merits.

If your goal is to become an executive, broadening your experience is a career enhancer. A person who held positions in sales and manufacturing would have broad experience. Breadth could also come about by experience in different industries, such as retailing and mining, or by holding positions in different companies. Being assigned to different teams, projects, and committees is another natural broadening experience. Conducting a job search within your company can often lead to a broadening experience, such as working with marketing people after having worked primarily with accountants. Another approach to broadening is to self-study different aspects of the business.

Rely on a Network of Successful People

Networking has already been described as a major assist to finding a job. Members of your network can also help you by assisting with difficult job problems, providing emotional support, buying your products or services, and offering you good prices on their products or services. On the negative side, being excluded from informal networks in your company can block your career advancement. The starting point in face-to-face networking is to obtain an ample supply of business cards. You then give a card to any person you meet who might be able to help you now or in the future. As the recognition of the importance of networking for career advancement and career finding continues to grow, new suggestions emerge. One such suggestion is to hold brunch or dinner parties at your home, and invite an interesting cross section of guests.[33] Professional and trade groups, such an association of bankers or sales professionals, are ideal for networking and are found in virtually every city.

While first developing your network, be inclusive by inviting any plausible person into your network. Later, as your network develops, you can strive to include a greater number of influential and successful people. One reason that playing golf persists as a networking technique is that so many influential and successful people play golf.

Social networking Web sites such as MySpace, Facebook, and even YouTube can often be used to find members for your professional network despite their social emphasis. A couple of years ago there were already 40,000 MySpace groups devoted to companies or coworkers, and 8,000 work-related networks at Facebook. A strictly professional site such as Linkedin is directly targeted toward making professional contacts. Millions of professionals turn to Linkedin to swap job details and contact information, often for recruiting purposes. To use these social networking sites for professional purposes, you will need to create an online profile including your résumé. An example of successful online networking is that a graphic designer named Angela Glenn developed a contact through a blog that led to the formation of a new advertising agency.[34]

Posting your own blog and visiting the blogs of other people can also be a source of valuable contacts. Be prepared to go through hundreds, if not thousands, of message exchanges before making one good contact. Converting some of these virtual contacts into in-person meetings will enhance the effectiveness of social networking on the Internet.

Skill-Building Exercise 16-5 provides suggestions for systematically building your network.

Work with a Mentor

In Chapter 11, mentoring was presented as a way of helping people grow and develop. Here I reemphasize that having a mentor can facilitate career advancement. Ideally, a person should develop a small network of mentors who give advice and counsel on different topics

such as job advancement opportunities and how to solve a difficult problem. Many people who receive exceptional promotions within their own firms, or receive excellent job offers from other companies, are chosen by their mentors. At the root of mentoring is the ability to attract and build a relationship with a person who is more experienced and talented than you.

A mentor can help the career beginner overcome hurdles such as being disappointed about the first job, such as not being listened to or receiving enough feedback. Another disappointment might occur when a recent grad anticipates that all workers will be fired up and eager to help the company. Yet on the job, the grad might encounter workers who are bored with their work. The newcomer might ask a mentor in a senior position, "Did you go through this? Is this normal? When does it all change, if at all?"[35]

SKILL-BUILDING EXERCISE 16-5

Building Your Network

From a career standpoint, networking involves developing a list of personal contacts who can help you achieve goals, and whom you offer something of value in exchange.

Networking is a career-long process, but the time to begin is now. Quite often the people who have been in your network the longest become your most valuable contacts. To begin networking, or systematizing the networking you are now doing, implement the following steps:

Step 1: Write down the type of assistance you are seeking for the next several months. Perhaps you need leads for a job, advice about getting ahead in your industry, or help with a difficult computer problem.

Step 2: List all the people who might be able to provide you the assistance you need. Among them might be fellow students, former employers, neighbors, and faculty members. Prepare a contact card, or database entry, for each person on your list as if they were sales prospects. Include relevant details such as name, position, major, e-mail address, phone numbers, postal address, and favorite pastimes. (Setting up a table with a word processor would work quite well for list and entries, or use a spreadsheet.)

Step 3: Identify an action step for making contact with the potential network members. Quite often the initial contact will be by e-mail. Gently mention that you would enjoy a telephone conversation or face-to-face meeting if it fit the contact's interest and

schedule. You might also be able to think of creative ways to make the initial contact in person, such as attending professional meetings, or talking to a neighbor while he or she is washing a car or doing yard work.

Step 4: Identify how you might be able to help each person in your contact list, or how you can reciprocate. For example, if a marketing person gives you an idea for a job lead, you can become part of his or her company's *guerilla marketing team* (you say nice things about the company product to friends and in public, or use the product in public). Sometimes the best approach is to ask the person who becomes part of your network, what you can do to reciprocate.

Step 5: Maintain a log of all the contacts you make, and what took place, such as an agreed-upon face-to-face meeting, or specific assistance received. Indicate how you responded to the assistance, such as, "I visited my contact's company Web site, went to the career section, and included her name as a person who is familiar with my work." Write down carefully your plans for reciprocity. Make a check list for whether you remembered to thank the person for any courtesy he or she extended to you.

Step 6: Update your log weekly, even if the activity requires only a few minutes of your attention. A network of helpers is a dynamic list, with people entering and exiting your network frequently. Each week ask yourself, "Whom can I add to my network this week?"

Find a Good Person–Organization Fit

Assuming that you have the luxury of selecting among different prospective employers, it is best to work for a company where your personality and style fit the organization culture. As implied at several places in the text, an **organization culture** is a system of shared values and beliefs that influence worker behavior. You have to study the culture through observation and questioning to understand its nature. A good starting point is to ask, "In order to succeed, what is really expected of workers?" You might find out, for example, that pleasing customers and being honest is the path to success.

A **person–organization fit** is the compatibility of the individual and the organization. Job interviews represent a good opportunity for evaluating a person–organization fit for both the applicant and the employer.[36] During a visit to the company to learn whether a culture tends to be formal or informal, you might observe the formality of the people and the emphasis on procedures such as a lengthy document to obtain a travel reimbursement.

The compatibility in question often centers on the extent to which a person's major work-related values and personality traits fit major elements of the organization culture. Following this idea, a person who is adventuresome and risk taking would achieve the highest performance and satisfaction in an organization in which adventuresome behavior and risk-taking are valued. Conversely, a methodical and conservative individual should join a slow-moving bureaucracy. How much an organization emphasizes individual effort versus teamwork is another important area for person–organization fit. Workers who enjoy teamwork would fit better in a teamwork-oriented culture.

Person–organization fit can also include superficial aspects of behavior such as physical appearance and dress. For example, a person who dresses like a Wall Street investment banker might not feel comfortable working in a high-tech firm in California where jeans and sandals are standard work attire. As a consequence of not feeling comfortable in your work environment, you might not perform at your best.

The consequences of a person fitting both the organization and the job have been systematically researched based on 25 studies. One of the conclusions reached was that commitment to the organization (a willingness to stay) was strongly associated with the person–organization fit. The study cautioned that it is not always easy for the job applicant to diagnose the fit in such areas as the conformance between the ethics of the individual and the company. When the topic arises, the hiring manager might be less than candid in explaining the company's true ethics.[37]

An interesting twist on person–organization fit is that it is more strongly linked to job satisfaction when the worker does not perceive a good fit between his or her needs and the characteristics of the work environment. This conclusion came from a study of 300 participants in a 12-week internship program.[38] An example of such a mismatch between needs and the work environment would be to want a job heavy on interaction with people, yet the job holder spent most of the workday isolated in a cubicle. So if your job is a little disappointing, fitting in with the company takes away some of the sting.

organization culture

A system of shared values and beliefs that influence worker behavior.

person–organization fit

The compatibility of the individual and the organization.

BACK TO THE OPENING CASE

Ellis Rowe has not only used internal networking to obtain new positions, he also uses internal networking to solicit ideas that will help him perform better. One of Rowe's contacts is four levels below him, yet because they have connected before, the person feels comfortable calling Rowe and saying, "Do you have five minutes?" Once or twice a month the contact submits an idea to Rowe, and the latter listens carefully for ideas that could help the business.

Take Sensible Risks

People who make it big in their careers usually take sensible risks on their journey to success. Sensible risk taking means about the same thing as *moving outside your comfort zone,* because you stretch your capabilities but do not plunge recklessly into a new venture. Among these risks would be to work for a fledgling company that offers big promises but a modest starting salary, or to take an overseas assignment with no promise of a good position when you return. Purchasing stock in start-up companies is sometimes a sensible risk, if you do not absolutely need the funds for living expenses. Fran Briggs, a motivational speaker and author says, "If you plan to advance in your career, experience fulfilling relationships, earn more money, and achieve your goals sooner, you must plan on taking the respective risks."[39]

Emphasize Relationships to Combat Being Outsourced

A major concern of many workers is that their job will be *outsourced* or *offshored* to a lower paid worker in a country where a competent worker will perform the same job at lower pay. As companies throughout the world struggle to stay competitive in a global economy, more and more jobs are outsourced. Call center and IT positions are the most frequently outsourced but so is a variety of design work, some legal research, and medical diagnostic work. The positions least likely to be outsourced are those requiring the physical presence of the worker and cannot easily be done remotely. Examples include nursing, real estate selling, teaching, funeral technician, massage therapist, and hairstylist. Managing people requires a physical presence, but not if your workers' positions have been outsourced.[40]

Another way to decrease the chance of your job being outsourced is to make relationship building a key part of your job, whether or not you are performing mostly technical work. An obvious part of relationship building is to be physically present in the workplace, so working from home might make you more susceptible to your job being outsourced.[41] A real estate agent with hundreds of personal contacts cannot be replaced by a Web site. And an information systems specialist who performs hands-on work with internal clients cannot be replaced by an IT specialist working 7,000 miles away in another country.

In short, good interpersonal relationships will not only advance your career but also help you preserve your position through the turmoil of technological change.

SELF-ASSESSMENT QUIZZES IN OVERVIEW

Self-Assessment Quiz 16-1 measures qualifications sought by employers. As you move through your career, it is helpful to reflect on whether you are strengthening your standing on many of these qualifications. For example, you might ask yourself if you are making progress in developing judgment and common sense, and teamwork skills. Self-Assessment Quiz 16-2 measures a more subtle qualification or characteristic—being a proactive personality. Initiative taking, providing you do not go well beyond the limits of your authority, is a quality welcome in most organizations.

Concept Review and Reinforcement

Key Terms

career path, 359

personal brand, 363

proactive personality, 364

organization culture, 369

person–organization fit, 369

Summary of Key Concepts

Recommended job-hunting tactics include the following:

1. Identify your job objectives.
2. Be aware of qualifications sought by employers.
3. Identify your skills and potential contribution.
4. Develop a comprehensive marketing strategy.
5. Use networking to reach company insiders.
6. Use multiple online approaches.
7. Smile at network members and interviewers and be enthusiastic.
8. Smooth out the rough spots in your background.

Job hunting almost always requires a résumé. A length of one page is recommended for a less experienced person, and two pages for a more experienced person. Résumés should emphasize skills and accomplishments. Be aware of the problems of identity theft and scams associated with online résumés. Video résumés can be important, as well as creative formats. A résumé should almost always be accompanied by a cover letter explaining how you can help the organization and why you are applying for this particular job. Comparing job requirements to your qualifications can be helpful. Screening interviews, including computer-assisted ones, precede a full job interview. A general guide for performing well in an interview is to present a positive but accurate picture of yourself. More specific suggestions include the following:

1. Be prepared, look relaxed, and make the interviewer feel comfortable.
2. Avoid talking too much during the interview.
3. Establish a link between you and the prospective employer.
4. Ask perceptive questions.
5. Be prepared to discuss your strengths and developmental opportunities.

6. Be prepared to respond to behavioral interview questions (examples of job behaviors).
7. Show how you can help the employer.
8. Use body language that projects confidence and decisiveness.
9. Practice good etiquette during the interview, including during a meal.
10. Send a follow-up letter.

The vertical, or traditional, career path is based on the idea that a person continues to grow in responsibility with the aim of reaching a target position, such as becoming a top-level manager. A vertical path is based on the traditional employment contract. A vertical career path should be related to the present and future demands of one firm or the industry. The horizontal career path is less predictable, and emphasizes lateral moves with an opportunity to gain more experience and increase job skills. A horizontal path is closely linked to the new employment contract that offers shared responsibility for career growth. Receiving rewards for good work rather than for rank fits the horizontal career path. Career paths should have contingency plans.

Improving interpersonal relationships assists career advancement. In addition, the following strategies and tactics are relevant:

1. Captitalize on your strengths and build your personal brand.
2. Be passionate about and proud of your work.
3. Develop a code of professional ethics.
4. Develop a proactive personality.
5. Keep growing through continuous learning and self-development.
6. Document your accomplishments.
7. Project a professional image.

8. Perceive yourself as a provider of services.
9. Develop depth and breadth.
10. Rely on a network of successful people.
11. Work with a mentor.

12. Find a good person–organization fit.
13. Take sensible risks.
14. Emphasize relationships to combat being outsourced.

Check Your Understanding

1. Identify four situations in a career in which conducting a job campaign would be necessary or desirable.
2. During a labor shortage (when there are more positions open than qualified applicants), why is it still important to have good job search skills?
3. What is your evaluation of the effectiveness of a job hunter using the Internet as his or her only method of finding a job?
4. In what ways might video résumés both help and hinder a company attain the goal of having a diverse workforce?
5. Why is a vertical career path still the dream of so many workers?

6. Give an example from your own life in which you behaved as if you were a proactive personality.
7. In what way do political tactics assist career advancement?
8. How might a person use a Webcam to help build and sustain a network?
9. Assume that you are attempting to create a personal brand. What key features about yourself do you would feature in your personal brand?
10. What is the most useful idea you picked up from this chapter about either conducting a job campaign or managing your career? Explain your reasoning.

The Web Corner

http://www.JobHuntersBible.com
(Career guru Dick Bolles guides career changers and suggests actions to take after they have exhausted Internet job sites.)

http://www.Vault.com
(Wealth of information about career advancement, job finding, and occupational profiles.)

http://www.mentoringgroup.com
(Suggestions for having a good mentoring relationship.)

Internet Skill Builder: Finding a Job Efficiently

So many job boards exist on the Internet that conducting a Web-based job search can be baffling. A direct approach is to visit Yahoo! Hot Jobs (on the front page of http://www.Yahoo.com) and enter three specific job titles of interest to you. You will be directed to loads of job opportunities closely matching the job titles you entered. It may be helpful to enter variations of the same job title, such as both "office manager" and "administrative assistant." Your assignment is to identify five jobs for which you appear to be qualified. Even if you have no interest in conducting a job search, it is informative to be aware of job opportunities in your field. Seek answers to the following questions:

1. Do I appear to have the qualifications for the type of job I am seeking?
2. Is there a particular geographic area where the job or jobs I want are available?
3. How good are opportunities in my chosen field?

Developing Your Human Relations Skills

Interpersonal Relations Case 16.1

Why Isn't My Résumé Getting Results?

Billy Joe Wentworth was working in the family business as a manufacturing technician while he attended career school. Although he got along well with his family members, Billy Joe wanted to find employment elsewhere so he could build a career on his own. Billy Joe's job objective was a position in industrial sales. He compiled a long list of prospective employers from personal contacts, classified ads in newspapers, and job openings on the Internet. Billy Joe clipped a business card with a brief handwritten note to each résumé. The note usually said something to the effect, "Job sounds great. Let's schedule an interview at your convenience."

After mailing out 200 résumés, Billy Joe still did not have an interview. He asked his uncle and mentor, the owner of the family business, "Why isn't my résumé getting results?" The résumé is shown in Exhibit 16-1.

Case Questions

1. What suggestions can you make to Billy Joe for improving his résumé? Or does it require improvement?
2. What is your evaluation of Billy Joe's approach to creating a cover letter?

EXHIBIT 16-1 Résumé of Billy Joe Wentworth

BILLY JOE WENTWORTH
275 Birdwhistle Lane
Cleveland, Ohio 44131
(216) 555-7512 (Please call after 7 P.M. weekday nights)
Billyjoe@wentworth.com

Objective
Long-range goal is Vice President of sales of major corporation. For now, industrial sales representative paid by salary and commission.

Job Experience
- Five years experience in Wentworth industries as manufacturing technician, tool crib attendant, shipper, and floor sweeper. Voted as "employee of the month" twice.
- Two years' experience in newspaper delivery business. Distributed newspapers door-to-door, responsible for accounts receivable and development of new business in my territory.

Education
- Justin Peabody Career College, business administration major with manufacturing technology minor. Expect degree in June 2010. 2.65 GPA. Took courses in sales management and selling. Received a B+ in professional selling course.
- Cleveland Heights High School, business and technology major, 1994–1998. Graduated 45th in class of 125. 82% average.

Skills and Talents
Good knowledge of manufacturing equipment; friends say I'm a born leader; have been offered supervisory position in Wentworth Industries; real go-getter.

References
Okay to contact present employer except for my immediate supervisor, Jill Baxter, with whom I have a personality clash.

Interpersonal Skills Role-Play 16-1

Helping Billy Joe with His Résumé

One student plays the role of a friend whom Billy Joe consults about his job résumé. Billy Joe is quite proud of the résumé, and is looking for encouragement and support.

The friend consulted, however, attempts to be objective and professional whenever he or she offers assistance. Run the role-play for about eight minutes. Outsiders can judge if Billy Joe is on the road to being helped.

Interpersonal Relations Case 16.2

The Brand Called Brandy

As Brandy Barclay navigated the challenging highways toward her job interview in Los Angeles, she rehearsed in her mind the importance of communicating that she is a unique brand. "I have to get across the idea that I am special, even if my brand is not as well established as Godiva Chocolates or Dr. Pepper. This administrative assistant position at the hotel and resort company will be a good way to launch my career and brand."

An excerpt of her job interview with the hiring manager Gloria Gomez follows:

Gomez: Welcome, Brandy, I am pleased that you made it through the online job application and the telephone screening interview. Tell me again why you would like to join our hotel company as an administrative assistant.

Barclay: Oh, I really don't want to join you as an administrative assistant. I would prefer a vice president job, but I have to start somewhere. [Smiling] Seriously, I like the hotel field. It fits my brand called "Brandy." I am a great support person, and a great people person. I'm so unique because I'm great with details and great with people.

Gomez: Tell me specifically, what key strengths would you bring to this job?

Barclay: As found in my brand called "Brandy," I am high info tech and high touch. I'm a whiz at Microsoft Office Suite, and I'm sweet with people. Kind of catchy, don't you think? Come to think of it, have you seen my business card? It contains loads of

details about my skills and strengths on the back. The card is laminated so it will last, and it contains my photo, and even is like a hologram with a 3-D look.

Gomez: Yes, Brandy, I do have your card. You gave one to the receptionist, and she gave it to me. And why do you keep referring to yourself as a brand? Is this just a gimmick to get you noticed?

Barclay: Being a brand is the modern way to tell you that Brandy Barclay is one of a kind. I've got a skill set that is hard to beat. Besides, I want to build a reputation fast that will propel me to the top as an executive in the hotel field.

Gomez: On your trip to the top, what do you plan to do for us as an administrative assistant?

Barclay: I will live up to the brand called Brandy by getting the job done big time. Just ask me to do something, and it will be done. Don't forget, I will be building my brand image while in this beginning assignment.

Gomez: Now let's talk about details like the job assignment, salary, and benefits.

Barclay: Fine with me. We have to deal with the mundane at some point.

Case Questions

1. How effectively is Brandy Barclay presenting herself as a brand?
2. What suggestions can you offer Barclay for presenting herself as a brand more effectively?
3. What suggestions can you offer Barclay for conducting herself better during her next job interview?

Glossary

action plan A series of steps to achieve a goal.

active listener A person who listens intensely, with the goal of empathizing with the speaker.

aggressive personality A person who verbally, and sometimes physically, attacks others frequently.

assertiveness Being forthright in expressing demands, opinions, feelings, and attitudes.

behavioral feedback Information given to another person that pinpoints behavior rather than personal characteristics or attitudes.

behavior modification An attempt to change behavior by manipulating rewards and punishments.

brainstorming A group problem-solving technique that promotes creativity by encouraging idea generation through noncritical discussion.

brainwriting Brainstorming by individuals working alone.

burnout A condition of emotional, mental, and physical exhaustion in response to long-term stressors.

business etiquette A special code of behavior required in work situations.

career path A sequence of positions necessary to achieve a goal.

carpal tunnel syndrome A condition that occurs when repetitive flexing and extension of the wrist causes the tendons to swell, thus trapping and pinching the median nerve.

challenge stressors Those stressful events and thoughts that have a positive direct effect on motivation and performance.

character trait An enduring characteristic of a person that is related to moral and ethical behavior.

charisma A special quality of leaders whose purposes, powers, and extraordinary determination differentiate them from others. (However, people besides leaders can be charismatic.)

coaching A method of helping workers grow, develop, and improve their job competence by providing suggestions and encouragement.

cognitive factors The collective term for problem-solving and intellectual skills.

cognitive restructuring Mentally converting negative aspects into positive ones by looking for the positive elements in a situation.

cognitive style Modes of problem solving.

collectivism A feeling that the group and society should receive top priority, rather than the individual.

communication The sending, receiving, and understanding of messages.

compromise Settlement of differences by mutual concessions.

concern for others An emphasis on personal relationships and a concern for the welfare of others.

conflict A situation in which two or more goals, values, or events are incompatible or mutually exclusive.

conflict of interest A situation that occurs when a person's judgment or objectivity is compromised.

confrontation Taking a problem-solving approach to differences and identifying the underlying facts, logic, or emotions that account for them.

consensus General acceptance by the group of a decision.

constructive gossip Unofficial information that supports others, is based on truth, and respects confidential information.

corporate athletes Workers who engage in high-level performance for sustained periods.

cross-functional team A work group composed of workers from different specialties, and about the same organizational level, who come together to accomplish a task.

cultural fluency The ability to conduct business in a diverse, international environment.

cultural intelligence (CQ) An outsider's ability to interpret someone's unfamiliar and ambiguous behavior the same way that person's compatriots would.

cultural sensitivity An awareness of and willingness to investigate the reasons why people of another culture act as they do.

cultural training A set of learning experiences designed to help employees understand the customs, traditions, and beliefs of another culture.

cycle-of-service chart A method of tracking the moments of truth with respect to customer service.

crew A group of specialists each of whom have specific roles, perform brief events that are closely synchronized with each other, and repeat these events under different environmental conditions.

defensive communication The tendency to receive messages in such a way that our self-esteem is protected.

defining moment Choosing between two or more ideals in which one deeply believes.

deliberate practice Strong effort to improve target performance over time.

denial The suppression of information we find uncomfortable.

developmental need A specific area in which a person needs to change or improve.

difficult person An individual who creates problems for others, even though he or she has the skill and mental ability to do otherwise.

diversity training Training that attempts to bring about workplace harmony by teaching people how to get along better with diverse work associates.

effort-to-performance expectancy The probability assigned by the individual that effort will lead to performing the task correctly.

emotional intelligence Qualities such as understanding one's own feelings, empathy for others, and the regulation of emotion to enhance living.

empathy In communication, imagining oneself in the receiver's role, and assuming the viewpoints and emotions of that individual.

employee network (or affinity) groups A group composed of employees throughout the company who affiliate on the basis of group characteristics such as race, ethnicity, gender, sexual orientation, or physical ability status.

empowerment The process of managers transferring, or sharing, power with lower-ranking employees.

ethical screening Running a contemplated decision or action through an ethics test.

ethics The moral choices a person makes. Also, what is good and bad, right and wrong, just and unjust, and what people should do.

expectancy theory A motivation theory based on the premise that the effort people expend depends on the reward they expect to receive in return.

extreme job A situation in which the incumbent works at least 60 hours per week in a position that usually requires tight deadlines and heavy travel.

feedback In communication, messages sent back from the receiver to the sender.

fight-or-flight response The body's physiological and chemical battle against a stressor in which the person tries to cope with the adversity head-on or tries to flee from the scene.

frame of reference The fact that people perceive words and concepts differently because their vantage points and perspectives differ. Also, a lens through which we view the world.

g (general) factor A factor in intelligence that contributes to the ability to perform well in many tasks.

Galeta effect A type of self-fulfilling prophecy in which high expectations lead to high performance.

group decision making The process of reaching a judgment based on feedback from more than one individual.

group norms The unwritten set of expectations for group members.

groupthink A deterioration of mental efficiency, reality testing, and moral judgment in the interest of group solidarity.

hindrance stressors Those stressful events and thoughts that have a negative effect on motivation and performance.

impression management A set of behaviors directed at enhancing one's image by drawing attention to oneself.

incivility In human relations, employees' lack of regard for each other.

individual differences Variations in how people respond to the same situation based on personal characteristics.

informal learning The acquisition of knowledge and skills that take place naturally outside a structured learning environment.

intelligence The capacity to acquire and apply knowledge, including solving problems.

intermittent rewards Rewards given for good performance occasionally, but not always.

interpersonal skill training The teaching of skills in dealing with others so they can be put into practice.

intuition An experience-based way of knowing or reasoning in which the weighing and balancing of evidence are done automatically.

law of effect Behavior that leads to a positive consequence for the individual tends to be repeated, whereas behavior that leads to a negative consequence tends not to be repeated.

leader–member exchange model A theory explaining that group leaders establish unique working relationships with group members, thereby creating in-groups and out-groups.

leadership The ability to inspire support and confidence among the people who are needed to achieve common goals.

learning style The way in which a person best learns new information.

mentor An individual with advanced experience and knowledge who is committed to giving support and career advice to a less experienced person.

message A purpose or idea to be conveyed.

metacommunication To communicate about your communication to help overcome barriers or resolve a problem.

microinequity A small, semiconscious message we send with a powerful impact on the receiver.

micromanager One who closely monitors most aspects of group members' activities, sometimes to the point of being a control freak.

mirroring Subtly imitating someone.

moments of truth Situations in which a customer comes in contact with a company and forms an impression of its service.

moral intensity In ethical decision making, how deeply others might be affected by the decision.

motivation An internal state that leads to effort expended toward objectives; an activity performed by one person to get another to accomplish work.

motivational state Any active needs and interests operating at a given time.

multiple intelligences A theory of intelligence contending that people know and understand the world in distinctly different ways and learn in different ways.

negative affectivity A tendency to experience aversive emotional states.

negative reinforcement (avoidance motivation) Rewarding people by taking away an uncomfortable consequence of their behavior.

negotiating Conferring with another person to resolve a problem.

networking Developing contacts with influential people, including gaining their trust and confidence. Also, contacting friends and acquaintances and building systematically on these relationships to create a still wider set of contacts that might lead to employment.

noise Anything that disrupts communication, including the attitudes and emotions of the receiver.

nominal group technique (NGT) A group problem-solving technique that calls people together in a structured meeting with limited interaction.

nonverbal communication The transmission of messages through means other than words.

nurturing person One who promotes the growth of others.

organization culture A system of shared values and beliefs that influence worker behavior.

organizational citizenship behavior The willingness to go beyond one's job description without a specific reward apparent.

organizational politics Gaining power through any means other than merit or luck.

participative leadership Sharing authority with the group.

peak performance Exceptional accomplishment in a given task.

perceived control The belief that an individual has at his or her disposal a response that can control the negative aspects of an event.

performance-to-outcome expectancy The probability assigned by the individual that performance will lead to outcomes or rewards.

personal brand For career purposes, what makes you unique, thereby distinguishing you from the competition.

personality Persistent and enduring behavior patterns that tend to be expressed in a wide variety of situations.

personality clash An antagonistic relationship between two people based on differences in personal attributes, preferences, interests, values, and styles.

personal productivity The amount of resources, including time, you consume to achieve a certain level of output.

person–organization fit The compatibility of the individual and the organization.

person–role conflict The situation that occurs when the demands made by the organization clash with the basic values of the individual.

political correctness Being careful not to offend or slight anyone, and being extra civil and respectful.

political decision-making model The assumption about decision making that people bring preconceived notions and biases into the decision-making situation.

positive self-talk Saying positive things about yourself.

positive reinforcement Increasing the probability that behavior will be repeated by rewarding people for making the desired response.

positive visual imagery Picturing a positive outcome in your mind.

power The ability or potential to control anything of value and to influence decisions.

proactive personality A person who is relatively unconstrained by situational forces and who brings about environmental change.

procrastination Delaying action on tasks that need to be done for no good reason.

protégé The less experienced person in a mentoring relationship who is helped by the mentor.

Pygmalion effect The phenomenon that people will rise (or fall) to the expectations that another person has of them.

rational decision-making model The traditional, logical approach to decision making based on the scientific method.

role ambiguity A condition in which the job holder receives confusing or poorly defined expectations.

role conflict The situation that occurs when a person has to choose between two competing demands or expectations.

role overload Having too much work to do.

role–person conflict A situation that takes place when the role(s) your organization expects you to occupy is in conflict with your basic values.

s (special) factors Specific components of intelligence that contribute to problem-solving ability.

self-efficacy The confidence in your ability to carry out a specific task.

self-esteem The overall evaluation people make about themselves, whether positive or negative.

self-managing work team A small group of employees responsible for managing and performing technical tasks to deliver a product or service to an external or internal customer.

sexual harassment Unwanted sexually oriented behavior in the workplace that results in discomfort and/or interference with the job.

social intelligence An understanding of how relationships with bosses and colleagues, family and friends, shape our brains and affect our bodies.

social loafing The psychological term for shirking individual responsibility in a group setting.

stress An adaptive response that is the consequence of any action, situation, or event that places special demands on a person.

stressor The external or internal force that brings about stress.

strong customer orientation A set of individual predispositions and an inclination to provide service, to be courteous and helpful in dealing with customers and associates.

summarization The process of summarizing, pulling together, condensing, and thereby clarifying the main points communicated by another person.

support network A group of people who can listen to your problems and provide emotional support.

synergy A situation in which the group's total output exceeds the sum of each individual's contribution.

team A small number of people with complementary skills who are committed to a common purpose, set of performance goals, and approach for which they hold themselves mutually accountable.

toxic person One who negatively affects others because he or she dwells on the negative.

training The process of helping others acquire a job-related skill.

triarchic theory of intelligence An explanation of mental ability holding that intelligence is composed of three different subtypes: analytical, creative, and practical.

type A behavior A behavior pattern in which the individual is demanding, impatient, and overstriving, and therefore prone to negative stress.

universal training need An area for improvement common to most people.

unwritten boundaries Dividing lines of behavior appropriate to different roles.

upward ethical leadership Leadership displayed by individuals who take action to maintain ethical standards although higher-ups engage in questionable behavior.

utilitarian predisposition A belief that the value of an act's outcomes should determine whether it is moral.

valence The value, worth, or attractiveness of an outcome.

value The importance a person attaches to something.

virtual office A place of work without a fixed physical location, where the output is communicated electronically.

virtual team A small group of people who conduct almost all of their collaborative work by electronic communication rather than face-to-face meetings.

win–win The belief that after conflict has been resolved both sides should gain something of value.

workaholism An addiction to work in which not working is an uncomfortable experience.

work–family conflict A state that occurs when an individual's roles of worker and active participant in social and family life compete with each other.

References

CHAPTER 1

1. *Dale Carnegie Training* brochure, Spring–Summer 2005, p. 12.
2. Joanne Lozar Glenn, "Lessons in Human Relations," *Business Education Forum,* October 2003, p. 10.
3. Research cited in Bob Wall, *Working Relationships: The Simple Truth About Getting Along with Friends and Foes at Work* (Palo Alto, CA: Davies-Black, 1999).
4. George B. Yancey, Chante P, Clarkson, Julie D. Baxa, and Rachel N. Clarkson, "Example of Good and Bad Interpersonal Skills at Work," http://www.psichi.org/pubs/articles/article_368.asp, p. 2, accessed February 2, 2004.
5. Edward Muzio, Deborah J. Fisher, Err R. Thomas, and Valerie Peters, "Soft Skill Quantification (SSQ) for Project Manager Competencies," *Project Management Journal,* June 2007, pp. 30–31.
6. The model presented here is an extension of the one presented in Thomas V. Bonoma and Gerald Zaltman, *Psychology for Management* (Boston: Kent, 1981), pp. 88–92.
7. Gary P. Latham, "The Motivational Benefits of Goal-Setting," *Academy of Management Executive,* November 2004, pp. 126–127.
8. Roger B. Hill, "On-Line Instructional Resources—Lesson 3, Interpersonal Skills," http://www.coe.uga.edu/~rhill/workethic/less3.htm, p. 1, accessed March 17, 2005.
9. Nancy Day, "Informal Learning Gets Results," *Workforce,* June 1998, pp. 30–36; Marcia L. Conner, "Informal Learning," *Ageless Learner,* 1997–2005, http://agelesslearner.com/intros/informal.html, p. 2.
10. Paul Cornell, "The Growth of Informal Learning Environments," http://www.steelcase.com, 1996–2007, Steelcase, Inc.
11. Morgan W. McCall, Jr., *High Flyers: Developing the Next Generation of Leaders* (Boston: Harvard Business School Press, 1998).

CHAPTER 2

1. Excerpted from Carol Hymowitz, "Business Is Personal, So Managers Need to Harness Emotions," *The Wall Street Journal,* November 13, 2006, p. B1.
2. Marvin Zuckerman, "Are You a Risk Taker?" *Psychology Today,* November/December 2000, p. 53.

3. Remus Ilies and Timothy A. Judge, "On the Heritability of Job Satisfaction: The Mediating Role of Personality," *Journal of Applied Psychology,* August 2003, pp. 750–759.
4. Robert R. McRae and Juri Allik, eds., *The Five-Factor Model of Personality Across Cultures* (New York: Kluwer, 2002).
5. Roger R. McRae and Paul T. Costa, Jr., "Personality Trait Structure as Human Universal," *American Psychologist,* May 1997, pp. 509–516.
6. Lawrence R. James and Michelle D. Mazerolle, *Personality in Work Organizations* (Thousand Oaks, CA: Sage, 2002).
7. "Which Traits Predict Job Performance?" APA Help Center, http://www.apahelpcenter.org/articles/article.php?id=33, accessed March 22, 2005.
8. Nicole M. Dudley, Karin A. Orvis, Justin E. Lebiecki, and José M. Cortina, "A Meta-Analytic Investigation of Conscientiousness in the Prediction of Job Performance: Examining the Intercorrelations and the Incremental Validity of Narrow Traits," *Journal of Applied Psychology,* January 2006, p. 51.
9. Gregory M. Hurtz and John J. Donovan, "Personality and Job Performance: The Big Five Revisited," *Journal of Applied Psychology,* December 2000, pp. 869–879.
10. David V. Day, Deidra J. Scheleicher, Amy L. Unckless, and Nathan J. Hiller, "Self-Monitoring Personality at Work: A Meta-Analytic Investigation of Construct Validity," *Journal of Applied Psychology,* April 2002, pp. 390–401.
11. Gerald L. Blakely, Martha C. Andrews, and Jack Fuller, "Are Chameleons Good Citizens? A Longitudinal Study of the Relationship Between Self-Monitoring and Organizational Citizenship Behavior," *Journal of Business and Psychology,* Winter 2003, pp. 131–144.
12. Jeff Joireman, Dishan Kamdar, Denise Daniels, and Blythe Duell, "Good Citizens to the End? It Depends: Empathy and Concern with Future Consequences Moderate the Impact of a Short-Term Time Horizon on Organizational Citizenship Behaviors," *Journal of Applied Psychology,* November 2006, p. 1315.
13. Michael Mount, Remus Ilies, and Erin Johnson, "Relationship of Personality Traits and Counterproductive Work Behaviors: The Mediating

Effects of Job Satisfaction," *Personnel Psychology*, Autumn 2006, pp. 591-622.

14. L. A. Witt, Lisa A. Burke, Murray R. Barrick, and Michael K. Mount, "The Interactive Effects of Conscientiousness and Agreeableness on Job Performance," *Journal of Applied Psychology*, February 2002, pp. 164–169.

15. Carl J. Thoresen, Jill C. Bradley, Paul D. Bliese, and Joseph D. Thoresen, "The Big Five Personality Traits and Individual Job Performance Growth Trajectories in Maintenance and Transitional Job Stages," *Journal of Applied Psychology*, October 2004, pp. 835–853.

16. Cited in David Stipp, "A Little Worry Is Good for Business," *Fortune*, November 24, 2003, p. 68.

17. Isabel Briggs Myers, *Introduction to Type®*, 6th ed. (Mountain View, CA: CPP, Inc., 1996), p. 10. (Revised by Linda K. Kirby and Katharine D. Myers.)

18. An example of this research is John W. Slocum and Donald Hellriegel, "A Look at How Managers' Minds Work," *Business Horizons*, vol. 26, 1983, pp. 58–68.

19. Myers, *Introduction to Type®*, p. 42.

20. Brian S. Young, Winfred Arthur, Jr., and John Finch, "Predictors of Managerial Performance: More than Cognitive Ability," *Journal of Business and Psychology*, Fall 2000, pp. 53–72.

21. Robert J. Sternberg, *Beyond IQ: A Triarchic Theory of Human Intelligence* (New York: Cambridge University Press, 1985); Bridget Murray, "Sparking Interest in Psychology Class," *APA Monitor*, October 1995, p. 51.

22. "Speed, Driver's Age, Cited in Japan Crash," Associated Press, April 26, 2005.

23. Howard Gardner, *Intelligence Reframed: Multiple Intelligence in the 21st Century* (New York: Basic Books, 1999).

24. Charles G. Morris and Albert A. Maisto, *Psychology: An Introduction*, 11th ed. (Upper Saddle River, NJ: Prentice Hall, 2002), p. 11.

25. Sharon Begley, "Critical Thinking: Part Skill, Part Mindset and Totally Up To You," *The Wall Street Journal*, October 20, 2006, p. B1.

26. Daniel Goleman, Richard Boyatzis, and Annie McKee, "Primal Leadership: The Hidden Driver of Great Performance," *Harvard Business Review*, December 2001, pp. 42–51.

27. David A. Morand, "The Emotional Intelligence of Managers: Assessing the Construct Validity of a Nonverbal Measure of 'People Skills,'" *Journal of Business and Psychology*, Fall 2001, pp. 21–33.

28. Research cited in "Managing Emotions in the Workplace: Do Positive and Negative Attitudes Drive Performance?" Knowledge@Wharton (http://knowledge.wharton.upenn), April 21, 2007, p. 2.

29. David C. McClelland, "How Motives, Skills, and Values Determine What People Do," *American Psychologist*, July 1985, p. 815.

30. Jean M. Twenge, *Generation Me* (New York: The Free Press, 2006).

31. "Get Ready for 'Millennials' at Work," *Manager's Edge*, January 2006, p. 1.

CHAPTER 3

1. Excerpted from Laura Egodigwe, "Working It Out! How a Young Executive Overcomes Obstacles on the Job," *Black Enterprise*, January 2007, p. 55.

2. Michelle K. Duffy et al., "The Moderating Roles of Self-Esteem and Neuroticism in the Relationships Between Group and Individual Undermining Behavior," *Journal of Applied Psychology*, September 2006, p. 1067.

3. April O'Connell, Vincent O'Connell, and Lois-Ann Kuntz, *Choice and Change: The Psychology of Personal Growth and Interpersonal Relationships*, 7th edition (Upper Saddle River, NJ: Pearson/Prentice Hall, 2005), p. 3.

4. "Better Self-Esteem," http://www.utexas.edu/student/cmhc/booklets/selfesteem/selfest.html, 1999, p. 2.

5. Ibid.

6. Randall Edwards, "Is Self-Esteem Really All That Important?" *The APA Monitor*, May 1995, p. 43.

7. Research reported in Jeffrey Zaslow, "The Most-Praised Generation Goes to Work," *The Wall Street Journal*, April 20, 2007, p. W7.

8. David De Cremer et al., "Rewarding Leadership and Fair Procedures as Determinants of Self-Esteem," *Journal of Applied Psychology*, January 2005, pp. 3–12.

9. Eugene Raudsepp, "Strong Self-Esteem Can Help You Advance," *CareerJournal.com* (*The Wall Street Journal*, http://online.wsj.com/careers), August 10, 2004.

10. Research reported in Melissa Dittman, "Study Links Jealousy with Aggression, Low Self-Esteem," *Psychology Today*, February 2005, p. 13.

11. Jon L. Pierce, Donald G. Gardner, Larry L. Cummings, and Randall B. Dunman, "Organization-Based Self-Esteem: Construct Definition, Measurement, and Validation," *Academy of Management Journal*, September 1989, p. 623.

12. Nathaniel Branden, *Self-Esteem at Work: How Confident People Make Powerful Companies* (San Francisco: Jossey-Bass, 1998); Timothy A. Judge and Joyce E. Bono, "Relationship of Core Self-Evaluations Traits—Self-Esteem, Generalized Self-Efficacy, Locus of Control, and Emotional Stability—with Job Satisfaction and Job Performance: A Meta-Analysis," *Journal of Applied Psychology*, February 2001, pp. 80–92.

13. Duffey et al., "The Moderating Role of Self-Esteem and Neuroticism," p. 1069.

14. Research reported in David Dent, "Bursting the Self-Esteem Bubble," *Psychology Today*, March/April 2002, p. 16.

15. Quoted in Carlin Flora, "The Measuring Game: Why You Think You'll Never Stack Up," *Psychology Today*, September/October 2005, p. 44.

16. Cited in Julia M. Klein, "The Illusion of Rejection," *Psychology Today*, January/February 2005, p. 30.

17. Research reported in Melissa Dittmann, "Self-Esteem That's Based on External Sources Has Mental Health Consequences, Study Says," *Monitor on Psychology*, December 2002, p. 16.

18. Research mentioned in book review by E. R. Snyder in *Contemporary Psychology*, July 1998, p. 482.

19. Daniel L. Aroz, "The Manager's Self-Concept," *Human Resources Forum*, July 1989, p. 4.

20. "Better Self-Esteem," pp. 3–4.

21. Ibid, pp. 4–5.

22. Cited in "Self-Esteem: You'll Need It to Succeed," *Executive Strategies*, September 1993, p. 12.

23. Raudsepp, "Strong Self-Esteem Can Help You Advance."

24. "Building Self-Esteem: A Self-Help Guide," http://mentalhealth.samhsa.gov/, p. 2, accessed September 7, 2007.

25. Marilyn E. Gist and Terence R. Mitchell, "Self-Efficacy: A Theoretical Analysis of Its Determinants and Malleability," *Academy of Management Review*, April 1992, pp. 183–211.

26. George P. Hollenbeck and Douglas T. Hall, "Self-Confidence and Leader Performance," *Organizational Dynamics*, Issue 3, 2004, pp. 261–264.

27. Jay T. Knippen and Thad B. Green, "Building Self-Confidence," *Supervisory Management*, August 1989, pp. 22–27.

28. Quoted in "Entrepreneurs Need Attitude: Power of Being Positive Can Help You to Succeed in Spite of Setbacks," Knight Ridder, September 16, 2002.

29. D. Brian McNatt and Timothy A. Judge, "Boundary Conditions of the Galeta Effect: A Field Experiment and Constructive Replication," *Academy of Management Journal*, August 2004, 550–565.

30. Price Pritchett, *HardOptimism: Developing Deep Strengths for Managing Uncertainty, Opportunity, Adversity, and Change* (Dallas, TX: Pritchett, 2004), p. 16.

31. Frances Thornton, Gayle Privette, and Charles M. Bundrick, "Peak Performance of Business Leaders: An Experience Parallel to Self-Actualization Theory," *Journal of Business and Psychology*, Winter 1999, pp. 253–264.

CHAPTER 4

1. Cliff Edwards, "Death of a Pushy Salesman: More Outfits Are Using 'Empathy Training' to Help Sales Reps Get Into Customers' Heads," *Business Week*, July 3, 2006, p. 108.

2. Diane Brady, "*!#@ the E-Mail. Can We Talk?" *Business Week*, December 4, 2006, p. 109.

3. Ritch Sorenson, Grace DeBord, and Ida Ramirez, *Business and Management Communication: A Guide Book*, 4th ed. (Upper Saddle River, NJ: Prentice Hall, 2001), pp. 6–10.

4. Steven Pinker, *The Stuff of Thought* (New York: Viking, a Member of Penguin Group [USA] Inc., 2007).

5. Sue Morem, "Nonverbal Communication Help for Salespeople," http://www.careerknowhow.com/ask_sue/nonverbal.htm.

6. Jeffrey Jacobi, *The Vocal Advantage* (Upper Saddle River, NJ: Prentice Hall, 1996).

7. Quoted in Joyce M. Rosenberg, "Don't Take Voice Message for Granted," Associated Press, February 21, 2006.

8. Eric Krell, "The Unintended Word," *HR Magazine*, August 2006, p. 51.

9. Robert Lee Hotz, "How Your Brain Allows You to Walk in Another's Shoes," *The Wall Street Journal*, August 17, 2007, p. B1.

10. Jared Sandberg, "'It Says Press Any Key. Where's the Any Key?'" *The Wall Street Journal*, February 20, 2007, p. B1.

11. Mark Henricks, "Can We Talk? Speaking Up About the Value of Dialogue," *Entrepreneur*, January 1998, p. 82.

12. Sharon Lund O'Neil, "An Empowered Attitude Can Enhance Communication Skills," *Business Education Forum*, April 1998, pp. 28–30.

13. *Aspire*, November–December 1998, pp. 3–4; Interview by Alyssa Danigelis, "Like, Um, You Know," *Fast Company*, May 2006, p. 99.

14. Jean Mausehund and R. Neil Dortch, "Communications—Presentation Skills in the Digital Age," *Business Education Forum*, April 1999, pp. 30–32.

15. For more details, see Brian Fugere, Chelsea Hardaway, and Jon Warshawsky, *Why Business People Speak Like Idiots* (New York: Free Press, 2005).

16. Joann Baney, *Guide to Interpersonal Communication* (Upper Saddle River, NJ: Pearson/Prentice Hall, 2004), p. 7.

17. Susan M. Heathfield, "Listen with Your Eyes," About.com: Human Resources, http://humanresources.about.com, 2007.

18. The information in this section is from Holly Weeks, "Taking the Stress Out of Stressful Conversations," *Harvard Business Review*, July–August 2001, pp. 112–119. The quote is from p. 117.

19. Deborah Tannen, *Talking from 9 to 5* (New York: William Morrow, 1994); Tannen, "The Power of Talk: Who Gets Heard and Why," *Harvard Business Review*, September–October 1995, pp. 138–148; Daniel J. Canary and Kathryn Dindia, *Sex Differences and Similarities in Communication* (Mahwah, NJ: Erlbaum, 1998), p. 318; John Gray, *Men Are from Mars, Women Are from Venus* (New York: HarperCollins, 1992).

20. Cited in Kris Maher, "The Jungle: Focus on Recruitment, Pay and Getting Ahead," *The Wall Street Journal*, October 19, 2004, p. B10.

CHAPTER 5

1. Josh Hyatt, "The Soul of a New Team," *Fortune*, June 12, 2006. pp. 134, 135.
2. Conference Board report cited in "CEO Leadership Skips Teamwork, Article Says," *Rochester Democrat and Chronicle*, February 17, 2002, p. 1E.
3. Jon R. Katzenbach and Douglas K. Smith, "The Discipline of Teams," *Harvard Business Review*, March–April 1993, p. 112.
4. Deal E. Yeatts and Coyd Hyten, *High Performing Self-Managed Work Teams: A Comparison of Theory and Practice* (Thousands Oaks, CA: Sage, 1998), p. xiii.
5. Rudy M. Yandrick, "A Team Effort," *HR Magazine*, June 2001, p. 138.
6. Claus W. Langfred, "Too Much Trust a Good Thing? Negative Effects of High Trust and Individual Autonomy in Self-Managing Teams," *Academy of Management Journal*, June 2004, pp. 385–399.
7. "Shepherding Communications When the Flock Is Scattered," *Flexible Workplace Management*, sample issue, 2001.
8. Arvind Malhotra, Ann Majchrzak, and Benson Rosen, "Leading Virtual Teams," *Academy of Management Perspectives*, February 2007, p. 62.
9. Shelia Simsarian Webber and Richard J. Klimoski, "Crews: A Distinct Type of Work Team," *Journal of Business and Psychology*, Spring 2004, pp. 261–279.
10. Carol Hymowitz, "A High-Seas Race Can Tell Tales about Executive Roles," *The Wall Street Journal*, August 9, 2005, p. B1.
11. Matt Bolch, "Rewarding the Team," *HR Magazine*, February 2007, pp. 91–93.
12. "When Committees Spell Trouble: Don't Let Individuals Hide Within a Group," *WorkingSMART*, August 1998, p. 1; Ross Kerber, "For Abigail Johnson, a Leadership Test," *The Boston Globe* (http://www.boston.com), August 21, 2007, p. 1.
13. Irving L. Janus, *Victims of Groupthink: A Psychological Study of Foreign Policy Decisions and Fiascos* (Boston: Houghton Mifflin, 1972); Glen Whyte, "Groupthink Reconsidered," *Academy of Management Review*, January 1989, pp. 40–56.
14. Martha A. Peak, "Treating Trauma in Teamland," *Management Review*, September 1997, p. 1.
15. "R. Meredith Belbin," in *Business: The Ultimate Resource* (Cambridge, MA: Perseus, 2002), pp. 966–967; Belbin, *Management Teams* (London: Elsevier Butterworth-Heinemann, 2003); Belbin® Team-Roles, http://www.belbin.com/belbin-team-roles.htm.
16. From a review of Meredith Belbin, *Management Teams,* by Colin Thomson, appearing in http://www.accountingweb.co.uk, accessed April 14, 2004.
17. "Fly in Formation: Easy Ways to Build Team Spirit," *WorkingSMART*, March 2000, p. 6.
18. "Score a Perfect '10' on Teamwork," *Manager's Edge*, May 2006, p. 1.
19. Pamela Lovell, "Healthy Teams Display Strong Vital Signs," *Teamwork,* sample issue, the Dartnell Corporation, 1997.
20. Glenn M. Parker, *Cross-Functional Teams: Working with Allies, Enemies, & Other Strangers* (San Francisco: Jossey-Bass, 1994), p. 170.
21. Mary J. Waller et al., "The Effect of Individual Perceptions of Deadlines on Team Performance," *Academy of Management Review*, October 2001, p. 597.
22. Mark G. Ehrhant and Stefanie E. Naumann, "Organizational Citizenship Behavior in Work Groups: A Group Norms Approach," *Journal of Applied Psychology*, December 2004, pp. 960–974.
23. Daniel G. Bachrach, Benjamin C. Powell, Elliot Bendoly, and R. Glenn Richey, "Organizational Citizenship Behavior and Performance Evaluations: Exploring the Impact of Task Interdependence," *Journal of Applied Psychology*, January 2006, pp. 193–201.

CHAPTER 6

1. "Spacecraft Will Examine Mars in Greater Detail Than Ever Before," http://mars.jpl.nasa.gov/mro/spotlight/20040706.html, accessed July 6, 2004.
2. Felix C. Brodbeck et al., "Group Decision Making Under Conditions of Distributed Knowledge: The Information Asymmetries Model," *Academy of Management Review*, April 2007, pp. 459–460.
3. Andrew E. Schwartz and Joy Levin, "Better Group Decision Making," *Supervisory Management*, June 1990, p. 4.
4. Michael Mercer, *Absolutely Fabulous Organizational Change* (Lake Zurich, IL: Castlegate, 2000); Duncan Maxwell Anderson, "Hidden Forces," *Success*, April 1995, p. 1.
5. Kay Lovelace, Debra L. Shapiro, and Laurie R. Weingart, "Minimizing Cross-Functional New Product Teams' Innovativeness and Constraint Adherence: A Conflict Communications Perspective," *Academy of Management Journal*, August 2001, pp. 779–793.
6. Stuart D. Sidle, "Do Teams Who Agree to Disagree Make Better Decisions?" *Academy of Management Perspectives*, May 2007, pp. 74–75. The Sidle article is a review of S. Schultz-Hardt et al., "Group Decision Making in Hidden Profile Situations: Dissent as a Facilitator for Decision Quality," *Journal of Personality and Social Psychology*, no. 6, 2006, pp. 1080–1093.
7. David A. Garvin and Michael A. Roberto, "What You Don't Know about Making Decisions," *Harvard Business Review*, September 2001, pp. 110–111.
8. Leigh Thompson, "Improving the Creativity of Work Groups," *Academy of Management Executive*, February 2003, p. 99.
9. "Future Edisons of America: Turn Your Employees into Inventors," *WorkingSMART*, June 2000, p. 2.

10. R. Brent Gallupe, William H. Cooper, Mary-Liz Grise, and Lana M. Bastianutti, "Blocking Electronic Brainstorms," *Journal of Applied Psychology*, February 1994, pp. 77–78.
11. Owen Thomas, "The Three-Minute Huddle," *Business 2.0*, April 2006, p. 94.
12. Allen C. Bluedorn, Daniel B. Turban, and Mary Sue Love, "The Effects of Stand-Up and Sit-Down Meeting Formats on Meeting Outcomes," *Journal of Applied Psychology*, April 1999, pp. 277–285.
13. Howard Baker, "Promoting Interaction and Teamwork with Electronic Mail," *Business Education Forum*, October 1994, pp. 30–31.
14. "Introduction to Groupware," http://www.usabilityfirst.com/groupware/intro.txl.
15. Erika Packard, "Meetings Frustrate Task-Oriented Employees, Study Finds," *Monitor on Psychology*, June 2006, p. 10; Steven G. Rogelberg, Desmond J. Leach, Peter B. Warr, and Jennfer L. Burnfield, "'Not Another Meeting!' Are Meeting Time Demands Related to Employee Well-Being?" *Journal of Applied Psychology*, January 2006, pp. 83–96.
16. Several of the suggestions are based on Rachel Zupek, "Horrible, Terrible Meeting Mistakes," http://www.CNN.com, August 29, 2007, pp. 1–3.

Solutions to the Problems in Skill-Building Exercise 6-2

1. The solution to Seven Tennis Balls in a Tube is to simply fill the pipe with water and the balls will float to the top. For the Too-Low Truck, carefully deflate the four tires about 2 inches, and then drive through the tunnel under the bridge. Harley management solved the Aging Members of HOG quite nicely by developing a motor tricycle that has become popular. However, Harley has also made other modifications of their models to make them easier for older people to control, such as being more comfortable and less powerful.

CHAPTER 7

1. Michael L. Diamond, "Employers Finding Equality Gives Zest to Diversity," *Asbury Park Press* syndicated story, February 4, 2007.
2. Margaret M. Clark, "Religion vs. Sexual Orientation," *HR Magazine*, August 2004, pp. 54–59.
3. Arvind V. Phatak, *International Dimensions of Management* (Boston: Kent, 1983), p. 167.
4. Robin J. Ely, Debra Meyerson, and Martin N. Davidson, "Rethinking Political Correctness," *Harvard Business Review*, September 2006, p. 80.
5. Quoted in "Leveraging Diversity at Work," *Hispanic Business*, November 2006, p. 70.
6. P. Christopher Earley and Elaine Mosakowski, "Cultural Intelligence," *Harvard Business Review*, October 2004, p. 140. The example is from the same source, same page.
7. Earley and Mosakowski, "Toward Culture Intelligence: Turning Cultural Differences into a Workplace Advantage," *Academy of Management Executive*, August 2004, pp. 154–155.
8. Ann Pomeroy, "She's Still Lovin' It," *HR Magazine*, December 2006, p. 60.
9. Scott B. Button, "Organizational Efforts to Affirm Sexual Diversity: A Cross-Level Examination," *Journal of Applied Psychology*, February 2001, pp. 17–28.
10. Charlene Marmer Solomon, "Global Operations Demand That HR Rethink Diversity," *Personnel Journal*, July 1994, p. 50.
11. Mansour Javidan, Peter W. Dorfman, May Sully de Luque, and Robert J. House, "In the Eye of the Beholder: Cross Cultural Lessons in Leadership from Project GLOBE," *Academy of Management Perspectives*, February 2006, pp. 69–70. Similar were dimensions were described in Geert Hofstede, *Culture's Consequences: International Differences in Work Related Values* (Beverly Hills: Sage, 1980); updated and expanded in "A Conversation with Geert Hofstede," *Organizational Dynamics*, Spring 1993, pp. 53–61. Dimension 8 is not included in this research.
12. Study reported in Bradley S. Klapper, "Report: U.S. Workers Are the Most Productive," Associated Press, September 2, 2007.
13. Lee Gardenswartz and Anita Rowe, "Cross-Cultural Awareness," *HR Magazine*, March 2001, p. 139.
14. Ellyn Ferguson, "Many Firms Seek Bilingual Workers," Gannett News Service, May 13, 2007.
15. Daren Fonda, "Selling in Tongues," *Time*, November 26, 2001, pp. B12–B13.
16. Paraphrasing of citation in Ferguson, "Many Firms Seek Bilingual Workers."
17. Carolena Lyons Lawrence, "Teaching Students How Gestures Communicate Across Cultures," *Business Education Forum*, February 2003, p. 39.
18. Roger E. Axtell, *Gestures: The Do's and Taboos of Body Language Around the World* (New York: Wiley, 1990).
19. Siri Carpenter, "Why Do 'They All Look Alike'?" *Monitor on Psychology*, December 2000, p. 44.
20. Mei Fong, "Chinese Charm School," *The Wall Street Journal*, January 13, 2004, p. B1.
21. P. Christopher Earley and Randall S. Peterson, "The Elusive Cultural Chameleon: Cultural Intelligence as a New Approach to Intercultural Training for the Global Manager," *Academy of Management Learning and Education*, March 2004, p. 106.
22. Kathryn Tyle, "I Say Potato, You Say *Patata*," *HR Magazine*, January 2004, p. 85.
23. Linda Noeth, "Turn Being Different into a Constructive Experience," *Rochester Democrat and Chronicle*, September 23, 2007, p. 2E.
24. Joanne M. Glenn, "Wendy's International, Inc.—Managing Cross-Generational Diversity," *Business Education Forum*, February 2000, p. 16.

25. Gillian Flynn, "The Harsh Reality of Diversity Programs," *Workforce*, December 1998, p. 29.
26. Kathryn Tyler, "Cross-Cultural Connections: Mentoring Programs Can Bridge Gaps between Disparate Groups," *HR Magazine*, October 2007, pp. 77–83.
27. Tyler, "Cross-Cultural Connections," p. 78.

CHAPTER 8

1. Jared Sandberg, "Shooting Messengers Makes Us Feel Better but Work Dumber," *The Wall Street Journal*, September 11, 2007, p. B1.
2. Michael R. Frone, "Work–Family Conflict and Employee Psychiatric Disorders: The National Comorbidity Survey," *Journal of Applied Psychology*, December 2000, pp. 888–895.
3. Michael T. Ford, Beth A. Heinen, and Krista L. Langkamer, "Work and Family Satisfaction and Conflict: A Meta-Analysis of Cross-Domain Relations," *Journal of Applied Psychology*, January 2007, pp. 57–80.
4. Timothy A. Judge, Remus Ilies, and Brent A. Scott, "Work-Family Conflict and Emotions: Effects at Work and at Home," *Personnel Psychology*, Winter 2006, pp. 779–814.
5. Joyce M. Rosenberg, "Equitable Time-Off Policies Avert Staff Conflicts," Associated Press, September 3, 2007.
6. Kathryn Tyler, "Beat the Clock," *HR Magazine*, November 2003, p. 103.
7. Judith Sills, "When Personalities Clash," *Psychology Today*, November/December 2006, p. 61.
8. Dominic A. Infante, *Arguing Constructively* (Prospect Heights, IL: Waveland Press, 1992).
9. "Workplace Violence," http://www.osha.gov, p. 1, updated July 20, 2007.
10. Study reported in Deborah Smith, "I/O Conference Examines Army Special Forces, Workplace Incivility," *Monitor on Psychology*, June 2003, p. 11.
11. Christine M. Pearson and Christine L. Porath, "On the Nature, Consequences and Remedies of Workplace Incivility: No Time for 'Nice'? Think Again." *Academy of Management Executive*, February 2005, pp. 7–30. The definition of *incivility* is from the same source, p. 7.
12. Comment made by John Derbyshire in a review of Lynne Truss, *Talk to the Hand* (New York: Gotham, 2005), *The Wall Street Journal*, November 5–6, 2005, p. P8; Loretta Chao, "As Workloads Increase, So Does Office Rudeness," *WSJ.com College Journal* (*The Wall Street Journal Online*, http://www.college-journal.com/), January 23, 2006, p. 1.
13. Kenneth Thomas, "Conflict and Conflict Management," in Marvin D. Dunnette, ed., *Handbook of Industrial and Organizational Psychology* (Chicago: Rand McNally College Publishing, 1976), pp. 900–902. Some of the information about when to use each style is from Dean Tjosvold, *The Conflict Positive Organization* (Reading, MA: Addison-Wesley, 1991).
14. Simon, cited in Mark Liu, "You Can Learn to Be Less Accommodating—If You Want To," *Rochester Democrat and Chronicle*, April 25, 1999, p. 1C.
15. Robert R. Blake and Jane S. Mouton, *The Managerial Grid III* (Houston, TX: Gulf, 1985), p. 101.
16. "7 Steps to Conflict Resolution," *Executive Leadership*, June 2007, p. 7. As adapted from The Common Sense Guy Blog, by Bud Bilanich, http://www.commonsenseguy.com.
17. The first three suggestions are from Connirae Andreas and Steve Andreas, *Heart of the Mind* (Moab, UT: Real People Press, 1991). Suggestion four is from Deb Koen, "How to Handle Criticism at Work," *Rochester Democrat and Chronicle,* June 20, 2004.
18. "Conquer Conflict with This Technique," *Manager's Edge*, September 2007, p. 5. As adapted from Maria Broomhower, "Dissolving Conflict through Reframing," http://www.conflict911.com.
19. Jared Curhan, Hilary Anger Elfenbein, and Heng Xu, "What Do People Value When they Negotiate? Mapping the Domain of Subjective Value in Negotiation," *Journal of Personality and Social Psychology*, Vol. 3, 2006, pp. 493–512.
20. Deepak Malhotra and Max H. Bazeman, "Investigative Negotiation," *Harvard Business Review*, pp. 72–78.
21. Mark Diener, "Mad Skills," *Entrepreneur*, April 2003, p. 79.
22. Steve Alper, Dean Tjosvold, and Kenneth S. Law, "Conflict Management, Efficacy, and Performance in Organizational Teams," *Personnel Psychology*, Autumn 2000, pp. 625–642.
23. Maria Rotundo, Dung-Hanh Nguyen, and Paul R. Sackett, "A Meta-Analytic Review of Gender Differences in Perceptions of Sexual Harassment," *Journal of Applied Psychology*, October 2001, pp. 914–922.
24. Remus Ilies, Nancy Hauserman, Susan Schwochau, and John Stibal, "Reported Incidence Rates of Work-Related Sexual Harassment in the United States: Using Meta-Analysis to Explain Rate Disparities," *Personnel Psychology*, Autumn 2003, pp. 607–631.
25. Hilary J. Gettman and Michele J. Gelfand, "When the Customer Shouldn't Be King: Antecedents and Consequences of Sexual Harassment by Clients and Customers," *Journal of Applied Psychology*, May 2007, pp. 757–770.
26. Jennifer L. Berdahl, "The Sexual Harassment of Uppity Women," *Journal of Applied Psychology*, March 2007, pp. 425–437
27. Jennifer L. Berdahl and Celia Moore, "Workplace Harassment: Double Jeopardy for Minority Women," *Journal of Applied Psychology*, March 2006, pp. 426–436.
28. Chelsea R. Willness, Piers Steel, and Kibeom Lee, "A Meta-Analysis of the Antecedents and Consequences of Workplace Sexual Harassment," *Personnel Psychology*, Spring 2007, p. 141.

29. Kathleen Neville, *Corporate Attractions: An Inside Account of Sexual Harassment with the New Sexual Roles for Men and Women on the Job* (Reston, VA: Acropolis Books, 1992); Joanne Cole, "Sexual Harassment: New Rules, New Behavior," *HRfocus,* March 1999, pp. 1, 14–15.

30. Jathan W. Janove, "Sexual Harassment and the Three Big Surprises," *HR Magazine*, November 2001, p. 123.

31. Robert McGarvey, "Hands Off! How Do the Latest Supreme Court Decisions on Sexual Harassment Affect You?" *Entrepreneur*, September 1998, p. 86; Cole, "Sexual Harassment: New Rules," p. 14.

CHAPTER 9

1. Case history collected in Rochester, New York, January 2008.

2. Bill Bill Bradley, "Whatever the Score—Bounce Back," *Parade Magazine*, October 18, 1998, p. 6.

3. Joseph A. Raelin, *Creating Leaderful Organizations: How to Bring Out Leadership in Everyone* (San Francisco: Berrett Koehler, 2003).

4. George P. Hollenbeck and Douglas T. Hall, "Self-Confidence and Leader Performance," *Organizational Dynamics*, no. 3, 2004, pp. 254–269.

5. Shelley A. Kirkpatrick and Edwin A. Locke, "Leadership: Do Traits Matter?" *Academy of Management Executive*, May 1991, pp. 26–27.

6. Daniel R. Ames and Francis J. Flynn, "What Breaks a Leader: The Curvilinear Relation between Assertiveness and Leadership," *Journal of Personality and Social Psychology*, Volume 92, 2007, pp. 307–324.

7. Survey cited in "What Are the Most Important Traits for Bosses?" *Employee Recruitment & Retention*, Sample Issue, 2006.

8. Reported in "Developing Trust Pays Off," *Manager's Edge*, April 1999, p. 9.

9. Douglas R. May, Adrian Y. L. Chan, Timothy D. Hodges, and Bruce J. Avolio, "Developing the Moral Component of Authentic Leadership," *Organizational Dynamics*, no. 3, 2003, pp. 247–260.

10. Anthony Bianco, "The Rise of a Star," *BusinessWeek*, December 21, 1998, p. 63; "AmEx's Ken Chenault Talks about Leadership, Integrity, and the Credit Card Business," Knowledge@Wharton (http://knowledge.wharton.upenn), April 2005, p. 2.

11. Bruce J. Avolio, Jane M. Howell, and John J. Sosik, "A Funny Thing Happened on the Way to the Bottom Line: Humor as a Moderator of Leadership Style Effects," *Academy of Management Journal*, April 1999, pp. 219–227.

12. Bill George, Peter Sims, Andrew N. McLean, and Diana Mayer, "Discovering Your Authentic Leadership," *Harvard Business Review*, February 2007, p. 129.

13. Dale E. Zand, *The Leadership Triad: Knowledge, Trust, and Power* (New York: Oxford University Press, 1997), p. 8.

14. Studies on this topic are reviewed in Timothy A. Judge, Amy Colbert, and Remus Ilies, "Intelligence and Leadership: A Quantitative Review and Test of Theoretical Propositions," *Journal of Applied Psychology*, June 2004, p. 548.

15. John Menkes, *Executive Intelligence: What All Great Leaders Have* (New York: Collins, 2006).

16. Gina Chon, "Chrysler Challenge: Burnish Image," *The Wall Street Journal*, August 24, 2007, p. B3.

17. Bill Breen, "The Clear Leader," *Fast Company*, March 2005, pp. 65–67.

18. Quoted in Brian M. Carney, "Of Tax Cuts and Terror," *The Wall Street Journal*, June 30–July 1, 2007, p. A7.

19. Daniel Goleman, "What Makes a Leader?" *Harvard Business Review,* November–December 1998, p. 92; Goleman, "Never Stop Learning," *Harvard Business Review*, January 2004, pp. 28–28.

20. Robert A. Eckert, "Where Leadership Starts," *Harvard Business Review*, November 2001, pp. 53–61. The quote is from page 54.

21. Richard Boyatzis and Annie McKee, *Resonant Leadership* (Boston: Harvard Business School Press, 2005).

22. Jay A. Conger, *The Charismatic Leader: Behind the Mystique of Exceptional Leadership* (San Francisco: Jossey-Bass, 1989).

23. Jack and Suzy Welch, "It's Not about Empty Suits," *Business Week*, October 16, 2006, p. 132.

24. Luisa Beltran, "Standout Performer," *Hispanic Business*, April 2007, p. 26.

25. Michael E. Brown and Linda K. Treviño, "Socialized Charismatic Leadership, Values, Congruence, and Deviance in Work Groups," *Journal of Applied Psychology*, July 2006, p. 955.

26. Suggestions 7, 9, and 10 are from Roger Dawson, *Secrets of Power Persuasion* (Upper Saddle River, NJ: Prentice Hall, 1992), pp. 181–183.

27. A. Skogtad et al., "The Destructiveness of Laissez-Faire Leadership Behavior," *Journal of Occupational Health Psychology*, January 2007, pp. 80–92.

28. "Bring Out the Leader in Everyone," *Managing People at Work*, sample issue, 2000, p. 4.

29. Jon R. Katzenbach and Douglas K. Smith, "The Discipline of Teams," *Harvard Business Review*, March–April 1993, p. 118.

30. "Pump Up Your Leadership Style," *Manager's Edge*, March 2007, p. 3. Adapted from Patricia Fripp, "Leadership Lesson 2: 'I'm Glad You Asked,'" http://www.fripp.com.

31. "Bring Out the Leader in Everyone," p. 4.

32. "What It Takes to Be an Effective Team Leader," *Manager's Edge*, March 2000, p. 6.

33. Terri A. Scandura and Chester A. Schrieisheim, "Leader–Member Exchange and Supervisor Career Mentoring as Complementary Constructs in Leadership Research," *Academy of Management Journal*, December 1994, pp. 1588–1602; George

Graen and J. F. Cashman, "A Role Making Model of Leadership in Formal Organizations: A Developmental Approach," in J. G. Hunt and L. L. Larson, eds., *Leadership Frontiers* (Kent, OH: Kent State University Press, 1975), pp. 143–165.

34. Francis J. Yammarino, Alan J. Dubinsky, Lucette B. Comer, and Marvin A. Jolson, "Women and Transformational and Contingent Reward Leadership: A Multiple-Levels-of-Analysis Perspective," *Academy of Management Journal*, February 1997, pp. 205–222.

35. This issue is treated at length in Bruce J. Avolio, *Leadership in Balance: Made/Born* (Mahwah, NJ: Earlbaum, 2005).

36. Jon R. Katzenbach and Jason A. Santamaria, "Firing Up the Front Line," *Harvard Business Review*, May–June 1999, pp. 116–117.

37. William D. Hitt, *The Model Leader: A Fully Functioning Person* (Columbus, OH: Battelle Press, 1993).

38. Manuel London, *Leadership Development: Paths to Self-Insight and Professional Growth* (Mahwah, NJ: Erlbaum, 2002).

39. Cheryl Dahle, "Natural Leader," *Fast Company*, December 2000, p. 270.

40. Michael E. McGill and John W. Slocum, Jr., "A *Little* Leadership Please?" *Organizational Dynamics*, Winter 1998, p. 48.

41. Bill Breen, "Trickle-Up Leadership," *Fast Company*, November 2001, pp. 70–72.

CHAPTER 10

1. "Travel Incentives Shown to Grow Sales," http://www.martizetravel.com/travel-toro.html, 2007, p. 1.

2. Gerald Kushel, *Reaching the Peak Performance Zone: How to Motivate Yourself and Others to Excel* (New York: AMACOM, 1994), p. 66.

3. Piers Steel and Cornelius J. König, "Integrating Theories of Motivation," *Academy of Management Review*, October 2006. pp. 895–896.

4. Research summarized in "One of These Seven Things Will Motivate Any Employee in the Company," *Motivational Manager*, sample issue, 1998 (Lawrence Ragan Communications, Inc.).

5. Fred Luthans and Alexander D. Stajkovic, "Reinforce for Performance: The Need to Go Beyond Pay and Even Rewards," *Academy of Management Executive*, May 1999, p. 52.

6. Steven Kerr, *Ultimate Rewards: What Really Motivates People to Achieve* (Boston: Harvard Business School Publishing, 1997).

7. "Simple Rewards Are Powerful Motivators," *HRfocus*, August 2001, p. 10.

8. "5 Ways to Create Team Motivation," *Manager's Edge*, November 2007, p. 4.

9. Martin Booe, "Sales Force at Mary Kay China Embraces the American Way," *Workforce Management*, April 2005, pp. 24–25.

10. Jennifer Laabs, "Satisfy Them with More Than Money," *Workforce*, November 1998, p. 43; Charlotte Garvey, "Meaningful Tokens of Appreciation," *HR Magazine*, August 2004, pp. 101–106; 10. Adrian Gostick and Chester Elton, *The Carrot Principle* (New York: The Free Press, 2007).

11. "Time Your Praise to Make It Last," *WorkingSMART*, June 2000, p. 2.

12. "Ten Sentences That Will Help You Retain Your Best Employees," *Employee Recruitment & Retention*, sample issue, 2004 (Lawrence Ragan Communications Inc.).

13. Andrew J. DuBrin, "Self-Perceived Technical Orientation and Attitudes Toward Being Flattered," *Psychological Reports*, vol. 96, 2005, pp. 852–854.

14. The original version of expectancy theory applied to work motivation is Victor Vroom, *Work and Motivation* (New York: Wiley, 1964). A scholarly update of the theory is presented in Steel and König, "Integrating Theories of Motivation," pp. 893–895.

15. Alexander D. Stajkovic and Fred Luthans, "Social Cognitive Theory and Self-Efficacy: Going Beyond Traditional Motivational and Behavioral Approaches," *Organizational Dynamics*, Spring 1998, p. 66.

16. Steve McShane, "Getting Emotional about Employee Motivation," *Currents* (published by McGraw-Hill), September 2004, p. 1; Amir Erez and Alice M. Isen, "The Influence of Positive Affect on the Components of Expectancy Motivation," *Journal of Applied Psychology*, December 2002, pp. 1055–1067.

CHAPTER 11

1. Elisa Ludwig, "Trade Secrets," *PM Network*, July 2007, p. 36.

2. Alina Tugend, "Why Is Asking for Help So Difficult?" *The New York Times* (http://www.nytimes.com/), July 7, 2007, p. 1.

3. Elwood F. Holton III, "New Employee Development Tactics: Perceived Availability, Helpfulness, and Relationship with Job Attitudes," *Journal of Business and Psychology*, Fall 2001, pp. 73–85.

4. Jeffrey Keller, "Associate with Positive People," a supplement to the *Pryor Report*, 1994.

5. Monica C. Higgins and Kathy E. Kram, "Reconceptualizing Mentoring at Work: A Developmental Network Perspective," *Academy of Management Review*, April 2001, pp. 264–288.

6. Ludwig, "Trade Secrets," p. 38.

7. Donna M. Owens, "Virtual Mentoring," *HR Magazine*, March 2006, pp. 105–107.

8. Anne Field, "No Time to Mentor? Do It Online," *BusinessWeek*, March 3, 2003, p. 126; Stephenie Overman, "Mentors without Borders," *HR Magazine*, March 2004, pp. 3–85.

9. Tammy D. Allen, Lillian T. Eby, and Elizabeth Lentz, "Mentoring Behaviors and Mentorship Quality Associated with Formal Mentoring Programs: Closing

the Gap between Research and Practice," *Journal of Applied Psychology*, May 2006, pp. 567–578.

10. Based mostly on Kathy E. Kram, *Mentoring at Work: Developmental Relationships in Organizational Life* (Glenview, IL: Scott Foresman, 1985), pp. 22–39; Erik J. Van Slyke and Bud Van Slyke, "Mentoring: A Results-Oriented Approach," *HRfocus*, February 1998, p. 14.

11. Steve Trautman, *Teach What You Know: A Practical Leader's Guide to Knowledge Transfer Using Peer Mentoring* (Upper Saddle River, NJ: Prentice Hall, 2007).

12. Stephanie C. Payne and Ann H. Huffman, "A Longitudinal Examination of the Influence of Mentoring on Organizational Commitment and Turnover," *Academy of Management Journal*, February 2005, pp. 158–168.

13. "Coaching—One Solution to a Tight Training Budget," *HRfocus*, August 2002, p. 7; Sharon Ting and Peter Scisco, eds., *The CCL Handbook of Coaching: A Guide for the Leader Coach* (San Francisco: Jossey-Bass, 2006).

14. Editors of *Managers Edge, The Successful Manager's Guide to Giving and Receiving Feedback* (Alexander, VA: Briefings Publishing Group, 2004), p. 14.

15. Anne Fisher, "Turn Star Employees into Superstars," *Fortune*, December 13, 2004, p. 70.

16. "Coach Your Employees to Success with This Plan," *Manager's Edge*, May 2000, p. 1.

17. "Coach with 'Could,' Not 'Should,'" *Executive Strategies*, April 1998, p. 1.

18. Andrew J. DuBrin, *Leadership: Research Findings, Practice, and Skills*, 5th ed. (Boston: Houghton Mifflin, 2007), p. 311.

19. Bruce Tulgan, "The Under-Management Epidemic," *HR Magazine*, October 2004, p. 119.

20. This one item is from John M. Ivancevich and Thomas N. Duening, *Management: Skills, Application, Practice, and Development* (Cincinnati, OH: Atomic Dog Publishing, 2006), p. 282.

21. Kent W. Seibert, "Reflection in Action: Tools for Cultivating On-the-Job Learning Conditions," *Organizational Dynamics*, Winter 1999, p. 55.

22. Career Track seminar, How to Deal with Difficult People, 1995; Fred Pryor Seminar, How to Deal with Unacceptable Behavior, 2007; Kenneth Kaye, *Workplace Wars and How to End Them: Turning Personal Conflicts into Productive Teamwork* (New York: AMACOM, 1994); Jared Sandberg, "Staff 'Handfuls' and the Bosses Who Coddle Them," *The Wall Street Journal*, October 8, 2003, p. B1.; Darnell Morris-Compton, "How to Unmask Workers Who Cheat," *Indianapolis Star* syndicated story, March 13, 2005.

23. Jathan Janover, "Jerks at Work," *HR Magazine*, May 2007, p. 111.

24. Leigh Buchanam, "The Bully Rulebook," *Inc. Magazine* (*Inc.com*), February 2007; Patrick White,

"Sometimes Office Jerks Finish First," *Detroit News* (*detnews.com*), July 23, 2007.

25. Quoted in Jessica Guynn, "Bullying Behavior Affects Morale as Well as the Bottom Line," Knight Ridder syndicated story, November 2, 1998.

26. Nando Pelusi, "Dealing with Difficult People," *Psychology Today* (*psychologytoday.com*), 2006.

27. "How to Deal with 'Problem' Workers," *Positive Leadership*, sample issue, distributed 2001; Martien Eerhart, "Top 7 Ideas for Dealing with Difficult Employees," http://top7business.com/archives/personnel/050499.html.

28. John C. Maxwell, *Winning with People: Discover the People Principles That Work for You Every Time* (Nashville, TN: Nelson Books, 2004), pp. 1428–1429.

29. Janover, "Jerks at Work," p. 117.

CHAPTER 12

1. Daniel Goleman, *Social Intelligence: The New Science of Human Relationships* (New York: Bantam, 2006); Carol Hymowitz, "Business Is Personal, So Managers Need to Harness Emotions," *The Wall Street Journal*, November 13, 2006, p. B1.

2. Hymowitz, "Business Is Personal," p. B1.

3. Amos Drory and Nurit Zaidman, "The Politics of Impression Management in Organizations: Contextual Effects," in Eran Vigoda-Gadot and Amos Drory, *Handbook of Organizational Politics* (Northampton, MA: Edward Elgar, 2006), p. 75.

4. "Career Article 103: Getting Along with Your Boss," http://www.seekingsuccess.com, 2002–2006, p. 2.

5. Terry Bragg, "Nine Strategies for Successfully Playing Office Politics," http://www.tbragg.addr.com, July 15, 2005, p. 1.

6. Tamara E. Holmes, "Admitting When You're Wrong," *Black Enterprise*, May 2007, p. 124.

7. "Get Rid of 'Yes Men,'" *Manager's Edge*, Special Bulletin, Spring 2006, p. 2.

8. Daniel Yi, "For Many Employees, Fitness Has Its Prize," *The Los Angeles Times* (http://www.latimes.com), March 12, 2007.

9. "Nu-Living Weight Management–Microsoft Program," http://www.nu-living.com/microsoft, May 24, 2007.

10. William L. Gardner III, "Lessons in Organizational Dramaturgy: The Art of Impression Management," *Organizational Dynamics*, Summer 1992, p. 45.

11. Kenneth J. Harris, K. Michele Kacmar, Suzanne Zivnuska, and Jason D. Shaw, "The Impact of Political Skill on Impression Management Effectiveness," *Journal of Applied Psychology*, January 2007, pp. 278–285.

12. Jim Rucker and Jean Anna Sellers, "Changes in Business Etiquette," *Business Education Forum*, February 1998, p. 43.

13. Rucker and Sellers, "Changes in Business Etiquette," p. 45.

14. Paula Gamonal, "Business Etiquette: More Than Just Eating with the Right Fork," *Ravenwerks Business Etiquette Blog*, http://www.ravenwerks.com, accessed October 24, 2007.

15. This section of the chapter is based on *Keying In*, January 1996, pp. 1–8; Rucker and Sellers, "Changes in Business Etiquette," pp. 43–45; Letitia Baldrige, *The Executive Advantage* (Washington, DC: Georgetown Publishing House, 1999); "Culture Shock?" *Entrepreneur*, May 1998, p. 46; Ann Perry, "Finer Points of the Meet and Eat," *Toronto Star*, http://www.thestar.com, January 2, 2004; Blanca Torres, "Good Dining Manners Can Help Bet a Bigger Slice of the Job Pie," *Baltimore Sun*, April 5, 2005; Erin White, "The Jungle: Focus on Recruitment, Pay and Getting Ahead," *The Wall Street Journal*, November 2, 2004, p. B8. The quotes are from the same sources

16. James F. Thompson, *The Cubicle Survival Guide* (New York: Villard, 2007).

17. "Disability Etiquette," *Human Resources Forum* (a supplement to *Management Review*), June 1997, p. 3; "Helping Today's Blind Children Become the Winners of Tomorrow," American Blind Children's Council (flyer), 2002.

18. Jared Sandberg, "How Office Tyrants in Critical Positions Get Others to Grovel," *The Wall Street Journal*, August 21, 2007, p. B1.

19. Anne Fisher, "The Trouble with MBAs," *Fortune*, April 30, 2007, p. 49.

20. Deb Koen, "Jittery About Networking? Know the Etiquette," *Rochester Democrat and Chronicle*, April 14, 2002, p. 4E.

21. Brian Hilliard and James Palmer, *Networking Like a Pro* (Atlanta, GA: Agito Consulting, 2003, p. 52).

22. Judith Sills, "How to Be a Rising Star," *Psychology Today*, March/April 2006, pp. 38–39.

23. Sills, "How to Be a Rising Star," p. 39.

24. "Managing Your Boss—How to Play Your Cards Right," *Monster Career Centre, Monster.com* (http://www.monster.com), vol. 4, 2002, p. 2.

25. James D. Westphal and Ithai Stern, "Flattery Will Get You Everywhere (Especially If You Are a Male Caucasian): How Ingratiation, Boardroom Behavior, and Demographic Minority Status Affect Additional Board Appointments at U.S. Companies," *Academy of Management Journal*, April 2007, pp. 267–288.

26. Marshall Goldsmith, "All of Us Are Stuck on Suck-Ups," *Fast Company*, December 2003, p. 117.

27. Research reported in Jeffrey Zaslow, "The Most-Praised Generation Goes to Work," *The Wall Street Journal*, April 20, 2007, p. W7.

28. Tom Rather, *Vital Friends: The People You Can't Afford to Live Without* (New York: Gallup Press, 2006).

29. Quoted in Anita Bruzzese, "On-the-Job Friends Improve Workplace," Gannett News Service, August 21, 2006.

30. Shelia Murray Bethel, *Making a Difference* (New York: Putnam's Sons, 1989).

31. Lea Winerman, "Have Your Heard the Latest?" *Monitor on Psychology*, April 2006, p. 57.

32. Gary M. Stern, "Small Slights Bring Big Problems," *Workforce*, August 2002, p. 17; Joann S. Lublin, "How to Stop the Snubs That Demoralize You and Your Colleagues," *The Wall Street Journal*, December 7, 2004, p. B1.

33. Cindy Krischer Goodman, "More Employees Finding the Net Works," *Miami Herald* (*Miami Herald.com*, http://www.miamiherald.com), October 24, 2007, p. 1.

34. Carol Hymowitz, "Personal Boundaries Shrink as Companies Punish Bad Behavior," *The Wall Street Journal*, June 18, 2007, p. B1.

CHAPTER 13

1. Quoted in Mark Hendricks, "Paying in Kind: How Can You Ensure Employees Give Service with a Smile?" *Entrepreneur*, February 2006, p. 82.

2. Quoted in Ryan Chittum, "Price Points: Good Customer Service Costs Money. Some Expenses Are Worth It—and Some Aren't," *The Wall Street Journal*, October 30, 2006, p. R7.

3. Leonard L. Berry, Eileen A. Wall, and Lewis P. Carbone, "Service Clues and Customer Assessment of the Service Experience: Lessons from Marketing," *Academy of Management Perspectives*, May 2006, pp. 43–57.

4. Paul R. Timm, *Customer Service: Career Success Through Customer Satisfaction*, 2nd ed. (Upper Saddle River, NJ: Prentice Hall, 2001), p. 8.

5. Quoted in Deborah Alexander, "Keep Tops Intact, Workers Urge," *Rochester Democrat and Chronicle*, December 1, 2006, p. 9D.

6. Quoted in Lin Grensing-Pophal, "Building Service with a Smile," *HR Magazine*, November 2006, p. 86.

7. Barry M. Stow and Jerry Ross, "Stability in the Midst of Change: A Dispositional Approach to Job Attitudes," *Journal of Applied Psychology*, August 1985, p. 471.

8. Sue Shellenbarger, "Domino Effect: The Unintended Results of Telling Off Customer-Service Staff," *The Wall Street Journal*, February 5, 2004, p. D1.

9. Lance A. Bettencourt, Kevin P. Gwinner, and Matthew L. Meuter, "A Comparison of Attitude, Personality, and Knowledge Predictors of Service-Oriented Organizational Citizenship Behavior," *Journal of Applied Psychology*, February 2001, pp. 29–41.

10. Alex M. Susskind, K. Michele Kacmar, and Carl P. Borchgrevink, "Customer Service Providers' Attitudes Relating to Customer Service and Customer Satisfaction in the Customer–Server Exchange," *Journal of Applied Psychology*, February 2003, pp. 179–187.

11. Craig A. Martin and Alan J. Bush, "Psychological Climate, Empowerment, and Customer-Oriented

Selling: An Analysis of the Sales Manager–Salesperson Dyad," *Journal of the Academy of Marketing Science*, no. 3, 2006, pp. 419–438.

12. Hui Lao and Aichia Chuang, "Transforming Service Employees and Climate: A Multilevel, Multisource Examination of Transformational Leadership in Building Long-Term Service Relationships," *Journal of Applied Psychology*, July 2007, pp. 1006–1019.

13. "The Chairman of the Board Looks Back," *Fortune*, May 28, 2001, p. 70.

14. Richard B. Chase and Sriram Dasu, "Want to Perfect Your Company's Service? Use Behavioral Science," *Harvard Business Review*, June 2001, pp. 78–84.

15. Karl Abrecht, *The Only Thing That Matters* (New York: HarperCollins, 1992).

16. Susan Okula, "Customer Service: New Tools for a Timeless Idea," *Business Education Forum*, December 1998, p. 7; Robert F. Gault, "Managing Customer Satisfaction for Profit," *Management Review*, April 1993, p. 23.

17. Amanda C. Kooser, "Crowd Control," *Entrepreneur*, August 2003, pp. 33–34.

18. Adapted from "For Extraordinary Service," *The Customer Service Professional*, October 1997, p. 3.

19. Lorna Ducet, "Service Provider Hostility and Service Quality," *Academy of Management Journal*, October 2004, pp. 761–771.

20. D. J. Cran, "Towards the Validation of the Service Orientation Construct," *The Service Industries Journal*, vol. 14, 1994, p. 36.

21. Dot Yandle, "Helping Your Employees Give Customers What They Want," *Success Workshop* (a supplement to *Manager's Edge*), November 1998, p. 1.

22. Patricia B. Barger and Alicia A. Grandey, "Service with a Smile and Encounter Satisfaction: Emotional Contagion and Appraisal Mechanisms," *Academy of Management Journal*, December 2006, pp. 1229–1238.

23. Steven Gray, "Flipping Burger King," *The Wall Street Journal*, April 26, 2005, B1.

24. Ryan Chittum, "Price Points: Good Customer Service Costs Money, " p. R7.

25. Michelle Conlin and Andrew Park, "Blogging with the Boss's Blessing," *BusinessWeek*, June 28, 2004, p. 100–102; Mike Sansone, "Purpose Driven Blogging," http://www.conversations.com, 2006.

26. Daniel Akst, book review of *Hug Your Customers* by Jack Mitchell (Hyperion, 2003), appearing in *The Wall Street Journal*, November 14, 2003, p. W9.

27. Research cited in "Service Facts," *Customer Service Professional*, October 1997, p. 1.

28. Hwee Hoon Tan, Maw Der Foo, and Min Hui Kwek, "The Effects of Customer Personality Traits on the Display of Positive Emotions," *Academy of Management Journal*, April 2004, pp. 287–296.

29. Donna Deeprose, "Helping Employees Handle Difficult Customers," *Supervisory Management*, September 1991, p. 6; Chip R. Bell and Ron Zemke,

"Service Breakdown—The Road to Recovery," in *Service Wisdom: Creating and Maintaining the Customer Service Edge* (Minneapolis, MN: Lakewood Books, 1992).

30. Patrick J. Kiger, "The Art of the Apology," *Workforce Management*, October 2004, p. 62.

31. Jan Norman, "Caring about Clients Helps Companies Handle Crises," Knight Ridder story, December 3, 2000.

32. Hal Hardy, "Five Steps to Pleasing Difficult, Demanding Customers," *First-Rate Customer Service*, no. 1, 2005, p. 1.

33. "Customer Problem Clinics," in *Making . . . Serving . . . Keeping Customers*, Dartnell, Chicago:.

34. Timm, *Customer Service*, p. 43.

CHAPTER 14

1. Mark Henricks, "Well, Honestly!" *Entrepreneur*, December 2006, pp. 103-104.

2. Linda K. Treviño and Katherine A. Nelson, *Managing Business Ethics: Straight Talk About How to Do It Right* (New York: Wiley, 1995), pp. 24–35; O. C. Ferrell, John Fraedrich, and Linda Ferrell, *Business Ethics: Ethical Decision Making and Cases,* 4th ed. (Boston: Houghton Mifflin, 2000) pp. 13–16; Anita Bruzzese, "Tools Take Ethics to the Real World," Gannett News Service, May 16, 2005.

3. Thomas M. Jones, "Ethical Decision Making by Individuals in Organizations: An Issue Contingent Model," *Academy of Management Review*, April 1991, p. 391.

4. Linda Kelbe Treviño, "Managing to Be Ethical: Debunking Five Business Ethics Myths," *Academy of Management Executive*, May 2004, pp. 69-72.

5. Scott J. Reynolds, "Moral Awareness and Ethical Predispositions: Investigating the Role of Individual Differences in the Recognition of Moral Issues," *Journal of Applied Psychology*, January 2006, p. 234.

6. Data from Ethics Resource Center and Kronos, Inc., reported in Sue Shellenbarger, "How and Why We Lie at the Office: From Pilfered Pens to Padded Accounts," *The Wall Street Journal*, March 24, 2005, p. D1.

7. Treviño and Nelson, *Managing Business Ethics*, pp. 47–64.

8. Data reported in "McAfee Anti-Piracy Information," http://www.networkassociates.com/us/antipiracy_policy.htm, accessed May 25, 2005; "Software Piracy," http://blog.ndiyo.org, May 1, 2006.

9. Edmund L. Andrews, "Interior Official Assails Agency for Ethics Slides," *The New York Times* (http://www.nytimes.com, September 14, 2006.

10. Nanette Byrnes, "The Comeback of Consulting," *Business Week*, September 3, 2007, p. 66.

11. "O'Leary Admits Lying, Quits," Associated Press, December 15, 2001.

12. Joseph L. Badaracco, Jr., "The Discipline of Building Character," *Harvard Business Review*, March–April 1998, pp. 114–124.

13. Edwin A. Locke, "Business Ethics: A Way Out of the Morass," *Academy of Management Learning & Education*, September 2006, pp. 328–330.

14. Treviño and Nelson, *Managing Business Ethics*, pp. 71–75.

15. Scott Sonenshein, "The Role of Construction, Intuition, and Justification in Responding to Ethical Issues at Work: The Sensemaking–Intuition Model," *Academy of Management Review*, October 2007, p. 1030.

16. Sonenshein, "The Role of Construction, Intuition," p. 1033.

17. Daniel J. Brass, Kenneth D. Butterfield, and Bruce C. Skaggs, "Relationships and Unethical Behavior: A Social Network Perspective," *Academy of Management Review*, January 1998, pp. 14–31.

18. Cited in Jean Thilmany, "Supporting Ethical Employees," *HR Magazine*, September 2007, p. 106.

19. "Extolling the Virtues of Hot Lines," *Workforce*, June 1998, pp. 125–126; Daryl Koehn, "An Interview with William Griffin," http://www.stthom.edu/cbes/griffin.html (Accessed May 27, 2005).

20. "The Optima Awards: They've Got Game," *Workforce Management*, March 2005, p. 44.

21. Mary Uhl-Bien and Melissa K. Carsten, "Being Ethical When the Boss Is Not," *Organizational Dynamics*," Issue 2, 2007, p. 197.

CHAPTER 15

1. Chris Penttila, "Time Out," *Entrepreneur*, April 2007, p. 71.

2. Cait Murphy, "The CEO Workout," *Fortune*, July 10, 2006, pp. 43–44.

3. Norman B. Anderson, "Toward Reducing Work Stress," *Monitor on Psychology*, February 2008, p. 9.

4. Jeffrey R. Edwards, "A Cybernetic Theory of Stress, Coping, and Well-Being in Organizations," *Academy of Management Review*, April 1992, p. 248.

5. Lea Winerman, "Reducing Stress Helps both Brain and Body," *Monitor on Psychology*, October 2006, p. 18.

6. Research reported in Christine Gorman, "6 Lessons for Handling Stress," *Time*, January 29, 2007, p. 82.

7. *British Medical Journal* study reported in "Trop de Stress au Travail Double le Risque de Mourir d'une Crise de Coeur," *Journal de Montréal*, 18 octobre, 2002, p. 7. [Too much work stress doubles the risk of dying from a heart attack.]

8. Jeffery A. Lapine, Nathan P. Podsakoff, and Marcie A. Lepine, "A Meta-Analytic Test of the Challenge-Stressor–Hindrance-Stressor Framework: An Explanation for Inconsistent Relationships among Stressors and Performance," *Academy of Management Journal*, October 2005, pp. 764–775.

9. Gillian E. Hardy, David Woods, and Toby D. Wall, "The Impact of Psychological Distress on Absence from Work," *Journal of Applied Psychology*, April 2003, pp. 306–314.

10. Quoted in "An Ounce of Prevention Beats Burnout," *HRfocus*, June 1999, p. 1.

11. Christina Maslach, *The Truth about Burnout* (San Francisco: Jossey-Bass, 1997). See also Dirk van Dierendonck, Wilmar B. Schaufeli, and Bram P. Buunk, "The Evaluation of an Individual Burnout Intervention Program: The Role of Equity and Social Support," *Journal of Applied Psychology*, June 1998, pp. 392–407.

12. Research reported in Deborah Smith Bailey, "Burnout Harms Workers' Physical Health through Many Pathways," *Monitor on Psychology*, June 2006, p. 11.

13. M. Afalur Rahim, "Relationships of Stress, Locus of Control, and Social Support to Psychiatric Symptoms and Propensity to Leave a Job: A Field Study with Managers," *Journal of Business and Psychology*, Winter 1997, p. 159.

14. Steve M. Jex and Paul D. Bliese, "Efficacy Beliefs as a Moderator of the Impact of Work-Related Stressors: A Multilevel Study," *Journal of Applied Psychology*, June 1999, pp. 349–361; Steve M. Jex, Paul O. Bliese, Sheri Buzell, and Jessica Primeau, "The Impact of Self-Efficacy on Stressor-Strain Relations: Coping Style as an Explanatory Mechanism," *Journal of Applied Psychology*, June 2001, pp. 401–409.

15. John Schaubroeck and Deryl E. Merrit, "Divergent Effects of Job Control on Coping with Work Stressors: The Key Role of Self-Efficacy," *Academy of Management Journal*, June 1997, p. 750.

16. Jeffrey R. Edwards and A. J. Baglioni, Jr., "Relationships between Type A Behavior Pattern and Mental and Physical Symptoms: A Comparison of Global and Component Measures," *Journal of Applied Psychology*, April 1991, p. 276; related research reported in Etienne Benson, "Hostility Is among Best Predictors of Heart Disease in Men," *Monitor on Psychology*, January 2003, p. 15.

17. Research reviewed in Nadja Geipert, "Don't Be Mad: More Research Links Hostility to Coronary Risk," *Monitor on Psychology*, January 2007, pp. 50–51.

18. Peter Y. Chen and Paul E. Spector, "Negative Affectivity as the Underlying Cause of Correlations between Stressors and Strains," *Journal of Applied Psychology*, June 1991, p. 398.

19. Families and Work Institute survey reported in Adam Geller, "Survey: Third of Americans Overworked," Associated Press, March 16, 2005.

20. Sylvia Ann Hewlett and Carolyn Buck Luce, "Extreme Jobs: The Dangerous Allure of the 70-Hour Work Week," *Harvard Business Review*, December 2006, pp. 49–59.

21. William Atkinson, "Causes of Workplace Stress," *HR Magazine*, December 2000, p. 107; Michele Conlin, "Is Your Office Killing You?" *Business Week*, June 5, 2000, pp. 114–128; "Sick Building

Syndrome," http://www.doctorfungus.org, January 22, 2007, p. 1.

22. The data on vision and carpal tunnel syndrome are from the Computer Vision Syndrome Center reported in Anita Bruzzese, "Computer Users Often Strain Eyes," Gannett News Service, September 13, 2004; Christine A. Sprigg et al., "Work Characteristics, Musculoskeletal Disorders, and the Mediating Role of Psychological Strain: A Study of Call Center Employees," *Journal of Applied Psychology*, September 2007, pp. 1456–1466.

23. Study reported in Deborah Smith Bailey, "Longer Train Commutes Are More Stressful, Study Finds," *Monitor on Psychology*, September 2006, p. 12.

24. Larry Copeland, "Drivers Rising Earlier to Beat the Traffic," *USA Today* syndicated story, September 16, 2007.

25. Edward Hallowell, *CrazyBusy: Overstretched, Overbooked, and About to Snap—Strategies for Coping in a World Gone ADD* (New York: Ballantine Books, 2006); "Zen and the Art of Thinking Straight," *Business Week*, April 3, 2006, p. 116.

26. Richard S. DeFrank and John M. Ivancevich, "Stress on the Job: An Executive Update," *Academy of Management Executive*, August 1998, pp. 56–57.

27. Jan de Jonge and Christian Dormann, "Stressors, Resources, and Strain at Work: A Longitudinal Test of the Triple-Match Principle," *Journal of Applied Psychology*, November 2006, pp. 1359–1374.

28. Richard Corliss, "The Power of Yoga," *Time,* April 23, 2001, pp. 54–62; Stacy Forster, "Companies Say Yoga Isn't a Stretch," *The Wall Street Journal*, October 14, 2003, p. D4.

29. Lisa Belkin, "Some Respect, Please, for the Afternoon Nap," *The New York Times* (http://www.nytimes.com), February 25, 2007, p. 1.

30. Lea Winerman, "Sleep Deprivation Threatens Public Health, Says Research Award Winner," July/August 2004, p. 61.

31. Katherine Ellison, "Mastering Your Own Mind," *Psychology Today*, October 2006, p. 75.

32. Quoted in "How I Work: A.G. Lafley," *Fortune*, March 20, 2006, p. 74.

33. Gorman, "6 Lessons for Handling Stress," p. 80.

34. "A Put-It-Off Personality," *Psychology Today*, January/February 2007, p. 42; Data reported in Jared Sandberg, "Fans of Procrastination Say It Boosts Control, Self-Esteem," *The Wall Street Journal*, February 9, 2005, p. B1.

35. Maia Szalavitz, "Stand & Deliver," *Psychology Today*, July/August 2003, p. 50.

36. Cited in "A Put-It-Off Personality," p. 42.

37. Shale Paul, as cited in "Tips to Keep Procrastination Under Control," Gannett News Service syndicated story, November 9, 1998.

38. Dru Scott, *How to Put More Time in Your Life* (New York: New American Library, 1980), p. 1.

39. Cited in "The Voices in Your Head," *Entrepreneur*, July 2000, pp. 105–107.

40. Christopher Percy Collier, "The Expert on Experts," *Fast Company*, November 2006, p. 116.

41. David Allen, *Getting Things Done* (New York: Penguin, 2001, 2007).

42. Curtis Sittenfeld, "She's a Paper Tiger," *Fast Company*, August 2002, p. 34.

43. Quoted in Adrian Wooldridge, "Why Clean Up Your Desk? Delight in Disorder Instead," *The Wall Street Journal*, January 2, 2007, p. D7. Book review of Eric Abrahamson and David Freedman, *A Perfect Mess* (New York: Little, Brown & Co., 2007).

44. Meni Koslowky and Abraham Sagie, "Correlates of Employee Lateness: Some Theoretical Considerations," *Journal of Applied Psychology*, February 1997, pp. 79–88.

45. Survey cited in Michelle Conlin, "Do Us a Favor, Take a Vacation," *Business Week*, May 21, 2007.

46. Anne Fisher, "The Rebalancing Act," *Fortune*, October 6, 2003, p. 110; Andrea Kay, "Avoid 'Traps' to Gain the Free Time You Need," Gannet News Service, January 10, 2005.

47. Brenda Goodman, "A Field Guide To the Workaholic," *Psychology Today*, May/June 2006, p. 41; Mildred L. Culp, "Working Productively with Workaholics While Minimizing Legal Risks," Passage Media syndicated story, 1997.

48. Tony Schwartz, "Manage Your Energy, Not Your Time," *Harvard Business Review*, October 2007, pp. 63–74.

49. "Secrets of Greatness: Marissa Mayer," *Fortune*, March 20, 2006, p. 68.

50. Cited in Jared Sandberg, "To-Do Lists Can Take More Time Than Doing, but That Isn't the Point," *The Wall Street Journal*, September 8, 2004, p. B1.

51. Penttila, "Time Out," p. 73.

52. The scientific information about multitasking is reviewed in Claudia Wallis, "The Multitasking Generation," *Time*, March 27, 2006, pp. 48–55. See also Joshua S. Rubinstein, David E Meyer, and Jeffrey E. Evans, "Executive Control of Cognitive Processes in Task Switching," *Journal of Experimental Psychology—Human Perception and Performance*, January 2000, Vol. 26, No. 4, pp. 763–769.

53. Research from the University of Oregon reported in "The Problem with Extreme Multitasking," *The Wall Street Journal*, February 12, 2008, p. B4.

54. Quoted in Claudia Wallis and Sonja Steptoe, "The Case for Doing One Thing at a Time," *Time*, January 16, 2006, p. 76.

55. Amy Dunkin, "Saying 'Adios' to the Office," *Business Week*, October 12, 1998, p. 153; Sue Shellenbarger, "When Working at Home Doesn't Work: How Companies Comfort Telecommuters," *The Wall Street Journal*, August 24, 2006, p. D1; E. Jeffrey Hill, Brent C. Miller, Sara P. Weiner, and Joe Colihan,

"Influences of the Virtual Office on Aspects of Work/Life Balance," *Personnel Psychology*, Autumn 1998, pp. 667–683.

56. Survey cited in "Average Worker Slacks for 1.7 Hours a Day," http://www.miamiherald.com, August 27, 2007.

CHAPTER 16

1. Laura Egodigwe, "Power Play: Using the Network," *Black Enterprise*, May 2007, p. 63.

2. Emily Steel, "Job-Search Sites Face a Nimble Threat," *The Wall Street Journal*, October 9, 2007, p. B10; John Zappe, "Recruiting Firms Setting Up Shop in Second Life," *Workforce Management*, March 26, 2007, p. 4.

3. Cited in Sarah E. Needleman, "How Blogging Can Help You Get a New Job," *The Wall Street Journal*, April 10, 2007, p. B1.

4. "Kat & Dale Talk Jobs," King Features Syndicate, April 14, 2002.

5. "Checking Credit of Job Candidates Drives Concerns about Civil Rights," *Christian Science Monitor*, January 19, 2007.

6. Chris Pentila, "Risky Business," *Entrepreneur*, September 2003, pp. 78–79.

7. Edward A. Robinson, "Beware—Job Seekers Have No Secrets," *Fortune*, December 29, 1997, p. 285.

8. M. P. McQueen, "Why You Should Spy on Yourself," *The Wall Street Journal*, April 21–22, 2007, p. B1.

9. Joann S. Lublin, "Silence Is Golden Rule for Résumés of People Who Have Broken It," *The Wall Street Journal*, October 2, 2007, p. B1.

10. Peg Thomas et al., "Resume Characteristics as Predictors as an Invitation to Interview," *Journal of Business and Psychology*, Spring 1999, pp. 339–356.

11. Douglas MacMillan, "The Art of the Online Résumé," *Business Week*, May 7, 2007, p. 86.

12. Dana Mattioli, "Who's Reading Online Résumés? Identity Crooks," *The Wall Street Journal*, October 17, 2006, p. B9.

13. Sarah E. Needleman, "Special Résumé Looks Can Do Quite a Job at Getting You Noticed," *The Wall Street Journal*, August 21, 2007, p. B6.

14. Data presented in Lisa Takeuchi Cullen, "Getting Wise to Lies," *Time*, May 1, 2006, p. 59.

15. Jim Pawlak, "Keep Job Application Cover Letter Short," http://detnews.com, April 15, 2005.

16. Sarah E. Needleman, "Speed Interviewing Grows as Skills Shortage Looms," *The Wall Street Journal*, November 6, 2007, p. B15.

17. Joann S. Lublin, "Talking Too Much On a Job Interview May Kill Your Chance," *The Wall Street Journal*, October 30, 2007, p. B1.

18. Quoted in Eileen Alt Powell, "Research, Practice Can Lead to a Stronger Job Interview," *MiamiHerald.com* (http://www.miamiherald.com), p. 1.

19. Anne Field, "Coach, Help Me Out with This Interview," *BusinessWeek*, October 22, 2001, p. 134E2.

20. Diane Brady, "Yes, Winning Is Still the Only Thing," *Business Week*, August 21/28, p. 52.

21. Alison Maitland, "Flexible Careers May Be Key to Worker Retention," *Financial Times* syndicated story, October 21, 2007; George Anders, "What Is Success, Anyway?" *The Wall Street Journal*, September 18, 2006, p. R10.

22. Marcus Buckingham, *Go Put Your Strengths to Work* (New York: Free Press, 2007).

23. Jeninne Lee-St. John, "It's a Brand-You World," *Time*, November 6, 2006, pp. 60–61.

24. Jack and Suzy Welch, "Get Real, Get Ahead," *Business Week*, May 14, 2007, p. 100.

25. Richard Boyatzis, Annie McKee, and Daniel Goleman, "Reawakening Your Passion for Work," *Harvard Business Review*, April 2002, pp. 86–94.

26. Jeff Bailey, "Devoted Work Wins Customers Willing to Pay," *The Wall Street Journal*, October 14, 2003.

27. Scott E. Seibert, Maria L. Kraimer, and J. Michael Crant, "What Do Proactive People Do? A Longitudinal Model Linking Proactive Personality and Career Success," *Personnel Psychology*, Winter 2001, pp. 845–874; Scott E. Seibert, J. Michael Crant, and Maria L. Kraimer, "Proactive Personality and Career Success," *Journal of Applied Psychology*, June 1999, pp. 416–427.

28. Douglas J. Brown et al., "Proactive Personality and the Successful Job Search: A Field Investigation with College Graduates," *Journal of Applied Psychology*, May 2006, pp. 717–726.

29. Cited in Cheryl Dahle, "Showing Your Worth Without Showing Off," http://www.nytimes.com, September 19, 2004; http://www.bragbetter.com.

30. Philip L. Hunsaker, "Projecting the Appropriate Image," *Supervisory Management*, May 1989, p. 26.

31. Quoted in Louise Dobson, "Skirting the Line: In the Office, Wardrobe Mistakes Can Be Disastrous," *Psychology Today*, July/August 2006, p. 13.

32. Quoted in "Taking Charge in a Temp World," *Fortune*, October 21, 1998, pp. 247–248.

33. Anne Fisher, "How to Network—and Enjoy It," *Fortune*, April 4, 2005, p. 38.

34. Jessica E. Vascellaro, "Social Networking Goes Professional," *The Wall Street Journal*, August 28, 2007, p. D1, D2; Ed Frauenheim, "Social Revolution: Social Networking Technology Is Colliding with the Workplace—Whether Employers Like It or Not," *Workforce Management*, October 22, 2007, p. 1.

35. Erin White, "The First Job Blues: How to Adjust, When to Move On," *The Wall Street Journal*, July 25, 2006, p. B7.

36. Daniel L. Cable and Timothy A. Judge, "Interviewers' Perceptions of Person–Organization Fit and Organizational Selection Decisions," *Journal of Applied Psychology*, August 1997, pp. 546–561.

37. Amy L. Kristof-Brown, Ryan D. Zimmerman, and Erin C. Johnson, "Consequences of Individuals' Fit at Work: A Meta–Analysis of Person–Job, Person-Organization, Person–Group, and Person–Supervisor Fit," *Personnel Psychology*, Summer 2005, pp. 281–342.

38. Christian J. Resick, Boris B. Baltes, and Cynthia Walker Shantz, "Person–Organization Fit and Work-Related Attitudes and Decisions: Interactive Effects with Job Fit and Conscientiousness," *Journal of Applied Psychology*, September 2007, pp. 1446–1455.

39. Quoted in Robyn D. Clarke, "Rewards of Risk Taking: How to Move Out of Your Comfort Zone," *Black Enterprise*, March 2006, p. 105.

40. David Wessel, "The Future of Jobs: New Ones Arise, Wage Gap Widens," *The Wall Street Journal*, April 2, 2004; Peter Svensson, "Hands-On Jobs May Be the Safest," Associated Press, July 9, 2004.

41. Jack and Suzy Welch, "The Importance of Being There," *Business Week*, April 16, 2007, p. 92.

Index